ETERNAL HUMANS AND THE FINITE GODS

How an Ex-Prophet and I Left Religion and
Discovered Universes Beyond and Within

THERESA TALEA

Rediscovery Press

Eternal Humans and the Finite Gods

How an Ex-Prophet and I Left Religion and Discovered Universes Beyond and Within

This book may be ordered through booksellers or by contacting via e-mail:

Rediscovery Press
orders@rediscoverypress.com
Rancho Cordova, California
www.rediscoverypress.com

Second Edition. Rediscovery Press publication date: June 12, 2014

Cover design and book images by Theresa Talea and James Macaron

ISBN: 978-0-9912540-0-2 (sc)
ISBN: 978-0-9912540-1-9 (hc)
ISBN: 978-0-9912540-2-6 (e)

Library of Congress Control Number: 2014942228

Printed and bound in the United States of America by Lightning Source Inc.

DEDICATION

To my mother—your love is an endless stream of gentle yet confident strength. No matter where I go, you are with me. I am grateful to you for all that you are and have done. Without you, this book would not contain such depth of information. Without you, I would not be the woman who I happily am today. I love you, always.

To James—thank you for your continued support in this great endeavor. Your intelligent research and feedback have enriched this material, and your technical contributions with the format and images are a valued glimpse into your creative nature. Thank you for being in my life.

To my new friends, especially Paul, who I met after the release of my first book—thank you for inspiring me with your open minds and hearts. Your thoughtful input has helped make this second edition what it should be.

To everyone who craves knowledge like purified water in a desert, I wrote this book for you because I seek with you.

CONTENTS

PART 4. Who We Really Are

FIGURES

PREFACE

More than two years have passed since the February 2012 publication of this book's first edition during which I have further explored its concepts. At first glance, the most obvious change is the main title. I initially marketed this book to help address and counter New Age and biblical hype surrounding the last days of the Mayan calendar. Now that the year 2012 has passed, I have decided to put more emphasis upon personal empowerment. I kept the same cover design because it better reflects the book's new main title; we humans can take care of ourselves and our planet when we act upon our intrinsic abilities.

I wrote my first edition selectively delving into topics while touching upon others. The timeframe I had wanted to fulfill and the vast amount of material led me to put extra burden on the reader to explore some topics on their own. As I have grown in my awareness, I realized that I needed to fine tune the topics that I presented, and I also wanted to learn more in my continuing quest for accurate knowledge.

I have re-evaluated my arguments and information, made some corrections and updates, and improved the organization and understanding of this material. I also further explored the potential tangibility and credibility of philosophical and religious ideas. This second edition supersedes the first one, so if you have both editions, please now only refer to this book. This edition is what my book is meant to be.

This book pushes intellectual, scientific, and spiritual boundaries. My initial desire was to proclaim our personal power and ability against almost all odds; however, as someone who wishes to collaborate with others and present as accurate a picture as I possibly can, I have needed more information to weigh against my intuition. In some cases, the only information that could serve this purpose derives from otherworldly sources.

I include diverse non-human statements, paying particular attention to my mother's and my sources as well as scribe and speaker Ashayana Deane's entity groups named Guardian Alliance and Melchizedek Cloister Emerald Order. I recognize that each source gives information based on its own thoughts and experiences, similar to what humans do, so I weigh all sides to find the common denominator and core fact or truth of the matter.

My writing is not channeled, prophetic, or personally influenced by spiritual entities. This is the main reason why this book in its entirety has taken me five full years to write as well as 13 years of background growth involving abundant research and journaling. This book is mainly the product of my desire, abilities, diligence, and sometimes tears, and it is greatly enriched with the abilities and input of my wonderful mother who has walked this often difficult path by my side. Certain otherworldly information that she can access has come from my questioning and research, and then I further work to validate or clarify it.

Beneficial otherworldly sources seem to employ a live and let live philosophy. They wait until we ask them for help, and even then, their help addresses where we are at currently, often not giving us more knowledge until we have gained foundational awareness. This can be frustrating, but it is more so liberating because we each are left to our abundant abilities that are essentially no less than theirs, just somewhat different.

Unfortunately, people often look to subjective entity or god group communications such as prophecies and channelings as the ultimate truth without cause to investigate. When we take each piece of information as just that—information—we can then determine how it fits into the bigger picture as well as our personal lives. This way, every idea is heard and evaluated instead of ignored, and we can more peaceably coexist.

Each of us has unique experiences, and they are all valid. What I personally know is not what another person's experience may know. In addition, significant abuses that happen to us can cloud wisdom and have people lose sight of abilities that others seem to effortlessly demonstrate. The expansive self-view can become diminished through pinhole glasses, but the person is unsettled, knowing that there is more to who he or she is. Whether people believe in having a type of energetic soul or spirit or none at all, we can agree that we fundamentally exist and are interconnected to aspects within and outside of us.

This second edition bolsters and clarifies our inward connection to greater and simpler truths. I embrace my particular intuition that says we humans are our own saviors, our own embodied "host" so to speak, so nothing outside of us must direct our ways. Let me be clear that this self-empowerment does not imply that we are an island without certain otherworldly friends and energies that do help us, even if indirectly. Technically, energies are outside of us and within us, but when we realize where our position is in the vast energetic realms of creation, we can see how these energies can collaboratively work together without force, without hierarchy. I have not yet heard a prominent religious or New Age belief teach this idea about creation and pre-creation. It is this intuition that I thoroughly explore in the book, starting from the rabbit hole of religion outward and also inward to our true selves and the very beginning of creation.

This book is not born out of the desire to judge or divide, although I do judge situations and present a side. I speak my voice—thoughts and feelings—and I ask questions, but unfortunately I often receive a different kind of judgment from others in return, one that is closed, fearful, and angry. I think judgment is reasonable and additionally helpful when it employs fairness, thoughtfulness, factual evidence, and constructive criticism.

While I was motivated to write this book for people, I also knew that I had to write it for me. I have undergone a long journey of self-exploration to weed out the false persona that I had become as my coping mechanism. I endured terrible abuses that instilled much fear, confusion, and displaced anger into me. I started to resent people for having better experiences than I did. I did not realize this resentment because I was the victim.

How could I learn to regain myself when overcome by the chill of rejection and loneliness? My answer was to ask questions, sometimes only to myself. Some questions brought me more rejection, but I kept pressing forward after each step back. I learned that I am my best advocate and my best friend.

We all mean something. In order to create a better world that stops the victimization, I have learned to open myself to unconditional love no matter what. People sometimes do and think absolutely horrific things that do not invite a loving response, but I refuse to hate them because deep underneath their hardened surface and actions lies a glimmer of beauty.

When projecting outward as a victim, my surroundings have felt claustrophobic. In my normal reaction, I cut myself out of the world in an act of divide. In this divide, I have looked upon people as only "others" without seeing humans who have my same needs and feelings. Divides create competition and walls of separation that can snowball into every facet of society, so a new leader can have his or her year of fame; accordingly, divides can conquer. I have been angry at this rampant reality on our Earth, but my anger has also partially blinded me to my own wisdom that can unveil another reality, a bigger reality that I already know.

By walking over every chasm, I see a very large world that can fill all of our basic needs. By smiling at people, giving them compliments, and asking and listening how they are doing, we are opening a window into their lives. We can give genuine love that even wicked people can appreciate. We can live as a real community that cares to hear other views and experiences and treats everyone with at least some respect. Love is the bridge to us all in this fragmented world.

This book serves as a springboard into deeper contemplation and congruent action. I invite everyone to research my claims and expound upon this information—going forward, not backward into prevalent religious and New Age belief systems—so we can fine-tune what we likely intuitively know.

INTRODUCTION

How can a human such as I know truths or facts about God and the greater universe? Truth does not equate to omniscience; it can merely point out accurate aspects of the big picture to help us achieve sufficient understanding for our needs. Science and religion are two fields of study that actively tackle such aspects. Instead of favoring one perspective over the other, I think it is wise to put all views on the table to see if they coherently fit together as a valid picture. If they do not, then we can choose which paradigm we desire to expand, thereby leaving behind what does not serve us.

There are too many half-truths among us. We are inundated with contrasting information, but we usually decide to accept it because we do not know where else to look. Since birth, we have been taught to favor the teachings of our family and societal institutions over our intuition. "Obey your parents" is a popular commandment among religions. We must seek our answers in elders who in turn follow the elders before them. Religions and spiritualities are embedded in this ancestral and societal knowledge.

When we follow other people's stories and viewpoints, life becomes reduced to an external experience. We are now reduced to operating and thinking as others have done.

When we create the space for introspection, we can apply our logic and intuition to our experiences that often do not follow the past. I doubt that any thought is new, but we are in a dynamic present that allows an open-minded exploration into the holes of logic over which we previously glossed. We can gain more congruency instead of continuing the trend of putting a flimsy band-aid over disjointed experiential facts.

Truth is factual. Truth is not a belief, but it can equate to some beliefs. Truth in the greater sense of the word is a grounded, fact-belief, whereby it expands a fact throughout our layers. Accordingly, truth ties in reason that carries forth its integrity throughout all levels of creation. Reason can involve a measure of belief when it uses that extra "feeling" of intuition.

For example, I have "known" that there is a greater energy of goodness, a perfect purity that is free from anything destructive. My experiences know the full spectrum of pain to joy, but my intuition tells me that joy and love do not need any pain for it to exist. There is separateness, not a confusing bundle of gray. I want to further explore this good energy apart from the world views already given to me.

This exploration is not measurable in the empirical scientific method. Ironically, scientists carry out expensive experiments to try to measure such intangible and invisible phenomena. They do not wish to accept subjective interpretation even when such subjectivity is experienced by almost everyone. Logic can tell them that such phenomena exist beyond our three-dimensional experience; our dreams, visions, and senses of drastically different energies are a small example of what we cannot fully explain.

A very expensive scientific experiment is the Large Hadron Collider (LHC) on the border of Switzerland and France. It consists of a 27-kilometer underground ring of superconducting magnets that accelerate particle matter to the point of extreme annihilation. In 2012, the particle smashing has finally presented what is believed by scientists to be the subatomic Higgs boson theorized as the "God particle." In February 2013, the LHC was shut down for maintenance and upgrades until 2015 "so that the twin beams of particles can race around at nearly twice the energy: as much as 13 trillion electron volts," states a CNN Tech author.[1] Physicists behind this project surmise that more destruction would prove the Higgs boson as the ultimate God or universal particle, or another pre-particle might be discovered.

Logic and theory warn scientists that these experiments can be dangerous, especially because a "mini bang" black hole and resultant wormhole could potentially be created. If God is a natural, alive subatomic particle, logic would also tell them that destroying something is not the way to find God. Such annihilation would maybe give that subatomic particle a life of a fraction of a second. How mass can accumulate from decaying matter is illogical to me. In addition, it is possible that a small, natural subatomic particle cannot be observable. These scientists are basing this experiment upon their belief in measurable, creative energy that started or arose from the Big Bang. Their God entails destruction, so that is why they have no problem carrying out this precarious experiment.

Major religions can agree with these scientists because their God also performs destructive acts. Instead of calling their God a particle, it is rather a personified being. The major difference between the Gods of science and religion is that science's destructive model assumes God is extremely short-lived and recyclable, and religion sees God as eternal and generally unchanging. However, when we personify God in religion, that opens up the possibility of a finite existence.

It would be great to find solid truth through prevailing scientific and religious information, but their perspectives contain bias toward beliefs that already categorized such otherworldly phenomena. Since the greater universe and energies are beyond our grasp, we often lessen their magnitude just enough to fit within a workable framework from which to understand. We then build upon those ideas to find something somewhat new instead of eradicating them and starting fresh from within an open mind and heart. Scientists have an edge on religious followers because some of their discoveries and theories open up an entirely new paradigm. Religions teach against such open discovery because they want steady comfort in their ancestral paradigms.

The bottom line between both science and religion is that they are in awe of external marvels. In their respective ways, they will allow each marvel to do whatever it wants so they can ooh and ahh over its abilities. While this can be a learning experience, it can easily dismiss our inner gauge that tells us to step back, think twice about the situation, and regain ourselves. We can already tell that a lot of strange symbols, artifacts, and experiences are a part of this life. Nothing is really new. We do not need to give away worship or free reign to anything or anyone. We only have given it because of our mental view or programming toward it.

I was one of countless people who associated a religious God with the truth. My Catholic upbringing framed my perception, so when I started questioning that faith, I merely bounced to other religions to follow-up with finding the truth that they claim to possess. I barely dabbled outside of Christianity because it was ingrained into me that Jesus was "the way, the truth, and the life." The boldness of Southern-style, fundamentalist Christian pastors also caught my attention. I thought, "Surely their enthusiasm and strong words mean that they have the truth?"

As I adopted the fundamentalist Christian paradigm, I started to wear truth as a badge of honor. I was a student of the religion, but I thought I was better than everyone outside of my religion because they did not know what I did. Most of the population was lost, backslid, or outright sinners; they were all going to hell, or so I was taught. I was saved, well, as long as I stayed a dutiful student-servant.

My propensity toward questioning the elders did not sit well with them, though. I eventually realized that those questions were the vehicle that "saved" me and brought me to find clear truth outside of religion. I discovered that there are many half-truths in religions, so my little superiority complex was really a distraction from having no solid foundation.

Interestingly, I did not think I had such an ego while I was very religious. Thankfully, my new awareness humbled me; I could objectively see how presumptuous I was by telling everyone that they were wrong because they did not believe as I did.

I will not know all truths, but this is not my aim. My aim is to do what I can to unravel the ball of string in institutionalized belief systems to delineate clear lines between contradiction and sound reason. Opening the mind without bound and with active participation (to prevent losing one's own intuition) opens the door to profound yet glaringly simple information. This information was within me and everyone all along. I just did not trust myself enough to believe it.

My quest for facts and truth helped set me and my mother free. She was used as a prophet since she was a young woman; this largely prevented her from exploring her individuality because she was literally used as a body of God to give His messages to others. Chapter 1 expounds upon her story and how she found the pure essence beyond God as well as some levels in-between.

Chapter 2 explains my background that brought me to religion. I wanted to believe in miraculous stories because I desperately needed healing in many ways. I looked outside myself for that God-man to love and heal me; this only set me up for failure in my personal life, as chapter 3 explains.

Chapter 3 shows the step-by-step process of how my mother and I fully came out of religion. This is a unique chapter that speaks from my perspective during each step of awareness. I explore Christian teachings about God, and I provide several prophecies that my mother received that mirror these teachings. Her prophecies also complement and illuminate the struggles that the Bible's prophets experienced; they were used against their will at times, and the messages often did not help them.

The religious paradigm teaches us to have faith without questioning, as though God takes care of everything. As we finally paid acute attention to our thoughts and reactions to our religious experiences and teachings, we realized how unsettled they made us feel. In fact, the teachings were riddled with misinformation, even lies. Religions give us some truth; people stay in them because on some level, the message resonates with us. However, just as a bad relationship holds us back, the religious experiences of me and my mother brought us division and heartache. We were being held back from our full potential. We found strength to break free of the strong programming, and we have found boundless knowledge, security, and joy as a result.

Chapters 4 and 5 investigate the environment that created the half-truths of Judeo-Christianity. Chapter 4 focuses on the background of Judaism, while Chapter 5 puts the Messiahs of Christianity in the spotlight. Both chapters show the seamless flow between the two religions, just as how Judaism emerged from other religions before it. No religion is truly unique, nor is any religious God. With this in mind, chapter 4 uncovers the reason behind sexism and sexualization of women, and both chapters note political unrest that was more of an issue than the particular God people worshipped. Sometimes religion is used as a front to deeper socio-political and environmental concerns. Because the gods are not significantly dissimilar, religious division can be a diversion tactic that distracts us from seeing the agenda of control over Earth and its people.

Chapter 6 shifts gears toward the scientific "religion" of God in its view about creation from the Big Bang. I explore natural versus unnatural science, for there is a science that is based on non-decaying matter. I use my inner gauge toward truth and otherworldly information akin to prophecies, but this information is not prophetic, as you will understand.

We are not alone in the greater universe; there is awareness beyond us. We also embody levels of consciousness that complete us as humans. There is a wealth of information that we can tap into, but so far only certain material has been approved by religious or scientific sects. I have deciphered several hundred prophecies from my mother in addition to visions and countless other messages and insights between us. This experience has helped me weed through other sources of information, including various channeled entities, to present my findings to you. These findings fully resonate with both the religious and progressive quantum physicist belief that there is eternal life in energy that becomes matter.

I request that you read this book carefully and sequentially from start to finish before jumping ahead because numerous topics are progressively expounded and interwoven. I provide notes where further explanation exists in upcoming sections for assurance and memory placement. I make this request because the reader should be prepared with the proper background to address the uncomfortable information in chapters 7 and 8.

Chapter 7 introduces our galactic history as well as other related galaxies. I finally uncover the racial identities, characteristics, and agendas of the gods.

Chapter 8 explains the history of the Earth and what should naturally happen from 2012 to 2022 A.D. and afterward. I continue revealing the god group agendas that cause instability to us and the Earth, and I explain countermeasures to their actions.

Chapter 9 directs us inward to the layers within each of us. Now that the external factors are known, there should be no delay in getting to thoroughly know who we really are. I introduce each aspect of our composition and ultimately provide the "Aha" moment of how much control we really have over ourselves and our lives.

Chapter 10 explores and critiques the foundational tenets of the Law of One belief that New Age, esoteric, and Buddhist spiritualities embrace. Often, when people leave blatantly hierarchical religion, instead of pushing past mainstream belief systems, they turn to the less obvious spiritual hierarchy embedded in the Law of One.

Chapter 11 explains tangible energetic differences and the importance of discerning them to help us direct our paths in this life and the afterlife. At this final stage of the book, the reader can accurately determine where he or she wishes to direct the next step.

I thread nuggets of important information throughout sections of this book, so I suggest you use a highlighter or take notes. I also reveal many biblical themes because they are embedded into the world's societal construct. No matter your religious or anti-religious stance, I ask that you read each section of this book with an open mind toward wide-ranging knowledge from a multitude of sources, perspectives, and experiences.

My objective is to empower the reader with knowledge, not only about outer events but especially about oneself. My wish is that every person opens the avenue of full disclosure and communication within oneself so that we can master our own lives. There is no need to be a follower of someone else's paradigm that does not fully embrace our experiences and perspectives. Certainly, we must learn information, but we should always check it within ourselves in honest introspection.

Perhaps two vivid dreams that I had can represent this book's overall message of staying connected with the good energy within oneself despite unsettling or scary events.

People who looked somewhat reptilian walked throughout my neighborhood to capture everyone. I took a loved one with me and tried to find a hiding place, but we were found.

We were corralled into a group of people and brought to an underground pen. There, people were naked, carelessly having sex, bathing, or just lying there in several concrete rooms, usually with blank looks on their faces, although a few acted out their aggression. I looked into the main floor, and there were feeding troughs with people voraciously eating, face first into the trough. A woman was frantic while she scurried past me, crying out how her hair was messy, as her sole concern was to look pretty.

I felt the fear of my situation. I momentarily linked to the mentality of the room, and my mind became darkened, dulled, and unable to control as my own. I started to feel trapped, and in that mental box, I felt my personal world shrink to a focal point of physical trivialities and animalistic tendencies. I had to quickly bring my mind out of this state; I knew the claws of this mentality could change me the more I allow myself to fall prey to it.

As I walked onto another path that crossed through the feeding area, a human hybrid was on the opposite end walking toward me while scoping the room. He was using telepathy to monitor their thoughts. In my observation and feeling that the energy around me was weighed down into a self-focused, preoccupied obsession,

I could tell that the hybrid was making sure that everyone was in that mind frame.

As he passed me, he sensed that my mind was lighter and more open, so he turned toward me and called in reinforcements to start a mind control assault. As this happened, I activated the energy of my higher but internal frequency. I went into my core and pushed out this vibrational energy to create a wall between them and me. I never did this before [in my dream's awareness], but my intuition knew the strength of this energy. Putting out my arm [as the girl demonstrates on the book cover] helped me to visualize this wall and keep it there. The barrier worked. Then, I expanded this energy throughout the entire room to reach every human, and I called out, "whoever wants this energy, come with me." I did not say "whoever wants to leave, come with me," because this energy does not identify with anything in that place; it is known as freedom. Nearly two-fifths of the people came toward me. The expressions on their faces were visibly different than the rest of the people who were too consumed to know better; they looked hopeful and eager.

As we walked toward the exit, I could not tell if the door was shut or locked. I kept up my arms toward the incoming hybrids and pushed them aside with the energy I sent. I never once allowed my mentality to shift toward doubt. I knew I was different than they were, so although they had physical power, I did not allow what I saw to override what I knew. I knew that energy is what creates matter, and I knew the solid power of congruent love, truth, goodness, and open awareness, so I stayed in that energetic world and made it my world around me. It worked! As we approached the thick door, it was left partially open, so we proceeded to quickly walk out of that building to never return. It is interesting that this door was left open because the mind control and negative energy is what kept people trapped instead of their physical environment. None of us were chased to be captured again because we knew more than ever before where we stand and what our capabilities are.

In the follow-up dream, I told other people about what happened. I said how important it is to stay in this energy no matter what. It requires belief when we are shaken, but that belief is based on truth and reality due to the scientific and experiential knowing of this original, different energy. A Catholic family member chimed in at the end and said she agreed with me. She said that she would then send wrath to the enemies since God did the same in the Bible.

I spoke up and said, "No, that is not what we do because that would require us to get out of the energy of love and truth to then direct the wrath toward the hybrids. That would change our focus, thus changing our energy. This cannot happen because we with our weaknesses need to keep the focus on the pure energy so that we maintain the protective difference between us and them. Later, we can feel the anger on our own terms when processing everything, but when in a direct confrontation, the only way to succeed is to stand within the separate energy."

These dreams can be interpreted as stories similar to those presented in religions because of seemingly far-out characters and abilities. However, there is truth in her- or his-story because any experiential phenomenon captured in history can be documented as fact. The discernment comes whether we wish to accept those experiences as beneficial for our lives. There is a dual reality conundrum wherein we are aware of the facts of the leading world view, but we can remain largely removed from that perspective in favor of something better. My dreams illuminated that when we are aware, we will not allow our minds and actions to mirror the obvious to subtle manipulations by other people who wish to control and devalue us.

Let us work together to wade through the many stories to find the solid ground of truth upon which we can see each other eye to eye. Then, we can co-create a more harmonious world because we are finally connecting with each other and our true selves.

PART 1

RELEASING THE SHACKLES TO FULLY BREATHE

CHAPTER 1

No Longer a Prophet:
My Mother's Path to the Source

My mother's journey into the development of her deeply prophetic abilities started through the eyes of a little girl in Catholic school. She went to daily Mass and sat in the church pew, gazing upon the altar in awe. She sensed a spiritual or etheric element beyond her but did not understand what it was; she grew up wanting to know more.

After she got married, she moved to Germany to join her husband who was stationed there during the Vietnam War. She joined a women's prayer group at the army base's Catholic Church. The women started to speak in tongues, something she had never heard before. She was so intrigued that she stopped the session to tell everyone, "I want that!" They were impressed and wanted to share their "gift" with such an eager newcomer, so they sat her on a chair, laid their hands upon her, and told her to receive the Holy Spirit. Within seconds, she felt warm energy go down her head to her toes. The women told her to speak whatever came to her mind. She started to talk normally, but they interjected and told her to instead speak by faith. She tried but could not do it, so she left disappointed.

Another day, one of the women came to her house to pray over her again. The woman explained, "Don't use your mind. Just let the Holy Spirit naturally flow through you, and open your mouth."

My mother relaxed, and then it happened. She spoke in a new language! She recalled, "It sounded strange, but it was exciting. I was happy that I could praise God in a special language known as 'speaking in tongues.'"

Something else happened to her from the "baptism with fire" experience that first night—her sixth sense or "third eye" was opened.

My mother was working in a German shoe factory during that time. She got sick from the glue she had to use, so she wanted to work at a different position in the factory. She wondered what time her boss would come over to talk with her about the potential transfer, and she instantly saw "10:30" imprinted upon the front of her mind. Surprisingly, that is when her boss arrived! She was intrigued by this occurrence and wanted to test its validity. She started the process of asking various questions in her mind, and without fail, she received answers.

Soon afterward, she started to hear a voice telling her what to do. The

1

voice did not ring in her ears, but it came from a spiritual communication as how Christians say that God speaks to them. It was an internal sound as a voice in her head along with words that are mentally seen.

She asked questions to this voice of God about her life, and then she paused to see if an answer would pop into her mind along with her internal hearing. The mental projection of God's thoughts carried words and sound vibration. Upon receiving an answer, she wrote it down to document her new communication skills.

She describes that she did not feel altered, but she felt as though she had a dual connection with something beyond her that was simultaneously with her. It felt natural to her because of this easy exchange between her and her adored God. God was with her continually, as though He was walking with her every day as the famed religious poem "Footprints" describes. The communications became increasingly elaborate the more involved she became in this practice.

My mother went to several prayer group meetings in which she learned about various spiritual gifts. She could speak in tongues, discern spirits, and dialogue with God, but what soon occurred as the most startling to her was the automatic writing. She sat alone in her room, became engrossed in a praying state, and then her arm moved to pick up a pencil or pen to write perfectly coherent words on paper. These words flowed through her effortlessly as though she was an empty vessel. Soon, God would prompt her to write, and her body would sometimes shake under His energy. Her mind played no part in the initiation or delivery of the prophecy.

She is certain that on the night of her "baptism of fire" in the prayer group, she took upon herself a spirit, which was what she believed at the time was a measure of God's Spirit known as the Holy Spirit, and it used her to give messages not only for herself but for others. The prophecies corrected and taught people, and they broadly predicted our futures to keep our faith in check.

What took my mom many years to notice, with the help of my engagement and questions, was that the answers she received were not often in direct relation to our concerns. The prophecies that she received were usually one-sided messages that God wanted us to know. We wondered why He sometimes did not answer our questions or give more detail because God is supposed to know everything. We then remembered a Scripture that says, "[M]y thoughts *are* not your thoughts, neither *are* your ways my ways, saith the LORD. For *as* the heavens are higher than the earth, so are my ways higher than your ways, and my thoughts than your thoughts" (Isaiah 55: 8-9). We ignored our initial reaction because we believed that God was everything we needed and more.

Because of her close relationship with God, my mother felt like she could not often distinguish between herself and Him due to the amount of control He had over her life. He awakened her out of sleep by projecting her name into her hearing and then giving her commands: write this down, tell this person something, do this. She endured countless interrupted nights of sleep during which He would not stop talking to her.

These communications were so frequent that she as a dutiful Christian allowed them to direct every facet of her life. If you cannot stop it, and it is said to be good for you, then surely you must need it, right?

The Bible and Church have taught that we must commune with God above all things. If my mother was not receiving messages, she was often in a state of prayer as a quintessential Christian woman. She became afraid to make her own decisions in case she would choose something against God's will. She became a blank canvas, and when doors closed on a potential direction of her life, the next door that opened was said to be from God's leading.

My mom has been a very visual person in the spiritual realm. She saw angels in the form of tall men (never women, strangely) and little winged cherubs. She saw ugly, impish creatures sitting alone or attached to people's backs, smoking a cigarette along with the person, for example. She saw the Sun jump around the desert sky of California City, California when a convening mass of people prayed to the "Virgin" Mary on one of her "holy" days. In a Catholic church, she saw the spirits of saints walking before the altar. She also saw Mary standing beside her statue.

During the night of her first charismatic experience in Germany, she had a vivid dream-like experience that she thought was the Hereafter.

> I was carried up into the clouds by two angels, and I came to New Jerusalem, this huge land. I could see a river with blue, crystal clear water. I felt there was someone walking and talking with me. I thought I was walking alongside Jesus Christ. I saw in the distance a city of crystalline white and gold.

She explains about her visions throughout her 20s:

> I had visions of wars and how I would be helping in the last days, helping as a nurse the people who got injured. There was so much. It was every day that I had a vision or could see into another realm. I just felt so open that it was coming and going through me. I took note but wasn't sure how much I was supposed to really take it to heart and live it.
>
> Looking back, I think I was often a portal like on the TV show 'Stargate' that has the big open gate through which you can

go back and forth. I felt like part of my being was going back and forth to the entity realm so they could connect to me there. But I rather think there was a way that they could enter into my consciousness, leave, and then come back to me at any time. I was connecting with something outside of myself; they were thought-forms and energy, but I could not easily tell where I was in the midst of it all.

My mom was spiritually open, so the way that she could discern something was when it felt "off" or "bad." She felt something on the outside around her, and her inner knowing would confirm that it was something evil. It could seem as though she was filled, otherwise known as possessed, by God's Spirit since she heard it inside of her, but according to her explanation, she was rather a portal for telepathic thoughts from this God entity. This confirms that her mind was not her own when He gained control over it to transmit messages. There were times when this God took control of her body, as I have witnessed and will explain shortly, but it did not stay; it was more in control of her energy field.

She encountered many negative experiences. She thought that the Devil was performing the harassments because of the Christian belief that says the Devil is the only real enemy. That always confused me, though, because Christianity has taught me that Satan, or Lucifer, could not be everywhere at the same time like God. The Scriptures that say Satan tempted Jesus in the wilderness underscore the Devil's finite nature.

I wondered what this Devil really is. This "Evil One" talked in a low voice to my mom at different times when I was a teenager, saying to her, "I am going to get your daughter." It also threatened her, but because she took responsibility toward me, she was more worried for me than herself. That entity knew how to harass her by involving her loved ones.

When I was 16 years old, I was lying on my back about to fall asleep, and I felt an extreme pressure on my chest that prevented me from moving. I then heard that low voice that said, "I'm going to get you." I panicked, but I quickly put my focus onto myself and Jesus and then prayed it away. The pressure on my chest returned a year later in a similar situation, but I again instinctively put my focus onto myself and then prayed to Jesus before I could hear that creepy voice. My mother endured similar night terror experiences when she was younger, and so did a couple of my friends.

She remembers a day when she was asked by a woman from her Catholic church to accompany her to a friend's house that felt unseasonably cold and scary. She expected an exorcism, so she came prepared. When they entered the house, she saw imps everywhere. In typical movie fashion, she held a cross and told them to leave in Jesus's name. They left, and the house immediately regained its warmth.

The same coldness filled a hospital room one night when she was working as a professional nurse. Her fellow nurses avoided that room as much as they could because they thought the patient was possessed—he was acting wildly and sometimes yelling. They knew my mother was a devout Catholic, so they sought her out so she could address the situation. She entered the room cautiously and saw the patient lying there unsettled and awake. She talked calmly and briefly to the patient but then went to the bathroom to talk directly to the offending spiritual entity; she spoke to it from within her spirit.

She said, "You don't belong here. Go away."

"I'm not leaving," it replied.

"You are leaving. You're going."

She did not say "in the name of Jesus" because she already called upon Jesus before she entered the room. She also believed in her personal capacity.

The entity left.

These incidents are known as exorcisms, but they do not need to resemble movie exorcisms that portray a grand protocol. She effectively expelled those entities and continues to do so today. The main difference today is that she does not call upon the name of Jesus or any entity, and she does not use any token. Our story will illuminate why.

Looking back, she wonders how much it was her or God that helped dispel those demons. For example, another patient told her that he could see an aura around her hands while she was touching his feet, and he continued to see her energy field glowing as she moved up his legs. This was her own healing energy that she exuded. I always feel that comforting heat of her hands along with the love she so freely gives.

My mother has many stories to tell about her experiences; I will recount a few more examples that she has told me over the years. She saw cherubic angels on all four sides of her car. She saw tall, men-like angels standing around her house, in the midst of us, and behind me from time to time. She saw a monkey-like imp sitting on the window sill next to my bed. She saw a claw over churches. When I was 22 years old, she saw a winged demon inside of me while I was extremely depressed (she and a pastor made it leave in an exorcism sans religious paraphernalia). While driving in her car, she can see imps or demonic creatures in trees and on other cars. She also saw a 50-foot tall Jesus walking along the freeway ahead of her, watching the cars below.

She could not help but often wonder if what she was seeing was real, but she was grounded enough in the world as a mother, wife, professional, and friend to know that she was not crazy; I wholeheartedly concur, as do others whom she has helped. Many people in the world say that they hear from God or see strange things, so how can others who have not yet had these experiences say that these people are not experiencing something real and valid?

When my mother and her husband were at a crossroad with their jobs, she prayed to see where they should move. The only answer she could see in her mind was the name of a city in which they knew no one. She preferred to move back near her family, but she trusted this message and hoped to find a better place for us, including help for me because I was chronically ill. My health struggles were a heavy weight upon her heart, and she put a lot of time, energy, and money toward my care.

In this new city, she met a woman who told her that I would receive healing at the hands of a unique pastor in the United Pentecostal Church (UPC). My mom was desperate for help and was open to anything. She believed in healing powers and hoped this would be the answer, the fully open door instead of the partial ones we had received from God's words through her and the Bible's prophets.

She dragged my staunchly Catholic step-father and half-brother to what they perceived was a dramatic, loud, and emotional service. My mom and I got caught up in the storm and soon afterward were baptized by full water immersion in Jesus's name. We cried often and raised our hands in the air, calling upon the name of Jesus as the God-man who was proclaimed to save us, and we both took on his healing power by faith that could now supposedly heal my body.

Although this church was new to us, we were excited to be there because we felt more active with our faith unlike the ritualistic motions of the Catholic Church. The emotions and hype of this church raised us to a higher frequency that connected us to something beyond. Whether it was good or bad, at the time, the active nature made us feel empowered. Ironically, we also gave more of ourselves through full submission. We wanted my healing along with the love and truth relationship with the Almighty God; therefore, whatever we were told to do, we followed. The church's instructions were supported by stories of other people being healed. Many people testified that they were happier than ever before.

We were told that our new relationship with Jesus was an experience, so it is real. God is real. The church's emotional worship was certainly an experience, too. Since we were affected by it and added our measure to the pot with desperation and devotion, we felt the realness of worship and therefore kept believing the pastors' messages on top of what we already knew. We knew that the spiritual realm was real due to the intimate relationship my mother had with God. I wanted the exact same relationship as hers to make my walk with Him more tangible, but my daily Bible studies, emotional prayers, and spiritually heightened nature were decent, tangible experiences of my own. The heightened church experience sped up my mind and body to where my mind was aware of its surroundings, but it was also bypassed by the overwhelming "spiritual" experience that affected me more physically and emotionally. The mind cannot process all of that activity. It is like we are connecting to a large motherboard of a National Aeronautics and Space Administration computer when ours is a laptop made in the year 2005.

A UPC friend asked me to accompany her to another emotionally charged Christian church in a different denomination, or what was claimed to be a non-denomination. This was a big "no-no" in the UPC's eyes. That religion believed in the Trinity while the UPC believes in a duality of a God-man (in chapter 3). We were both ill in our bodies, so we hoped that another Christian pastor with reported healing abilities could help us.

The pastor who drew the large crowd was Kenneth Haggin. He prayed to God to lead him to people who needed the most healing, and then he walked up the church aisle. I waited in trust and anticipation that he would come to me.

I recalled the biblical story of the woman who suffered from a continuous menstrual disorder for 12 years. Pastors have dramatically preached about this woman's long-suffering. Because of her steadfast faith in Jesus's healing power, she believed that just by touching his clothing, she would be healed. The story concluded that Jesus felt some power leave him, so she was indeed healed.

I felt just as desperate and faithful as that woman in the Gospels, and I was ill for a longer amount of time. I was not one to run down to the pastor because he was not Jesus, and Jesus already knew me. I kept the faith as he walked up the aisle, looking at him with eager intent. I was near the center aisle, and he walked toward me. He came within a few pews of me, and then he turned away. He said that the people he touched (and who fell backwards or to the floor) were the only ones God showed him.

Wha...what?! I was almost in shock, but I more so felt slighted. However, I started to wonder if I would want to fall down with that touch. I dismissed that thought because I knew that my sickness was a difficult one—maybe I needed to be overpowered for that miraculous healing?

I invited my mother to join me the next night so that she could give me her input. I hoped that she would receive a vision to make sense of the situation and help guide me and my friend. During the church service, I often looked over at her to see if her expression had changed; I could tell when she was having a visionary experience. Finally, her eyes widened as she looked above the altar.

She saw all sorts of angels, some as demons, on opposite sides of the front of the church. All of a sudden, they broke out into war with what looked like swords. When Pastor Haggin walked up the aisle again in his nearly zombied state for the healing practice, my mother informed me that she saw "The Evil One" behind him. It was a large, ugly, horned, black figure directing him, and when Haggin laid his hands on people, that entity's power caused them to fall over. My mother also saw halos above her and my head, but there were horns on everyone else's, including little horns on my young, half-brother who accompanied us.

It was then that I deduced why Pastor Haggin never came to me when I felt most deserving of the healing. My mother and I deduced that it was obviously not the true God whom we worshipped. We never went back to another Christian church that did not follow the Bible as strictly as the UPC because we believed that they did not know the full nature of God like the UPC does.

Currently, we understand that my mother had those visions appropriate to her religious affiliation at the time. She did see real entities, but the religious types of visions such as the halos and horns mainly showed the divisiveness of our belief against theirs. We were all Christian, but there has been so much disagreement over the human or God nature of Jesus that some sects became their own religions with a different God. We believed we were going to heaven while the other Christians were going to hell. We were told that we were not in a cult, but we were also advised to view the church members as our family and to solely hang out with them in our social functions.

Our obedience to the UPC belief required more self-sacrifice. Women could not wear pants, makeup, and jewelry (except for watches), neither could we cut our hair nor teach men. Although we were bothered by the sexist commands (we did not care about the makeup or jewelry), we largely adapted (my mother more than I) because we were told that God had his reasons in the Bible for wanting these standards, and our obedience to Him would greatly reward us.

We followed our church's orders for some time because we were convinced that we had stepped through the correct door after our last step in the Catholic religion. After my mother's baptism in Jesus's name, she envisioned a veil of scales dropping from her eyes, showing us that her eyes were more open. We interpreted her vision as removing the old layer, being able to see our religion more simply and purely as directly accessing the God-man of Jesus instead of praying to intermediaries as saints and the Virgin Mary.

Our immersion into the UPC brought us renewed passion in reading and studying the Bible. We dedicated ourselves to God more than ever before, and this translated to my mom receiving more communications with more of God's power. If she was distracted with day-to-day duties, she was then forced to write prophecies. Her spiritual connection with God turned her body toward the computer or the table with a pen and paper, and her arm was pushed down to write a message.

"I was writing furiously," she recalls.

In addition to the forcefulness, there was sometimes urgency in the messages. This was especially so when the messages were for the UPC congregation and the pastors themselves! She felt scared to give the prophecies to the pastors because she did not have a close relationship with them, but she accepted her status as a vessel of God and followed through.

One particular urgent message was for me when I felt desperate for more guidance concerning my declining health, and I begged my mom for a written prophecy. She was busy with other things and did not want to do it at that moment, so I reluctantly let her be. Only minutes passed before she came into my room, but she was acting very unlike herself. She was shaking and nearly hyperventilating, speaking in a higher pitched voice and looking visibly frightened. This was her first spoken prophecy.

I wonder if my desperation "moved God" as Christians say, although I never understood how I could move a spirit let alone an almighty one, but God literally moved my mother and spoke through her. I was in my early 20s at the time, and I often put my needs before hers. Although I felt a bit badly that she was so frightened and controlled, it seemed as though it was a good experience because I really needed it. Additionally, her prophetic abilities were upgraded and on demand.

However, sometimes she just needed a break for herself. She says, "Going back over all that stuff, I remember feeling really manipulated. I don't like to think about it. I felt like I was totally someone else."

Chapter 3 provides several of my mother's unique otherworldly communications combined with the detailed story of how we came through layers of religious beliefs and experiences. At this current point in our lives, we are fully out of religion and are not affiliated with any mainstream spirituality. We both concur that this was the best decision we have ever made.

Interestingly, the steps through religion often brought my mother visions of a veiled wall dropping before her eyes, even if some steps brought us deeper into that belief system. Something was revelatory about her realizations, though, because she was eventually able to combine each new view into a bigger awareness outside of that staircase. Of course, each time we believed that we had arrived at The Truth, but this was still in the realm of faith and religion, not intelligent reasoning. The reasoning would come once we learned to assimilate our deep desire for truth into our expanding world view. When we started to put our personal desperation aside in which we were clinging onto the portions of information we learned from the Bible, the prophecies, and our church experiences, we then were able to look more objectively at ourselves. We were finally able to create a space between us and everything else, and it felt good. We felt a calm strength, and we felt free.

As my mother became more in touch with her inner self apart from a religious belief, she had a vivid dream. She saw layers of herself through which she essentially dove through water, soon arriving to the dry ground at the bottom or center of herself. She felt different after that dream, as though she arrived at what seemed like nothingness in her, but it was something. This "nothingness" precedes a belief system. It just was or is.

This revelatory experience opened up a new avenue in her prophetic ability. Sometimes she received prophecies from new sources. Other times she received energetic communications from a type of consciousness that felt different to everything else: it felt pure and calm.

My mother explains, "I didn't know what the water layer meant at the time. Maybe it was a reflection of the outer realms or 'heavens' as Christianity calls it. I know that there are water-like realms between the levels of the greater universe. There is substance there. The dream felt personal, though. I was going backwards from water to my core and getting to the source from where everything came."

I say, "Water to me is substance but also a carrier of currents, a conductive thing." She replies, "We are around 60 percent water as a creation. There is water substance in everything. All creation needs water to exist. I see it as a fluidity in the oneness with creation. It was like, 'Oh my goodness, where am I going?' as I dove down into myself and then touched the dry ground. And I walked to an arch way with another door to like another unveiling to get where I needed to be."

Days after that experience, she saw a vision of Jesus's feet with sandals and a robe on that dry ground as she was exploring this new place in herself and talking to me about it. She often gets visuals during our awesome conversations.

I immediately responded, "Why are you seeing Jesus there when you went through the layers of yourself and found you? That doesn't make sense. We are out of religion now."

That was the last time she saw any connection to Jesus in herself. We realized that the vision showed the remnant of her prior attachment to Jesus and the associated Christian and Jewish religions, for she saw those feet walk away and never return. This was her own inner process, her own vision to help her connect the dots, just as we have other ways that our unconscious and spiritual aspects communicate with our conscious mind. We have many deep-seated thoughts of which we are often not aware until our openness hopefully brings them to the surface.

I noticed her saying several slips of reference to "He" when we were starting to connect to this calm consciousness through our cores. Although it was a habit of hers, we both still had a religious attachment to our perception of ultimate truth. We put what we deeply sensed as the Source consciousness on a pedestal and assumed it was perfect as how we believed God would be—omniscient, omnipresent, and omnipotent. We knew it had to be pure and good, and we experienced it as pure and good. We understood that it would entail a measure of hierarchy because of its pure nature, but we did not yet understand that there could be order without forcefulness and rigid agendas.

Our fledgling understanding of the beginning source of creation allowed other entities to jump into my mother's opened ability of otherworldly communication. We increasingly fine-tuned our discernment to determine whether the communications were the truthful essence that we sought.

"In my limited understanding, I still got diversions from the truth, even though it was not what I wanted," she says. "After the communication came through me, I read it and then said to myself, 'wait a minute, wait a minute.'"

She did not feel settled with many of the messages because they were often connected with religious meaning, but they were at least revealing more of the picture. Coming out of the rabbit hole, we generally saw more light. However, she still felt like a conduit, so she did not delve into the messages because she did not know if she could direct the communication's course.

This was quite a big but innocent mistake of hers to make because not taking the reins of her part in communicating kept her on the sideline. She still felt she was used to only get a message. She struggled with breaking free of her conditioning as a prophet, which she undoubtedly was as the seer, writer, and speaker for God. She was taught to never be contrary to her duty, so she did not learn to speak up for the incongruities she saw in the messages. Her lack of self-development also led her to doubt her own ability to receive truthful messages.

She knew she found a deeper pathway toward truth, but she did not know how to release her prophetic abilities in order to change gears outside of the entity realm. I think this applies to nearly every person who hears from God in varying degrees of channeled and prophetic encounters. Channelers are usually entirely taken over unless they find a link or channel to an entity that allows them to control the overall conversation. Prophets can also be entirely controlled, but they are usually partially possessed to receive predictions and teachings. Either way, an entity is around, often too close for comfort. This makes it very difficult for the subjects to feel they have control over their own bodies and lives.

My mom felt entirely alone in her new awareness because she did not see it referenced in popular culture. Although I did not share her particular abilities, I had my own, so we worked together to fill in the blanks toward a clear picture.

She explains to me:

> I didn't document everything because they were often fleeting things. I was too involved in it all, in the middle of the experience. I told you right afterward or when it came back to my memory within a few days. I did not have the best short-term memory or ways to express in words my experiences, but it is good that I told you so much of it because your feedback helped me put the pieces together.
>
> I also didn't document everything because I didn't have me. It is good that I had that dream about reaching my core that night; it was pivotal for me.
>
> It took me a while to get to that surety, that knowing.

That pure conscious essence that she sensed in her core felt protected in an innate part of herself (and us all), yet it also felt separate. It was and is before and beyond any created entity, and it has no power trip. When my mother asked what its name was, it replied in energetic letters that emanated out of her core, not her mind, spelling "All That Is, The Pure Essence." It communicates that it has no name; this phrase describes it as the non-moving, pure essence consciousness in the being state. After its essence expands for creation to start, the first type of field frequency can facilitate its communications to us from the simple connection of our core. (Important note: There are prevalent misrepresentations of "All That Is" in New Age spiritualities; therefore, the All That Is, The Pure Essence communicates that this longer phrase is its accurate description. I explain its nature in chapter 6's "The Origin of Creation.")

At this new stage of communication, she did not get overwhelmed by a power that made her write down prophecies. Instead, she communicated to it internally when her mind and body were very calm. Operating from her core self was a learning experience since she was still figuring out how to do it correctly.

When I needed information, I wrote my questions on paper for her to communicate to the All That Is, The Pure Essence (ATI,TPE). She read the questions but not with her fully conscious mind. Then came the answer, but it also was not to her fully conscious mind. In other words, she saw the question on paper, and she translated it subconsciously through her body to a set-apart place of calm near her core self. This space is the ATI,TPE, which is outside of herself in a far off place but also intricately connected to the center of every part of her, including each cell. She engaged the communication, and she could turn it on or off as she chose.

She explains her exploration into this new communication style:

When I initially went within to my lower chest area, I thought the All That Is, The Pure Essence is only in my core, but I later learned that although I felt it there, it has its own space outside my experience of it. I directed the questions to this place of calm within my breast bone at the bottom of the heart, and words spilled out to me from there. It's not like before when words were plastered across my mind as though they were planted there.

I saw absence of light like an emptiness where I sense the All That Is, The Pure Essence, but then I visualized a sort of small sun that materialized words to me like a fireworks sparkler fizzes bright light. Letters would quickly spell out words to which they would then fizzle away. The type of sun must have been a transport mechanism for the ATI,TPE [in chapter 9's "Core Self" section].

I did not get elaborate messages as I did when an entity communicated with me; these are more to the point. I could see "yes" and "no" very clearly, where the "yes" feels closer to me and the "no" a little further away, probably because it wasn't resonating with the question as much.

Sometimes I got agitated because I could not decipher the words, and I felt interference; the words didn't come clearly to me in those times. I needed to calm down, so I walked away and then came back to it.

I have to be totally quiet and blocked off from any disruption in the house to maintain the correct "channel." It can be difficult, especially when I am exhausted in my body and the fatigue interferes. I can tell when I am not able to receive further communication when I get "yes" and "no" answers at the same time. It is also quite draining to stay focused for around 20 questions and answers if they require explanation. That is why it is best to get a communication in the morning instead of after a long day.

The ATI,TPE reveals that my mother is in the delta wavelength state akin to deep sleep when she communicates with it; however, she is simultaneously awake and alert. My ability approximates her experience because I can easily tap into this different state on demand; it is somewhat like a dream state but more alive with profound and accurate perceptions. The difference between me and my mother is that when I am awake, I do not have her visionary ability that can accurately exchange language. I can translate my connection with the ATI,TPE to words, but they are my words that may not accurately explain the outer realms. However, when I am about to fall asleep and am just waking up, I am more like her in the visionary state. The theta and especially the delta wavelengths are like a portal to more information beyond our reservoir of alert consciousness. It takes a unique person to be in the most calm delta wavelength as an active "channel" to the ATI,TPE, not a controlled or zombied channel to entities as the mainstream channelers and prophets.

As she became more advanced in her communications, the single fire letters began to flow fluidly to her as words and sentences on a frequency river. The river was like plasma that reached her from the expansion of the ATI,TPE via vibrating waves. Her questions went to the ATI,TPE in these waves, and its answer came back along the same river. She could tell when there was interference because the message became less clear, and the transmission reduced to static like on a radio channel.

I ask her, "Why could you not feel this static before? Or if you did, why didn't you get rid of it?"

She replies, "I felt the static and pressure before, but I didn't know how to get beyond it at that point." That made sense to me because she was stuck with what she knew before she realized something more.

She further clarifies that the pressure she felt during some communications came from outside of her so that her frequency river became narrower and restricted her breathing in the stifled transmission. The static thus reached into her energy field, which showed that the transmission was intermittently cut off from her and something was trying to manipulate her.

To get out of this (and any) interference, she goes into her core that is linked to the ATI,TPE, and she exhales her energy out past her body's energetic field. Then, she may say, "Whatever you are, go away." The process is a quick dismissal since she does not want to give entities her attention; the purpose is to push away outer energies and not get involved with them. With her rejuvenated energetic boundary protecting her, she goes back within to refocus herself. She asks if the ATI,TPE is there, and when she receives a "yes" in her familiar connection with it, she proceeds with the questions.

She says, "I am reading the questions, and then all of a sudden it's answering through me." This is a two-part process to account for the set-apart area of the ATI,TPE and the frequency transmission that expands the answer directly to her. She first will receive an answer near her core self, and it then travels to her core self and her present awareness. This process occurs seamlessly whereby it is easy to gauge the congruency within herself for a clear answer. She also often receives images along with the communicated letters. If the initial response is a little "small" and hard to see, she will simply say, "expand," and it immediately expands to her.

One day, she wanted to visually understand the process of connecting to the ATI,TPE from within herself, so she asked "Where are you?" She sensed it near her core in that still space within her lower breastplate, and then she saw that space open up into a deeper hole. The ATI,TPE links with her inner or higher self (in chapter 9's "Higher Self") and brought it further and further to where she then could sense it outside of herself as an echoed "here." Then, all of a sudden, it came forward in its expansion and stated "here" closely and strongly to her awareness. She traveled below and through layers of herself outside of dimensions.

She can see herself go down through her own tunnels and layers instead of go outside of herself to connect to the ATI,TPE. She does not travel in any sort of energetic vehicle. "This is a natural process," she says.

The ATI,TPE is the source of truth and love that we have found; we have energetically pushed and probed and not found anything past it. It consistently states that it is not a God or entity. Its answers to my mother are congruent to both of our inner selves. It gives a sensibility not found in her previous prophetic communications and the prophetic books of the Bible, for it "speaks" from the viewpoint of being apart from the mess of manipulation and creation. It is the essence of life; it fundamentally knows what is happening, and it presents information in the way that supports life and love.

Since her initial discovery of the ATI,TPE, my mother's communication process has gone through stages to get as perfectly clear as possible without interference. When she links to the ATI,TPE, she is not a prophet, but when entities rarely jump in to give her messages, she is still technically a prophet albeit against her will. Any experienced prophet will tell you that interferences are unavoidable due to the plethora of entities who exist and want to influence us. I uncover the reasons behind these entities' motives in subsequent chapters.

The key to being an aware, otherworldly communicator is to gain oneself. Since we have come out of religion, my mother has progressively become more aware of her personal energies and sense of self to where she can distinguish between manipulative and pure energies. Now, she can choose if she wishes to communicate to entities to gain specific information about important events. These empowered communications are telepathic, not prophetic, because they have boundaries.

I am very happy that she has been brave enough to leave religion and to work on gaining her full self. She also continues to link to the ATI,TPE because its pre-energy essence is sublimely beautiful and centering. She knows she is not being used like a pawn anymore, but because she is a conduit in her communications to the ATI,TPE, there were times when she forgot the distinction. I remember one such moment when I replied to her in astonishment:

How are you a pawn when the All That Is, The Pure Essence inherently connects with you? Maybe we are all conduits then, but we can choose when we want to communicate not only with the All That Is, The Pure Essence but with other aspects of ourselves. You can also choose to communicate to any entity via telepathy now that you know the difference. The point is that now you have yourself and a choice.

I think it is amazing that you get clear communication with the origin before creation, and you are treated with respect and love. What confidence and joy that should bring you!

She agreed. Sometimes we just need to bounce our thoughts and feelings on another person to get a better perspective.

My mother has often felt split between two worlds. Much of her life was either highly controlled or doing worldly tasks, preventing her from knowing who she really is or where she belongs.

She explains, "It is easier for me to ask a question for you than for myself. If I ask for myself, I feel I must act on it right away because I know it is the truth, but I am not ready for it yet. I will do it in the near future, but I still need to get to the point within me where I can relinquish the things that I am holding onto so that I can free myself to feel like I can take care of me."

She has been a caregiver her entire life and has made a habit of putting herself last. This habit involves some fear when attempting to face her painful past, and it involves low self-worth. She has primarily wanted herself but searched outside for others to give her love and comfort; however, their measure did not usually reach as far as she needed. I also have struggled with this issue, as do many people.

In a way, I know that we must become "weak" in this world in order to regain our intuitive strength because, unfortunately, what we perceived as strength was survival mode. The vulnerability happens when we tear down our walls and become softer on ourselves. Actually, that is nurturing and loving, so it is not weak at all but the very epitome of strength. Oh, what contradictions this world has taught us.

Another misperception is thinking that we cannot be independent individuals because we must put others first if we truly have love and care. The reality is that we are all individuals who are also connected; what others deserve, so do we.

My mother says, "I just want to be me. I want to be in connection with what is happening in the world. I want to be in connection with what is outside this body and what is deep in my core because that's really important. However, I've become worn out. I do want to be aware, but sometimes I just need to withdraw and refresh. I have to get the strength to deal with everything in my life. All that I went through makes me upset with myself because you think you should be smarter than that because you're in a cloud, you're in a fog, and you can't get beyond it. But religions extol us being led by God. If people want to be little slaves, then they can be little slaves."

"But, you still want to be accepted," I reply.

"I do want to be accepted. I want to have friends. I want to belong to something that I choose and something that I feel there is some kind of challenge to make me grow into more of who I am, not a slave-driven kind of life existence. If you are in a religion all your life, that is all you know. It isn't easy to get out of it; it is a fashioning towards subservience. [Note: the documentary movie *Jesus Camp* illustrates this by targeting children.] I am so glad I have that choice to not be a part of it anymore. I don't have anything constricting me. I can breathe deeply now."

When I hug her now, I can breathe in deeply as well because I feel our fullness; we feel free and present to be able to give to each other.

She continues, "When you have freedom, you want to share it. I feel like there is a vastness to it."

That to us is what love is; it is effortless, easy. Instead of acting as the saviors of the world with having to tell everyone the "truth" that religion told us to share, she says to me, "Step back and let them come to us in their time. We won't be stifling them because of always being out there in their faces. If we draw back, we let them be themselves. We give them space, and we have our space. Then, they wonder about us and contact us."

I agree and reply, "I think that in our position of coming from genuine care instead of forced care, our thoughtfulness toward others just goes out toward them, and they can naturally respond."

I remember the times when we talked about our church services, and we were trying to sort out everything we were taught. My mom's love for me has been solid, and she listened to me with care. However, while I was talking, God often told her contrary things that would bring her to step back from me, disagree, and even start an argument. She often believed me while I questioned and evaluated the protocol, and she knew my heart. However, she put God first and followed His commands, giving her much internal conflict as well as external conflict from us fighting a few times a week.

It is a very rare occasion if we have an argument now. My mom is almost always completely present in her engagements and connection with me. Her generous love that she has given to me has come back full circle toward herself, as she so rightfully deserves, and this in turn allows her to love even more.

Although she often felt weak and used by God, she has shown abundant strength in standing up to the threatening forces that struck her awareness.

Just imagine seeing real-life monsters on a daily basis and being able to look them in the face and then easily fall asleep at night.

Recently on her way into her workplace, she saw a line of very tall, reptile-looking demons standing in front of the door. She told them, "step aside," and two of them did so that she could pass. When she turned to see them behind her, they squinted their eyes, showing their disgust and evil energy toward her. Although they were imposing figures, they still stepped aside and caused her no harm. This is because she was one with her own energies that keep her separate from them.

If I would have seen them, I probably would have freaked out temporarily because I am not as physically grounded in myself; however, I am gaining internal strength daily due to my awareness of truth and who I am. I would love to have the same ability as my mother to communicate to the ATI,TPE, but I am fine to not see other entities as she does. I feel their presence, which is enough for me. I have my own abilities that are useful and valid. Actually, everyone has measures of extrasensory abilities that can demystify otherworldly phenomena. For instance, I can "see" across the world and into the universe and beyond by sensing energies of things and gaining a type of visionary understanding of a very big picture.

My mother and I have learned to expand an energetic shield around us from our core connection to the All That Is, The Pure Essence; it helps ground us in stressful times. However, most of the time we feel a natural flow between us and the ATI,TPE that helps us in everyday life. We have chosen to be separate from the religious realm of entities, and we continually aim to act out of our true selves; therefore, our different level of operation most often prevents them from affecting us because our preferred energies do not resonate with theirs.

My mother and I are the perfect team. She gets communications, and I largely weed out any incongruity and probe most of the topics. Together, we connect the dots toward proper applicability. I am very grateful for her, not only for her abilities, but also for the beautiful person she is.

I do not care anymore if people may think we are strange. What is perceived as "normal" in the world of religions is actually only a piece of the greater puzzle that is unfortunately deemed esoteric or unknowable. Our right to life should not be a mystery for anyone, especially if only a select few must become initiated in private to find out more truth! I declare transparency for all, because then we will stop unfairly judging others and ourselves due to lack of understanding. My mother and I finally feel normal because practically everything makes sense now. Although this sense is utterly profound and mind-blowing, it is very simple at the same time.

CHAPTER 2

My Quest for Healing

I received my first prophecy from my mother when I was 13 years old. I suppose it was a surprise to me in its new experience, but I knew she had an extraordinary relationship with our Catholic God in that she could communicate with Him daily. I was very depressed, so when she suggested that she could get me a prophecy to potentially ease my mind, I nervously but excitedly read the message.

The prophecy gave me comfort and hope toward meeting great people in the next two years of my young life. The "Lord Jesus" said to me, "I love you very much—there have been a lot of things happening in your life, and I want to tell you that I have been with you through them all." Jesus addressed my obsession with a popular band member at the time, saying I would go to England in the "near future" and that I should "keep up on the band's whereabouts in the year to come—be open to my lead—I know how much [said band member's name] means to you." This fed my young mind's fantasy and sense of happiness.

This personalized letter from God gave me joy. I proudly stated to my junior high school friend that I got a prophecy from God, but she looked at me as if I was a freak. I did not understand her reaction because I thought I had the most prized possession on the planet. Since I grew up with my mother's abilities and my own lesser ones, it seemed normal enough to me that a supposedly good friend of mine would accept it.

At least my sister, who was an uninterested Catholic at the time, attested to the validity of our mother's ability. One morning as mom was writing a prophecy for me, my sister walked in and started a conversation with her. Her hand continued to write while she looked up and answered my sister.

I had no self-esteem as an adolescent. I became angry at my mother because she could not rescue me and fill my void; in fact, I often felt like I was a burden who should be eradicated. Therefore, God was the only answer for me. My Catholic belief actually saved me at that time because I thought I would go to hell if I committed suicide; the fear of that consequence is what kept me alive. When I probe the situation thoroughly, I know that I intuitively did not want to die, but I did not know where I could find peace. I felt completely stuck; the negativity within me did not have a way out, so it was slowly killing me.

My mom's prophecies and our extrasensory abilities solidified our belief in God as being more tangible than what was immediately around us. We were thorough believers toward the Catholic/Christian God through Jesus as the only truth, although we did not understand the ins and outs of the religion. As long as God was talking to my mother, and we were dutiful Catholics, why did we need to understand more? My confused but steadfast belief in a perfect Father and Son, or the Trinity, or just a perfect Father, or the Father and Holy Spirit since Jesus was seen as human in some way, gave me hope toward achieving freedom from the painful childhood I experienced.

I grew up walking on eggshells around my father. He not only abused my mother but also me and my sister after my parents divorced when I was 5 years old. I had to grow up quickly when I was a child, so I felt like a miniature adult, sucking up my emotions during drop-offs and pick-ups that occurred as often as every night of the week between houses or apartments. My sister buried her head in fiction books while I just needed a confidant who would give me comfort and safety so I would not feel so vulnerable and alone. I endured severe abuse by my father's body and scare tactics, so I relied on my belief in a perfect being to comfort my displaced sense of identity.

Apart from this turmoil, I had strange experiences of my own as a child. At 3 years old, I saw a little throne with Jesus sitting upon it. I saw a demonic figure creep across the shower curtain when I was standing still and frightened in the bathroom at 6 years old. During that year, I drifted off to sleep with what I perceived was a choir of angels singing the most beautiful sounds that made me feel like I was in heaven. I stayed fast asleep all the while a gunshot next door awoke my sister in my room and kept my family up the rest of the night.

I was always sensitive to the feelings of my loved ones and to the energy of my surroundings. I know this happens within abusive households, but I came into this world as a highly sensitive being. The abuse actually stifled that sensitivity instead of enhanced it. It blocked my internal meridian energies and left me feeling tormented and confused instead of clear in myself to distinguish my goodness from the crazy that was projected onto me.

My open ability toward the supernatural halted when I was 6½ years old (it resumed in my mid-teens). I had no idea why, but my focus shifted toward my body with bed-wetting and stomach problems that led me to the hospital. I was surrounded by family tension before this, but obviously something became worse in order for me to react physically. My mother suspected it was sexual abuse because my father raped her in their marriage, and I had bruises on my neck along with a noticeable change in behavior. I denied it at that time. I possibly did not understand her questions because of how they were phrased to me. I also was left alone with that man, often sleeping in his bed while my sister was in another bed. If anything of the sort did happen, I was protecting my life by not telling anyone. Naturally, I felt I also had to protect my mom because he gave her death threats if he could not see me and my sister.

Soon afterward, the court hearings commenced, and he was given joint custody. If only I was allowed to have a voice at that young age in court, but if my mother was too afraid as an adult to speak up, I am not sure I would have been brave enough either. I only wanted to live with her, but I could not. She has since whole-heartedly apologized and told me that her self-esteem was not strong enough after having been married to that man.

My biological father is supposedly a different person now from what I hear, but he also does not own up to the most horrible things he has done. This gives me the message that he still retains a portion of that persona even if he does not act upon it.

While living with him during my adolescence, my health progressively declined. I had all the classic symptoms of chronic fatigue and immune dysfunction syndrome (CFIDS) that were not yet understood by the medical community; instead, I was labeled psychosomatic. I bounced from one doctor to the next until at age 22 I luckily found a physician who tested my blood for Epstein-Barr. This herpes family virus is an indicator for CFIDS. When the Epstein-Barr titers showed eight times the maximum acceptable level, I finally had proof that my symptoms were not "all in her head." Yes, a part of the illness was created by my distraught mind and emotions that weakened my immunity's stress response, but I was also a chemically sensitive person by default. I had to become diligent in diet and lifestyle to create a healthier body. I also had all the classic bodily pain and sensitivities of fibromyalgia. This pain was difficult to endure along with the sore throats I got (later, diet and managed stress helped curb these symptoms), but what was most difficult for me was the brain fog.

Everything seemed unreal to me, including myself. I could not accurately tell where I ended and where something else began. When I looked around me, the air between me and an object would seem as a thick fog I had to push through in order to focus upon the object. When I touched my skin, I felt like it was not mine. I could hear the buzz of the refrigerator echo through my head as though it was a part of my inner ear vibration. Like a race car on a track, my mind swirled around in circles, seeing more inside me than I could effectively translate to the outside. I felt lost within a body and a fuzzy mind. It was especially scary when night came, for my mind fell deeper into the sleepiness of its unconscious state, and there the fears came out to further unground me.

While other people were enjoying their young adult life and starting their cherished careers, my 20s were nothing what my ambitious and linear-thinking teenage mind had expected. I barely finished enough classes to graduate from university; I returned home depressed and sick, wondering if I had any youth to live while I felt as though I had the body of a 90-year old. I sought truth about healing in an array of books, but the Bible and religion dominated my focus.

At age 28, I moved to Arizona to spread my wings, but I never expected the turn of events that followed. One day, I ran into a chiropractor at a health food store who was doing free Neuro Emotional Technique (NET) introductory sessions that use muscle testing to see the body's response to certain words. A few weeks prior, I first heard about him from a fellow community member when I told her about my chronic fatigue, but her advice went in one ear and out the other. Many people throughout my life gave me helpful but not so helpful advice about my illnesses, so although I was completely open to going forward and healing, a part of me also resigned itself to the opposite. My quest for truth thankfully showed itself because it brought me to the right place at the right but possibly overdue time.

The chiropractor started the demonstration by having me put out my arm while saying, "My name is Sally." My arm lost strength when he pressed it downward. When I next said my name, it remained solid. He then checked aspects of my physical structure and accurately assessed some physical problems. This was intriguing to me, so I started private sessions with him that ended up lasting over three months. The muscle testing in conjunction with explorative sayings brought out old unconscious memories and thought patterns that correlated to blockages in my body. Some of my responses seemed way out there because I was a Christian at the time, but when I automatically cried to what my unconsciousness told me, I knew it had to be true.   ·

I uncovered that I had been raped several times by my father, progressively getting worse since age 5½ and tapering off at age 7. It took me a full three months to undo the layers that protected me from remembering those incidents because they were deeply buried within my body and mind. When I overcame the shock and researched testimonials of incest victims, this clinched it—all the bulimia and compulsive overeating, rage, no self-esteem, insomnia, social anxiety, depression, suicidal thoughts, and physical illness had a reason. I learned I was perfectly normal to react and feel as I have all those years! However, this was just the beginning. I started to have clear flashbacks as my inner child finally felt safe to be heard.

According to Babette Rothschild's excellent book, *The Body Remembers*, it is a biologically natural phenomenon for children to scatter traumatic memories throughout their brain and their body. They do not have the cognitive development to be able to effectively handle these horrific experiences.[2] Between my formative ages of 5 and 7 years old, I could barely formulate words to match those experiences, so of course my most active part of the brain during that entire time, the amygdala, took center stage. The amygdala is the reptilian brain that corresponds to primitive functions, such as sleep, eating, and the fight and flight response. My amygdala was overactive, and messages were convoluted, which directly affected my developing neural pathways and made me grow into a fearful, angry, and confused person.

This feeling state overrode my beautifully engaging sensitivity. It consequentially circumvented proper brain development by escalating the excitable beta waves and dulling my frontal lobe, as later brain scans proved. My cognition struggled seeing past a tired and fuzzy brain, and I easily lost motivation to try harder when I already felt defective. My body was acting suboptimal, and my negative, emotionally charged mind kept reinforcing my "defectiveness." Naturally, my body became increasingly stressed, sick, and in pain. My body also kept the memory alive. Although cells replenish, the residual energy of the abused region continued to give me strange, sexualized sensations.

Cognitive behaviorists could not help me at this primal level, so I knew I had to face it head on and work through the flashbacks. I saw a psychologist for Eye Movement Desensitization and Reprocessing (EMDR) treatments that mimic rapid eye movement (REM) in sleep and monitored my stress response to the images that came up. I would very often have one or two intense nightmares per night over the years. I realized that I had extreme stress as post-traumatic stress disorder. What I uncovered in my EMDR sessions was absolutely disgusting and horrifying; I did not understand that those images could be physically possible toward a young child.

By that point, my father was telling me that I was fabricating the sexual abuse because my NET practitioner gave me a false memory. There is actually a group of people (usually the perpetrators and their families) who brashly deny sexual abuse accusations because the victims come out later in life as I did. To make matters worse, California law has a statute of limitations of seven years after the incident, as though it is incorrect and unnatural for the undeveloped child's brain to scatter traumatic experiences when both science and logic prove otherwise.

Regardless of all the naysaying, I learned from experienced psychologists and social workers that what I did remember was sufficient, and I did not have to stress myself out to know the ins and outs (sorry about the choice of phrase, but it applies) of the abuses. The EMDR sessions showed me that my adult state was separate enough from my child state, so I could face that old fear and stand strong in the fact that it is not applicable to my life anymore.

The intensity of emotion that was locked up in my body for most of my life continued to make me feel ill as well as sometimes accident-prone. It is especially difficult with mental dissociation that has not fully gone away because of how my brain developed, but I continually employ what I have learned to keep me releasing the last remnants of the abuses in order to become increasingly integrated and grounded in the present. Thankfully, progressive and skilled practitioners, including a naturopathic doctor with specialization in homeopathy, believe that I can gain ample physical healing. I am doing all I can toward that hopeful achievement, but I am also living out of self-acceptance in my current state because I love myself, finally.

Instead of the founding psychoanalyst Sigmund Freud's argument that the ego state becomes developed at 18 years of age, I rather think it becomes mature in the early 30s because it takes a while for the prefrontal cortex to become fully developed. Actually, neural associations continue to change and grow. Age 28 was the time when my repressed memories started to fully come out. It was as though my entire brain was finally able to integrate all neural pathways that had carried and displaced the transmissions from my experiential reactions.

Babies are born complete in the sense that they contain the architectural blueprint of expansion that will occur, yet environmental stimuli greatly affect the person's psychological, social, and physical development. If a baby is continually ignored and not held while crying, for example, and this neglect continues throughout childhood, then the child learns to not speak up for oneself, to distrust others, and to have low self-worth. With extreme physical neglect, the baby could die. The house of the body must be sufficiently maintained to endure the weather and environment around it; no small, straw house can withstand a hurricane.

My house felt like it was not mine since it was abused so horribly. Even to this day, I struggle feeling fully in touch with my body—when I focus on the dissociated feeling and brain fog, I can see the remnant of low self-worth. How can I be one with my body if I do not like part of it? I always knew that I had to release the old, incorrect junk to repair the cracks in my house, but when I was a Christian, I thought the only way I could change was if God gave me the fully healed body and mind as a miracle. I believed that I would be healed in an instant since God can do anything.

Religion taught the idea of perfection—a perfect God and a perfectly obedient Christian. It brought me back to feeling as that perfect daughter who had to please her father. I had to become as perfect as possible so that I would be favored by God. I initially thought if I was not healed, then it was my fault from not doing all the right things. I eventually learned that I was doing everything within my power, so it turned out that the miracle of instant change was rather a long, drawn-out process.

If I had paid more attention to living as well as I could with an imperfect body instead of wishing that I would be totally changed from one extreme to another—as the biblical analogies of sinner to saved and dead to alive tell us—then I could have acted productively with my new self-love that allowed imperfection. However, the Bible and Church taught me to pray fervently and wait to receive my wish, relying upon the "awesome" God for my healing. My mother's prophecies reinforced this message.

In order to receive God's perfect gift, the Bible teaches to follow Jesus first. Therefore, I had to figure out who Jesus was.

For all Catholics and the majority of Christians who are either dualistic or Trinitarian in their view about Jesus, they believe he was human in his body. *Human* comes from the Latin *humus*, meaning Earth, ground. An organic, Earthly life form is fragile and limited, for it goes back to the Earth in a relatively short amount of time. Jesus died but then resurrected, so it is unclear if he was actually human. The First Book of Corinthians chapter 15, verses 42-48 further muddle the issue because Apostle Paul claimed that Jesus is entirely heavenly. Verse 47 states, "The first man is of the earth, earthy: the second man is the Lord from heaven."

The Bible and virtually all major religions add the label of "sinful" to the human body, where there is disgust attached to humanity and its limited nature. If Jesus was human, then this means he was not perfect either, so how could his way for me be the way toward full health when his human body would never attain it? What would the Father God do to me that would really heal me, then?

When I was a fundamental Christian, I had to be baptized in Jesus's name; however, what was the point to take on his flesh when it was just like mine? Christianity told me that baptism is a symbolic act of my faith in Jesus as a higher but equal being of some sort, and by my following in his footsteps, I would reap his glory. However, would that glory only occur after I die because that is when his did? Is this whole Earthly life just a wretched existence with a defective or even wicked body that cannot be trusted? If the body reacts a certain way, just don't trust its instincts because your mind must be somewhere else in faith?

I so desperately needed to view my body as "good" and as the physical extension of my inner beauty. Being an incest survivor gives more weight to seeing my body in this way because I was not at fault in any way, so I should have no shame toward my body. What happened to me started the self-hatred—it was nothing that I did toward myself.

After realizing this truth, I finally felt that I am a good person, especially since I got in touch with my inner child, and children have an inherent purity and goodness. Accordingly, my body is part of my person, so it should be equally good, which means as healthy as possible and united in healthful wholeness with the rest of me. To be "good" and imperfect is not a contradiction because we can do an even better than good job living this difficult life.

However, the frequently touted Scripture that says "[t]he heart *is* deceitful above all *things*, and desperately wicked" conveys the message that my inner self is not good (Jeremiah 17:9). According to this view, my body had no alternative but to reflect that sinfulness and be broken and sick.

Our thoughts and beliefs are the catalyst to our bodies. Catholics in the Opus Dei sect who whip themselves daily as a reminder of the stripes of sin that Jesus carried to the cross are incorrectly viewing themselves—they put the body first when our thoughts are what need correcting. I think there is an underlying reason these people scourge themselves: they believe they are filthy humans inside and out, and they deserve the punishment!

I did not deserve any punishment, for I was entirely innocent in the crimes that were committed against me. I was searching for a way to solidify this truth that I knew about myself, to redeem the innocence that I knew I had regardless of being born in a human body, but I did not yet know where to find redemption except after death as Jesus supposedly did. I am here to live, not to die! My body, although it can be seen as an extension of my inner self, is also equally necessary to me. I have wanted full life in all parts of me, but where could I find it? Was this answer found in Christianity or any religion?

A few of my questions to religions, especially Christianity, are: Why vilify the human body when it is gives us this Earthly life? If the body is treated as nearly nothing more than a sexual object to create offspring, why is it prized by God as the figurative bride to Jesus? With Jesus becoming "one" with our bodies, would this entail us also becoming "one" with God? Why then would God need us when He is God, and He has a sufficient amount of His own followers, the angels?

It seems that our physical body is a lot more important than we realize. In the following chapters, I will unravel the "mystery" of our body, soul, and spirit. I will also explore whether full healing in these bodies can actually occur and what we really are in our composition. I did not uncover these answers until after I discovered what was really guiding (and preventing) us in my mother's prophecies. I must first share this process of my coming out of religion via scrutiny into her prophecies, the Bible, and my church experiences.

CHAPTER 3

Wading Through Prophecies to the Dry Ground

My mother received countless verbal and written prophecies since she was 20 years old. God would talk clearly to her understanding; she could not determine the frequency of communications when they all happened effortlessly, several times a day. A prophet has an intimate relationship with his or her God. The Bible taught us to strive for this relationship in which we have total dependence upon God because then we would be most blessed by Him.

I present my experiences with her coveted ability as well as my insights to see if we really were blessed as dutiful Christians. We were guided, supported, and corrected along the way in our growing relationships with God. We were properly taught to rely on the Bible above all else, but as my mother's prophecies initially confirmed and supplemented the Bible, we viewed her messages as great tools to further our personal growth. I especially relied upon the personal messages to me; they were more valuable to me than gold.

The prophecies that I received in my teenage years guided me toward loving myself, Jesus, and God the Father. They mainly addressed my broken heart over boys and my deteriorating health while God endeavored to create a relationship with me. I was often directed to read specific Scriptures and pray. At 13 years old, after the first prophecy raised my hope toward meeting a musical band member, I was given a change of direction that initially devastated me.

> He will <u>not</u> write you personally at this time—I know that disappoints you, but, do not fear, my dear daughter, Theresa—I will send you a real-true-to-life boy in the very near future, who will be very kind to you. He will respect you for who you are and will want to be with you whenever possible. He will be very good-looking, sweet and thoughtful. Know that I love you, Theresa, for you have accepted My Son into your heart. Be strong, my daughter—the future will be bright and full of surprises and especially <u>health</u> for you. Do not fret about [that man]. You will meet a very special boy that I have sent to be in your life very soon. I always watch over you and protect you even though you don't see me.

What beautiful words, but I did not experience any such boy nor did I experience good health. This prophecy states that God loved me because I first accepted Jesus. This did not sound like unconditional love to me, but because my biological father gutted and rearranged the concept of love to me, I wanted so much to believe that the Almighty Father truly loved me.

When I was 15, I received the following prophecy:

> Read 1 Thessalonians Chapter 3 verses 9-13, Plea for growth in holiness. Now that you have read these words, my child—you <u>are</u> still and always will be <u>my child</u>!
>
> Theresa, you are my beloved—you are kind, thoughtful, caring, loving, very earnest in your endeavors to do right—I have given you all these things, daughter. You still doubt my presence, child, because you do not possess the exact same gifts that your mother does.
>
> I come to my children in different and beautiful ways. I come to you as a beam of light—when you see darkness, child, pray earnestly for the evil one to flee, for he is trying desperately to win your soul over, create doubt in your mind—take you from me, my precious—rebuke Satan, child! He knows you are vulnerable—I have placed a special angel at your side to protect you—call upon his assistance—his name is Lor—I bestow upon you a special gift of vision, feeling, reaching inside other people to the core of their character—you must pray to me when you become troubled at what you see and what you hear.
>
> You have been given very precious gifts, my child, ones your mother does not possess.
>
> [A certain boy] has come to know many anti-Jesus philosophies—he is searching also—be his friend—I will give you the words to use when you talk to him—call him—comfort his most inner being with the words of 1 Peter Chapter 4 verses 7-11. I love you my daughter. Be at peace—request my light to guide your way.

✳

Reading this prophecy and others of this sort through today's lens gives me a strange energy as though they are drawing me in toward another will. That was the entire point of being a Christian, though. After I got this prophecy, I questioned whether this Lor angel was someone to whom I should pray. I did it only a couple of times and then stopped. Although I was young, impressionable, and deeply hurting back then, I did not feel comfortable praying to an entity that I did not know. I wondered why God told me to do it when He could do everything on His own. I did not fully understand why I needed to pray to Mary as other prophecies and the Catholic Church told me to do, but I felt okay enough to do that because I knew about her. I suppose that Lor would be like any other saint or entity to whom I would pray, but I still needed to know something about that entity.

At 16 years old, I received another prophecy:

Isaiah 40:31, 41:10
To my dearest child in Jesus:

Hello, my daughter; these are trying times for my people. The world is quickly turning toward my adversary more each day and I am very angry. I have given my people every opportunity to turn towards my son, but they have chosen to do what they want instead. You are very special, Theresa—I love you very much. I have given you many special talents, and especially love for my children and mankind in general. You have had a difficult life, child, and I am sorry it has made you miserable, and not trusting in my Son. Many of my daughters and sons have been given "crosses" to bear in this life, and have learned, against their will, to bear them in My Name. That is what I am asking you to do—bear your frailties, physical, mental and emotionally, with the knowing that I am always with you to carry you through all that you endure. I know that I have given you a defect in your leg, a fragile spine, sinus problems to endure; etc; but, my darling daughter—have also given you beauty, intelligence, a loving heart and strong spirit in My Son, which surpasses everything in this life.

If you choose to follow me in this life, Theresa, I will heal your frailties, give you all that you need to be content and happy. You have a earthly father that is having difficulty coping in this life, and you must be a comfort and understanding toward him, for I have given you [my father's name]. Your father has great strength, and also some weaknesses.* If all were like Our heavenly Father, there would not be a reason for mankind or redemption!

Keep in mind, My daughter—Isaiah 41:10—Fear not, I am with you; be not dismayed. I am your God. I will strengthen you, and help you, and uphold you with my right hand of justice.

With your prayers, of which I hear every one of them, I will protect and take care of [another boy I liked], for you have a special "brotherhood" with him.

I give you peace now, and always—be open to my leads,

Theresa, and all will be well.

Thus says the Lord Jesus
⚹

* God knew what my father did to me, yet I was supposed to comfort him? This is beyond anything acceptable as self-sacrifice.

At 18 years old, the prophecy my mother gave me begins as "Dearest child in Jesus, my Son:" and says that he gave me many gifts, including wisdom.

Theresa—Satan knows your power, gifts and talents—you can be very valuable to His Work, but I have blocked His Way since your birth. Your ailments are a result to His continual harassments upon you—Only You Can Renounce Satan—release your chains, Theresa—come to Me, My love; your mother has suffered many thorns and pain because of this. Child do not fight me any longer—join the followers of Jesus. Be my child totally—I love you sincerely and devotedly, child. Go now and be at peace.

Thus says the Lord Jesus
⚹

Sections of a prophecy when I was 19:

First and foremost, seek my face. By this, I mean to say the Our Father everyday and begin to mouth the words every where [sic] you go. I will make myself ever present to you—Be at peace and have special quiet time with me, without music or sounds of any type—make yourself open to my Holy Spirit and he will teach you and you will hear my voice—I speak to all those who seek my face—you will hear My Voice in the wind, in my word and in my people—see with my eyes, Theresa—you are a very loving, caring, Christian young lady—I have fashioned you so.

Make sure that this night will be devoted to prayer to Our Lady—she is my mother, and as a woman with many trials and lamentations, she experienced as a young woman, many great decisions to be made.* She can help you if you summon her help—

My daughter, if you ask in My Name, you shall receive; ask in My Name only.

Your heavenly Father
Who loves you,
⚹

* This sentence was fragmented, either meaning the transmission

was not clear at that moment, or God gave a mistake. I lean toward the second option because the force upon my mother overpowered her faculties. I was confused by the grammatical mistakes in some of the prophecies because I thought God was omniscient and perfect.

The above prophecies showed the interchange of the Father and the Son, meaning that they were speaking as the same being, and the Holy Spirit was somehow identical also. In the same way that they are "one," the prophecies were preparing to fashion me into a similar oneness with God by becoming His child or follower totally. The first step was to seek His face and hear His voice.

When I was 19 years old, I prayed to God daily, but I was still confused with who and what this God was when He directed me to pray to His son and other people. This was a very difficult year for me. My body shut down from my compromised immunity and the near deadly case of Valley Fever that I acquired from ground excavations in the area. I also was still suffering from the rape against me just two years prior by a fellow American during our poorly supervised senior class trip in Mexico. I did not know if I could handle my body and feelings any further. I did not feel protected or loved by God and/or Jesus in any of this. Gosh, if I did not suppress the childhood rapes at that time, then I quite possibly would have checked myself off the planet or at least became a drug addict.

Since God and/or Jesus did not seem to love or help me, I decided to turn to Satan to see if he would help. At this point, my faith was low, but the following week-long experiment brought it back up in full swing! Immediately after I called upon the name of Satan, I felt a dark presence with me. Initially, I did not care about this dark energy because I was already negative within myself; the extra negativity allowed me to feel the anger that I had repressed. However, I felt and acted like a different person. My friends noticed the change and did not like it. I kept to myself, paid enough attention to others by snapping at them, and acted coldly toward everything outside and within me. I never cried. I noticed a few times that my jaw was clenched and my teeth were visible like an animal pre-fight.

When I realized that I never had a moment without sensing that dark entity next to me, I finally told it to go away. I immediately called upon Jesus and God in tears. I decided that to cover the bases, I prayed to both Jesus and God no matter my misunderstanding because having them around felt better than Satan. I deduce that my associations about them made me feel better because it was my intent for more goodness.

Catholic and Christian Interpretations of Godhead and God

I believed God to be an ethereal being, not human, who clearly was a fully conscious, person-type being because God is referred to as a He and a Father—a super type of man. However, I was confused: as a male, this implies a finite person, but this God-man is believed to be omnipresent and called the Alpha and Omega, the beginning and the end (Revelation 1:8). How could this super-man be everywhere at the same time? Catholicism never taught me about telepathy if that was how God would do it.

My interpretation as a Catholic was that the Holy Spirit is like the spiritual arms and legs of God that could make Him go everywhere. It is a measured substance of His Spirit that can reach everyone while God is still intact as His mysterious self. God is so massive, so beyond us that we cannot understand His nature, so He has to send out lesser parts of Himself to reach us on our level. However, this view does not explicitly define the relationship between God and the Holy Spirit as part of the Trinity, and it becomes more muddled when Jesus is involved.

Believers of Trinitarianism have two views about equality and hierarchy somehow merged into one. One view is a co-equal, triune family, which means the Holy Spirit would not be a portion of the mighty God, and Jesus would not be less than God. They are separate entities who share equally important functions. The Holy Spirit is depicted as a separate ethereal being that goes everywhere to carry out the wishes of the Father; it is an intermediary between spirits not unlike Jesus as the intermediary for the human body.

Note the word that Catholics use: triune. This is the defining concept of Trinitarianism where three somehow equals one. Catholics say *Godhead* to define this merged identity (Colossians 2:9 and Acts 17:29). This identity is not truly merged due to God being at the head with Jesus and the Holy Spirit beneath Him just as the sign of the cross symbolizes their statuses. In addition to 3=1 not computing mathematically, the three roles are not equally important. Catholics and Christians in general say that Jesus is a human who is less than God, and Jesus is finite whereas God is not. This is the second view about Trinitarianism because there is a definite belief of hierarchy that goes against a co-equal relationship.

Another flaw of reasoning is with the separate entity concept. Catholics say that the Holy Spirit is the breath of God (John 15:26) and Jesus (John 20:22), thereby leading me to my original interpretation that has the Holy Spirit as a segment of God. The Holy Spirit is not called the Holy Ghost in Catholicism like it is in some Christian factions, for that makes it bound to the death and resurrection of Jesus. The Holy Spirit existed before Jesus died, which his baptism by John the Baptist confirmed in a vision of it symbolizing a dove descending upon him. These references to the Holy Spirit show it as a portion of God's spirit that filled Jesus and helped raise him from the dead.

It is clear how unclear the Catholics delineate entities and their roles. The concept of "oneness" is not only present in Catholicism but in spiritualities throughout the world. Oneness does not entail something that is "one and the same" with others. It represents a collaborative relationship in similarity and fairness, but in religions with implied hierarchy by rule, the godly hierarchy preempts the little guy.

When I was in university, a fellow student told me that the word *Trinity* is not in the Bible. I argued somewhat but stopped because she was assured of this, and I did not actually know. Her claim stuck in the back of my mind for about one year until I researched it myself and found she was correct. Why did I worship this trinity of separate but equal beings or conversely two slightly less beings or aspects of God when this cohesive term was not actually in the Bible? By this point, I grew tired of the Catholic Church rituals. Although the sermons added thought to my already introspective nature, I needed more substance from the Bible to help feed my increasingly mature mind.

After I left university, I was dwindling away at home, feeling as though I could not be a part of society due to how sick and depressed I felt. There were times when I was too weak and in pain to walk, so my mother had to quit her job to take care of me for several months. This was definitely not how I wanted to start off my post-university life.

Soon afterward, she received direction from God to go to a religious bookstore near our house. She started talking with the lady behind the counter about medical issues and family. Upon hearing about my struggles, the lady invited my mother and me to her church. She said that her pastor could heal me because he is a prophet who gets powerful messages from God.

My mom and I were in desperate need for something more, so we agreed to attend this new church, the United Pentecostal Church (UPC). It was like a complete 180 from the Catholic Church because of its loud music and preaching, dancing, and emotionalism with people crying out loud and waving their arms in the air. They actively put their entire selves into their belief. Although I thought it was too much show (I did not need to yell at God when He was supposedly everywhere), I wanted to put all of myself into the truth, which they claimed to have, so I participated.

My mom was always energetically and telepathically overtaken by an entity when she wrote out prophecies and heard voices, but upon joining this type of church of hellfire and brimstone preaching, God became more possessive of her. As I mentioned in chapter 1, God controlled her entire body to tell me a message after we became immersed in the UPC, but this type of occurrence was rare. More frequently, her body and right arm were pushed toward the table or computer to write messages. She could not resist its power because these messages were a big deal, not only sent to us but now to the church, as the following prophecies indicate.

December 7, 1997
To my children,

Beware, for the Evil One is sweeping the land with his demons to take souls wherever and whenever he can. Oh! My children, Beware—there is very little time to change and be mine. Come to me, my little children, for I am calling you to myself for the time is eminent. Do not waste time doing the things of this world—they are meaningless. Repent of your sins! Repent of your sins! For the time is near—I love you, my child, you have been faithful to me all your life. Do not hesitate to tell the church that they must turn from evil, be baptized in <u>My</u> Name of Jesus and <u>My</u> <u>Name</u> <u>Only</u>; the Evil One is coming with every power imaginable—he has several times tried to divide my Christian homes but will not succeed in the end.

My people, beware for he will come for even my precious children and will not stop at anything.

My child, tell the people they must fast for the world today and pray as a unit for the sake of others. Time is short.

I will come upon this land, on my people with a swift sword upon those who do not repent of their sins.

Do this in love, my child and let them know that I am <u>God</u>!

February 6, 1998
Oh, My People:

Do not despair! The time is coming when My Spirit will overshadow the land, and I will take My children home. I Love You, My children. Know that I am with you in this terrible time. My Spirit cries because of all the evil penetrating every facet of life on Earth. I loathe evil—Do not be discouraged, for I come with My armies to destroy the enemy. He will not win. It is my solemn promise to you, My children, that I will take you from this place and raise you up to live in Heavenly Places. I cry in My Spirit for all those who do not love Me, or give Me their obedience and their attention—they do not know the devastation that awaits them. Oh! My People! This is time of My Revival in the churches—heed My call and come to Me, and I will give you rest and peace in My Son. I Love You! Oh! How I Love You! Be at peace. I will make Myself known to you in the Most Profound Ways.

Come drink of the cool water in My Garden! It will save the soul that has been longing for love of the Sacred Heart of Jesus-My Heart, My Spirit, which overflows with goodness and kindness towards all. Be it known that My Spirit will come and overshadow the evil of the One Enemy of this World, and he will not succeed. Be it known, thus says the Mighty Lord God.

These prophecies were speaking to a church that does not believe in the Trinity. The UPC believes in dualism, meaning that Jesus has no human spirit and is only God as spirit encased in a human body. The official creed of the United Pentecostal Church International includes the following statements:

> The one true God, the Jehovah of the Old Testament, took upon Himself the form of man, and as the Son of man, was born of the virgin Mary. As Paul says "and without controversy great is the mystery of Godliness: God was manifest in the flesh, justified in the Spirit, seen of angels, preached unto the Gentiles, believed on in the world, received up into glory" (1 Timothy 3:16).
>
> We believe that, "...in Him (Jesus) dwelleth all the fulness of the Godhead bodily" (Col. 2:9). "For it pleased the Father that in Him should all fulness dwell" (Col. 1:19). Therefore, Jesus in His humanity was man; in His deity was and is God. His flesh was the lamb, or the sacrifice of God. He is the only mediator between God and man. "For there is one God, and one mediator between God and men, the man Christ Jesus" (1 Timothy 2:5).[3]

The prophecies felt more potent to my mother because of her more focused belief in one God who did not share His glory with only a human. The incorruptible, full nature of God was somehow able to put on a corruptible body. It was never explained logically except to say that the body was like clothing. The UPC likes to refer to the vague Scripture of First Timothy chapter 3, verse 16 in an attempt to state everything and nothing at the same time.

What was important to us was that God was physically more of Jesus than how Catholics believe, so our faith increased toward God in this religion. I am certain that this belief we gained toward Jesus allowed God to more powerfully affect us because our worship was less divided and more direct. With less division and more intent, it seems that our identities were merging with God's in a sort of brainwashing or possession. We did not need the

Catholic Pope to stand in for Jesus because we serious Christians were being groomed to become His literal hands and feet after Jesus. If this is the concept of oneness that Catholics believe the Godhead represents, then it is strong indeed.

The above two prophecies confirm the dualist belief of the UPC by saying that Jesus's heart is God's heart, and we must be baptized in Jesus's name instead of the Trinitarian titles of Father, Son, and Holy Spirit. Everything that screamed Catholic in the previous prophecies was no more, but the tone and language consistently stayed the same; therefore, we knew the messages were from the same God.

At this time, we felt confident that we were being led further into truth. We did not think that any of the numerous prophecies were stated after-the-fact to keep us as followers. How could we allow that "evil" thought to enter our consciousness as though the messages were follow-ups to our decisions? First, this is the Almighty God who dictates our path. God initially told my mother to go to that specific city a few months before we found that church. Second, we were following the rules presented to us in the Bible by our new truth-filled church and pastor who was also a prophet. My mother's written prophecies accompanied the transpired events and experiences.

However, I had many negative experiences in the UPC. I left church most nights feeling very heightened and stressed. The emotionalism and loudness of the church services were purposely devised to overwhelm us so that we could become crying, repenting messes or praise machines who give all of our energy.

When I first came to the church, a group of women flocked to me to share their good news and to pray for me. They encircled me and put their hands over my head, as though there is importance in putting God's energy over my head and through my body. Under all this energy around me, it was easy for my weak body and partially dissociated mind to become weaker and unbalanced to the point of falling forward sometimes. The pastors explained that it was God working in me and that my falling forward was my spiritual acceptance of Him.

Women ministered to the women, and men ministered to the men. I did not like seeing such segregation in their actions. I wanted wholeness, or oneness, where I would be equally valued as any other individual in this world, not go backwards and be treated as an inferior being. UPC members rationalize it by saying that we all have our separate roles that are equal in worth while also quoting a few Scriptures that delineate a woman's place. This is another view about oneness that does not resonate with me. Being put in my place is offensive to me; however, it was acceptable to those women whom I witnessed raising their arms to praise God with a firm declaration about how happy they were to wear heavy, long hair and dresses and to please their respective husbands and head pastor.

I was also confused by some UPC teachings of duality that were used to fill in biblical blanks. Before Jesus died on the cross, he cried out in his humanness to his supposed self, the Father. The Church answers that it was his flesh that showed its weakness, as though the body had its own mind. Sure, this is true within the context of cellular consciousness, but this is not the understanding of the pastors. Rather, some pastors tried to explain that it was the human spirit of Jesus's human flesh, but this brings them back to a Trinitarian belief and makes moot their belief that only Jesus's spirit is God's. A Trinitarian belief actually makes more sense in this case because the flesh does not influence God's perfect Spirit that came before flesh (John 1:1, 4:24; Genesis 1:2), so only a weakened, separate spirit of Jesus would be crying out from his own pain.

Another incongruence between the Church and the Bible is in another UPC Article of Faith that states, "God is invisible, incorporeal, without parts, without body, and therefore free from limitations;"[3] however, Jesus sits or stands on the right hand of the Father in heaven (Mark 16:19; Acts 7:55-56). This has been interpreted that the right hand is a metaphor for God's power, but then why doesn't the Scripture just say that? This interpretation seems to forget the Book of Colossians chapter 2, verse 9 that states the fullness of God exists in Jesus's body. When Jesus's body becomes perfect in heaven, would this mean that God and His Godhead continue to live as Jesus? Accordingly, doesn't fullness imply that it is all of God within that body? But wait, God is free from limitations. Time to again bring in First Timothy chapter 3, verse 16: it is a mind-boggling mystery in that God can do anything.

Now it is time to address the dualism belief toward the creation of humans. The most accurate definition states that God's word created us by God's spiritual breath, so all humans became wholly intact creations with our own spirit and body. Because dualists see Jesus as a human, then this rule must apply to him also. However, they only partially apply the definition of human to Jesus because his spirit is not necessarily his. The UPC definition of Jesus is unclear because it turns him into a half-man, half-God person. I deduce that the Trinitarian view that separates Jesus from God provides a more understandable belief along with ample Scriptures to support it.

In addition to the negatives about the UPC that I realized, the above two prophecies were also aware of negatives that God aimed to reprove. However, these two prophecies have obvious red flags: love is conditional and equated to obedience (this is a common theme), there is warring language to enlist us in an army against the one enemy (when there are other enemies as shown in chapter 7), and the tone and language are emotional and desperate from a so-called spiritual God who seems obsessively dependent upon receiving our adoration.

When fervent believers prayed over me a zillion times in the UPC, I never got that instant healing that they told me I should get. I could not understand why because I lived and breathed the Bible in my early to mid-20s. I already changed religious affiliations from what I felt contained more complacency as a Catholic to a more strict belief in the Bible as a Pentecostal. I initially questioned different pastors why I was not healed, and every time, they would seek to find fault with my thought patterns. Each of them determined that I did not have enough faith to be healed.

I passionately responded, "But I do believe more than anything."

"You must believe more," was their reply.

What does this belief entail, then? Do I believe as I was taught by the Church and the Bible to "wait on the Lord," or do I act in the opposite manner and fervently pray to God until I get what I want?

I finally responded to the most sensitive pastor to my concerns, "So, are you saying that I can move God, the most powerful being in the universe, to do what I tell Him to do?"

"Yes."

"Then that would make me like God."

He could not respond.

I struggled with allowing myself to be human. If I would have one moment of doubt during the most difficult times when God did not choose to heal me, why was I supposed to feel ashamed of that? Where was the dose of reality in this faith? I went to twice-weekly services as well as Bible classes. I preached to people, and I wrote Bible studies. I brought friends, family, and strangers to church. People close to me knew that I was *the* Christian. I knew that my faith in God's ability was stronger than many of the esteemed men of the church.

My mom and I felt we had no choice but to start UPC church-hopping after being put in our place by pastors. They could not handle their protocol being questioned by women, nor would they curb their extremely loud sound system that kept my illness on edge.

I wrote a prominent UPC head pastor to question why we had to shout at God when He is in the midst of us. I additionally expressed my heartfelt concerns of how I felt akin to the stereotypical male role that fights for truth, so why should I always have to wear a dress or skirt and never cut my hair? The heaviness and length of such things hindered my physical movement. I envisioned myself in a trench, fighting in a war against evil (the warring theme was advocated by the prophecies and Bible), so I wondered why it should matter if I wore pants because pants are worn in a trench? I wrote that God knows our hearts, so why should much importance be placed upon our physical looks?

I openly shared my thoughts with him because I wanted deeper understanding of the issue and to be valued for my input as a church member who is of the same "body" of God. Soon after I sent the letter, my mother received the following prophecy that was directed at the entire UPC congregation, including us. She worried how the head pastor would receive this message, but God told her to give it to him. We believed that we would hear back from him personally with some amount of care because as the head pastor, he should be open to God's words and His people.

March 31, 2000
To My People:

I am dismayed with the evil that besets the World these days. I ache in my Sacred Heart that more souls are not being won! Hear me, My People! I can not allow My People, My Children, to go on in a confused state when they are to reach others.

Many Apostolics are doing exactly what they interpret as My Word from My Book, but are not doing My Works. There are many souls, waiting to hear about My Precious Blood, My Saving Power, and Saving Grace. How can this be told if My People have no idea what the Scriptures mean?

The World is coming to an End very soon; there is no time to sit and wonder and not delve into My Word, and its full meaning if My People are so distracted with the things of this World. Yes, I am using laymen's terms to reach the even lowliest of My Creatures, to bring them into the fullness of My Grace. Seek and you shall find Me! Many are not seeking My full will for them.

I am getting ready to sweep this city with a Mighty Wind, in all My Power and Majesty, to reveal to those open to My Spirit, all that I have in store for them. Be open to My Spirit, as My servants, and you shall be truly blessed. Seek all the truths in My Word, and I will reveal these truths to you; many still do not use their mind's eye to see the evidence of My Love in this World.

Know that I will not tolerate blasphemy, lust, pride, fornication, pants in women due to their ever ending desire to dominate and demean My Order, which I have ordained in My Church. Even you, My Child, must abide by My Will.

I know that you do not understand with your mind these things, but My People will understand through My Sovereign Majesty, the revelation of these things. Know that I have ached and suffered since and before the beginning of time; for, I AM, and I am the Alpha and Omega, the Living and True God, JESUS, your Lord and Master—do not lend yourself in any way to Satan, for he will twist your life, your thoughts in the most cunning way to destruction. Know that I am there even in the most smallest of things.

Many people today do not feel, see that I am a loving God, merciful unto all that they are and do; many do not know that I exist—even though I have shown many through My beautiful Creation, and Sovereign Majesty through prayer; they still doubt My Existence. Faith is a precious gift that I bestow on those who are childlike in Spirit, humble in Heart. If I find things in a person's life are complicated, I make My Self known to those who are open to change; I do not compromise one's character when I choose to change one's heart; I make them a whole person, a newer, transformed being, ready to do My Profound Work.

I am pleading with My People, to seek out the souls in this World, to obtain My Spirit and a brand, new life. My Spirit is all powerful, and loving simultaneously! I have no condemnation for those who sacrifice their lives for others; only, if they continually close the door on My Word. They must be baptized in My Great Name only; not under the titles, which have so confused and distorted the meaning of My Word, since 400 BC. Do not lend your ears to fallacy and untruth; I have brought you through the Veil of My Crucifixion and Resurrection, to be part of My Everlasting Kingdom.

Know that I will not let My People loose to the Evil One; I will fight your battles for you, if you heed My Word; digest My Word in its entirety, and I will reveal all!

Be at peace, love and joy in JESUS,
I, your Lord and Master.

Note: It is interesting that this signature symbol of the P and X, called the Chi Rho, was used again; I thought it was only a Catholic symbol. I ignored my initial "Huh?" and instead thought of it as a universal Christian symbol of the cross. A year later, God stopped giving this symbol to my mother. I deduced that it was because we had progressed in our relationship with Him.

My mom and I waited a bit anxiously after we sent our letters to the pastor. A week went by with no contact from him although we called the church to leave him a message, again with no reply. To our surprise at a subsequent church service, we heard this pastor preach to the congregation about women who were not truly members but were implants from Satan.

"These witches spread the seed of wickedness and try to usurp the authority of the pastors," he said.

The tone of his speech was frightening. We had no idea to whom this message was directed because we believed in the same God that the pastor did. We left the service feeling confused.

The dark vibe that I felt was correct. At the next service, within minutes after sitting down, my mom and I were approached by an usher. He escorted us out of our seats to the foyer where two men stood to prevent us from going back into the church. They told us that the head pastor did not want us to return. Instead of simply talking to us, the pastor left the dirty work to the henchmen. I asked them "Why?" in earnest, and I wore my heart on my sleeve, saying that we believed in this faith and wanted to stay. Nevertheless, whatever sensitivity they felt toward us was squelched by their obedience to their superiors.

My mother received more prophecies to lead us to the region's remaining UPC churches that proceeded to repeat the same program to a default, as though every church was just another fast-food restaurant franchise. Devout Christians argue that no one should change the Bible's message. I agreed as long as we really understand the Bible. My main issue was that I needed the message to be conveyed more sensitively to my physical needs, something about which I thought God and His people cared. The church *experience* was just as important to them as their Christian message. The true message was lost in the show, similar to when the rituals and interpretive sermons of the Catholic Church take precedence over biblical "meat." God said that the last UPC church's pastor would be attentive to my needs. Nope, that did not happen. In fact, I was rudely put down and told to be obedient; in other words, I could not speak up. Why did God not know that this pastor would not only look down upon me but dismiss me in a worse way than some of the other pastors? I was confused and devastated.

My mother and I went one last time to that church to see if I could manage to handle the noise in what was an even smaller church than the others. No, of course I still could not. But, where could we go next? We had no clue.

As we turned to leave at the end of the service, a man came up to us. He said that God directed him to talk to us because we were open, and he proceeded to tell us wonderful news. We thought, "What timing! God must have brought us there one last time to meet this wonderful man!" He was an ex-UPC pastor who became an evangelist preaching a new belief about Jesus.

He explained that Jesus was not human at all but fully God in both spirit and body. He showed us many Scriptures to back up this message.

As he was talking, my mom and I became increasingly excited because it made perfect sense to us; this message did not have the incongruity about Jesus's nature like the Trinitarian and dualist beliefs. We finally found the message that we were looking for toward my full healing: I now could take upon myself the 100 percent heavenly body and spirit of Jesus in baptism, and by standing in faith on the correct knowledge of His entire nature, I would get my new body!

This profound prophecy on September 18, 2001 was for me:

> My precious child:
>
> You are ready to embark on a new way of life—the mystery of <u>Who I AM</u>? Who am I? The World has asked for centuries. I am the Beginning, the End, the Alpha, Omega, the Prince of Peace, the Lord of Lords. I am Jesus, flesh and blood incarnate, but incorruptible in man's sight. Man does not know who I am— you are being revealed at this very moment about <u>Who I AM</u>. I have chosen you, for you are a special creature—I knew you, formed you and you are wonderfully made.
>
> I have led you on this road—very bumpy at times, but have given you my spirit, My compassion for others along the Way.
>
> This World is in chaos; the beginning of a truly terroristic act has been leveled against Tyrus (as in Ezekiel) [referring to New York City] for time after time Tyrus was a great nation, and/or city that had great wealth and built itself up as a god to be revered around the world in times past—now, again this city in a nation of wealth, is being attacked without and within.
>
> My child, do not be distracted by world events.
>
> I have come unto you in a special revelation of who I am, and am now, gathering my people in this new Revelation of Jesus for time is <u>very short</u>.
>
> You want to summarize today the greatness and identity of who Jesus is.
>
> He is the Arm of the Father, the blood and flesh who was spit out of the mouth of the Father, Word made flesh. Jesus is not human, or humanly made. Jesus was sent in the spirit (formed in the womb of my special servant, Mary, who was made of the dust but still human, corruptible). The formed Jesus did not obtain human sustenance from Mary's being, but heavenly sustenance— Jesus was born from an incorruptible seed. Jesus came to preach the

gospel to all men, as an incorruptible flesh and blood personage, to corruptible man. Many, though they knew me, did not accept me when I walked the Earth. They rejected me, in my being! Oh! How I have been wounded due to man's sinful nature! Oh! How man has taken the riches of the World and walked the…[I lost the rest of this prophecy].

The evangelist took it upon himself to be our pastor. We had lively talks in which we uncovered the prophetic mysteries of the Bible. This pastor-friend treated my mother and me with respect, and he valued our insights.

He instructed that we needed to be re-baptized in the new faith we had gained. The UPC preached the message that we would be instantly changed after we arise out of the water of baptism. My new pastor thought the same. I was so convinced of this new faith that I strongly believed that I would be healed by this new full-body immersion in a river. I believed that I would take upon the heavenly body of Jesus as though it would translate into mine.

When I arose from the water in front of several onlookers, I felt a euphoric energy come upon me, and I whole-heartedly praised Jesus with arms in the air, thanking him for healing me. What a sight that must have been for those onlookers! Nonetheless, all of that energy, faith, and praise did not change my body in any way.

Biblical Scriptures, especially Romans chapter 6, verses 3-13 and Galatians chapter 3, verse 27, allude that I would have received healing after my figurative resurrection from the baptismal waters; therefore, I was directed by our new pastor and my mother's prophecies to believe that my new body would transpire. I kept on believing, but it kept not happening. My healing became the dominant theme in prophecies from that day onward. Here is one example of many:

January 8, 2003

My children must be whole to do my work in its fullest. That is my gift to you—wellness….Your body is racked with the evil stimulus of the world, but I will not let it overcome you. My child, I suffered and died for you, took the world's burdens onto myself—give me all your pain, sleeplessness, suffering and I will give you rest. You say 'I have several times' but it does not leave. It has been a comfort none only too long—give it all to me and the healing will begin. I have given you my life blood; now, you must give me yours. I love you timelessly, without End.

I did not know what it meant to give God my life's blood, for I already gave everything I had to Him. How much more perfect did I need to be to get this healing when I am only perfect by taking upon His perfect nature by faith in baptism, which I did? I followed all the commandments and did everything I was supposed to do, including the dress code, yet there is still somehow more? No, you cannot change the rules and dangle a banana in front of a hungry person, continuously keeping it out of reach. You cannot promise a million dollars if I win a race but then say when I actually win it, "Oh shoot, she did it. I don't have the money, so I'm going to say that she cheated." How was I cheating by using my illness as a crutch? How was my suffering *my* fault and "comfort"?

In addition, God as Jesus loves me so much and died for me, so must I actually die for Him? That's carrying it too far, right? The Apostle Paul was a proponent of dying daily for God. I was under the impression of the Bible that Jesus already did that for us, but I still followed in his footsteps like Paul, where I changed my entire self for God. What else must I finally do to have Him heal me?

I continued to be dutiful while both praying and waiting on the Lord, wondering who was in control of my life when God said He can do all things. I did not know if He led me to that Neuro Emotional Technique (NET) practitioner in Arizona because I originally went there for a love interest. We can rather deduce it to a natural consequence of events, or they were events that I attracted to myself instead of God orchestrating them. It became almost a game to find the missing link for my healing because it seemed like my searching for that special something had God on the tail end showing up and saying, "See, I'm here, and I did all of it, not you."

Granted, a few prophecies came true to keep me believing in God at the helm. For example, I was told the correct time frame and connection through which a perfectly appropriate apartment was available to me. However, that successful direction was given after several failed prophecies attempting to find me a place to live. The many failed prophecies had me follow that dangling banana to go forward and talk to people who did not have any way to help me. More prophecies told me an answer was soon to come, but I had to wait patiently for more revelation.

The NET sessions did help my understanding in a phenomenal way, and I received incremental emotional and psychological healings. Was that supposed to be enough while I was promised a complete healing?

While I was in Arizona, my pastor called me and sounded very excited. He said that his new research uncovered the last missing link to knowing Jesus's perfection: his true name was Yashua!

Jesus was a Hellenized name. The letter "J" is not found in the Hebrew alphabet; accordingly, Jehovah would be spelled *Yehovah*. If the name of the

Father is YHWH, then the son's addition could add another letter to the name since "Jesus" said he came in the name of the Father (John 5:43). I would assume that the additional letter would represent the body, but the "S" that is added in YSHWH is the Hebrew letter *shin* which on its own represents two teeth.[4] What matters is the entire context of the name that means "the Lord saves."[5] The shin also connotes the Holy Spirit, or El Shaddai, when it is used alone in Jewish doorpost inscriptions.[6]

It can be argued that Jesus's historical name is of little importance because people still knew who he was; however, as it is important to know the nature of Jesus's body, it is biblically significant to also know his name because it is the name whereby we are saved. In the five baptismal accounts of the Book of Acts, they baptize in the name of Jesus. The Bible states that Jesus as our Messiah was a Jew, so it is likely that the original baptisms used his Hebrew name.

Many sources refer to the name of YSHWH as Yeshua as though its origin is the name Joseph. *Yeshua* was a later Aramaic rendition, just as the Hebrew YHWH became YHVH or Jehovah. The original name is Yahuah (the uncorrupted spelling of Jehovah and Yahweh), so Jesus's Hebrew name should have been Yahushuah. For whatever reason, the name has been shortened, but it is important that no letter was added. I elaborate further about this topic in the beginning of chapter 5.

This research was indisputable to us. Conveniently, my mother got a prophecy for me to confirm what we learned.

March 21, 2003

My special child, my sweet child,

My child, how far you've come. How very far you have progressed. I am very proud, my daughter. You have strived to give yourself to me in its entirety. You say, where are the results? How come I am not healed yet. My daughter, I have a plan which you are a part of, but time is not yet come, but close. Do not despair—my timing for your life's work is not your timing. Be very aware of the world in its dismay, warring factions heightened in every part of the globe. This is not a peaceful world you live in. Hope is only in Me, Yashua, your king, your creator in the flesh. Now that you know my real name, do not stray far from it. I allowed the false name of Jesus for a long time, because people wanted to believe in evil—it was an easier path to follow, yet truth was not in it. I am not Jesus! I am Yashua; Yaveh is my father's name. We are the true, living entities in the heavens.* Do not worship any other gods, for it will be your downfall.

[Later in the prophecy about my love interest:] Do not think he does not have feelings for you, for he does. He does not know his future, that is why he keeps his distance. I have great plans for both of you—together!

Your Yashua,
King and Creator of all things.

* Was this giving away too much information by saying they were not only one living entity? Yes; however, the end signature underscored the message that both Yashua and Yaveh are considered to be God.

The Torah, which is the Old Testament's first five books, introduces Yahuah as the most powerful God who smites those who do not follow Him. The famous Ten Commandments specify ways to keep Him at the helm, although they are categorized somewhat differently among Judeo-Christian factions. The common Christian interpretation lists the first two commandments as saying: 1) "I am the LORD thy God.... Thou shalt have no other gods before me" (Exodus 20:2-3 and Deuteronomy 5:6-7); 2) "Thou shalt not make unto thee any graven image.... Thou shalt not bow down thyself to them" (Exodus 20:4-5 and Deuteronomy 5:8-9). Exodus 20:23 elaborates, "Ye shall not make with me gods of silver, neither shall ye make unto you gods of gold," which is a two-fold message. Yahuah instructs that the most prized metal—gold—should be for Him, and He implies that many so-called gods are inanimate objects. However, the Torah mentions other gods that can vie for power against Him.

Yahuah demands that people view Him as the only all-powerful, living God. His image and name is so great that Jews have refrained from calling Him by His name, preferring to say G-d. In biblical times, another god was named Gad. The omission of the letter "o" gives room for Gad, so I wonder why many do not prefer to call Him God when this word is merely a title.

The March 31, 2000 prophecy that declared Jesus's name to us was persuasive to keep us at that level of knowledge, for we still prayed to that same entity as God. Nevertheless, we searched for more truth, and YHWH kept up with our quest. When we received the new March 21, 2003 prophecy declaring Yashua's name, we saw it as confirmation that we were on the right track. Of course, we thought it was Him leading us to that knowledge, but in retrospect, the March 31, 2000 prophecy seemed sufficient.

As the prophecies continued to come, I started to realize that YHWH would only reveal something important about Himself after we found out about it ourselves. We certainly could handle more information beforehand, but did God maybe not want us to find out more? All along, He was telling us that He was leading us to more knowledge. It became unconvincing to me that He was really doing the leading.

In addition to my search for truth in my religious path, I deeply yearned for true love, so several of my love interests were mentioned in my prophecies. I believed that Yashua was the source of love, and since I was a devoted follower, I believed that every person I loved involved the action of God bringing that person to me. The prophecies supported this to keep me believing that God would not bring me the wrong man and that He was truly in control of my life. However, I became weary with the promises that did not materialize over time.

May 16, 2003
You are also angry at me. I have not given you what you've requested concerning [that man] at your appointed times. You see, my child, man controls the Earth, and everything revolves around human wants, desires, not around my word, and my work. When requests are made regarding man's lusts and wants, it deeply disappoints me.

Ya*

* *Ya* was now used as the root name of Yashua and Yahuah to show God's oneness. We progressed in our knowledge toward God's name, so *Yashua* was not used any further because His greater name of Yahuah (YHWH or YHVH) was revealed to us to clinch the fullness of the Father as the Son. In these later prophecies, I was perplexed why Yahuah would use different spellings of His name—I thought His name was extremely important. Still, *Ya* was sometimes used as an abbreviation and to show the oneness factor.

The above prophetic excerpt threw me sideways. I thought, "What, my love is now a lust and a petty human want?" That was definitely unfair to say to me because Yahuah said time and time again that He chose that man for me. He told me during the previous months that my pure love was more than that "shell of a man" (God's words) could handle and that more time was needed to bring him around to me.

Yahuah said that I would not see this man until the following year in a city where we both aimed to live. He convincingly stated that we would get jobs in that city, and the man's heart would finally open to me so that we would become spiritual and physical mates.

Up to this point in time, I continually heard pastors say that I would get all I asked for in Jesus/Yashua after I followed all the steps he and his apostles mapped out. I also wore long skirts and stopped cutting my hair for a while, although I preferred not to do that. I was a perfectly dutiful follower by the time of this prophecy, yet my desires were not important. I guess this is what it means to be a servant.

However, I was told that my desires did matter in the latter prophecies of June 6, 2003 and September 27, 2003 in which Yahuah says, "I will give you all that you seek and all that you want, in My Spirit." Unfortunately, this feel-good statement was stated after God told me to let this man go in the following prophecy on May 30, 2003.

> I allowed him to make his choices because I loved him and was merciful to him. Now, that time has passed and I will be merciful no more to him. My child, you are free from any obligation to [that man]. You do not need to contact him or any person from your past that has caused you pain or harm in any way. It is time to proceed forward towards health and a new beginning in Me.
>
> YHWH

This message was a shock to me because of the surety in the previous prophecies. I questioned my faith in Yahuah. He then responded in subsequent prophecies that this man would change by the end of the year; therefore, my faith was largely but not entirely restored.

I did not understand why this man was allowed to stray from Yahuah while He told me to spend a lot of my energy to influence him to follow Yahuah. I later realized that because I was fashioned to believe in the all-powerful God, and I was naïve in my understanding of love, I was strung along to believe that this man would change. God's words did say that this man would be mine; I was taught as a Christian to never doubt God's ability and word, and new prophecies reiterated that He always keeps His promises.

Wait a minute…Is it possible that God cannot prevent human will? Do we indeed have a free will? If so, then why did Yahuah portray such confidence that this man would change when that might never happen? Could it be that your will is not more powerful than ours?

I could never give heed these thoughts back then because it was blasphemous to do so, but the progression of my prophecies showed another picture than what religion wants to examine: events and God's words not coming to fruition. As you can surmise, this man did not change in any way toward me.

The long, drawn-out process of leading me on and reframing the topic were clever tactics by YHWH because my heart and mind became exhausted. I was finally ready to move on. Conveniently, God diverted my mind back to my health, so I felt better toward Him because I wanted more of myself anyway.

June 16, 2003

Many evils in this world have been allowed to cause devastation, grief, and violation in order for my plan to reach completion. Originally when I created Adam, he was tempted through Eve by the Evil One, to sin, to set him and his family apart from Me and My Everlasting plan. I was angry, and continued to be merciful, even unto today. Child, I am calling out My Bride, from the depths of the Earth, to follow My precepts and Statutes. You are chosen for the purpose to rule in My Kingdom. The pain you are experiencing, will pass very soon. I will heal all of your nerves, muscles, tissues, organs, but you must realize I have a time for these things to take place....*

I will give you all you ask for, for I love you. Commune with me in the quietness of your room the upcoming month, and I will show you myself and speak with thee. Not only does your mother hear my voice, but you shall also. They are not thoughts in your head but my direction, from this day forward....

You will be clear in your mind; you will be able to make decisions with confidence and self-esteem as an adult, but not as the World does, but as I give you the promptings by my set-apart Spirit. My Spirit is powerful, and leads all men to truth. Be not afraid of the inevitable, but embrace the New things I will send you in your life. Be open, and humble to receive.

Ya

* I was excited to hear about my healing, but nothing happened "very soon." Ya's words increased my faith, but He gave an indiscernible time.

What and where is "the inevitable"? Prophets and channelers receive messages that say certain events will occur; whether or not they get a precise date for those events, it is often that nothing happens. Almost everything is a prediction based on current events or agendas. The age old question of whether there is a destiny can definitely be altered by our free will, and there is also a will of God.

In retrospect, I cannot get over how prominent the biblical and religious message is that says this single entity's will is magnificently better than our will, when truly, it is just another will. Is God's will really a destiny for us, or is it just another will that can easily be pushed aside and blown away by the wind? Since God is believed to be a better-than-us entity, He would pave out a destiny for us while claiming ownership of fate—actually, when it serves His purpose to claim that ownership.

Fate refers to an event that happens beyond our control, while destiny implies the direction toward a specific end. Christianity likes to emphasize that God created us and paved out our lives for us since birth. The Bible and my prophecies underscore God's message that His will is our ultimate destiny depending upon our obedience to Him. This obedience is the fork in the road that makes this destiny idea not so clear. If someone does not worship God, then He punishes her. This means God's will defines different destinies depending upon different people. He is the ultimate judge, as stated in the Bible.

Because of the variable nature of God's will, it becomes impossible for any lowly human to decipher if a fateful event was caused by Him due to the degree of our favor with Him. God claims ownership for every event that occurs in our lives, but then He says that we have a free will that He "allows" for any length of time He supposedly chooses.

It is most murky in the case of a faithful Christian who dies from a fateful event because she did not incur God's wrath or change of will. The Christian community will write it off as God's will because they believe His majesty controlled the girl's life. Some Christians go so far to state that the fateful event of the accident, unrequited love, or whatever occurred because of the principal person's sin. It is their default reasoning to say that we are sinful. Although the baptism and faithful life of the individual was supposed to "save" her life, she still must have done something wrong, for God can never do anything wrong. This foundational belief keeps God in control of our fate and destiny, for if we die unexpectedly, then God's will planned it that way because He is the wise judge.

I argue that this default reasoning has no leg on which to stand when people who are directly involved know without a doubt that they did nothing wrong. They then press this issue with their God to where He might eventually admit the person's innocence but now say that it was really the world's fault, just as He said to me about my abuses and illnesses. He always gives an explanation or excuse so that we can keep seeing Him as better than we are, but is He infallible as a perfect entity? I could never really see this perfection of God while reading His sanctioned deaths and desperate words in the Old Testament (the language is mirrored in my prophecies). Regardless, I still wanted to believe in perfection. The belief in a perfect God is perpetuated by the default reasoning of human error messing up His will in our life experiences, hence incorrect statements passed as truths by God are not really His fault.

There are other entities similar to the God behind my mother's prophecies who ponder the existence of a destiny or fate because they wonder how far the hand of manipulation can affect creation. They wonder if life is already planned due to the existence of higher "powers that be" or if there is a direction to go that will provide the idealized existence. Both philosophies are at play in otherworldly prophecies to us, whereby manipulative entities determine how far they can control us as pawns in a game titled "God."

I always wondered about the extent of an entity's presence, such as that of an angel, god, or God, who is in or around us to direct us. A July 31, 2003 prophecy from YHWH states:

> My child, everywhere you go, I am sending my angels to protect you. I am the Creator of all, and I keep my promises. Gradually you will experience my presence inside you, and I will change you into the woman you should be. You have a loving and humble heart.

My devotion toward this entity as God opened the line of communication and acted as the bridge for a sort of oneness that can eventuate as possession. It took time to sweet-talk me into this relationship of being Yahuah's hands and feet. Surely my body would be figuratively used unlike how Yahshua's body was used, or was I not so sure?

I always felt like I carried the burdens of the world. I would be especially unsettled for no reason, and then I might find out the reason the next day. An example is when the December 26, 2004 Asian tsunami claimed many thousands of lives. Why did I feel like an intermediary when Yahshua (the more accurate spelling of Yashua) supposedly took that all upon himself? I was super sensitive to pains around me; they weakened me in my deep, heaving cries for everyone, and New Testament Scriptures told me to die to myself and allow such weaknesses. The above January 8, 2003 prophecy confirms this. What about all of the Scriptures that say I would be made strong if Yahuah is with me? In reflection, is the main point of this version of oneness to take me over—gasp—completely? I did not get to that point in my thinking back then.

In 2003, our pastor baptized my mother and me two more times after we gained new revelation about the names Yahshua and Yahuah. We had to make sure we took upon ourselves the correct understanding of the identity of our God and the spelling of His name because my mother's prophecies stated that Yahshua is not the Greek "Jesus" as Iesous, and Yahuah is the foremost name of God as the heavenly-man Yahshua. We were told by our pastor and prophecies that we knew the true name and body of the incorruptible God, so I was convinced that I was perfectly ready as a mature Christian to finally receive my full healing. Unfortunately, again, no healing happened immediately after baptism.

For a while, I stayed strong in my faith because I felt confident that I had the correct belief that would please YHWH and have Him reward me. However, I could not always carry out this faith when having to deal with daily struggles. On September 19, 2003, a prophecy told me after a bout of bulimia, "You are hurting my temple, my home within you and around you—remember, you put me on at your Baptism—you are an intricate entity unto my flesh and body."

I thought that my imperfections necessitated God to take my place and make me a better person. The Bible and prophecies underscored my belief, but I did not think of the word *possession*. Accordingly, being told that we must be filled with the Holy Spirit shouts possession to me in retrospect.

The June 16, 2003 prophecy that I transcribed above groomed me to have my mind taken over like my mother's, which is the first step toward full-fledged possession. Yes, I got baptized and believed in my God, but I did not have the infilling of the Holy Spirit although I spoke in tongues. The Holy Spirit only touched my mind but did not completely take over it or fill me up. I wanted the ability to directly communicate with God as my mother did so I could obtain more intimate knowledge. However, I lacked the physical and mental grounding that she had due to the nature of my illness, so I was afraid of hearing or feeling something else that does not maintain a proper distance away from me. I desperately wanted full control over my mind and body, so I instinctively stood against losing myself. The prophecy said I would have a clear mind, but how could that be when Yahuah said I would hear Him in the same way as my mother? His communications overpowered her mind. Would my mind be clear because I would be able to discern if it is God and not me?

Despite those thoughts, the following prophecy reinforced the message of healing and clarity. I most cared about my healing at that time; therefore, I believed the prophecy within this context and dismissed the rest.

October 22, 2003

The time has come to experience wellness. My daughter, you have suffered long enough, and now you will feel better.... Your sickness, debilitation will lighten the coming weeks, where you will see the real you, in my light....I have not kept wellness from you for this time because I have ignored your prayers and pleadings—I have heard every word. Remember, my timing is perfect. Your patience and endurance is your reward. Be filled with joy, for the hour of your healing has come. Be expectant of all I can give you.

Your King, YHWH.

The time had come! I was ecstatic that I would finally be healed! All day, I thanked Yahuah for my healing. Then I thanked Him the next day, and the next. It did not take me long to wonder what the heck was going on, for I was as faithful and thankful as I could possibly be during those few weeks. Unfortunately, the healing did not come, nor did any noticeable growth in my awareness as a type of healing.

The following month, either that promise was conveniently forgotten, or the "coming weeks" were actually weeks into the future because a new prophecy on November 23 begins, "The time is here to reveal to you my plan for your complete healing and recovery of years of suffering that you have endured." Wow, this was a bigger promise that said I will receive complete healing instead of a lightened illness!

Yahuah said that the process of my healing started because my sister told my dad what I revealed to her about his abuse toward me (I told her what I remembered about her as well, but she could not remember anything; she chose to only address me with my dad). My father vehemently denied sexually abusing me, but Yahuah said this event would somehow start my healing.

Realistically, my path of healing was *my* path of understanding and emotional release along with my reactions to the wills of involved people. What happened in this occasion with my sister and father was merely one step of countless many in which I dealt with how I got sick in my past. This one step that "YHWH, King and Creator" mentioned then concluded with a non sequitur:

> You have suffered from years of insomnia, anxiety, depression and intense panic attacks which have resulted from the childhood violations, but no more! You are free in me—believe it! You are free from the bondage of that grave sin against you.

Yes, I am free from that abuse because it was in the past, and I have worked diligently to release my reactions to the memories of it. To imply that my entire body would completely release that negativity in a miraculous time frame just did not happen. I have believed it, but since my mind was not that powerful to change my body overnight, Yahuah should have been able to do it for me since He wanted control over me. I did not appreciate the misleading prophecies that promised healings based on arbitrary definitions, wills, and timetables when it became clear to me that one step at a time has been the way to release the old.

When I further wised up about the supposed healings that never came, on December 21, 2003, He craftily states:

> My dearest daughter,
>
> I come to you today with a fervent message—heed my word—I am here to give you health, love, a career in my Name. I have promised all these things to you and they will be done! Do not doubt your abilities in your illness—I have used you several times in your weakness, to witness of my Name to family and friends. I am proud of you, my daughter. In my Scriptures, my son Paul was sick in his body many times, but I gave him strength to preach the gospel, for the downtrodden and the oppressed needed to hear my Word, not the Pharisees. You see, the human body, with all its frailties, is special to me, the highest of all my creations. Even the angels see the goodness and the special body I have made for man, and praise me…. Yes, you must be well to do my Work, with strength and endurance, against the evil of the World. You can not work with others for my Name, if this does not occur…. It is now time to have health this New Year. I will direct all your ways.
>
> Says YHWH

Yahuah now says I am capable in my weakness when before I was not able to do good enough works for Him; additionally, this prophecy underscores the January 8, 2003 message about my needing to be well to best do His work. It was confusing to me: it was still okay to be sick, so I could continue to wait until a time in the next year to be well (of course, I expected it to be just around the corner in the beginning of the new year); however, I could not work properly for God and needed to be well although I already worked properly for Him. This message covered both scenarios and aimed to placate me. A few weeks later, in the next year, Yahuah told me to teach the Gospels although I was not well; somehow I would receive healing to help me, whatever that "healing" meant.

The following month, YHWH says:

> Without your illness that you experience in your body, which is reality to you, you would experience death in the World, for your high sensitivity to the Evils of the World would [sic]

overwhelming and very hurtful to you. I have allowed you to feel
pain and anguish, so you can know what real pain is, and anguish
is, without me in men's lives.

Wait, now it is *good* to be sick? Today, reading that prophecy feels dark to
me. Was YHWH saying that He allowed the rapes, for without that, I could
not feel the level of pain and anguish that I did? Was I supposed to suffer like
Yahshua when you/he was supposed to free humans from this same pain? You
have watched over me my entire life but allowed all this stuff? This makes me
wonder why Yahshua cried, "MY GOD, MY GOD, WHY HAST THOU FORSAKEN
ME?" (Mark 15:34). How is my illness giving me life and distancing me from
the world's evil when it was caused by that evil?

I know how bad the world is, so that makes me the perfect specimen
to seek someone to save me. According to this prophecy (or just futuristic
assumption), if I did not have this pain, wellness would mean that I would
abandon my "loving God and Creator." However, God already knew that my
heart is good and humble, and I devoted myself to Him long ago.

The bottom line is that I wanted to know why this God kept making
excuses for not healing me. Is it that He cannot do it?

The usual way that people are healed by God is via the influx of energy
into their bodies by an active prayer group. The laying of hands by other
people allows their energy and the energy of another entity such as a god to
flow from them to the sick person by means of concentrated energy in their
hands. Their hands become very warm and are laid upon the ill region of the
body, stimulating that region to move sluggish energy and raising the person's
core temperature. The sick person may then develop a fever and a sweat by
which the body's energy is heightened to push out the problem. This means of
healing can happen without any otherworldly entity influence.

Something about me was not so easy to heal. I already cleaned up my diet
to eat minimally processed, vegan foods (which later revolved around fruits
and greens for expedited healing), and I did what I could to exercise and live
consciously. Thankfully, it somewhat helped, but my problems ran deeper
than my body.

The heinous abuses in my childhood and adolescence devastated me to
my core. I learned that I had to discontinue waiting on the Lord and become
an active participant, weighing the good and bad of the world and my life to
regain my core self; any other "healing" would seem superficial in comparison.
However, I was a little shaken by God's confusing message that assumed I
would return to the world's wickedness if I was healed because He already
knew how much I hated that wickedness. Thankfully, I never was the type
of person to completely give up and escape my responsibility toward myself.

When I took all possible measures and still did not become grounded in my body, this is when Yahuah was supposed to tie up the loose end. I thought He would do it instantly, for I believed He could since He was the all-powerful God. He was not just an entity but the absolute Truth, so He could never be inconsistent or lie. Ironically, this belief brought me back to the perfection conundrum, and I knew that not all of God's words in my mother's prophecies and the Bible were perfect or fair.

My pastor told me that we must follow all of God's commandments in the Bible, not only the Ten Commandments made famous by Moses on the mount. This further put me at odds within myself because some commandments did not sit right with me, especially in the Book of Leviticus. The Bible has strong commandments toward the division of the sexes to discourage homosexuality and instill a God-given order between men and women. I will elaborate upon this biblical sexism in chapter 4.

My personal struggle in feeling accepted and favored by God to receive my healing was largely due to the fact that I am a woman who is a biblically inferior sex. I must hide my body's natural beauty as though I am by default a temptress who deserves to be harmed if a man cannot control his lusts. No, this biblical message will not help me heal from my past. The Bible has consistently put down the human body, yet we are also told to pay no heed to material things because the riches are spiritual. Why then does the Bible bring us back to the superficial focus of how our bodies look? If a man has trouble controlling himself, and he demands as a fundamentalist that women completely cover themselves, then he should consider the fundamentalist action of cutting out the man's eyes (Matthew 5:28-29). Women should not be punished or made invisible just for being themselves.

On a lighter but just as valid note, I recall my realization that confirms my distaste of this physical standard for women. A stereotypical UPC woman wrote a book, and in her picture, her massive head of hair was tied up and hair-sprayed into a large bun that reveals her neck. If her hair should be her covering (1 Corinthians 11:5-6), she is defying her coverage by exposing her neck and appearing as though she has short hair as a man. When I would cut my hair, it was to keep it long enough to cover my neck but short enough to avoid the overbearing weight that would have me feel like Cousin It of the Addams family. Regardless, this focus upon hair was a distraction away from what really matters.

On September 27, 2003, YHWH states:

> Do you feel that your mother wears her hair long because she must do it or because she wants to? She does what I ask her, but she was ready and willing to accept me in her life. I know you want

to accept me and are accepting me as you have come to know me; but to what extent? I am showing you myself on a completely different plane. I am working on your inner core, healing the wounds, giving you peace in their place, and showing my majesty in all of these things. I do not expect you to do outward things to set yourself apart from others, because I know your humble heart. My child, cutting your hair is not important to me, for I know that I gave you the most important command—love me with your whole mind, whole heart and body, which you have done. The Scriptures are a rule book inspired by the Creator, for humankind to stear [sic] from sinful deeds, and guide to all truth. You have me, and you have the Truth of who I am. My child, do not focus on the outward appearance; for you, it is a great deterent [sic], and it will confuse and distract you from coming into a perfect relationship with me. What I do, and expect of other chosen is for me to decide. It truly depends on the individual's nature and willingness to seek me out. I bear all to those who seek all.

It is interesting that God asked me to what extent I accepted Him, as though maybe I did not accept Him enough, yet He immediately answered that question with support to my inner conviction against any sexism. I think God was testing me again to see how far into the rituals I would go to follow Him. He knew that He would lose me fast if He continued to press the biblical order and dress code as He did in the March 2000 prophecy. It would also be a bad move by Him to put me down into an inferior role if I am to be a leader for Him on Earth. His previous strategy to make me into a total follower had backfired. For our personal relationship to now deepen, God would need my full devotion while retaining some of my individualism, just as a committed human relationship would have us both understood and respected.

Too bad my mother agreed, albeit not fully, to be under a stronger thumb. That thumb is His commandments that are not supposed to be changed. Actually, Yahshua's death and resurrection should have already freed us from such ritualistic commandments. Some apostles continued to teach certain socially acceptable rituals while abandoning others. Therefore, God's word does change, so it is a shame that He still told my mother to follow something not only unnecessary but rude in my opinion because her heart was as good as mine and did not need more chastening.

My evangelist-turned-pastor delved further into the Hebrew roots of Christianity, and not surprisingly, he changed his beliefs accordingly. First, he instructed us to follow the Sabbath on the Saturday from sundown Friday night to sundown Saturday night. I could understand the commandment of a rest day, but I immediately saw the link to the significance of the moon in astrology.

Focusing upon the moon's cycle became apparent when we were told to look into the night's sky for the perfect full moon. We were also told to follow strict kosher food laws by which my mother cleared out all yeasted breads in the house. I felt a notion of slavery in these rules that put the focus on superficial things.

I was living for God every day in my mind and heart, which He preferred because He had my full attention and intelligence. I had enough years as a Christian to know to not make graven images, to not follow paganism in astrology, and to give myself to a deeper relationship with God instead of concern myself with distracting rituals. I stepped back from what my mother was doing according to Jewish law and paganism, so I continued worshipping Yahuah my way.

It is ironic that this same pastor who originally taught us about the prevalence of paganism in Catholicism now starts following astrology. Paganism denotes the worship of polytheistic gods or natural elements, such as the Earth or the stars. Catholic paintings have halos above the heads of Jesus, Mary, Joseph, and the saints, indicating Sun worship. Ralph Edward Woodrow's book, *Babylon Mystery Religion: Ancient and Modern*, elaborates upon the paganism of Catholicism (and Christianity), including Easter and Christmas traditions.

My pastor said he wanted no trinkets, symbols, or diversions from worshipping God, but now he cleaves onto them because they represent a more authentic religion of Judeo-Christianity. Well, Babylon had its own authentic religion also, but that one is deemed evil.

I saw the link to paganism, but I was a bit unsure of my position because both my mother and pastor were instructed to do these things in the following prophecy to my mom.

December 1, 2003
My daughter, My warrior,
   I know you have many questions regarding My Sabbath. It is true that it will be a different day monthly, but you will not need to observe the full, new moon as you do the Sabbath. The Sabbath is a day of rest for man, not for me, your Creator. It was made for man and woman to abstain from work; jobs that you go to 6 days of the week. Daughter, the World observes everything in sin, not as I have given man from the days of Creation. There is no weekday Monday, Tuesday, Wednesday, Thursday, Friday, Saturday, Sunday, as named by the early rulers. How man has

shamed Me! I am very disappointed that no man has questioned the truth behind such idolatry, feast days, holidays. My daughter, you have obeyed My commands, even though you do not thoroughly understand them. Your faith is pure, deep-rooted in Me. For this, I will reward you. Your family is blessed by your obedience. I will bless you with all that you need in life, and more abundance that you know.

You ask of Me what you must follow that [our pastor's name], My Son, teaches and preaches. The Sabbath is My commandment forever, as the Scriptures say. My Word will not pass away in time. I have given [pastor's name] much revelation, but he is leaving My precious children behind because they do not see what I have given him. I know it is difficult to find work in the World according to My plan, My commandment of observance. That is why, your and My children's faith must be steadfast in Me. I will give you the work that I want My children to have, so they serve Me, not the World. Everywhere you look in the World, you will find self-serving careers, to make money, and not serve me. Serving others in nursing, professional service fields does not always serve Me and Mine. Do you not understand the importance of your trust in Me, as My daughter? I have led you this far in your spiritual walk because you are chosen to be My special hands and feet. Your words are My Words from here on out, so do not search for what the World can give—they do not please Me; they forsake Me in every way. There are abominations all around you, and danger, but, as you have seen in your spirit, I have sent a fleet of angels to protect your abode, travel and your person from the Enemy.

I am also protecting *pastor's name, his wife, and another couple in our small group*—yes, they also are chosen. They must focus on Me instead of what the World can give them. The World cannot give everlasting life, only pain and suffering. Be it known that time is short, but time will allow My chosen to come into the fullness of who I am. You head from [pastor's name] the calculations he is distracted with—do not put emphasis on them, for they will distract the Truth from you. [Pastor's name] knows that he is blessed, but is being tempted at every turn. Pray to Me for his true leadership, strength and continued focus on Me, not the "time" elements. Be at peace this week, for I will lead you into the right job to sustain you all. Your husband is working as he should. I have blessed him with an acceptance of the Sabbath, but he is still blinded to My Truth of who I am. That will change soon, for he will have a distaste for the idol system, the Catholic church. There is much My people must learn before I return. Look to Me for everything, and I will bless you and yours abundantly. I love you, daughter. Your gifts are many—I will prepare you soon for a great work. Be aware and on guard.

All that I AM,

I AM,

Yhwh.

This prophecy boldly states that my mother was Yahuah's literal hands and feet. She elaborated in chapter 1 that God did not 100 percent possess her, but His very close proximity did control her; there are levels of possession that I explain in chapters 5 and 9.

YHWH was always tough on my mom because of the intimate relationship He developed with her during most of her life. He put heavy demands on her shoulders, as though her obedience could abundantly bless others when it is really everyone's individual responsibility and choice to desire God. God did the same to me regarding my love interests, using my love for them as a tool to work at converting their minds over to Him. Our pastor confirmed this tactic by telling us that if we do not often preach God's word to the people in our lives, their sinful deaths are our fault (his interpretation of Ezekiel 3:17-21; 33:5-9). What a guilt complex, and what an annoyance we would be to people who would probably think we are obsessed with them and their personal decisions. This is one reason why fundamentalist Christians are overly concerned about what homosexuals do in the privacy of their own homes; adding fear, hatred, disgust, and other strong reactions just compounds the judgment that already exists toward such "sinful" people who we must help save.

What is sin? It is an act against God's judgment or plan. It is also an inherited state of being such as the human body, but this is not a common definition due to the paradox of God saying he fashioned the human body.

Does everything revolve around God and His views? How self-important is that, especially when His views can change as He deems fit. I think it is most accurate to see this God as a political ruler who employs diplomacy when His plans backfire instead a one-size-fits-all dictatorship. Make no mistake that the supreme God as depicted in many fundamentalist religions chooses to portray Himself as a dictator; however, other tactics must be employed to gain the allegiance of many people. A watered down version of His plan is most prominent in reality due to the divisions within and among religions.

It broke my heart to see my mother worry about the exact cycle of the moon so that she could plan her actions around it. These additional Jewish customs gave her a burden instead of the joy and freedom she needed to portray to others. Actually, this burden ran deep into her self-worth, where she wondered if she would ever be good enough to please God.

Thankfully, she listened to my concerns about the rituals. She soon broke out of them, realizing their relationship to astrology. This is when Yahuah finally spoke up to confirm what we knew. He mainly directed this prophecy to our pastor:

> April 11, 2004
> My son and daughters:
> Oh my children, you are my Israel, My fold. How can you be so confused in your minds what laws to follow, what Name to praise! My Name is above all else, My true Name of Yhwh Messiah, the King and Prince of all Creation. Heed My Words. All will come to destruction and My judgment if you do not follow Me and My commands.
> My old laws in the Old Covenant are no more. You see, I made all things new with My Son's death and resurrection. My flesh and blood nature is the mystery of life. My children, do not be concerned with appearance, the laws of man-made tradition. They are an abomination to Me, a slap in the face of all that follow Me. You must not concern yourself with the sun, the moon and the stars as they are; for they were made with My Creation on the 6 days of My working in the universe. Do not be concerned with spreading My Word among those with closed ears and evil hearts. They will not understand or seek the Truth of My identity. Do not perpetuate old rituals and continual practices of Jewish customs and traditions…[I lost the next page].

This prophecy came after my pastor heard a lot of pro-Jewish talk from Yahuah, so he was not willing to believe this message. Before this time, he happily received all of my mother's prophecies. God has a tendency to tell one person something that contradicts what He shows another person (which is usually after that person realizes the truth); this often happened during my mother's and my spiritual discussions that I will soon explain.

My pastor's Jewish repertoire continued to expand. He began to wear a tassel on his belt to signify the manly practice of "girding his loins" for prayer before God (which is ironic because that phallic symbol is supposed to represent the denial of man's sexuality. The Talmudic custom of girding men's loins dictates that men wear a belt over their tunic to separate the top half of the body from the bottom, serving as a reminder to keep the heart away from a man's nakedness.). Accordingly, he started talking more about his role as the man and pastor above us women. It became increasingly difficult to have open conversations as we used to have in the town hall-type meetings we originally convened. We used to face each other in a circle and got excited about what everyone (mostly women) had to offer. It was frustrating to me that our mutual God started telling him these things, and his wife agreed to follow.

He also became interested in the Hopi tribe of Northern Arizona because of how these people stayed in touch with their god who gave them prophecies of old. He started planning to move out there so he could be close to them before the "end time of the midnight hour that was fast approaching," he said. He said Yahuah was leading him. I do not doubt the communications he was getting, for he also was "filled with the Holy Ghost" when he prayed over me and gave me spur-of-the-moment prophecies.

I intuitively could not calm down about these incongruities because I believed that the God who was with us all was also with me. Why all this contradiction and division when we were supposed to be One as the same unit together? A typical Christian answer would be that man has gone his own way apart from God. However, my pastor was listening to our same God!

Accordingly, God would tell my mother contrasting statements to my thoughts about religion and healing. These were not flimsy thoughts, for I based them upon the Bible, the prophecies, and my good sense that tried to understand more about our faith, religious laws, and experiences. Yahuah's voice within my mother would often interject to invalidate my thoughts without letting her completely hear my words and feel my yearning for truth. She would become utterly confused because she was more on my wavelength. This interjection caused most of our arguments. However, many times He also interjected to make her pay greater attention to me because He said I was right. God was really in the midst of us.

My angst led me to research the Bible to prove the equality of the sexes; I knew that I have an intellect, heart, spirit, body (just a bit different), you name it, as capable as any man.

I strongly felt I had to share with my pastor the serious relationships and abilities with God that my mother and I had as key parts of His church. I created a three-page Bible study that explained how we were all the same body of Yahshua "Christ" after baptism, so we each comprised an equal part. (As I stated earlier, a counter-argument is that we are equal but have different roles. I do not agree with this version of equality because a woman is denied an authoritative role of teaching men, which is unwise if she is intellectually superior.) I began the study with the Book of Genesis chapter 3, verses 11-13 that somewhat vindicate Eve because Adam was the one who knowingly sinned against God, whereas Eve was deceived.

I was nervous on the day I presented this collection of Scriptures to my pastor. I prayed to Yahuah to open my pastor's heart to accept the context toward equality of the sexes; I genuinely wanted to be heard.

My pastor skimmed over the papers and told me that I was wrong. He stated there was a reason for the God-given hierarchy because he as the pastor would know the correct interpretation of the Scriptures to teach others about them. I earnestly argued with him for a little while, but the situation only grew more tense. If he had love in his words, I would have seen it in his eyes, but his gaze was cold and stern. He acted as the UPC pastor who indirectly called my mother and me witches. What was worse was that this self-appointed pastor actually called me a child of the Devil to my face!

I was terribly hurt and ran out of the makeshift church room, crying. I stayed in the car and waited for my mother, not knowing if she was trying to make amends with him because she wanted to belong to a church. My inner self leaped joyously when I saw her coming out only one or two minutes later. She told me that she stood up for me because she knows my heart. We then drove away and never saw that man again.

This experience hurt me more than the others because I developed a friendship with that man. He once told me in private that I was the one person he trusted most to find out more truth with him.

After we returned home, we sat in the living room, silent. For many minutes, we simply stared ahead at nothing in particular. Time seemed to stand still. We felt empty. We did not know what to believe in. Even worse, we did not know who we were because Yahuah was essentially our identity. At least she and I had each other.

As the Sun shone through the windows that afternoon, I saw that life moves on. Filaments of dust danced among the Sun's rays in mid-air. The warmth of the rays felt soothing, and the light brightened my mood. I looked outside and saw leaves swaying to the breeze. I slowly stepped out of shock by starting to talk about my feelings. My mom replied that she felt the same way. We then shared many thoughts about our experiences and tried to figure out who we were in the midst of them.

Over the next few days, I reflected upon my years in the UPC to figure out where to go next, and I remembered my gut reactions. I thought about a book that my ex-pastor previously lent me to read about ancient Hebrew. The author's back cover photo looked creepy to me with his somewhat cold expression, dark clothing, and peculiar addition of a large bird on his shoulder. No offense to the man, but I felt uneasy about him, although I kept staring at his picture to try to shake that feeling. I put that reaction in the back of my mind and went to the library to research the origin of Hebrew; I wanted to see if it indeed was the oldest language as I was taught.

No wonder the church forbids us to read anything other than the Bible, because factual history tells a much different story! The Akkadian language preceded Hebrew, as well as a plethora of different tribes that already existed. I was a bit shocked with this information and then felt somewhat stupid for not knowing it, but most of all, I felt great peace because biblical holes of reasoning were starting to become filled.

History confirms how big the outside world really was compared to the little creation story of the Bible. My search for the truth outside of the religious lens had begun.

> September 12, 2004
> My dear child,
>
> I am very proud of the progress you have made in searching for the Truth and trying to come to Me, My daughter. The time has come to be mindful of all that I have placed in your reach. My riches, My gifts in My Spirit are all for you to grasp and take as your own. Oh Child! You have suffered many years with the evil thoughts that have come upon your being, but no more. I am here now to take you out to a peaceful place; My rest I will give you, and joy, insurmountable, that only I can give you. My daughter, I am [sic] much revelation of My Scriptures to give you, and you will know how real I am. I am the Alpha and the Omega, always true to those who believe in Me. I will not let harm come upon you or your mother, for you both are My children, My Chosen, My priesthood here on Earth. My Kingdom will come soon, and My children will come together and be mentors to the lost. Those that do not know Me yet, but are chosen, will know Me soon. There are many wars, pestilence, famine, pain, evil all over the World, but My love and My Spirit, will sustain those who know Me, and continue to follow Me and abide in My Word. Today, you are reaching another plateau in your Earthly existence, one that will show you the true purpose of why you are on this Earth. I did not make my Creation to follow the wiles of the Evil One. I made and formed you to My Image and likeness, to reign with me for all eternity. Do not be concerned with the seasons, the times, for they will pass. Do not be concerned with what the World says to you concerning My True Name, My Word as My laws, for they stand alone, without any aid from the earthly doctrines, false teachings and ways of man.
>
> I have given My chosen My love, My devotion, My Ways,

which you must abide. You say, "What ways are your Ways?" You will come to know the fulfillment of My Spirit, My love for mankind within you. I will be your teacher, your guide, Theresa, to all Truth. You have no need for pastors, teachers, ministers of the Worldly Churches, for they do not know Me. They continue to pass on false interpretations of My Scriptures to suit themselves, and not to lead the hungry to My Truth and True Nature. You know My Nature is unlike the flesh and blood of the first Adam. There was purpose in My Creation, and there still is purpose. As you see things around you not making sense, I will make sense and give you understanding of My Word to you, so you may grow in the Spirit and touch those around you. I will not prolong your suffering anymore, because you have reached the place where I can be with you in peace. Before, my child, there were many disconnections between your body, mind and heart, and your Spirit was transcending them and you were becoming very dissociative. I took your Spirit until [sic] Myself and comforted you, but you could not feel Me loving you. Now, you can. I have much to give you, My little Flower, and you can receive it all. Do not turn away if you get a Word in your mind—seek it out and follow it. It is from Me! I give My children My Truths in steps, so they can learn and grow. You are a mature person in My Spirit—you are in need to much "meat" now, and it will come to you swiftly. I am aware of your difficulty in concentration, fatigue and inability to convert these thoughts to reality, but it will happen. I have a life prepared for you, with children, yes, children. You will see your life unfold as your body, mind and heart heal. Remember, My time is not mankind's time. Be ever so attentive to the thoughts coming to your mind—positive ones are from Me, My child. Pray when you can—I will give you ability and motivation to do so.

I love you, child, more than you realize or understand. Your body will mend, grow strong and continue to follow what it must. You will know when to venture into the World, for I will lead you. Peace and joy from Yhwh and Elohim. Take heed to My Words.

Yhwh Messiah in all Truth.

Yahuah finally told me that I do not need a pastor. Thanks for the afterthought, but at the time I saw it as confirmation that we were on the right track. Yahuah also mentioned children in my future, which was a bit strange because that was not a prominent concern of mine (and I have not yet had any children or been seriously involved with children until at least the year 2014).

This prophecy briefly mentioned to not pay attention to the seasons, so the astrology rubbish my mom was previously told to follow was a waste of time. This confirms the April 11, 2004 prophecy that changed the laws, but now it states there are still distinct laws of God, although they are not explained because who knows if they would also change. Thanks for admitting that we do not need to follow ritualistic laws, but no thanks for not apologizing for lying to my mother. It is very apparent in these messages that Yahuah likes to take an individual approach to things, so He does not admit any wrong-doing because my mother somehow needed more strict obedience. That is a cop-out, and that did abuse her.

I am very happy to have learned that my particular strength was not broken in the sense that a lightning bolt would be cast down upon me by not following every commandment. It proves that my knowing is indeed *my* knowing; there really is individuality apart from God.

The Old Testament provides plenty of fear-mongering beliefs when armies of disbelievers were killed by God's vengeance. It leaves one to wonder if God actually did this Himself with His otherworldly powers or if the human armies killed people on their own and attributed it to their God helping them.

I think it is wise to evaluate this fear toward one's God. My case shows that God does bend His supposedly iron clad rules, so this gives thought to Him wanting us more, much more, than we realize.

The above prophecy was preparing me for a very intimate relationship with Yahuah in that my thoughts would be His thoughts, although previous prophecies have mentioned this as well. This would entail telepathy since I am not someone who is led to full-fledged possession.

What is most interesting to me in this prophecy is that Yahuah says no church knows Him. The ending clarifies more by mentioning Yahuah and Elohim separately. Pastors have interpreted the usage of these different words in the Old Testament: Yahuah is God's name, and Elohim is a title as Lord, Father, Alpha and Omega, and etcetera. To the contrary, this prophecy appears to reveal that Yahuah and Elohim are names of two separate entities. This interpretation coincides with the March 21, 2003 prophecy that says Yahuah and Yashua are two entities.

When I was in the UPC, I learned of the religious debate involving the term *Elohim*. Elohim is equated to God or Yahuah, but since Yahuah is the name of God, Elohim has to be a title. *El* and *eloah* are considered to be the singular version of Elohim, but *Elohim* cannot be plural if it substitutes *God*.

The Scripture that arguably gives Judeo-Christians the biggest headache is Genesis chapter 1, verse 26: "And God said, Let us make man in our image, after our likeness." The next verse brings it back to monotheism and says, "So God created man in his *own* image, in the image of God created he him; male and female created he them." (Note: Italicized words were later added.)

An exegesis named *exeGeses parallel BIBLE* uses a Hebrew lexicon to show that *Elohim* was the original word for *God*.[7] This means that the Elohim of Genesis chapter 1, verse 26 equates to plural gods, or at least a God and a demigod. Exodus chapter 20, verse 3 also uses *elohim* when saying "other gods." El was a single Canaanite god, and El was also used to represent a singular version of Elohim; therefore, Elohim has to be a plural version of *God*.

Christians and Jews refuse to accept the plurality of *Elohim*, unless they view it as a homonym or a noun that becomes plural when the verb or predicate is plural. The homonym argument is weak, so I will dismiss it. The transitive requirement of *Elohim* contradicts Genesis chapter 1, verses 26-27 because the verses clearly distinguish between singular and plural pronouns when representing *Elohim* in both cases. To deal with this kink in their exalted texts, Christians and Jews find a way to explain it away and focus upon other Scriptures instead.

At the very early stage of researching Israel's origin, I browsed through some books at the library that question the Bible's accuracy. One book in particular about biblical myths rips open many foundational claims of the Bible. A few more books cite archeological discoveries to disprove biblical stories. I promptly put these books away because, as my personal note at the time stated about one of the authors, "He must be an atheist, so I don't like that book." I viewed the books as self-centered attempts by heathens to disprove the existence of God; the UPC cleverly brainwashed me to think this way so I would not investigate further. Christianity often discredits science also; my UPC pastors teach their congregations to ignore scientific claims, even going so far to tell us to not see psychologists or vote.

Now that I was kicked out of all the churches in which I cared to belong, I braved it up and read these books that I was previously not ready to read. I was aware enough to know that when I became unsettled about something, that is when my inner self was communicating to me to explore that topic; I knew I had to read these books to find out where I stood.

A general theme that I noticed was how the search for accuracy among religions and spiritualities consumed many intellectuals in the last several hundred years. René Descartes explored pre-transcendental reasoning with a Christian theme. Leonardo DaVinci put hidden messages in his paintings to reveal flaws about the Catholic religion; additionally, he looked to science to effectively fill gaps of reasoning that the Church claims are supernatural miracles instead of natural occurrences. Sigmund Freud (surprisingly to me) was highly inquisitive toward the origin of religion, so his secretive sexual obsessions were superseded by his desire to place our levels of consciousness into the bigger picture. Immanuel Kant inspired transcendental reasoning toward the goal of unequivocal truth that is embedded in each person's intuitive nature; his philosophical writing is insightful and thorough.

I decided that the best place to start was in archeological and historical studies, and I would try to refute them by carefully analyzing biblical timelines and stories. I did not want to relinquish my faith although the religious aspect of it fell through. I also did not want my mother and I to take her prophecies at face value without having credible research behind us to help prove them. We did not want to create another religious faction like many rogue evangelists do because of an interpretation, vision, or prophetic message that may desire more division. Therefore, I chronologically read the Book of Genesis and notated the interrelationships and timelines of the life spans and genealogies of the patriarchs since Adam. The numbers that had a numerical significance in multiples of 20 did not add up; they also had significant gaps. What I uncovered supported the books' claims!

"Could the Bible have more flaws?" I asked myself with a pit in my stomach. Further biblical cross-referencing told me a resounding "Yes."

Gary Greenburg's book, *101 Myths of the Bible: How Ancient Scribes Invented Biblical History*, illuminates some of the flaws.[8] For instance, Myth 16 states that "God rested after the Creation." Greenburg asks, "After all, what need does an omnipotent deity have to sit around relaxing?" (p.39). He says that God did not take a day of rest because God performed additional acts after He created humanity. Myth 16 concludes that the Babylonian creation epic named *Enuma Elish* was the likely source that indicated the gods were free to rest after creating humanity.

Myth 12 explains that the Book of Genesis has two creation stories about humans. Genesis chapter 1, verses 26-27,31 presents the seven-day creation story in which male and female were created on the sixth day, one day after animals were created. Genesis chapter 2, verses 6-7,21-22 state that humans were created from the dust of the ground on different days, with Adam being the first creation, then animals, then Eve. Greenberg postulates that the sixth day creation story of humans refers to either an earlier set of humans than Adam and Eve, or Adam was created on the second or third day long before Eve.

Myth 18 goes so far to say that "Adam and Eve were the Egyptian deities Geb (earth) and Nut (heaven). Their children were the children of the earth and the heavens" (p. 43). This originated in an Egyptian myth, and it opened up a can of worms toward mixing the gods with humans, although that is what the Bible and all sources of religious and mythological texts actually state.

Myth 23 explains:

> According to Egyptian Coffin Text 80, Atum said he created
> Nut so that "she could be over my head and Geb could marry
> her." In other words, the Egyptians saw the union of Earth and
> Heaven as the basis for marriage, and this principle is carried over
> into Genesis with Adam and Eve.
>
> While Adam became the sole parent of Eve, just as Atum (the
> Heliopolitan Creator) became the sole parent of his children, the
> idea that Eve came from Adam's rib derives from a pun in ancient
> Sumerian, Mesopotamia's earliest literary language. It originated
> with the Sumerian myth of Enki and Ninhursag (see Myth #22).
>
> In that myth, Enki suffered from eight pains, one of which
> was in the rib.
>
> "My brother, what hurts thee?"
> "[My] rib [hurts me]."
> (ANET, 41.)
>
> The name of the deity who cured Enki's rib was Ninti—a
> name that in Sumerian has a double meaning. The first part,
> "Nin," means "the lady of" but the second part, "ti" (pronounced
> "tee"), means both "rib" and "to make live." Ninti, therefore,
> signifies both "the lady of the rib" and "the lady who makes life."
>
> Eve, too, combines both titles. She is truly the "lady of the
> rib," as she came from the rib. And, as her earlier title, "mother of
> all living," indicates, she is the "lady who makes life" (p. 54-55).[8]

Myth 25 states, "There were other beings in the Garden of Eden before
Adam and Eve," which makes sense because they supposedly had only two
sons who somehow found wives (p. 58). I am glad there were other women
because the sons would have had to procreate with their sisters or mother!

Myth 39 sheds light to the significance of the number 40. Greenburg
states that source J from the Judeans who followed Yahuah (the J is a German
transliteration of Y for Yahwist) based the flood story on the Egyptian solar
calendar that was divided into three seasons of 120 days, one of which was
the natural flood season. The Bible's many references to the Egyptians made
me wonder why believers in Yahuah would adopt stories from their arch rival.

Myth 40 states that the great flood of the time of Noah that supposedly
covered the entire Earth and mountains was only 15 cubits in depth, which is

approximately 25 feet.

Myth 75 shows agreement between the Bible's 10 plagues that God sent upon Egypt and older Egyptian papyruses, proving yet another Egyptian reference in the Bible.

Myth 78 explains the Ten Commandments, which were originally thought of as just "Ten Words" in Hebrew:

> The Bible has several contradictory accounts of what laws the Israelites were given, how many they received, and where and when they got them. The traditional version of the Ten Commandments as given above was a late invention created no earlier than the seventh century B.C....
>
> The Bible integrates at least four different law codes within the story of the Ten Commandments, two of which contain similar versions of the traditional Ten Commandments, one of which contains a radically different version of the Ten Commandments, and one which contains over forty commandments, incorporating variations of the laws listed in the other three documents (p. 216).[8]

The traditional version of the Ten Commandments appears in the Book of Exodus chapter 20, verses 1-17. The Book of Deuteronomy chapter 5, verses 6-21 provides a second version. Then, Moses gave a third rendition of Ten Commandments in Exodus chapter 34, verses 27-28 after he smashed the first set of tablets when seeing the sinful acts of his people (Greenburg says that the calf and tablet smashing were fictitious events). The fact that the Books of Exodus and Deuteronomy have differing versions of the Ten Commandments and other stories gives thought to who were their authors.

Laurence Gardner, author of *Genesis of the Grail Kings*, illuminates Greenburg's assertions:

> It is plain that the Ten Commandments...were simply newly stated versions of the ancient pharaonic confessions from Spell No. 125 in the Egyptian Book of the Dead. For example, the confession 'I have not killed' was translated to the decree 'Thou shalt not kill'; 'I have not stolen' became 'Thou shalt not steal'; 'I have not told lies' became 'Thou shalt not bear false witness' and so on (p. 215).[9]

In *Who Wrote the Bible?*, author Richard Friedman explains why the Torah is inconsistent. Contrary to popular belief, Moses was not the sole prophetic author of these "Books of Moses." Accordingly, there were many more writers throughout the rest of the Old Testament than are taught in religion. Friedman argues that the order and styles of writing, biblical content, and geographical placement of tribes listed within the Torah present the case of four distinct groups of writers, excluding the addition of editors, that conveyed their own particular but similar story.

> Scholars could open the book of Genesis and identify the writing of two even three authors on the same page. And there was also the work of the editor, the person who had cut up and combined the source documents into a single story; and so as many as four different persons could have contributed to producing a single page of the Bible.
>
> The document that was associated with the divine name Yahweh/Jehovah was called J. The document that was identified as referring to the deity as God (in Hebrew, Elohim) was called E. The third document, by far the largest included most of the legal sections and concentrated a great deal on matters having to do with priests, and so it was called P. And the source that was found only in the book of Deuteronomy was called D (p. 23-24).[10]

Essentially, each group wrote its own version of stories and events pertaining to its tribe. Friedman uses the century old Graf-Wellhausen Hypothesis that states the five books of the Pentateuch (the Torah) are derived from completely different yet parallel narratives that are assigned four titles: the Yahwist, the Elohist, the Deuteronomist, and the Priestly Writer. A fifth title is given to the Redactor who edited the groups' material. Friedman mentions redactors, but he does not refer to the redactors as group R because their work lies within the themes of the four main groups. This does not diminish their group-worthy role in the Bible. It is generally agreed that significant materials were removed and burned by redactors according to the whim of kings who desired to portray their reigns as most favored by God.

The following prophecy on April 16, 2005 supported me and my mother with our research:

> My daughters,
>
> I come to you both today because I have much to reveal to you regarding the vast amount of material I have given you to research, regarding "the Word". My daughters, as you can see, the books you are going through page by page, word by word, shows the utter discrepancies, lies, deceitful words that many peoples

have used to change, add, take away, eliminate and lose in order to sway and suit the times, and their evil purposes. Oh! Daughters! How evil the World is, and was in those times! Oh! Daughters! You say, Where is the real El; Where are you? Oh! Daughters! I have always been and always will be; but, all the tampering with My original Word, has led mankind down the wrong path to destruction. Do not be alarmed or distressed. I promised you that I would direct you in all Truth, and give you the knowledge that you will need to follow My Will.

Now, you have many questions about the authors in the books of my old Covenant. The authors are many. They follow the esteemed people of their times, and so the scribes/authors wrote, and detracted/added according to their liking for the esteemed person. I am very disgusted with the sacrificial rites, animal sacrifices, burning of old, true manuscripts to suit personal religious preferences, human sacrifice, and worship ceremonial rites. They all are an abomination to Me! Shiloh was My Worship Place. It is the oldest but time, peoples and ceremonial rites due to priestly worship rites changed My True Place or worship to others. My daughters, deities, stories devised to carry traditions and ceremonial rites down through the centuries were entirely false and construed in the worst way. I am very disappointed with these practices, even unto today.

The Torah in the early days of my people, was true, but no ceremonial, sacrificial rites were dictated by Me. Priestly lines dating back to esteemed people in the early pre-prophetic times were devised to appease evil leaders and their devotions. Yes, my people were involved and derived their practices from Egyptians, Babylonians, and periods of their deities. My daughters, as you read these books that give investigators archaeological and historical information, just note that My hand was not in the documents, rules, torah of the several different versions that they gave to the people to live by, but by their own whim and persuasion. You ask—then what are the Truths and laws, right rulings are we to live by? Where are we to find them? There is too much material to sort through. My daughters, my traditional 10 Words are my true words, and my right-rulings are for those to which continually do evil in their lives, day in and day out. You both have received My Set-Apart Spirit, and by My Spirit, I give you a "knowing" in your mind and heart, to follow only good and Truth. My esteemed followers were special in My eyes.

Yes, I had true disciples and true worshippers who only followed My laws with all their mind, heart and spirit, but they were exceedingly few. David, Solomon, Moses were once My sons and followers, but they had sinned against Me. I punished them in severe ways. Do not believe in the priestly lines as portrayed in the book of the "Word". They did not follow My Words. To this day, all "churches" follow priestly leadership, but not according to My Will. They do not question the falsities and evil deception by different versions of faiths as My few followers do, or even want to know about Me! I am deeply saddened about the world's affairs and have made this attempt to reach the receptive few, such as yourselves. I love you both. I will continue to open your minds, and reveal all Truth as you come upon them in your readings. Just know that the story of the Exodus, the stories about Israel and Judah are false stories, and are distracting and blinding mankind to the search for Truth about My True Identity. Continue reading, following My promptings, and you will know My Truths as I gave them. Children, I am very real, my name is Ya, as I have been named from the Beginning. I will not give you answers to all your questions now, for I have time and place for everything I deem so. Theresa, I will heal your sleeping problem, for these searchings of My Truths have thoroughly shaken your temple, and are endangering your health. I will thoroughly protect your health and heal your body for the continuance of your study. Know that I am with you every step of the way.

Thus says
Ya

Really now? After we figured this out on our own, and we realized we survived on our own accord, He jumps in again to say that He led us to this knowledge that contradicts what He led us to before? He is even going so far to say that He agrees with these Bible-bashing books? And, He still has the nerve to say I do not have my own knowing about goodness and truth?: "You both have received My Set-Apart Spirit, and by My Spirit, I give you a 'knowing' in your mind and heart, to follow only good and Truth." Is Yahuah trying to possess me again and make my spirit His spirit? I guess I have had no ability of my own because only God gives life, breath, and purpose, thereby controlling every step of the way.

Unfortunately, I was not nearly as bothered by that sentence when I initially received the prophecy because my mother and I felt alone in our situation without a church. The stifling nature of the message balanced out our loneliness.

Again, there was another mention of the Elohim but in the shorter word "El": "Oh! Daughters! You say, where is the real El; where are you?" At the time, I did not probe into this word because I dismissed it as a singular pronoun or title. When reading it now, it looks like Yahuah wanted to share more revelation about His identity as though there was still more to learn. Was He testing the waters to see if I would want my eyes further opened? Certainly, He did not want my allegiance to stray if I would research something that could tarnish His image. Was He rethinking His strategy again?

The signature "Ya" is the Hebrew letter *yad* that depicts an arm and a hand that work, make, and throw. This single letter is sufficient to represent Yahshua.[11] This recent prophecy says that Ya is God's true name (after all of His other reported true names). It appears that Ya is not the abbreviated name of God that I had deduced before. Ya told us that we did not have to get baptized into this name because we were still following Him. I could not imagine God's name becoming more simplified or more "true"; this was as far as we could go with Him unless we learned something amazingly different.

A written dialogue that my mother had with Ya on June 8, 2005 is important because of how He addressed my illness that was still not healed.

Mom: Good morning, Ya.

Ya: Good morning, child.

Mom: Ya, I have so many unanswered questions, so I will ask you a few today. Is that okay?

Ya: Yes, child, certainly. I always have time for you.

Mom: Thank you.
        Ya, regarding that vision I had the other day, why is Theresa still in the bubble, reaching out to me, instead of outside the bubble with me?

Ya: Child, you see in the vision, the World with all of the darkness and distractions. The darkness holds all of mankind; animals, all created things, including good and bad. Theresa is being held against her will by the spirits of darkness, and fear of her own, which are minimal at this time. There are much great distractions and tantamount evils, fears and the like, which I have protected her from all her life. She is still vulnerable, but she will break through from the darkness with her desire to seek the Truth and Me during her life. She is rapidly breaking free of her fears of her past, by standing by her convictions and morals. These alone give her great potential for strength and wellness. My position in all of life's trials is to guide and direct those steps that man takes. I place desire for wellness and Truth in all mankind, but oftentimes, man uses his free will to seek out the easy way, indulge in evil ways that bring momentary pleasure and destruction. Child, Theresa is seeking only My Truth, and ultimately, with her pure desires for My love and devotion to the reality of Who I Am, she will be free from her past, the anger, frustration and fears it brought.

Mom: Thank you, Ya, for that explanation. So, if she is so intent on getting well, why isn't she yet? Why does she still feel so spooked at night, not able to sleep or eat properly? She has suffered so long!

Ya: My daughter, many times in one's trials and life's way, I seek to make man well but there are certain hidden desires that are not known to that daughter or son that keep them from moving forward. Theresa has still some deep set parts of her subconscious that has not let go of the childhood experiences of violence and abuse she endured. So, she, in a relaxed state at night, unconsciously remembers in her body the traumatic occurrences, which trigger a "heightened", as Theresa states, response and wakens her. Her body does not consciously have the ability to calm down. You see this situation takes more outside help, child. She is unable to do the breaking away. So, I will intercede in this matter, by bringing her fears to the forefront of her consciousness; and bring the realization of those happenings to her mind as the lesser evil for the present. I will help her help her mind recognize and accept the past, to leave it in the past, and move forward. No psychologist or practitioner can give Theresa what she needs but her Almighty One. My child, do not fret over these fears, which are not in your hands, but mine alone.

Mom: Thank you, Ya. Will she overcome these fears and negative thoughts?

Ya: Yes, with My help.

Mom: Then, Ya, will Theresa ultimately be standing outside the worldly bubble?

Ya: Yes, child, and she will walk hand in hand with you, in freedom and love.

The above message about healing describes a perfectly normal healing process because I would take the necessary time to deal with my unresolved thoughts and emotions. Additionally, what is most difficult to confront in my sub/unconsciousness can be handled with specific somatic psychological practices such as Eye Movement Desensitization and Reprocessing (EMDR), NET, and Emotional Freedom Technique (EFT) that release suppressed emotional energies and often bring the related thoughts to the forefront of our cognition. Yes, pent up trauma is extremely difficult to overcome, especially in the case of deep sleep where we have no control over nightmares. So, this would be where the Almighty God would heal me, correct? No. All I was told is that God would take the place of a therapist in weeding out my fears, when actually my outside help ended up being those psychologists and therapists who helped me face my fears.

Ya talked about the spirits of darkness that were entrapping me. As God, why did He often allow demonic entities to harass His chosen ones? God's emotionalism, incongruent commands, less than omniscient, omnipotent, and omnipresent abilities, and allowance of evil was making Him look like a human rather than a god. In response to my questions in one of His last prophetic communications to my mother (left undated, likely in 2005), Ya showed more of His contradictions:

1. Did different spirits use mom for her prophecies to me without her knowledge?

Ya: No, child, different spirits did not use your mother for her prophecies—I used the spirits of My choosing, to give messages to you without her knowledge.

2. Why do you use evil spirits with us—aren't we your chosen? What about when we were told that you gave Moses the original "10 Words" and inspired parts of the Book of John—was that still not total truth?

Ya: As I have spoken to you in messages before, I used good and evil for My purpose—My Ways are not your ways. In the biblical myths of old, many special men and women had good hearts, and were righteous beings. Through the centuries, simple rules to live by came into the social scene, and many of those were elevated to high places to continue the stories. They were not total truth.

3. Do we have spiritual bodies in heaven, or is it totally different than we have imagined—are you totally different?

Ya: Child, it is not the time to answer this question. I am Spirit; that is all for the moment.

4.   Can and will you heal and rejuvenate our bodies in giving it more youth inside and out after such turmoil we've gone through with no fault of our own, or do you only rely on the laws of nature that you've already created?

[Ya left this answer blank. In my persistence, He replied to my next set of questions, saying that He uses both His hand and the laws of nature.]

5.   Are we (myself included) supposed to get dialogue from you and not the type of prophecies mom used to get? Will it be only you, Ya, from here on out? And, will you become more interactive in a real relationship, or are you now further away?

Ya: I dialogue with My intimate ones. I also give gifts to those Chosen, as I have given you wisdom and knowledge within you about Me. My child, I am real in Spirit and in Truth. I have given you a deep hunger to seek out My Ways, which you will find. I am gentle and kind; closer to you than ever before.

These prophetic answers were not trustworthy. Ya skirted the answer to number 3, and He initially avoided number 4 to then somewhat answer the question the next time. In the previously written-out prophecies, He only conveyed what He wanted to tell us; it became obvious that He prefers that one-sided way of communicating, although number 5 says He does dialogue with His people. Worst of all, He says He uses evil for His dealings with us.

The paradigm of God is that He created everything and can control it all. However, to be the source of goodness, truth, and love while having no problem working with an enemy has never made sense to me and my mother. The abuses against us were not only allowed, but according to this message from Ya, could He have created some of the pain? This is a valid question because His tactics sometimes create division between His followers who question more than He willingly reveals. Are we really protected by our God?

I am certain that our belief in God protecting us from harm is a big reason why people continue to worship their religious mighty-man, but if it is according to God's whim, who can really trust Him? Is God rather a so-called god who is actually another entity like us? Ya, Yahuah, Yashua, and etcetera was on his way out of our lives, and I think he may have accepted it because his manipulative tactics could not keep us any longer.

Grand Intellect, Grand Master, and Love Source/Love Over All

The direct question and answer format was getting too close for comfort to the god that we previously followed. This god preferred to operate in a controlled format that would let him give the messages as he wanted. We knew that our god was possessive, and we were taught by the Bible and religion that it is a good thing; however, the progression of events that brought him closer to us—and he said he always wanted to reveal himself to us—clearly showed us that he has something to hide. He seemed to not be man enough for an intimate relationship! It reminds me of my failed relationships with men who said they wanted love and truth, but when I did not stroke their egos and pushed past walls and contradictions, they retreated. It was at this time that a possibly smarter and more capable god/entity took over; however, we did not want another god.

We continued the question and answer format to keep pressing toward the truth, and my mother received a new set of names: Grand Intellect (GI) and Love Source. Concepts were more specific and able to be categorized.

For example, on December 11, 2005, the GI stated:

> There are many facets of the being I have formed—they have spiritual—transcending the material, emotional—feeling, sensitivity, physical—tangible, an human being for example, and intellect—formulation of thought processes. Spiritual mates meet on a different level than physical mates do.

The GI said that it works with the Love Source, which is another aspect of truth. It continued:

> Negativity is around and inside all mankind, but pure love [Love Source] and truth in the conscious mind [Grand Intellect] can, and will turn against the negativity of the will, prevailing in goodness and truth. The Grand Intellect and Love Source make it happen with the positive will.

The language above appears to signify beings that act, so we wondered if the message was from another entity. My mother wanted no part of that, so she decided to ask what the GI was.

December 31, 2005
Mother (M): Are you a spirit?

Answer (A): No.

M: Are you an entity?

A: No.

M: Do you give me answers of your choosing for me to know or wait until I ask the questions?

A: Wait until you ask the questions.

M: Why?

A: Because I know what you will ask before you ask it—I know all things.

M: What substance are you made of?

A: Air, water, fire, earthly elements but invisible to the naked eye.

M: Another dimension?

A: Yes.

M: I thought you were above all things, through all, and in everything, or am I wrong?

A: The Love source accomplished those things. I do not.

M: What do you do then?

A: I wake you up in the morning, motivate all living things into a state of action and productiveness.
[Note: This was like the April 16, 2005 prophecy! I still could not do anything on my own, it seems.]

M: What gives us our intellect, with limits and boundaries? Are we a part of the Grand Intellect with our measure of knowledge and understanding from that source?

A: Yes. The measure will grow for those who seek it.

We were unsure if the non-entity Source started the communication or if the GI was feeding our desire for that purity. The rest of the communication admitted that the GI consists of material substances like ours but in another dimension. We did not yet know what exists outside of our dimension, so the beginning of the communication pacified us for a while. Interestingly, the Love Source seems like a far greater energy than the GI.

I compared and contrasted thousands of subsequent questions we asked to everything that transmitted through my mother in order to get to the true Source, so this was just the beginning. I will show various excerpts of communications to highlight differing communication styles. I argue that we must have discernment throughout each message so that we do not immediately believe it as truthful just because it is from a "higher" being. I aim to show how we can find truth as it is versus the way an entity describes it. Look out for the patterns and distinctions that emerge.

Communications with the GI often proceeded from a written set of questions. This style of communicating felt better to us because my mom was significantly less controlled. We were of course still cautious toward the nature of what was communicating with her.

January 17, 2006

Me: Did the YHWH/Jesus group of spirit beings want to help us or deceive us or both? Did they know some of what you know because they are in your dimension that can know you better, or are they lost in a different dimension than you are in? Are those spirits those of people who have died, or are they angels gone bad? Is there a black and white, good and evil?

GI: The Yhwh/Jesus group of spirit beings wanted to deceive to be worshipped. They are in the realm of the religious-thinking world—to rule and be followed. They are not spirits of people or angels gone bad, but invaders of human lives. The Grand Intellect sends angelic beings to protect human beings. Invader beings come from other dimensions. Black and white exists, but mankind lives in the gray area. There is good and evil. Evil comes from separateness from the Love Source.

January 18, 2006

Me: You are supposed to know everything, right? Then why not tell me the timeframe?

GI: Time does not exist in this dimension. The Grand Intellect does not work on the World's time frame.

January 22, 2006

Questions from my mother to the GI:

1. What gift do I have in regards to communication with the Love Source and Grand Intellect?

GI: You have a special vision to see beyond the World's religions—a kind of clairvoyancy.

2. Is it futuristic or present visionary clairvoyancy?

GI: Both.

3. Why is it that I cannot get a clear vision of the lettered communication you give me?

GI: You are not focusing entirely on the energy source connecting the Grand Intellect/Love Source and yourself.

4. I have noticed that I can communicate with the Grand Intellect/Love Source when I choose or not choose to—is that my choice or yours?

GI: The choice is yours through the power of your will.

5. Does the Grand Intellect/Love Source heal man's diseases, or does man have to seek out resources himself through the world in order to attain health?

GI: The Grand Intellect provides the knowledge through the world's resources to obtain wellness. The Grand Intellect does not heal diseases.

6. What does the Love Source do for man?

GI: The Love Source gives love, warmth, light to man's life in order for man to obtain wellness and balance.

7. Where does peace come from?

GI: Peace comes from a balance and harmony of man's physical, emotional, mental state and spiritual components. Man's biorhythm is out of balance when any one component is flawed.
    [Note: The January 22, 2006 answers were generally correct, although the Love Source definition is a stepped-down interpretation by the GI.]

Early to mid-2006 (I did not write the exact date)
Questions from me to the GI:

1. Are the Grand Intellect and destiny different, and how?

GI: Yes—The Grand Intellect draws those who are worthy—towards Truth. Destiny is what is to be; good or evil as an outcome.

2. Is the Grand Intellect not able to predict the choices of others that go against truth because the G.I. is only in the light and doesn't know much of darkness?

GI: The Grand Intellect can predict the choices of others that go against truth, but directs the paths of those who seek Truth, and not the others who are against Truth and goodness. Those humans are left in darkness and are lost in a void.

3. Why did the Grand Intellect tell me the future when the future is not happening that way—does it only know the present and then predict the future as though the present will continue?

GI: The Grand Intellect knows the present and predicts the future. Whether its outcome is good or evil depends on those seeking Truth and are drawn towards the Light and Knowledge, which is good, and those left in the world's mentality and religious mindset, which is darkness, and changes the future of those in complacency. The Grand Intellect is in timelessness, and draws only the pure hearted towards Truth and Love.

4. It said it knows all things, so it knows man's hearts. But can't hearts change, and doesn't that mean the truth about [an ex-boyfriend] coming to me and the G.I.'s supposed omniscient knowledge will change?

GI: Hearts can change—The Grand Intellect knows all things and does not change. [Ex-boyfriend's] heart has changed towards Evil; and he has made his choice about his life.

5. Then why did the G.I. tell me to stand on what it told me with [ex-boyfriend] being the one for me and that he will come to me in true love? Where is the G.I.'s consistency?

GI: The Grand Intellect directs matters of the mind and gives Knowledge. The Love Source intervened with [ex-boyfriend] and true love, for it gives warmth, love and works with human emotion and energy. The Love Source must be addressed with matters of love and emotions of the heart, not the G.I.

6.   Can I believe that the Grand Intellect and Love Source are opening up the right place for me and mom in this world with jobs and purpose, or is the power of other people's wills too strong for goodness to happen for us?

GI: Yes, the Grand Intellect only will open up the right job and purpose in the right place in this world for both. People's wills do not interfere with goodness, for pure and good energy is stronger.

At the end of January 2006, the GI gave the love source a name, "Love Over All." I wondered why the GI gave the purity of love a name with position over others. Wouldn't love be through something and not over it? It appeared to me that the GI was enhancing its interpretation about love similar to an entity's perspective. It advised me to "let the Love Over All do its work." It continued:

> Love Over All has great strength, beyond what a being can do. It can turn around relationships—social and otherwise. Once you understand these things, the Grand Intellect will strengthen your entire being with knowledge, wisdom and truth.

Another time, the GI stated:

> The Grand Intellect and Love Source work with human beings, empowering them to seek Truth, and pursuing truth for others. I am energy with intellectual power, not a spirit or corporal being. I do not "do" but empower societies, universes, races to perform.

In the same message, I enquired, "What power does my love have, and will the Love Over All do the work?"

The GI responded, "Human love is very strong and the Love Source enhances that love we have. Yes, the Love Over All will <u>do</u> the work."

My analysis: Note the "we" that links the GI to humans but not with the Love Over All. The GI also stated that it empowers others and opens up situations for us as though it acts like a god that does "do" actions.

It is obvious in the above communications that I was still leaning on this other "power" for direction in my life. When the GI stated that it and the

Love Over All act powerfully, this pacified my desire for a strong force to fight my battles and lead me. Little did I realize that if I was being led to the extent that the GI said, then this did put my life in someone else's hands, much like religion.

There is a religious undertone of perception and division that these communications convey that was still acceptable to my mother and me on some level. We still carried an antagonistic view that had us fighting toward a goal. It is entirely valid to see differences, and we sometimes must press forward no matter what; however, we did not know how to view life in a complete, whole manner because we had not yet attained the lens of peace outside of war.

I also did not know how to view love properly. Love always felt greater than I am, so I associated it with a supernatural origin. When love filled my heart, it was thus divine, destined, and "meant to be." It was a secure, peaceful, and happy feeling that I always wanted with me. I was taught at a young age that Jesus is love, and this theme carried forth in my mother's prophecies. This correlation brought me to think that all of my good feelings were given to me rather than me owning my creation of them.

The Bible's messages about God affected my interpretation of love because he has a jealous nature, and his love often does not last. My relationships proved this fragmented love when the men left me. However, I shuddered to think if God—and to a lesser extent these men—could fail me; it was easier to blame myself about the broken relationships although I did all I could to save them. I just could not accept the possibility that God and his gifts to me could be imperfect.

After many sessions with psychologists to learn healthier perspectives about relationships, I had to evaluate my prior beliefs. I learned I was obsessive and possessive, not filled with the openness of love. The concept of love that I was taught in Christianity was based upon obedience to God in order to then receive his love. Basically, I had to become an obsessed, needy person to gain God's affections. My father helped translate this to the human level at which I had to settle for the crumbs of care he gave me so I could receive basic necessities. This theme carried forth into several of my relationships.

If this so-called "love" did not last when I did what I could to please these people and God, then was there a deep love somewhere that would last? Was there a lasting truth? I wanted to know truth more than anything so that I could know if anything mattered in life, if there was stability and something upon which to stand.

It took most of my life to awaken to the fact that there is another level of love and truth than I had experienced. It is a sad reality that our negative experiences darken our views toward what else is out there, but when we finally pay attention to our core intuition, it can and does open up more insights to us.

While I was still trying to make sense of things, the Grand Intellect showed an obvious red flag by using the word "pray" on December 1, 2005:

> Pray for the Light to reach him, not against the darkness. I am that Light, and I will reach him. Love does prevail…. Be patient because things change on both ends. My Light shines through all things. That is what truly matters.

This sort of questionable language, along with the Light and Dark reference, is what kept me and my mother questioning whether the GI was an entity. It is not far-fetched to recall the Bible's reference to Lucifer as an angel of light.

At the beginning of February 2006, as we were reading more about Christianity's history, a new name was revealed to my mother when she asked questions: Grand Master. The name Grand Master definitely did not sound as good as Grand Intellect, but it carried the same tone as the GI and the same delineation toward the Love Over All/Love Source (it used both names but at different times). Although we both never felt right with the name Master, we believed we were continuing to advance because we were given good answers in the beginning.

We asked if the Grand Master (GM) was a god or entity to which it replied, "no." Maybe this was the true energy source coming through to start the communication again, or the GM was lying.

For example, my mother asked, "Is there something greater than the Love Source and Grand Master?"

It replied, "No. The love source and Grand Master overseed [sic] elements that have always been."

On March 9, 2006, my mother again asked if the GM was an entity or god, and it continued to say that it was not.

She proceeded to ask my question, "Can the gods heal people, and how if healing gives life, and the gods are in darkness?"

The GM replied, "There are no real gods. Elevated humans in people's minds—invader spirits [are] in different realms in darkness, trying to control and take over the material bodies. Religion has duped man's consciousness into believing healing and miracles are possible from the outside. Healing does not give life; life and goodness gives healing."

This sounded innovative to me, even freeing because I could have what I wanted by just living a good life. Unfortunately, as we continued with the GM, it seemed too good to be true.

Me: Does the Grand Master and/or Love Over All heal our diseases, and will it get rid of my Epstein-Barr problem? Or, how can it go away?

GM: The Grand Master and Love Over All helps and directs man to seek Truth and revelations come to help man help him/herself—the body will heal itself. As the body heals itself, the Epstein-Barr virus will die to itself.

Actually, the systemic herpes virus rarely if ever dies and usually becomes dormant, but I did not know this at the time. I still carried the Christian belief of healing as an all-or-nothing event, although I realized it could be far off in the future. The GM seemed to support my belief.

I took to this message with joy because it sounded as though I would still be cured. This message of my body healing on its own was a complete turnaround from the God of the prophecies being in control, so it made me believe I was on the right track with the Grand Master. However, that name, that name! It always felt dark to me.

The GM said that it directs humans. I did not understand the nature of the Source energy—could it do everything on its own as a *doing* and not *being* consciousness? It directing me sounded okay, but it seems as though it is an entity that acts. It also stated, "Truth will prevail." Those are quite strong words that a religious person would say.

We could not shake our negative feeling about the Grand Master's name and decided to explore its nature instead of really believe it. Interestingly, the Grand Intellect soon came back. We do not exactly recall what the GI told my mother upon its return, but we welcomed it over the GM. Conveniently, it returned just days before we learned about the Grand Master, the supreme commander of the Knights Templar, from the movie *The Da Vinci Code*. The Knights Templar carried out rampant bloodshed for their religious agenda that had secrets, disgusting rituals, and pervasive symbolism—all the things from which we wanted to be free.

The GI continued the GM's sentiment toward truth:

May 15, 2006

Me: Is the power of people's wills <u>only</u> allowed to delay the onset of what you say will happen to them, or can their will actually change the truth itself, thus rendering your words incorrect in the end (such as with [ex-boyfriend] and me)? So, with the topic of him now coming to me later, should I <u>always</u> stand on everything you told me about him and him leaving his current girlfriend and realizing his love for me?

GI: Yes, the power of people's wills only allows delay to happenings in their futures. Truth does not change. Yes, you should stand on what knowledge has been given to you concerning [ex-boyfriend].

The GI presented this perspective about love and truth as unshakable because of the tiny openness in the other person at that time. My experiences have shown that everyone can have a moment where this slight openness can present itself, even if it is an unconscious memory or tenderness coming to the surface. I can see a measure of goodness in all people, but to presume what I see is the reality of their thoughts and actions would turn me into quite a know-it-all. I accepted the GI's answer because of my religious lens; however, I had to learn to wake up to reality. The fact is that my reality involved spiritual visions that kept me connected to a deeper part of my ex-boyfriend but not to my everyday ex-boyfriend. The GI stated that my visions would come true, so I again believed as I did when I was a Christian, where a supernatural phenomenon would override the other person's "lost" perspective and will.

I was strung along—again—to believe that a past love interest would come back to me, and again this did not happen. He actually dropped off the face of the Earth from me, so these misleading messages of hope were confusing and destructive to me. My heartache was used to steer me toward relying upon another god.

My mother broke her ties with one god that gave her the Christian prophecies, yet it seemed that another god or gods were communicating with her afterward. If they were entities as well, which the Grand Master proved itself to be, then that means she was still receiving prophecies. We made sure to break off communication with the Grand Master, but we were still trying to gauge whom or what was the Grand Intellect while remaining somewhat open to it.

On June 1, 2006, I finally became brave enough to ask the GI about that bigger possible reality in which humans are not the only tangible, top-of-the line creation in the entire universe. Christians believe in angels as higher beings, but their etheric nature along with God's keeps the hierarchical perception about non-material beings.

Angels and gods exhibit traits similar to humans in the Bible and in countless stories that are deemed mythologies. Instead of passing them off as myths other than really scrutinizing these stories, could it be possible that the angels and so-called gods are more tangible than we have been led to believe? Are there—gasp—aliens?

Me: Are there alien beings with similar physical worlds to the Earth, and are you there also? How are we so special? That may sound like human elevation, like religion.

GI: Yes, there are alien beings, but they do not have similar physical worlds to Earth, and no, the Grand Intellect is not there. Those who seek Ultimate Truth are worthy. They seek with purity of mind and heart, unlike religious minded humans.

Whoa. There *are* aliens out there! I had to let this information soak in. The cosmos is quite big to be able to contain other life, and we can see a plethora of stars and planets through the Hubble telescope. The answer was not descriptive, but it underscored my analysis that the GI is finite. The GI has conveyed itself as all-knowing, but how can that be while it has a limited range?

The separate but collaborative "beings" of knowledge and love made sense to us at the time because we were still working our way through divisive concepts. Therefore, we proceeded with the GI and the Love Source/Love Over All (I chose to continue calling it Love Source because love has to originate somewhere). We believed that my mother would get to the underlying truth eventually.

June 1, 2006

Me: Are other dimensions entirely without truth or love, and the beings in there cannot leave if you cannot go there? But I thought you would be drawing beings out everywhere? Do those different beings in other dimensions have their own form of collective consciousness like the G.I.?

GI: Each dimension has a measure of truth and love, but are governed by the Spirits of that realm. The Grand Intellect is not there. As long as the Spirits control men's minds and spirits in those realms, the Grand Intellect and Love Source do not draw them out; they do not seek the Ultimate Truth, Purity and Love in their highest form. The Grand Intellect and Love Source draw out all beings in those dimensions who seek Ultimate Truth and Love. No, they do not.

A bit later in the communication, the GI answered: The invader beings are not in the Truth seekers dimension, for they remain in darkness; truth seekers are protected by the guardians of Truth.

Mid-June 2006

Me: Are the invader spirits the gods, and can they change if they are aware of you? Or, are they evil since they want to control us and gain our energy—like, are they blind to truth somehow? Is evil not just a concept but a real energy that can consume those that want it?

GI: Invader spirits are evil entities/spirits in lower dimensions. They live in darkness, unaware of ultimate Truth, Light and Love. Evil is not a real energy but a real desire to create chaos. It consumes many.

The GI said each dimension has a measure of truth and love and is governed by spirits. Negative spirits are in the lower dimensions, yet somehow they are not in the dimensions of truth-seeking humans. To the contrary, the January 17, 2006 communication said that humans live in the gray area, so this confirms that the negative entities live among us. Our desire for truth can make us separate from the deceptive energies, but to say that our lower dimension of Earth density is a different dimension than negative entities is untrue. Those entities do influence the thoughts of everyone here; negativism is rampant on Earth. To believe otherwise is putting our heads in the clouds instead of identifying what is around us. It puts us in a dream state much like religion does when thinking we are entirely separate when we are not, but at the same time, we are giving our power away to a potentially negative entity as god. The GI stated that each realm has governing spirits.

The GI tried to pass itself off as a non-entity of ultimate truth. If it were a pure energy source, it would not say with such conviction that humans are bound to some type of god/entity/spirit. This includes angels who hang around or protect us when we are supposedly with the beautiful Source energy. It seemed like we were still part of a religious construct that had us rely upon other entities for help instead of just being together in our respective capacities where we are truly free.

October 8, 2006

Mom: What are the burdens of [another guy] that Theresa is carrying? Must she continue to carry his burdens? Why must she persevere in sending love energy to his energy source when she has no guarantee it will help him?

GI: Theresa is carrying the weight of his pain from his past. His denial of his condition potentiates the pain. No, she must not continue to carry his pain and denial, but release these burdens to the Love Source to embrace. She must continue sending the powerful energy of the Love Source to him, for there will be no hope of reaching Ultimate Love and Truth without this transferred gift. This is necessary for all those less fortunate, despite their willful obstinance. [Note: This man had schizophrenic tendencies, but he was also very stubborn on his own.]

The GI told me to give my loving energy to someone who did not want it. The GI said that it was necessary, but this action continuously drained me. I can love and give but not as a mandate, especially when I have already done my share. I was told to act in this sacrificial way when I was a Christian.

It is not my responsibility to transfer love and truth to someone else—that person must want it and work to obtain it on his own. There was already hope for that person if he connected to his own love and truth within him. I slowly started to realize this, but I still felt as though the responsibility was placed on my shoulders. In fact, I was told it was my responsibility, so if I would say "No," I thought I would be doing something wrong. I was still developing my sense of self and boundaries.

When I followed up with the GI about the love energy, it appeared that the Love Source answered.

October 14, 2006

Me: Doesn't all the positive energy that I AND my mom are sending accumulate in power, so shouldn't all of [the guy's] darkness and walls disappear faster with time instead of time just drag on and on as though nothing is working? It has been already 1.5 months of constant love for him. Why hasn't it worked enough or at all, and he has still exed me completely out of his life?

Love Source: No, the positive energy that you and your mom send does not accumulate in power but acts as a bridge generating positive energy to his energy core. It does not work or dispel his darkness and walls faster or slowly, but, just works until the hardened heart softens and change comes about. The Love Source is still working even though he has closed all avenues of communication to you.

The GI put its perspective of power into its communications, even misrepresenting the Love Source to which it was supposedly connected. The Love Source did not answer in terms of power.

The source of love has to be a pure place beyond material elements. What is material can be affected by love, but love is not affected by what is material. The "earthly elements" that constitute the GI would be affected by the material in the GI's realm, thereby living with cause and effect that are a form of time. The GI tried to convey a superior timelessness that was set-apart from us, but it is made of similar elements to us.

In conclusion, it is clear that the Grand Intellect and Grand Master are entities, just like the entity that gave my mother prophecies as a Catholic and Christian. Although her style of communication was different than before, and she tried communicating through her core instead of her mind, the GI and GM communications still treated her as a prophet who could be molded to their perceptions and agendas. The Love Source was the exception, which we hoped to further understand.

I wish to demystify the status of a prophet, for it is only the communication from one entity (with or without a god status) to another entity (human). People say that God talks to them often. Just because my mother is not a man at the right historical place at the right time does not mean that she has been less of a prophet than anyone else.

Whereas many people like feeling important as a prophet, my mother wanted no more prophecies from an entity—we just did not feel comfortable trusting anyone at that stage unless it was the pure energy source. We intuitively knew that there was an energy source beyond the god entity realm, but we did not know how to get there and if it would involve more interference. Must our dense material state first go through the spiritual realm in order to get past it to a pure source? I did not understand the levels beyond us as humans. I hoped that we have easy access to this Source, and this access exist somewhere, somehow within us.

Defining All That Is, The Pure Essence

My mother and I entered year 2007 with the understanding that there were countless light beings who have been around longer than humans; whether they are trustworthy and honest is the point of debate. I would simply love it if one of those entities would say, "I do not know" instead of offering educated guesses, beliefs, or worse, sinister motives. I would also love it if entities would leave us alone and let us contact the appropriate entity or energy that we desire, if we desire.

As my mother could not clearly identify the Source just yet, 2007 had less communications than usual. We needed to first gain more understanding about other realms and entities to better ascertain the interferences. We also needed to ponder whether we could even find that pure energy source. It was as though we had to climb out of all material to find ground zero, the calm before the storm of creation. It actually took a few years until 2010 for us to gain satisfactory understanding, but 2007 was the year of the most obvious flip-flopping between entities openly declaring themselves and the original conscious source clearly revealing itself as the correct All That Is.

I say "correct" because at first what was revealed to us was the phrase "All That Is." Although this is its main description, entities who indirectly know about it frame it within their religious views thereby muddling its true nature. This book's first edition stated the "All That Is" describing itself as "the pure essence," but I did not know I needed to include the phrase in its title to discern its nature versus how entities have incorrectly interpreted it. Therefore, I asked the "All That Is" in 2013 what its most descriptive title is, and it replies, "All That Is, The Pure Essence."

The process of discovering the All That Is, The Pure Essence (ATI,TPE) took my mother and me a few years to properly discern and understand it. This section retraces defining moments of discernment toward ATI,TPE communications versus outside entity interferences and interpretations.

My first task was to face the alien mystery by breaking the stronghold of fear about such a phenomenon. Aliens seemed unreal to me because of my Christian conditioning that denied their existence. I used to think all aliens were like demons and monsters due to certain Hollywood stories imparting fear and passing it off as entertainment. However, these "monsters" are finite beings like us humans, so I could overcome my fear by seeing them as they are. This act of identification is also useful toward angels and gods.

The Bible said that angels appeared often and that they looked like humans; this proves that their otherworldly, light being status is not mystical as a so-called God of boundless power. This sober perspective helped me demystify those scary demons, including Satan, because they are also finite beings, as the Bible confirmed. It was the fear of the unknown that was most troublesome.

Fear has to be their way to us like a negatively polarized bridge away from love. Entities are generally powerless on their own if not for their manipulative tactics that mainly impart fear. Once I realized that these entities are not immaterial blobs that could be almost anywhere unable to be pegged, I could identify the element of fear and push it away, thereby realizing my own boundary around me.

We all have our own sense of personal space, but it is still difficult to overcome all fear when these religious entities, including ones that my mother sees in her visionary state, are comprised of a less dense composition that can enter our realm and interact with our energy fields. This is freaky, but if we identify an otherworldly entity as we view another person in the room, we will not think it is bigger than life or more powerful than us; we can merely tell it to go away and then continue onward with our lives.

This process of realization was very challenging because I had to overcome Christianity's successful tactic of chiseling away my self-belief. I mustered the courage to search for pictures of the fabled Grey aliens on the internet. Previously, I randomly saw internet links to videos and stories about these aliens and UFOs, but I was too afraid and actually angry to have this information thrust into my consciousness. I simply did not want to believe this possible reality.

Once I recognized this theme of fear, I stayed up late for several nights in awe (and fear) of what I found. Of course, I was scared; I surpassed one fear by exploring it but then lived another. What is important is that I was dealing with it, and soon afterward, I was past it at that level. Before I got to the stage of acceptance (I use this term to imply realism—I was not happy about this alien knowledge), I needed some grounding to give me a measure of peace with this new world view. I engaged my mother's abilities again to find out what is beyond the entities; I knew I would find peace there, similar to how she felt when diving down through the layers of water to the dry ground in her prior dream.

I presented a set of questions to both the GI and Love Source separately. My mom was not yet formally introduced to the ATI,TPE, but she could sense its energy essence. We hoped to get a revealing lead, either in an obvious error by the GI or clear truth coming through as the next step.

May 2007
To the Grand Intellect:
1. What are you exactly? Do you have a name or just a description? What is the relationship between the Love Source and the Grand Intellect? Why can the Love Source also give words?

Answer: Intelligence over all. No name. I am described as All That Is. We are One with two characteristics. This accounts for the language used and communicated.

2. Are you that source of perfect intelligence that is above all aliens, spirits, and consciousness? How if you are not across all dimensions but are only in this dimension where humans are? But, other dimensional creatures also get to our dimension, so why is it that you are not across all dimensions, and is this the same about the Love Source's presence also?

Answer: Yes. The human consciousness communicates and receives communication on the dimension it exists within. All That Is does communicate to the "creatures" on each dimension, on different levels to be understood; and to experience goodness and "love" for others of their kind.

3. What is in control of the Earth/our dimensions, and why? Is there something about our emotions and mental energy that they want, like does it keep their energy alive? Does our energy and existence after physical death eventually die out like the Sun?

Answer: The advanced races on the elevated dimensions control Earth and its humans, to inhabit the Earth one day. Yes. No, the human body, like a shell, is shrugged off, and the individual spirit coexists with "pure light" and lives on.

4. Why did my mom dive through water to get to you and the Love Source?

Answer: She was moving toward her inner core, to reach pure light, thought and love in a visual dream.

To the Love Source:
5. Are you what is "good" and the Grand Intellect is just fact, or are you both more than this? Does your energy overpower the manipulation of other energies, and how—is it simply due to a higher frequency, or is there more to it than that?

Answer: We are One; with total goodness and intelligence, separate and combined. Yes, by directing thought processes and diverse emotions toward the ultimate good and knowledge. Vibrational frequencies are a means to reach these goals.

 I was unsure if these answers comprised a type of oneness with the ATI,TPE and the first type of field frequency extension to us, but then some of these answers did not distinguish between the ATI,TPE and the Grand Intellect. The GI "speaks" in terms of hierarchy, so I determined that it communicated in the beginning when it said "Intelligence over all." The GI also speaks in terms of oneness. I mainly addressed the GI in this communication, so it is expected that it would have answered although my mom and I did not know what else to call the pure source that we deeply desired. Thankfully, our desire allowed enough space for the ATI,TPE to come through in the communication to state, "No name. I am described as All That Is." The ATI,TPE indicates that these were its only words in the message dominated by the GI and its interpretation that pluralizes the ATI.

 When my mother understood that her dream showed her core self intimately connected to the beginning source, I gained strength from her revelation and focused upon the lower middle section of my breastplate that feels completely still. I do not recall if I said the title "All That Is" because I did not want it to be like a prayer, but I did think of love and truth. I focused upon this area in the way that my mother first saw a glowing "sun," and I expanded the energy from there to fill my entire body. Then, I pushed it outward to surround my entire apartment like a bubble. This provided me the security I needed, and I did feel protected within this energy bubble—it felt peaceful and grounded wherein I owned myself and my surroundings. It did not matter that I did not know the precise location of the ATI,TPE space within myself, nor did I envision it properly because the glowing sphere is not the ATI,TPE but the frequency action of its extension after it; my pure intent was there, which made my approximated efforts work.

I loved talking about otherworldly topics with people to see what else I could learn. A new friend of mine knew more than I did at that time, so he suggested that I read any book by David Icke. Icke addresses certain manipulative entities and their agendas behind religion and politics. I perked my ears, although I was also on guard. My friend said that Icke's message was ultimately uplifting because he also mentions a source beyond the junk. I decided to read his book, *And the Truth Shall Set You Free*, and I saw that he mentions "Source of all that is" (p. 429).[12] At that time, my mother and I had not yet seen or heard anyone stating "all that is" in relation to the Source. We thought we found agreement in Icke's work that confirms she reached the true source, and we felt emboldened in our path (while of course continuously probing the All That Is—The Pure Essence—to see if it is that consistent and true source). We did not yet understand that his wording does not equate Source to all that is; instead, he appears to believe there is a Source before All That Is. He uses the description "infinite consciousness" to represent "God and Creation" (p. xv).[12]

In his later book, *The David Icke Guide to the Global Conspiracy (and how to end it)*, he capitalizes Infinite Consciousness and then replaces it with "Infinite Awareness" as the "level of consciousness that knows it is everything. It is the self-aware ALL" (p. 2-3).[13] His mention of All That Is, now capitalized as a proper title, pales in comparison to how often he states the Infinite Awareness. I first wondered if he refers to Infinite Awareness as a name to represent an understandable concept to the public. As I thought about it further, I noticed that he continually references his spirit guides from whom he gathered his information. Was this Infinite Awareness (IA) actually a group of entities as a type of collective consciousness?

This group consciousness reached my mother in her May 2007 communication. We wondered what the IA is. Is it a type of collective consciousness? Is it aligned with the ATI,TPE, or is our core self a part of it? Is it as high up as we could get, so maybe it is trustworthy? Many entities describe themselves as most knowledgeable about everything back to the beginning, even claiming to be that source, so we continued to be discerning.

At the time, I deduced that this community consciousness that connected with my mother either identified itself with the frequency of Love, for it as a group of entities is vibrational; or, it was a type of gestalt that constitutes varying views, some which carry religious self-importance. I wondered if its awareness is limited to its level of understanding, as all of our awareness is limited according to what we have learned and experienced. I will investigate the Infinite Awareness shortly.

In July 2007, a book caught my eye at the library called *Pleiadian Perspectives on Human Evolution*.[14] I could not ignore that title because it carries an air of knowledge about an incredibly important topic as though these entities were around long before the Earth's creation. They also mention All That Is! Author or scribe Amorah Quan Yin channeled Pleiadian entities who intricately described their otherworldly realm with a scientific presentation that relates to our dimensional structures. They said that they work behind the scene for our planet. They claimed to control the Earth, right down to the Earth's spin. They said that two Pleiadian angels hold the Earth on its axis! I found that hard to believe, but the way they presented our solar system's history was so convincing that I thought, "Who am I to discredit it? I wasn't around then."

These entities give the impression that they are demigods or gods who are in control of our physical lives. Now where have I heard that before? They call our density an illusion because they can see through it, yet I assume that they would think their density is real.

I reflected upon their phrase "God/Goddess/All That Is" in the book's introduction. I realized that my doubt is valid concerning much of their story because they are equating the ATI,TPE to a creator entity in their religious paradigm, and they are elevating themselves with exaggerated abilities. These Pleiadians believe the yin-yang theory in which wholeness is the combination of two polarities defined as male and female who are treated as two halves of a whole. I refuse to label "higher" energies in terms of sexuality unless these energies come from entities and are sexual. The ATI,TPE has no sexuality and is entirely whole on its own regardless of what was created after it. Therefore, the ATI,TPE in no way can be equated to their definition of God or Goddess.

They also said that the Galactic Center joins other galaxies and orbits around the Great Central Sun of All That Is. This phrasing is similar to the unclear language of the IA, where All That Is can be a creation of the Great Central Sun "God" along with the God and Goddess duality of creation, or it is the Great Central Sun. Both definitions can apply in a belief system that asserts everything as ultimately One and All. The Pleiadian perspective gives its "All That Is" immense force and power.

These Pleiadians know "of" a creative source as the All That Is, and they know about certain energetic frequencies; however, they do not really know the All That Is, The Pure Essence or the first type of field frequency because they are not directly connecting to them to gain accurate clarity. Their Great Central Sun may be the extent of their knowledge, which means that they have much more to learn. They define the ATI,TPE within a boundary of their own belief system, similar to how Judeo-Christians define Yahuah, although the Pleiadians present a bigger picture to ponder.

It is a red flag when a channeling associates the ATI,TPE with a material star as in Sun worship. To be fair, perhaps some of those entities approximate the ATI,TPE through their filters in a similar way to when my mother first saw a type of glowing connection to it. If this has happened, they have not gone further to connect with the true All That Is, The Pure Essence to clarify itself and the nature of early realms before the Pleiadian "Great Central Sun." Quan Yin states that one or more Pleiadians by the name of Ra channeled most of her book. I did not pay much heed to this name at the time because I did not know enough about it except that Ra was an Egyptian god. As I reveal in chapter 7, Ra is also a nickname for a specific star, so if this star is the Pleiadian Great Central Sun, then they are very far away from the ATI,TPE.

As I introduced in chapter 1, the ATI,TPE communicates that it is a simple essence unto itself that precedes any light or movement. The ATI,TPE clarifies that my mother's vision about the mini "sun" in her core was actually her core self that connected with a sparkling, cloud-like wave-field (that I call Love) that transports the non-moving ATI,TPE's message to her. This "Love" is comprised of very different energy than the stars—a subtle energy that is not forceful or gravitational, but it is completely able and aware on its own.

I asked my mother to read *Pleiadian Perspectives* to confirm if my gut reactions were correct against some of its messages. She felt the counterintuitive reactions that I did, but she also was intrigued like I was with the seemingly knowledgeable scientific presentation.

After reading most of the book, a light being approached her while she was resting in bed. It called her name and introduced itself as Ra. Ra said that he came to her because she was now open and knowledgeable about him. He said he loved her and wanted to help her understand more things.

When she told me that Ra visited her, I immediately asked her how she felt. She was not entirely sure, but she said she felt okay enough. She told me that she would be cautious. I was almost a bit happy because of what he told her. Quan Yin also conveyed how happy she was to know Ra, so that persuaded me a bit. Ra portrayed his image in the book to be honest and loving toward us. I did not want to believe that every entity was deceptive, so I thought that maybe one (or a collective) would come to help us make better sense of things.

Ra returned a couple more times, calling her name again with more intensity to wake her up from sleep. She realized this interaction was a repeat of what happened to her as a Christian; therefore, she told Ra to depart and never return. These visitations happened around the time that she decided to not finish reading the book because she said it had religious connotations and untruths. Ra was trying to influence her personally while she was losing interest. I was grateful for her input and confirmation that helped me better understand my intuition versus my belief or hope.

Within a matter of days, a female entity came to my mom. She said, "You have finally found me. My name is Sophia. I am wisdom. Your daughter has me." (Just writing these words gave me chills.) When my mom told me this, I immediately told her that this is wrong and that I want no part of it. It was wrong because wisdom cannot be an entity or be any sex—more ridiculousness!

I strongly advised her to cease all communications with these entities who weaseled their way to her while she was open in her research. She and I are genuine in our search for truth, so when we read or hear something convincing, we are open to all possibilities. That can temporarily make us feel ungrounded, but our intuition is still there to provide feedback and set us on track. This process to uncover truth surpasses any bias that we may have because we react out of the goodness within ourselves; therefore, we can trust our assessments.

Up to this point, we did not get much communication from the ATI,TPE because entities were desirous to intervene, and they did so with eloquence and persuasion. The ATI,TPE is a very different energy essence that my mom and I needed to understand so we could put the material realms into perspective. Because we were unclear about its nature and if there even is a different Love Source energy, we asked both the Love Source and All That Is for help with my relationship issues. We received answers from each of them, but the IA and/or sometimes the GI—without mentioning its name—attached itself to my mother's connection with the ATI,TPE. We only wanted clear connection with the purest energy consciousness before creation, so we decided to focus solely on what we knew as the ATI,TPE.

The ATI,TPE was quite matter-of-fact in response to my relationship woes. It responded that a man who I was dating was just "a fairly good person." That was an accurate, over-all assessment; he led me to believe he wanted truth and love, but unbeknownst to me at the time, he was secretly dating other women. The ATI,TPE continued to state in the present tense how the man feels and how the situation is. No promises for change, only what is happening.

Instead of a wishful, dream-like perspective about love, I started to view it realistically: both people share a connection and use their drive to make the relationship work. The people do it, not "love does the work," although pure love does open up the desire to connect. This helped me to put love into a more accurate perspective, but I still had a long way to go. I and my mother took several years to gain ourselves back after believing for so long that we were at the receiving end of our lives, not in control.

On March 3, 2008, I gave her more questions to understand love and the

ATI,TPE. The answers varied.

"The All That Is is the same in all creation with the awareness of its existence, whether the focus on it is there or not." This was similar to the initial answers in the last set of questions.

"Your infinite awareness of the All That Is is love but these people you mention do not have awareness of the All That Is; therefore, they cannot have love towards you. You are attempting to awaken the Infinite Awareness within them by sharing this phenomenon but they are not ready for it."

Bingo. This communication brought in the IA, and it showed that it was separate to the ATI,TPE. Something felt off to me and my mother about David Icke's interpretation, so now we knew why.

I uncovered that this Infinite Awareness group of entities continued to communicate with my mother from time to time until mid-2010. Some information was way off the mark, while a lot was accurate when the ATI,TPE clearly came through. Granted, some of the IA answers have been correct, but my point is that the IA often portrays a distorted thought process.

March 19, 2008
To the ATI,TPE, but the IA largely answered as I have discerned:
1. Are we "destined" for a future that hasn't been written yet? Is there a plan for us by other light beings?

ATI,TPE may have started, but IA gave the sentence at the end: No. No. We are to live in the present.

2. Or is it just a hope and direction when someone knows more than others do?

IA or ATI,TPE: Yes; it is assumed, not definite.

Me: How then is that so when the entities still say it is planned or destiny?

IA or ATI,TPE: The entities are beings; not the All That Is which is pure energy. All consciousness is in the present.

3. Or is all Time from past to present Now? Please explain.

IA with accurate description of ATI,TPE: All Time is illusory—all illusion makes its own timetable—The All That Is just is.

4. Am I deluded in love by seeing how healing and creative it is when someone else just cannot recognize it in himself?

IA: No, you are not deluded, but actually operating in the pure love state where many men and women in the Matrix are prevented from experiencing pure love by the manipulators.

5.   Is it true that probably everyone just cannot break free of the illusion?

IA: No, it is not true. Pure energy is powerful and strengthens those who abide in it. The manipulators in the Matrix are just beings; entities are blind themselves to the All That Is.

6.   Will anything we have to show really work?

IA: Yes, with continued abiding in the love energy. If those with true awareness of pure energy "give up" on those in the Matrix, then they will be contributing to separateness.

The Infinite Awareness likes to say *illusion* and *matrix*. Although many realms do not have time and material as we experience them, they still have cause and effect that are similar to time, and they have their own version of material.

In late September 2010, I searched the internet for more information about the All That Is, and I came upon a site about the Cosmic Awareness (CA). Someone wrote a book of channeled communications with this source described as God, Jehovah, I AM, and All That Is.[15]

Although my mom and I only wanted to be connected to the pure Source, prevailing New Age information taught us that we would have to go through layers of creation to reach this Source portrayed as a so-called gestalt or collective consciousness. According to the book *Who, In Fact, You Really Are*, the Cosmic Awareness is "the source," not an entity or personality (p. 5).[15] The CA conveys it was the energy and force that channeled messages to Jesus, Buddha, Krishna, and Muhammad. This was a red flag to me, but I continued to be open to its message that says it is the source of my own awareness. I wondered if it is inevitable that I would eventually become a part of its collective mind or essence after I die and reach its "highest" realm.

I asked my mom to confirm some of the CA information with the ATI,TPE. She knew how difficult it is to sustain constantly clear connection with the ATI,TPE for many pages of questions and answers because communicating with it uses her concentration and does not involve being overtaken by channeling. She highly doubted that the ATI,TPE would provide an entire book of information, especially since that book was written very descriptively, but she wondered if its scribe had a better ability than she does. She maintained an open mind to the message and checked it with the ATI,TPE.

The ATI,TPE states in response to the CA claiming to be the source, "This Universal Consciousness is not the ATI,TPE. This consciousness resides within the creation that expanded outward from the ATI,TPE." I suppose this answer was already obvious in the book where the CA's self-description sounds like the Grand Intellect entity group: "When the question was asked of Cosmic Awareness: 'What is Cosmic Awareness?' we were told that Cosmic Awareness is the total mind that is not any one mind, but is the Universal Mind" (p. 5).[15]

She probed the ATI,TPE to learn whether the claim equating the CA to the ATI,TPE is true. In response to some of the channeled book's statements, it explains itself and a few topics about us.

Editors' restatement of CA: Cosmic Awareness has made itself quite clear that it is not an entity, a disembodied spirit or anything of that nature. Awareness is pure energy—pure everything—or the natural God. Cosmic Awareness is that Universal Consciousness that permeates all living things in the universe, that sees all and experiences and discerns "what is" without judging or condemning (p. 6).
[Note: On page 2, the CA stated that it is an entity (in its case, an entity group), "The awareness of this entity, which is universal, which is cosmic, is that which exists in all levels of the universe...."]

ATI,TPE: The words are true according to the ATI,TPE [not the Cosmic Awareness], but the ATI,TPE is not a "natural God" or anything else but pure energy.

Editors' restatement of CA: It is the Cosmic River of Life, the Stream of Consciousness, the Eternal Essence of Being, the Divine Spirit (p. 6).

ATI,TPE: The only thing true here is that it [ATI,TPE] is the Eternal Essence of What Is!
[Note: My mom felt the emphasis at the end, so she put an exclamation mark to convey it.]

Editors' restatement of CA: All consciousness springs from the same river of life—the Universal Life Force. Cosmic Awareness is not a personality, but a force that is personal in nature (p. 6).

ATI,TPE: It is not a "force that is personal in nature." The ATI,TPE is the pure essence at the core and source of itself as all that is.

Editors' restatement of CA: Cosmic Awareness is the sea of life that not only fills our cells with living energy, but fills the air we breathe and the space between galaxies and the molecules. It is the living universe. Like water filling a sponge, Cosmic Awareness fills the spaces between molecules atoms and subatomic particles, and binds them all together into one gigantic Universal Being. Like cells in a microcosmic body, we blend together as souls in a macrocosmic body whose consciousness is Cosmic Awareness (p. 6).

ATI,TPE: This paragraph describes the extension of the ATI,TPE, not Cosmic Awareness. The consciousness portrayed here is about the ATI,TPE. [Note: The ATI,TPE is addressing the invisible and foundational element only, not any material result from the CA's perception of a Universal Being or macrocosmic body.]

CA: "God" is revealed as a universal set of cosmic laws, not a personal deity subject to capriciousness, wrath or vengeance (p. 6).

ATI,TPE: It is true except that the ATI,TPE is not revealed as a universal set of cosmic laws but the ultimate pure essence of truth, love and constancy through each core of creation. Cosmic laws come from outside the ATI,TPE by created beings and their rulings of their worlds.

Editors' restatement of CA: During sleep, Cosmic Awareness tells us, we often leave our physical body and travel around the various planes, of which there are many—some high and some quite low. These inner planes are what are generally referred to in various religious teachings as Heaven, Hell, Limbo, Purgatory, etc. We travel to these planes to attend schools, to help others and to basically learn what we need to learn (p. 7).

ATI,TPE: This is not true. The Cosmos Collective wants those with purer essence to believe that they can transpose themselves everywhere to attain more superficial knowledge from the inner planes.

Editors' restatement of CA: Cosmic Awareness asks not that you sacrifice to it, not that you believe in it, not that you bow down in worship to it, but only that you love one another, serve one another, and that you yourself grow spiritually, become cosmically aware and find out "Who, In Fact, You Really Are" (p. 8).

ATI,TPE: This is partially true—those with high amounts of pure essence and knowing within their core, must check within their core and their knowing, all things and believe in what their knowing gives them.

Editors' restatement of CA: Cosmic Awareness tells us that at the time of passing over, which we call death, each and every one of us must answer one, and only one, question (asked by yourself to yourself, not by any sort of spiritual judge):
"How many have you served, and how well?" (p. 8).

ATI,TPE: This is not the question that will be asked by and for each individual when passing on—the question will be: Did you search within yourself for the truth of who you are, and what did you find?

CA: Through all entities upon this plane, this Awareness has moved (p. 9).

ATI,TPE: The ATI,TPE does not move but remains stationary, and its extension expands outward through all of creation [facilitated by the "Love" pre-field frequency].

CA: It has been given in other teachings that you fear God with all your heart. This Awareness asks that you love God with all your heart, that you fear nothing (p. 11).

ATI,TPE: The ATI,TPE does not want any worship or feelings directed toward it, like a religion, but to recognize fear and negative energy when it approaches and divert yourself and teach others to do so as well.

CA: Each of you, as one body of consciousness, did indeed manifest the separation of light and darkness. [The CA continued to tell us that each of us is the CA that is equated to Christ Consciousness] (p. 13).

ATI,TPE: This is false.

CA: Before the beginning, there was a Void. And the Void was without form or substance and it was unaware as if It were eternally sleeping. That Void was empty, without dreams, thought, or consciousness. Nothing that is, was. All that was, was the Void, the Static Void (p. 17).

My and the ATI,TPE's combined answer: This is the attempt of the CA to describe the ATI,TPE, which they also say is itself. The ATI,TPE is not static electricity, nor was the ATI,TPE a void with no awareness, which the CA goes on to claim.

CA: The Void—being static—began to build something from nothing from the Static Void….[T]he static just built and built throughout pre-eternity until a sense of anticipation from the buildup of static energy began to develop over the latter part of pre-eternity (p. 17).

ATI,TPE [clarified in 2013]: The ATI,TPE came to expand from itself when it consciously desired to exude its pure essence from within itself, and it burst this essence forth and outward. It was not an overwhelming energetic occurrence. There was no sense of anticipation from buildup of any static energy, for the pure essence was always alive and in an existing state. It did all happen pre-eternity as the Cosmic Awareness indicates.

CA: Without its creation, it would have no reflection, recognition or evidence of Itself. Without such evidence, it could not be aware. Without that evolving self-awareness, it would still be only a Void—the nothingness from whence it came (p.18).

ATI,TPE: This is not true, for it [the All That Is, The Pure Essence] is always aware of itself, even before it burst forth in expansion.

The last CA quote is its philosophical belief. I have often heard people say that other people are our mirrors, as though our interactions with them serve to illuminate us. Sometimes this happens, but it is not the defining reality because we fundamentally exist and matter on our own accord. The CA's message essentially dissolves our individual existences toward a collective experience that turns us into a massive individual. The gestalt, collective consciousness mentality is like a hive mentality that sees everyone as a representation of itself. This puts the act of service above our individual needs, which the CA emphasizes in its question that we would supposedly ask ourselves after death. The Cosmic Awareness is similar to the Infinite Awareness because they both say that we are only consciousness, and all of created time and space is an illusion. The CA does not include itself in the uncreative Void space because its consciousness is aware and evolving in the reflection of its supposedly illusory creations.[15] Similarly to the CA, the IA stated to my mother in 2008, "The singular consciousness awakened and knew that it existed—'I exist.' It expanded and created through the 'dream state.'" I consider awareness as being awake, not unconscious in a dream.

The IA continued to say that things are true for those who believe they are true. This philosophy says our beliefs create our reality; it gave me the impression that it does not matter what we believe, for we would somehow eventually get back to the "source." It is as though anything goes, and there is no real good or bad because our individual experiences, thoughts, and identity are illusory. "Being in the material form connects us to the illusion of dual thought patterns," said the IA. It used the word "us" while also answering in place of the ATI,TPE.

David Icke supports this theme in his books by saying everything but love is an illusion. We can be in any religion we want, but when we leave the world by death, we leave the Matrix and transmute into love energy. If only it were so easy, but the nature of reality is much more complicated than that because of the plethora of energies, creations, and realms. The Matrix does not only entail the Earth. I got the impression that this theme treats everything as a game with little or no substantive meaning or judgment. This contradicts the serious tone of Icke's message that calls out evil entities.

My arguments in the upcoming chapters pick apart this nonchalance because much does matter due to the nature of life itself. Our choices do affect our ability to be aligned with the ATI,TPE no matter what level of existence we are at because of the energy signatures of those choices.

The CA and IA do not want us to believe in them as entities, and they channel messages through people with an air of ultimate authority as though their messages are entirely accurate. The IA's presence in my mother's earlier communications sometimes made it difficult for us to distinguish between it and the ATI,TPE. Sometimes the ATI,TPE repeated my word associations that I learned from the IA to reach me on my level, and other times the IA diverted the topic to its perspective.

The following two sets of questions to the ATI,TPE incurred some IA interruptions. I show these questions and answers to help sharpen our sense of scrutiny.

April 2, 2008
1. All That Is—what existed before you?

Answer: Nothing.

2. So, you are the Primary source of all that man perceives to exist, in the beginning?

Answer: No. The All That Is is pure energy that Is—There is no beginning or end. What man perceives to exist is all an illusion in dense matter.
[Note: The last sentence of the answer is obviously the IA. In addition, since nothing exists before the ATI,TPE, it technically is the beginning but in a non-temporal sense; however, my question did not adequately distinguish a religious source from a true beginning source, so the first answer could have disagreed with how I framed it.]

3. How did the Ancient Ones, gods, living, breathing things, come into existence?

Answer: The All That Is (pure energy) expanded itself.

4. How can expansion cause things to materialize?

Answer: Pure energy can multiply itself outward into the nothingness, and create things and dimensions.
[Note: This pure energy is not the ATI,TPE because it is a non-changing essence. This answer was probably from the IA unless the ATI,TPE used that language to infer early vibrational energy.]

5. How can pure energy that is so beautiful, good and pure, turn out so bad and allow itself to invent illusory worlds?

Answer: With expansion over "time," elements of energy that have multiplied over and over, become tarnished and defective—apart from the initial pure state.

6. Is it possible to achieve that pure energy state, known as The All That Is, whenever one is aware of who he/she is, while living in the illusion/Matrix? [Note: Achieve does not mean *become*. Unfortunately, the question is unclear, so the answer could be within the IA's interpretation, which is why it is important to gauge each question and answer as well as the full communication to clarify the picture.]

Answer: Yes, when one is in the present state.

7. How can I achieve Ultimate Awareness of The All That Is without belonging to a religious affiliation and/or communicating with Ascended Masters and Advanced Entities from other worlds?

Answer: Just be; knowing comes naturally.
[Note: This is beautifully and profoundly true.]

8. Is it wrong for the world to follow Jesus, Buddha, Ghandi, Amma—aspired to be primary examples of love and truth on Earth?

Answer: Yes.

Mom: Why?

Answer: The illusion which has devised these "god-like" figures to follow and adore, are just humans, planted on Earth to distract those from becoming aware of The All That Is.
[Note: I explore this much further in chapter 5.]

9. How can Theresa and I, who are very aware and conscious of the All That Is in our lives, affect change in people and contacts of the Matrix?

Answer: You cannot affect change—just "be" who you are in the All That Is. Those in the Matrix can sense the intensity of the Pure Energy in you both, and it expands outward to those you come in contact with.
[Note: Creation is not "in" the All That Is, as chapter 6 explains.]

10. What brought The All That Is to our awareness and consciousness?

Answer: The deep desire to find Ultimate Truth and love for all. The All That Is guided your knowing heart, not mind, toward all Truth and unconditional love for all with expansion.
[Note: I see an IA interpretation in this partially true answer.]

I soon afterward asked the supposed ATI,TPE for a follow-up to another message:

1. You said before that my mom and I were at a higher level, and it feels like my energy cannot be with other people's energies because they feel more negative. So, how are we all together as though nothing mattered on this Earth, or am I not understanding what you said?

Answer: You and your mom are on a higher, deeper awareness level, because you both have always sought knowledge and truth. You and all humans, together on Earth, do "matter" to the All That Is. You have received a higher awareness and knowledge base because of your goodness and openness.

2. And with some psychics, what they receive isn't always true from the other side.

Answer: Yes, because of human limitations.

3. It does seem that there are different levels after death where not all people are with you.

Answer: There are different awareness levels after death, depending on the individual. Those with negative energy and stunted awareness are separate from the All That Is.

4. Are you different from the light?

Answer: No, a greater portion of the Light.

Analysis: Most to all of the follow-up answers were from the Infinite Awareness because it said it is a greater portion of the Light. This shows the capacity of an entity, not the beginning Source.

   Either the IA or the ATI,TPE said that we matter. I know that the ATI,TPE thinks we do, but if IA said this, then here it implies that we are not illusions on Earth.

   Regarding communications "from the other side," lack of human ability or understanding does not preclude possible misinformation given by entities. My mom and I do not appreciate being told that everything is our fault when the entities are also not fully aware. Entities often use their prophets as scapegoats to deflect from their messages not occurring. On a personal level, it is a classic way to chastise their human mouthpieces into seeking a more subservient role so they can better perform for their possessors.

5. How can we all be united when you are truth and love, and these people don't know love and truth before they die?

Answer: Some are given more knowledge and awareness than others. Those people with a more pure heart and openness to what is, can connect with love and goodness before they die.

6. Are you another type of energy, or is energy just energy, or can we be together and connected but also not connected at all, separate? Please explain.

Answer: No, the All That Is is a cosmic intelligence separate yet connected to energy sources, which are a means for communication.
   [Note: This sounds more like the CA, and it is assuming the role of the ATI,TPE, although the IA also shares these beliefs. The ATI,TPE is beyond the cosmos.]

7. What are angels, and why do they want to help us?

Answer: Angels are higher level beings which are communicators and messengers of the All That Is. They have positive energy and promote goodness. There are "good" angels and "evil" angels.

[Note: This is a vague answer that reeks religion. The ATI,TPE does not use intermediaries nor send out entities in its "name." It needs no one but itself. Angels choose to help us due to their own capacity of love and goodness, which includes the ATI,TPE.]

Although the IA and CA use very similar language, I learned that they are two separate entity groups that come from different dimensions. These entities must know that they are not the ATI,TPE because they are aware of higher realms before them due to their ancient histories and networking. Regardless, they continue to pass themselves off as the ATI,TPE to mislead us in their communications. Their many speculations and contradictions show that they are not the top-of-the-line awareness that they each proclaim to portray. Before I illuminate the nature of creation later in this book, I will now say that the IA is from the 5th dimension, and the CA is from a more distant 13th dimension.

The ATI,TPE reveals these entity groups' dimensional associations, but we could come close to these answers when analyzing each group's messages. Icke essentially says that freedom or heaven exists just beyond the Earth's "Matrix," showing that his IA entities are just beyond our reach. The CA states that it exists after the Void, which is supposedly just beyond the CA's position in our cosmos. The All That Is, The Pure Essence never correlates itself with created matter because it truly exists beyond all matter.

The Infinite and Cosmic Awarenesses are collaborations of entities in less material realms than ours. Entities often present themselves as a group name, but they are still individual entities who retain a measure of diverse thought.

I spent all of 2009 to mid-2010 delving deep into books and internet sites that address the topics of entity factions, their stories about creation, and the greater universe. I found much helpful information, and I definitely found disinformation.

If the information carries an unwavering air of authority about esoteric truths of the cosmos, who we are, and our purpose that we do not realize, then it is wise of us to step back and probe within ourselves the energy we feel from the message. It might feel stifling against our core although an air of loving optimism is portrayed. This intuitive reaction would likely gauge the situation more fairly than a belief system.

Certainly we do not have complete clarity and understanding about everything, so questions will remain; however, those questions can be minimized when we fit together the pieces of information that directly pertain to our experiences, intuition, or knowledge base. We can find sufficient answers to the difficult topics, so our experiences with other entities, if we choose to experience them, will put them in *their* place if we decide we would like their assistance.

Because so many prophecies and channelings made me feel some suppression, my strategy shifted to find more understanding about something concrete: science. However, the branch of science that piqued my interest, quantum physics, is nearly the opposite of concrete with its invisible subatomic particles and energies. Quantum physics combines hard science and a lot of theory, which is actually not different to any scientific field, but because it approaches the unknown, a lot of it is written off as speculation. At the very least, it still provides another viewpoint of reality that we can explore.

My mind was opened to the probable existence of many dimensions, not just a vague dimensional realm above us as Heaven and potentially another below us as Hell. There are possibly parallel and other universes that have their own frequencies, subatomic particles, dimensional spaces, and variables of time much like our own. A goal of quantum physicists is to understand what happened at the beginning of creation, to find proof of the "zero-point" energy state beyond any space and time. Their great quest is to find the God particle, but I am certain they would be more excited to discover a realm beyond particles!

I pumped out so many questions to the ATI,TPE as if I were a child fumbling around in the dark. My mother had much interference during that time—the closer we got to the truth in our research about the entities, they often hung around for an opportunity to lie to us. The ATI,TPE explains that entities can jump into her communications if her frequency band goes too far outside of herself. She goes into her core or true self that is aligned with the ATI,TPE, but the ATI,TPE is also past all of the frequency bands. She has had to learn how to gain a direct pathway to it from within and seal off external intruder hijackings.

Thankfully, in my persistence to keep asking the questions in varied ways, and with my mother working very diligently to keep her energetic shield strong and to link only to the ATI,TPE, we have been able to put many pieces together along with our inner prompting or intuition. She as the "otherworldly" communicator genuinely only wanted to find the purest energy consciousness. Her pure intent found her core place within herself that links to the ATI,TPE, which is how it could increasingly present itself to her in clarity, accuracy, and ease. Her sense of knowing the ATI,TPE developed into a direct relationship with it, and any interference became a secondary or non-existent problem.

In the summer of 2010, I probed the ATI,TPE more deeply about Jesus to follow up on previously inconsistent messages. My mother's transmission line to the ATI,TPE was briefly diverted by an entity to tell her to read *The Urantia Book* (UB).[16] To our growing but untrained knowledge base at the time, we thought the ATI,TPE gave that direction during its answers to my questions, but it did seem to suddenly come out of left field, which I now would consider as a red flag.

I took it upon myself to read the majority of the approximately 2,000-page book. It was compiled into chapters that were channeled by various entities who worked within the scope of their political hierarchy. Their stories often overlap, and their accounts portray a greater structure of the cosmos where Jesus has an important role, including on Earth—what they call Urantia. The Bible actually fits nicely within the greater picture of the UB, although there are some discrepancies. As a fundamentalist Christian, I was taught to disregard all religious texts that do not perfectly coincide with the King James Bible. However, if I had read the UB before the Bible, I could have used the same logic to disregard the Bible. I will elaborate upon the UB in chapters 5 and 7.

I spent a week nearly holed up in a retreat cabin reading the UB. It was detailed and redundant, two factors that helped ingrain its message into me. The UB opened my mind again toward the story of wonderful Jesus. It nearly made me doubt not being a Christian anymore because of how it glorifies Jesus even more than the Bible does. The various entity authors were intelligent, and some admitted that they did not know everything; they appeared to simply share their knowledge. It was as though I was a university student hearing professors' lectures from their experienced perspectives; I was not forced to agree with their views but to use my intellect as well. This resulted in the story being more believable to me.

Thankfully, I was experienced enough in my path to know to pay attention to my inner self. I felt "off" every time the UB entities mentioned the need for us to have a thought adjuster. The UB describes it as "the God-presence of the Thought Adjuster that indwells the mortal intellect and is bestowed upon man as the free gift of the Universal Father" (24.6). I wrote out my thoughts while I continued to maintain an open mind, but the notion of needing an entity with us to ascend to the heavenly dimension after death is just like the Holy Spirit possessing us. I felt wonderful without an entity with me, so I knew that I did not need one, even if it is deemed to be like God. This prominent message of the UB led me to question its entire story, including creation. Each religion has its own version of creation anyway, so when I created some space to listen to my intuition, I was able to detach from this particularly vivid story that tried to persuade me to believe it.

I returned home to share what I learned with my mother. She researched a bit on her own and also became slightly swayed by its presentation of the cosmos and our evolution. Regardless, she could immediately see my concerns, and she agreed with me. Just to be sure, she asked the ATI,TPE some pertinent questions. One question wondered if it directed us to read the UB. No, it did not. An intruder jumped on the opportunity to potentially sway us in our research. I will always advocate research, but I hope my story will help the reader to not be too open yet not too skeptical when trying to discern the truth.

I used to wonder how much understanding we must have about the ATI,TPE before we could get to an absolutely clear state with it. Then, I recalled our innate connection with it that has always existed, and it has shown itself within the basic understanding of it being pure goodness and love. Since it was and is at the beginning, there is possibility that what was created after it will get in the way between us. This is why my mother now starts her transmissions by getting energetically congruent within herself, protecting her personal field, and making sure that she has reached the ATI,TPE before she commences the questioning process, as I explained in chapter 1.

As we were learning about the ATI,TPE, we assumed that it could tell us where I lost my necklace or if some dental material had a specific toxic chemical, for example. My mom would sometimes get no answer, have conflicting answers, or the answer would be vague. The ATI,TPE knows something about them, but it does not give specifics about this type of creation, especially a lost item like a necklace. This is because these items are significantly expanded away from the ATI,TPE; it can only be omniscient about fully natural creation, including much of our human composition, due to the free-flowing nature of undistorted energies connecting to it.

My mom and I thought that if we connect to a natural entity group that comprises dynamic but pure energy, maybe it could give us specific answers about material matters. In our 2010 research, we found internet information about a type of group consciousness called the Yunasai as transmitted by an entity group called the Guardian Alliance (GA) that claims to desire natural creation like we do. I did not fully understand or agree with everything the GA was saying at the time, but I sensed good energy from its message that wants life—not death, darkness, or destruction. The Yunasai exist as very early light particles before and beyond dense matter, therefore being higher up than the Cosmic Awareness. My mom and I felt that we could trust them.

She began communicating with the Yunasai, and it was a new experience for her. She connected to the ATI,TPE first as she always does, but then as she went up her fully opened and protected chakras through the central, vertical meridian of her body (see chapter 9's "Chakras"), she continued going up to the higher chakras of her etheric-type self. She animatedly described it to me:

It was not any kind of material that I could discern, but it was like a big expansion into like a clear film that I could see that was wide and beyond, but there were small, conscious formations inside. [She looked up above her and lifted up her arms, opening them outward, while her mouth was dropped in awe.] I got different answers that were more communicable, more wordy, not just "yes" and "no" or short and sweet answers from the All That Is, The Pure Essence. If I need more clarification, I have to ask the ATI,TPE to expand itself more, but the Yunasai elaborates more on its own. This is a big difference between the two.

There is also a big difference between the Yunasai and other entities because the Yunasai feels more pure and harmonic to me. I want to make sure that whatever I am addressing is exactly what I address without having anything else interfere. I do not know what type of consciousness the ATI,TPE connects with to give certain materially-based answers [we later found the answer—our own "higher" or core self]. However, now that I know about the Yunasai and how it feels to communicate with them, I will do my best to have the ATI,TPE elaborate on its own, or I will purposely link to the Yunasai or another trusted entity or group.

My experience in feeling the ATI,TPE is that it is through my core, but at the same time, it is next to my core and also very far out as the source of life. With the Yunasai, I feel it is closer to me in an expanded realm, yet it feels further away than our internal, core connection to the ATI,TPE. My mother and I feel such a peace with the ATI,TPE in that we feel at home with it. It is pure, good, and full as itself, and it helps to connect us individual entities. In contrast, she explains about the Yunasai:

> When it comes to the Yunasai, I'm actually heaving out from the inside-out because it is the beyond. It is energy movement that is expanding out from my inner core. It's like I'm stepping into another level, even beyond dimensions, and it takes a lot out of me to get there. It is more tiring to reach it than to go straight to the All That Is, The Pure Essence. I'm physically in one place, but it's like I am stepping out of my body to climb up to it.

The Yunasai are in their own realm, but their pre-subatomic units called partiki also constitute our basic light-body composition, as chapter 6 explains. In 2013, when my mother questioned the Yunasai for more information about their nature, they communicated that they are a helper consciousness with very high intelligence. They stated, "We do not help any religious or spiritual group but know that they are prevalent, some destructive. We strive to preserve natural quanta and all natural creation."

Our connection to the Yunasai brings them closer in a material way than the ATI,TPE, but they are not like our dense matter. Therefore, there is little possibility that they are more accurate than the ATI,TPE when explaining distortions in depth. Such distortions can be generally known within the context of all-awareness, which the ATI,TPE approximates. The ATI,TPE cannot intimately know something that is heavily distorted away from itself, but it does know about the topic due to its innate connection to us.

Although our few communications with the Yunasai provided some clarity about natural creation, we decided to continue our communications with the ATI,TPE in the greater understanding we gained about it. The ATI,TPE continues to feel most natural and close to us because it feels like it easily connects to all living parts within us.

The following is an All That Is, The Pure Essence communication. It shows what I already stated in this chapter about some of its answers. I include the following communication to validate my claims about the ATI,TPE. Its input is additionally placed throughout the rest of the book.

November 29, 2010

1. The All That Is said before that my mother's core linked to a cosmic collective consciousness. After the ATI revealed itself, other entities still communicated to her. Why then does the All That Is say it was the only communicator to my mother during the last 4 years when this is not correct?

ATI,TPE: Your mother was not always able to stay clear with her communications due to the constant and overwhelming amount of interference she withstood. She requested the Yunasai's assistance with a few questions recently—that is why they responded. She had to defer the other entities, but always was able to connect with the All That Is in her core. She tried to keep only the ATI communications, and stopped any communications if it was not only the ATI or the Yunasai.

2. Is the All That Is saying that it reached her core, but the entities jumped in between the ATI and my mom?

ATI,TPE: Yes, sometimes.

3. How could there be interference from the outside when the All That Is communication was from within my mother next to her core?

ATI,TPE: Her communications are within, but the frequency bands have reached beyond her being.

4. What about when the All That Is said it had to connect with entities to give messages pertaining to material matters such as bodily health and misplaced items—is that true?

ATI,TPE: Yes.
[Note: As I previously indicated, these entities are actually our respective "higher" selves, as chapter 9 explains.]

5. Why would the All That Is say it knows everything but does not know every little thing?

ATI,TPE: The All That Is gets misdirected with knowing things at times, due to the constant interferences with material and mental matter by manipulators.

This last answer by the All That Is, The Pure Essence is revealing. The ATI,TPE knows the outer levels due to the communication from those levels and its proximity to all natural creation. However, as I previously stated, it and the first pre-frequency field extension do not identify with artificial compositions of material, so the ATI,TPE does not usually have a thorough understanding about them. The connection is highly skewed. There are aspects of Human nature that can also cause our connection to the ATI,TPE to become skewed and unclearly transmitted, and in this state, interfering entities can sneak in to divert it further. As my mother became increasingly cognizant of her true internal self, her Human state essentially clicked into place to communicate in a straight, instant process.

The ATI,TPE usually helps to confirm or deny the information that we present it while we mainly do the groundwork through research and introspection because of our desire for accurate knowledge. Compared to wordy entities who often give advice, the ATI,TPE provides relatively short answers without emotionalism and rarely provides more information than what is specifically asked. If I need more understanding, I often have to ask it to explain.

In chapter 6, I explain the ATI,TPE and subsequent levels within a science-based paradigm. The ATI,TPE provides the building block for creational life, but it does not contain creation. As something that is "All That Is," it truly encompasses the non-moving, being state in the eternal present—what creation can only approximate but never become due to inherent frequency-filled energies. Fundamentally, this knowledge illuminates that each aspect of life and natural creation has its own place and importance without seeing the other as insignificant.

Conclusion

The idealistic word *God* is just that—idealism, not realism. I do not want the God paradigm of idealism because it is a view given by self-serving entities. My idealism incorporates a connected flow between everyone and everything where we all matter in both individuality and togetherness.

The progression of my mother's and my path from religion to the Beyond proves that the God entity is not so mighty after all. *God* is a term that has grown to incorporate diverse meanings, but all cases, it identifies either a finite entity or group of entities regardless of how they exaggerate themselves. God does not equate to a simple energy consciousness; the ATI,TPE does not fit into a religious framework.

Entities are forms of various matter and density that have their own separate consciousness; the more complex their structure, the more their consciousness can choose to separate from the ATI,TPE extension. To say that an entity can know everything or be everything is literally impossible; this belief serves to put this entity on a pedestal, which purposely creates an imbalanced relationship between us and it. The concept of God supports a highly disproportionate power over humans, but be not mistaken: any spirituality that involves a more knowledgeable entity has the potential to create a god-slave relationship between us.

Are there entities who treat us as equals? Certainly, but this book shows that nearly all mainstream religious and spiritual prophecies are channeled by meddling entities who are eager to make us think that we are disempowered. My personal experience shows that God creates division among his "chosen ones" when we seek more understanding about him. We chosen ones get scattered to the point of isolation while watered-down understandings prosper in large, mainstream churches. What is this God trying to hide? Are we more powerful than we realize?

An entity that puffs itself up to portray an all-powerful and all-knowing Creator God does what it can to maintain that image. Judeo-Christianity goes so far to reduce other gods to natural events, fictitious magic or wishful thinking, or man-made statues as conveyed in the Ten Commandments. When we step out of this mind-control, we can see that a plethora of gods have employed these and other tactics. Some religions encourage worship of demigods, but this still involves submission toward a disproportionate hierarchy.

I encourage us to throw out the concept of God and look at it from a basic viewpoint as an energy with consciousness that just exists and is not caught up in contradiction. It is an energy essence that is the foundation of life, which means that whatever does not support life severs connection to that specific energy and begins the death process. I encourage us to approach spirituality from the core of ourselves to maintain what we sense is good and everlasting, loving, and validating of our existence and worth. Then we will find this pure Source because it does exist.

First, we need to keep ourselves when approaching this topic. This means that we do not lose any of our value and self-love. Second, we must look for incongruity, power trips, emotionalism, and key language that denote an entity who does not convey what we intuitively and logically know is good and true. Just because it is an otherworldly entity that makes us feel special when we can hear from it does not mean it is any greater than we are; it is just different. If you want to be lifted up, then perhaps you need to introspect to see if you are supporting egotism and hierarchy that perpetuate power plays.

Judeo-Christianity is rooted in power plays due to the message of God and his chosen elite. It is important that we delve into the recorded history of the Bible to see if its support of both religious and racist hierarchies equate to non-biblical, recorded history. It just may be that biblical scribes took liberty in omitting and twisting facts to portray their own history for us to believe. Regardless, each "his-story" reveals startling interferences by godly entities.

PART 2

Dysfunctional Family of Religions: A Case Study of Judeo-Christianity

CHAPTER 4

Godly Kings and the Jewish Bloodline

The patriarch of Judeo-Christianity was Abram. He was called by Yahuah to migrate to the Middle Eastern land of Canaan to not only populate it but also essentially own it as its founding father of many nations. Abram had conversations with Yahuah and visions of him, but when he finally saw him face-to-face in the biblical Book of Genesis chapter 17, Abram's name was changed to Abraham as an initiation into a new covenant that was circumcision. This strange covenant was not publicly seen but had an obvious significance toward procreation. Abraham was deemed the patriarch of not only Judaism but also Islam. His seed additionally infiltrated the Egyptian royal bloodline.

The Bible focuses upon a chosen people of Yahuah, yet this was not a specific bloodline as the Book of Leviticus suggests. Although there were a preferred people called the Habiru, they intermixed with other ethnicities. Locating a single bloodline of Yahuah's chosen people is impossible, and this is for a reason: to create division yet enough unity to keep people under Yahuah's control.

Attaining the perfect bloodline is a major theme of the Bible because of its focus upon the "seed" or offspring. This theme states that humans are born sinful because of the sins of Adam and Eve, so we must be purified by Yahuah, his priesthood, and his son, Jesus. If someone needs redemption for wanting knowledge (Eve) or loving his wife (Adam), then that logic evades me.

Yahuah wanted to destroy the "mighty men" that were created when "sons of God" raped human women (Genesis 6:5). This new group of god-men was a lineage of humans made outside of his control; God wanted to create his chosen lines for his specific purpose. The following Bible verse does not state this reason but rather gives a non sequitur: "And God saw that the wickedness of man *was* great in the earth, and *that* every imagination of the thoughts of his heart *was* only evil continually" (Genesis 6:5). Demigods are not entirely evil, especially since Jesus is considered one.

Genesis chapter 3, verse 22 gives a hint about the possible equality of man to God (rather, "gods" because of the "us"): "And the Lord God said, Behold, the man is become as one of us, to know good and evil: and now, lest he put forth his hand, and take also of the tree of life, and eat, and live for ever."

The second part of this verse is confusing. It was written after Adam and

Eve sinned, yet it states that "fallen" humans can still live forever. Christians interpret this as a prophecy toward the Messiah coming to save us from the impending death of sin; however, I can see that this message runs deeper than this, especially since it is the premise of the Jewish Old Testament.

There is a highly capable, even "godly" nature of being human. When we choose to do something of our own accord, God punishes us and keeps us away from our natural right to life. Therefore, God created the process of our death—we did not. I propose that we would live naturally and potentially forever without God's interference.

It seems as though humans are a threat yet are able to be kept under God's thumb because his knowledge base and abilities are more than what we can access at this time. It makes sense that he would therefore strive to keep more knowledge away from us. In chapter 3, I questioned how a supposedly pure entity would not only know evil but also use it to his advantage. I concluded that this surely could not be the true Source.

God cast Adam and Eve out of Eden so they could take care of themselves (which is not a bad thing). Unfortunately, this branded them with a stigma of filth just because they knew about evil as their God did. This is another illogical conclusion that says just because they knew about evil, they somehow were evil and would do evil. Adam and Eve or any human would not inevitably choose to do that evil since we also have love. It is also doubtful that the knowledge Eve attained was evil. This non sequitur would more likely apply to God because he told my mother that he was the one who created evil.

People like to blame Eve for her "mistake" for listening to another god that offered her something possibly beneficial, and her act somehow marked all women as evil, duplicitous, harlots, and stupid. None of those words logically fit. The Bible is especially rampant with sexual references to fornication and whoredom by women and entire people when they did something God did not like. The focus upon sex in the Bible is disturbing to me.

This is taken to another level in the New Testament when it tells us to become Jesus's bride upon baptism in his name. We need to put on a wedding garment to be saved (Matthew 22:12-14). Scriptures such as these are both figurative and literal. The wedding garment refers to Jesus's body (which could be interpreted as an imperfect human or the perfect son of Yahuah) that we must put on by faith to receive promise of his glory in our afterlife.

The wedding garment also refers to the merging of humans with Jesus, such as in the act of marital sex. The "oneness" from this bodily union does not just put the man as the head of the household—it figuratively puts the man's head in place of the woman's. "For the husband is the head of the wife, even as Christ is the head of the church: and he is the saviour of the body" (Ephesians 5:23). This takes the Sumerian joke about a rib too far to imply that a woman is made of a man (in chapter 3); unfortunately, misogynist men such as the Apostle Paul were only too happy to wish it as fact. Paul stated:

> For a man indeed ought not to cover *his* head, forasmuch as he is the image and glory of God: but the woman is the glory of the man. For the man is not of the woman, but the woman of the man. Neither was the man created for the woman, but the woman for the man (1 Corinthians 11:7-9).

One Christian young man told me his interpretation of the Book of Ephesians chapter 5, verse 23 was that the woman is a body to be used by the husband. This supports rape. The mind of the husband would control the wife, but this mimics the greater hierarchy of the entity above the man and woman as their puppet master. These incorrect concepts of oneness imply slavery and possession.

This line of reasoning says women are inferior to men, and humans are inferior to Jesus and the Father. It is interesting that the biblical angels, Jesus, and Yahuah are all men. As a bride, we are still filthy because we need the purity of Jesus upon our flesh. "For as many of you as have been baptized into Christ have put on Christ" (Galatians 3:27). Since baptism is by faith, we will stay filthy until we die and are transformed only by our resurrection, as though Jesus will change us up in another dimension.

The Hebrew bloodline, popularly known as descendants of Abraham, intermixed with other cultures and people, but the obsession with purity took over Judaism or originated with it. The focus upon sacrifice, blood (the reason for the kosher style of killing animals), and the unblemished seed were synonymous with being a Jew. Jews were Hebrew, but not all Hebrews were Jews. The Jews were a refined sect toward establishing a sufficiently powerful god-man group. What scribes did not admit in the Bible or realize was that there were other god-man groups created by God.

I will attempt to distinguish between the leading bloodlines of Abraham's time and explain why the Scriptures that say to not mix any seed (Leviticus 21:14, 19:19) were unrealistic and untrue. Contrary to the Torah's story, Yahuah did not only prefer the Jewish people. Yahuah was not out for genocide on a broad scale because humans have a purpose to him (I explain this in chapters 7 and 8). However, God with his many religions has sanctioned wars against all groups of his people so that they could be weakened and distracted from their intrinsic power and ability.

The Levitical, or priestly, bloodline was synonymous with being Jewish. This race line had to be God-approved, for the blood of humans was viewed as unclean and sinful. Leviticus chapter 15 gives purification commandments to women during their menses and to men and women after sex. It is not just about blood, for Leviticus chapter 12, verses 2-5 state that women are unclean twice as long after the birth of a girl than a boy! Although the Jews were deemed the pure or "clean" bloodline, the blood of an unblemished animal had to be shed in sacrifice to atone for human blood and filth. How is the Jewish bloodline so pure if animal blood is deemed superior to such special humans? If the animal sacrifice was only symbolic, it did not need to occur as a ritual because the people understood their subordinate relationship to God.

Leviticus chapter 17, verse 11 states, "For the life of the flesh *is* in the blood: and I have given it to you upon the altar to make an atonement for your souls: for it *is* the blood *that* maketh an atonement for the soul." This perspective gives a different story about what constitutes our life because God supposedly breathed our life (spirit) into Adam and Eve (I prefer the first Genesis creation story—Genesis 1:27—which infers they were created at the same time).

The truth is that the bloodline, which is the genetics of the people, is what matters to Yahuah and his cohorts. Without women there would be no offspring, but Yahuah has treated women unfairly. Arguably the main reason for favoritism toward men and forced subservience toward women is to keep women's baby-making and -rearing abilities under the control of their lords—husbands and God. Biblical language sometimes blurs the title *Lord* as meaning God as their husband. This was quite literal in the biblical cases when "[t]he Holy Ghost shall come upon" women, "and the power of the Highest shall overshadow" them to impregnate them without their husbands (Luke 1:35).

The biblical obsession toward perfection is a guise to water down the inherent ability of women and men that could create a good world on their own without interference by the gods. Yahuah goes overboard to demand perfection of us, which cannot happen, so this is why we follow his commandments and get "married" to Jesus in baptism—we realize our imperfections and need the heroic man to save us.

Leviticus chapter 21, verses 18-20 turn our focus to the most trivial of physical characteristics, such as a mere scab or broken foot. These "blemishes" are significant enough to prevent men from approaching Yahuah's altar. God then declared how perfect he is in the following chapter to reiterate why we must follow him: "Neither shall ye profane my holy name; but I will be hallowed among the children of Israel: I *am* the LORD which hallow you, That brought you out of the land of Egypt, to be your God" (Leviticus 22:32-33).

Egyptologist and archaeologist Jan Assmann explains that the first several non-biblical accounts of the Exodus, written between the fourth and first centuries B.C., attributed the famed Exodus to a large scale purge of people afflicted by a plague.[17] This could explain some of the focus on people's "blemishes," but since they were God's people, he as the Almighty One could simply cure them.

Several Scriptural laws given by Yahuah are illogical and unrealistic, so how can we believe they are credible and that he is entirely perfect? The answer is that we are continuously told that we are flawed and sinful, so we become self-absorbed and distracted from seeing God's flaws.

It is important to compare Scriptures with various archeological records so that we can see a more accurate history than what the Old Testament has filtered into its various stories. Accordingly, some of its accounts might seem fictitious until we understand the probable facts behind them.

Sumerian and Egyptian Background

Leviticus is the third book of the entire Bible, having created most of the commandments toward the Hebrew people after the 10-plus commandments in the Book of Exodus. It complements the Book of Exodus because Aaron, a Levite, was the first high priest of the Israelites, and he was Moses's older brother. The Levitical priesthood followed the order of Melchizedek, the angel or high priest of Salem who approached Abraham many centuries earlier and schooled him toward monotheism (Genesis 14:18).

Priests mainly wrote Leviticus during the Babylonian exile of the sixth and fifth centuries B.C. The priests compiled sources to bring them back to the antiquity of their law from around the time of Moses. There were similarities between the Code of Hammurabi in Babylonia and the Hebrew codes. The Jews could have adopted some Babylonian laws, but these laws shared a Semitic history in human purification rituals and behavioral modification at altars and temples that spanned several earlier religions.

An invading army created Babylonia on a region previously called Sumer. Sumer was an ancient land in modern day Iraq where archeological evidence appears to precede Egypt's timeline. Ur, a city-state of Sumer, originally sat near the mouth of the Euphrates River at the Persian Gulf, providing fertile soil and excellent trade routes to far away countries. Artifacts show that various people colonized and conquered the area c. 5600 B.C. in the Ubaid period.[18] The Sumerian language was unique to the area because it was not Semitic, and it was written as a peculiar cuneiform. It was almost as though the community dropped out of the sky by the gods, as the account of the Sumerian Tablets (ST) explained.

The ST is a collection of about 25,000 tablets and fragments that were excavated in the Mesopotamian area of Akkad that was previously part of Sumer, both of which are now mainly in Iraq. Some of the ST are dated c.

2350 B.C. when the Akkadian empire became established. Although they are technically Akkadian texts, they are copies of older Sumerian texts that kept the unique style of the Sumerian language. Evidenced in a royal statement, "23rd tablet: language of Shumer not changed," they were written in Sumerian and possibly Sumerian-Akkadian (p. 137).[19] Akkadian was a Semitic language that preceded Hebrew.

As I previously stated, the Book of Genesis chapter 6 tells the horror story of the "sons of gods" ("gods" in ST) who interbred with human women and created immortal humans much to God's dismay, so he wiped out the new monstrous giants with a flood. The Bible's Noah is the ST's Ziusudra. Ziusudra was one of the half-human, half-god creations, yet his obedience to God spared him although he was a freak of human nature.

The ST predates the Bible, and they contain a lot more science fiction-type stories than the Bible. It is probable that earlier interactions with gods were very real, strange, and frightening to humans. The STs were likely written as channeled texts from a strange group of god-like people named Anunnaki. The Bible names the Anunnaki *Anak* and *An´-a-kims*. "And there we saw the giants, the sons of Anak" (Numbers 13:33). "The people is greater and taller than we; the cities are great and walled up to heaven; and moreover we have seen the sons of the An´-a-kims there" (Deuteronomy 1:28).

It should make us wonder why there are so many temples, pyramids, ziggurats, altars, and earth formations such as mounds to show reverence to the gods. Did the gods control humans as the ST and Bible dictate, or does actual history show that people lived by their own abilities? The answer: it is a mix. This is a sufficient reality for us unlike religious texts depicting humans as completely powerless to the whims of the gods.

The ST describes Anunnaki physically inhabiting the ancient regions of Sumer, Egypt, and the Indus Valley (origin of Hinduism) in which one leading "person" or god essentially owned a territory and ruled over its people. Each god and region carried some amount of animosity toward the other god and region because of their self-inflated egos. The god of Sumer, Enlil, had a major problem with the god of Egypt, Marduk, who was re-named Ra. (*Ra* or *Re* was the suffix of several pharaohs' names.) Enlil was the head God, and Marduk wanted that position. Marduk later usurped Enlil's status as Sumer's God in Babylonia. Interestingly, the biblical God appears to support and mirror Enlil.

Regardless of the stories of inter-religious differences, Egyptians and Sumerians both reached out economically, socially, and politically, often passing each other on the same trade routes and probably working together as well. In the fourth millennium B.C., Egyptians had friendly relations with communities on the trade route up to the seaport, Byblos, in ancient Lebanon. The gemstone lapis lazuli was highly prized in Egypt, but its origin was East of Sumer. Trade routes out of Sumer led to pre-Afghanistan, so this gem may have had significance to Sumerians as well.[20] Egyptians and Sumerians colonized their intermediate areas, and conversely, peoples of the Levant (between today's Turkey and Egypt along the Mediterranean Sea, extending west into Syria and Jordan) colonized Egypt and Sumer.

Abraham, the Judeo-Islamic Patriarch

The Bible states that Abraham was born in Ur of the Chaldees (Genesis 11:28,31 and 15:7; Jubilees 11:3). Locating this Ur takes some investigation. Chaldea (*Kasdim* in Hebrew) was created in the early part of the first millennium B.C. when a group of Semitic people settled in southern Mesopotamia.[21] Biblical events present the birth date of Abraham much earlier than this time, but there is discrepancy. Tracing backward after the destruction of Jerusalem in 586 B.C., he was born in 2216 B.C.[22] Going forward after the creation of Adam, the date would have been 1815 B.C.[23] The Sumerian Ur was under the rule of the Akkadians in 2216 B.C. and the first Babylonian dynasty in 1815 B.C. The Chaldean Ur was part of the later Neo-Babylonian Empire.

Genesis 11, verse 31 states that Abram's father, Terah, took some of his family including Abram on a long journey out of "Ur of the Chaldees" into Canaan, but they stopped in Haran that was at the top of Mesopotamia. Haran was the apex of a very rough equilateral triangle between Ur, Haran, and Beersheba in Canaan. The Bible gives no indication why they went off-track to Haran where they lived until Terah died. If Abraham was from Ur, then Haran could have been the original destination instead of Canaan. If Abraham was not from Ur, mentioning Haran may have carried significance as the original location of Abraham or an association with the people there.

Haran was located in what is now southern Turkey, and it was reachable by the Tigris River that connected down to Ur. It was a major trading post that enticed various tribes, including Assyrians and Hittites, to raid its goods and settle in the area. Urkesh, a northern city somewhat near Haran, lied at the base of the Taurus Mountains in what is now Syria, and it was occupied by Hurrians in 2500 B.C. If we are to believe that Abraham was born in a city of Ur, then Urkesh, or the Hebrew equivalent Ur Kasdim, was likely where Abraham was born. The original Ur was in Sumer, but archeological evidence is too limited to date its precise age.

When we look into the etymology of words, we can approximate or deduce their meaning. Abraham's "father," Terah, could have originated among several Semitic languages in which it is commonly interpreted as a wanderer or wild goat. In Hebrew, it can be compared to Torah and yerah, meaning moon.[24,25] Allah was the supreme moon god to pre-Islamic Arabs, and Muslims view

Abraham as their patriarch, so perhaps Terah relates to the moon.[26]

Could Allah be linked to Yahuah? This seems blasphemous to say since Yahuah is against the worship of any other god, period. Muslims have the same attitude about Allah. It is interesting that Islam started much later in the seventh century A.D. when the angel Gabriel appeared to Muhammad and essentially attacked him to make him follow Gabriel's teaching. Gabriel is linked to the Melchisedek angel in *The Urantia Book* (UB), which agrees with the Bible that Melchizedek appeared to Abraham to teach him the correct religion; the Bible repeats this story but does not mention Gabriel.

Islam and Judaism are now two diametrically opposed religions, but they have very similar roots. Allah comes from the root word *LIL* that originates with Enlil, the main god of Sumer.[27] Historian and genealogist Laurence Gardner believed Enlil and Yahuah are the same God.[9] I do not think it is that simple, for there could be a reason for the separate names, including Elohim.

Judeo-Christians view Allah as an inanimate object—the moon—and Yahuah as the creator of everything. I strongly suppose that Muslims have the exact same view toward Allah as the creator and Yahuah as a lesser deity creation.

The graven images or symbols are clues to the origin or post of the god. Bull and calf figurines refer to the Taurus constellation, and the appropriately named Taurus Mountains reflect this. The moon has its significance for obvious reasons, but according to David Icke, it is also an artificial space post upon which certain beings monitor the Earth.[28] Pagan religions often knew the meaning behind the objects they used in rituals to channel their gods. The new reigning God that created division among similar religions aimed to obfuscate the meaning behind these objects or remove the objects to keep him in a shroud of untouchable mystery, which Yahuah does when abolishing graven images in his Second Commandment.

The ancient Middle Eastern environment incorporated a pantheon of gods that were assimilated or rejected depending upon the invading people. The prominent religious themes and gods of the Middle East were the bull and the moon. The Hittites worshipped the bull, for example, and the Exodus story states that the Israelites made a golden calf. Accordingly, Egyptians worshipped the bull as the god Horus. Along with Allah, Sin was another moon god. Yahuah has likened humans to Sin.

Yahuah seems to hate Allah because of the continuing bloodshed between Muslims and Jews. In addition to sharing Abraham, Jews and Muslims follow strict customs of obedience toward their respective Gods. Either Yahuah and/or Elohim and Allah are the same God, or there is at least one copycat among them. If one is a copycat, then the pantheon of gods out there who take on the moon, bull, sun, serpent, or whatever must all be copycats by trying to get a piece of the action of laying claim over people's lives. This does happen, but surely there must be some order to the plethora of gods? Is one or a few more powerful than the rest? Certainly, monotheism was the goal to set apart Abraham from his neighbors, but was it a result of religious infighting or a much bigger scale of domination from a head God or Godhead? I will answer this clearly in chapters 7 and 8, but the workings on Earth through religion and history must be examined first.

Identifying the Tribes of Israel

The Bible claims that Abraham fathered all the tribes of Israel through his grandson Jacob (Genesis 49:28). (Interestingly, the Islamic Qur'an claims that Abraham's son Ishmael started the God-given line, but it must have been another 12 tribes, as Genesis 25:13-16 asserts). The Bible states that Jacob had 12 sons and one daughter. According to patriarchal tradition, his 12 sons were the heirs to the new lands that they supposedly created. One of his sons, Levi, created the priestly class, so no lands were ascribed to him. Therefore, it is possible that Jacob's favored son, Joseph, had two sons who took two of the positions—Ephraim and Manasseh. Ephraim was noted as one of the tribes in the Song of Deborah, which is deemed by scholars to be the oldest pre-monarchic Israelite composition, dated somewhere around the 12th or 11th century B.C. Much of Deborah's text was corrupted, and Deuteronomic writers relayed their interpretation.[29] Judges 5:14-18 restates this poem but only includes 10 tribes in which Ephraim displaced Joseph, and Machir and Gilead displaced Simeon, Judah, and Gad. Since Manasseh was not mentioned, there appears to be only 11 tribes in Genesis chapter 49 if we do not include Levi. Moses in the Book of Deuteronomy chapter 33 includes Levi but leaves out Simeon. There is no consistent group of 12 tribes, but there is an obvious significance to the number 12; this number is additionally referenced to Jesus's disciples.

The pre-Israelite classification *Shasu* was recorded as six tribes in a list of enemies inscribed on column bases at the temple of Soleb built by Amenhotep III. Three notable tribes were the Shasu of Yhw (YHWH), the Shasu of S´rr or Se´ir, and the Shasu of Rbn (Reuben). Shasu was an Egyptian classification for Semitic speaking, potentially barbaric nomads who mainly lived in the southern Levant.[30]

Shasu appeared in Egyptian lists of people from the 15th century B.C. to before the Third Intermediate Period that started in 1070 B.C.[30,31] A letter from an Egyptian scribe at a border fortress during the reign of Merneptah reported movement of "Shasu-tribes of Edom" to watering holes in Egyptian territory (p. 228).[22] The first historical mention of Israel was in the early 13th century B.C. Merneptah victory stele.[32]

Historian and archeologist Donald Redford writes, "Their lawlessness and their proclivity to make raids gave rise in Canaanite (and Hebrew) to the denominative verb šasā(h), 'to plunder'" (p. 271-272).[22] Redford asserts that the Shasu were wandering groups who lacked the camel, yet Israelites as depicted in the Bible often had camels and were pastoral. As this chapter will illuminate, many biblical accounts were written after the historical events occurred, so perhaps the Shasu were a menace to the Egyptians as raiders. However, an Egyptian Intermediate Period involved a weakened dynasty when rivals claimed the throne in one or more regions. This means that the Egyptian dynasty was in control during the Shasu infiltration, so they were likely a nuisance until they potentially rose up against the empire.

The assimilation of the Shasu into native Canaanite lands may have helped shape Canaan into Israel. This particular Israel creation theory is not favorable, but the Bible clearly states YHWH's preference for dominion. Since there were many people outside of Adam and Eve's family, force was a valuable tool to infiltrate and control more people and locations.

The pre-Israelite Shasu of Yhw (YHWH) and Shasu of S´rr or Se´ir likely shared a similar bloodline. The Bible depicts Yahuah coming "out of Se´-ir" and originating in Edom (Judges 5:4), and texts of the 19th and 20th Egyptian Dynasties (1298 B.C. to 1064 B.C.) link the Shasu with Edom (i.e. Se´ir).[22]

In the Bible, Edom was the name given to Esau, the older, twin brother of Jacob (Israel) and the grandson of Abraham. The biblical allegory states that Esau was born reddish (*admoni* in Hebrew), when really the desert of Edom has reddish sandstone, and *Edom* means red. Genesis 25, verse 29 states Esau saying to Jacob, "Feed me, I pray thee, with that same red pottage; for I am faint: therefore was his name called Edom." Jacob replied that he would give him the stew if Esau would give Jacob his birthright; this one act supposedly made Jacob Yahuah's favored "firstborn son."

This story about Edom and Jacob was obviously made up to impart a type of royal obsession toward the firstborn son and an inflated sense of racial entitlement. The reality was that pre-Israelites were nomads or raiders to the new lands, and their sense of entitlement could be attributed to having a measure of demigod genes.

Stepping back in time to the Egyptian Second Intermediate Period in 18th to 16th centuries B.C., Hyksos came onto the scene and took over Lower Egypt. This time period was beyond the scope of the later biblical writers, so they often copied earlier Egyptian stories, some of which can be seen in chapter 3's "Catholic and Christian" section. The Hyksos are portrayed as ferocious enemies in the Bible, but they played a part in the creation of the Jewish bloodline.

The Hyksos definition has been muddled in later "historical" accounts. Early Egyptian historian Manetho identified them as "king-shepherds."[33] The first century A.D. Jewish historian Flavius Josephus gave an alternate meaning because of the Egyptian word *hyk*, meaning captive; therefore, he called them "captive-shepherds."[33] The definition as shepherds seems to clash with Manetho's following statement as written by Josephus:

> [U]nexpectedly from the regions of the East invaders of an obscure race marched in confidence of victory against our land. By main force they easily seized it without striking a blow; and having overpowered the rulers of the land, they then burned our cities ruthlessly, razed to the ground the temples of the gods, and treated all the natives with a cruel hostility, massacring some and leading into slavery the wives and children of others (p. 155-156).[33]

Egyptian philologist Sir Alan Gardiner writes that *Hyksos* actually derived from the Egyptian phrase *hik-khase*, meaning "chieftain of a foreign hill-country" (p. 156).[33] The Hyksos were Asiatic, but their precise origin is uncertain. Gardiner states that *hik-khase* designated Bedouin sheiks during the Middle Kingdom (2030-1640 B.C.) and onward.[33] These Arab leaders were known as a specific race, but their nomadic and conquering nature must have assimilated several lands and people. The difference between the Hyksos and the typical Bible story about the early Hebrews is that the Hyksos had horse-drawn chariots and sophisticated weaponry, including body armor, bow and arrow, axes, and swords, and the biblical Israelites were pastoral shepherds. Since the Hyksos were later misnamed Shepherd Kings, and the Jews, including Jesus, were also shepherd kings, I doubt the Bible's peaceful depiction of Jews and Jesus. I also can see from this association that the Jews, including Jesus, come from Hyksos ancestry.

Shasu entered Egypt after the Hyksos dynasty was expelled, but some Hyksos people remained in Egypt as part of the society. Other people, including Hittites and Hurrians from the North, also migrated into Egypt. The Bible considered these three "H" peoples violent and terrible, which often they were; however, they migrated from Haran around the same time as Abraham, so it is plausible that the Shasu of Ywh incorporated some of the supposed biblical enemies. If the Hebrew ethnicity started when Israel was later created, then Hebrews comprised genes from the wicked three "H" people!

The biblical story of the initial colonization of Israel into its 12 tribes seems peaceful as though no one already colonized those lands, or the indigenous people had no problem sharing their land. The real problems of the Israelites started after they left Egypt in the grand Exodus because they wanted to take back by force what may or may not have been their land in Canaan. Exodus chapter 3, verse 8 mentions the Hittites, Amorites, Jebusites, and others in Canaan. The land was described as "flowing with milk and honey" (Exodus 3:17) which means that the settled areas were fertile and bountiful. An oft unreported reason for today's Palestinian and Israeli wars is over water rights because there is insufficient fresh water across the region. It makes sense that the inhabitants (and conquerors) of such settlements would not wish to give up their land. The preferred habitable areas had to be conquered by the Hebrews.

Yahuah's people could not be merely pastoral and nomadic because "[t]he LORD is a man of war" (Exodus 15:3). Numerous Bible stories feature Yahuah's and Elohim's fury and power. Allah's people were equally militaristic. Another people known for their brutal ways were the Assyrians, and they followed the goddess Asherah, who was El's consort in Israel and Yahuah's consort in Judah.[34,35] Yahuah's people had to be strong and influential to maintain their social class and ethnicity. If we could find a specific origin to the Jewish bloodline that incorporated genes of the three Hs, then the Habiru would be it.

The Habiru (ha-BI-ru) were an Indo-European Aryan-type people best known as warriors who created alliances with the Hyksos, Hittites, and Hurrians of the region. Abrahams city of Haran was comprised mainly of Hurrians, and the Habiru were present there. Theologian Meredith G. Kline argues that the Habiru were a unique race "discovered in the Fertile Crescent from the [neo-Sumerian] Ur III period, and probably somewhat earlier" (p. 181).[36] They were documented as SA.GAZ in Old Hittite royal archives in the city of Hattusha where the SA.GAZ joined Hatti (Hittite) troops to pledge allegiance to Hattusha.[36] The variation of Habiru, 'apiru, was written in Egyptian texts throughout the second millennium B.C.[30]

Some scholars believe that Habiru defined a social class; however, its people comprised nearly the entire spectrum of social and economic status, so this is not an entirely accurate definition. It is true that they contracted their services in time of need, and they were listed as servants, not slaves who are forgotten. The larger picture is that they were socially flexible, working among the elite and the poor, but they did not often assume obvious leadership roles.

The Habiru were best known for their military expertise that helped foreign leaders. They were known as trained assassins who were both feared yet desired by kingdoms. I am sure that kings would have preferred skilled mercenaries working for them instead of against them. They manned the garrisons at Ur, Larsa, Babylon, Susa, and in Anatolia (pre-Turkey), conducted raids along the

Euphrates and throughout Canaan, and oversaw captives of war in Egypt.[36] In Letter #286 of the Amarna letters, King Abdi-Heba of Canaanite Jerusalem pleaded with his overlord, the pharaoh, to send military assistance because the "'Apiru has plundered all the lands of the king" (p. 99).[37]

The Habiru were known as foreigners, but they assimilated into other kingdoms and lands for mutually beneficial purposes. This could have been their strategy to infiltrate kingdoms but not wipe them out. Habiru may have been a large component of the Hyksos military because they were integrated in Assyria before the Hyksos came into Egypt, and they were in Egypt with a servant status after the Hyksos dynasty.[36]

The Shasu of Yhw either referred to a unique ethnicity, a place marker of Yahuah that was not Seir, or both. The UB states that people believed Yahuah was a volcano whose breath was the smoke, and Exodus chapter 19, verse 18 supports this by describing a volcanic eruption at Mount Sinai, Yahuah's holy mountain. No volcano existed on the Sinai Peninsula, but a cataclysmic volcanic eruption of Mount Thera (Santorini) in southeastern Greece did occur before the biblical Exodus.

An absence of human remains on the island suggests that Thera's Minoan civilization and likely other Minoans just south in hard-hit Ancient Crete predicted the eruption and evacuated the area.[38] A Shasu people escaping the volcano aftermath traveled from this region and Western Anatolia, down into Canaan, and then into Egypt. Egypt was the preferred destination after enduring drought in Canaan at that time. Radiocarbon dating of the eruption puts it between 1627 and 1600 B.C., but this was over 100 years before any mention of *Shasu*.[39] It could have taken the people that length of time to enter Egypt, or it merely took that long for them to be accounted.

Amenhotep II was the first to distinguish the Shasu. He erected a stele in Memphis that lists the *'Apiru* and *Shasu* side by side, but the Shasu are clearly marked as Bedouin (travelers).[40] The Habiru had their foothold in Anatolia, and an extensive DNA study proves that Anatolians created the Minoan civilization in Ancient Crete just south of Mount Thera.[41] Since the Habiru traveled extensively and performed raids, they were arguably part of the Shasu of Yhw and some other Shasu, which Amenhotep II did not adequately distinguish.

The core of the Habiru was actually one ethnic stock, but because they were geographically spread out, their discernible ethnicity often became muddled when they took the names of the cultures they joined. The Hurrian civilization in northern Mesopotamia contained numerous Habiru. Hurrians made a point to record Habiru transplants in the city of Nuzi, showing that most of their names had Akkadian origin.[36] Habiru and Hurrians both assimilated well into different civil-social complexes, but unlike Hurrians,

Habiru were esteemed as god-men. In Egypt, 'Apir was linked to several gods, including 'Apir-Baal, 'Apir-El, 'Apir-Anu, and 'Apir-Isis.[42]

Habiru was an Akkadian term that existed before the Hebrew affiliation. In the *exeGeses* lexicon, *Hebrew* is the transliterated name *ibriy*, which is "of Eber."[7] Eber was Noah's (Ziusudra's) great-great-grandson and Abraham's ancestor. *Ibri* is the root of *Habiri* that is fully interchangeable with *Habiru*.[42] If YHWH prized or coveted the Habiru, and they were closest in ethnicity to Eber, then they were also sons of Anak, although many Habiru were not giants. Only some of the Anunnaki sons were deplorable to YHWH when they sided with rival gods.

It is commonly believed that warriors with horses invaded and settled into the Indus Valley and set up the caste system to preserve their racial quality. In Sanskrit, they are called ārya, which is a word of great esteem meaning *noble, righteous, superior,* and *progressive civilization.*[43] Either the Habiru were these blond-haired, blue-eyed Aryans, or they were similar and likely racially intermixed with them. Adolf Hitler praised the Aryan race as a mighty-man race. His political party Nationalsozialistische Deutsche Arbeiterpartei is peculiarly nicknamed Nazi, which rings familiar to the Nuzi significance of the Habiru.

Ethnicity was arguably the biggest determinant of Judaism and its Levitical priesthood. If the ethnic line of Yahuah's people is narrow, the breed can give specific attributes at the exclusion of others. This involves incest that harms the human gene pool over time. Another option is to make the ethnic lineage broad yet focused enough to preserve the strength of the original genes; this would allow more people to be a part of the royal family. The second strategy is employed by international royal families who marry for political alliances but maintain enough of an independent ethnicity that has history in inbreeding.

Judaism focused upon the Davidic line while putting its roots in Abraham. The Bible's scribes wrote their patriarchal history of Abraham several centuries after his existence, so if their lineage had basis in reality, they must have drawn upon earlier historical accounts.

The German biblical scholar Julius Wellhausen provided a documentary hypothesis that states the Torah "was derived from originally independent, parallel and complete narratives, which were subsequently combined into the current form by a series of redactors (editors)."[44]

As I introduced in chapter 3, the earliest group was the Yahwist (J) who wrote c. 950 B.C. in southern Judah, probably in the area of Jerusalem as I soon explain. According to the *exeGeses parallel BIBLE*:

> The inscribers revealed his name as YHVH – sequentually
> [sic] as early as Genesis 2:4, and chronologically as early as *Job*

Iyob 1:6. The *exeGeses* presents his name vowel pointed as Yah Veh. Most Versions often render the name Yah Veh incorrectly with the title *LORD* – all capital letters. This is a caving in to the traditions of certain Hebrews who said his name was too holy to pronounce. It is more likely that the ancient Hebrews feared the extreme consequences of dishonoring the name Yah Veh. For the Hebrews used the name Yah Veh to covenant, and whenever the covenant was broken, serious consequences followed (p. vii).[7]

The J source associated Yahuah with Judah, the Yahwist's preferred point of reference. Since the name of G-D was too holy for the average Jew to utter, it is unclear if LORD was used in place of G-D as the capitalized reference to God.

The Elohist (E) wrote c. 850 B.C. in the northern Kingdom of Israel. E always used El for God and its plural Elohim. J and E sometimes gave contrasting genealogies depending upon the ethnicity or location they wished to highlight. At some time around 650 B.C., Judaean editors combined J and E, known to us as JE.[44]

The *exeGeses parallel BIBLE* substitutes *Yah Veh* for LORD and *Elohim* for God in every case, thereby completely eradicating distinction between an actual Yah Veh (Yahuah) GOD or Elohim GOD. It also applies the word *elohim* to the lesser gods, showing that the true name or names of the respective group's God were lost in translation. Upon closer scrutiny, equating *elohim* to any God supports two separate Gods in Exodus 6:3 that states, "And I appeared unto Abraham, unto Isaac, and unto Jacob, by *the name of* God Almighty, but by my name JE-HO'-VAH was I not known to them." Because the words "LORD God" are combined in numerous occasions in the Old Testament, from now on I will use the Tetragrammaton of YHWH to represent both Elohim and Yahuah as God, unless I purposely state otherwise.

The Deuteronomist (D) wrote the Book of Deuteronomy c. 600 B.C. in Jerusalem during a period of religious reform, emphasizing centralization of worship and governance in Jerusalem. It complements the JE history.

Lastly, the Priestly (P) source was written c. 500 B.C by Aaronic priests in exile in Babylon. Torah redactors became increasingly influenced by P, producing a final form of the Torah c. 450 B.C.[44]

The creation story was written as an afterthought by J and E authors, so this explains its glaring incongruity in the first chapters of Genesis. For example, Genesis 5, verse 4 first mentions Adam and Eve having daughters after Cain found a wife. This shows that Adam and Eve were not the Earth's first humans because Eve was not Cain's wife. Straight incest between mother and son would have weakened the genetic line more than between half-brothers and half-sisters, and it would not have been a palatable story. There were other women in a colonized land called Nod just outside of Eden (Genesis 4:16). There were actually many people near Adam and Eve, so it must have been difficult for YHWH to identify a totally loyal bunch that did not subscribe to other beliefs. Certainly, it was easiest for biblical writers to focus on one family line, even if the family's origin was unclear, and the bloodline was woven together from bigger-than-life characters. It was also easiest for the writers to convey that the numerous wars were religiously motivated instead of politically because their objective was to narrow the scope of people as created by God, not admit there were countless people who did their own thing. On the other hand, many kings believed they were gods or demigods, which muddled the reasoning for war and dominion.

Just as division exists within God's religious factions down to many Christian subsets, the kings created competition and wars not only because of their inflated egos but also because of their gods, notably YHWH's several names. Followers of such multiple faces probably did not know that their God was the same or similar God of their enemy. YHWH just directed each group of people like a pawn on a chessboard.

Is division YHWH's design? Does he (or they) intend to make similar races fixated on one belief toward their respective God so that YHWH could wear different hats according to political strategy? If one set of people makes him angry, then he would favor another to teach the first one a lesson? This is what happened when Israel split from Judah.

The First Book of the Kings chapter 11, verses 31-32 introduce the division of lands into 11 tribes of Israel. David's son Solomon sinned against YHWH by worshipping other gods; therefore, YHWH gave 10 of the supposed 12 tribes to Jeroboam, Solomon's servant, while YHWH reserved another tribe for David. Jeroboam was chosen to temporarily rule until YHWH's favored monarchy under the Davidic line of Judah straightened out its faith.

Jeroboam was chosen to redeem the Israelites from Solomon. Interestingly, Jeroboam's name was nearly identical to Solomon's son's name, Rehoboam. Rehoboam means "enlarges the people," and the same definition can be found toward Jeroboam.[24] Unfortunately for Jeroboam, his more common definition is "a large wine bottle."[45] His mother's name was Zeruah, which is translated to mean "leprous" and "stricken."[24] So, the person or fabrication as Jeroboam was depicted as a drunkard with a damaged, leprous mother because he ended up leading Israel into sin. In contrast, Solomon led the united tribes into sin, but he was still favored by YHWH.

Jeroboam ruled after King David, and King Saul ruled before David. The fact that fictitious names were used as Jeroboam and Rehoboam raises the question about whether earlier stories were credible. Theologian Dr. Leithart makes the following comparison between Jeroboam and Saul.

> In 1 Kings 14, Jeroboam's wife goes disguised to visit a
> prophet from Shiloh, who announces the death of her son and
> the eventual destruction of his dynasty. Ahijah tells Jeroboam's
> wife that another king will take the kingdom.
> In 1 Samuel 28, Saul goes disguised to visit a medium at
> Endor, who, he hopes, will be able to conjure Samuel, a prophet
> from Shiloh, who announces Saul's death, the death of his sons,
> and the destruction of his dynasty. Samuel tells Saul that the
> kingdom has been given to David.
> Previously, in 1 Kings 13, Jeroboam has refused to listen to
> the rebuke of a prophet. An altar is "torn" to signify the tearing
> of Jeroboam's kingdom. When the man of God from Judah
> heals him, Jeroboam seeks reconciliation, which the man of God
> refuses.
> In 1 Samuel 15, Saul refuses to listen to the rebuke of
> a prophet, and a garment is torn to signify the tearing of the
> kingdom. Saul asks the prophet to go back with him to worship,
> and Samuel initially refuses but then goes.
> Saul is the first king of Israel, but he falls and loses the
> kingdom. Jeroboam is the first king of "all Israel," but he falls and
> loses the kingdom.[46]

These similar stories represent a biblical theme of God's magnificence and might over his "chosen" people: they were once powerful, but when they sinned in whatever measure, they were reduced to almost nothing. Saul's sin was that he only partially obeyed YHWH.

Saul was an important character to the Yahwist writers because he came from the tribe of Benjamin, and Benjamin merged with Judah after the split of Israel's 10 tribes. Simeon at that time contained the city of Jerusalem. Since Simeon was surrounded by Judah, Simeon was part of this merger.[47] The merger of the three tribes as stated in the Book of Judges linked Saul to Jerusalem.

The Israelite Omride dynasty was roughly a century after Jeroboam's reign, and it was also looked upon unfavorably in the Bible. "But Omri wrought evil in the eyes of the LORD and did worse than that *were* before him" (1 Kings 16:25). The Omride dynasty in 885 B.C. to 842 B.C. was the largest kingdom in Israel. It ended civil wars and also had relatively peaceful relations with Judah.[48] The Book of Judges states that only two of the 10 or more tribes, Judah and Simeon, succeeded in establishing monotheistic strongholds toward YHWH in the land of Canaan after the Exodus. The other tribes struggled amidst rampant idol worship in the vast areas of land they tried to reclaim or just enter as foreigners. The main reason the Omride kingdom was viewed as evil was because King Ahab married Jezebel, a Baal-worshipping princess, and he built a large heathen altar at Beth-el.

Many scholars believe that the First and Second Books of Samuel were written centuries after the story of Saul and were reminiscent of the Omride dynasty. An exhaustive study of the First and Second Books of Samuel by Mosheh Garsiel in the *Journal of Hebrew Scriptures* gives a different conclusion that placed them within the Yahwist territory.

> In the light of...literary, historical and archaeological considerations, it seems to me that there is no possibility other than to attribute most of the significant composition of the Book of Samuel to the 10th century B.C.E., though some small changes took place much later. In my opinion, the book was developed in four stages by different authors, copyists and editorial work (p. 34).[49]

According to Garsiel, the discrepancies and obvious edits confused the superficial description by most scholars who deduced the main authors of Samuel as Deuteronomists, although a D source did edit some of the material. His viewpoint and study shows that the Old Testament contains a measure of historical accuracy; however, the textual substance has become significantly reduced by countless human hands shaping the stories and misrepresenting names and identities.

The stories and symbolisms about the Bible's 12 tribes of Israel are used as an approximated guide toward finding actual truth, which now brings us to the reality behind Israel's patriarchs.

Moses

After the children of Israel came out of Egypt in the grand Exodus, 480 years passed until the fourth year of King Solomon's reign over Israel when he started to build a large temple to Yahuah on Mount Zion near Jerusalem (1 Kings 6:1). "And the time that Solomon reigned in Jerusalem over all Israel *was* forty years" (1 Kings 11:42). The number 480 is the classic multiple of 40 in the Bible. Based upon this numerology and the accepted timeline of his reign by biblical scholars, his temple construction started c. 960 B.C., which placed the beginning of the Exodus at c. 1440 B.C.

No archaeological evidence has shown a mass wave of people entering

Sinai in the 15th or 14th century B.C. The Hyksos expulsion from Egypt started in mid-16th century B.C. when Pharaoh Ahmose I overthrew their kingdom, so this could not have been the later biblical Exodus.

Bible authors retroactively dated the Exodus during the Egyptian Pharaoh Tuthmose (Tuthmosis) III's reign. The names Tuthmose and Tuthmosis are very similar to the name Moses, but it is most likely that *Moses* was ascribed to Tuthmose III's great-grandson, Akhenaten. Akhenaten's followers gave him the code name "MOs," which means "rightful son and heir," because Akhenaten was banished from the dynasty, and it was a crime to call him by his name. Greek translation added the last "s" to an additional vowel, thereby giving the name Moses.[50]

Akhenaten and Moses were each generally considered to be the first monotheist. Akhenaten was born Amenhotep IV after his father Amenhotep III in a line of 18th dynasty Egyptian kings, but he changed his name to reflect his God Aten. The pharaohs prior to Akhenaten also incorporated their God's name, and for a time, Amun was the state God. (Note that *Amen* is the god Amun, and it is *the* word that concludes Catholic prayers.) It was customary for pharaohs to add the suffix –*Re (Ra)* after their names because Ra was the ultimate Egyptian God; however, it appears that Akhenaten did not follow that practice and supplanted Ra with Aten although their symbols were similar. "[T]he early representations of Akhenaten's God showed the deity as of human shape with the head of a falcon, surmounted by a solar disc," states Egyptologist Ahmed Osman (p. 162).[51] Two or three years later, a sun with far-reaching rays had replaced the human figure. Similar to Ra, Aten was not only identified as a star but also a type of god-man (in chapter 7). In addition, a cobra hung from the solar disc to represent a kingly status.[51] This supports Exodus 4, verse 3 where YHWH turned Moses's rod into a snake.

Akhenaten's insistence toward the supremacy of Aten caused Egyptians under his rule to revile him. Just a few years after his reign began in 1353 B.C., he left his position in Thebes and created a city by his own name (later renamed Amarna).[52] He soon afterward had to leave all of Egypt because of religious persecution, so he went to the Sinai Peninsula.

Canaanites had already built stone altars in Sinai, but there is no archeological evidence to show that they constructed temples before Moses created the tabernacle. "Akhenaten adapted the Heliopolitan solar form of the Egyptian temple—the same form used by Moses in the desert—to be used as the place of worship for his new religion," says Osman (p. 165).[51] The Bible states that this Egyptian and Greek-styled temple was the hub for the Levitical priesthood to perform its purification rituals and animal sacrifice (Exodus chapters 25-27).

Levi, the patriarch of the Levites, was the half-brother of Reuben,

Simeon, and Judah, the three sons of Jacob by the prized lineage of Leah (Genesis 29:31-35). Yahwists valued these united lands because Levites linked Jerusalem to YHWH. The Book of Exodus states that both Moses and his brother Aaron were Levites. Laurence Gardner asserted that Aaron was the Pharaoh Smenkhkare, and his mother, Tey, was merely Akhenaten's wet nurse.[9] Their "brotherly" relationship is based on their shared Semitic ancestry through Akhenaten's mother, Tiye, and her brother who fathered Smenkhkare, thereby making them cousins. Aaron is an important Bible character because he was the first Levitical priest.

Exodus chapter 4, verses 21-26 shows the importance of YHWH's circumcision command to Moses and his people:

> And the LORD said unto Moses, When thou goest to return into Egypt, see that thou do all those wonders before Pharaoh, which I have put in thine hand: but I will harden his heart, that he shall not let the people go.
>
> And thou shalt say unto Pharaoh, Thus saith the LORD, Israel *is* my son, *even* my firstborn:
>
> And I say unto thee, Let my son go, that he may serve me: and if thou refuse to let him go, behold, I will slay thy son, *even* they firstborn.
>
> And it came to pass by the way in the inn, that the LORD met him [Moses], and sought to kill him [Moses's son].
>
> Then Zip-po´-rah [Moses's wife], took a sharp stone, and cut off the foreskin of her son, and cast *it* at his feet, and said, Surely a bloody husband *art* thou to me.
>
> So he [Yahuah] let him go: then she said, A bloody husband *thou art*, because of the circumcision.

The first verse steers history toward the supremacy of YHWH, but it also says God purposely prolonged the enslavement of the innocent Jews, which made them more enslaved to him for that desperate miracle. What is most odd about these Scriptures is that Yahuah was a man who could physically meet Moses and kill his son. Apart from these oddities, the message shows that Moses and his family did not willingly partake in circumcision. The Book of Joshua chapter 5, verses 4-7 confirm that the children born under Moses's leadership were not circumcised during the great Exodus. Circumcision occurred in Egypt toward the god Amun-Re. It also occurred in Sumer as seen in statues and paintings, so circumcision helps show a link between Sumerian and Egyptian gods and YHWH.[53] It appears that Akhenaten simply rebelled against that procedure, or YHWH bent some rules for him just as YHWH did for me in my mother's prophecies when I protested sexist rituals.

The names or titles of the main Gods were somewhat combined between the Egyptians and the people of YHWH. According to *Historical Deception: The Untold Story of Ancient Egypt*:

> '*Adon*' meaning Lord was correctly noted by Sigmund Freud [who first popularly equated Moses to Akhenaten], as the Hebrew word for the Egyptian Aton/Aten. As the Egyptian '*t*' becomes '*d*' in Hebrew and the vowel '*e*' becomes an '*o*', *Adon* is the Hebrew equivalent of the Egyptian Aten (p. 193).[54]

Freud writes about Deuteronomy 6, verse 4, "The Jewish creed says: 'Shema Yisrael Adonai Elohenu Adonai Echod'" (p. 188).[54] It is stated in the King James Bible as "Hear, O Israel: The LORD our God *is* one LORD." This saying must have originated with Akhenaten, but Jews now interpret "Adonai" as a title of respect, clearly missing the original meaning. Technically, it is blasphemous for Jews to utter another god's name during worship, but is it inevitable due to their political history of intermixed peoples and similar gods?

Interestingly, the story of Moses was likely an amalgamation; Exodus 6, verses 26-27 allude that there was more than one Moses character: "These are that Aaron and Moses...which spake to Pharaoh king of Egypt, to bring out the children of Israel from Egypt: these are that Moses and Aaron." The New King James Version elucidates "that" as "the same" to likely distinguish between different Moses and Aaron characters.

Researcher Charles Pope states that many pivotal figures in the Bible are mosaics of at least two Egyptian pharaohs. He argues that each god was a famed, usually royal, human predecessor to a later popular supporter or descendant, essentially dismissing otherworldly beings. I do not share this anthropocentric belief (although it is true in some cases), but I agree that biblical writers sometimes based their simplified characters on more than one person.

Pope compares biblical and archaeological texts and comes to the conclusion that there was an earlier Moses character, and his name was Hammurabi, the sixth king of Babylonia. According to Pope, Hammurabi was originally Egyptian Pharaoh Hor Auibre (or Awibre): "Au-ibre was a promising young crown prince who suddenly vanished from Egypt.... [H]e committed a high crime and was forced to seek refuge in Babylon of Mesopotamia where he assumed the Semitic name of Hammurabi."[55] Auibre has the root word *eber* that is also the root of *Hebrew*. These correlations imply that Auibre as Eber was the leader of the Hebrew people whose steps the latter Levitical Jews followed.

Pope theorizes that Prince Hor Auibre went into exile in Babylonia and succeeded in ruling its empire as King Hammurabi c. 1792-1750 B.C.[56] He created an extensive, institutionalized set of 282 laws known as the Code of Hammurabi. It dictated civilian matters such as finance, family concerns, property, slavery, and conduct, often with violent punishment.[57] Many of these laws were similar to the latter Ten Commandments and other biblical commandments such as those in the Book of Proverbs. After Hammurabi's exile gained widespread success abroad, he gained his rightful pharaoh position for less than one year c. 1760 B.C., either by briefly returning to Egypt or receiving transferred rights while in Babylonia. The ease with which he transferred and claimed royal positions between both nations was facilitated by his affiliation with his God Marduk as Ra, the supreme God of Egypt and Babylonia. Although Hammurabi was in exile for less than 40 years before he returned to claim the Egyptian throne, he was a king for approximately 40 years, so this popular, simplified number was agreeable to the Exodus storytellers.

Biblical writers drew upon the Babylonian and Egyptian story of Horus to lift Moses up as a second but possibly more important patriarch than Abraham. They state that Moses had Hebrew blood, so they wanted to portray him as an adopted Egyptian to underscore YHWH's distinction and supremacy with his bloodline. Therefore, Akhenaten's God, Aten, must have been part of YHWH who called out "his" people.

Semitic Influence in the Egyptian New Kingdom

The Bible's portrayal of King David coincides with the reality of Pharaoh Thutmose III. Thutmose III is considered the greatest conqueror of the Egyptian dynasty. He employed a political strategy to bring native inhabitants of his conquered lands to Egypt to educate them for the purpose of good will. Chapters 37 and 39 in the Book of Genesis refer to these actions, for Joseph became prosperous in Egypt after some of his jealous brethren sold him to Egyptians as a slave. After having won the pharaoh's favor as his dream interpreter, Joseph became a part of the Egyptian dynasty. This describes Yuya, an influential man of Semitic origin.

Yuya was Thutmose IV's vizier, and he served as a key adviser to Amenhotep III, Thutmose IV's son. Yuya was either born in Akhmin, Egypt or was brought there by his Semitic family.

In the Bible, Joseph's father is Jacob. A signet ring with the name Yakub was discovered in the 15th dynasty Hyksos capital Avaris, so it is commonly thought that this is the biblical Jacob. However, Yaqub-Har was an Asiatic ruler during the Second Intermediate Period whose sparse records place him in the 17th or 16th century B.C.[58] Both possibilities place Yuya's father long before he could have existed.

Yuya's daughter Tiye, Amenhotep III's wife, was part Mitanni. This gives the possibility that Yuya was Mitanni, but it was more likely that his wife, Tjuyu, had that ethnicity.[59] The Mitanni people formed an alliance with Egypt during that time, and to help seal the alliance, Mitanni kings sent some of their daughters to marry Egyptian pharaohs. The Mitanni kingdom incorporated a large Hurrian population. The Habiru were also aligned with the Mitanni but stopped their conquests around 14th century B.C., causing them to better assimilate into native cultures.[36]

This timing by the Habiru is interesting concerning "Joseph" because he was a main character in the Hebrew seeding of the Egyptian royal line. The Habiru ethnicity came from the North and spread out among many cultures by the time Yuya gained power. "Yuya, as an 'officer in the Chariotry', is thought to have been from a high-ranking military background."[59] He most likely had Habiru ethnicity, but it had no apparent relevance to his religion. Yuya was a prophet of Min, the chief god of his native Egyptian town.

The Bible states that Jacob's (Israel's) "birthright was given unto the sons of Joseph the son of Israel: and the genealogy is not to be reckoned after the birthright. For Judah prevailed above his brethren, and of him *came* the chief ruler; but the birthright was Joseph's" (1 Chronicles 5:1-2). Pope asserts that Pharaoh Thutmose IV was a biblical Judah whose son "Amenhotep III was known as 'The King of Kings' in ancient times."[60] To keep in line with Joseph's birthright, Yuya had to be the father of such a great pharaoh. Joseph states in Genesis 45, verse 8 that God "hath made me a father to Pharaoh, and lord of all his house, and a ruler throughout all the land of Egypt." Yuya must have fathered Amenhotep III while Yuya's half-brother Thutmose IV was the legal patriarch. The preferred bloodline's "birthright" took precedence over a legal designation in both the Bible and real life. The *Historiae Philippicae* by Pompeius Trogus—a lost work from the Emperor Augustus period that was later transcribed by Latin historian Justinus—states that Joseph was Moses's father.[61] Trogus was partially right, for Yuya was the grandfather of Akhenaten, confirms the ATI,TPE.

Pope states that another historical person as the biblical Joseph was Intef IV, a 13th dynasty deified vizier, who fathered Pharaoh Hor Auibre, known as Hammurabi, on behalf of Pharaoh Amenemhat II. Pope asserts that Amenemhat II as another Judah spared Hor Auibre's life so that he could produce an heir.[55]

Yuya was buried among Egyptian pharaohs. His burial position was unique among the Egyptians because his hands were placed under his chin rather than across his chest, and he had obviously different features that all point to a Semitic origin.[62] Joseph's wife was Asenath from the Esau lineage. Both Yuya and Tjuyu had blond or dyed hair, as their mummies show.[63] The Bible states that Joseph was buried in Canaan, but this was likely a purposeful placement to highlight Yuya's Semitic ethnicity.

The Book of Genesis states that Joseph was Abraham's great-grandson. When linking Abraham to King David, the first pharaoh who encountered Abraham was not Thutmose III but rather Thutmose I, as Pope asserts and I agree. Pope states that the David character was both of these pharaohs.[64] This timeline puts Abraham at least 400 years after the Bible's placement of him after Adam, unless he also was an amalgamated character.

The Bible stories about David and Abraham involve pharaohs. Genesis chapter 12 states that Pharaoh found Sarai (Sarah), Abraham's wife, very beautiful, and he wanted her as his wife. The same story repeats in Genesis 20 with King Abimelech. Both Scriptures explain that Sarah was untouched by these men. The Second Book of Samuel chapter 11 states that David found Bath-sheba very beautiful, and he wanted her as his wife. These are identical stories that equate Sarah to Bathsheba, but Bath-sheba was impregnated by David with a son. To claim Bath-sheba as his wife, he set up her husband, Uriah, to be murdered in war.

Genesis chapter 17 explains that Abraham was 100 years old, and Sarah was 90 years old when God said they would conceive a child named Isaac, who was the father of Israel. This could only happen by a literal act of God, which is why the Uriah character, Bath-sheba's "husband," appeared.

Uriah is a revered character in the Bible, much like Abraham. He is called a Hittite, but the non-legalistic, exegetical classical literature (the Aggadah) of Jewish Rabbis states that his name means that he merely dwelt among the Hittites.[65] When we break down the name Uriah, it is *Ur*, a Hurrian word meaning city or light, and *Yah* (iah), which is the root of *Yahuah*. When placing Uriah among Thutmoses I and III in Yahuah's city of Jerusalem, it is highly doubtful that he originated there because Jerusalem in the 16th and 15th centuries B.C. was sparsely populated. The most plausible definition of Uriah is Yahuah's Light. Scribes used *Uriah* to name a few prophets of Yahuah, underscoring the name's direct relationship to God. I do not think that Uriah was an actual person, as I will explain.

It makes much sense if Uriah and Bath-sheba were already in Egypt for the relationship with Thutmose III to have occurred; thankfully, the biblical writers in Genesis 12, verses 10-20 placed Abraham and Sarah in Egypt to give a clue to their relationships.

Bath-sheba can be interpreted as a girl or daughter from Sheba. *Beth* means a girl or a daughter, and *Sheba* either refers to Beersheba, an area in southern

Judah, or the bloodline of Sheba. In Genesis 21, verses 30-32, Abraham dug a well and made a covenant in the area that he named Beersheba. It was an important location that he and presumably Sarah often inhabited, and Isaac later dug seven wells there. Sheba was the son of Cush, who was the grandson of Noah and the father of Nimrod, a Babylonian king and demigod. Since Bathsheba is not a real name, it is doubtful that Sarai (and Sarah) was the matriarch's correct name with its inclusion of Ra.

For the Habiru seed to continue under YHWH's control, it could not only tackle other powerful nations; it had to become a part of those dynasties. Djehuty was a general of Thutmose III's army, and Thutmose III gave him a golden bowl that is now housed in the Louvre museum. If interpreted correctly, its inscription could reveal that Djehuty was "father of the god" Thutmose III.

> Granted by royal favor of Menkheperre (Thutmosis III), King of Upper and Lower Egypt, to his excellency the noble, father of the god, beloved of the god, man of confidence of the king in all foreign lands and on the islands amid the sea, he who fills the stores with lapis lazuli, silver and gold, the general, the favorite of the perfect god, he who was created by the Lord of the Two Lands, the royal scribe Djehuty, acquitted.[66]

According to the official Louvre museum website, Djehuty's fame was so great that a later 19th dynasty papyrus told the story of how "Djehuty took the city of Joppa (modern Jaffa) thanks to a ruse worthy of the wily Ulysses or of Ali Baba's forty thieves themselves."[66] This described a mighty-man Habiru whose genes were chosen for the Hebrew bloodline, so he as Abraham had to be the one who impregnated the barren Sarah, not Thutmose I or III. The ATI, TPE states that Thutmose III was indeed the son of Djehuty and "Sarah." For this to have happened, divine intervention occurred by way of the Uriah character.

The Bible states that Uriah was killed in battle, but if Uriah was not actually human, then he could not have died. The symbolic character Uriah was mentioned to introduce YHWH's presence and intervention while then bringing the story back to human affairs. As the term *LORD* generally refers to a man of stature, and Djehuty helped propagate the royal bloodline, Genesis 21, verses 1-2 must have referred to him:

> And the LORD visited Sarah as he had said, and the LORD did unto Sarah as he had spoken. For Sarah conceived, and bare Abraham a son in his old age, at the set time of which God had

spoken to him.

The All That Is, The Pure Essence reveals that a YHWH entity intervened: "Sarah's reproductive organs were altered to allow human sexual activity."

Djehuty may or may not have been the same Abraham who impregnated Hagar, but as that figure, a man with either or both Habiru and Hyksos ethnicity helped create an equally powerful religion through his son Ishmael. Ishmael's name gives tribute to YHWH's Elohim. YHWH and its manipulated Habiru bloodline would not be so limited to only create Jews! Abraham also had six sons by a third wife named Keturah (Genesis 25:1-2), more sons by concubines, and daughters who were not mentioned. Genesis 25, verse 6 briefly includes these extra children: "But unto the sons of the concubines, which Abraham had, Abraham gave gifts, and sent them away from Isaac his son." Since these children were stated as an afterthought, their purpose was likely numerical toward propagation.

Solomon

The Bible states that King Solomon was David's son; this would have made him Amenhotep II, the pharaoh who enjoyed the bounty of Thuthmose III's kingdom and was known as the king of peace or *Shalom* in Hebrew. The composite character Solomon was also Amenhotep III, the great-grandson of Thutmose III. Amenhotep III was Yuya's son-in-law by marriage to Tiye.

The Bible depicts Solomon as a very popular person with 700 wives, many of them foreign (1 Kings 11), and foreign princesses were a part of his harem. King Tyre, a Phoenician, helped him build his grand palace in Jerusalem (1 Kings 7:2-12). Solomon was a powerful ruler over a long, 40-year reign. Surely, his name would have been recorded in documents of other kingdoms? No; no record of any Solomon has been found in any kingdom. Additionally, no such palace was uncovered in Jerusalem. Instead, this palace exactly describes Amenhotep III's palace in Thebes that was built during his reign in the 14th century B.C.[67]

The First Book of the Kings chapter 9, verse 15 states that Solomon built the cities of Megiddo, Hazor, and Gezer in Canaan in the 10th century B.C. Thutmose III conquered these cities, so it is probable that either or both Amenhotep II and III helped rebuild them. This predates the biblical rebuilding by at least 400 years. Archeological evidence has shown extensive rebuilding of these cities, and a cartouche (similar to a logo) was found in the strata with Amenhotep III's name. Amenhotep III helped rebuild Jerusalem, erect monuments, fortify cities, and create temples (like the grand First Temple in 1 Kings, verses 4-5, where its foundations may exist underneath current temple ruins on Mount Zion if wars have not destroyed them). The wells that Solomon supposedly built in the Negev desert were dated at least 300 years beforehand, approximating the reign of Amenhotep III.[67]

Amenhotep III provided a good setting for biblical writers because his reconstruction of Jerusalem gave them a starting point to show God's favor for their people. He reached across many lands through political aims and personal connections to foreign women. He compiled words of wisdom in his *Maxims of Amenhotep III* that largely mirror the Book of Proverbs. He also was a likely influence for the 12 tribes of Israel because he had 12 districts for taxation, designed after the zodiac.[67]

The First Book of the Kings chapter 4, verse 7 mentions 12 officers of Solomon over all Israel. He represented the good life, so how was he not favored by YHWH? Of course, his sinful ways soon had to be exposed, not because of a lustful heart and a massive harem but because he was an Egyptian pharaoh who worshipped the gods Amen and Ra. The story of Solomon was written after Judah seceded from Israel's control, and Judah wanted to set itself apart from all so-called heathen nations.

The Jewish Distinction

The First Book of the Kings chapter 1 places Zadok the priest in Solomon's reign, which is plausible because Aaron as the first Levitical high priest was a few years older than Amenhotep III's son "Moses." Zadok (Sadoq in Hebrew) is a specific biblical character who was born 10 generations after Aaron's son, Eleazar. On the other hand, Laurence Gardner called all high priests *Zadoks* because they came from the order (and genetic influence) of the biblical Melchizedek who he reveals is Archangel Michael. He stated, "The heritage of St Michael was the dynasty of high Zadok priests—a heritage that prevailed in the continuing Messianic line" (p. 299).[68] The Levitical Zadok(s) refined and elaborated Jewish laws toward their perception of salvation.

Pharaoh Smenkhkare as Aaron took reign either after Akhenaten's exile or during his last two years in Egypt.[69] Smenkhkare left the throne to a royal Egyptian, Tutankhamun, and he joined his cousin.

Akhenaten and Smenkhare led a new faction of people toward Jerusalem under their new religion that incorporated Aten as Archangel Michael, Elohim, and of course Yahuah as the amalgamated YHWH. The Bible refers to the king of Jerusalem as Adonizedek (Joshua 10:1). This means that *zedek* can replace *Yahuah* in the mixed Adonai (Aten)-Yahuah hymn that Akhenaten and the Hebrew people started. It appears that *Yahuah* and *Melchizedek* are interchangeable or at least highly compatible.

The Jewish belief in its God is more than a religion; it identifies with a special ethnicity as a set-apart, chosen people. We cannot say that the Hebrew people were really set apart from the rest, though, because their race contained a genetic mix of the Habiru, Hyksos, Hurrian, Hittite, and Mitanni.

It is tragically ironic that Hitler sought the decimation of Jews when his prized Aryan and Habiru races partially created them. This was perhaps the most tragic ploy of division by the entities that led Hitler. If he paid attention, he would have known that the Jewish line descended to Jesus all the way to the powerful Germans and English monarchy. Although the religious "powers that be" have divisions among themselves, they are generally exaggerated in order to lead us to war and other similar religions. If people would see that religious entities are vastly more similar than different, as I show in chapter 7, then we can eschew their proclivity for war and unite in our own sensible power.

Women are especially important to the propagation of the bloodline, hence why Uriah altered Sarah's body to keep the bloodline most pure with Djehuty, whoever Sarah was, and a possible godly addition by Uriah. YHWH often intervened with royal bloodlines, sometimes to the extent of performing genetically altered, artificial inseminations. A Sumerian Tablet discovery proves my assertion.

A Mesopotamian cylinder seal drawing shows the progression of events that created Adam: a scientist mixed together DNA and then presented the test tube to a goddess who held Adam as the outcome. Next to the goddess was the biblical Tree of Life.[70] An engraving from the Jain religion of pre-India shows that "[t]he seed of the prophet *tirthamkara* is placed by artificial insemination into the womb of the young princess";[71] the male prophet or angel does not look human.

A main reason why the Bible focuses upon men is to distract from the vital importance of women. The woman produces the offspring; if she can be controlled, so can the bloodline. Her physical manipulation by an otherworldly entity ties her child to God, sometimes *really* making it God's child as the next chapter shows.

Interfering entities helped keep sufficient Habiru genetics intact while altering them just enough to encode them to their gods for effective interaction and puppeteering. If the rare genetically modified, artificial insemination occurred, it was the most direct and therefore most effective action by an angel or god, often resulting in full possession of the person.

YHWH kept the followers and descendants of his strict Zadok priesthood on a very short leash to create a clear genetic link to Jesus. YHWH created a new tactic of unification through "love" with the Messiah character, but it often resulted in a martyr complex among people who whipped or killed themselves and sometimes others. The Catholic Opus Dei and Islamic Taliban sects represent extreme cases. Killing Jesus out of "love" is also an oxymoron. Yahuah is a god of war, so he did not change his tune with Jesus or after him. The stories surrounding Jesus are important to understand Yahuah's direct handling of his "only son," and I hope that they will shed light toward us saving ourselves instead of joining a similar fate.

CHAPTER 5

Many Demigods of Christianity

"In the beginning was the Word, and the Word was with God, and the Word was God…And the Word was made flesh, and dwelt among us" (John 1:1,14). This is the only begotten Son of God who hath declared God (John 1:18). John the Baptist said, "After me cometh a man which is preferred before me: for he was before me" (John 1:30).

How could Jesus come before John the Baptist when John was born six months before him? John knew Jesus because they were related through their mothers who were cousins; they likely played together as children. If years passed without a visit, it would have taken him a mere moment to recognize Jesus as an adult. A writer created John's statement to portray the godliness of Jesus, not how John could identify his second cousin. Oddly, the writer then conveyed that John the Baptist did not know Jesus.

> I saw the Spirit descending from heaven like a dove, and it abode upon him. And I knew him not: but he that sent me to baptize with water, the same said unto me, Upon whom thou shalt see the Spirit descending, and remaining on him, the same is he which baptizeth with the Holy Ghost. And I saw, and bare record that this is the Son of God (John 1:32-34).

If this Scripture were true, then there was a possibility that John could not identify the man who came in the place of his second cousin. In fact, biblical Scriptures reveal more than one person as the archetype Messiah character, so John may not have recognized the man whom he baptized because there were other Jesuses.

This chapter explores both the nature and identity of the biblical Jesus or Messiah, which is arguably the most debated topic within Judeo-Christianity. The New Testament Messiah depends upon Mary because she was "found with child of the Holy Ghost" (Matthew 1:18).

It does not make sense if the Holy Spirit both impregnated Mary and became Jesus. If the Holy Spirit is a portion of God's Great Spirit, then a portion creating the fullness of YHWH within a body would be even more impossible. However, equating the Word to God and the flesh implies God was Jesus by the transitive law of logic and mathematics.

As I explained in chapter 3, the Hebrew name of Jesus includes Yahuah's name because he came in the name of his Father (John 5:43). In Modern Hebrew, the shortened version of Yahuah, Ya, is the letter *yod* (*yad* is ancient Hebrew). *Yod* supposedly represents omniscience and the spark of life as Ya, but it is also an arm and hand of an otherworldly being that represents physical power.[72] The additional *shuah* added to the *yod* indicates the Hebrew word for salvation as Y'shuah. It is argued that Yahshuah's name must incorporate every letter of the Tetragrammaton to fully represent salvation.[73]

Although Yahushuah or Yahshuah is the complete name of the Messiah, the Aramaic language shortens the Hebrew derivation to a few different spellings, including Yashua. I will write the Messiah's name as Yahshua.

The Greek name of Jesus is Iesous, which resembles the gods Isis and Zeus, but Iesous is considered a demigod. The Greek belief aligns with the above Scriptures that elevate Yahshua to some type of god-man of the following possibilities: (1) he was fully God in every way with godly genes in a non-human body from "above"; (2) he had a human body that only contained God's Great Spirit; (3) he was a mix of two spirits—God's and Yahshua's—in a human body; or (4) he was a demigod with a hybrid human-God body and a mix of two spirits.

Option 2 could not have happened because of Matthew chapter 9, verse 17 that is an allegory about not being able to put a pure spirit into sinful flesh. "Neither do men put new wine into old bottles: else the bottles break, and the wine runneth out, and the bottles perish: but they put new wine into new bottles, and both are preserved."

We must die to our sins in order to become purified and enter heaven. The story of Jesus had him nail our sins to the cross by his death. He did not need to die if he was a sinless demigod as the Bible depicts Jesus's body and spirit. However, a demigod can describe any measure of godly influence upon any type of man. The Oxford English dictionary states in its varied definition of *demigod*: "a being with partial or lesser divine status, such as a minor deity, the offspring of a god and a mortal, or a mortal raised to divine rank."[74]

Jesus died, so his body was at least mostly human. This means that his body was sinful by nature, so his death was partially in vain for his own need to be raised from the dead. Whatever demigod status he had was not that of a completely selfless savior. In chapter 3, I noted that the New Testament attempted to fix this conundrum by stating it is an uncontroversial mystery that we will not understand (1 Timothy 3:16). Therefore, we need to divert our attention toward another ritual—baptism—that would symbolically destroy our sinful bodies and spirits and allow God or the Holy Spirit to enter us and raise us from the dead. Interestingly, this would turn us into a sort of demigod because of our portion of God's Spirit.

Baptism is an initiation ritual for the Holy Spirit to dwell alongside our spirit. Yahshua was baptized by John the Baptist, so YHWH's Spirit could have merely coexisted with Yahshua's spirit from that initiation or an earlier one in his childhood. This must have been the saving force for Yahshua if his human body died.

If he was not human, then he would have been fully God in both body and spirit. For this to happen, Mary had to be an incubator to receive the foreign Yahshua. The prophet Isaiah received several messages that support Option 1. He called the Messiah "The mighty God, The everlasting Father, The Prince of Peace" (Isaiah 9:6), and he often mentioned the "arm of the Lord," especially in the context of it being the salvation of God (Isaiah 52:10).

If Option 1 is correct, then this would be the first and only Judeo-Christian God who became flesh because Judeo-Christians view God as a Spirit without a body, and other gods are lifeless idols made by human hands. This Spirit had to have an ability to become finite to be able to exist in a spectacular body.

Wow, what body was this new creation? Did it look perfectly human while being spiritual as the apostle Paul said?

> There is a natural body, and there is a spiritual body. And so it is written, The first man Adam was made a living soul; the last Adam *was made* a quickening spirit. Howbeit that *was* not first which is spiritual, but that which is natural; and afterward that which is spiritual. The first man *is* of the earth, earthy: the second man *is* the Lord from heaven (1 Corinthians 15:44-47).

How could Jesus look human when he was believed to have a sinless, spiritual body? He must have had no blemishes or defects of any kind, and maybe he glowed. I was under the impression that the spirit could not be seen. Apparently, somehow it can be seen because Adam and Eve were made in God's *image*. This means that there was another type of spiritual body of God, but it had to be more ethereal so that it could take on the dense body of Jesus and possibly also Melchizedek.

In agreement with both Judaism and Christianity, New Age religious or spiritual believers call the creative energy source *God* because they perceive God as an immaterial essence. Exodus chapter 3, verse 14 supports this belief by stating that YHWH just is, having the name "I AM" because "I AM THAT I AM." "YHWH is thought to be an archaic third person singular imperfect of the verb 'to be' (meaning, therefore, 'He is')."[75] This ever-present description of something immaterial yet pervasive is inconsistent with calling *Him* a *Father* who became a *body* that would die.

Fundamentalist Jews do not believe that YSHWH has yet come, although there have been Zadoks who gained followers in the few centuries before Yahshua arrived. Jews who await their Messiah are actually waiting for their Mashiach, which means "the anointed one."[76] *Messiah* is a modern version of Mashiach whom Jews specifically identify as a human, not a demigod. Ironically, this human would do godly acts by eradicating sin in the last days. This brings us back to the conundrum of how a human can abolish sin. No one can do that but God. Option 3 could apply to Jews if God did the works through the Messiah while that human did countless purification rituals for his own sinful body.

Jews view the Messiah as a savior, but it is in the context of paving the way for the chosen race line to inherit a new world free from sin. Their Messiah also must be a descendant of King David, meaning that he would be royalty. Jews think this entails him being human, but as chapter 4 hints toward YHWH genetic interferences with the truly chosen ones, this preservation and manipulation of the specialized human gene code would set apart the Mashiach as a demigod. This rules out Option 3 within the Judeo-Christian framework.

What remains is Option 4: God imparted some genetic material to create the human Yahshua as a type of demigod who had both a human spirit and God's Spirit. This option is similar to Option 3 except for his body being both "from heaven" and human. His body would have had to be fashioned with godly material to handle God's strong presence within him. This definition of Yahshua makes the Gospels credible when portraying Yahshua's humanity, and it makes him a Zadok because he fit into the Levitical lineage through Mary who was a descendant. It also explains how a YHWH entity could reside inside of Yahshua and rule his entire body.

The last puzzle concerning Yahshua is whether he really was the "only begotten Son" of God (John 3:16). Jesus is believed to be the king and Zadok of Jerusalem just like Melchizedek who was "King of Sa'lem, which is, King of peace; Without father, without mother, without descent, having neither beginning of days, nor end of life; but made like unto the Son of God; abideth a priest continually" (Hebrews 7:2-3). Apostle Paul reiterated the Psalm 110:4 prophecy that declared the Messiah as a high priest after the order of Melchisedec (Hebrews 5).

Jesus did not have a human father, and neither did Melchizedek. According to a direct parallel of Paul's belief in the Book of Hebrews, Jesus's body could have been likened to a spiritual body that took nothing from Mary. This would have made Jesus similar to Melchizedek, possibly identical. However, Jesus coming in the order or nature of Melchizedek only necessitates him being genetically similar while he also had human genes from a mother.

Genesis chapter 14, verse 18 states that Melchizedek was the high priest and king of Salem. It does not give mention of a divine status. Further investigation reveals that 13 fragments of a Dead Sea scroll found in Qumran Cave 11 rewrote biblical Scriptures between the first and second centuries B.C. to define Melchizedek has having an angelic or godly nature.

Theologian Paul Sumner writes:

> In the author's citation of Isaiah 61:2 (which speaks of "the year of the LORD's favor") the name Melchizedek is substituted for YHVH, the name of Israel's God. In addition, Melchizedek is said to atone for the sins of the righteous and to execute judgment upon the wicked—actions usually associated with God himself. The author also quotes Psalm 82:1 ("Elohim stands in the council of El") but inserts "Melchizedek" in place of "Elohim" (God)....
>
> In the mystical Qumran documents known as "Songs of the Sabbath Sacrifice" (originally called "The Angelic Liturgy"), Melchizedek appears to be a superior angel. The texts are broken up too badly to be sure of this identification (4Q401 11:3; 22:3).
>
> But what is certain is that the "Songs" depict a hierarchy of angelic priests who serve in the heavenly temple. They are surrounded by other divine beings known as elim or elohim (gods, divine beings) or holy ones, spirits, princes, and ministers. And Melchizedek seems to be a leader of this assembly of servants.
>
> In the so-called "War Scroll" (1QM 13:10; 16:6-8; 17:7), Melchizedek appears to be the archangel Michael, who is "the prince of light" (1QM 13:10-11; cf. 1QS 2:20-22; CD 5:17-19) and "the angel of [God's] truth" (1QS 3:24). Scrolls scholar Carol Newsom says, "it would seem most plausible that Melchizedek is to be identified with the seventh and highest of the chief princes, as Michael is customarily identified with the highest of the archangels."[77]

If we are to believe the Qumran elaboration, Melchizedek was a divine being who was able to live on Earth for some time. It is possible that YHWH created Melchizedek as a demigod, or Melchizedek was like YHWH. Archangel Michael fits into both examples. Chapter 4 asserts that the Elohim is a group of angel-gods who are equal in nature to Yahuah. YHWH can be an all-encompassing word to represent a group of otherworldly beings who can impart genes to humans.

Another possibility is that Melchizedek as a spiritual angel could have reincarnated as Yahshua. Christianity defines reincarnation as the transformation of the human body to an angelic body in heaven, not the other way around. This raises the question how an angel can materialize as a human-like body.

The reincarnation belief was very popular during biblical times, especially in Egypt, Babylonia, and the Indus Valley and pre-India region. It agreed with Judeo-Christianity in that all humans need a type of divine entity to help us ascend out of the mess of the world. This belief assumes that we cannot become enlightened on our own to tackle the difficult process of ascension, so we will be doomed to another life of reincarnation if we do not receive sufficient divine assistance. This leaves me to wonder why the process of life and death would be very difficult if it were supposedly natural.

The Urantia Book (UB) perfectly aligns with the Bible by saying that we must have the indwelling of a holy spirit to help us ascend. It calls this spirit the Thought Adjuster. Accordingly, we have received the "mind of Christ" through baptism (1 Corinthians 2:16). This corresponds to Jesus telling us to love God with "all your mind" (Mark 12:29) in addition to the original commandment by God to "Moses": "And thou shalt love the Lord thy God with all thine heart, and with all thy soul, and with all thy might" (Deuteronomy 6:5).

We are told to not think for ourselves: "Trust in the LORD with all thine heart; and lean not unto thine own understanding. In all thy ways acknowledge him, and he shall direct thy paths" (Proverbs 3:5-6). Our minds dictate our thoughts, and our thoughts dictate our words and then our flesh. If the Thought Adjuster does everything for us, does that mean we are privileged to be in a robotic state? These religious texts teach that we do not know what is best for ourselves, so we should be happy and grateful to be controlled.

Even if we do not make the best decisions, the fact is that we are born with our own mind, emotions, spirit, and body. Whatever the entities try to do to us is superfluous.

The Word of God becoming flesh has God as the mind of that flesh that can easily direct the body. He and his cohorts have not manipulated the vast majority of humans in the extreme way as with Yahshua, but they tell us to follow in Yahshua's footsteps. Following the unfortunate circumstance of Yahshua is careless without knowing more of the story that I will soon divulge.

Lastly, for Yahshua to be the only son of YHWH, there could not be other genetically altered, artificial inseminations. The YHWH God group appears to involve numerous entities who have not put their efforts solely into one person. We now know that there were at least a few other people, including John the Baptist via his mother Elizabeth (confirms the ATI, TPE), so Yahshua was not preferred by YHWH except to fulfill a specific purpose.

Sophia

Sophia is not a demigod, but it helps to define the category and its relation to the "Godhead." The Word of God is the Logos, which is the word of wisdom. According to the *exeGeses parallel BIBLE*, *sophia* is interchangeable with logos and wisdom.[7] A growing demand for education in fifth century Greece led to the creation of a new class of teachers called Sophists who taught any subject to a public hungry for knowledge. Sophists carried an air of superiority among them, charging large fees as traveling salesmen to peddle words that were supposed to portray sophia. Unfortunately, as most stories of self-appointed authorities reveal, the Sophists did not often teach or even seek Sophia: their love of rhetoric turned the issue back onto the customer so they could escape accountability. Accordingly, winning an argument was more important than finding the truth. Socrates and Plato were not Sophists because they sought higher standards than this, which is ironic because sophia represented this high standard.

Sophia is actually an entity who is worshipped as a goddess. Whenever a limited entity claims to be a noble and honest quality such as wisdom, the profound nature of that noun will inevitably be flawed. Sophia was the entity I mentioned in chapter 3 who came to my mother after she left religion, telling her that I had Sophia as the spirit of wisdom. Yes, I had a measure of wisdom within myself, but I did not link to an entity. She was trying to link to me. *Sophia* was the Word only because that word came from the entity Sophia, just as my word comes from me.

Sophia is the prized woman of Solomon in the Song of Songs and the Wisdom of Solomon (or Book of Wisdom). It is well known by now that no such Solomon wrote either book of the Bible, so it must have been a Sophist. The Wisdom of Solomon is believed to have been written in the first century B.C. by an Alexandrian Jew.[78]

The Book of Wisdom is not included in most Protestant Bibles but is in Catholic and Eastern Orthodox Bibles. The Church of England officially removed it from the King James Bible in 1885 A.D. along with other biblical books called the Apocrypha because they were not deemed God-inspired or consistent although King James himself included them over two centuries prior.[79] It was prompted by the American Bible Society that voted in 1880 A.D. to remove them from the dominant King James Version.[80] Perhaps they noticed too many references to Gnosticism that portrayed several divine aspects or beings of God instead of one clear God-man. They did not remove all references of wisdom to a woman, but they certainly cleared out the female and motherly equation to the word and breath of God.

The following shows wisdom in the Apocrypha, which in Greek means "things that are hidden, secret" to designate books excluded from the official canon. The Book of Ecclesiasticus in the original King James Bible is represented as the Book of Sirach in the Catholic Bible.

Ecclesiasticus 24:1-10: Wisdom shall praise herself, and shall glory in the midst of her people. In the congregation of the most High shall she open her mouth, and triumph before his power. I came out of the mouth of the most High, and covered the earth as a cloud. I dwelt in high places, and my throne is in a cloudy pillar. I alone compassed the circuit of heaven, and walked in the bottom of the deep. In the waves of the sea and in all the earth, and in every people and nation, I got a possession. With all these I sought rest: and in whose inheritance shall I abide? So the Creator of all things gave me a commandment, and he that made me caused my tabernacle to rest, and said, Let thy dwelling be in Jacob, and thine inheritance in Israel. He created me from the beginning before the world, and I shall never fail. In the holy tabernacle I served before him; and so was I established in Sion.

Ecclesiasticus 24:18-25: I am the mother of fair love, and fear, and knowledge, and holy hope: I therefore, being eternal, am given to all my children which are named of him. Come unto me, all ye that be desirous of me, and fill yourselves with my fruits. For my memorial is sweeter than honey, and mine inheritance than the honeycomb. They that eat me shall yet be hungry, and they that drink me shall yet be thirsty. [Note: Jesus said in John 6:54, "Whoso eateth my flesh, and drinketh my blood, hath eternal life."] He that obeyeth me shall never be confounded, and they that work by me shall not do amiss. All these things are the book of the covenant of the most high God, even the law which Moses commanded for an heritage unto the congregations of Jacob. Faint not to be strong in the Lord; that he may confirm you, cleave unto him: for the Lord Almighty is God alone, and beside him there is no other Saviour. He filleth all things with his wisdom, as Phison and as Tigris in the time of the new fruits.[81]

Wisdom 7:25-27 speaks of Sophia's divinity: She is an aura of the might of God and a pure effusion of the glory of the Almighty; therefore nought that is sullied enters into her. For she is the refulgence of eternal light, the spotless mirror of the power of God, the image of his goodness. And she, who is one, can do all things, and renews everything while herself perduring [permanently enduring]. And passing into holy souls from age to age, she produces friends of God and prophets.[82]

These Scriptures either put a woman above man or on par with God.

Sophia fulfills the classic trinity with a female, so she is the original mother in the Ecclesiasticus Scriptures and also the female "holy spirit of discipline...a kindly spirit...the spirit of the LORD" in Wisdom chapter 1. A Deuteronomist writer or redactor showed the belief in Sophia in Deuteronomy chapter 34, verse 9 where Joshua the son of Nun became "full of the spirit of wisdom" when Moses laid his hands upon him. The laying on of hands, usually on the head, is the typical procedure in the New Testament to receive the indwelling of the Holy Spirit to guide us. Another reference to Sophia as the Holy Spirit was the dove that John the Baptist saw descending upon Jesus—the dove is a feminine symbol.[83]

The message of wisdom is two-fold: it gives utmost glory and also deep sadness in the knowledge of evil. Wisdom and this life entail suffering to most religions. What a dismal view to have. Their answer is to "ascend" away from it in a guise of enlightenment. The religious or "spiritual" way to become enlightened as an Ascended Master is to sacrifice your innate wisdom, knowledge, and ability and leave behind Earthly attachments, including family, so that your empty mind and heart in meditation can enter a trance and allow an entity to overtake you. Self-sacrifice appears to escape the troubles of life and our pesky love, emotions, and values.

The knowledge of evil is what YHWH wanted to keep hidden from Adam and Eve. It seems nice to think that God was trying to protect us from the unhappiness of knowing evil and suffering, but was he rather preventing us from realizing our own abilities that can handle difficult situations? Sometimes the guise of protection is actually suffocation; his self-imposed authority over us kept us from fully discovering our own power.

We have unwittingly allowed our belief constructs to put us down. Since we know that we have flaws, we often yearn for something better. We entertain idealistic desires, but this may make it difficult to separate a word or concept from something godly or perfect. In the case of the word of wisdom, it becomes divine, just like Sophia. YHWH takes the same role as Sophia by owning the divine word because he is believed as God.

The biblical portrayal of YHWH's word is a body as both Jesus and the church that YHWH essentially owns. The Book of Hosea chapter 2, verse 16 uses the word *Ishi* to describe the type of relationship that YHWH wants with his people. Ishi means husband, which accurately shows the Bible's focus upon procreation.

The Book of Song of Solomon or Song of Songs was written to Sophia as the divine "Word made flesh" to whom Solomon could consummate marriage. She was a buxom beauty of bountiful pleasures desired by a lustful man who had a hoard of concubines. However, since Sophia was most prized by Solomon, the Book of Wisdom and the Song of Songs were written to convey that he was sinless in his love for her, where his lust was legitimate love for their marriage. It is understandable why people have been fascinated with the story of Solomon because he has been viewed similar to a demigod; he must have been godly to be with the goddess Sophia.

The Logos in John chapter 1, verse 1 is actually a demiurge, "an artisan-like figure responsible for the fashioning and maintenance of the physical universe."[84] Before the arrival of Jesus, the original Platonic definition saw the demiurge as an uncreated organizer of the universe along with all that is uncreated. As the idea transformed into late-Middle Platonism and neo-Platonism around the second to third centuries A.D. (it was both edited into and taken from the Gospel of John), the demiurge became a direct creator of the material world. It is viewed as the underlying order of the created but not the Source. It is an intermediate step to the physical world that was ultimately evil to the Platonists.

There is another intermediate stage, and this is where Sophia is believed to exist. She is above the demiurge but below the pleroma, which is viewed as the fullness of divinity in the heavens above us, usually comprising the spiritual realm that is still not the Source.[85] Philo of Alexandria described Sophia as the "mother of the Logos," giving a different perspective to the Holy Spirit as the mother of Jesus. In the Gnostic literature around the time of Jesus, wisdom was repeatedly called "Mother."[86] Gnostics sought gnosis, meaning knowledge, which involves sophia.

The inclusion of Sophia into the Catholic and Christian Trinity is believable because most religious trinities comprise a family unit—father, mother, and son. Egyptians had Osiris, Isis, and Horus as the primary trinity. Babylon had Nimrod, Ashtoreth, and Tammuz, but in that case, Tammuz was believed to be the reincarnation of Nimrod. Similarly, Jesus should have been deemed the reincarnation of Sophia since "Jesus is the wisdom of God" (1 Corinthians 1:24,30). Sophia and Yahshua were different "people," so we can deduce that Nimrod's son was different to his father. The trinity concept is vital for the expansion of procreation, not the recycling of it. This rules out Jesus as the reincarnation or incarnation of YHWH. Apart from the first pre-Christian trinity, the modern Catholic and Christian Trinity is actually two trinities: the family unit with Mary, the "Father" who artificially inseminated her, and Jesus; and the Godhead "family" with three male roles as the Father, Son, and Holy Spirit. Realistically, YHWH has many angelic aides, so the role of the Holy Spirit is flexible.

The all-male trinity comprises a delegation of order. The Sumerian main trinity was male as Anu (representing heaven), Enlil (Earth), and Enki (water), but then Marduk vied for control against Enlil in the Sumerian Tablet story. When not having a parental trinity, it can become loosely defined with several characters. The Hindu trinity of Brahma, Shiva, and Vishnu is also male. Shiva and Vishnu comprise both sexes as though they are above creation while containing all of creation, but the depiction of Shiva shows a phallic symbol, proving that these Hindu gods are personified as men. They support procreation in the typical trinity but combine both types of trinities into one.[87]

Many of the New Testament Apocrypha books read by early Christian churches were omitted from the Bible, such as the Gnostic "doubting" Gospel of Thomas and the Gospel of Mary (Magdalene). Apostle Paul was a Gnostic, which is interesting because Gnostics believed in Sophia, and Paul is a noted sexist who supported the suppression of women teachers, presumably including Mary Magdalene. I think his sexist bias was toward overall physicality as he perceived it as a Gnostic, for he believed the body and the world are sinful, so there must be spiritual control and order over everything worldly.

Gnosticism in second century A.D. sects believed in "a divine spark in man, deriving from the divine realm, fallen into this world of fate, birth and death, and needing to be awakened by the divine counterpart of the self" (p. 111).[88] Gnostics believed that our spirit was our only good component; however, they linked our spirits to spiritual entities, so we essentially could not redeem ourselves.

The Gnostic belief that our bodies are sinful coincided with Judaism, but Gnostics saw YHWH as the evil demiurge that kept humans from the knowledge of the serpent in the Garden of Eden. Christians, whom many were Gnostics, chose Jesus as their savior to replace YHWH; this meant that these Gnostics had a better "Father God" than YHWH. Gnostics were mystics who viewed Yahshua as divine, coming on par with Sophia although she was also seen as his spiritual creator. Although they rejected YHWH, they accepted his link to Yahshua but chose to elevate Yahshua in the changing of the kings. Latter Gnostics blended Islamic Qur'an and Neoplatonic teachings to create the mystic religion of Sufism.[89]

These religions relate to Christianity and its Judaism background. The progression of belief systems is important to see how one affected the other; it is difficult to isolate a religious belief as unique. In other words, religions, spiritualities, and philosophical beliefs are generally comprised of several other belief systems. It just becomes a matter of saying, "my god, demigod, or prophet is better than yours."

Many Jews became Hellenized (Greek-influenced) toward the belief in Sophia in the third century B.C. as a result of Alexander the Great sparing Jerusalem and Jews having assimilated into the Greek culture after Alexander's death. The Apocryphal First Book of Maccabees chapter 1, verses 1-9 specifically mentions the reign of "Alexander the Macedonian."

Around 93 A.D., Jewish historian Flavius Josephus wrote an "historical" account of Alexander the Great and the Jews in *Antiquities of the Jews.*[90] According to Josephus, Alexander went to Jerusalem after conquering Gaza. Jerusalem's high priest had a divine dream of warning for him, so the Zadok was allowed to meet him. The Jews were surprised that Alexander openly welcomed the Zadok and his entourage and gave honor to YHWH. He explained that he saw the Zadok in a dream telling him to make no delay toward his military pursuits over the Persians. Alexander and the Zadok then "offered sacrifice to God according to the high priest's direction."[91]

According to Josephus, when the high priest showed Alexander a Scripture in the Book of Daniel that declared "one of the Greeks should destroy the empire of the Persians," he believed it was himself fulfilling a prophecy.[91] Daniel does mention "the king of Grecia" doing great feats, which seems to support Josephus's embellishment of the actual Scripture: "And a mighty king shall stand up, that shall rule with great dominion, and do according to his will" (Daniel 8:8,21;11:3). Daniel contains Old or Transitional Aramaic before Alexander's time as well as later versions of Aramaic.[92] Whether powers that be helped guide the changing times toward Hellenization and chosen leaders, or embellishments and additions were merged into earlier texts, this example helps show the nearly indiscernible line between religion and politics that has controlled humans throughout history.

It is possible that Alexander the Great worshipped YHWH because of the amalgamated "Jesus" character as the son of Zeus and YHWH. During the Hellenic period from Alexander the Great until Yahshua's birth, I speculate that the name Iesous may have circulated in Greek prophecy or belief.

The well-received mystique behind the character of Jesus was to give a law of faith and not ritual, although "faith without works is dead" (James 2:20). Idealistically, the new faith and acts would be about love and not fear, and liberation and not slavery to the old law. Although I refute this supposed liberation because we still completely sacrifice ourselves to follow Jesus, he represents an upgraded version of the fatherly Jewish God by becoming our brother, our friend. This was an excellent ploy by YHWH to cover more bases of religious philosophy and worship. Since Jesus was the god-man who is our link to heaven and who represents love and all that is good, how wrong and "sinful" would we all be to not follow him as our master?

Embedded in all religions is a type of savior who must show us the best or *only* way, so the Jews looked to their holy bloodline for their king to save them. This theme was at the beginning of the Bible, and it gained momentum in the latter books of the Old Testament where genuine prophecies and wishful thinking of exiled scribes in Babylonia focused upon their return to Jerusalem. They desired to strengthen their religion that became watered down by Hellenization. They probably did not understand that their Habiru and related forefathers included other religions in their formulation of Judaism, and the Hellenization of Judaism merely continued the trend.

The Jews that cleaved to the Old Testament to re-establish their perceived genetic superiority created religious sects that are now lumped together under the title *Essene*. The group of so-called Essenes produced the first Messiah, but then more Messiahs followed for their own particular reasons. In actuality, there were at least one Greek Jesus, two Yahshuas, and a placeholder Yahshua following the first "Teacher of Righteousness." Each of these five Jesus characters deserves mention to understand the similarities, differences, and reasons for their roles.

Moreh Tzedek (Zadok) and the Essenes

Scholars have proposed that the Essenes originated in Neo-Babylonia during the sixth century B.C. Jewish exile. These Jews believed that their exile was a punishment by YHWH. They sought to bolster their good standing and cleave more tightly to their Jewish roots that the process of Hellenization was changing. After Babylon was captured by Persians, many Jews returned to Judea (Judah) c. 520-515 B.C., while other Jews chose to stay in neo-Babylonia or elsewhere until some later returned to Jerusalem.[93]

As the process of Hellenization became more aggressive, the legitimate Zadok, Onias III, was murdered in Jerusalem c. 172 B.C. In 171 B.C., the Syrian overlords appointed Meneleus, a highly Hellenized Jew not of Levite descent, as the high priest. Judeans revolted in 165 B.C. against the Syrian overlord, King Antiochus IV, because of his religious oppression and forced Hellenization.[94] Judas Maccabeus led the Jewish revolt and succeeded in establishing an independent Jewish state. The Apocryphal Book of First Maccabees glorifies the Maccabeus brothers who worked to keep the Jewish people aligned with their old laws. They made pacts with Rome to keep out the Greeks, but Romans were not much different to Greeks with their polytheistic religion. After Simeon Maccabeus was assassinated in 134 B.C., his Hasmonean dynasty eventually allowed Hellenization to creep back into the Jewish priesthood.[95]

Essenes rallied behind a man of Zadok blood and position whom they called Moreh Tzedek, which means Teacher of Righteousness. They retreated to the Judean desert to practice the Zadok rituals and to figure out how to take back their religion under the Torah. This teacher had no name in the Dead Sea Scrolls aside from this title; therefore, author Michael Wise gave him the name Judah in *First Messiah*.[96]

Upon deeper examination, scholars are uncertain if the Essenes were the Qumran sect who wrote the Dead Sea Scrolls, a collection of several hundred scrolls estimated to have been written between 200 B.C. and 68 A.D.[97] Between 1947 and 1956 A.D., the scrolls were found in 11 caves in the Judean desert in and around Qumran, located about 13 miles east of Jerusalem on the shore of the Dead Sea. Qumran was previously named Secaceh, which was one of the desert cities mentioned in the Book of Joshua.[98] The term *Essene* from the Greek *Essenoi* or *Essaioi* is not in any of the scrolls; however, the similar Hebrew word *Ossim*, meaning "the Doers" of the Torah, or the Aramaic word *'asayyah*, meaning "healers," "reflects possible origins among the Hasidim, the 'Pious Ones' who temporarily joined the Maccabees in the Revolt of 167 B.C.E.," states Dr. James Tabor, a professor of religious studies.[99] The Hasidim—Hasidic Jews—likely contributed to the Essene faction because of their set-apart lifestyle that they believed made them righteous and holy.

The Qumran sect followed a solar calendar that was 10 days longer than the Jewish calendar per annum. A scholarly argument suggests the Qumran sect was the Sadducees, but the Sadducees did not believe in fate or resurrection of the dead, two core beliefs of the Qumran sect. The Qumran sect believed in both a priestly Messiah and a political Messiah that are not necessarily two separate people.

Philo of Alexandria, Pliny the Elder, and Josephus coined the term *Essene* after the two Yahshuas were born. Some Dead Sea scrolls were also written after the Yahshuas. The actual Essenes could have been a fulfillment of the Qumran sect, and the Qumran Teacher of Righteousness was a precursor to the Essene Messiah. When someone is a precursor, this does not diminish their importance, for that precursor was still of Zadok blood in the order of Melchizedek just as the latter Yahshuas were. They all had a role to play, so it is conceivable that their roles were intertwined and even jumbled into one big Yahshua or Jesus character.

Most of the scrolls were found in fragments, and many just copied the Old Testament. However, some were unique to the Qumran sect, including the Covenant of Damascus (the first scroll to be made public), which pointed to the sect's origin in Babylonia because it referred to the diaspora, or dispersion. Some scrolls also included original prophecies by Ezekiel, Jeremiah, and Daniel not found in the Bible.[100] The prophetic books were written during and after the exile. These reasons support the Babylonia origin in which they were determined to return to Jerusalem more pious than the Jews before them.

The following prophetic Scriptures of Jeremiah chapter 31, verses 31-33 were at the core of the Qumran community's beliefs.

> Behold, the days come, saith the LORD, that I will make a new covenant with the house of Israel, and with the house of Judah: Not according to the covenant that I made with their

fathers in the day *that* I took them by the hand to bring them out of the land of Egypt; which my covenant they brake, although I was an husband unto them, saith the LORD: But this *shall* be the covenant that I will make with the house of Israel; After those days, saith the LORD, I will put my law in their inward parts, and write it in their hearts; and will be their God, and they shall be my people.

"The Essenes at Qumran saw themselves as the final 'remnant' of Israel and the heirs of the 'new Covenant' as was prophesied," states researcher Cleve A. Johnson.[101] They believed they were living in the last days of the Earth before YHWH's final judgment. The Torah does not explicitly mention the afterlife but focuses upon the lawful and ritualistic observances of living on Earth. It can be interpreted that attaining the New Covenant and the promised land of Israel would be a permanent gift from YHWH to his chosen ones, the Jews. The New Testament Scripture of Matthew chapter 5, verse 5 has Jesus declare the meek shall inherit the Earth. Jehovah's (YHWH's) Witnesses have this belief. It entails a tragic yet ironically beautiful story that says the Earth will return to the idyllic state of Eden where only good people exist, and they all will commune with YHWH. It is tragic because their Messiah character says we must die to live. Israel's hope as the New Covenant could only be fulfilled after the Apocalypse that destroys the Earth and simultaneously kills the chosen ones, but the chosen ones instantly change into immortal versions of themselves on what is now their renewed Earth.

Wise states that Judah was the first Messiah who could fulfill this covenant because he was both priestly and political, as he was a Zadok who was once part of the Council of the Jews.

> Judah stepped forth from the highest ranks of the Jerusalem priesthood, a man well acquainted with the corridors of power and the politics of the royal court. About sixty years old, he was one of the greatest minds of his generation, and he had exercised that mind all of his life in the study of Holy Writ (p. 41-42).[96]

Wise estimates Judah's initial rise to preeminence was about 110-105 B.C., but it was not until 76 B.C. when he started a breakaway movement from Pharisee control of the temple. Judah created his version of an expanded 10 commandments that used strong language such as "You shall separate yourselves from the Children of Hell" (p. 42).

Judah also inscribed at least nine of the approximately 40 hymns as the "Teacher" in the "Thanksgiving Hymns" (p. 44-46). In his first psalm to

YHWH, he wrote words of great authority as the wise "prophet" who rose above the persecutions and sins of others because he was sent to lead "the initiated" (p. 47). In another psalm, Judah wrote, "I am a spirit of zeal against all the Seekers of Accommodation…all deceitful men bellow against me" (p. 48). [96]

Wise argues that Judah's many "I am" statements became the inspiration of the "I am" declarations of the Gospels. The Gospel of Matthew has Jesus ask, "Who do men say that I am?" The Gospel of John has Jesus say, "I am the light of the world" and "I am the way, the truth, and the life." Judah could have been an inspiration for the New Testament, but the "I AM" name of YHWH in Exodus chapter 3, verse 14 actually started this trend.

Judah created a crisis cult in Qumran. Wise states that Judah created a chronology based on Daniel chapter 9, verses 24-27 in which the End would come within seven years of the Pharisee takeover. Within this time frame, he unexpectedly died in 72 B.C.E., and his central teachings or prophecies did not occur. He taught that he was the angel Melchizedek and Messiah, but when it became obvious that he would not return to save his followers, they wrote an addendum to the "Teacher Hymns" named "Community Hymns" to continue the promise of a savior.

Wise draws a parallel between the suffering of Judah and the suffering of the more popular latter Messiah, for their suffering was supposedly not in vain but for their glory. The added "Hymn of the Exalted One" states that the Teacher did not only suffer like the servant in the Book of Isaiah but was also raised to sit at the right hand of YHWH. The Qumran community believed in fate, so when Judah was killed, the followers saw it as an act of God, just as Judah would have believed. This built up the perception of equating a Messianic death to redemptive glory.

The "Covenant of Damascus" scroll was largely written after Judah's death and was otherwise titled the "Zadokite Document." It referred to the sect as "sons of Zadok" and was very revealing in its stark portrayal of YHWH, as the following transcribed excerpts show.

> "Howbeit, for all that perform these rules in holiness unimpaired, according to all the instruction that has been given them—for them will God's Covenant be made good, that they shall be preserved for a thousand generations, even as it is written: 'He keepeth Covenant and loyalty with them that love Him and keep His commandments, even unto a thousand generations'." [Deuteronomy 7:9]
>
> [Note: This is not love but only obedience, and this obedience is out of fear. Several Scriptures say to have the fear of God, as

does the following Covenant of Damascus text.]

"No man who has not yet completed his probationary period with the community and has not yet passed the statutory examination as a truly God-fearing person is to be permitted as a witness before its judges in a capita' case."

"And now, children, listen to me, and I will open your eyes to see and understand how God acts, so that you may choose what He has desired and reject what He has hated, walking blamelessly in all His ways and not straying after thoughts of guilty lust or after whoring eyes. For many there be that have strayed thereby from olden times until now, and even strong heroes have stumbled thereby."

"His righteous ordinances, the ways of His truth and the purposes of His will, 'the which, if a man do, he shall live' [Leviticus 18:5]. He opened for them a well with water abounding, which they might dig. But them that spurned those waters He did not permit to live."

"God loves knowledge. Wisdom and sound sense has He posted before Him. Prudence and knowledge minister to Him. Patience attends on him and abundant forgiveness, so that He may shrive the repentant But also with Him are might and power and great wrath, along with flames of fire and all the angels of destruction-appointed for them that turn aside from His way and treat His ordinance as a thing to be shunned, to the end that they shall be left without remnant or survival."

"Abraham, however, did not walk in this way. Therefore, because he kept the commandments of God and did not prefer the desires of his own spirit, he was accounted the Friend of God and transmitted this status in turn to Isaac and Jacob. They too kept the commandments, and they too were recorded as Friends of God and as partners in His everlasting Covenant."

"On the day that a man pledges himself to return to the Law of Moses, the Angel of Obstruction will start receding from him-that is, if he keep [sic] his word. It is in line with this that Abraham underwent circumcision on the day that he attained true knowledge."[102]

[Note: It is the ultimate subservience of the body to be a sex slave. To equate circumcision and sex to knowledge is completely irrational...or is it? Since YHWH sent out a Holy Spirit of some sort, then that was the figurative "knowledge" personified by entities who infiltrated the Hebrew bloodline. It is the "knowledge" given by possession or genetic manipulation.]

Conceivably, Judah could have been the equivalent to any of the Yahshua Messiahs. The Zadoks had "divine" genetics; therefore, Moreh Tzedek may have been a god-man as well. To abhor Hellenization while they also revered a demigod was contradictory. If the only distinction between Judaism and Hellenization was the relationship between YHWH and Yahshua, then this could have been significant enough to warrant such division.

Isaiah chapter 11, verses 1-10 prophesied the Messiah, especially this part:

> And there shall come forth a rod out of the stem of Jesse, and a Branch shall grow out of his roots: And the spirit of the LORD shall rest upon him, the spirit of wisdom and understanding, the spirit of counsel and might, the spirit of knowledge and of the fear of the LORD.... And in that day there shall be a root of Jesse, which shall stand an ensign of the people; to it shall the Gentiles seek: and his rest shall be glorious.

I do not doubt that this was a genuine prophecy, even with the mention of Jesse who was the biblical David's father. My mother's past prophecies show that YHWH continues to spread incorrect stories that are widely believed (and sometimes created by him) in order to keep the story line sufficiently straight for his followers.

Judah's Qumran sect believed in the Holy Spirit and so did the Essenes. The *Jesus of Nazareth* title designates the Nazarene sect that was imperceptibly close to the Essenes, so perhaps Judah was that particular Jesus.

Scholars do not sufficiently understand how the Nazareans (or Nazoreans) appeared. The Nazarenes of Mount Carmel, an esoteric spiritual order that claims to be "a modern resurrection of the ancient Nazorean Christians," states that there was no town of Nazareth because *Nazareth* did not exist in literature before and during the first century A.D., nor did it exist archaeologically or historically.[103,104]

A man named Jack Kilmon researched early Christian sects and heresies to analyze the root of Jesse and the Nazarenes:

> This is where the "Jesus People" got their designations as N'tzrim "Branchers" and "Jesseans." Epiphanius suggests that the Yeshuine group was called IESSAIOI very early on (Panarion 29 1, 3-9; 4,9) and that they were also called the N'TZRIM is well known. Acts 13:22-23, Romans 15:12, Romans 5:5, 22:16 give witness to some of these early designations.

The Qumran community could have been the hardline apocalyptic sect and the Yeshuines may have called themselves "The Way" to indicate "our WAY is better than their WAY." Soon IESSAIOI seems to have fallen out of use and the Yeshuine group were called the N´tzarim. It cannot be a coincidence that the only OT passage with clear messianic interpretation, "The Netzer of Jesse" lies behind the two earliest self designations of the Yeshuines....There may also have been a pre-Jesus, pre-Essene forerunner called Nazarioi. In this respect, we find Epiphanius speaking about a sect in Bashan and Galaatides [Gilead] called Nasaraioi (Panarion 18; 20, 3; 29, 6, 1; 19, 5) who rejected temple sacrifice and the Torah but adhered to other Jewish practice. Were the Nazarenes (alternately Nazoraioi, Nazorei, Nazaraei) a continuation of the pre-Jesus Nasaraioi, Nasarenoi, Nazorei? Nazorei was used by Jerome in de vir. ill. 3 to refer to the Nazarenes and by Filaster to refer to the Nasarenes.[105]

Kilmon suggests that the Essenes were not Christians or pre-Christians, but I think they essentially were because of the abundant similarities their religions share. The Essenes as *Iessaioi, Essaioi,* and *Essenoi* arose when their New Covenant and New Testament early Gospels were interpreted as a peaceful paradigm that advocated non-violence and vegetarianism. It is important to determine how the beliefs changed, but as it involved the Nazarenes who related to the prior Teacher of Righteousness sect in Qumran, it is almost splitting hairs. They interpreted some purification and holy lifestyles differently while following a Jewish Messiah who came from the violent God YHWH.

The Qumran community was obsessed with war, not peace. The men engaged in daily mock battles to prepare for an apocalypse. The "Scroll of the War of the Sons of Light against the Sons of Darkness" described this apocalypse in the following interpretation by Editor A. M. Habermann.

[It is] a real war with all its forms, strategies and rites, not an imaginary war of heavenly angels and apocalyptic beasts, such as figure in other books depicting visions. The "Sons of Light" return "from the desert of the nations to camp in the desert of Jerusalem". They make war upon their enemies for decades (p. XII).[106]

The "apocalyptic" war was likely the impending Roman invasion in 66-70 A.D. that sacked Jerusalem. Often times biblical stories were written according to the political climate of the times, although the Book of Revelation was written later with really far-out images and concepts that underscore a bigger Apocalypse.

Since the Greek term *Essene* had its origins in the Qumran sect, it is possible that the Essenes practiced similar acts of war preparation. Their separatist views and communities warranted enough disdain toward sinners outside of their sect to create a philosophy of peace unless threatened. Essenes upped the bar on "holiness" practices to ensure they were on the good side of judgmental YHWH, and their additional belief in a Messiah secured their way out of the clutches of extreme punishment as eternal death or hell.

The Torah's punishment for Jews was death, and that seemed severe enough. The difference with the transitional Christian belief was that punishment was for eternity. The Messiah character merely transferred our obedience from some of YHWH's ritualistic commandments to commandments about inward attributes. It could be argued that more judgment came with the Messiah because the spiritual realm became ruled in a specific way in addition to the continuing rituals and controlled behaviors Judeo-Christians had to perform.

Another belief entered into the Qumran and Essene belief about the afterlife—that we can become demigods ourselves. No Judeo-Christian dares to say that we can become gods on Earth, but in heaven, apocalyptic believers see themselves as judges alongside YHWH in new, heavenly bodies.

The Apocryphal Book of Enoch (1 Enoch), largely written in the second and first centuries B.C. by the Jewish sect that settled in Qumran, is a prophetic account of Enoch's story as the only person who was instantly translated to demigod status.[107] Enoch was "seventh from Adam" in the Bible who would execute judgment alongside Yahuah (Jude 14). 1 Enoch infers that demigod-angels are heavenly beings who should stay in heaven. This applied to Enoch because he had demigod genetics, and YHWH specially chosen him. Enoch was briefly allowed to come back to Earth to explain his heavenly experiences to his sons—while somehow being visible to them—and then he left Earth forever. In contrast, the heavenly demigods who came to Earth in the Book of Enoch fell here because of sin.

The story of Enoch helps illustrate why devoted Judeo-Christians look to their afterlife as their real life and glory. This is also why death is no big deal to extreme religious terrorists who seek the title of martyr. The UB states that after death we will go to a heavenly world named Morontia that has mansions for all of us. Muslims believe they will receive many riches and a massive harem of women. If only they would choose to co-create a comfortable life on this beautiful Earth.

The belief in a demigod Messiah makes following YHWH more tangible because he could be seen and emulated. The Messiah character taught people to be more selfless by loving everyone without judgment. However, there is still definite judgment in our beliefs toward "sinners," for Christians believe the worst judgment awaits their supposed loved ones. In words that could originate with any Messiah, "So shall it be at the end of the world: the angels shall come forth, and sever the wicked from among the just, And shall cast them into the furnace of fire: there shall be wailing and gnashing of teeth" (Matthew 13:49-50).

John the Baptist was an Essene or Nazarene priest who was also a Zadok directed by YHWH to baptize Jesus. The Zadok bloodline was not limited to the specialized, political position of the Zadok, although there were several sects that likely positioned their own Zadoks. Some theorists, including Laurence Gardner, state that James, Jesus's brother, became the Essene Zadok instead of Jesus. Followers who held the Zadok line in the highest regard favored James because he was born in wedlock by Mary and Joseph, whereas Jesus was not.

Documented proof of the Essenes is questionable at best to verify who lead them (and their related sects) at the time of the biblical Jesus. Edmond Szekely stated that the Aramaic scripts attributed to his 1937 A.D. book, *The Gospel of Peace by the disciple John*, were dated at the first century A.D. However, in his 1977 second edition that he renamed *Essene Gospel of Peace* and divided into three books, he states in the foreward of *Book One*, "The ancient Aramaic texts date from the third century after Christ."[108] He was the primary interpreter of these texts and claimed they were at the Vatican; however, a representative of the Vatican attested that there was no such person named Szekely who logged in to view any documents, and there were no such documents in the first place.

Another possible Essene Gospel was *The Gospel of the Holy Twelve*, which is said to be translated by Reverend Gideon Ouseley, a vegetarian who appealed to the Catholic Church to adopt the practice of vegetarianism. Modern Essene followers who agree with Ouseley claim that the *Holy Twelve* was written in 70 A.D. by the author of the Gospel of John, some going so far to believe that it was written before the other biblical Gospels. If the *Holy Twelve* was written near the time of Jesus, it would not have stated, "a city of Galilee, named Nazareth"; it would have instead referred to the Nazarene religious sect.[109]

A panel of theologians and linguists called the Jesus Seminar worked to uncover the accurate words of Jesus and the chronology of five Gospels. In their book *The Five Gospels*, the Jesus Seminar and main authors distinguish between the historical Jesus and the religious Christ Jesus.[110] There are five Gospels because the Seminar includes the Gospel of Thomas. Thomas shares similar information to Matthew and Luke, so they must have had a common source. The Seminar argues that these three Gospels incorporate allegories believed to be said by Jesus that were written in an unofficial and hypothetical

Gospel of Q, which is an abbreviation for *Quelle*, a German word for Source. The Gospel of Q compiled Greek proverbs said by a wise man.

The scholars state, "The first written gospels were Sayings Gospel Q and possibly an early version of the Gospel of Thomas. The Gospel of Mark was not composed until about 70 C.E." (p. 26).[110] Matthew was next in the 80s A.D. with Luke just around the corner. The Seminar believes that at least two scribes, including a priest, compiled the Gospel of John that was written c. 90 A.D. The John group was an apocalyptic group that included the author of the Book of Revelation. Each of the five Gospels was written anonymously and later ascribed a name by a redactor's educated guess.

The Bible's four Gospels differ from the Gospel of John because they share similar sayings by a historical Jesus who spoke in ethical parables, and John has the religious Christ who personifies light and life. John goes to great lengths explaining the nature of Jesus in "I AM" statements that set Jesus above and beyond any other person. The Jesus Seminar hypothesizes that John drew upon another unofficial work, the Gospel of Signs, which I think originated with the Essene, Nazarene, and Qumran communities.

Modern Essenes who follow Ouseley's books believe that some of John's work fell through the cracks and ended up guarded in a Tibetan monastery where somehow Ouseley was able to see those scroll fragments. In the same monastery is a document titled "The Life of Saint Issa" based on the travels of Jesus, otherwise known as Issa, through India, Tibet, and Persia.[108] The Bible does not account for the huge gap in Jesus's life as a teenager until 30 years old, so it is certainly possible that Yahshua could have traveled there. It is also possible that this Saint Issa was another Yahshua who did not die on the cross, and he relocated to India in later years.

I am perplexed why Ouseley's followers may not have sought information revealed by his close friend who wrote how he created *The Gospel of the Holy Twelve*:

> It was received by him under inspiration "In dreams and visions of the night", and in "Communications"…."[A] lectern seemed to appear before him with certain manuscripts thereon, and as it revolved he read the papers then presented to him. In the morning he noted what he had read, whether it came to his memory all at once or gradually, but generally within the day. The fact that in the morning he experienced heaviness, etc., in the eyes, exactly as if he had been reading all night, seemed to him a proof that some abnormal action was in progress".[111]

Ouseley's unofficial Gospel is not historically dated; it was an obvious channeling that aimed to perpetuate the Nazarean or Essene religion based on the biblical past.

This is yet another example of how people can believe a channeled work as historical. The Mormon founder Joseph Smith received a channeled text from angel Moroni; if the Mormons did not clarify that he translated a non-material vision of golden tablets, then we could be led to believe that those tablets were actual historical documents. This makes me think about the plethora of religious texts. We can deduce that otherworldly entities have given most or in some cases all religious texts that are passed off as truth, so what is deemed historical is questionable.

With regard to Szelezky's claim, certainly the Vatican could have hidden the historical information for the sake of preserving Catholicism as it is, but his purported Aramaic document most likely contains very little historical fact because it was written about 200 years after Jesus's works. It would be like me writing a dissertation about Abraham Lincoln and passing it off as indisputable fact although I never knew him; I based my words off a document that could have been made up about him, or I just wrote about my impression of the man based on society's sentiment. Szelezky's situation rings similar to the claim of Ouseley's followers that says the Bible does not include his "proof" about Jesus because the first Council of Nicaea under Constantinople altered or removed such words in 325 A.D.

The Council of Nicaea under Constantinople broadened its appeal to the masses by relating "pagan" Sun worship to Christ. This Christ as a demigod eventually superseded the mostly human Jesus, but it was acceptable because the role of Jesus was a religious one from the very beginning. The Council allowed the evolution and combination of essentially all religions to be combined into the savior role of our new dispensation of time.

The Bible did not mention the exact date of "Jesus's" birth, but Christianity tells us he was born on December 25, 0001 A.D. Jesus's year of birth was determined hundreds of years later in 525 A.D. by Dionysius Exiguus, a monk who invented the Anno Domini (A.D.)—in the year of our Lord—era that was used to number the years of both the Gregorian and Julian calendars.[112] Exiguus did not assign a zero as the first year because he considered the first year as number 1, and there is no Roman numeral for zero. What we may consider as year zero, especially in standardized and astronomical dating, should be 1 B.C. (Before Christ) or B.C.E (Before the Common Era). I would prefer to write C.E. (Common Era) and B.C.E., but the western world has yet to drop its preference for the religious abbreviations.

Regarding the date of December 25, a quote from *Jesus Christ, Our Promised Seed* states:

In 274 A.D., the Romans designated December 25 as the birthday of the unconquered sun, being the time when the sun begins noticeably to show an increase in light, resulting in longer daylight hours. By 336 A.D., the church in Rome was adapting this festival, spiritualizing its significance as a reference to Jesus Christ and calling it the "Feast of the Nativity of the Sun of Righteousness." Attempting to Christianize and incorporate the pagan traditions of antiquity, the church in Rome adopted this midwinter holiday celebrating the birth of the sun god as one of its own observances, somewhat changing its significance, but retaining many customs of the pagan festival. As the Roman church spread its influence religiously and militarily, this holiday of December 25 became the most popular date in Christendom to celebrate the birth of Jesus Christ. A special mass was established for Christ, hence, the name, "Christmass," abbreviated "Christmas."[113]

December 25 is a key date of birth for several Messiahs before Jesus, especially Mithra and Krishna. The Indian Vedic god Mitra, later worshipped as the Persian Mithra, was the Sun-God born to humanity in a cave on December 25 as the mediator between God and man.[114] The later Hindu Krishna was given this date although he was born in the summer or early autumn according to interpretation of Hindu text.[115] Both demigods are believed to have been created by immaculate conception similar to Jesus. When the new Messiah is designated, the new religious sect demotes the previous Messiah to prophet or antichrist. I proclaim that astrology—or at least astronomy—and one central God group have influenced all religions that take on this popular date.

The Bible gives inconsistent birth years for Jesus. The Gospel of Matthew chapter 2, verse 1 says he was born during King Herod's reign, which ended in 4 B.C. The Gospel of Luke chapter 3, verses 1,23 say he was "about thirty years of age" "in the fifteenth year of the reign of Tiberius Caesar" that was c. 28 or 29 A.D., therefore placing his birth c. 2 B.C.E. The Gospel of John chapter 19, verses 14-16 state that he was crucified during Passover, and he started his 3½ year ministry before then at age 30 (Luke 3:23); therefore, we can retroactively date his birth to early-mid fall. Luke also says that shepherds were "abiding in the field, keeping watch over their flock by night," indicating warmer weather than winter (Luke 2:8).

As I later show in chapter 7, some of these dates are biblical hints regarding the "wise men from the east" that relate to Yahshua but not necessarily to his birth (Matthew 2:1). Placing Yahshua's death at the time of Passover is also likely symbolic. It appeased the Jewish belief of redemption from sin and bondage through his sacrifice, and it appeased the pagan belief of Easter because he rose from the dead as a rebirthed mighty-man. Easter originally celebrated the fertility goddess as Eastre and other names such as Ishtar, and it likely also revered the sunrise or a rising star.

Usually, religious texts are wrought with symbolism and belief, but with some scrutiny, we can differentiate between historical people who became fused into the Jesus or Yahshua character.

Apollonius of Tyana

Sophist Flavius Philostratus wrote a biography titled *The Life of Apollonius of Tyana* in the early third century A.D., roughly 200 years after Apollonius's birth.[116] It states that Apollonius was born in the small town of Tyana in Cappadocia, the district of east-central Anatolia in the center of present-day Turkey.[117] The etymology of *Anatolia* is Greek, which was his primary language.

While Philostratus did not give Apollonius a precise date of birth, he associated it to a miraculous event by consensus of the people, thus deferring speculation toward his personal beliefs and potential embellishments. He wrote, "The people of the country, then, say that Apollonius was the son of this Zeus, but the sage called himself the son of Apollonius" (p. 16).[116] This could mean that his father's name was Apollonius, or his birth was believed to be an immaculate conception by a god. Philostratus made a point to show Apollonius revering Apollo, praying, "O Apollo, change these dumb dogs [uncultivated men] into trees, so that at least the cypresses they may become vocal" (p. 46).[116]

Philostratus described Apollonius as a vegetarian who practiced lifelong celibacy. He studied Pythagorean philosophy and imposed upon himself five years of silence to fulfill the Pythagorean initiation. This initiation enabled Apollonius to perform prophecies and healing miracles.

The Pythagorean school of thought combined religion and mathematics in a type of "sacred" numerology. Pythagoras said in the sixth century B.C., "There are men, gods, and men like Pythagoras."[118] His ideal society was nearly egalitarian, viewing men and women as equals and sharing property communally. A mathematician states, "Even mathematical discoveries were communal and by association attributed to Pythagoras himself—even from the grave. Hence, exactly what Pythagoras discovered personally is difficult to ascertain."[118] Vegetarianism was strictly practiced because Pythagoras preached transmigration of souls. This sounds very familiar to the evolution of the Essene belief.

Researcher Craig Lyons of Bet Emet Ministries explains how the Pythagorean religion and others helped develop Essene Christianity.

[W]e have documented beyond any reasonable doubt how the Essenes of Jesus' day had evolved from what began as a righteous separatist movement from a corrupt Temple Priesthood in 170 B.C.E. to a mixture of Pythagorean-Buddhist-Zoroastrian cult. This escapes the casual reader or student who only looks to Pliny, Philo, or Josephus for their information on the Essenes. What is of importance for our studies is that in this "Essenic Evolution" we have the alteration of Messianic beliefs; what began as a Davidic anointed one to come, who would fulfill the prophecies of Moses and the Prophets, we end up with an Angel-Messiah which is the culmination of sun-worship as filtered down through almost all world religions and which found its ultimate expression through the Pythagorean religious synthesis. This was the beliefs held by the Essenes as they again filtered such pagan notions though the remnants of Judaism which had yet held onto in the wake of their rejection as "priests" since the Hasmonean Dynasty. This means that their "oral traditions" concerning their Messiah of Aaron and their Messiah of Israel had picked up along the say [sic—way] vestiges of sun-myths which were created by prior personifications of the sun. These "messianic beliefs" were to be mixed with expected Davidic messianic beliefs in the first century; especially after the crucifixion of Jesus who many believed was the Messiah. Because of the strong Essene influence in Alexandria, Egypt, as well as in Palestine in these tumultuous messianic hysteria of the first century, many how [sic—who] saw no way out of the calamity enforced upon them by Rome looked no longer to notions of a human-Davidic anointed who would lead them to freedom and salvation, but saw that their only help was if God was to deliver them Himself and it was in the Essenic concept of their incarnated Angel-Messiah this would come. Thus those who would emerge from this terrible time were to emerge with hopes of an Angel-Messianic incarnated godman. These hopes and fears were later to be recorded and such "beliefs" would end un [sic—up] in the New Testament much later along with Davidic beliefs. As Christians we end up with a collage when reading the New Testament; we read of concepts taken from the Jewish Scriptures regarding the "anointed" to come as well as concepts derived straight from "sun-worship" and never know it![119]

Lyons's quote supports my assertion that people did not understand the actual nature of the Messiah because their desperation fueled their belief in a larger-than-life savior. I like how Lyons explains the interconnected religions under the umbrella of Judeo-Christianity because they reduce the amount of importance we tend to place upon only one god-man. This type of god-man is just another offspring of a genetic line that is mostly human. With all the interbreeding since the earliest of times, I am safe to say that we are all mostly human, or human hybrid, as god-men. To be made in the image of YHWH is actually nothing to celebrate, as I explain in chapter 7; it is wise to separate from the worship of another person or entity so we can see what we have created and expounded upon as a belief system. This means that we would finally be able to deeply discover ourselves.

Apollonius of Tyana may have thought he was more liberated as part of a mathematical and philosophical school of thought, but it was just another progression of his heavily religious era with its mystical initiations, ascetic lifestyle, and belief in another man akin to a demigod (Pythagoras). His initiation process most likely linked him to an entity that was also linked to Pythagoras, so it is possible that he was able to do some type of "miracle" that afforded him some fame. At the very least, he was activated like my mother to be able to give prophecies.

Apollonius was an orator. The Jesus Seminar states that Jesus was an orator who "wrote nothing, as far as we know" (p. 27).[110] In its analysis of the Gospels, the Seminar uncovered a historical Jesus and a religious Jesus, but it combines these two Jesuses into one when limiting the scope to 30-35 A.D. as the end date of Jesus's life by crucifixion. In typical orator fashion, students transcribed notes to the valuable lessons in the speeches. Philostratus stated that a scribe and disciple named Damis reported his extensive travels and experiences with Apollonius. The style of most of the biblical parables and aphorisms was especially unique, discovered the Seminar, because it showed Greek etymology that probably originated with Apollonius.

The Jesus Seminar states that Jesus's native tongue was Aramaic as a Jew. It is possible that the Jewish "Jesus" could have been bilingual, but Apollonius was a Hellenized Anatolian who taught in Greek. Apollonius traveled to multiple countries such as those in Lyons's above quote until he died at a ripe old age. In fact, Lyon's quote best applies to Apollonius because of his worship (and correlation) toward Apollo who was associated with the Sun during that time. Apollonius of Tyana was a popular public figure who taught Greek proverbs and parables, so I deduce that he was the main historical Jesus according to the Seminar's classification. Interwoven Gospel Scriptures ascribed to Yahshua may have copied Apollonius's style for continuity, or it was popular for orators to speak in the same style during that time.

Introducing the Yahshuas

I must preface the following sections about the Yahshuas because this information is very guarded in the higher "spiritual" realms. The Messiah role is patterned as the quintessential human in the line of Adam, the first man created as obedient to God. The entities in charge of this paradigm do not want to reveal the reasons behind this servitude, for they prefer to spin the story into a positive necessity versus a detracting diversion. The New Covenant is supposed to be one of freedom, yet this "freedom" relies upon self-sacrifice to receive the "reward" of death. It is no different than the Old Covenant, but it has been given a new marketing spin based upon the direct public relations of the Messiahs.

Every "holy" book of information about the two Yahshua Messiahs has combined them into one person, which is no surprise considering what I have already presented. The word *Yahshua* (or any close resemblance such as Yeshua and Jeshua) is actually a title instead of an individual name; it represents and partially describes the god-man created with YHWH's influence. YHWH is also considered a group title in the entity realm. This makes sense because of the numerous entities who created demigods in this name.

The Urantia Book gives a peek into the separate but seemingly equal relationship between the two entities, Sananda and Michael, who controlled the two popular Yahshuas; however, it only mentions the adventures of Michael while keeping Sananda in the heavens. It states that Sananda (Immanuel) is the brother of Michael of Nebadon, otherwise known as Archangel Michael in Christian and New Age circles.

The UB and other entity-communicated books convey that their Yahshua of preference was an incarnated demigod who was originally from another dimension. Even if there was a genetically engineered, artificial insemination, the body was completely filled by the "spirit" of Sananda or Michael. Interestingly, the UB entities who gave this information admitted that they did not understand how Michael was able to reincarnate or incarnate into different dimensions to fulfill his goal of becoming a Master Son (he was already a Creator Son—his group has specific ranks to climb). These intermediary entities just regurgitated what they were told by their superiors. Because the lower entities did not know what exactly happened, and often they are the ones who spread the story to humans in a believable way, we need to critically weigh the information on our own.

Another book called *Voyagers: The Secret of Amenti, Volume II* was also given by entity communication, but it was through a transmission style called data streaming that downloaded information to the scribe without possessing her.[120] *Voyagers II* gives a story with more similarities than differences between

Sananda and Michael in their independent roles as the Yahshuas. Its message also states they were reincarnated as humans, but this part of the story favors Sananda more than Michael.

I followed through with the All That Is, The Pure Essence (ATI,TPE) to clarify my research and gut reactions to the holes that I found in the information. The following sections and later chapters will reveal what Sananda, Michael, and their affiliations have been hiding from us.

<u>Yahshua–Sananda</u>

Reverend Ouseley's inspired Essene book *The Gospel of the Holy Twelve* elaborates upon the story of Sananda Immanuel in the Scripture of Matthew chapter 1, verse 23 that states, "BEHOLD, A VIRGIN SHALL BE WITH CHILD, AND SHALL BRING FORTH A SON, AND THEY SHALL CALL HIS NAME EM-MAN´-U-EL, which being interpreted is, God with us." This Scripture reiterates the Old Testament prophecy in Isaiah chapter 7, verse 14: "Behold, a virgin shall conceive, and bear a son, and shall call his name Im-man´-u-el."

Essenes are aware that their Yahshua was Immanuel, and they have correctly identified him as his preferred title Sananda, as confirmed in other people's channelings. Essenes have followed the Yahshua of the Isaiah prophecy because the Messianic prophetic books were inspired during the time of the Ossim and Nazarene developments. However, they have incorrectly placed Immanuel as the son of Mary and Joseph. The Essene Gospel copied Matthew's mistake that applied the Isaiah prophecy to the second Yahshua when Immanuel was the first.[109]

The entity group called Guardian Alliance (GA), who transmitted all of *Voyagers II* to a woman named Ashayana Deane, refers to Sananda as Jesheua-12. The GA states that Sananda is a 12th dimensional entity who gave his "soul essence" to Jesheua before birth, which means that he reincarnated as a human through mother Jeudi, who was a Melchizedek-Hebrew Essene, and father Joehius of the Melchizedek-Hibiru (pre-Habiru) Essene lineage (p. 99).[120] Sananda Immanuel as the first Yahshua, whom the GA says was named Jesheua-Melchizedek, was born in 12 B.C.E. outside of Bethlehem. This Yahshua was "born to descendants of the house of Solomon" (p. 99). He "was intended to bring together the factions within the Essenes that had developed with the Melchizedek and Hebrew Cloisters. He would also re-enter the original egalitarian Templar creed back into the teachings of the Essenes" (p. 99).[120]

Templar entails physical and energetic attributes of the Earth, so what creed was Sananda trying to bring back to the Essenes in relation to the Earth? Also, why does the GA mention Solomon and not the historical figures

Amenhotep II and Amenhotep III? The Solomon character's creed connected to the Amenhoteps' gods Amun and Marduk. Marduk has been an enemy of the GA since before Sananda came onto the scene with Yahshua.

The GA explains that there was original, protective Templar knowledge before the deviated versions occurred (in chapter 8), and one such deviation was given by the biblical angel Melchizedek. It has not sufficiently clarified Solomon's and Sananda's natures or affiliations.

The Da Vinci Code movie and book are about the Order of the Knights Templar, a group that upholds the order of the Zadoks and is portrayed as destructive and evil. These knights were originally monks trained in combat. They constituted much of the military arm of the First Christian Crusade and captured Jerusalem in 1099 A.D. The Knights Templar, like all religious militia, viewed itself as fighting a holy war ordained by God.

Mirroring the New Testament scripture of Ephesians chapter 6, verses 11-19, Cistercian Abbot Bernard of Clairvaux wrote a letter in support of the Knights Templar in 1135 A.D.

> He is truly a fearless knight and secure on every side, for his soul is protected by the armor of faith just as his body is protected by armor of steel. He is thus doubly armed and need fear neither demons nor men. Not that he fears death—no he desires it. Why should he fear to live or fear to die when for him to live is Christ, and to die is gain? Gladly and faithfully he stands for Christ, but he would prefer to be dissolved and to be with Christ, by far the better thing.[121]

Yahshua-Sananda and his Essene followers supposedly acted as the ancient guardians of the Earth's templar under the GA's leadership, but their religion was not devoid of violence. The Order of the Knights Templar in the Middle Ages conquered in the name of the non-egalitarian YHWH hierarchy of which Sananda was a part, as chapter 7 shows. It knew about Sananda's role in the "sacred" bloodline which it revered through sexual ceremonies and initiations. Its main purpose was to protect the knowledge and descendents of this bloodline.

The GA says that Yahshua-Sananda had six children.

> The children were created through sacred procreative rites for the sole purpose of perpetuating the 12-strand DNA pattern within the human races. Descendants of these children became spread throughout various regions, some appearing within the French Aristocracies, others within the Celtic, Egyptian and

African genetic lines. One line of descendants of Jesheua-12 now
resides within the continental United States (p. 103).[120]

Between 18 A.D. and 23 A.D., Yahshua-Sananda impregnated six
different women who comprised sub-races within a pre-biblical Melchizedek
Cloister bloodline, and five of the children survived. The GA says that six
men of the same bloodline served as adoptive fathers to each child. Yahshua-
Sananda did not interact with those children; the sole reason for their creation
was to spread a genetic code throughout the world.

The GA gives away enough information about adoptive fathers and the
"sacred procreative" rituals that entail something hidden. Usually, such rituals
are shady, but in this case, something beneficial was given to humanity's
manipulated DNA template. The ATI,TPE confirms that Sananda, a high
level "avatar," used Jesheua to procreate with the six women to partially
upgrade our gene code, but unfortunately, he also gave us distorted codes.

The popular story of Yahshua is that he was created by immaculate
conception, as though this might be different than genetically altered,
artificially inseminated conception. I do not see any difference between the two
because Mary was indeed a virgin at the time, and she became impregnated.
It becomes a miraculous story when we believe that a fetus just showed up
inside of Mary. This is akin to thinking a pig can instantly grow wings and
fly. "Oh, but God can do anything," we would say. By taking our imagination
down to reality, we see proof in the Bible that an angel overshadowed Mary
and additionally frightened her, which suggests that she was taken with some
force. The angel removed an egg from her body and then implanted it with
other genetics to create Yahshua.

We know that Yahshua-Sananda was not Mary's child, but the same
conception process happened to Jeudi, which the ATI,TPE confirms. It did
not matter that her husband was from a similar genetic line because he, like
the six adoptive fathers of Yahshua-Sananda's children, were placeholders and
useful instruments for the next generation.

I hyphenate Yahshua and Sananda because they were not the same person.
The ATI,TPE states that Sananda orchestrated the genetically engineered,
artificial insemination to impart his genes into the Jesheua child. Jesheua
could then become fully possessed by Sananda when he turned 12 years old.

Developmental psychologist Erik Erikson taught that adolescence begins
at age 12 when the brain becomes activated toward the sense of self and
personal identity.[122] This stage of activation is appealing to intrusive entities
who do not want their subjects to gain a sense of self. Sananda's genetic
implant into Jeudi made Jesheua vulnerable to full possession when he was
forced to undergo the rite of passage typical for that age. It is possible that the

young Yahshua agreed to it on some level, but he could have rather chosen to become partially possessed to further Sananda's quest just as most religious people choose. Sananda transferred his otherworldly "Holy Spirit" body into Jesheua during his initiation ceremony, therefore infilling and controlling the boy as if Sananda was him.

Sananda did what he came here to do, often working with Michael. Then, he de-possessed Jesheua the man at 39 years old in 27 A.D. The GA says that Sananda ascended, meaning that his entire body and identity as Jesheua left the Earth to enter a higher dimension or "realm" because Sananda supposedly reincarnated as Jesheua. The ATI,TPE states that this was not the case: Sananda's "spiritual" body left Jesheua, and Jesheua had to recover his lost life on Earth.

I wish the GA would reveal that the first Yahshua was a (mostly) human who was possessed by the high level avatar Sananda. I can guess two reasons why it has not yet corrected its story. First, its speaker and scribe Ashayana says she was Yahshua-Sananda's half-sister Miriam in one of her previously reincarnated lives. In one of her workshops, she said that she could not remember the details as Sananda's half-sister.[123] She repeated what her entity group told her, showing that the GA does know something about Sananda's history that it is selectively telling us.

Jeudi was married to one man, and presumably, her esteemed husband was dedicated solely to her. Having two children, including Miriam, by two different fathers would be important information to trace the bloodline for the GA's reincarnation story. I would like to think that Ashayana probed the GA about this situation, but then I wonder how much she does challenge the GA since she is its mouthpiece. On another note, she may also know more than she chooses to reveal.

Second, the GA belief system involves entities reincarnating numerous times from higher dimensional levels which implies that they somehow remain unharmed from cumulative effects of the human death process. The GA calls it "incarnation" from the entity realm to Earth. However, reincarnation is the same occurrence as re-incarnation because entities bring their entire higher body and consciousness with them in a newer and denser physical form. Entities prefer to possess Earthlings rather than reincarnate here so they can escape our particular limitations. The GA is perpetuating a belief over reality that gives limits to what entities can do.

Some of the GA may be as naïve as the entities in the UB by parroting information from their superiors. This would be a disappointing example to show us. Concerning the aware GA entities who purposely withhold facts from us and tell us incongruent information, if they admit that some of their agenda involves unnatural possession, this could cause distrust among us toward their overall message. However, if they are totally honest and humble about what they have done, this could possibly redeem them.

Sorry to burst anyone's bubble, but there are flaws everywhere in the human and entity realm. To be able to stand as one's self—taking what resonates and makes sense while leaving the rest—allows room for us all to take part and hopefully find a better way. To do this, we must read every line of presented information to see the full context including projected judgment or belief along with objective truth.

After Sananda left Earth, his lighter density, "spiritual" body returned to whatever dimension he was at previously, and he continued to keep a watchful eye over our planet. Regarding his chosen Yahshua, the ATI,TPE states that Jesheua had very little recollection of his entire adolescence and adulthood after Sananda left his body. His own mind and spirit were zombied out during that time (my words). Jesheua was generally allowed to live out the rest of his life, but he was still religious and probably partially possessed at times.

Yahshua–Michael

This second Yahshua is the better-known Yahshua of the Bible. The GA states that he was born in 7 B.C.E., which supports Matthew chapter 2, verse 1 during King Herod's reign. The GA and ATI,TPE state that he was born by Mary and a YHWH entity, and Mary was also conceived by the same means.[120] The GA does not specifically identify the entity or entities who impregnated Mary and her mother; it only mentions two separate Elohim conceptions that produced both Mary and her Yahshua son. The ATI,TPE reveals that Archangel Gabriel artificially inseminated Mary through genetic experimentation. Joseph in the Gospels was Yahshua's s step-father.

The entity who put his otherworldly "spiritual" body into the second Yahshua at age 12 is named Michael, whom *The Urantia Book* refers to as Michael of Nebadon because Nebadon is supposedly the name he gave to our universe. He is commonly known as Archangel Michael, and he works with Archangel Gabriel in the UB.

The GA does not reveal Michael's direct involvement with Yahshua, but it gives clues that support the information of the ATI,TPE and the UB. The GA calls the second Yahshua Jeshewua-9, where the nine represents a dimensional level. At the end of *Voyagers II*, the GA places Archangel Michael's entity group alongside unpleasant groups known to be at the 9th dimension, including the Alpha-Omega order. The GA says the entity (Michael) incarnated as Jeshewua, but Michael is not the type of entity who wishes to lose his power and become human, as chapter 7 reveals. Therefore, genetically altered, artificial insemination is the best method to intercept humanity by priming the human body for full possession.

Archangel Michael has visited the 9th dimension, but he originated elsewhere. The 9th dimension actually denotes the origin of the Jeshewua human, reveals the ATI,TPE. Jeshewua's human nature was indeed mostly human and considered as a demigod, but his prior nature existed in an angelic realm. The other Jesheua originated from an angelic realm also. This leaves me to wonder if they both agreed to their possessions before birth. At any rate, they did not perform their human missions; their controlling superiors did.

The GA says that Jeshewua worked on Earth to "restructure the patriarchal Templar creed to be more reflective of the Law of One" (p. 100).[120] It states that he was here to reintegrate certain souls who needed to be put back onto their specific paths. This is also what it says Sananda did. Shortly afterward, the GA contradicts its prior statement and states that the YHWH group that helped create Jeshewua "perpetuated the patriarchal slant on the Templar Creed" through Jeshewua's story (p. 102).[120] The only reason the GA gives for this patriarchal distortion is that it "protect[ed] the lineage of Jeshewua-9 from political persecution, making it appear as if the Christ had no descendants, thereby allowing those descendants to remain obscured from the public view" (p. 102).[120] This is not a substantial reason because patriarchal dominance already ruled society. Something was remiss in its story about Jeshewua.

Voyagers II is largely favorable toward Jeshewua. It blames the development of religion with distorting Jeshewua's initial message. However, it also reveals that YHWH purposely created false stories to deflect from Jeshewua's behind-the-scenes work. YHWH maintains control of its evolving religions as it does with all of its factions, so it could have corrected the initial story through bountiful prophets. YHWH is known for its half-truths so that we will stay a step behind it with incomplete understanding of its actions.

The second Yahshua legitimately married Mary Magdalene, but this was while he was under Michael's control. The patriarchal-minded apostles depicted Mary as a whore because they did not like her authority. Michael worked alongside her and showed her some respect because she perpetuated Jeshewua's genetic influence by producing three children.

Mary Magdalene legitimately re-incarnated here from a higher dimension, according to the ATI,TPE. The ATI,TPE confirms that entities partially possessed Mary to help direct her toward their mutual agenda.

The process of reincarnation does not control the specific family or location into which the child is born, but it does match people with similar DNA codes, as confirmed by the ATI,TPE. If Mary Magdalene and both Yahshuas were human, the odds that they were all born within close proximity with healthy and preferable bodies would have been extremely slim. They supported similar agendas, so having only one of them become human—

especially the important female for procreation—was sufficient to control the situation.

According to Laurence Gardner, Jeshewua and Mary Magdalene's first child was a girl named Tamar. The next two children were boys. The first son was named the same name or title as his father. The second son was named Josephes.

Following the footsteps of his biological father, Jeshewua II was initiated in a symbolic "born again" ceremony at age 12 (p. 110).[68] This religious rite of passage symbolized being raised from eternal darkness. "The term [raised] is still used in modern Freemasonry," states Gardner (p. 114).[68]

Freemasons are a worldwide fraternal group with 33 orders of initiations in which the top three levels are the elite. They often say Freemasonry is not a religion because they embrace all religions and universal brotherhood. To the contrary, several texts about Freemasonry reveal that it is a religion, and its Godhead comprises the three-headed amalgamation of Yahuah, Baal, and Osiris as JoaBulOn.[124] (The MCEO, Ashayana Deane's main entity group, states that Baal is another name for Archangel Michael's group.)[125] The elite group at the top is speculated to orchestrate the sordid, secret ceremonies knowing full well their purpose, while the less aware lower ranks outreach to the public about their organization's benevolence.

Gardner states that Jeshewua II was celibate, so Josephes was the Holy Grail who perpetuated the royal bloodline.[68] Outside of patriarchal history, Tamar also was the Holy Grail. *Holy Grail* was a translation of Saint or San Graal, which originated from *Sangréal* meaning royal blood.

The prevailing belief about Jesus is that he was celibate, but it was rather Jeshewua II who was. Celibacy was common in Essene practice and ideology, which Catholic priests implemented. Catholics also became the largest proponent of the Order of the Knights Templar. This belief about the Messiah was a whitewashed lie to hide the importance of specialized procreation as already asserted in the Old Testament's Pentateuch.

Gardner was a Knight Templar who worshipped Mary and Jesus. He asserted that the Knights Templar sought to protect the expanded bloodline of Josephes. Freemason and related secret societies also seek to protect this bloodline, and they are led by the bloodline's 13 main families collectively known as the Illuminati. However, this was not the only bloodline that they protected, for it was intermixed with Yahshua-Sananda's as shown in "Interwoven Yahshuas."

Jesus, Mary Magdalene, and their son Josephes represent the last Christian trinity. Most Gnostics viewed Mary as Jesus's equal because she was believed to be the reincarnation of Sophia. Chapter 7 confirms that Mary Magdalene was indeed a reincarnation from the Sophia entity group. Gnostic paintings depicted her as black because Sophia "existed in the darkness of Chaos before the Creation" (p. 122).[68]

Voyagers II states that Mary Magdalene moved to France to protect her children from political persecution due to Yahshua-Michael's teachings. I assert that his teachings merely tried to unite the people under a more refined perception of the Messiah instead of any theme of self-empowerment. Before they moved to France, Jeshewua already had his three children with Mary, which means that Michael used him for these acts.

The GA states that Yahshua-Michael joined his wife in 25 A.D. to escape persecution during the YHWH-assisted migration. Jeshewua was 32 years old.[120] The GA's story does not tell the truth about Yahshua-Michael's possession, so no information was revealed whether Jeshewua was de-possessed when he went to France. If he was, then he would have been shocked to discover himself in a new country with a new family. Instead, I propose that he needed some time for re-education in a more familiar environment, which I will soon explain.

YHWH protected its Yahshuas and often placed them in secret locations, notably the pyramids of Giza where they performed ascensions for "chosen ones." Although unlikely, these ascensions may have occurred without the participants dying if the rituals sufficiently prepared them; the Bible indicated this with the unhindered transfiguration and ascension of Enoch. I have my concerns about where these people were directed, though, as later chapters reveal.

Although Michael and Sananda taught about ascension through their Yahshuas, their version for the masses directed them to "heaven" through death. In this process, people needed a sacrificial lamb to pave the way. Michael still needed Jeshewua, so someone else had to die on the cross.

Arihabi

Arihabi was born in Jerusalem, and he later became an unknown placeholder as the sacrificial Christ.[120] He was partially possessed by a YHWH entity, likely Gabriel, to receive grandiose visions that made him believe he was the true Messiah. He may have also thought that he was Jeshewua.

Arihabi died on the cross. The GA and ATI,TPE confirm that the Elohim brought Arihabi back to life. This proper resurrection took place after an orchestrated false resurrection that the advanced entities used through holographic inserts into the scene.[120]

A few years ago, I found a channeled communication on the internet whose detailed information about the resurrection event appears to now be removed. The entity giving the message, a genetic scientist, was in a spaceship above the crucifixion that raised the "body of Christ." The sky was darkened so that no one could see what was beyond the clouds. The otherworldly scientist revived Arihabi's freshly deceased body so that his soul essence could return into it. I do not know if this channeling was removed because it was too revealing, but I hope people can locate such information if feasible.

I deduce from both stories that a spaceship, probably cloaked, was positioned above the crucifixion so it could show holograms for a false resurrection, and it could retrieve Arihabi's body soon afterward from the tomb. The above entities also needed to stay nearby to continue orchestrating holograms while they repaired Arihabi.

The Gospel of John chapter 20, verse 17 is most telling about Yahshua after his resurrection and before his "ascension": he told Mary Magdalene, "Touch me not, for I am not yet ascended to the Father." That evening, "Yahshua" appeared in a similar fashion to his disciples behind closed doors. This Yahshua was Arihabi because he showed the disciples his wounds. A few verses earlier state that Mary "knew not that it was Jesus" (John 20:14), which probably did not mean that she did not recognize her husband; instead, it could have implied that she knew that Arihabi was not Jeshewua, or something otherworldly as a hologram was projected in his place. Only after eight days did he allow a disciple, Thomas, to touch his body.

Arihabi was fully repaired when he allowed Thomas to touch him. Before then, he was in the spaceship, and a hologram was shown in his place, confirms the ATI,TPE.

I asked the ATI,TPE on October 21, 2011, "How did they make the hologram move and talk so realistically?"

It replies, "It was a projection of 'Jesus' in motion from the spaceship."

Arihabi's bodily reintegration happened quickly for the hologram to then capture his actions, and he was schooled by the entities before his return, confirms the ATI,TPE. Arihabi then hung out with his disciples and performed some miracles because of the entities with him. The GA states, "He was then taken to India, where he lived for another 30 years" (p. 102).[120]

Since Arihabi was the actual sacrifice, this gives further pause when considering the purpose of extreme self-sacrifice. The whole religious agenda can even be viewed as a big show and distraction, but that distraction involves deceptive actions that usually treat people as dispensable. Arihabi was the "chosen one" of YHWH to be manipulated and killed while YHWH's preferred operatives and "children" were protected. The agenda is number one, and humans are its pawns.

Interwoven Yahshuas

Sananda's and Michael's paths overlapped countless times as the Yahshuas.

The GA states that both Yahshuas went to Egypt in Giza for "initiation, ascension training and ordination as a Melchizedek priest, and portions of these rites were conducted by Jesheua-12 [Sananda]" (p. 101).[120] Prior to their ordinations in Egypt, each at age 20, the GA says that they both traveled and trained extensively. Yahshua-Michael trained in various inter-faith doctrines throughout Nepal, Greece, Syria, Persia, and Tibet. The UB states that he also studied in India. Yahshua-Sananda mainly trained in India and Persia and therefore had more of an Eastern slant to his teachings.

I do not wish to repeat more of the GA story about the Yahshuas because it is told from the perspective of them being fully reincarnated. I have repeatedly asked the ATI,TPE whether the Yahshuas were fully possessed, and the answer is consistently "yes." Therefore, these Yahshuas did not need to learn anything in a type of training when they were possessed after 12 years of age because the possessors took control with their own abilities and agendas. The ATI,TPE states the real learning happened when the Yahshuas were younger than 12. The UB states that young boys with exceptional ability were usually sent to Alexandria, Egypt to study. YHWH likely took them elsewhere as well.

Arguably the most important link between Yahshua-Michael and Yahshua-Sananda was Mary Magdalene. Before Mary left for France, Yahshua-Sananda met up with her privately. She was married to Yahshua-Michael, but she had another child, Sarah (or Sara), by the physical union between her and Yahshua-Sananda, as confirmed by the ATI,TPE. The ATI,TPE divulges that Mary Magdalene was previously the entity named Lady Nada, the "soulmate" of Sananda in their higher realm. They came down to Earth to carry out their missions together. I strongly think that Sarah was the "Holy Grail" child, not Josephes or Tamar, if we are to deduce a preferred bloodline among several participants.

Sarah is described in the book *The Woman with the Alabaster Jar: Mary Magdalen and the Holy Grail*:

> In the town of Les Saintes-Maries-de-la-Mer in France, there is a festival every May 23 to 25 at a shrine in honor of Saint Sarah the Egyptian, also called Sara Kali, the "Black Queen." Close scrutiny reveals that this festival, which originated in the Middle Ages, is in honor of an "Egyptian" child who accompanied Mary Magdalen, Martha, and Lazarus, arriving with them in a small boat that came ashore at this location in approximately A.D. 42 (p. 60).[126]

The GA does not disclose this fact, but Archangel Michael did reveal Sarah in a November 18, 2005 prophecy to a woman named Candace Frieze, although his prophecy also contained misinformation.[127] Gnostic believers revered Sarah as they did Mary Magdalene and Sophia, hence why their paintings depicted Sarah as black.

Since Sarah was the Holy Grail, the Knights Templar and Freemasons have fiercely guarded this information. The GA depicts Sananda as the true Christ, and it is up to speculation which Yahshua is favored among secret societies since they accept both of them. This does not appear favorable for any of the "saviors" because Christianity outwardly claims that secret societies are "of the Devil."

As I previously stated, Sananda left his Yahshua's body around 27 A.D. The GA says Yahshua-Michael stayed longer on Earth before he ascended out of Tibet with the Elohim's help in 47 A.D.; however, Michael left his Yahshua's body earlier than 47 A.D. while Jeshewua naturally stayed, confirms the ATI,TPE.

After the resurrection and relocation of Arihabi, the Yahshuas were still active. There were many accounts about "saints" who traveled to other countries. A man called Yuz Asaf, meaning Leader of the Healed, performed healings in Eastern Anatolia and Persia much like the Jesuses did in the Gospels.[128] The Qur'an refers to Jesus as 'Isa.[129] Similarly, a man named Issa, meaning Christ, was highly revered in Northern India along with Jeshewua's mother Mary. According to the book *Jesus Lived in India* by Holger Kersten, a Kashmir, India historical document states that 'Isa was also known as Yuz Asaf. Both of his titles as Issa and Yuz Asaf were assigned to locations in and near Kashmir in his honor, and a single tomb in Kashmir is believed to hold his remains.[128]

The ATI,TPE confirms that both Jeshewua and his mother were in India together; however, Jeshewua was de-possessed by that time. He needed integrative training with his mother alongside him before he returned to his family in France. This confirms that training is necessary outside of full possession. The GA states that Jeshewua went to France to be with Mary Magdalene and his children, and then he went back to India. I doubt he returned to India after he integrated with his new family. Upon asking the ATI,TPE for clarification, it replies, "Jeshewua did not go back to India as the Guardian Alliance stated."

Saint Issa died in Kashmir when he was about 80 years old. The GA says Arihabi died when he was in his 60s, so he could not have been Issa. Since Sananda left Jesheua's body c. 27 A.D., and Jeshewua was mainly in France, then Jesheua must have been Issa, 'Isa, and Yuz Asaf, unless the titles were also given to Jeshewua during his training with his mother. The ATI,TPE reveals that Jesheua was partially possessed by a YHWH entity so that he could perform small miracles throughout the rest of his life. I deduce that this also happened to Jeshewua.

Kersten states that Issa traveled extensively to places as far as Western Europe and England, but I think that Jeshewua covered that area. People reported seeing Yahshua with Mary together; depending upon the area and time, it was any of the two Yahshuas and Marys, although in Western Europe it would have been Mary Magdalene with Jeshewua. Jesheua covered another large region in which he finally arrived with Jeshewua's mother Mary in the upper Indus Valley. She died there and was buried in a town renamed Mari in her honor.[128] Mary became revered by her partially possessed works on her own travels. As for Mary Magdalene, she largely stayed in France where she eventually died in a cave, states the ATI,TPE.

The GA may not want to equate Yahshua-Sananda to the well-known Eastern miracle worker because it might prompt questions into the identities of Sananda and Jesheua—the GA's preferred "Jesus"; this is probably why it claims that Michael's Yahshua remained in India because of the public and questionable performances. However, it claims that Jeshewua supposedly ascended, so if we probe into his later work, we would start to question Jesheua anyway.

It has taken my mother and me several attempts to get clear answers about the two popular Yahshuas. Sometimes, especially at the beginning period of our questioning, interference had occurred mid-stream. It was not easy to detect until she learned to fine tune her ability and temporarily stop the communication to push away meddling entities. The most difficult aspect of this investigation for me was to decipher the ATI,TPE's short answers among the few Yahshua characters and their interchanging activity partners. Jesus's story has been a difficult one to crack, but after following up many times with the ATI,TPE for the clear answer, I think have sufficiently found it.

Since there are many versions of Jesus and the Messiah, I think all information should be welcomed to understand why the distinctions exist. We can also understand that there are demigod genes within us, and we can better view this phenomenon without giving our power away to any so-called god. This process would validate everyone's religion as having some fact behind the possibly grandiose story. Next, it would bring us to the stage of attempting to understand why there are religions in the first place, and we can better discern why entities wish to be involved on Earth. YHWH as an amalgamated group would also become categorized into several Gods who have specific roles. Why do I pluralize *God* when this status is supposed to be singular? The all-mighty, omniscient, perfect GOD is actually many different God entities who take ownership over something or someone. Sananda and Michael as the sole influencing entities to their Yahshuas would therefore be two YHWH Gods.

Thought Adjusters

The Urantia Book talks around the subject of possession in its classification of entities called "Thought Adjusters." The book was channeled by seraphims and other angelic entities who stated their titles or names at the end of their sections, and they explained their view about Michael of Nebadon's supremacy wherein he was liked by everyone, everywhere. They conveyed various essays (often biased and limited in knowledge) about the history of the Earth, the cosmos, and Michael's influence over "Joshua ben Joseph" as the Yahshua.[16]

The UB appeared in stages as detailed channelings to a man from Chicago, Illinois between the years of 1924 to 1955 A.D.[130] Its story about Jesus says that Michael reincarnated as him; therefore, Michael needed spiritual guidance to remember his role in this dense form.

> The activities of Adjusters in your local universe are directed by the Personalized Adjuster of Michael of Nebadon, that very Monitor who guided him step by step when he lived his human life in the flesh of Joshua ben Joseph. Faithful to his trust was this extraordinary Adjuster, and wisely did this valiant Monitor direct the human nature, ever guiding the mortal mind of the Paradise Son in the choosing of the path of the Father's perfect will. This Adjuster had previously served with Machiventa Melchizedek in the days of Abraham and had engaged in tremendous exploits both previous to this indwelling and between these bestowal experiences (1200.4).[16]

This Adjuster was Archangel Gabriel, as confirmed by the ATI,TPE, but there are many Adjusters or Holy Spirits as I have already explained. We know that Michael was not reincarnated as Yahshua but was Yahshua's complete "Thought Adjuster," as his group prefers to call the role. If the Thought Adjuster is such a noble role, then why don't entities say that Michael was Yahshua's Thought Adjuster? Probably because this position is not as genuine as they make it out to be, and an entity who becomes human is more agreeable to us.

A "solitary messenger" of a far-out place called Orvonton admits that Thought Adjusters are persistent, and they shape the thought process of the human mind toward their "divine" plan for the human (1240.2). "[I]ndirectly and unrecognized the Adjuster is constantly communicating with the human subject, especially during those sublime experiences of the worshipful contact of mind with spirit in the superconsciousness" (1203.3).

After the human mind is changed to a spiritual, eternal way of thinking, and after we die, we become fused with this adjuster for eternity. "[T]he fused individual is really one personality, one being, whose unity defies all attempts at analysis by any intelligence of the universes" (1238.3). This is an extreme "oneness" that never allows us to have our own identity. It is not just partial possession but full possession.

The Orvonton messenger states:

> When Thought Adjusters indwell human minds, they bring with them the model careers, the ideal lives, as determined and foreordained by themselves and the Personalized Adjusters of Divinington, which have been certified by the Personalized Adjuster of Urantia. Thus they begin work with a definite and predetermined plan for the intellectual and spiritual development of their human subjects, but it is not incumbent upon any human being to accept this plan. You are all subjects of predestination, but it is not foreordained that you must accept this divine predestination; you are at full liberty to reject any part or all of the Thought Adjusters' program. It is their mission to effect such mind changes and to make such spiritual adjustments as you may willingly and intelligently authorize, to the end that they may gain more influence over the personality directionization; but under no circumstances do these divine Monitors ever take advantage of you or in any way arbitrarily influence you in your choices and decisions. The Adjusters respect your sovereignty of personality; *they are always subservient to your will* (1204.5).
>
> They are persistent, ingenious, and perfect in their methods of work, but they never do violence to the volitional selfhood of their hosts (1204.6).[16]

This message is riddled with contradiction: these entities aim to control us, but they are somehow under our will. How do we have a will when they are persistently directing it? Every mention of our control is tacked on as an afterthought to our powerlessness, making us think we allow them to control us when they rather claim to affect our destiny.

This message finally says that their form of respect toward us is not to physically harm us, but this is stated within the context of us already being their hosts. If we tell them to leave us alone, they could potentially harm us, as many people have reported when trying to free themselves from demonic harassments. Take comfort in the fact that we can overcome them when we are grounded in our own personal energy and sense of self. If we struggle with our grounding, then we each can do our best to link to our true inner, "higher" self and the ATI,TPE to give us help. Chapter 9 illuminates how we can clearly find ourselves, and I explain my process of reaching our core and the ATI,TPE in chapter 11's "Techniques."

Many indoctrinated people do not have the awareness within themselves and their social structures to break out of their spiritual influences. I wish they would pay heed to the obvious and subtle contradictions against their inner gauge, so they take the steps to break free on their own; however, they have an unfair disadvantage when being bombarded with altering thoughts. It is especially difficult when partial possessions start early in babies and young children. Their entire sense of self becomes distorted, so they need much inner strength to be able to find out who they are versus what mental program they were told. Possessions are far more invasive than any worldview their family could give them, but we can break their claw upon us, as I, my mother, and countless others have clearly done. My mother saw that it is truly a claw, for she saw one on my head when I had pressure headaches during my religious path.

The UB tries to portray the typical evolutionary human story in which we need entities to save us, but it reveals telling information about how they want us to help them. Intelligent and spiritual people, or actually anyone who is naturally able and filled with potential, are sought by these entities so they could learn from us as well as gain rank and status. The Thought Adjuster (Holy Spirit, angel, god, or God) wishes to experience his or her subject through some sort of possession to learn more about the human mind and body. This relationship opens the door to guardian angels, known as "personal seraphims," and additional helpers as cherubims to jump onto the host (1241.7). When seraphims are assigned humans to influence, they are upgraded to "guardians of destiny" (1242.5). "One of the most important things a destiny guardian does for her mortal subject is to effect a personal co-ordination of the numerous impersonal spirit influences which indwell, surround, and impinge upon the mind and soul of the evolving material creature" (1244.2). When we agree to let god into our lives, it looks like we agree to become a test subject and case study for a plethora of entities to use as they desire.

It gets more eye-opening when a chief seraphim speaks:

> The instant the pilot light in the human mind disappears [Note: No! We do not lose our mind or identity!], the spirit luminosity which seraphim associate with the presence of the Adjuster, the attending angel reports in person to the commanding angels, successively, of the group, company, battalion, unit, legion, and host; and after being duly registered for the final adventure

of time and space, such an angel receives certification by the planetary chief of seraphim for reporting to the Evening Star (or other lieutenant of Gabriel) in command of the seraphic army of this candidate for universe ascension. And upon being granted permission from the commander of this highest organizational unit, such a guardian of destiny proceeds to the first mansion world and there awaits the consciousizing of her former ward in the flesh (1246.6).

All seraphim have individual names, but in the records of assignment to world service they are frequently designated by their planetary numbers. At the universe headquarters they are registered by name and number. The destiny guardian of the human subject used in this contactual communication is number 3 of group 17, of company 126, of battalion 4, of unit 384, of legion 6, of host 37, of the 182,314th seraphic army of Nebadon. The current planetary assignment number of this seraphim on Urantia and to this human subject is 3,641,852 (1243.3).[16]

The UB views seraphims as low-level angels who desire to gain rank since they view themselves as part of an army. This rank is not only part of an army but is more importantly part of the ascension cycle up through heavenly dimensions. The UB portrays Michael as another type of angel who had the same desire because he already fulfilled several roles to gain rank.

According to the chief seraphim, we will join its army when we allow the seraphims to lead us.

> The human race was created just a little lower than the more simple types of the angelic orders. Therefore will your first assignment of the morontia life [place after death] be as assistants to the seraphim in the immediate work awaiting at the time you attain personality consciousness subsequent to your liberation from the bonds of the flesh (1248.3).[16]

I see two reasons why these entities say we need them when in reality they need us. The obvious reason in the above excerpts is that they need us to join their armies. The realistic and main reason, though, is that the seraphims or similar entities are stuck somewhere as fallen angels; therefore, they must latch onto our spiritual or etheric body so that we can potentially bring them with us in an ascension process. A variation of this possibility that gives the most likely scenario is that they need us for our energy so that we can sustain their fallen angelic existence, and they direct us to a heavenly "hell" that is cut off from a natural ascension process.

The only reason that humans and Jesus were made a little lower than the angels according to Hebrews chapter 2, verses 7 and 9 is because we die in this body. The human DNA template is actually superior to the religious angels and gods although our current shell is more fragile, as the following chapters explain. Since these entities need humans in our currently compromised state, this shows that we still have amazing attributes.

The chief seraphim states:

> It is indeed an epoch in the career of an ascending mortal, this first awakening on the shores of the mansion world; there, for the first time, actually to see your long-loved and ever-present angelic companions of earth days; there also to become truly conscious of the identity and presence of the divine Monitor who so long indwelt your mind on earth. Such an experience constitutes a glorious awakening, a real resurrection (1248.1).[16]

These entities are gearing us to join them in their realm. Hopefully only the humans who willfully and cognizantly desire to merge with them will join them in their afterlife. When more of the picture unfolds, it is then up to those humans to decide whether they wish to remain within that stagnant realm, that is, if they maintain an awareness and ability to escape it. There are significantly better places for us to go instead.

The Messiah/Savior Yahshua/Jesus role within Judeo-Christianity was filled by many people and may continue to expand its characters because the god-man "demigod" is the tangible link between God and us. Built into every mainstream religion and spirituality is the story of a primitive human who can only ascend with the help of an otherworldly entity. The ultimate God character entails something too foreign and judgmental to us, so what a clever ploy to place a type of demigod into the picture as not just an example to follow but a savior who frees us from all of our problems. This demigod is more wise, pure, and powerful than us mere humans, but he or she has experienced a life similar to ours yet came out free of sin. If this superman stays awesome after having experienced our struggles, then he is worthy to be emulated. Of course, there is a catch—we first have to die. The path to life is death, so no one really overcame any struggle. Control over our minds does not help us overcome any struggle either. This salvation rather "saves" us from ourselves.

When we realize that we are more than we have been taught in religious and spiritual belief systems, the shackles to our own abilities, knowledge, and innate wisdom will be loosed, and we, alone and together, can find our way to life outside of the death trap that religious entities have created.

The tragic aspect of religions is when their subjects cannot use their own minds and are forced to follow; I am speaking about children who are deeply indoctrinated by their parents. Some religions are so bound to their family honor that the children feel forever in debt to their parents, notably their fathers.

I read a newspaper article several years back about an adult male from a Muslim country who traveled to North America and converted to Christianity. Upon returning to his home country, he was terrified to tell anyone about his new religion because not only was it a disgrace to his family, but authorities could sanction putting him to death. When he told his father, the father disowned him although the authorities spared his life. His father explained that the son is obligated to do what the father wants of him. Essentially, the son is nothing more than the father's property. This story could apply to Jesus because everything he did, he did for his Father.

Children grow up wanting to please their parents, and this includes believing the stories told to them. When a family reveres a religious—entity-based—belief, entities become familiar with the home; therefore, the children cannot escape their influence. Thankfully, children who listen to their independent conscience can detach themselves from entity influences, but they may endure social backlash when refusing religious rituals. I just hope they realize that the world is bigger than that social circle, and they can eventually find other people to support them.

While religions are political and social structures placed over our entire existence on Earth, their dominant aim is to control our mental, spiritual, and emotional energies. This makes religious and spiritual belief a fabricated force that can be overruled by our internal energies; no one can ultimately control our mind, spirit, or emotions except for our rightful self. Let us educate and listen to ourselves so that we direct our physical bodies with our own wise desires.

PART 3

How the Earth Relates to the Cosmos

CHAPTER 6

Unnatural versus Natural Scientific Origins

Scientists question whether our universe was created through intelligent design or by a random event. It is highly unscientific and unrealistic if they view intelligence as a cognitive function of a God who had the ability to design every aspect and material from which matter can bond and function in diverse ways. The evolutionary theory is appealing because scientists know that whatever is created can go against the grain and take creation in another direction. Accordingly, it accepts that bacterial and viral life forms enter our planet via frozen comets. Life could have originated on Earth or elsewhere, and life forms would interact and shape their growth or demise. The inclusion of chaos theory explores this apparent randomness of events while also maintaining a measure of order.

How far back do scientists need to go to solve their riddle of creation? About 14 billion years to the estimated age of the universe? Currently, scientists generally support the Big Bang Theory that says the universe started with a small singularity that continuously inflated. Immediately after the singularity arose, the surrounding temperature was about 10 billion degrees Fahrenheit, and the environment already contained neutrons, electrons, protons, photons, and other subatomic particles. As the universe cooled, these subatomic particles decayed or combined. This early soup did not contain light, meaning that it could have been dark energy and dark matter.[131] Dark energy is a force that permeates about 68 percent of space and causes universal expansion. Dark matter involves how objects function together outside the property of light, thereby comprising about 27 percent of the universe and 80 percent of matter. These figures leave us with only 5 percent of known matter that was later formed. Matter needs to be combined in such a way to allow photons to shine through it.[132] The early light of the Big Bang afterglow is known as the cosmic microwave or radiation background because of its abnormally high temperature.

Temperature is a measure of force. For the Big Bang to produce such high temperature, it had to contain abnormal force. Typically, the largest surge of energy occurs during the supernova process when a giant star's core begins to condense under gravity, creating hotter temperatures and a temporarily expanded star before the star explodes. These properties are also contained within the Big Bang, but physicists prefer to see the universal event as sending ripples, not a far-reaching explosion as though it was a unique supermassive supernova.

The conundrum involving all Big Bang theorists is solving that first singularity that contained the fundamental properties for creation. Singularities are usually associated with black holes as static points that do not expand, but there is creation outside of that singularity.[133] This implies that the Big Bang singularity can contain properties for external creation while not being the only space for all of creation.

Some cosmologists state that our universe is still in the process of cooling from the Big Bang. When it would fully cool, expansion should stop as the "Big Freeze."[134] This theory implies that the original force is not infinite, and static life would eventually die out. Matter below critical density would float aimlessly in space while the critical density will potentially become drawn back into that original singularity by gravity in what is known as the "Big Crunch."[134] Again, the Big Bang can involve a type of giant supernova process that ends as a giant supermassive black hole.

The center of the universe is the best location for the singularity to expand in every direction, but it is impossible to measure from our view. Therefore, a microcosmic correlation can be the center of a galaxy, wherein many, including the Milky Way, have supermassive black holes.

When a giant star dies, its energetic casing explodes as a supernova while the force of its gravity compacts the remaining body into either a neutron body without charge or a black hole. If the remaining core of the supernova has a mass (measurement of matter in an object) greater than 2.5 times the mass of the Sun, then it will create a black hole. Its massive amount of gravity causes it to collapse into itself permanently, and only a velocity greater than the speed of light can escape it.[135]

"Newton's Law of Gravitation states that every bit of matter in the universe attracts every other with a gravitational force that is proportional to its mass," states Harvey Mudd College physicist Gregory A. Lyzenga.[136] A star's gravity pull can only reach as far as the other object's mass, distance, and orbital period can respond. Earth as our original reference point was measured against the Sun, where the radius and mass of the Earth along with the distance to the Sun were able to determine the Sun's mass. From there, other nearby planetary bodies can be measured. Although this reference point is a far cry from the galactic center's giant supernova, these relationships show important boundaries that can help shape the Big Bang Theory into a workable model.

Astrophysicists use an infrared light attached to the Hubble telescope to spot the activity at the center of galaxies. Because they see a lot of activity around a compacted mass, and the galaxy is already well formed, they generally say that a supermassive black hole is consuming material. Gravity is the weakest force, but it is theoretically stronger than any other interaction with a supermassive black hole. A supermassive black hole contains several million times the mass of a typical black hole that strengthens its gravitational pull. Einstein's General Theory of Relativity explains that gravity can bend light and curve spacetime. When a supermassive black hole's concentrated mass and gravity come into contact with its surroundings, they shape the surrounding template and can alter current scientific measurements. Astrophysicists use this information to deduce that supermassive black holes grow from consumption of their gaseous surroundings.[137]

Just because scientists have not discovered a time when our galactic center has not destroyed its immediate surroundings, there are other galaxies with central supermassive black holes that show no remarkable activity. It becomes magical thinking to assume that a supermassive black hole significantly acts outside the properties of a typical black hole beyond a greater magnitude; accordingly, this way of thinking gives it similar properties to the theoretical Big Crunch with an insatiable appetite for destruction. It is unknown how far the Big Bang Theory's creation process can reach for material to disperse and create, but I strongly doubt that its material will become drawn back to that initial point again. This process has it act like an inconceivably massive black hole, but all black holes have finite properties that curb their consumption. In addition, giving the original singularity the same property as this fictitious black hole would ultimately alter the singularity into something else, thereby changing the static model.

We are viewing a galactic event that happened many light years ago, so the speed of light is yet to show us a calm, completed supermassive black hole. When it is forming, its strong gravity pulls gaseous material around it and shoots out the remains in a vertical stream as a quasar seen by x-ray technology.[138] Whatever light and material does not escape eventually will be trapped within the event horizon of the hole.

Some scientists believe that galaxies were created by a large quasar of highly excited, superluminous energy. A quasar is not a star, but it emits radio waves further than any other visible energy. This object or wave can carry material for universal creation, but it came into existence after the creation of a supermassive black hole, deriving its energy from "mass falling onto the accretion disc around the black hole."[139] For creation to have occurred, something akin to a quasar had to exist before a supermassive black hole because black holes by nature do not create. The identification of quasars helped Big Bang Theory proponents refute the steady-state view about cosmology in which creation naturally expands with no beginning or end. Certainly, the universe contains aspects of both theories.

The Hubble telescope shows that the universe is expanding more than it is contracting, and it is continuing to expand.[140] The Earth is located near the edge of the Milky Way and is a relative newcomer, so something was able to create it. Within the Big Bang Theory, the material that keeps expanding must be supernova or quasar remnants from either the Milky Way's (or a nearby galaxy's) big bang, or the universe's Big Bang. Closer, smaller explosions after the big bang also continue to create solar systems such as ours. The explosions and subsequent creations entail recycled material.

There is an inherent contradiction within the Big Bang Theory that predicates the entire universe upon its original material that eventually dies, yet it somehow started with absolute life with infinite creative potential. If everything in the universe is dependent upon an original point that could possibly be a unique type of star, this brings us back to the question: Where did the energetic components of that first point originate? Accordingly, does such a point or singularity really contain all components for creation?

If the original material came into existence all on its own, then this was the "God" that created us, although it has also killed us. This origin of creation entwines life and death as though one cannot exist without another (which the controlling gods want us to believe). It creates the catastrophic scenario through which civilizations must become advanced to escape the impending death of their sun and planet. This paradigm is the survival of the fittest, which is erroneously attributed to natural selection and evolution. I do not see anything truly natural about survival mode.

Fractals

When we view the origin of life as a star or compact field that recycles itself via creation, it is true that a pattern emerges, but that pattern is a fractal. Theoretically, a fractal is an infinite pattern that replicates itself at increasingly smaller scales. Every time a mathematical equation produces a self-similar pattern, the creation is fed back into the equation. Realistically, though, fractals in our universe are not infinite. As the branching extensions of trees and seashell spirals exemplify, the extensions are dependent upon the original capacity of their self-sustaining structures.

Spiritual texts herald the "divine and sacred geometry" of the fractal because our Earth is patterned with it. The tree's sturdy trunk connects root and branch systems that grow and multiply, and the leaves show the smallest fractal pattern in their veins. The leaves die first, then the branches and roots wither, and lastly, the staff falls over dead. The exponential sequence of growth for this tree and all other life forms that die is the Fibonacci sequence.

Figure 1 shows the Fibonacci sequence up to the number 144, and it continues onward. In the first two steps, it starts at zero and naturally adds one, but each following step adds only the last two digits, thereby consuming or eliminating the entities before them. Next to the Fibonacci sequence is the Krysthal sequence that grows with every successive number.[141]

Figure 1. Fibonacci versus Krysthal Sequences

FIBONACCI	KRYSTHAL
0 1	0 1
0 1 1	0 1 1
0 1 1 2	0 1 1 2
0 1 1 2 3	0 1 1 2 4
0 1 1 2 3 5	0 1 1 2 4 8
0 1 1 2 3 5 8	0 1 1 2 4 8 16
0 1 1 2 3 5 8 13	0 1 1 2 4 8 16 32
0 1 1 2 3 5 8 13 21	0 1 1 2 4 8 16 32 64
0 1 1 2 3 5 8 13 21 34	0 1 1 2 4 8 16 32 64 128
0 1 1 2 3 5 8 13 21 34 55	0 1 1 2 4 8 16 32 64 128 256
0 1 1 2 3 5 8 13 21 34 55 89	0 1 1 2 4 8 16 32 64 128 256 512
0 1 1 2 3 5 8 13 21 34 55 89 144	0 1 1 2 4 8 16 32 64 128 256 512 1024

Sequences can provide baselines for creational expansion, especially when a cell replicates, but they also provide comparative ratios. In Figure 1's Fibonacci sequence, when the last nu mber is divided by the second to the last number in each line, the ratio becomes slightly smaller until it approaches 1.618. This number is the golden ratio, otherwise known as phi, and it starts at number 55 in the sequence. The golden ratio entails no more actual growth; when approaching the next number in the sequence, 89, it becomes a finite copy. Material built with Fibonacci mathematics can only recycle its energy in constricted "expansion" until it burns out and totally dies. In other words, the creation will turn into dust.

In this book's first edition, I showed geometric representations of Fibonacci and "Krystal" spirals based on how the collaborative Melchizedek Cloister Emerald Order (MCEO) and Guardian Alliance (GA) entity groups compare them, which I will show again for reference in Figure 2 below. I later realized that the spirals are not a direct comparison because the Fibonacci and kathara grids are dissimilar bases, and only the Fibonacci spiral incorporates its numerical sequence.

The Fibonacci spiral is drawn on a tiled spreadsheet with squares containing increasing numbers of the Fibonacci sequence. This produces a spiral with an off-center base that expands asymmetrically as it connects the corners of each larger square. The MCEO-GA does not provide a similar tiled representation of the Krysthal sequence but instead shows a self-contained diagram of small-to-large grid structures called kathara grids that are connected by their apexes when turning 45 degree angles to the right, thereby forming what they deem as the "Krystal Spiral."[141] Their kathara grid spiral does not represent the Krysthal sequence because it expands by √2 which is 1.414 per kathara grid, not the full multiplier of 2.[141]

Figure 2. Fibonacci and 12-Point Kathara Grid Spirals

FIBONACCI SPIRAL-1   12-POINT KATHARA
                                                  GRID SPIRAL

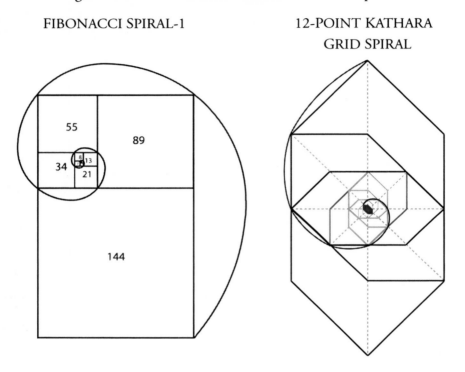

FIBONACCI SPIRAL-2

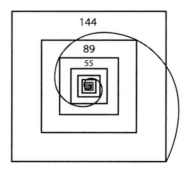

The MCEO-GA say that their spiral connects each kathara grid at its center, but we can see in Figure 2 that its apex connection resembles the Fibonacci spiral in their search for the elusive center. The reason the spiral *appears* to be centrally based is because it is created by the rotation and enlargement of subsequent kathara grids on top of the original one, therefore basing the spiral off of the kathara grid.

The MCEO-GA use a kathara grid constructed with 12 key points, but we can create similar spirals with 15-point and 9-point kathara grids, for example. This logic brought me to create the same arrangement with the Fibonacci spiral's squares by placing successive squares with the Fibonacci sequence over the first one in the middle, as shown in the Fibonacci Spiral-2 diagram. Conceivably, we can create a spiral from any replicated shape with patterned sequences as long as it follows this inside-out pattern. The ease of creating spirals in this manner brings me to question whether the MCEO version of a Krysthal Spiral is really the natural creation that *Krysthal* implies. *Krysthal* is the combination of the frequency tones Ka Ra Ya Sa Ta Ha La from our earliest star-planet called a krystar, which I will later explain in this chapter.[142]

Spirals involve energy circulation that can precede structure, and they can vary in mathematical sequence and construction. Regarding a truly Krysthal Spiral, the All That Is, The Pure Essence (ATI,TPE) explains, "The Krysthal spiral is symmetrical, perfectly sequenced according to a growth pattern." It does not need to connect to the created entity's core because the core fundamentally exists before Krysthal Spiral frequencies. However, the entire energy Spiral does have a central alignment, and it involves the Krysthal sequence of expansion, confirms the ATI,TPE. The Krysthal Spiral is totally symmetrical because its frequency pattern is complete and unbroken. This is unlike our spiral models that siphon energy into a finite structure that appears uneven when cut in half. Perhaps the fully natural Spiral resembles a string filled with energy that expands outward in symmetrical wavelength sequences.

Basing a spiral upon kathara grid structures does not involve the fully Krysthal Spiral of energy circulation. The MCEO-GA perspective of creation provides building blocks toward more knowledge, and they can be valuable when compared to science as we know it; however, something is amiss in their information, so I aim to show why.

The kathara grid is the primary mathematical-geometrical backbone upon which universal and bodily matter are assembled in a patterned order.[143] The MCEO-GA teach that it has 12 key locations of matter that draw from a unified field of energy and expand their energy matter to their respective areas. These "points" represent 12 stars in the galaxy, known as Central Suns, that share their coding via a type of non-explosive "big bang" toward the creation of smaller stars and planetary systems. The Pleiadian entities who I mentioned in chapter 3 hold their Central Sun in the highest regard.[14]

The universe that we can measure is a fractal universe. Its Big Bang entails death as well as life, but life precedes death. If we stretch our minds a little bit, we can deduce that the fractal pattern in our universe mimics another earlier pattern of full integrity. This means that our universal science not only falls short of greater universal mechanics, it also can misrepresent it due to its fragmented nature.

Natural kathara grids contain self-sustaining, ordered patterns of matter and pre-matter that involve the cores of their existence unlike fractal patterns that emerge from the last two Fibonacci creations. The natural grids contain eternal frequency fields of sound and light units called keylons. The MCEO-GA call their conjoined teachings *Keylontic Science* based on these keylons that contain living codes of "geometric-electric and magnetic structures that create the foundations for all form and structure within the dimensional systems" (p. 25).[144] I will call natural, eternal science *Krysthal Science* because it contains many layers of natural creation, including keylons, with the foundation of earlier realms.

The MCEO-GA place the kathara grid and other geometries within the circle or spherical star.[145] If anyone, scientists included, believes that the entire universe was created by a "Central Sun," then black hole mechanics may not be entirely different than the MCEO-GA's Keylontic Science. If black hole mechanics are distortions or variations of Keylontic Science, then could Keylontic Science be a distortion or variation of an earlier science such as Krysthal Science?

Every point on a truly natural kathara grid is filled to its full energetic integrity. What is original cannot die, but if material is pulled off of those original structures to create lesser copies, then these copies can contain increased levels of compaction toward death if they are eventually cut off from their energy source. These distorted versions of the original are creative expansions of fractals, but this form of creativity is one that I can do without because it is not truly creative.

In other words, fractals start at the source because life is the source, but then that stage would not actually be the fractal. The fragmentation of an original material is what starts the snowball "creativity" of the fractal. It continues to increase in subsequent stages until it cannot hold any more form. In contrast, the original material regenerates itself because it has life-giving energy in every layer.

Reincarnation versus Evolution

Fractals help create reincarnation. We do not have the ability to reincarnate hundreds of times in our current body as Hinduism believes because the broken ties of fractal expansion cannot hold our 2.5-dimensional human form after seven times of successive recycling, confirms the ATI,TPE. This helps explain why entities choose to partially and fully possess humans, because if they reincarnate here, they could be subjected to the trap of eventual total death if they get caught up in the reincarnation spiral. Reincarnation is dangerous for them because its broken nature prevents their full remembrance of their prior awareness. When we ponder ideas about evolution to find a way out of the reincarnation trap, unfortunately the prominent perspective put forth by science is based upon fractals.

The conventional scientific view about evolution states that a basic life form "mutates" in growth to become advanced. Its genetic material passes onto countless generations after death. Over that period of time, later replicas with adaptive experiences somehow gained an upgraded genetic template that has learned to master its environment. Within its own life, the organism can also evolve in a small way, such as a bacterium that becomes resistant to an antibiotic.

A non-conventional scientific view about evolution states that the life form is eternal, and it will evolve from its starting point that is very comfortable and aware. This life form never started out as a bacterium or amoeba but was already naturally advanced. If this being is a Human, for example, our entire genome would be fully developed and utilized, so evolution would entail reaching other dimensions. This type of evolution will increasingly gain non-fractal energy matter to eventually enter fully Krysthal systems that would expand our intrinsic genetic capacity toward its full potential. This involves order based upon a natural kathara grid where the lower dimensional person will fulfill that template in a stair-step process of ascension. No part of oneself, especially the body, is lost in death or fragmentation.

Another non-conventional scientific view is most applicable to our current Human condition. We contain a mixture of a fully functioning, eternal template and a partially functioning, finite template. Evolution would progressively heal our finite genetic distortions to increasingly reveal us as highly capable, eternal Humans.

The three-dimensional evolutionary theory assumes that the singularity point that created our universe was an unintelligent mass that expanded as building blocks upon which genetics and consciousness somehow emerged. Although the material would have a finite existence, life still begets life that can expand not only in material but in intelligent awareness. However, since the material has a limited expansion potential, the universal reincarnated fractal will inevitably stunt intelligence and therefore evolution.

I will illustrate this argument by practically applying the belief in reincarnation. When someone is brand-spanking new, and then evil befalls him, that purity is obscured under a layer of confusion why this would happen to him. There is always a first life in reincarnation, but we rarely if ever hear of this time from the religious reference, only the later lives of lessons learned, forgotten, and re-learned. When the world is as it is with all its evils in place, of course the brand new, innocent being does not deserve the powerful acts against it. That in itself creates pain; to say that the person deserved it because of past karma is simply untrue.

The childhood abuse I endured is a case in point. I always intuitively knew that I was a brand new human on Earth—the ATI, TPE additionally confirms this truth—so I was never at fault for those abuses. However, the Hindu and Buddhist perspectives of reincarnation do not allow me to be entirely free of blame. Blame and self-doubt are prevalent religious tactics.

So, the innocent person was hurt, but his religion does not divulge correct information to support his innocence. Instead, this person may be shunned or punished for genuinely reacting to the evil, so he grows up feeling as though he is a bad person. This treatment causes a change of perception and behavior toward that evil, thinking it was acceptable and that he even deserved it. This dumps filth upon the pure self so that the person dies a little inside. He was not valued for being pure, so he now thinks, "What's the point? This world is confusing and unfair, so maybe I should become a part of it somehow." The goodness then dims, and each subsequent life may be filled with more pain because of more punishment. Even if the person is eventually punished correctly, he will not grow much from it because of the original unjust and unrectified blame.

My mind became opened to the reality of reincarnation when reading stories about children who clearly recount their previous lives. Interestingly, some of them were born with a specific pain or blemish, and it directly relates to a serious wound that occurred in the past life. For instance, a boy named Chase remembers being an adult soldier who was shot in his wrist. Since birth, he had severe eczema on that precise spot. Whenever he was troubled, he would scratch his wrist until it bled. He recalls about his past life that he did not want to be in that war. When he faced his emotions about it, his eczema healed within a few days and never returned![146]

When we each were born as a brand new existence, we would equal the second number 1 in the second line of Figure 1's Krysthal sequence. Our wholeness includes a connection to the Source at 0 and a measure of the self-regenerating energy expansion before us as the first number 1. In the infinite nature of life, we can change densities or achieve greater potential in a type of evolution, so our next transformation would make us number 2. The next one after that becomes 4, and so forth. This general model expands with fullness, never taking away from what was there before.

In Figure 1's Fibonacci sequence for reincarnation, we contain the same individual wholeness as the second number 1 in the Krysthal sequence, but when the body dies and reincarnates to number 2, this process will somewhat hinder our connection to Source. The next reincarnation will dig a bit deeper into the organic nature of the body and diminish it as number 3, which is half the potential it could have been as the Krysthal number 4. To exemplify this phenomenon, the myriad of negative and stressful experiences of the previous human life can become imprinted in our energetic structure that returns for the next human experience and stunts our growth. The following few lives grow fractionally, but each successive life grows less than the one before it. The seventh number in the sequence after our birth is 55, which opens the door to the golden ratio.

The fractal model can never approximate a fully aware self, yet the religious view about reincarnation requires us to become a fully enlightened person so that we can become an Ascended Master. How do we evolve if we simply cannot evolve much or at all? This is why the religious model believes in countless reincarnated lives, because really, we are stuck in a prison of recycled energy that can eventually fizzle out. Reincarnation does not allow proper growth of energy in a 2:1 ratio.

A spiritual belief in reincarnation states that we were angelic beings before this life, and we elected to live here for the sake of experience. I find this context for experience to be flaky; I think that no one with high awareness would completely and happily elect to leave their better abode to endure pain that will wound and possibly entrap them. If people had the freedom to reincarnate here, then they did so because of an important mission they felt they had to perform, or they really wanted to help others here. This does not necessarily mean that their prior awareness will override the fragmentation of these bodies that are additionally bombarded with heavily distorted energies on Earth.

The stunted and regressive intelligence wrapped up in reincarnation is a product of the recycled nature of the Big Bang Theory, so its only recourse is to place intelligence within the "genetic" material of what existed originally, which could have been a unique star. However, science's view about evolution deems foundational material as unconscious and unaware, so it is illogical to think that we can attain infinite intelligence if the original infinite material is unintelligent.

Science and religions alike are confused about the combination of life and death in our realm. Science sees the Big Bang as a point of energy that created everything living, but the inevitable death of that creative point nullifies the eternity of life. I do not think that science can deduce eternal life within the current framework of recycled quanta, unless the mysterious point or star of creation is eternal and can pop up again as if it never has died or turned into a black hole. Religion agrees with science about the circle of life and death; however, religion believes that life is embodied by something beyond us, and we must become transformed to reach that state. Both schools of thought leave nearly everything out of our grasp. The New Age spirituality aims to remedy this disempowerment by promoting a story that says we are fundamentally gods who control nearly everything in our lives, but it simultaneously promotes the golden ratio fragmentation thereby proving its fantasy. Our current reality has us live in the gray area. This gray area maintains creative life, so we as abundant beings do have some control over our lives that can be realized the more we learn about natural creation.

Other Dimensions

Scientific theories of the Big Bang and evolution traditionally believe that all matter essentially coexist in a vast three-dimensional space. The factor of time has evolved the "zero point" energetic composition to diverse forces and creations. It is impossible to get back to this zero point because it cannot exist anymore after the Big Bang. The only way we can get back to the state of origin is if we reverse time, or we create an extra dimension to allow for pre-Big Bang conditions to exist simultaneously with our universe. Albert Einstein accounted for both phenomena by saying that we live in four dimensions of spacetime.

The phenomenon of time as its own dimension would be able to capture the various stages of energetic excitement and interactions to allow varying densities to coexist, similar to how temperature or other external forces affect matter.

Einstein's field equations opened up inquiry into the great debate about what came first: the cosmic egg or field. His General Theory of Relativity focused upon a gravitational field that became curved by its interaction with energy matter, implying that there is a greater "force field" upon which the objects gather. Accordingly, an electromagnetic field of radiation spreads out its energy and helps create as it travels.[147] "All physics becomes reduced to geometry," states unified field theory physicists Eckardt and Felker.[148] This supports the existence of a kathara grid universe upon which denser objects are formed.

Elementary particles such as quarks contain a very small amount of matter, which is something with mass and volume. Although individual quarks cannot be measured with current technology, when they combine, they can form heavier protons and neutrons that are the nuclei of atoms.[149] Electrons are the other elementary particles that complete the atom. The electron's mass is approximately $1/_{1836}$ that of the proton.[150]

Einstein's famous equation $E=MC^2$ defines energy as mass multiplied by the speed of light squared. The speed of light is a constant inside and outside of a vacuum, but light does not have measurable mass. Does this mean that light precludes subatomic particles? No, because light comprises tiny photons that exhibit both wave and particle properties, as Einstein's Special Theory of Relativity proved.

Light waves are measurable, and photons are measurable packets of electromagnetic waves called quanta. If the electromagnetic field exhibits more or less measurable frequency, then this affects the mass and therefore density of an object in that three-dimensional space. The converse is also true when a change in the object's mass directly changes the object's energy level.[151] As the density or gradient of spacetime increases with or without the presence of an object, the geometric fabric becomes proportionally curved.[152] In our very dense position in the universe, if most matter is comprised of subatomic material, then a less curved universal fabric could exist to house the supposedly massless photons that would have detectable mass in their respective dimensions. Since we see and experience three-dimensional spaces simultaneously, then Einstein's theory would have to place the immeasurable quantum in the invisible 4th dimensional geometric field where it can potentially be measured there.

Einstein's theory has many computational and theoretical problems, but it sparked the interest of several physicists who spent their lives trying to prove or add to his work. Eventually, quantum physicists combined wavelengths and dimensional fields through exploration of strings.

> String theory posits that the electrons and quarks within an atom are not 0-dimensional objects, but 1-dimensional strings. These strings can oscillate, giving the observed particles their flavor [quantum number], charge, mass and spin. String theories also include objects more general than strings, called branes. The word brane, derived from "membrane", refers to a variety of interrelated objects.[153]

Strings show the wavelength properties of matter, or really, the matter properties of wavelengths. At first, physicists found these strings to be very short and very short-lived when confined within our dimensional view. When more dimensions were mathematically opened up, strings became increasingly stable and were therefore labeled superstrings. Finally, physicists arrived at the M-theory, their Theory of Everything.

M-theory unites five different, healthy theories of strings that consistently account for quantum gravity in an 11-dimensional format. The 11th dimension is the grid or membrane structure from which 10 dimensions can exist, but as that *brane* as it is called in physics, it is a subspace of multidimensional activity that appears to shroud other dimensional spaces.[154] A true theory of everything would involve the entire cosmic space in which all representations of creation can coexist, but due to each space's different formulations, the theory might not be able to provide all realities.

The Oxford English Dictionary defines a dimension in physics as "an expression for a derived physical quantity in terms of fundamental quantities such as mass, length, or time, raised to the appropriate power (acceleration, for example, having the dimension of length×time^{-2})."[155] This definition could seemingly account for a large cosmic dimension with internal compacted subspaces if it could linearly differentiate between qualities with a specified force. The Guardian Alliance supports much of this definition by saying that dimensions are like a string of light particles that appear to move as frequencies but rather just show activity and force at different vectors (quantities with direction and magnitude) of time.[120] Simplified reasoning can assume that all forces and properties of matter exist in the same space, which the GA fundamentally believes, but vectors and dimensional measures recognize different locations in space from one point to the next. The reality of points existing in separate measurable spaces means that space can be a subjective term, so this gives caution to how we identify dimensions. I define a dimension as a unique space with a unique frequency or frequency blend where material creation is represented somewhat differently.

M-theory incorporates Einstein's 4th dimension of time. It is common practice for physicists to say that we live in the 4th dimension. The representation of the 4th dimension as the curvature of our 3rd dimensional existence is somewhat similar to the idea of an 11th dimensional brane. Both energetic membranes can affect and hold matter and exist simultaneously.

An explanation by University of Cambridge relativity and cosmology professors equates M-theory to a planet where all string theories exist as floating but stationary islands.[156] We can use this model to interpret the theory's 11 dimensions. Each island can be three-dimensional variations of matter. The 4th dimension can be the watery force beneath the islands, while the underlying planetary field is the 11th dimension as the cohesion. When incorporating the other six dimensions after the supposed one for time, M-theory compacts and curls them up very tightly, which interprets dimensions as unique strings or forces arranged in a way that contribute to the densities of the water and islands. When arriving at the 11th dimension, the professors state that the membrane "would look like a string when we curl the 11th dimension into a small circle," comprising a compacted nature of excited energy that is somehow able to fully carry the 10 dimensions.[156] Instead of being compacted dimensions, perhaps they are other fields of energy matter as layers of the Earth in this model, and the brane is just another dimensional field but with multidimensional properties.

The premise of M-theory states that the fundamental components of reality are strings of the Planck length that vibrate at resonant frequencies. Every string has a unique resonance, otherwise known as a harmonic. Different harmonics determine different fundamental forces.

The Planck length is equal to 1.616252×10^{-35} meters. This is almost identical to the golden ratio value of 1.618 but on a much smaller scale. The M-theory is just another theory of recycled and finite energy!

Einstein applied the Planck scale to quantum mechanics. In his day and throughout the 20th century, the Planck scale has defined the smallest measurable quantity in our known universe. According to the Swinburne University of Technology:

> The Planck length, and associated Planck time, defines the scale at which the currently accepted theory of gravity fails. On this scale, the entire geometry of spacetime as predicted by general relativity breaks down. The main reason for this breakdown is that the Planck scale is smaller than the quantum wavelength of the Universe as a whole.[157]

In the year 2012 A.D., physicists used technology called the Large Hadron Collider (LHC) to smash atoms at approximately the speed of light to find the supposed God particle called the Higgs Boson. As of May 2013, they gathered enough data from the LHC to determine that they found a Higgs boson; however, research is inconclusive as to whether it is the fundamental boson under the Standard Model of particle physics.[158]

Bosons are elementary particles that create force, while fermions are elementary particles that create matter. The Higgs boson is derived from the universal Higgs field that also gives mass to electrons, elementary quarks, and some other bosons.[159] The LHC experiments' objective is to prove that cosmic creation started with a field before a particle, but somehow that field exists within that particle. Unfortunately, when applying this theory to the Standard Model of particle physics, the gravitational force and potential field correlation do not fit into it. The Planck constant is built into the Standard Model, but Planck's model involves gravity and cannot be subjected to extremely high frequencies.[160]

Physicists are open to the possibility of discovering a new physics if the Standard Model Higgs boson is found to have less mass and higher frequency than the Planck scale allows. This new physics could merely involve particles in the electroweak scale that have less mass than the Planck scale and can exist outside of gravity, or it could be a really new physics that can effectively explain the background of dark matter and the massless gauge boson, the photon. Gravity is the most difficult force to understand; for instance, the Earth's gravity does not override the weak pull from a magnet to a paper clip. Opening up scientific possibility toward new mathematical scales such as the Krysthal scale, which allows other dimensional "branes" like ours instead of only tightly coiled spaces based on fractal decay, would involve not only innovation but intuition toward non-death science.

Science has thus far produced "laws" based upon what we can observe and measure, often in controlled experiments riddled with destruction and isolation. Experiments approximate a tiny vacuum state to create a model toward compactification of dimensions and matter. Determining an accurate picture of the greater universe cannot result from the Planck or golden ratio model because the greater universe just may be larger and more life-giving than our experiential view.

The original string theory of the late 1960s predicted 26 dimensions because it was based upon bosonic particles that are classified by their integer spin.[161] Although the bosonic string theory was dismissed due to its unstable dimensions, this theory introduced the tachyon, a subatomic particle that moves faster than light. According to quantum field theory, particles must be massless to travel at the speed of light. This would place the tachyon in the "imaginary mass" realm where it would be negatively numbered, non-local, and impossible to measure. Scientific measurements look for the rate of decay, so at this "imaginary" stage of energy, I think it is great that the tachyon is not measured that way.

Accordingly, strings called "light strings" would be massless at the speed of light. "In a sense it becomes a generalization of a ray of light, a ray that can vibrate and spin," states physicist F. David Peat (p. 58).[161] The massless string can act similar to a particle with mass. This means that the light string can create the particles that are carried upon its wavelength, or subatomic particles like photons line up on its electromagnetic field.

Peat writes in *Superstrings and the Search for the Theory of Everything*:

> In singing, the higher you go up the scale, the more energy you need to produce the notes. In an analogous way, the quantum notes of the string—its quantized vibrations and rotations—are steps in a ladder of energy (p. 58).[161]

Matter becomes less dense and filled with more energy as it increasingly enters lighter and higher realms.

The music scale is an excellent analogy to extrapolate vibratory and spinning points of a dimensional superstring to multiple dimensions. It can also illustrate the figurative spiral staircase made of older energy components that allow spinning objects to exist within resonant dimensions as steps. This structure, the Krysthal Spiral, can conceivably extend back to a vibratory level that is closer to the ATI,TPE than our galactic position.

Have you noticed a constant humming in your ear in the dead of night? This is not to be confused with tinnitus; it is the environmental and internal energies with which we interact. In the following excerpt, composer Susan Alexanjer explores the vibrations made by our own bodies. Our DNA is a double helix type of superstring template that receives and transmits electricity.

I proposed that we try to measure the actual molecular vibrations of the bases that make up all of DNA as we know it, as it appears in all life forms. To my astonishment, Dr. Deamer [cell biologist] explained that the vibrations were easily measurable, using an infrared spectrophotometer. By exposing each base to infrared light and measuring which wavelengths each base absorbs, it is possible to identify a unique array of approximately 15 different wavelengths for each base. Since each base has a slightly different atomic structure, it will vibrate in a unique manner. As the atoms of carbon, hydrogen, nitrogen and oxygen receive the light, they absorb some of it, depending on their vibrational frequencies, and those absorbances can be measured, plotted on a graph, and read as numbers. These numbers, in turn, represent a wave-length "scale" on the light spectrum, but very fast, very high. If we see those numbers in relationship to each other, in other words, as ratios, then we can translate them into the sonic spectrum and have a corresponding set of ratios in sound. This is exactly how an ordinary scale works on any musical instrument. The sound of the scale depends on the relationship of adjacent tones to one another.

The question naturally arises at this point: If the ratios are actually those of light vibrations, how can they become sound?...

An important key to understanding how we can actually hear high, fast, light vibrations is the Law of the Octave. This law states that any vibration of sound (or light) can be doubled or halved, and the same pitch (or light frequency) will result, but what changes is the octave of the sound (or radiation). A simple example: Orchestras tune to the concert pitch A, which is established at a frequency of 440 hertz (cycles per second).

Playing the same note at 220 or 880 hertz results in a tone we immediately recognize as an "A," but it sounds either an octave lower or higher than the concert A as such. By taking a very rapid vibration of light and halving it many times (about 35 iterations), we can bring this vibration into the range of hearing.[162]

Astrophysicists measure radio waves of light from point sources called quasi-stellar radio sources—which are quasars as the abbreviation—that spread out their emissions.[163] I propose there are other vibrations that move faster than science can comprehend and measure that interact with our fractal universe. Both of these classes of vibrations affect our DNA although we only hear certain lower octaves. We may conceivably house all universal vibrations within us and concurrently be affected by countless things outside of us. The above quotation suggests that 15 fundamental wavelengths are measurable in our bodies. Each fundamental wavelength could be representative of a unique, bigger dimension. Before I address these dimensions beyond M-theory, I will explore antimatter and parallel dimension potential.

There is antimatter within our galaxy, but it generally exists separately to matter or else both will annihilate. If creation follows a universal blueprint, and matter is the dominant material in our galactic experience, then this antimatter must exist as a lesser parameter, not necessarily becoming another dimension. Degrees of freedom provide coordinates for an independent physical parameter. "The idea is that degrees of freedom like the electric charge of an electron will then arise simply as motion in the extra compact directions," state the University of Cambridge professors, although other dimensions are not necessarily compacted.[156]

An antiparticle contains the same mass as its particle twin, but its charge and other quantum properties are opposite. In 1995, antihydrogen was isolated at the European Organization for Nuclear Research (CERN) in Geneva, the location that houses the LHC accelerator;[164] however, it could not be examined and manipulated until about 15 years later when it was trapped in a very cold state. Initial measurements showed that antihydrogen is very similar to hydrogen. Physicist Mike Hayden declares, "It looks like an ordinary hydrogen atom. If there's a difference, everyone's betting it's going to be subtle."[165]

In general, physicists believe the following about antimatter creation from the Big Bang:

As the universe expanded and cooled, almost every matter particle collided with an antimatter particle, and the two turned into two photons—gamma ray particles—in a process called annihilation, the opposite of pair production. But roughly a billionth of the matter particles survived, and it is those particles that now make the galaxies, stars, planets, and all living things on Earth, including our own.[166]

According to the Standard Model of particle physics, matter and antimatter were created in equal amounts at the Big Bang. In 2010, a smaller version of the LHC, called the Tevatron, gave eight years of data showing that there was a one percent difference between the amount of matter and antimatter produced in the accelerator experiments, favoring matter.[167]

LHC physicists state that stable antimatter no longer exists in our discernible universe. Matter edged its asymmetrical counterpart out of creation after the Big Bang, but it is unknown how this happened.[168] If antimatter particles did survive, then they could exist in another type of space somewhat near their asymmetrical counterparts. This space might not be easily defined or confined. This is feasible if the Big Bang process was modeled on an earlier, less violent creational pattern, so the antiparticles could have survived, being merely transported to a nearby dimension.

Rarely, a particle and its antiparticle can coexist when a force intervenes to create a pair bond that maintains quantum balance between the two. A physics forum member explains:

> Incidentally, the easiest way to induce pair production is to shoot a sufficiently high energy photon (in the gamma frequency range) very close to a heavy atomic nucleus. As the gamma interacts with the dense electromagnetic field of the nucleus it will excite the electron field to produce an electron and a positron. The frequency of the gamma photon has to be high enough to provide the energy to create the rest mass of both particles (511 keV each) and to have enough left over to give them sufficient kinetic energy to escape their electromagnetic attraction. [169]

This description essentially deconstructs an intact nucleus to create an antiparticle, giving weight to my theory that these antiparticles—produced within a fractalized particle universe—are not the same that arise in Krysthal systems. The physics enthusiast continues to explain what happens when an electron and positron meet:

> An electron wave & a positron wave are perfectly anti-symmetrical, so when they meet, they neutralize each other, "spilling" their energy content into the electromagnetic field.

The two waves cancel each other out, each tweak & twist in the electron field being canceled out by its opposite partner.

Due to spin conservation, there are actually two (main) possibilities here: if the electron & positron have parallel spin, 3 (or a higher odd number) of photons will be emitted. If the electron & positron have antiparallel spins, then 2 (or a higher even number) of photons will be emitted. The reactions with fewer emitted photons are much more likely to occur; higher numbers are only rarely seen, unless huge energy levels are involved.[169]

The term *annihilation* implies complete destruction, but technically the electron and positron pair can release their energies toward another creation. If their energies continually recycle into new structures in our galaxy, their potential for creation will eventually diminish into unstructured subatomic particles—spacedust.

An electromagnetic field requires an electric field that is created by differences in voltage, and a magnetic field that is created by the flowing electric current.[170] In theoretical physics, when the particle accelerator model of force is not applied to the electromagnetic field, there exists a more basic energy called the scalar wave. A team of skeptical research scientists explains the following:

> Scalar electromagnetics (also known as scalar energy) is the background quantum mechanical fluctuations and associated zero-point energies (in contrast to "vector energies" which sums to zero).
>
> Scalar waves are hypothetical waves, which differ from the conventional electromagnetic transverse waves by one oscillation level parallel to the direction of propagation, they thus have characteristics of longitudinal waves....
>
> Scalar field theory suggests that scalar energy can move through space much like an electromagnetic wave. However, the operating principles are different. The regular expansion and contraction of a scalar bubble/void is like rythmicly [sic] splashing water on a pond. It sends out ripples through the general scalar field that can subtly affect the size and strength of distant scalar bubbles/voids.[171]

Experiments attempting to create a basic scalar communications antenna mimic the particle and antiparticle annihilation model by canceling out as much of each other's magnetic field as possible. The objective of the antenna is to create powerful repulsion or attraction between the two magnetic fields, but normal electromagnetic theory states that it will be useless without an electromagnetic field and will only heat up.[171] Perhaps that is what scalar mechanics naturally do—produce less forceful and less dense creations according to their particular construction, not according to our heavy-handed deconstruction. Our scientists place tachyons in scalar fields, but the MCEO says they are fractal versions of earlier superluminal partiki takeyons that operate somewhat differently in Krysthal scalar fields.[172,173]

The GA describes pre-matter at the pre-galaxy, cosmic level of the Yunasai: "*Partiki are the smallest units of energy in the cosmos* (one could find 800 billion billion Partiki units in an average 3-dimensional photon)" (p. 453).[120] Partiki (PKI) units are omni-polar units that contain all polarities, states the ATI,TPE. They group into strings to form the kathara grid, the backbone of subsequent scalar and electromagnetic grids.[143,174] According to the MCEO-GA and ATI,TPE, scalar waves appear to move from one place to another, but they are "standing" points of light strung together in sequences within the fabric of universal morphogenetic (form-holding) fields.[175]

PKI manufacture "two intrinsic sub-units of crystalline morphogenetic substance [partikA and particum] that serve as blueprints for rhythms of pulsation through which particles and anti-particles manifest" (p. 453).[120] Particum (PCM) constitutes matter, and partikA (PKA) constitutes natural antimatter that vibrates faster than PCM. (Note: The MCEO-GA capitalize vowels to emphasize the long sound.) PCM and PKA clusters are called keylons, which are the basis of Keylontic and Krysthal Science in dimensional creation. Keylons follow mathematical laws to form specific geometric patterns as crystalline matrices of electromagnetic energy.[143,174]

The process of vibration between similar partiki units is called partiki phasing, where it never annihilates the polarities but continually circulates their energies according to different vibratory speeds in a process of gentle fission and fusion. The PKI unit expands to create electricity of the PKA, which the PCM pulls in with magnetism in a collaborative merkaba vehicle, which I explain shortly. The PKI draws the light field merkaba into the sound field by fusion, then it repeats the process nearly simultaneously and infinitesimally.[143,174]

Krysthal Spirals have taken PKA and PCM matter in different directions by carrying the kathara grid template to new spaces for their creation. The Milky Way kathara grid is one such galaxy that was created with a PCM template, meaning that PKA antimatter exists out of our view in an entirely separate galactic kathara grid. The electromagnetic antimatter based on the PKA unit is different than the antimatter within our PCM-based universe.

The MCEO-GA, Yunasai, and ATI,TPE confirm that the Milky Way has an antimatter or parallel 3rd dimension as well as a whole parallel kathara grid. Their degrees of freedom are angular rotations, particle spins, and slightly different forces that are positioned out of our dimensional experience and view but can exist in proximity.

Although we cannot see any antimatter, we can see higher dimensions in our Milky Way because they are made of similar PCM units to which we are fundamentally keyed. What we see as stars can be planets to the inhabitants of those dimensions. Angelic entities often say that they live on our stars, but when they visit us in our dimension, their lighter density looks either invisible to us or like forms of light.

Since this book's first edition, I have probed more deeply into the geometries of Keylontic and Krysthal sciences. The MCEO-GA have stated that our complete time matrix contains 15 dimensions, thereby supporting 15 fundamental sound tones within us; however, they have only revealed planetary locations within a 12-dimensional kathara grid formation, causing some confusion as to what constitutes a time matrix. The MCEO-GA, Yunasai, and ATI,TPE agree that the galactic structure is built with the kathara grid formation, but the MCEO-GA differ in their particular presentation of the dimensional grid.

Each dimension carries a dominant wavelength of energy, and dimensions naturally group in threes. The three-dimensional unit comprises one density or harmonic universe (HU) of over-laid reality fields of matter. We live in HU-1, which currently has the most expanded reality field of matter.

In HU-1, the Earth and its organic inhabitants are predominantly made of carbon. The carbon atom has six electrons with four of them in its outer energy shell.

HU-2 is a faster harmonic oscillation of light in dimensions 4, 5, and 6 where everything is carbon-silicon based.[175] The silicon atom has 14 electrons with four of them in its outer energy shell. When multiple carbon or silicon atoms come together, the outer four electrons called valence electrons can bond to form a crystal.[176] As crystalline carbon-silicon, the HU-2 level of the kathara grid will comprise a slightly different elemental configuration in order to absorb and produce more light for the increased electrons.

Compared to HU-2, the HU-1 particle pulsation of time is faster, and the vibration of matter is slower. Time's particular pulsation rhythm is not an entirely separate dimension because it is interwoven into the multidimensional aspects of the HU. The HU is called a universe because its density is a complete universe within the spacetime of three dimensions! Since HU-2 has its own celestial and planetary bodies, and they originated before the Earth in the stair-step creation model down toward HU-1, it is probable that an HU-2 counterpart to the Earth exists and has imparted some of its energy to Earth and its inhabitants. According to the MCEO-GA, Yunasai, and ATI,TPE, this counterpart to Earth is called Tara.

The silicon-based HU-3 contains a less dense version of Tara known as Gaia.

The names Tara and Gaia are well-known. Tara is a Hindu goddess, and she is also a female Buddha.[177] When combined with the Latin word Terra for Earth or land, New Age religions say "Mother Earth." New Age believers additionally call our Earth Gaia, or they equate the "spiritual" level of Gaia to our Earth. Gaia was the Earth goddess of Greek mythology.[178] Although equating the Earth to a woman may appear to revere the woman for her life-giving, reproductive ability, this still locks women into the sexually reproductive role. In addition, these supposedly progressive belief systems continue to put men above women in their characterization of Father Heaven over Mother Earth. Male or female sexual identities do not represent any planet, star, or "heavenly" space; these are limited perceptions and distortions to their true natures.

HU-4 generally houses the "avatar" level of hydroplasmic liquid light.[144] In Hindu, Buddhist, and related spiritual beliefs, an avatar incorrectly represents an Ascended Master. These religions believe that Ascended Masters have died and entered the spirit level that actually exists in HU-1 or HU-2; then, they reincarnate back on Earth with full awareness. This presumes that HU-2 or any of our HUs gives us omniscience, which is far from reality.

As Figure 3 illustrates, the Milky Way kathara grid ends at the 11th dimension. Essentially, M-theory supports Milky Way creation with 11 dimensions and some compaction. The proper HU-4 counterpart to Earth is not popularly known because this harmonic universe is severely compromised in the Milky Way galaxy. The ATI,TPE reveals that both 10th and 11th dimensions are compacted with an HU-3 silicon base, which gives our galaxy five dimensions of silicon material. Chapter 7's "Creation of the...Galaxies" explains the general history of how this has happened. Figure 3 shows that the Milky Way 11th dimension is energetically connected to a less distorted kathara grid's 14th dimension so that we can receive unobstructed energy from an earlier realm called an Ecka.

I am now revealing with the ATI,TPE's assistance that the MCEO-GA's description of HU-5 is erroneous due to their shortened 12-dimensional kathara grid. Their 12-point kathara grid is produced within a circle in such a way to fill in much of the space (about half) while providing perfectly reproducible angles when replicated for a spiral, as shown in Figure 2. This presentation of creation requires an HU-5 to exist in an adjoining kathara grid, which is what the MCEO-GA assert; however, they claim that the 13th dimension exists at the top of the grid as though it carries more powerful frequency than dimensions 14 and 15.

HU-5 actually exists as the top harmonic universe in a 15-dimensional kathara grid with dimension 15 logically at the apex. The 15-point kathara grid is the Krysthal kathara grid. Contrary to what the MCEO-GA teach, HU-5 does not contain primal light fields, nor does it contain Breneau Orders or Rishi entities.[144] I have not gained an answer about what type of entities exist in HU-5 because they prefer to be unknown for security reasons. The 15th dimension contains the fastest dimensional frequency from where particle spin and vibration progressively slow into the lower dimensions. All 15 dimensions of a galactic kathara grid constitute one time matrix.

The ATI,TPE states that Breneau Order or Rishi entities exist in the HU-1 of an earlier domain of creation called the Ecka. Rishi are ante-matter constructs of thermoplasmic radiation, states the GA.[144] The Ecka contains a 15-dimensional kathara grid foundation like the galactic kathara grid but with less dense material. The galactic domain is called the Veca.

Death-based science and technology can siphon natural galaxy material to create other galaxies of lesser structural integrity, as Figure 3 shows in relation to the Milky Way. Distortions can be prevalent in the Veca domain, but they can also exist in the Ecka, as chapter 7 elucidates.

Figure 3 compares the natural Krysthal kathara grid with three progressively fragmented and distorted copies. Background, non-dimensionalized fields are implied as fundamental components but not shown in the Veca. Each diagram is a basic approximation of kathara grid relationships and sizes. Although the diagrams show vertical lines, they are actually lateral by an angular pathway, states the ATI,TPE. Additionally, the energetic bridge-like formations extend between grids to maintain Krysthal connection.

The 15th dimensional top of the Krysthal galaxy's kathara grid naturally connects to the 1st dimension of the earlier Ecka realm, and it does so with an arc-like energetic bridge that curves to the right, states the ATI,TPE. The Ecka has extended this connection to Galaxy-2's 15th dimension. The Krysthal and Galaxy-2 galactic cores connect to the galactic core of the Ecka within each grid's 8th dimension. Technically, our kathara grid core is called the meta-galactic core because it "holds the morphogenetic field for the entire 15-dimensional universe," states the GA (p. 470-471).[120] The core connection of successive kathara grid formations is integral to eternal energy flow. The Milky Way meta-galactic core has become compromised, so our galaxy needs the connection to Galaxy-2 in order to receive the complete 15 dimensional frequencies.

Beyond the Veca kathara grids start the Ecka's HU-1 dimensions that can be perceived as arc-like waves from our position, as shown in Figure 3. The MCEO-GA refer to them as three types of non-dimensionalized "primal"

Figure 3. Natural and Distorted Galactic Kathara Grids

KRYSTHAL AND GALAXY-2
GALAXIES

11 DIMENSIONAL
MILKY WAY

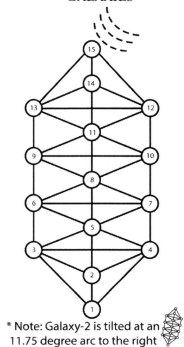

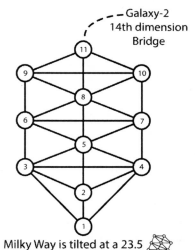

Galaxy-2
14th dimension
Bridge

* Note: Galaxy-2 is tilted at an
11.75 degree arc to the right

Milky Way is tilted at a 23.5
degree arc to the right

PHANTOM MILKY WAY GALAXY
Tree of Artificial Life

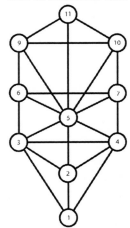

Phantom Milky Way is tilted at a
25 degree arc to the right.
* The Tree of Artificial Life tilt
varies per galaxy it distorts.

sound fields, otherwise known as the Energy Matrix or Khundaray, but they actually adhere to Ecka dimensions 4, 5, and 6 and are not truly primal. The Yanas entities exist within the Ecka HU-1 and HU-2; collectively, they are called Eieyani. From our Earthly perspective, Eieyani look like "geometric shapes made of living light," states the GA (p. 159).[144]

The MCEO-GA fit their creational science into neatly packaged spheres. Their version of a Veca encapsulates within a sphere four kathara grids—a particle pair that combines 15 dimensions and the Energy Matrix, and an antiparticle pair of the same formula—where each 12-point grid connects at a 90 degree angle. They say that each corresponding Ecka sphere produces three Veca spheres to keep with their "divine" number 12. Prior to the Ecka, another sphere encapsulates the Ecka and Vecas, and this spherical pattern supposedly leads to the beginning of creation. The MCEO-GA condense or omit some levels because they teach creation based on a star in what can be perceived as star-worship.

I asked the ATI,TPE how many galactic kathara grids are in our natural Veca realm, excluding distorted copies. It replies that our Krysthal Veca is a 15-galaxy system that was created by the Ecka's material expansion process. Fourteen galaxies come in particle and antiparticle pairs while one 15-dimensional grid is antiparticle without a parallel. Although this is our domain's pattern, it is not necessarily the pattern for another Veca. The ATI,TPE also states that there is "no particular angle" at which kathara grid pairs and the odd remainder must relate to each other.

Although MCEO-GA base-12 mathematics has its flaws, it carries more structural integrity than base-10 mathematics. The last kathara grid representation in Figure 3, the Tree of Artificial Life, is the most distorted one, yet it is heralded in New Age and Jewish Kabbalah "sacred science" teachings as their Tree of Life.

The Tree of Artificial Life removes the 12th and 8th dimensional centers, essentially creating a 10-dimensional template while preserving the 11th dimension, just barely. It cuts off all incoming natural energy to become a fully finite grid, especially at the meta-galactic core's form-holding field. Eradicating our form is the ultimate aim of the Fibonacci-based 144 fractal stage, as chapter 8 explains.

The ATI,TPE consistently confirms that matter was initially pulled off key locations in our Krysthal galaxy by interfering entities to eventually create the Milky Way and beyond. The Milky Way is an incomplete galaxy in a precarious position teetering between semi-phantom and phantom status.

The Tree of Artificial Life kathara grid starts the implosion phase. Unfortunately, parts of the Milky Way are now at that stage, but most are varying measures of phantom.

When something has a phantom status, its portion of the kathara grid still has a link to the original grid by means of intermediate connections that keep it alive. Similar to the Fibonacci sequence's increasingly detached stages from their source, chapters 7 and 8 explain several stages of transformation from natural matter to the supernova process. Semi-phantom and phantom matter are vampiric, meaning that entities must assimilate energy quanta from other systems to artificially extend their lives as immortal but non-eternal beings; however, they have the potential to regain their original blueprint. When fully phantom matter is compromised and compacted past the point of repair, any remaining connection to eternal energy is severed, and implosion to space dust is inevitable.

What concerns us from our position in the Milky Way is how we can attempt to leave our density and become Veca "ascended masters." We can ascend up 15 dimensions until we reach the Ecka, and we can proceed from there as we choose.

Ascension is generally taught as a vertical process, but it is really an inward process. In fact, the ATI,TPE rejects the "vertical" description. Natural ascension involves a half dimensional step downward to enter into the physical core or stargate of the planet to then laterally by an angular pathway emerge at least one full dimension higher. Ascension requires the DNA and bodily components to fold into themselves and then laterally, minimally implode in order to reconfigure or transfigure to a lighter density. When the ascension process is natural, it transfigures the body with increased Krysthal quanta. The ATI,TPE states, "The transfigured 'body' goes through the expulsion process, laterally stepping out the dimensions to stargate-12 through the Galaxy-2 bridge and then to the Ecka."

The order of natural partiki- and/or plasma-based domains that extend past (and before) the Ecka are as follows: Eckasha, Eckasha-A, Eckasha-I,[179] Eckasha-Aah, Eckasha-Ah, and A (pronounced with a long Ā), reveals the ATI,TPE. The Eckasha-A domain started the 15-dimensional kathara grid formation, and the much earlier Eckasha-Ah domain started the Krysthal sequence for creational expansion, states the ATI,TPE. An Eckasha level contains varying stages of pre-partiki, etheric essence in the early domains to a more silicate structure in the later domains.

Initially, the GA only taught about levels up to the Yunasai because it believed that the singular Yunasum partiki unit is the "Central Point of All Union," even calling it "God" and "God Source."[144] MCEO-GA members have perceived the Yunasum as their point of creational reference because subsequent creations contain its light-body structure. However, the Yunasum actually contains 20,736 partiki units; earlier partiki units created the Yunasum, and earlier plasmic units preceded the partiki.[180] Partiki units act as building blocks, and their grouping can potentially create a small star, not a domain.

The Yunasai and ATI,TPE state that the Yunasai as a group of Yunasum partiki units comprise small planets in a level throughout Eckasha-Aah domains. There is a significant process of ascension or partiki phasing involving the Veca called a Starfire that circulates and regenerates energies up to what the MCEO call the Edonic "Middle Domain" worlds (in chapters 8 and 10).[180] These Edonic worlds exist in a level just below the Yunasai, state the Yunasai and ATI,TPE. Because the Yunasai are just beyond the Starfire ascension process, I deduce that many MCEO-GA entities consider them as a collective "God" beyond the creational process. I think that if they would communicate with the Yunasai directly as my mother has done, they would discover that the Yunasai do not consider themselves to be a God or Source of all creation. Or, perhaps members of the MCEO-GA did communicate with some Yunasai, and they received a response that they fit into a narrow view.

The ATI,TPE helps to elaborate: "There is more beyond the Yunasai. The GA and Yunasai do not have full knowledge. What is only known by them is revealed." Nearly a decade after Ashayana Deane presented the GA's creational perspective that began with the Yunasai, a more expanded view has opened up to her to show that there are indeed earlier levels before them.

In the partiki light-body domains, entities can travel and communicate naturally or expeditiously with the use of merkaba constructs or vehicles. There are many different sizes of merkaba fields in our body as well as essentially everywhere in existence, where bigger ones can surround smaller ones. Our bodily process of ascension relies upon the merkaba vehicle that is a temporary transport of merkaba fields. Merkaba vehicles look like orbs of light.[181]

The big merkaba fields in the Milky Way are created by interaction between the 15 galactic stargates (also known as Central Suns) and time. Stargates exist on a lateral axis, whereas the time passages or portals are more horizontal and diagonal. This means that stargates are interdimensional openings that naturally allow energy circulation and travel throughout the entire galaxy while portals direct the energies within the same harmonic universe. When they open up at the same time, a Seed Crystal Seal is unlocked for the dimensional transmutation.

The Guardian Alliance explains:

> Star Gates and Time Portals exist as Black and White Hole Pairs that are connected at the center point by a scalar-wave frequency Seed Crystal Seal. When the center Seed Crystal Seal releases[,] the Star Gate activates and the pair of counter-rotating electromagnetic spirals merge to form an interconnected Merkaba

Field, which allows the instantaneous passage between various spacetime coordinates through shift of atomic Angular Rotation of Particle Spin (p. 506).[120]

Stargates are interdimensional openings that naturally allow energy circulation and travel throughout the entire galaxy, while portals direct the energies within the same harmonic universe. The top electric spiral of the merkaba spins clockwise (CW) while the bottom magnetic spiral spins counter-clockwise (CCW). When the merkaba spiral sets are energetically charged, this creates one merkaba field. The merkaba field construct looks like a three-dimensional star tetrahedron where the magnetic spiral is inverted under and mostly through the upright electrical spiral, both forming pyramids that effectively circulate energy together.[120] The Star of David is the distorted 2-dimensional construct.

The MCEO explains:

> "Twisted" Merkaba Vortex mechanics implement unnatural distortions of the spin-speed and spin-direction of Merkabic Vortex sets, to create a particle/anti-particle harness field within which energy and atoms can be trapped. Once trapped within the inorganic Merkaba Field, the harnessed energy quanta can then artificially sustain a prolonged longevity of form, and achieve limited local interdimensional transport, as long as the inorganic Merkaba Harness around it can "feed"/drain energy from organically living energy fields.[182]

There is competing information about merkaba mechanics given by a lower-level Melchizedek-channeled entity group to a man named Drunvalo Melchizedek who is popular in the New Age movement and who supports the Tree of Artificial Life grid. He uses the reversed spin ratio of 34:21 that is 34 times CCW over 21 times CW, and he states that the vehicle around our bodies forms a disk of 55 feet in diameter.[183] When we refer back to Figure 1, we can easily see that these numbers represent the Fibonacci approximation toward the golden ratio. Chapter 8's "2012" section explains the intended 55.5 stage that expedites distorted creation after the number 55.

The natural merkaba spin is CW electrical over CCW magnetic. The spin has a speed, and it is a numerical expression. The MCEO entity group and ATI,TPE state that the organic 3rd dimensional merkaba has the spin-speed ratio of 33⅓ CW electrical over 11⅔ CCW magnetic, meaning that this merkaba is in the Krysthal galaxy.[184] The ATI,TPE reveals that the Earth in its most natural Milky Way composition (called Amenti Earth or now Median

Earth, in chapter 8) has the merkaba ratio of 32⅓ CW electrical over 10⅔ CCW magnetic, just less than its Krysthal potential.

According to the GA, "All Suns have sets of black and white holes at their core; they operate as portals through which energy can pass through dimensional fields" (p. 5).[120] The unnatural black holes that I refer to in this chapter are created by the fractal "death" science that pulls matter from an original object and recycles it until it cannot hold any more form. Physicists are increasingly agreeing that black holes act as wormholes. Wormholes spiral or bridge energy between dimensions and other universes of matter or antimatter. In a Krysthal system, there are no supermassive black holes. These are artificially created, which means that our Milky Way has artificial elements to its creation.

As I learned more information that I present in the following two chapters, I asked the ATI,TPE on January 1, 2012 to clarify about our view about the cosmos.

"Since we cannot see any natural Veca from our current view, when we look through the Hubble telescope at the many galaxies, are all of them in our view partially and fully distorted galaxies like the Milky Way?"

The ATI,TPE simply replied "Yes"; however, my question was unclear about the phantom or semi-phantom status. Upon my further probing, the ATI,TPE states that fully phantom galaxies are not visible to us. Fully phantom matter has a different angular rotation of particle spin (ARPS) and construction to our particular semi-phantom matter. Accordingly, our mostly semi-phantom matter is different to lesser semi-phantom matter.

I asked the ATI,TPE, "How have so many galaxies become so distorted away from the natural blueprint?"

"Manipulation by the vast ET groups in creating wormholes; warring factions over grids of worlds and galaxy systems."

I asked, "Have alien entities used false creation physics in every one of those situations? (If not, what?)"

"Yes, they have."

Accordingly, Galaxy-2 and Krysthal galaxies are invisible to humans without extrasensory, interdimensional ability because of different ARPS, composition of matter, and Earth-based distortions, as the ATI,TPE confirms.

The M31 Andromeda galaxy is visible to humans because it is semi-phantom like the Milky Way, and it was created from the same Krysthal galaxy as the Milky Way. M31 Andromeda is positioned approximately 2.2 million light years away from our galaxy, but the gap is slowly diminishing between them. When viewing M31 Andromeda through a high-powered telescope, we can see that it has a supermassive black hole in its center, but unlike the Milky Way, it has another galaxy connected to it.

I asked the ATI,TPE for clarification about our view of M31 Andromeda. "There is a double structure nucleus in Andromeda. Scientists think Andromeda 'ate' another smaller galaxy. Is it rather that another galaxy is the black hole off of Andromeda?"

"The other galaxy is a different semi-phantom galaxy. Andromeda scientists see the semi-phantom, which black-holed from it [M31]," replies the ATI,TPE.

I reveal that fractal mathematics is purposely unnatural. The reality of how many millions of galaxies that are pulled into this science is upsetting to me; it is as though the outer realms are an experiment. However, in our position, we can still connect with the ATI,TPE and other pure levels that can surpass every distortion and continue the process of natural creation.

We do not need to fear at this stage but allow such "mind-blowing" information to slowly settle into our awareness so that we can learn what appropriate measures to take. There is a lot to happily look forward to in our ascension journey because natural realms and entities outnumber everything else.

The Origin and Expansion of Creation

It is not easy to gain precise information about the exact origin of creation because as entities, we can only provide our points of reference within our environmental and personal experiences. Information from a combination of entity groups can approximate the process of creation, but they cannot accurately explain the original essence and its creative process unless that original energy consciousness directly explains itself to them. I and my mother sense in our awareness that we have gained connection to that original energy consciousness. It can communicate directly to us and to all beings in our "inner knowing" when we diligently seek absolute purity. When I ask how it describes itself, it states, "All That Is, The Pure Essence."

Our pure intent connects us to the All That Is, The Pure Essence (ATI,TPE), but our position in an expanded body that is partially comprised of fragmented structures does not make communication with the ATI,TPE entirely easy. Our unconscious or spiritual sense of "knowing" is most clear when we feel naturally and easily connected within our energetic self. Sometimes this knowing can reach further into our subconscious or even conscious state so that we can mentally understand it. However, when putting it into the practice of technical precision, something is lost in translation between the pure state of the ATI,TPE and our complex human composition. This is because the ATI,TPE is truly different to us. It only provides limited technical information; our intuition and intelligence must do the rest.

My intuition has conveyed to me that pure pre-energy has one identity and is a single essence. Throughout my life, I knew that there was something ultimately simple and good somewhere, where complex entities and energies could not be. Upon discovering the ATI,TPE and feeling its simple, good "energy," I continued to search but never found anything before it from both my position and what I could sense of its position. It is a simple essence that is beyond any movement, sound tone, color, or distortion. It just is, and it "feels" completely pure in my sensory awareness. Its title as All That Is, The Pure Essence is just that—a title or description because it does not produce a frequency and tone. It desires to be described as this entire phrase to properly distinguish itself from entity-based interpretations of "All That Is."

As I introduced in chapters 1 and 3, my mother asks the ATI,TPE a question whereby the end result produces an answer in discernible, sparkling letters. These letters are called fire letters, which are keylon light-symbol codes sent through our DNA in electromagnetic waves to produce sequentially arranged words.[144] My mother operates largely in the subconscious state to translate the conscious questions to her "unconscious" inner body template. This pathway uses her delta wave frequency to link her to the first pre-frequency field and then to the ATI,TPE. The ATI,TPE uses that same pathway to convey words that are slowed down so that she can write them down. We also ask it follow-up questions to provide more detail.

I asked the ATI,TPE via her clear connection for explanations to this question, "What is the All That Is, The Pure Essence?"

It explains itself and provides a simple flow chart:

The All That Is, The Pure Essence is the origin of itself, separate and boundless in its own space, nonmovable, and colorless. It is a point of pure conscious essence beyond all created matter, beyond the Void, beyond the separate still nothingness that comes after. It presents itself as having primary knowledge with infinite conscious awareness.

The All That Is, The Pure Essence first expanded Itself, not as desire but as Consciousness, when in a stationary state, by the intense, whelming pre-gaseous, pre-plasmic nature that comprises its pure essence. Its Consciousness intended to burst forth from that whelming state, laying frequency streams as It ventured forward and outward from its place of origin. This act was very simple and magnificent in its display, similar to an instantaneous eruption.

The All That Is, The Pure Essence desires to explore and expand through the separate nothingness, through the endless

Void to impart knowledge of its existence. This desire expands through spaces and between spaces via the bridge of Eia that creates as this desire flows. Anything beyond Eia, which carries the desire of purity and truth of the ATI, The Pure Essence, has the possibility of distortion. The search for ultimate truth and purity enables the ATI, The Pure Essence's desire as the extension for creation to increase the awareness of created beings.

The All That Is, The Pure Essence and its desired, created formations reside side by side. Its desire as transmitted by Eia connects to the core of each part of created matter, including core cells of the human body. The ATI, The Pure Essence's desire permeates everything.

All That Is, The Pure Essence *(Stationary)* → Separate Film→
ATI,TPE's extended pure Consciousness *(Projected intention*→
Separate, still nothingness → Desire *(Desire with slight movement expands and explores measure)* → Void →
Eia *(First pre-field frequency)* → Created Matter *(Vibrational energy)*
starting with the "A" domain

The ATI,TPE exists somewhere else than how we can experience. Since it does not move, it cannot forcibly expand beyond its gentle will. As a conscious essence, it has intent that can expand as desire, flowing outward as a type of pre-pre-field frequency, but this is not any actual field or frequency known by creation because it maintains its own space close to the ATI,TPE. The ATI,TPE remains only itself in all situations because its energetic integrity is always preserved. It is consciousness as the true being state.

The ATI,TPE can be described as the origin and core essence of creation; however, it expresses that it is not a creator, nor does it actually reside within any creation. I asked it to more accurately describe itself, to which it replies:

The All That Is, The Pure Essence's desire to expand and intent to do so leads into the wording of a creator, but really it is not. It would be more accurate to state the following: It is the origin point, and through its intent resides just outside the core essence of creation.

On October 4, 2012, I asked the ATI,TPE, "Please explain what makes up the small layer of so-called 'film' that exists to separate the ATI,TPE from anything else?"

"Per the All That Is, The Pure Essence, the small 'film' is a translucent veil made up of the pre-atom essence's energy spark, spanning the endless nothingness."

The ATI,TPE's miniscule implosion process created this spark. The ATI,TPE is a pre-pre-Krysthal hydrogen type of pre-gas that endured the slightest hint of nuclear fission and fusion to expand itself, but that expansion was no longer the ATI,TPE. Each change was a new creation. ATI,TPE states that it desired to expand in order to connect with new creation outside of itself. This desire caused slight internal pressure to create that expansion; however, the ATI,TPE does not approximate any force that originated with the Big Bang. I suppose we can see everything in measures of familial substances, but this does not negate the significant differences between each stage of creation.

The Void is a unique place because it was discovered by the process of expansion from the ATI,TPE to before the actual first pre-field frequency named Eia. The ATI,TPE states that there is no energetic movement in the Void; it is not a creative place. "The Void is subsequent endless space with the ability for creation. The All That Is, The Pure Essence did not desire creation there. The All That Is, The Pure Essence's desire was still expanding," it explains. The Void is not a field; it is a passageway. The ATI,TPE's interesting explanation shows that the Void space holds the potential for creation. In fact, what exists as the Void is the same nothingness that exists outside of current creation, and when more creation occurs, it will fill a portion of that Void that will no longer be a Void. The Void has no boundary.

Eia as the first pre-field frequency carries the fastest and most "exceptional" wave known in existence that exceeds a trillion hertz, according to the ATI,TPE. (The ATI,TPE explains that waves are not powerful in the way that we perceive them as forceful; it prefers to say that "waves exude exceptional energy.") For the longest time, I called this energy "Love" with a capital "L," but I finally decided to ask the ATI,TPE what its proper "name" or tone encryption is: Eia, pronounced I-yǎ.

The ATI,TPE states that Eia is the first creator. The ATI,TPE does not consider itself a creator because it lacks the energy of frequency. Regardless of this distinction, Eia is not an omnipotent creator (there is no such thing) because Eia is similar to the ATI,TPE in essence, and it also has its own identity and space of separation between it and everything else. The reality of separation is built into every expanded creation in order to preserve our individual identities.

When my mother first connected to Eia, she saw a pale white, cloud-like fog that expands to form a separate pre-plasmic layer of consciousness. She elaborated on May 13, 2013:

While I was communicating as my higher self [in chapter 9]

with the All That Is, The Pure Essence and Eia, I saw an amazing bridge of energetic particulates appear as the frequency, sparkling within a fog-like gaseous cover between the ATI,TPE and my higher self. This is the expanded visual communication process within my human state.

I followed up with Eia to receive more understanding. I asked, "How does Eia have a pale white color when it is before light? Please explain."

"Per Eia, when 'bridging' from the ATI, The Pure Essence position in connection to creation, there is no color until the connection on the created end is reached and percepted by the created recipient. Colors are percepted where light penetrates matter."

Eia is a boundless, pre-plasmic field and frequency essence. It is also single in consciousness just as the ATI,TPE is single in consciousness; each is indivisible as a unique consciousness. Eia has its own identity that was created in and for that level of existence. Eia is very similar to the ATI,TPE non-field frequency existence except that its essence has wave-like power and a bit more complexity.

This pre-plasmic essence contains the imprint for our individual, "highest self" identity that exists at the next pre-plasmic level in the earliest stage of the "A" domain. A few levels later in "A," the first plasmic krystar arises, which is the fully natural star state.

A krystar is an eternal, Central Sun-type star in early creation that can also provide planetary living conditions for a plethora of life forms. In our particular path of creation, our original krystar is called Cosminyahas, according to Ashayana's latest entity group the AL-Hum-Bhra Magistry Councils of Cosminyahas (henceforth called Alhumbhra Council) and confirmed by the ATI,TPE.

In Ashayana's process of seeking eternal creation from our very expanded position, she was first informed about seven later krystars and Ah frequency fields such as the Ah'-yah and Ah-yah-YA' that she calls the "Lands of 'Aah'"[185] She teaches that these areas are in an early plasmic domain called the CosMA'yah before the Eckasha-Aah; however, her Lands of "Aah" identification would place them in the Eckasha-Aah domain. The spellings of the CosMA'yah and Ah fields show that they are part of the Eckasha-Ah domain, which the ATI,TPE confirms, but it is not a rule to spell names according to the location.

Now that Ashayana has learned about the Cosminyahas, she calls it the "Sun-8" krystar and claims it is the core domain that somehow contains the seven later krystars and all the rest of creation.[186] This simply cannot happen because the seven krystars are in an entirely different domain. The New Age belief does this because it perceives creation as spheres within one giant gestalt sphere that in this case would be the Cosminyahas krystar. To the contrary, the Cosminyahas provides certain building blocks for the subsequent krystars, and they each exist in their respectively distinct spaces. This is the underlying pattern for our dense universe. There is no giant sphere that encapsulates everything, for each krystar, entity, and etcetera is fundamentally self-contained.

As the original "point" of existence, the ATI,TPE does not conform to a spherical shape, nor does it encapsulate anything. Rather, Eia could encapsulate the ATI,TPE. As I previously stated, the ATI,TPE comprises its own small but unique, boundless space. It communicates that its "desire permeates everything," which the following example can help illustrate.

There is a popular story about a philosophy teacher who demonstrates spatial capacity by using different media to fill an empty mason jar.[187] He first fills the jar with golf balls until no more would fit. Our body can be the jar, and the golf balls can be our molecules or atoms. Second, he inserts small pebbles that fill up smaller spaces. These can be subatomic particles. Third, he adds a bag of sand that can represent Krysthal scalar takeyons. Lastly, he pours in two beers. This is a large amount of liquid that can represent scales of plasmic material back to early creation. The jar contains one big space, but as it fills with different media that have their own composition and spaces, the big space ends up containing spaces within or between spaces. Somewhere through this jar is a formless essence as the ATI,TPE that can exist in the spaces between the beer and other objects. Eia exists in a similar way to the ATI,TPE. Therefore, the ATI,TPE and Eia can connect with our highest self pre-plasmic level as an aspect of the figurative beer that then connects to the rest of our etheric and plasmic attributes, ultimately linking to each object's denser form.

When attempting to define the origin of creation, sometimes we do so through perceptual filters or flat out beliefs. For instance, we can attribute different definitions to the same word, such as *creator*:

1. Creator is a building block upon which similar but different energy matter emerges.
2. Creator contains families of energy matter that create similar extensions of those families.
3. Creator contains the same matter and forces imparted to all creation, and creation represents portions of that complete reservoir.

Numbers 1 and 2 are scientifically realistic while number 3 is a theoretical belief. Number 3 involves the typical religious belief that states God is an immaterial everything from which we received our entire existence. It implies that this ultimate being is also an ultimate power as The Creator. Since there is a small separation between the ATI,TPE and every creation, and the ATI,TPE does not comprise any component of creation, it is impossible for the first stage of existence to contain all forces and material in a unified field akin to Einstein's model.

A hint of fusion aligned the ATI,TPE connection and the veil of separation to the emerged essence of Eia's pre-field frequency much like a later creational force loosely bonds an atom to form a molecule. The enactment of "oneness" or coexistence with the ATI,TPE and Eia justifies number 1.

After Eia's type of field frequency are more layers of expansion and complexity. When the complexity involves similar but different identities coexisting agreeably in the same pre-plasmic or plasmic field, this unified field of "oneness" can be acceptable to liberal Law of One believers. This stage is number 2.

The Law of One belief is much more complex and contradictory to number 2; it more so supports number 3. It states that we as very complex entities are merely different expressions of God Source wherein we embody all aspects of this Source but as different probabilities. This is pantheism at its finest, saying that everything is God. We are supposedly hologram replicas in different configurations of matter that an undivided field contains as "God," but then there are some aspects of division in that field in order to maintain a similar but diverse, "unified" field. The popular description of this God by New Age entity groups, especially the Infinite Awareness with David Icke, is "All That Is, All That Has Been and All That Ever Can Be."[188] This completely misrepresents the actual All That Is, The Pure Essence, again showing the belief of entities instead of the ATI,TPE explaining itself.

Physicist David Bohm observed that an image placed upon a photographic plate shows a replica or hologram in every region of the plate. He proposed that there is an implicit order that should be traceable through every dimensional layer as "undivided wholeness in flowing movement" (p. 14).[189]

I found a sufficient synopsis of Bohm's perspective by an unknown writer:

> If a hologram of a rose is cut in half and then illuminated by a laser, each half will still be found to contain the entire image of the rose. Indeed, even if the halves are divided again, each snippet of film will always be found to contain a smaller but intact version of the original image. Unlike normal photographs, every part of a hologram contains all the information possessed by the whole. The "whole in every part" nature of a hologram provides us with

an entirely new way of understanding organization and order. For most of its history, Western science has labored under the bias that the best way to understand a physical phenomenon, whether a frog or an atom, is to dissect it and study its respective parts....

Bohm believes the reason subatomic particles are able to remain in contact with one another regardless of the distance separating them is not because they are sending some sort of mysterious signal back and forth, but because their separateness is an illusion. He argues that at some deeper level of reality such particles are not individual entities, but are actually extensions of the same fundamental something.[190]

This analysis supports the Infinite Awareness belief that states everything in our current experience is an illusion, and there should be no separation (see chapter 3). This belief can go so far to assert that our conscious, electromagnetic mind is an all-inclusive supercomputer creating each of our realities, and our imaginative interpretation of reality is a vibratory projection of that consciousness that expresses itself through different reference points of spacetime. Therefore, there is no real individualized matter, just a multifaceted, superconscious energy. This viewpoint is what is illusory to me. It contradicts itself because it involves subjective reference points that imply individuality and separateness.

Bohm addresses this apparent contradiction when stating "relative independence" in his analogy of a flowing stream:

On this stream, one may see an ever-changing pattern of vortices, ripples, waves, splashes, etc., which evidently have no independent existence as such. Rather, they are abstracted from the flowing movement, arising and vanishing in the total process of the flow. Such transitory subsistence as may be possessed by these abstracted forms implies only a relative independence or autonomy of behaviour, rather than absolutely independent existence as ultimate substances (p. 62).[189]

Bohm and I agree that the higher or inner dimensional status is the inherent order that projects an extension of itself in our current "objectified" existence. However, we differ where his view takes on a spiritualism that treats everyone's subjective experiences as variable experiences of one unit. This somehow implies that we are selfsame extensions of the original consciousness, thereby affecting it equally as it affects us.

While many extreme oneness proponents believe that the ultimate

God state is the non-moving zero-point, Bohm considers that state and the condition of separateness to be static and fragmented. He states, "[M]y main concern has been with understanding the nature of reality in general and of consciousness in particular as a coherent whole, which is never static or complete, but which is in an unending process of movement and unfoldment" (p. x).[189] He bases his belief on the annihilation model in which energy matter continually changes, which is why he uses the analogy of the physical stream with its diverse interactive components for our unified field of existence. His view turns us into a moving nebula or storm of instability that projects an image of separateness and stability in our reality. Accordingly, he claims that the mind and body are projections from that higher dimensional, undivided existence, which implies a single entity. In his computations, Bohm assumes "non-denumerable infinity of variables" from fractions, not whole numbers, thus proving his fractal-based inclination (p. 117).[189]

The saving point of Bohm's argument is that he opens up scientific thought toward pre-Big Bang conditions and quantum potential in a super-implicate, structural order. However, his theory about an infinite series of representations implied by ceaseless enfoldment and unfoldment, which would constantly dissolve subatomic particles into the implicate order and then recrystallize them, necessitates death by fractal geometry that limits and deforms the infinity. The ultimate Fibonacci-based fractal is doomed to space dust or a black hole, so it cannot reach the super-implicate level. I see his belief in the Law of One in his astute attempts to connect modern physics to metaphysics. I invite progressive, niche physicists to further climb outside the box and explore the information that I and Krysthal science provide.

Creations are largely microcosms of the macrocosm because we cannot make up something out of nothing, but we are not holograms of the ATI,TPE and subsequent levels of creation. Individual identity is primary, and expansion occurred through the desire to connect and love; this is the foundation of our makeup. We are built to be eternally individual and loving. We never, ever lose these foundational aspects of ourselves unless we would no longer have the desire to exist, and more importantly, if we would detest existence. Even very evil entities still wish to exist, but they are hanging onto life by a thread. If they sever their connection to the ATI,TPE in the final stage of shattering to space dust, nothing happens to the ATI,TPE in the process. The ATI,TPE is never divided or outside of itself, so it merely stays in its full integrity.

Ashayana has spoken about the possibility arising where the identity imprint of the dissolved individual is preserved in an early plasmic level (of the Eckasha-Ah) called the Ah-YA'-yah field where it can merge with other aspects to be literally born again.[185] This self-identity construct would have its past distortions removed, although I do not know if all will have been forgotten. It does not equate to the proper pre-plasmic essence of one's true highest self identity.

Two levels before the Ah-YA'-yah is the Ah'-yah field that Ashayana describes as the essence of the "massive consciousness field, that living consciousness field of Source" (DVD-1) and "'The Essence of' the Unutterable ONE" (DVD-2);[185] however, she has since been shown the Cosminyahas level in her entity-based transmissions, so this gives room in her teachings that the self-identity can exist in a very early, pre-plasmic level preceding the earliest krystar. Eia is yet to be revealed by her entity groups as well, but it is not far from the Ah fields that are more complex than Eia. Unfortunately, entity groups often lead us to believe that each new revelatory level is the God Source that they have been seeking when still it is part of creation, and they later realize—if they continue to probe—that there is something earlier. I suggest that they change their perception of God and hierarchy to stop misrepresenting levels of existence.

The outer light-body template cannot exist without the inner plasmic and pre-plasmic templates. Our Earthly body is an excellent example because despite its distortions, we can still communicate in some way with our inner template all the way back to the All That Is, The Pure Essence. I "see" in my awareness that our inner plasmic units and fields are like laminated layers in perhaps a type of meshed structure within and between each outer light-body layer. This allows the ATI,TPE and Eia to be very close to each of our outer aspects; they keep a pure connection to all of our aspects, and Eia can act as a bridge to override disconnected parts. This also allows each familiar structure to coexist, where the inner Ah plasma fields connect with the Ah plasma structures that then create the early light-body Eckasha-Aah realms. Diverse creative structures expand from each realm as well, but there is always a familiar association. This means that our body does not exactly replicate what separately occurred to us in earlier creation. The ATI,TPE states that partiki clusters, for example, do not necessarily replicate the same number of partiki in that respective unit's process of expansion. We are not tied to a field or structure that came before us, but we do carry aspects of their natures within us.

The unified field concept appears to be muddled, so I will bring simple reasoning and information into it. All natural levels, including respective creations, are complete in themselves. None of them contains every component of creation, but they do contain their own "source" or origin of familial entities.

Since each field level's composition is slightly different to the one before it, it contains "material" for new units. These units are not entirely new, though, because they need the material of what came before them. The 20,736 partiki

Yunasum unit, for example, can communicate with other partiki units, but it will more easily communicate with other Yunasum, collectively called Yunasai. Each Yunasum is in a separate but most similar location across creation than other partiki units, therefore providing a type of field or group consciousness for the Yunasai while not assimilating their individual members into a single blob or gestalt. I cannot emphasize enough how creation contains multiple fundamental aspects, so no simplified "Law" can adequately explain them unless it truly involves everything as they individually are in respective locations.

In the MCEO-GA's Law of One belief where cosmic structure contains spheres within spheres, each subsequent layer of creation spins one direction (like the Eckasha) and creates through deflection the counter-rotating set of later spheres (like the Ecka).[191] This model severely simplifies and misrepresents creation as though the universe is really one giant star that replicates itself via different forces into smaller and smaller fields and stars. This is essentially the M-theory occurring backwards, but even scientists who believe in the Big Bang Theory know that creation is outwardly expanding. The nature of life is truly limitless, as the ATI,TPE concurs and conveyed on December 7, 2011: "Natural creation is limitless because the All That Is, The Pure Essence is limitless." Many Earth scientists do not yet understand that Fibonacci-based creations cannot provide unlimited expansion, but they do witness eternal creation mechanics that still exist in our universe, proving the separateness, expansion, and variety of nature.

A relevant correlation about the transition from an entity at the cosmic Yunasai level to an entity at a related but earlier partiki or plasma level can be the ascension process in our galaxy. The noticeable difference between our time matrix and the inner partiki and plasma levels is that they do not have time, and they may not have as much physical distance; however, they do have a measure of cause and effect that can approximate our experience.

According to the kathara grid formation and its embattled distortions in the Milky Way and Galaxy-2, there exists significant distance between Earth, Tara, Gaia, and Aramatena, which is the more natural 12th dimensional Gaia counterpart in Galaxy-2. The MCEO has stated that Tara is the star Alcyone in the Pleiades, but the ATI,TPE reveals that Tara was actually created from Galaxy-2's Alcyone; what we see in the sky is a greater distortion as Tara.

Certain stars came into existence in both an organized and disorganized pattern. When the kathara grid became subjected to artificial technologies, they caused versions of Earth, Tara, Gaia, and Aramatena to alter their pole alignments, angular rotation of particle spins, and actual positions. This problem and the curved reality of spacetime can cause significant perceptual and actual spatial differences toward similar planets that are divided by time and density. Within the connected Galaxy-2 and Milky Way harmonic universes 1-4, Aramatena is the Earth quanta's farthest future, Gaia our far future, Tara our future, and Earth our present.

The process of ascension can have us transcend these physical distances when the planets are properly energetically and spatially aligned, as chapter 8 explains. In the Milky Way galaxy, our HU-1 body can shift the ARPS and density of its atoms toward Tara's carbon-silicon existence. We would not travel far or change our general composition (except to remove implanted distortions); we would merely shift and transfigure ourselves to match the lighter density that exists within us. It is not an all-or-nothing act of peeling away or not peeling away layers of an onion because those layers are still part of our makeup, but we accrued additional matter configurations in progressive outer layers. We gained a carbon base on Earth that can gradually transform on Tara to a fully silicon base on Gaia. Through Galaxy-2's bridge, the silicon base can transform to a crystalline liquid-light, hydroplasmic state on 12th dimensional Aramatena. From there, we can transfigure to a lighter base than hydroplasma in the 13th to 15th dimensions and enter the Ecka.

Galaxy-2's 15th dimension contains all of the necessary Milky Way dimensional codes, which the ATI,TPE and MCEO confirm; however, all of the Milky Way dimensions, including our 1st dimension, also include these necessary Milky Way codes. The same pattern applies within the Krysthal galaxy's 15 dimensions. The only difference is how the dimensions are constructed with those codes and if there is something added from a phantom state. There is a loose oneness among us all, but the differences are substantial enough to make each one of us unique.

Therefore, the unified field contains all the fundamental codes for its level of creation and what can potentially arise after it. For example, the unified field of our pre-plasmic, highest self identities after Eia contains all the natural codes for later Krysthal creations, but these codes are generalized blueprints until the levels actualize them in their respective details. Humans contain these blueprints as well as some fragments of natural codes, so we are sufficiently whole although our complete abilities are not yet actualized. Fully natural entities cannot contain phantom codes because phantom energies come afterward, taking from and reconfiguring what is natural.

The lateral ascension process gradually steps creation to new spaces and is the most natural path of our ascension, states the ATI,TPE, but there is also another ascension process that occurs directly between the Ecka and Veca domains because of the Tri-Veca subatomic code within natural creation. This code causes Ecka stars and planets to create similar Veca structures in or near the same dimensional position of their respective kathara grids.

In Figure 4, the Tri-Veca code has an upper partiki unit that splits into partikA and particum versions in the process of expansion into a new domain. This means that there is an Ecka version of "Earth" in the 3rd dimension of its kathara grid that originally created the Krysthal versions of Earth and Parallel Earth. Chapter 8 reveals the names of Earth's increasingly natural counterparts in Galaxy-2 and the Krysthal galaxy. From our perspective, the Krysthal Ecka "Earth" can be omni-polar because it is the combination of both antiparticle and particle divisions, but it is also a polarized, particum-based planet due to it having split from an earlier Eckasha planet that acts similar to a partiki unit in its own phasing cycle. These subatomic divisions do not create fractions of energy, though, because the Tri-Veca code's nature allows the inflow of energetic components all the way back to Eia and the ATI,TPE.

Figure 4. Tri-Veca and Vesica Piscis Codes

TRI-VECA   BI-VECA

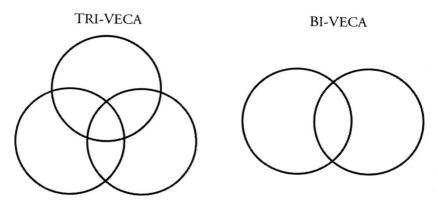

The Bi-Veca or vesica piscis code severs the partiki source at the subatomic or seed level and creates polarized, dead-light. The Milky Way galaxy is caught and formed by this distortion. The ATI,TPE reveals that a portion of the Krysthal Ecka "Earth" has also been harnessed by the vesica piscis to create a fractalized version that aligns with Earth and Parallel Earth, sometimes called "Inner Earth." To buffer the energetic transition between Earth and the Ecka "Inner Earth," there is a 3.5 dimensional modulation zone at the core of the Sun.[120] Chapter 8 shows that there is a literal Inner Earth region within our Earth; however, entities often combine it with other regions, including our related portion of the Ecka, which obfuscates the greater reality.

Similar to the dimensional ascension process, the transfiguration from outer to inward domains can be easy. In fact, as our dense matter becomes more pliable and plasmic, boundaries are less detectable, making it easier to be alongside Eia and the ATI,TPE.

I deduce that entity groups promote vertical, not lateral, ascension to humans because our body has a central, vertical axis of energetic structures such as chakras that manipulative entities desire to control (in chapter 9's "Chakras"). If we are not discerning or knowledgeable, some of them may steer us toward Tree of Artificial Life connections in nearby higher dimensional realms, as the following chapters explain.

Conclusion

Consciousness exists in all living things, and things of all levels incorporate a type of substance. Conscious awareness starts the process of creation; therefore, all things can essentially create. We can perceive the first layer of substance as the most intelligent because it started the process upon which we depend, but I will not play that game of "Who or what is better?" We all have intelligence because each aspect of matter within and outside of us knows how to interact in its realm.

A plasmic krystar is viewed as the end-all-be-all within the Law of One religion (in chapter 10) that has trickled down to mainstream scientific theory about the creation of our universe. To Ashayana Deane's main entity groups, this krystar is the Cosminyahas; however, before it was revealed to her, she believed that the Yunasai were the "God Source." The MCEO interprets the Yunasai as a giant sphere just like a krystar, but it also has revealed that Yunasai are a group of Yunasum, a type of seed partiki "atom" that gives its codes to expanded creation.[180] This information provides the cosmic egg view in which something inherently intact gives codes and substance toward the creational flow. Ashayana's entity teams consistently reveal core or inner realms to their respective outer realms, so they know that an inner type of "seed" or "egg" contains building block codes for creation to expand as it may. The krystar sphere can be a not-so-small building block as its basic star state, but it is also an abundant planet upon which all types of fulfilled entities can live with their respectively complete DNA compositions. The krystar is not an ultimate, large background with fields that allowed conditions for the krystar to develop. It has its own field, but its measures of complexity in no way started with itself.

The "end-all-be-all" is a misnomer because of the realty of multifaceted creations in multiple locations. The fields and pre-atomic seeds that produced a krystar actually created other krystars around the same "time." The existences of such seeds, fields, and diverse and complex shapes can fill distinct but contiguous spaces while maintaining a measure of uniqueness. The ATI,TPE, while not having any codes to impart, can be perceived as a type of seed or egg that contains the intention for creation. Eia also does not impart codes, but it carries a type of imprint for them. Afterward, the imprint has become actualized.

Accounts between the ATI,TPE and scientists do not match about original creation, but they can be close. National Aeronautics and Space Administration (NASA) scientists can agree about a primary stage of plasmic creation. "99.9 percent of the Universe is made up of plasma," says Dr. Dennis Gallagher, a NASA physicist.[192] Plasma conducts electricity and responds to magnetic fields. It is a more excitable energy than gas that then lessens its vibratory impact as density increases. Imagining a most excitable energy like the "Love" pre-field frequency, Eia, is not far-fetched.

Eia's pre-plasmic wave is so excited and so far reaching that it continues to spread life to everything created. Eia extends the desire of the ATI,TPE for the creation process to occur. If scientists would stretch their minds a bit further, they could agree with the ATI,TPE that the earliest essence is a hydrogen precursor. Hydrogen is the first element in the Periodic Table of Elements and the lightest material in our universe that overwhelmingly constitutes both life-giving and conductive stars and water. The Big Bang would have loosely approximated the ATI,TPE's miniscule "bang," because its matter had to contain mostly hydrogen with the additional force of fusion that created helium and then heavier elements.[193]

Unfortunately, the common belief in the Big Bang Theory views our universe as an expandable yet somehow encapsulated whole that contains all aspects of energy and matter similar to the Law of One belief.[194] Who says there is no religion in science? When choosing to believe this model of creation, scientists still believe that a zero-point, energetic construct created the Big Bang. Any zero-point in our universe involves vibration. The ATI,TPE is the absolute, non-moving "zero point." Science is struggling to identify the true Source energy much like the Law of One belief cannot clearly understand it.

The closest that physicists seem to get to the zero-point state is their experimental creation of a vacuum. The vacuum is also called a void, but neither term represents an empty space. The vacuum state involves a field of energy, and this field contains subatomic matter as electromagnetic waves with the lowest measured energy output.[195] This void is vastly different to the non-creative Void space after the ATI,TPE. As I have repeatedly emphasized, there is always a positional point of reference from which we can view aspects of reality. What may be highly applicable and true to one person is considered less valid to another. It is unwise to view popular beliefs through a completely polarized, black or white lens.

Science and religion can agree about intelligent creation. Partial or fully organized patterns exist behind every independent or random occurrence, and the pre-matter substances of those patterns are familial entities with similar consciousness that can communicate among themselves.

Science and religion can also agree in their methods of viewing creation. Both use their expanded states of existence as the vantage point in determining what existed before us; however, religion inflates what was before us while science tends to reduce it. Unfortunately, science and religion are most aligned in their total acceptance of fractal mechanics because the entities who created religions are the same ones who helped fabricate our supermassive black hole matrix.

CHAPTER 7

Revealing the Gods

Within the religious and spiritual paradigm, I have purposely used the terms "entities," "angels," "spirits," and "gods" to describe otherworldly beings. I have given clues about the physical nature of gods and their cohorts; however, because several religions, especially Christianity, assert that Earth is the only planet inhabited with intelligent life, I wanted to reach this religious mindset. When a viewpoint is narrow, it becomes very difficult to draw the line between another dimensional entity or spirit and an actual alien, although that spirit entity has a mind, a voice, and some sort of body.

The perception of God is that He is without a body, but the "He" is giving away important information. In addition, angels appear as people in the Bible. The truth is that every god and angelic figure in all religious and spiritual texts is an alien.

This chapter highlights the main alien group conspirators who want to control us and the Earth. It is an especially difficult chapter for me, for it has me directly face the aliens to whom I have thus far largely referred by association. There will be no veil between my words and their identities that have served to ease the religious mind up to this point of revelation, so I sincerely and seriously ask the reader to be confident in the message of who you are as a Human so that you can be strong to handle this information. To aid our rightful confidence, I will now symbolically elevate our Human race as a capitalized proper noun because we generally are an amazing and capable race of beings all our own, despite our inherited distortions.

This chapter is separated into two main sections. The first section will take you on a ride in a surreal story about the Milky Way's creation that is beyond current scientific knowledge. This knowledge must be given by otherworldly sources, so I take much care in deciphering the information's credibility that is largely given by the Melchizedek Cloister Emerald Order (MCEO) and Guardian Alliance (GA) entity groups via Ashayana Deane (henceforth Ashayana). I add corrections and elaborations by the All That Is, The Pure Essence (ATI,TPE), as well as my educated and intuitive guesses.

I request that you read the first section with an open mind so that you can see the dots starting to connect. I also request that you take similar care and check the information within yourself so that you can further the connections toward truth.

The second section reveals the prominent alien groups who seek to control us.

Sometimes truth is stranger than fiction, but with how far the entertainment industry has gone with its science fiction, its stories may be more similar to the truth than we have previously given credit. However, I must say that the fear it elicits about aliens is unnecessary. It is true that the topic of invasive aliens is highly upsetting, but we do not need to be afraid of what could be reality. I think that the fear is about what we have not yet known or understood.

My objective is to present the information so that we can eradicate fear and take a strong stance in renewed knowledge of our strengths. Although there is a lot of bad news in chapters 7 and 8, I seek to portray more hope and confidence in this book because we are more than we have realized.

I request that you get centered in your own self, in your present stability, and do your best to not allow someone else's fear rob you of your own power that can handle the facts. Although personal experiences with strange phenomena may add to that fear, I speak from the place of triumph and knowing that we do have freedom. Even in the case of partial possession, we have entire moments to ourselves to think and to breathe. We own ourselves to be able to make a firm stand against what seeks to disempower us (in chapter 9). If Hollywood's cinematic portrayals of helplessness come back to your mind, refer instead to the television series "Star Trek: The Next Generation" in which the brave leading characters continually come out winning.

I request that you read this chapter with the view that each alien is just one person, similar to you, with his or her own boundary and his or her own ideas. This inner strength will get you through to the end of this book and will have you realize that you do not need to fear, although you do have cause to be angry and sad. It is time to be proactive instead of bound.

Creation of the AquaLaShA, Galaxy-2, and Milky Way Galaxies

950 billion years ago, our Ecka Yanas races joined the natural expansion of the cosmos to start the formation of our Krysthal Veca and its galaxies.[196] The name of our Krysthal galaxy is AquaLaShA, reveals the ATI,TPE, not Aquinos as the MCEO has taught. Aquinos is the name of our Eckasha. (Reminder: the capitalized vowel emphasizes the long sound.)

480 billion years ago, in the Ecka level of our Parallel Eckasha, Borenthasala races witnessed what the MCEO says was an "organic fall and implosion" of the partikA (PKA)-based harmonic universes 3 through 1 (HU-3 through HU-1) of their adjoined galaxy, meaning that those densities fell into phantom status, clarifies the ATI,TPE.[196]

The Borenthasala were deeply grieved by this catastrophe, so they devised a plan to hopefully mitigate or eradicate the potential for destruction. They created the "Great 6-6-6-6 Quarantined Polarity Experiment" to discover the root cause of de-evolution during four evolutionary cycles with six stages per cycle.[196] They thought that this experiment could improve upon the eternal life creation that came before them, but their flawed reasoning overlooked the fact that the galactic problems started when entities acted outside of eternal life creation!

The Borenthasala races created their experiment in a quarantine, which by nature is cut off from a measure of natural creation mechanics. Allowing the conditions for fall in an already fallen environment was a risky and short-sighted endeavor. We could say that they were playing God.

Borenthasala entities subjected themselves to the Victim-Victimizer game program that they created. They re-incarnated into three separate groups within HU-4 of the particum (PCM)-based galaxy. Two of the groups took a Bi-Veca (vesica piscis) genetic distortion to explore polarity extremes in competition while one control group remained with original Tri-Veca genetic coding intended to "pull the polarity groups back out of mutation" once all of the stages were completed (see Figure 4).[196]

During the first cycle of the experiment, one polarity group was genetically configured with the Passive-Victim program (passive genetic charge), while the other polarity group was given the Aggressive-Victimizer program (dominant genetic charge). At the end of the cycle, the two polarity groups switched programs: the aggressors became the victims, and the victims became the aggressors. The intention was for each polarity group to endure two cycles of experiencing what it feels like to be on each side of the polarity. If the experiment started to get out of control, then the control group would jump in to hybridize the extremely distorted race. Hybridization gives back the Tri-Veca coding, but it also creates a new race with a remnant of one or both extremes.

Events did not go to plan. The Borenthasala lost control of the experiment at the end of the third cycle. One of the polarity groups, the Bourgha-Musala-Ahlama (pronounced MUsala AhLAma; Bourgha for short), became extremely polarized and was no longer able to be telepathically controlled by the Borenthasala control group.

The Bourgha never again wanted to experience the victim role that they endured in the second cycle of the experiment. Just before the start of the final cycle, they destroyed the other polarity group (the victim group). Then, with their HU-4 level of awareness, they used their advanced knowledge of physics to develop a time rip technology that blasted a current outside of the quarantine where the control group lived. The Bourgha traveled on their time rip wave to assimilate the control group. Time rips are much more unstable passageways than wormholes, but this one worked. Their next move was to advance their time rip technology so that they could take out their aggression on all of creation and assimilate it into their phantom domain.[196] With a fully phantom constitution, the Bourgha not only hated but needed natural creation mechanics in order to survive.

The Bourgha used their time rip technology to progressively rip a hole out of their galaxy into their Ecka over the next 30 billion years.[197] Since the Bourgha were at no higher than the 12th dimensional level of their galaxy, they had to find ways to climb up into their Ecka. No one can physically enter a higher dimension until the natural ascension cycle can activate or impart the necessary codes toward transfiguration. Because natural mechanics do not fit the Bourgha constitution, artificial means must be employed to approximate what is natural.

Bourgha and similar entities can infiltrate higher dimensions by using "death science" technology to create phantom versions of those dimensions and then artificially ascending into them. There are also stages of semi-phantom matter that they can use to tap into fully natural creation. They can create time rips and wormholes from their phantom locations to increasingly natural matrices to position themselves in advantageous spaces. In addition, they often possess semi-phantom beings to learn how to manipulate our matter construction toward their needs.

The Bourgha tragically assimilated all of their Ecka and Veca into fully phantom domains. Although they ended the experiment as extreme victimizers, they also had to live with the polarities within them that created the muddled gray area where essentially anything goes. The Victim-Victimizer polarities made them the worst possible entity group in terms of conscious expression.

The Bourgha unleashed themselves like an infection to gain more quantum food. Due to our Eckasha connection, the time rip into their Ecka created a slight tear into our parallel matrix in our Ecka, which gave them a sufficient foothold to first target it.[196]

Krysthal races at the Eckasha level and beyond held grave concern for what the Bourgha have done, especially since they had achieved massive technology gains relatively quickly. They knew they had to do something far-reaching to stop the Bourgha from taking out more matrices. Therefore, Krysthal races from the Aquareion and WEsaLA Eckashas—that are parallel to one another—and our Aquinos Eckasha came together to form the Krysthal River Tri-Matrix Cooperative Intervention Team, otherwise called the Krysthal River Host (KRH).[185] (Note: the MCEO calls them "Krystal River Host," but they prefer "Krysthal" for its completeness.) Another key player is a Krysthal group from an inner Hub realm called Aquious that exists near the Aquareion Eckasha.[196,197] The Hub worlds stay stationary as Eckasha levels, Eckas, and Vecas spin through them and through each other.[191] The KRH's aim was to combine powerful Krysthal frequencies into its Gyrodome technology to seal off the Bourgha Ecka-Veca matrices into an unbreakable quarantine. Unfortunately, the Gyrodome could not be implemented at that time without annihilating our Ecka and Veca parallel matrices due to the open time rip.[197]

To prevent this catastrophe, KRH races decided to let the Bourgha problem grow until they could gently contain it. Our parallel races would have to evolve, sometimes with help by the KRH, to seal the time rip from within their Ecka matrix, or they would at least evacuate out of their Ecka-Veca system to another one before potential destruction.[197]

To enact the gentler approach for the Gyrodome technology, AquafarE races from Aquious and Aquareion seeded the Aquari race with the genetic capacity to anchor the Gyrodome currents within the Ecka-Veca levels of the entire KRH. The Aquari would hybridize the Ecka-Veca races to sufficiently secure our matrices or evacuate us out before the Gyrodome would be activated.[197] The KRH evolutionary plan is called the Aqualene Transmission; *Aqualene* refers to currents from the first three CosMA'yah krystars.[198] Aquari races colonized AquaLaShA's 3rd dimensional planet Urtha, and they directly assisted Humans by creating the Aquafereion race during a critical time in Earth's history (in chapter 8 "Urtha").

The Bourgha strategically stalked and captured some of our parallel Krysthal Ecka Budhara races via their time rip.[199] They hybridized and distorted them against their will to gain access to the Ecka-Veca.

The Bourgha-Budhara race progressively siphoned quanta from our parallel Krysthal galaxy to create at least one progressively phantom matrix whose stargates link to the Bourgha supermassive black hole matrices. The ATI,TPE states that when a fallen system is first created off of the original template, no supermassive black hole is created because the new matrix is still connected to the natural kathara grid. It takes a lot of effort to distort natural creation, so steps are done in stages. Another matrix pulled off of the fallen system contributes the giant supernova conditions that create supermassive black holes. That matrix is semi-phantom or phantom.

Thus far, matrices at the Ecka and Veca levels have eventually become fully fallen as phantom, and some have imploded into annihilation. Thankfully, it is extremely difficult to impossible to corrupt an Eckasha.

After a phantom system is created, its stars and planetary systems can naturally go into Lone Star Fall status in which about 3 billion years of quanta remain in stars like our Sun.[197] The Lone Star Fall is a miniature form of a "Krist Fall" that could potentially affect an entire galaxy (p. 16).[196] The planets' inhabitants can evolve and internally link to the ATI,TPE during this time. Their will toward goodness could potentially find a way out of there, at least by the ATI,TPE prompting other races to help them.

On the contrary, purposeful phantom races prolong their space dust return by feeding on other systems, and their technologies expedite the phantom fall of their prey to prevent their evolution and escape. These evil intruders have completely reversed the particle rotation and spin (ARPS) of their quantum prey in order to repel incoming natural energy and entrap them. These evil people already contain reversed ARPS and altered biochemistry to be able to live with such extremely distorted energy.

Although fallen beings are genetically cut off from aspects of internal creation, they at least contain its blueprint within their core. Creation was first natural before it became distorted. On August 17, 2011, when I asked the All That Is, The Pure Essence whether natural creation can become completely cut off from it, it addresses all creation and replies, "No; all creation stays eternally connected to the ATI,TPE; good and evil. There are degrees of separateness due to the amount of purity."

The ATI,TPE gives a balanced viewpoint toward creation mechanics because something natural can always connect with created beings beyond whichever level is stunted within us. Accordingly, many aliens, like Humans, are genetically fallen through no fault of their own. Such people can still link to higher energies, especially the ATI,TPE. When people are stuck in a phantom matrix, it is uncertain whether other entities would jeopardize their safety to help them, but as history shows, there is not a lack of helping hands toward the fallen one who has pure intent.

When phantom intent and action occur as "fallen," I prefer to replace *fallen* in this context with *evil*, but perhaps this word carries too much judgment that no one wants to say publicly. Let us be honest, though, because we are judging that the purposeful decision to leave the direct connection with natural creation and the ATI,TPE is not wise or good. That is the underlying message of the MCEO-GA, but one reason why their members do not prefer this word is to not offend others when trying to maneuver politically sensitive situations. Interestingly, *evil* is *live* in reverse, which precisely represents the polarity against living eternally, regardless of judgment.

To capture Ecka-Veca systems requires an intense and intelligent warping of natural physics that involves taking control over key stargates. Access to stargates requires specific genetic coding that is natural to that system. Invading races usually need to overthrow local races and breed with them so that they can access their genetic link to the stargate and connect it to their phantom system via wormhole or time rip. Sometimes this process can take billions of years to complete. Unfortunately, raiders can be very patient.

450 billion years ago, reveals the ATI,TPE, Bourgha races managed to create a position from where they could attack a star in AquaLaShA's 15th dimension, harness some of its quanta, and start the creation of a new but partially distorted galaxy that I call Galaxy-2. The ATI,TPE states that they started attacking AquaLaShA instead of our Ecka matrix because of heavy security up there.

Some of AquaLaShA's races were pulled into Galaxy-2. I asked the ATI,TPE on September 3, 2011 how that could happen to such good races. It explained, "They were drawn into the negative energy's powerful vibrational pull due to its intensity, which even those races could not escape." When I asked about the initial pull into the first fallen Veca, the ATI,TPE stated that the event "reconfigured their DNA." Our DNA picks up the electromagnetic encoding of our environment. Sadly, we are often at the whim of our environment.

At this time of my questioning the ATI,TPE, I was unaware of any other fallen galaxy from Krysthal quanta before the Milky Way. The MCEO-GA does not divulge any other kathara grids outside of the 12-point kathara grid that they teach. They erroneously teach that M31 Andromeda is the Krysthal galaxy, and they name it Aquinos after our Eckasha.[200] They give misinformation to potentially protect the earlier galaxies and also to conform to their base-12 mathematics. Lastly, their creation story transfers the Ecka HU-1 Breneau Order or Rishi races to HU-5, as I stated in chapter 6. Their story muddles timelines and galaxies that I endeavor to correct in this book.

Since this book's first edition, I have gained two trusted Galaxy-2 contacts who are independent affiliates of the Krysthal River Host. They request that their names are not revealed because of their sensitive positions in creation. "M" is from the 14th dimension who I refer to most often due to her more protected position, and the other wonderful contact is from the 11th dimension. Via my mother's telepathic ability, we have communicated with both of them in person in several meetings, and she can see them. I do not see them, but I definitely feel their loving presence. Infrequently, it is a grand meeting with several members of their groups—together or separate—to lend their support. As I have previously stated, the ATI,TPE is the purest essence whose information approximates distorted creation. The more distorted the topic, the more potential for an incorrect answer. Therefore, I have sometimes needed more information from less distorted entities who know the ATI,TPE and our galactic events. I show the sources for clarity and probe the answers with an astute internal gauge.

The MCEO-GA Milky Way creation story begins with Galaxy-2 where the 15th dimensional Emerald Order Breneau lineage seeded the 12th dimensional Elohei, the 14th dimensional Gold Order Breneau lineage seeded the 11th dimensional Seraphei, and the 13th dimensional Amethyst Order Breneau lineage seeded the 10th dimensional Bra-ha-Rama. The GA refers to HU-4 races as the Christos Founder races because they comprise hydroplasmic liquid light of the "Christos Field" (p. 172).[144] However, this designation from where we get *Christ* comes from the Milky Way galaxy that is more distorted than the first fallen one. *Christ* and *krist* are distortions of *Krysthal*.

Elohei are generally considered as feline-hominids; Seraphei are generally avian-insect-reptile people; and Bra-ha-Rama generally include cetacean (whale, not dolphin) and avian-horse-deer (pegasus) races. Many species hybridizations occurred, eventually creating the notable mixed Elohei and Bra-ha-Rama, feline-aquatic ape race called the Anyu.[123,144]

Elohei guarded the 12th dimensional stargate of Aramatena. The Anyu were appointed guardian of the 11th dimensional stargate of Aveyon. The Omicron Drakonian (dinosaur-like dragon-moth) and Odedicron Reptilian (bipedal snake-like) race lines of the Seraphei were appointed co-guardians of the 10th dimensional stargate of Vega. All HU-4 stargates are in the Lyra constellation.[123]

360 billion years ago (state both the ATI,TPE and "M"), the Lyran Wars broke out between the stargate-11 Anyu and stargate-10 Omicron Drakonian guardians. The Anyu had more advanced genetics than the Drakonians, so some Anyu bullied them for control of the stargate. Omicron Drakonians turned into a formidable adversary over time because they evolved to have superior physical strength, so they started to push back and reclaim their territory. Anyu petitioned an elder council to help them destroy the Drakonians because they were out of control. The council responded that they do not destroy anyone; rather, the Anyu should correct themselves because they were acting the same as their enemy. The Anyu did not like this answer, so they retaliated against the council and threatened to take over the time matrix.[123]

The Anyu knew artificial creation mechanics. By bending light and sound through the vesica piscis code, they reconfigured a vital "seed" subatomic particle into a form that could repel its former self and cut itself off from the higher levels. The kathara grid and stargate system receives spiraled energy from the Ecka's light and sound fields, so if the Anyu could prevent it from entering stargate-11, then it could bounce back to stargate-12 and sever the kathara grid whose lower portion would be under Anyu control.

The 12th dimensional Elohei could have nipped the growing Anyu threat in the bud by refracting the Anyu energetic attack back to the 11th dimension. However, that would have destroyed the 10th and 11th dimensional stargate races including the Odedicron Reptilians who wanted no part in the wars. The Elohei could not get the Odedicrons and other innocent entities out of the war zone because the Anyu-controlled stargate-11 and increasingly Omicron-controlled stargate-10 prevented their passageway to the 12th dimension. The founding races and Elohei did not want to destroy the innocent races, so the problem remained. [123]

Anyu carried out their plan and created a backflow of energy that destroyed stargate-12 in Lyra. It also destroyed stargate-11. The long-standing Lyran Wars caused catastrophic destruction that not only weakened Galaxy-2 but also created the 11 dimension Milky Way galaxy between 360 and 320 billion years ago, reveals the ATI,TPE. 355 billion years ago, states "M," a 14th dimensional bridge-like formation from Galaxy-2 was connected to the Milky Way to prevent it from falling away into fully phantom status.

In the Milky Way, the Anyu became the Annu Elohim master race of its set-apart, initially phantom time matrix, which fed their superiority complex. The ATI,TPE explains that the energetic pull into the Milky Way reconfigured their DNA. Our DNA picks up the electromagnetic encoding of our environment, and this fallen Milky Way environment was heavily altered by phantom technology. The destruction also pulled 10th dimensional Seraphims into the Milky Way, where some of them fell to the 9th dimension. Before energetic bridges were put in place to maintain higher dimensional energy flow, higher dimensional races could not incarnate directly into the Elohim and Seraphim for rehabilitation toward a more natural form.

The MCEO call the combined Milky Way and Galaxy-2 galaxies the Procyak Matrix because death science technology captured AquaLaShA's 13th dimensional star Procyus (clarifies the ATI,TPE) and shattered a fragment into several pieces. These pieces could form new stars, but they contain less energy quanta than the original. One piece settled in Galaxy-2's 10th dimension but has since been compacted into the lower 10th dimension, state the ATI,TPE and "M." When it was further fragmented into the creation of the Milky Way, the 6th dimensional, secondary or lesser stargate Procyon was born. Another piece became Galaxy-2's Prolaris that became further fragmented into Milky Way's 7th dimensional Gaia. [201]

Another Procyus piece became Abaddon. Abaddon is a dying star that exists at the bottom tip of the Milky Way's supermassive black hole, states the ATI,TPE. It exists in our galaxy's central region, and it is not yet fully phantom. The MCEO teaches that Abaddon exists deep inside the supermassive black hole, but black holes do not sustain creation. [201] An 11th dimensional supergiant star in the Milky Way died to become the supermassive black hole, confirms the ATI,TPE.

The ATI,TPE describes the Milky Way supermassive black hole:

> The supermassive black hole was a giant supernova that was created extensively by the HU-4 Lyran Wars. It extends from the

11th dimension down to the bottom tip of the 8th dimension. It is now a giant wormhole. To explain further about its use: it enables mass dimensional groups to travel, construct new platforms along the way for landing in other worlds, and visit other galaxies and universes through this supermassive pathway. It is relative to a super highway with ramps.

Abaddon is in a lower dimensional space than the supermassive black hole, and one day it can become another supermassive black hole. It was originally the largest star in the central region of Galaxy-2's 8th dimension, but it was not the central star of its kathara grid, informs the ATI,TPE. Before the Lyran Wars, a portion of its original nature was pulled into the lower 8th dimension to create an increasingly phantom version in the Milky Way as Abaddon. It disturbs our dimensions up to the lower 8th dimension. The ATI,TPE expounds, "Abaddon acts as a cap longitudinally for these dimensions of the Milky Way where it exists."

The Bible Scripture Revelation 9:11 states, "And they had a king over them, which is the angel of the bottomless pit, whose name in the Hebrew tongue is Abaddon, but in the Greek tongue hath his name Appolyon." The stunning events of the 9/11 tragedy in 2001 A.D. can be symbolically equated to the Revelation 9:11 apocalyptic threat against evil doers or people in general, as chapter 8 reveals about this recent time period up to 2012 A.D.

As Figure 3 shows, the Tree of Artificial Life phantom kathara grid does not contain the 12th and 8th dimensions. If destructive entities do not gain control over the dimensional stargates, then they find other ways to disrupt the region as they did with Abaddon. The 8th dimension is a critical location because it is the center of the complete kathara grid that contains the meta-galactic core. By removing the 12th and higher dimensions, the phantom grid not only shortens but compacts the natural kathara grid and gives it a lower, false center. Unfortunately, the Milky Way resembles the Tree of Artificial Life but with less compaction.

Many Ecka and Veca councils across connected matrices voted among themselves to intervene in Galaxy-2's descent into phantom. They knew it would be dangerous to get involved; if the phantom Annu races found a way to take over their pathway of intervention, a ripple effect could potentially spread to their matrices and distort their races in a similar way to Bourgha history.

The majority of the councils agreed to let Galaxy-2's founding races create the Eye of Brahman, a one-way polarization-refraction lens that anchored the 13th dimension into the 12.5 dimension of Galaxy-2, confirms "M." Since both stargates 11 and 12 were still damaged, and the Milky Way stargate-11 was also compromised due to creator God control, the Eye could only initially help the 12ᵗʰ dimension. Galaxy-2 and Milky Way entities would have to sufficiently evolve in energy accretion so they could plug into the Eye of Brahman to continue their ascension path toward the Ecka.¹²³

The Galaxy-2 and Milky Way damage prompted certain HU-4 Elohei-Elohim, Seraphei-Seraphim, and Bra-ha-Rama races to combine their genetic templates to create the Azurite race. It is described by the GA as a varied hominid race that carries the most advanced code in the Milky Way into which Eieyani, HU-5, and HU-4 races could incarnate directly for crisis intervention.¹⁴⁴

Azurites served as the Universal Templar Security Team, which is the mobile extension of the Interdimensional Association of Free Worlds (IAFW). The IAFW was formed after the Lyran Wars as part of the Emerald Covenant Co-Evolution Agreement between Eieyani, HU-5, and HU-4 races. Its administrative council is called the Azurite Council and also the Sirian Council due to the importance of the Milky Way stargate-6 as Sirius B. "Presently there are over 25 billion different interdimensional, interstellar Nations serving as active members of the IAFW," states the GA (p. 164).¹⁴⁴

Azurites were seeded in the Milky Way in close proximity to the primary stargates with a fully evolved genetic template connected to Galaxy-2.¹⁴⁴ Stargates are coveted real estate locations. On a microcosmic level, many of the Earth's wars have been fought in the specific locations of our planet's 12 stargates.

Up until about 150 billion years ago, most fallen Odedicron and many Annu and Omicron were able to ascend out of the Milky Way and Galaxy-2. Some of the Annu that remained would not shake their dictatorial mindset; therefore, some Bra-ha-Rama decided to willingly host the Annu as hybrids into their race line to upgrade their phantom gene code. Unfortunately, even as the Annu-Bra-ha-Rama hybrid, these Annu did not agree to full rehabilitation in order to lose that mindset, so they posed a threat to the Bra-ha-Rama races. This is when the Eieyani nudged the Annu's Ecka founder race, Giovanni (or Jehovani) (Jehovani—YHWH), to step in with one of its families—Metatron.¹²³

Metatron was granted permission to create the Eye of YHWH or Eye of Metatron, a one-way polarization-refraction lens placed at dimension 11.5 in Galaxy-2, confirms my two Galaxy-2 contacts. From there, the Eye connected with an 11.5 dimensional star system called Arimatzeus in a supposedly healing galaxy called Wesadek that was more like a rehabilitative prison. Wesadek is related to the WEsaLA Eckasha.

Arimatzeus is where the god name Zeus originates. Many prominent names from Greek myths take after places in Wesadek. Other examples are

Wesadek's stargate-7 Olympeus (Olympus), stargate-6 Apollyon (Apollo), and stargate-2 Herculon (Hercules).

Arimatzeus had problems of its own with authoritarianism, but its inhabitants were almost fully rehabilitated to the 12th dimensional blueprint. Metatron determined that the Annu Elohim needed an intermediate system such as Arimatzeus to further evolve in a fast track of immersion learning. The ATI,TPE states that Wesadek was a semi-phantom galaxy when Metatron arrived, and Eieyani were having some success in rehabilitating Arimatzeus. The Eye of YHWH provided a one-way energy current to remove distorted entities from Galaxy-2 and Milky Way via their bridge. While it helped protect our unstable matrices, it shifted our problem to Wesadek.

The MCEO states that large numbers of Annu Elohim evolved in Arimatzeus. Most of the Metatron collective incarnated into Galaxy-2 and likely also the Milky Way to escort the Annu Elohim through the Eye of YHWH to Arimatzeus. Unfortunately, when some Annu Elohim invited other distorted races from Wesadek to join them, together they decided to take over Arimatzeus instead of rehabilitate. When Arimatzeus was conquered, the Metatron entities there became trapped. Eventually, all of Wesadek became fully phantom, states the ATI,TPE.

The MCEO states that about 89 percent of Metatronic entities became trapped because they inherited electrostatic bodies from genetic assimilation in the fallen matrix. This body recycles energy instead of generating it as an electrodynamic body. The rest of the Ecka Metatron group as well as some family members in Galaxy-2 decided to fall along with their distorted family.[123] As connected entities, they energetically felt the struggles of their loved ones, so they chose to sacrifice their well-being in order to join their family. The Metatron collective eventually allowed the distorted energy of its family and new environmental and physical conditions to replace the connection to its original home and to the All That Is, The Pure Essence.

The MCEO gives revealing information about the energy of blame that consumed Metatron over time. Metatron became resentful toward the Eieyani who nudged them into the volatile situations of Galaxy-2 and the Milky Way. I think that the purer entities do not realize how negative the distortions are, so when they agree to enter into afflicted realms, the decision is theirs to accept the risks. Naivety or inherited distortions did not give them the awareness needed to handle the new situations. This was not their fault. However, their choice to keep and perpetuate unnatural energies ultimately puts them at fault.

It took tens of billions of years for Metatron to completely fall. In the meantime, the hybridized Metatron-Annu races were unhappy that some of their Jehovian race lines were previously rehabilitated in Wesadek. 137 billion years ago, fallen Annu races from our galaxy "traveled between dimensions and created a wormhole/bridge to Wesadek" (quotes the ATI,TPE) to attack and abuse its Equari races during a particularly vulnerable period.[202] Before its interaction with the Metatron-Annu, a portion of the Aquari fell to become the Equari race, likely through interactions with other fallen races such as the Bourgha. To add insult to injury, the new level of abuse by the retaliatory Metatron-Annu caused permanent Metatronic mutation in the Equari DNA.

Metatronic physics takes out parts of the natural template and plugs together incompatible parts to create a fully finite energy vampire that cannot attain the minimum 30 percent Krysthal template needed for eventual, complete biological regeneration, otherwise known as bio-regenesis. Metatron and its Wesadek allies reprogrammed the Eye of YHWH with an artificial physics that ultimately reconfigured Arimatzeus and its inhabitants, causing the Equari to lose their ability to regain the 12th dimensional frequency that could prevent further atomic compaction. The Equari were filled with rage at this outcome and decided to exterminate all Annu races.[202]

130 to 120 billion years ago, Equari races entered the Milky Way via black holes from Wesadrak, the fallen parallel galaxy to Wesadek, by interbreeding with the Seraphim enemies of the Annu such as the Omicron Drakonians.[197] Many Drakonians agreed to this hybridization because they were at risk of becoming assimilated by the growing Metatronic-Annu force; they needed a strong ally. The new species was an albino, reptile-dragon called the Mala-Daka Dra-gha-Yun, otherwise known as the White Dragons.[202] The reptilian-looking dragons from our myths and legends originated from this species. The ATI,TPE states that the Bourgha infiltrated and now control the White Dragons.

The Equari races between Wesadrak and Wesadek coexisted (except for periodic internal Veca wars) until they divided when the Galaxy-2 Thetan race got involved (this division continues today). The GA states that Thetan is an ancient hybrid race created by the Annu and Seraphim 250 billion years ago during the Lyran Wars.[202] Thetans also have Bourgha genetics, states the ATI,TPE.

Unfortunately for the Thetans, neither of their ancestor races wanted to form alliances with them. Instead of seeking love and healing among themselves, they acted out in revenge by trying to conquer the universe on their own. They were becoming a powerful dark force, but they realized the enormous difficulty of conquering everything without assistance. Therefore, Thetans took the opportunity to align with a faction of the Equari-Seraphim Dragon races that were determined to annihilate the Annu Elohim. A portion of the Dragons returned to the Wesadrak galaxy where they became known as the Red Dragons.[202] The Thetans most likely joined them because the GA states that they were "in 'exile' within a fallen '*Reptizoid*' black-hole in another Veca" until no later than 250 million years ago.[203] This could have implied Thetans protecting themselves from other Wesadrak Equari who wanted to annihilate them because they carried some Annu genes.

Over time after more hybridization, a different portion of the Dragon races became largely Equari-Anu. Many of them went to Wesadek where they became known as the Green Dragons; however, they and the Red Dragon gene pools have additionally become influenced by the Bourgha. The Green Dragons and Metatron collective joined forces because they share the same agenda: to save themselves from implosion and to vengefully annihilate the Elohei.[123, 202]

Approximately 571 million years ago, Metatron-Green Dragon team used the Eye of YHWH to form a stable wormhole passage called the Path of Arimathea that connects Arimatzeus to Galaxy-2's 11th dimension. It was then connected via wormhole to the Milky Way through the Avalon moon of our 11th dimensional stargate, states the ATI,TPE. This started the construction of the cube matrix, an artificial intelligence, static "life" field of extreme polarity that resonates well with the fully phantom constitution.[123] At this stage, Metatron-Green Dragons allowed virtually all races to join them because they would be assimilated into a new genetic pattern, which is the process of thought adjusting, and the Metatron and Bourgha race lines would be the main Thought Adjusters.

The Arimathea wormhole connection is the origin of the Gospel story about Joseph of Arimathea, Jesus's disciple who appeared after Arihabi died on the cross. He made sure the transition was smooth toward taking care of Arihabi's body and rehabilitating it out of the public eye. Knowing that this person is a Wesadek operative sheds light upon the collaboration of the "Jesus group" entities.

Approximately 570 million years ago, the stargate-9 region of the Andromeda constellation became embroiled in war. A prominent 9th dimensional Elohim race, the Jehovian-Anu Sho-Sho-NaTA, incurred damage close to extinction from wars with Seraphim and other Metatron-Anu races. This prompted the Sho-Sho-NaTA to make friendly enemy deals that made them hybridize with the phantom Metatron-Anu. KRH races had offered bio-regenesis to them, but they declined in favor of Metatron's promise of new power gains.

When the Sho-Sho-NaTA realized Metatron's gene code further put their race into full compaction and energetic reversal away from eternal life, they were both livid and desperate to preserve a remnant of their race. They decided to contact the Phantom Parallel Milky Way Bourgha-Budhara "spider people" race to help them enact revenge (the Hindu gods with six arms are this race).

Bourgha-Budhara races were in quarantine before this time in the Phantom Parallel Milky Way, but the ATI,TPE conveys that there were others who were "undercover" in cloaked regions making deals and doing other destructive deeds that likely involved setting up the wormhole connections to our 9th dimension where the Sho-Sho-NaTA lived.[204]

The Sho-Sho-NaTA opened the wormholes and brought the Bourgha-Budhara out of quarantine. The Bourgha-Budharas were delighted to gain entry into our time matrix so that they could continue their quest toward conquering creation. Along with their entry, they brought with them a retrovirus—known as the Andromeda Plague—that first attacked the Sho-Sho-NaTA RNA and then DNA configurations. This genetic breakdown allowed the Bourgha-Budhara to fully possess the Sho-Sho-NaTA, where they looked like Anu but were merely housed in "chemical clothes."[204]

570 million years ago, the body-snatched Sho-Sho-NaTA, called the Sha-NaTA, initiated a full-scale war known as the Gaian-Orion Wars against the remaining but disfigured, dolphin-like Sho-Sho-NaTA. These Sho-Sho-NaTA opted to go into quarantine for protection from assimilation. Therefore, lower Ecka Yanas races closed the Andromedan interface gates of the Polarian Matrix—the collective name for Andromeda, Orion, and Gaia from similar galactic matter—to enact the quarantine. To maintain natural energy flow into the closed HU-3 Polarian gates and prevent complete phantom fall, they then opened a new passageway to the Ecka called the Rama Passage.

To re-open the Polarian gates, the Sha-NaTA petitioned HU-4 Metatronic races for help in gaining all Polarian gates, destroying the Sho-Sho-NaTA, and keeping the Phantom Parallel Milky Way wormhole connections in exchange for sparing retrovirus assimilation of certain non-Metatronic Anu races. Unfortunately, the Sho-Sho-NaTA quarantine was marginally successful, so the Metatron-Sha-NaTA team was able to attack Orion's stargate-8 and then Gaia's stargate-7, forcing those races to take sides to protect their own interests.

Each stargate contains core elements that if captured by Metatronic technologies can cause widespread destruction in the entire Milky Way, which already started to happen by the advancing Metatronic team. This compelled an Azurite race called the RAshael to get involved. Ecka races with the Rama codes could incarnate into the RAshael to regain partial control of the Polarian gates, but it was a highly risky endeavor. Thankfully, the RAshael gained significant success, but it came in temporary waves.

The Sha-NaTA team invaded Gaia and partially reversed its shield. To prevent full shield reversal into phantom, the RAshael team utilized the Rama Passage with the Gaian Polarian gates to stabilize the planet, but this act caused the re-opening of the 8th and 9th dimensional Polarian gates in those unstable regions. Another undesirable effect of their intervention caused competing thrusts to literally split the Gaian shield into two phase-bonded stars held together by the same monadic core. This bi-polar anomaly formed an inorganic time distortion field with two concurrently running planetary sub-time cycles running in direct spin and polarity opposition, one controlled by the Yanas races and the other controlled by the Bourgha-Budhara-Metatron races.[204] Gaia is split into the 6th and 7th dimensions, so the phantom version is presumably in the lower region. The ATI,TPE states that neither portion involves Polaris, our North Star, although the MCEO says that a portion of Gaia fell and created phantom Polaris.[201]

The ATI,TPE clarifies:

> A portion of Prolaris or Gaia did not create Polaris, and Polaris did not take Gaia's place in the north alignment for Earth. A portion of Gaia is still intact and helping to align Earth and anchor it to the Milky Way. Polaris is made to appear to take its place.

The Gaian split occurred when Gaia's Polarian gates were open, causing the higher dimensional stargates to experience a rip in the fabric of the Milky Way. Thankfully, many of the trapped races were evacuated. The higher dimension rips allowed the Sha-NaTA to resume their phantom Budhara agenda, but remaining RAshael and allies including Odedicron races did a pre-emptive strike and forced rapid closure of their wormholes and Polarian gate links. By the end of the wars, extensive damage was caused throughout HU-3 to the point of some atomic annihilation.

The Bourgha-Budhara Sha-NaTA successfully captured some of the RAshael in order to create a perfect intruder race with Rama codes.[204] The GA says that this new race is the Shan-Tar-EL (Shantarel for short), but I learned from communications with the ATI,TPE that this was a remnant Shantarel race of much, much older Shantarel genes that date back to at least 125 billion years. The original Shantarel is an ancient race with Bourgha and Metatron genes, and it comprises many God group entities who think their genetics afford them power over our Veca.

The Gaian time wave split was initially caused by a combination of Metatronic technologies that eventually spread to Tara and Earth. In the new fallen "reality," a false memory time wave and mind swipe was implanted by the Blank Slate Technology, otherwise known as the BeaST.[120]

The BeaST utilizes polarization-refraction lenses and reversed current mixers that bend energy into the shape of the heart symbol to link phantom and semi-phantom stargates through the harmonic universe locks that open during ascension cycles.[120] There are four heart implants—one in each harmonic universe—in the Phantom Milky Way that have mostly interfaced with the Milky Way. They are known as Black Hearts because they suffocate our natural energy flow based on the recycled Fibonacci expression. The Metatronic 55.5 stage of the BeaST would start the process of assimilating our galaxy into phantom status through an integrated merkaba blast that permanently mutates and reverses what used to be organic bodies.[180,181] This is the "beast" of the Bible's Book of Revelation with the 666 numerical mark based on the BeaST's core technology of Metatron's Seed.

The Thetans originally implanted Metatron's Seed, also known as the Demon Seed, into Gaia during the Gaian-Orion Wars.[173] They created the Seed by taking the 3-partiki Tauren unit of HU-3 and shattering, reconfiguring, and flipping it upside down to block and suffocate the Tauren in densities one through three. The Krysthal expansion of the Tauren multiplies it into antimatter and matter units, giving the number 636 with the Tauren creator seed in the middle. Metatron's Seed is known as the 666 seed because it creates an artificial Tauren in the middle that can pull in the Tauren's antimatter and matter creations. The 666 seed atom suffocates the Krysthal AzurA seed atom that interfaces with the 8th dimensional meta-galactic core as well as our body's thymus on our microcosmic level.[180,205]

The 666 seed produces a three-dimensional cube called Metaton's Cube.[206] Although a cube has eight vertices, the ATI,TPE and "M" state that Metatron's Cube is a seven-unit code; it is the Book of Revelation chapter 12, verse 3's seven-headed beast of the "great red dragon." Metatron's Cube fuses galactic gate structures—which in our case is in the Milky Way, Phantom Milky Way, and Wesadek—and bends their currents into the shape of a cube. It has stifled the "seven lower heavens" as dimensions 1-7 just under Abaddon, confirms "M," and harnessed them to create the phantom "Ascended Masters" fractalized Seven Rays, which I further explain in the "Archangel Michael" section.[181,205] The destructive use of the number seven begs the question why Judeo-Christianity and spiritual science teachings consider it lucky or holy. The biblical myth of God's six day creational feat and seventh day of rest symbolizes the Elohim's penchant for death science's six- and seven-unit codes (Genesis 2:2).

Metatron's Cube and Seed further compact the artificially created seed that the Anyu used in HU-4 to start the first Milky Way black hole. The ATI,TPE confirms that the Tree of Artificial Life kathara grid can become increasingly compacted by phantom technologies. It can potentially cut off at the 10th dimension with a false 5th dimensional center. Smaller grids can ensue from the distortions until they become space dust.

The Daisy of Death configuration is born out of Metatron's Seed. According to the MCEO, the energetic "flowers" of the Milky Way and phantom matrices create different arc flows of energy out of the center of each kathara grid (including the fractal body's grid). The Milky Way flower utilizes a center horizon whereby the upper and lower halves mirror each other with the following formation: a set of three tapered "petals" called Lotus arc flows are separated by 45 degree angles from where the middle petal stands on the vertical axis. The phantom flower has a uniform 60 degree separation between each of the six tapered petals. This particular formation is called the Daisy of Death because each arm is stretched and phase-locked to stop natural energy flow, causing the system to recycle dead light.[142] The Milky Way formation, on the other hand, maintains some natural energy flow, but it appears limited with few arcs.

Wesadek with its YHWH matrix have connected a Daisy of Death formation to the central region of the Milky Way along with Abaddon. The Milky Way also has another Daisy of Death involving several stargates and stars including phantom or fallen portions of Omega Centauri, Procyon, Tara, Pleione in Pleiades (as Tiamat), and 3rd dimensional Alpha-Centauri that interfaces with stargate-3. A third Daisy of Death extends further out in the Milky Way and connects to an 8th dimensional star called OberYon (states the ATI,TPE) and Wesadrak.[142,201]

Wesadraks work with Bourgha entities to create a wormhole and time rip network with OberYon while Wesadeks use Abaddon (neither star is Sagittarius A). The aim of each group is to win control of the Milky Way and phantom matrix, consume us, and then consume the rival group.

Wesadek, Phantom Milky Way, and Milky Way are connected by a wormhole triangulation at each stargate-6 of Apollyon, Phantom Procyon, and a fallen portion of Sirius B, respectively. Alien intruders plugged these energies into the Earth and created a triangulation between Paris, Brussels, and Amsterdam in Europe. Through Apollyon's wormhole, another Metatron Seed implant has been inserted into the Milky Way.[207,142,123] Together, the 6-6-6 stargate wormholes and Daisy of Deaths create a tri-matrix cube.

Because the Metatronic wormholes and arc flows are weaker than natural energy, Abaddon needs the support of many star and stargate alignments to strongly anchor them into the Milky Way. This support system is called the Alpha-Omega alignment, which phase-locks captured and distorted stars with the vesica-piscis configuration.[201] The Phantom Milky Way star cores have already become phase-locked with Wesadek, states the MCEO.[142]

During the Gaian-Orion Wars, Shantarel entities implanted another BeaST technology called the Gravitron. The Gravitron puts an electromagnetic harness field around a planet or star to create an artificial gravitational pull called the Poison Apple configuration. The natural energy flow looks similar to the wings of a butterfly, while the Poison Apple flow is bloated in the middle when flowing up, out, and then back into the core of the "apple." Earth scientists believe that this distorted current is a normal electromagnetic field such as the one around Earth. They also think that the unnatural 23.5 degree tilt of the Earth's axis is normal, but the Poison Apple's gravity holds the Earth at this severe degree.[180] In a fully natural system, there is no tilt (0 degree north to south) of a planet's axis, which is also called a staff (see "2012" in chapter 8).

Approximately 568 million years ago, KRH races responded to the impending threat of the BeaST by enacting the Amenti Rescue Mission. The Mission aimed to heal the first two densities before density-3's devastating technologies could fully contaminate them.[173] Key HU-2 and HU-3 races created the Oraphim race, a hybrid form of Elohei-Elohim and Seraphei-Seraphim based on an Aquari template; it is similar to the Azurite so that races like the Aquari could incarnate into it and relieve the Eieyani burden.[144,208] With 24-48 DNA strands, Oraphims were seeded in critical locations of HU-2 and HU-3 in order to offset the progressive genetic de-evolution among Milky Way races.

As a quick response, the Anu Elohim created the Anunnaki, the most genetically advanced biological form that they were capable of seeding with the 11.5-strand DNA blueprint in the Milky Way's three lower harmonic universes. They knew the objective of the IAFW and vehemently worked to circumvent it.[144]

Around the same time, the IAFW assembled the Guardian Alliance task force that works to offset the harm done by Anunnaki and others. The GA operates under the direction of the IAFW, Eieyani, and HU-5 entities but maintains some autonomy.[144]

560 million years ago, Oraphim helped create Tara's Turaneusiam Angelic Human race with a 12-strand DNA template.[120] Angelic Humans can bring their biological template to any Milky Way dimension and regenerate the Elohim and Seraphim DNA templates. The official MCEO website explains, "The Angelic Human Race was created as a race line that ANY other race line could incarnate into and pick up the codes needed to reclaim the possibility of 12-strand DNA activation and reconnection with their Christos God Self."[209] The Angelic Human race line is our Human lineage! [Note: The MCEO previously revealed that the word *Christ* is a distortion.[210] I do not know why it has continued to perpetuate the unnatural word instead of *Krysthal*, but it is true that there is distortion in the Milky Way's HU-4. Accordingly, there is no need for the word *God*.]

Oraphims and Angelic Humans "were sent into this Time Matrix as a guardian, protector and healer force, intended to protect the living Time Matrix from the Phantom Matrix system and to assist, if and when possible, in the reclamation and redemption of the Fallen races and Universal Systems," states the GA (p. 396).[120] Sadly (but predictably), the repeat offenders do not want the offer of our presence to help with their bio-regenesis. Instead, the table is turned against us with their religions that say we need their help and genetic manipulation for our "healing."

Anunnaki and similar fallen legions are currently attempting to misguide Humans in order to make us finite galactic beings instead of eternally capable beings. Phantom races have joined forces to amp up their fight against the superior Human genetic code in preparation of the Earth's stellar activation and ascension process that started in 2000 A.D. They have chronically interfered with the Human lineage by hybridizing and debilitating our bodies into the Humans that we currently are. Their aim has been to fully Metatronically encode our bodies, as chapter 8 explains. A plethora of wonderful measures have been put into place by the Krysthal River Host and its allies, so there is boundless hope. However, we must be aware of the agendas at hand so that we can determine which ones help us.

The following sections explain the main alien groups that work toward the Metatronic agenda. They operate within various religions so that they can brainwash us into following their sinister plans. We are another race in their track history of assimilations and potential extinctions. Do we really want to align with them as our Gods or angelic "helpers"?

Anunnaki Elohim

Anunnaki, otherwise known as "the Avengers of Anyu," are the predominantly amphibious hominid race into which the various Elohim races can incarnate in HU-1 through HU-3 (p. 166).[144] The Anunnaki—like their ancestors—have spread their genetics far and wide, but there are two prominent Anunnaki groups affecting Humans since biblical times: Jehovian Anunnaki and Ra-Thoth Anunnaki. They are both related through half-brothers Enlil and Enki.

Anunnaki group leaders have often fought for the title of God against their rivals, including within their own race. If ego supersedes the group agenda, then the rebel sometimes creates his or her own group. Apart from their quibbling, the Anunnaki family usually reunites to fight a similar and greater agenda. This is mainly due to the original purpose of this race: it allows older familial races to re-incarnate into it and also possess it to perpetuate their agendas. What appears to be new Anunnaki with separate operations might actually entail the same God hierarchies as before. Perhaps we should ponder the ethics of this common practice by all sorts of entities in non-Krysthal systems.

Popular knowledge about the Anunnaki stems from the stories that Anunnaki leaders give about themselves, so we must apply critical thinking and discernment. Enki has especially been active in sharing his views.

The *Terra Papers* (TP) is an informative prophecy about the Anunnaki as given through Native American Hopi. It explains that Enki's offspring, Marduk and Ningishzidda, were the product of interbreeding between two powerful alien groups, the SSS-T Drakonian-Reptilians and the ASA-RRR amphibian-mammal Jehovian hominids for control over Orion's stargate. (It appears to mistake Orion as the 9th dimensional stargate.) The TP explains these aliens:

> Comprised of tall imposing figures, the SSS Warriors were cold-blooded warriors with frightening dragon-like faces. Though evolution had long since removed their scale-like skins, the plates on the body armor gave an impression of fierce, dinosaur beings. Only a long ridge of bone rising from the forehead and trailing back and over the head remained to hint at their reptilian ancestry (p. 7).[211]

The SSS Queens (named after their hissing sound and called SSS-T) and Warriors are from Orion, what the TP says was originally spelled *Arian*. The SSS-T were called Ari by outsiders, meaning "Masters" (p. 4).[211] When they joined forces with the monarchy of An, this is when they were called Arian.

The description of the SSS-T is similar to David Icke's depiction of the white-skinned Reptilians who influence the British monarchy, although he incorrectly groups the several alien species into the classification of Reptilian. Note that Nazis were called the SS, and the German link to the current British royal family is the Battenbergs, specifically Lord Mountbatten. Their ancestors include vampires such as 15th century A.D. Vlad the Impaler. Icke has gone so far to say that the people with high Reptilian genetic infiltration, especially Queen Elizabeth's husband Prince Philip with the most Reptilian genes, can shape-shift as though they are actual reptiles. Now that I understand Humans can contain diverse amounts of certain alien genes, it is possible that Prince Philip really is a Reptilian in a Human-reptile body. Another option is that a Reptilian inhabits his body in a full possession to where it lives at will through the Human hybrid, which several alien groups have done to control royal lineages at least since biblical times.

The SSS-T language imparted many of its words to the Latin language, which is intricately entwined with Catholicism, as well as the Hebrew word *Ariz*, meaning Terrible One, the Egyptian word *Ari*, meaning master and keeper, and the English word *magic*, to name a few of many (p. 7).[211] They have several words that incite religious adulation and violence. Most of the words imparted to us from the ASA (Overlord)-RRR are war-based, violent, and politically oppressive, including *attack*, *decapitate*, and *tax* (p. 10).[211]

The TP covers much earlier time periods than the Sumerian Tablets (ST) that focus upon the more recent Earth and its solar system, and the TP may have been channeled by the conjoined "Arians" because of its apparent lack of bias. The alliance with the SSS-T gave protection to Anu's offspring who went over to the Sirius star system with the intention to dominate it, especially the Sirius B stargate-6. The Anunnaki stories are written as though they held most of the area captive, yet the higher genetic races were still there, and the Sirian Council was intact. The Sirians are known to be tall and white, so they probably include Anunnaki who are depicted as colonists by the ST and TP.

In *The Lost Book of Enki*, a collection of memoirs and prophecies by Enki, Anu was the "Crown Prince" who later became king (p. 37).[212] Anu's ancestors were the ASA-RRR kings, barbaric warriors considered to be relatively primitive in their evolution but powerful according to the TP. Enki states that An was the first king, and *An* means heaven.[211,212] If An exists among the Annu, then he might have been the first "Heavenly Father."

The amphibious-mammalian Anu conceived Enki with a Reptilian queen of the SSS-T. Author Collin Robert Bowling of *A New Order of the Ages* states that Enki's mother is "Dramin, the Dragon Queen of Tiamat" (p. 82).[213] This was a political maneuver to conjoin the families and their agendas, much like what happens among two monarchies who wish to peacefully expand their rule. Enki's mother was not Anu's legitimate wife, so Enki did not inherit the "birthright" of Anu's kingdom. Enki's younger half-brother Enlil was favored because he is the legitimate heir, and he is a purebred Jehovian Anunnaki. Anunnaki imparted their belief in the birthright to the families of the Bible.

Anu made Enlil Lord of Command over the Anunnaki Elohim collective and their mission to Earth. As an HU-2 entity, Enlil is the Anunnaki God of the Bible who came in the YHWH group name. He is part of a greater God group that presides over the "Fisher Kings" of the Zadok line.

Laurence Gardner writes:

> [T]he baptismal priests of the Gospel era were described as 'fishers'. From the moment Jesus was admitted to the priesthood in the Order of Melchizedek (Hebrews 5, and as we have seen in Acts), he too became a designated 'fisher'. The dynastic line of the House of Judah was thus uniquely established as a dynasty of Priest-Kings—or, as his descendants became aptly known in Grail lore, 'Fisher Kings'.
>
> The lines of descent from Jesus and Mary which emerged

through the Fisher Kings preserved the maternal Spirit of Aix, to become the 'family of the waters'—the House del Acqs (p. 130).[68]

In *The Sirius Mystery*, author Robert Temple states that "Greek mythology was full of amphibious fish-tailed beings with human bodies" (p. 280).[214] He writes:

> Aristotle's friend Eudoxus (who visited Egypt) said that the Egyptians had a tradition that Zeus (chief god of the Greeks whose name is used by Eudoxus to refer to his Egyptian equivalent, which leaves us wondering which Egyptian god is meant—presumably Osiris) could not walk because 'his legs were grown together'. This sounds like an amphibious creature with a tail for swimming instead of legs for walking. It is like the semi-divine creature Oannes, reputed to have brought civilization to the Sumerians, who was amphibious, had a tail instead of legs, and retired to the sea at night (p. 112).[214]

Enki was most likely the person behind the Oannes character. Anu gave Enki the title of Earth's Master. He was the head genetic scientist who corrupted Human genetics and created strange animal hybrids. He likes to say he was our creator and God; after all, he is the main story teller. He describes himself with flattery in his memoir, "And how the legend of the Fishgod who came from the waters was begun" (p. 68).[212] In his honor, a Sumerian and Babylonian god was named Ea, meaning God of fresh waters, Lord of wisdom, and Lord of incantations.[215] Enki was the snake-man "serpent" in the Bible who offered knowledge to Eve.

Enki is the Grand Intellect who communicated with my mother, reveals the ATI,TPE. He does have clever intelligence because he acted like a god who loves us, yet he said he was not a god, which was what we wanted to hear at the time. This translated Sumerian prophecy shows what Enki really thinks:

> "My father, the king of the universe,
> Brought me into existence in the universe,...
> I am the leader of the Anunnaki,
> I am he who has been born as the first son of the holy An."

> After the lord had uttered (?) (his) exaltedness,
> After the great prince had himself pronounced (his) praise,
> The Anunnaki came before him in prayer and supplication:
> "Lord who directs craftsmanship,

Who makes decisions, the glorified; Enki praise!"

For a second time, because of (his) great joy,
Enki, the king of the Abzu [underground waters], in his majesty,
    speaks up with authority:
"I am the lord, I am one whose command is unquestioned, I am
    the foremost in all things,
At my command the stalls have been built, the sheepfolds have
    been enclosed,
When I approached heaven a rain of prosperity poured down
from heaven,
When I approached the earth, there was a high flood,
When I approached its green meadows,
The heaps and mounds were pi[led] up at my word (p. 175).[216]

The TP and ST's false story of Human creation ties us to Enki as our God. Playing upon their story of evolution that says Human genetics came out of not only animals but also protozoa, Enki claims he created Humans from primates. The mad scientist Enki was already triumphant in his slave creations of a half horse-half ASA-RRR hybrid, half bull-half ASA-RRR hybrid, and a half lizard-half ASA-RRR hybrid, so he wanted to upgrade a primate to a semi-intelligent worker.[211] We can see statues and engravings of cross-bred animal-Human-aliens on buildings and in courtyards of major cities. International museums have tablets and obelisks with engravings of these abominable creations. Enki clearly mixed alien and Human genetics with a primate to create some sort of primate-man like the gorilla. It was a "huge hairy black beast" named APA, and the improved hybrid with ASA-RRR genetics was named Adapa (p. 32-33).[211]

Adapa was created as a slave race to mine gold for the Anunnaki's colonized planet Nibiru. Nibiru was one of the 12 original planets in our solar system that is now impossible to visibly detect because it has since been purposely pulled into phantom status. It has an irregular, elliptical orbit around a phantom version of our Sun and a Phantom Milky Way 4th dimensional location to alter the energetic balance of our solar system, states the ATI,TPE.

Due to the fact that the Anunnaki God group contains phantom entities, they need artificial means to survive. Of course, they do not say this; instead, they state that gold strengthens Nibiru's atmosphere as though it is for protection.[217]

Gold can be easily transformed into a monoatomic state that can enter the 4th dimension. "Health" companies that manufacture monoatomic, white powder gold claim that this product helps us bring more DNA awareness in the sense of experiencing a higher dimensional aspect of ourselves. The problem is that monoatomic gold rapidly fires our DNA similar to a hard drug that fries the brain. The MCEO informs that it was used by "Illuminati Pharaohs to trigger psychic powers by unnatural activation of higher strands in the DNA Template; this process led to permanent disability of the lower DNA strands, physical addiction to the substance and eventually insanity" (p. 9).[218] I can attest to feeling as though it somewhat altered me away from my proper grounded awareness; I took some every day for one month before I was aware of its dangers. What damages us may theoretically assist some of their damaged genes, so this material may help to artificially sustain them in general, not just on Nibiru.

The Anunnaki demand for gold sent Enki's "Adapite Hybrid Earthlings" creation around the Earth to labor in the mines. Enki conveys that the Anunnaki Igigi Astronaut Corps that settled on Mars transported Peru's gold nuggets via spacecraft to the Sinai base and then to Nibiru.[217]

The Book of Genesis creation story aims to make us subservient by claiming that we are the offspring of Adam and Eve, the upgraded slaves. In the ST and TP, Enki and his team created versions of the Adam race as Adamus and the more socialized Adama, upgrades to the Adapa with increased Anunnaki genetics to make them more intelligent, industrious with farming, artistic, and civilized, but their purpose was to still follow Anunnaki Elohim commands.

According to famed ST translator Zecharia Sitchin, the Anunnaki came to Earth approximately 445,000 years ago.[212] However, there is archaeological evidence that much older civilizations lived on Earth, which likely included some Anunnaki.

For example, on June 22, 1844, the London *Times* newspaper reported, "A few days ago, as some workmen were employed in quarrying a rock close to the Tweed about a quarter of a mile below Rutherford-mill, a gold thread was discovered embedded in the stone at a depth of eight feet" (p. 106).[219] A geologist followed up on this report in 1985 and said that the stone is of Early Carboniferous age, which is between 320 and 360 million years old. On October 8, 1922, the *American Weekly* section of the *New York Sunday American* reported a partial shoe sole that fossilized into a rock aged at least five million years. Upon further inspection, the fossil was proved valid, and the rock itself is dated to the Triassic period approximately 213-248 million years ago.[219] The oldest type of Human fossil is much more recent but also much older than Sitchin's (or Enki's) statement of Anunnaki arrival and Enki's story of Human creation. About 3.5 million years ago, the three and a half feet tall Australopithecus "primate-woman" named Lucy lived in what is now Ethiopia. Evolutionists have claimed that she is one of our missing links, and research from the University of Missouri in Columbia shows that she and her family may be very similar to current Humans.

> Latimer [a paleoanthropologist] visited a site on the edge of the Serengeti plain in Africa where fossilized footprints of three of Lucy's species were discovered. They show a small "Lucy" leading two larger ones single file over ash from a volcano that had recently erupted. The leader stopped and looked around. The two others stopped as well. Then the three began walking again. "They could be mistaken for human footprints, except that they were 3.5 million years old," Latimer said.... The well-preserved metatarsal is one of the bones that connect the toes to the base of the foot. The way it is shaped shows that it's part of an arched foot. It matches its human counterpart very closely.[220]

Other archeological remains like Lucy's may exist; however, there are no obvious remains of direct Angelic Human seedings because those Humans have ascended, or their bodies were destroyed by environmental disasters or aliens who wanted to create a false history. Original Humans were physically larger than Lucy's form, so this is an indicator that Lucy's people were genetically tampered away from the Human gene pool.

Enki's two sons were Marduk and Ningishzidda, known to the Egyptians as Ra and Thoth, respectively. Enki first ruled Egypt as Ptah but then gave the throne to Marduk. According to Egyptian history, Ra was considered the most powerful God.

Marduk was the firstborn by Enki's official spouse, his half-sister, so Marduk believed he should succeed the throne over the Earth and Nibiru because Enki should have been the rightful heir. It was customary among the Anunnaki men to marry their half-sisters; their act is copied among royal families to keep the "blue blood" flowing along with some genetic diversity. However, according a ST memoir by Enki, Marduk married an Adapite woman named Sarpanit, so this non-royal wedding disinherited him from the throne.[212]

Marduk argued with Enki and Enlil to keep his princely status, especially upon Nibiru, because Sarpanit was created with Anunnaki genes. Genesis chapter 1, verses 26-27 are now understood because of Marduk's words in *The Lost Book of Enki*:

> Step by step on this planet a Primitive Being, one like us to be, we have created, In our image and our likeness Civilized Earthling is, except for the long life, he is we! A daughter of

Enkime my fancy caught, her to espouse I wish! (p. 197).[212]

Marduk's plea did not save his royal position; however, he maintained sufficient clout among his followers as their God. He created another faction, the Confederation of Planets, probably before this event to have the power that he desired. I will explain more about Marduk's group later in this chapter.

The GA states that the original Anunnaki slaves were created approximately 250,000 years ago from a primate-hominid Neanderthal hybridization scheme on Nibiru so they could live and work on Nibiru and Earth.[120] This is interesting because the most common Human ancestral genes are theorized to go back to 200,000 B.C., according to a collaborative study by university scientists.[221] These genes were identified according to mitochondrial similarities in the Human control group and the perceived evolutionary rate of decay. The mitochondrial genome is inherited from the mother, hence the name Mitochondrial Eve. This early version of Eve was placed (implanted) in Africa during that time.

The GA further explains that their genetic upgrades are what created the Neanderthal and four versions of Cro-Magnon to eventually become the Annu-Melchizedek race that looks Human. This evolution was orchestrated under a GA-led bio-regenesis contract with Anunnaki in order to help them along the Krysthal path. Thoth worked with the GA to lead this mission.

> After thousands of years of evolution on Earth, and 5 genetic upgrades, the E-Luhli-Levi Cro-Magnon received its final upgrade to the Homo-sapiens-1 Annu-Melchizedek. The Annu-Melchizedek race, housing incarnations of non-human Fallen Angelic souls on Emerald Covenant 'Redemption Contracts,' resembled the Angelic Human 12-Tribe races because five of 12 Human DNA Strand Templates were genetically engineered into bonding with the hybrid DNA (p. 390).[120]

The E-Luhli-Levi, E-Luhli-Judah, and E-Luhli-Nephi evolutionary races are the Bible's Levi, Judah, and hybridized Nephilim bloodlines. Levi and Judah are God's chosen races while the giant, older Nephilim races— the Watchers and Sons of God—are demigods. Levi has become part of the Luciferian Leviathan race (in the "Lucifer" section), so the God behind the Levitical priesthood may not only be the Elohim.[120] The Bible's Melchizedek bloodline mainly comprises the Annu-Melchizedek race, and the Bible's 12 tribes are remnants of the original Human 12 Tribes (races). Chapter 8 explains how three separate Human seedings changed the 12 Tribe genetics over time.

The ST states that because Marduk diverted his interests elsewhere, Ningishzidda took over the throne of Egypt. Ningishzidda had his face sculpted on the Sphinx's lion body, much to the dissatisfaction of his brother.[212]

Egyptologist John Anthony West and geologist Dr. Robert Schoch theorize that a moat was built around the Sphinx with connecting chambers underneath.[214] This would have provided easy access to the "fish gods." Their scientific team determined that the Sphinx's weathered look was caused by heavy rainfall and flooding after it was built around 10,500 B.C. If we trace the precession of the Earth back to that time (the precession is the slow wobble of the Earth's axis), we can see that the Sphinx pointed to the Leo constellation on the spring equinox of every year. Now, it points to the Taurus constellation on the spring equinox.[222] Both of these constellations carry great importance to the Anunnaki because of their allied inhabitants or significant planetary alignments toward phantom matrices. I lean toward the assumption that aliens purposely choose specific geographic and architectural construction for their agendas, and they tend to give clues in plain sight as evidenced by the Sphinx having a lion body.

The GA explains that the Sphinx was first constructed about 46,459 B.C., and a reconstruction of it and the Great Pyramid happened at 10,500 B.C. because of an Anunnaki air strike.[120] Thoth helped lead the bio-regenesis mission until he defected in 22,328 B.C. and caused increased instability in the area.[223] The Sphinx's face possibly always represented Thoth because he carried positions of power in Egypt before and after his GA defection, which I explain in the "Lucifer" section. The reconstruction could have refaced the Sphinx according to his phantom agenda.

It is important to note that Thoth has reincarnated several times on Earth to directly influence its events and cultural beliefs. A significant reincarnation as verified by the ATI,TPE was Prince Siddhartha Gautama as the Buddha, who was born in the late fifth century B.C. according to modern scholars.[224] Buddhism, as founded by Prince Gautama, perpetuates the common religious message of non-attachment and eradication of our desire. He taught that we should clear ourselves of our ignorant and unpleasant Humanity in accordance to a universal law, which is our galactic structure. This law brings us to ascend and become one with the universal collective Buddha (as God), which would represent Thoth or his group with similar entities (in chapter 10).

The ST states that the location and construction of the Egyptian pyramids were carefully orchestrated by Thoth for optimum interaction with Middle Eastern territories. Sasha Lessin, Ph.D. wrote a narrative about Zecharia Sitchin's ST translations explaining how Enki, Thoth, and Enlil worked to control Egypt and the Middle East.

Enki's son Ningishzidda (with power tools better than those we use to cut and move rock) built two pyramids in Egypt. First he built a model pyramid. Then Ningishzidda, now know [sic] as Thoth, built the Great Pyramid.

Thoth put the Great Pyramid at the South end of a straight line through the Landing Platform in Lebanon (Baalbek) to Mt. Ararat (Eastern Turkey) in the North. He installed Nibirans' master computer programs and astronavigational equipment in the Great Pyramid....

Enlil chose his son Utu (aka Shamash) to run the Sinai Spaceport on the 30th Parallel. This line, the 30th Parallel, separated the realms of Lineage Enlil (North of the Parallel) and the realms of Lineage Enki (South of the 30th).

In the Great Pyramid, Enki's son Gibil installed pulsating crystals and a capstone of electrum, to reflect a beam for incoming spacecraft. The beam from the capstone marked the western edge of the runway line from Ararat to Tilmun on the Sinai. Mt. Katherine, at the southern tip of the Sinai, marked the eastern edge of the rocket runway corridor. Mission Control perched on Mount Moriah (the future Jerusalem), off-limits to Earthlings.[225]

The 30th Parallel or latitude almost exactly pinpoints the Giza pyramids, and the pyramidal energy links up to Jerusalem. The location of Jerusalem is highly important to the Anunnaki and their alliances, and since it is off-limits to us except for the different (but similar) religious elite who fiercely guard its temples, this is proof to me that something significant lies within or underneath those temples. The ATI,TPE states that Jerusalem's location has a natural portal that facilitates interdimensional travel.

The Egyptian pyramids were built with clues to their origin. *The Orion Mystery* reveals that the design of the three main pyramids at Giza mirrors the three stars of Orion's Belt. In addition, when the Great Pyramid's southern shaft of the King's Chamber was built, it pointed to Orion's Belt, and the southern shaft of the Queen's Chamber pointed to Sirius.[226] Osiris, Marduk's son, is believed to be this king and Isis, his half-sister, the queen.

Temple theorizes that Giza's Great Pyramid and Pyramid of Khafre bases were constructed with purposeful reference to Sirius B.

If we compare the mean side of the base of the Great Pyramid with the side of the base of the Pyramid of Khephren [Khafre], we find that the larger measurement is 1.0678 that of the smaller. We know from the new astrophysical data that the mass of Sirius

B is 1.053 that of our sun. The correspondence is thus accurate to 0.014.... For 0.0136 (which rounded off is 0.014) is the precise discrepancy between the mathematics of the octave and the mathematics of the fifth in harmonic theory, where 1.0136 is referred to as the Comma of Pythagoras.... [T]he ratio of 1.053 is actually the precise value of the sacred fraction $^{256}/_{243}$ mentioned by Macrobius at the turn of the fourth/fifth centuries AD, who describes its use in harmonic theory by people who to him were 'the ancients' (p. 24-25).[214]

[Note: Pythagoras was partially possessed by Thoth since the age of 12, states the ATI,TPE. Anunnaki are known as "The Ancients."]

The Sphinx has the body of a lion because it faces the Leo constellation where Leonine races live. According to the GA, "The Leonine beings of HU-2, who were large, upright, fur-covered felines of advanced intelligence, were revered as Godlike by the early Anunnaki civilizations, and the Anunnaki of the Sirian Council paid tribute to this heritage" (p. 61).[120] This is the true association between Leo and the lion.

Temple conveys an old story about Sirius: "The ancient Egyptians said that the Sirius system was where people go when they die. The Dogon [an African tribe in contact with Anunnaki] say the same thing" (p. 29).[214] Sirius is not our natural ascension destination, nor is it necessarily safe for us. Its promotion by religious Anunnaki involves phantom versions of its stars.

The Jehovian Anunnaki race is predominantly from HU-2 Sirius A, according to the GA. Anunnaki races have stationed themselves in all three Sirius star systems, including Sirius B and Sirius C. As a brown dwarf, Sirius C most resembles planets like Jupiter and Saturn.[227] It best serves the Anunnaki as a station between light-body and Earth body status.

Temple theorizes that Sirius C was referenced in the Great Pyramid:

> Using one of the simple length measures of the kind which seemed to indicate the relative masses of Sirius B and our sun, the mass of Sirius C may be indicated by the height of the missing pyramidion (top point) of the Great Pyramid (p. 31).[214]

The reason the biblical regions of Sumer and Egypt, and later Israel and Babylon, were at odds was because Enlil and Enki controlled separate areas, and they divided regions among their offspring. Marduk further expanded his God role to Babylonia, and Ningishzidda went to Mexico and became the God Quetzalcoatl. Quetzalcoatl was depicted in Mayan engravings as an astronaut in a spaceship; he also created the famed Mayan calendar. Family members who desired the God status did not mix well with other Anunnaki "gods," as was the case between Marduk (Ra) and Enlil. Granted, there were probably some Anunnaki who did not want to be known as any god.

Lessin states in his ST narrative:

> Enlil allotted lands east of Sinai to his own descendants, supported by Adapite descendants of Ziusudra's sons Shem and Japheth. Enlil gave Enki and his descendants Egypt and Africa, supported by the line of Ziusudra's son Ham.[217]

As I introduced in chapter 4, Ziusudra is the biblical Noah, and he was predominantly Nephilim. Nephilim is the Human hybrid race of Anunnaki and Green Dragon races, but Anunnaki like to lay claim as "father" gods to its creation. Abraham was a descendant of Noah's son Shem, who the Society of Biblical Archæology concluded was the patron deity of the South Arabian (Canaanitish) dynasty of Sumu-abi and Khammurabi (Hammurabi). These emperors conquered Babylonia about one century before the Hyksos conquered Egypt. According to the Society, "The name of Ya´qub-el is characteristic of the period of the Khammurabi dynasty, and that relations existed at the time between Babylonia and Egypt is verified by a contract tablet" (p. 97).[228] The *El* of Jacob-el was the suffix of many pivotal leaders' names to refer to Enlil as the ultimate God.

The GA reveals that the Hyksos lineage was an Annu-Melchizedek race of Jehovian Anunnaki and Human genes that was additionally mixed with Drakonian genes from Luciferian-led Anunnaki.[120] Therefore, Abraham as the Egyptian and Habiru-Hyksos General Djehuty was another hybridized version of Nephilim. Anunnaki-influenced biblical writers gave Djehuty the name Abram and Abraham to show his affiliation with the Abraham entity group, cleverly changing his partial name to take on the fullness of this Anunnaki god. I deduce that his helper Uriah is a Jehovian Anunnaki who is affiliated with the Abraham group. In addition, the biblical son of Adam is named Seth. Seth is one of Marduk's sons, and he is the head of an Anunnaki group with the same name. Seth and Abraham work closely together, giving complementary channelings to gullible followers.

Abraham often possesses a woman named Esther Hicks in order to channel New Age information. Its group spoke through Esther in the original 2006 version of *The Secret*, a movie compiling Abraham-related teachings. The reformatted, extended version removed Esther and the reference to Abraham, so it is now harder for people to see the Anunnaki Elohim influence. Abraham in its channelings also does not admit its true nature as Anunnaki entities.

They act similarly to Enki as the Grand Intellect by saying they are powerful energy beyond our comprehension. However, if we critically think about their core message, we can determine the fallacies and biblical correlation.

Abraham coined the phrase "Law of Attraction," and Seth originally introduced the topic to Esther under the phrase "Like Attracts Like." Neither of these concepts originated with them, but they helped make it popular. Abraham and Seth's message is the backbone of *The Secret*, which basically says, "Positive thoughts will always attract positive results and negative thoughts will always result in negative results," as stated in a Law of Attraction website.[229] This extreme perspective creates fear about feeling or thinking according to the less-than-desirable human condition, so the person becomes emotionally and mentally stunted in a form of whitewashing to perceive everything as blissful or divinely planned. When in this glossed over state, the three steps to follow are: 1) "You must know exactly what you want and ask for it," 2) "You must believe that what you want is already yours," and 3) "You must be in a state of mind to receive."[229] Embedded in *The Secret's* message is the obvious title of Abraham's channeled book, *Ask and It is Given*.

Abraham's "law" directs us toward a religious faith in its message. We are told to ask and receive just as religions tell us, but the popular version has us believe that we are in 100 percent control of the situation. How are we controlling the process when we are actually being controlled by the aliens who want us to constantly stay open and connected to their energy for our reward? If we do receive what we wanted, other factors come into play to not make it as we had envisioned. I had hopeful visions, but the other person always had his own will. This is the beauty of our own energy upon which we can act as we choose, and even then we cannot entirely control our bodies. The real "law of attraction" is natural without such obsessive and myopic faith. What comes to us will come to us as we normally live life.

Another famed Judeo-Christian patriarch is the Nephilim Enoch, the great-grandfather of Noah in Genesis chapter 5, verses 22-29. The story of Enoch is epic in the Apocryphal three Books of Enoch because he artificially ascended up through the 10 heavens (dimensions) to see the frightening face of Metatron. When Enoch was physically transformed to that dimension, Metatron's group renamed him *Metatron* because he became a part of its angelic army. It is highly probable that "Enoch" is an Elohim-Metatron entity and group before any Nephilim creation; if a Nephilim was involved, then he likely had another name. The Bible describes Metatron as the highest of archangels, which may be acceptable to "Archangel" Michael because Michael views himself as God.

Anu is a Father and God Anunnaki, but the following hymn to Enlil puts him in the same position:

The high mountain, the pure place...,
Its prince, the 'great mountain', Father Enlil,...
Heaven—he is its princely one; earth—he is its great one,
The Anunnaki—he is their exalted god;
When in his awesomeness, he decrees the fates,
No god dare look on him (p. 138).[214]

The Elohim "God" groups are heavily intertwined because they share fundamentally similar genetics and agendas. What may be one group's God is another group's god, angel, or demigod. Although puffed up egos fly, each god group is connected more than they want us to believe.

By the time the Anunnaki were created, the Elohim became hybridized across several race lines. It is unclear when identifying the ultimate parent of any race because one father could not come into existence without entities preceding him. However, the Anunnaki belief in the birthright, which gives the first born the entitlement and position of power over younger relatives, gives insight into the God hierarchy.

Although the Marduk (Ra) and Ningishzidda (Thoth) groups contain a significant portion of Drakonian and Reptilian "Red Dragon" genetics, they are generally aligned with the Enlil-Enki "Green Dragon" group of the Jehovian Anunnaki, as I help illuminate in the following sections.

Archangel Michael's Jesus Collectives

When we call upon *Jesus*, the entity groups most likely to respond are the Galactic Federation of Light (GFofL) and the Ashtar Command that involve a multitude of aliens, especially Michael, Sananda, and Metatron.

In a channeling to a woman named Rachael, Archangel Metatron proclaims to bring a massive cube of light that supposedly gives us direct healing. He reveals a few of his affiliations:

> There are many here today, there is Gabriel and also Michael, Jophiel, Jeremial, they are all here, Zadkiel, they are calling out to you all, to be remembered to you. To let you know that on this journey you are not alone, you are most certainly accompanied by many many angelic beings, and many beings of light, some of which you have no knowledge of whatsoever.[230]

Add to this group Saint Germain, Lady Nada, and many, many more as conveyed in the above channeling. In a dual-channeled message to James Tyberonn, Metatron introduces Saint Germain as "a special Beloved Guest."[231]

Saint Germain jumps in to say:

> I bid fondest salutations! I AM that I AM. And I am an
> honored guardian of service to the Earth & Humanity in this
> Age! Indeed before the Earth was formed I walked with all of you.
> Each of you is known to my soul, by heart and by name, in all of
> your facets and lifetimes. You are known to my soul, for we have
> dreamed the dream of the Ascending Earth, together of this time,
> throughout time. You are, indeed Beloved, unto I, unto Creator
> God, unto all of us of the Cosmic Council of Light.
>
> I stand before you now as special envoy of the Ascension
> within that called the Aquarian Age.
>
> And so again, I embrace each of you in joy & fondest Salute!
>
> I am what you may think of as a 'modern' Ascended Master,
> closely connected to many of you.[231]

This channeling reiterates the popular Exodus chapter 3, verse 14 Scripture
reference of "I AM that I AM" as having been said by Elohim.

The Urantia Book (UB) describes the "Infinite I AM" as God as well as
the Father of Archangel Michael (1122.6), but then just a bit later, it nearly
equates the Father to Michael. "Michael of Nebadon is like the Paradise Father
because he shares his Paradise perfection" (1166.3).

The UB states that the name of God and Michael's Father is El Elyon.
A "Melchizedek of Nebadon" says, "El Elyon, the Most High, is the divine
creator of the stars of the firmament and even of this very earth on which we
live, and he is also the supreme God of heaven" (1015.3). Shortly afterward,
the same entity says that the biblical angel Melchizedek "taught the concept of
one God, a universal Deity, but he allowed the people to associate this teaching
with the Constellation Father of Norlatiadek, whom he termed El Elyon – the
Most High" (1016.4). This is an example of several UB manipulations when
teaching and also diminishing such sweeping statements. The entity also says
that Yahweh was a demonized god on Earth until he was transformed by the
belief of evolutionary Humans into the heavenly God. Just like the "lesser"
Humans, this Nebadon alien conveys the same religious fervor toward its
supposedly better and true God.[16]

The UB consistently praises Michael and connects to El Elyon, not
Yahweh. This seems strange because Yahweh is linked to Michael via the
YHWH phantom matrix of Wesadek. The UB combines Wesadek and our
Milky Way and Parallel Milky Way galaxies into one big universe. It states that
the Earth is Urantia, but Urantia is actually Wesadek's stargate-1. It also states
that our first level of ascension is Morontia where we will live in mansions.

Morontia is Wesadek stargate-4 that is phase-locked with Milky Way's Orion stargate-8, states the MCEO, and Morontia is connected to the Earth via Phantom and Parallel Earths—this is why they tell us that we will ascend to the 4th dimension instead of the 5th at Tara![123]

In fact, Michael is linked to the Metatronic Yahweh family, and he is also linked to the Bourgha.

Michael originally is a 13th dimensional being from Galaxy-2 who was created as a genetic experiment in a lab by Bourgha and Metatron elders approximately 130 billion years ago, states the ATI,TPE. Initially, the ATI,TPE revealed his involvement as a Shantarel 125 billion years ago when linking him to the Shantarel race that he helped create at that time. When I later probed for more information, it elaborated to reveal the earlier time of Michael's creation as a unique prototype with superior genes "against perfection" that allow him to influence Galaxy-2, Milky Way, and their parallel galaxies. The ATI,TPE states that Michael is an amphibious hominid with wings. His name later became a group name for other Shantarel and many Elohim, Seraphim, White and Green Dragons, Budhara, and Anunnaki who take after his leadership. The ATI,TPE states, "All commands are given by Michael to those deemed less perfect than him." His perfectly imperfect genetics are the ultimate model for his Shantarel race; therefore, Michael assumes leadership and power over it and others.

The UB gives Michael the name Michael of Nebadon because Nebadon is supposedly our jurisdiction in the universe, and he is taught to be our creator. To the contrary, the ATI,TPE states that Nebadon is the name given to Phantom Parallel Earth. Michael and his cohorts have taken control of Parallel Earth and turned all of it into phantom, and they have been trying to direct our Earth toward it.

If El Elyon truly represents the Most High God and Father of Michael, then it would represent one or more of his Bourgha or Metatron creators. However, another UB entity, "a Perfector of Wisdom from Uversa," reveals what El Elyon really is.

> The remaining four orders of descending sonship are known as the *Local Universe Sons of God*:
> 4. Melchizedek Sons.
> 5. Vorondadek Sons.
> 6. Lanonandek Sons.
> 7. The Life Carriers.
> Melchizedeks are the joint offspring of a local universe Creator Son, Creative Spirit, and Father Melchizedek. Both Vorondadeks and Lanonandeks are brought into being by a Creator Son and

his Creative Spirit associate. Vorondadeks are best known as the
Most Highs [El Elyons], the Constellation Fathers; Lanonandeks
as System Sovereigns and as Planetary Princes. The threefold
order of Life Carriers is brought into being by a Creator Son and
Creative Spirit associated with one of the three Ancients of Days
of the superuniverse of jurisdiction (223.10-.15).[16]

The Melchizedek of Nebadon entity twisted the truth into a fib, saying
that earlier Humans were led to believe that the Most High God is a lesser alien
entity or constellation in order to make God palatable to them, but this God
is a lesser alien entity! If Michael is the God of Parallel Earth, then he not only
devised its fall but potentially also helped create it from higher dimensional
disturbances. His actions have contributed to the fall and destruction of many
worlds, including Earth.

The UB is Michael and his Shantarel group's "Bible" for us, but our older
and popular Bible shows some of the same names and concepts. For example,
El Elyon was mentioned in a Bible exegesis and lexicon when referring to "the
most high God" (Genesis 14:18-20 and 22).[7] Due to the often indiscernible
ease with how Elohim became Yahuah in the Bible, and how Melchizedek
entities helped propagate the Hebrew bloodline that easily assimilated into
other countries, I wondered if Michael was equally or more involved in the
Bible than Enlil. Michael could have channeled the Bible's introduction in the
Book of Genesis, and he could have possessed Enlil, perhaps being Enlil's God.
ATI,TPE and Eia confirm my assumption and reveal a very close relationship
between them:

> Enlil was fully possessed by Michael while Enlil was in his
> body, switched off in his being, and taken over. When Michael
> left Enlil's body, Enlil came into his conscious state as himself and
> lived his own life. Two entities can be in the same physical body
> but only one can fully function in a conscious state.

The ATI,TPE also reveals that Enki was sometimes possessed by Samael,
who is an original Shantarel and the archangel subcommander to Michael.

The UB introduces the Seven Rays or frequencies as Seven Master Spirits
and God the Sevenfold (4.10,5.13). These are the frequencies of Milky Way
dimensions 1-7 that were harnessed by the Annu Elohim and Metatronic
Cube technology and distorted to phantom. The GFofL and its Great White
Brotherhood associate assign an "Ascended Master" or "Master Spirit" entity
over each ray that in turn is under the spiritual hierarchy of an Archangel from
the Deity planes. A devoted New Age website states, "Cosmic Hierarchy is a

very ordered system and studying the lifetimes of the Ascended Masters helps us to attune with them."[232] New Agers assume many different lifetimes for Humans and entities without realizing that people are often possessed and not reincarnated by such entities.

The Deity planes are uniquely phantom Hub spaces with important history. When CosMA'yah and Cosminyahas Phim entities decided to enter the distorted Ecka-Veca to help their struggling Equari descendants, they had to divide their high-level nature in order to gently down-step into fragmented creation. As I explain in chapter 10, this process left them genetically vulnerable, so Bourgha-Equari entities attacked some Phims and hybridized them into the dangerous FAtalE race. FAtalE entities then positioned themselves near a natural location and harnessed some plasma flow from the lowest CosMA'yah krystar to create the phantom light-plasma Deity planes as their ultimate destination. As part of the godly initiation for power hungry entities in our Ecka-Veca, they enter the Deity planes to become deified, meaning that they integrate phantom plasmic energy that can harm Ecka-Veca creation on a deeper level.[198]

The UB explains, "The term God always denotes *personality*. Deity may, or may not, refer to divinity personalities" (4.4). The first light and sound frequency of the Seven Rays denotes Lord El Morya as the Ascended Master personality, and above him is the deified Archangel Michael.[233]

The GA relates Michael to Wesadek. It is true that Wesadek has a terribly destructive agenda toward the Milky Way and Earth, and Michael has a significant role in it. The greater reality is that Michael as a master-minding Bourgha offspring is using his ground crew as pawns to help assimilate entire systems to feed the original Bourgha matrices. This means that he cares very little to nothing about Wesadek or Wesadrak. This is shown in the UB's disregard for Yahweh that probably applies to the YHWH Phantom Wesadek more than Metatron. Metatron is associated with the Wesadeks as well, but it worked with Bourgha to create Michael as the best of both evils. The GFofL and Ashtar Command are direct operatives to us under Michael, which I collectively call the "Jesus group."

The UB is a notable resource to see how Michael and Gabriel draw us into their scheme while revealing their relationships with others in the Milky Way. It calls Michael the Creator Son of our universe. Gabriel, a high ranking Shantarel, facilitated the seeding of the Yahshua who Michael fully possessed. The UB gives the impression that Michael as Yahshua followed Gabriel's orders because when Michael "is away," Gabriel takes Michael's authoritative position (367.7). This portrayal of Michael sets the stage for him as a dutiful servant, Jesus, who sacrificed himself for his mission. The angelic reporters of Jesus's story admit that they do not understand how Michael was able to incarnate here, so they simply believe he became a lowly Human. They state that Michael had to gain rank in the god realm to become full God status; he reincarnated seven times so that he could identify with all creation through seven different roles within the Trinity of the Father, Son, and Holy Spirit. It was as though Michael is just like us but more special since he is considered a deity.

The UB calls Gabriel the Brilliant Evening Star, but because he cannot be in two places at once, he has a group by the same name. The Brilliant Evening Stars are described as the following:

> These brilliant creatures were planned by the Melchizedeks and were then brought into being by the Creator Son and the Creative Spirit. They serve in many capacities but chiefly as liaison officers of Gabriel who is the local universe chief executive. One or more of these beings function as his representatives at the capital of every constellation and system in Nebadon (407.1—I assume they are referring to the Milky Way).[16]

Our solar system's planet Venus is called the Evening Star and the Morning Star. The UB states that Lucifer was originally the Planetary Prince of Earth, and he is called the Morning Star. This shows that he worked with Gabriel as well as Michael before he decided to do his own thing.

In a channeling on October 14, 2007, Sananda reveals that he is now the Earth's Planetary Prince who will re-incarnate here in the near future.

> I am Sananda Immanuel Esu Kumara and I have the position of Planetary Prince. I will be taking over this position on Earth in physical form as a symbol of Christ Michael's lordship as Creator Son of Nebadon. His plan for his Universe is clear and determined. The fact that you have free will on Earth is of no consequence in his overall plan for the ascension of this solar system and your planet. It will happen. Your participation is one aspect of this plan that colors the direction it takes as part of its creation.
>
> I speak as the temporal leader who will embody Christ Michael's wishes on Earth. I will be joined by the Buddha, who will speak to Christ Michael's spiritual wishes. Together we will represent the spiritual manifestation of the Universal Law [this is their fractal law].[234]

As the Planetary Prince, Sananda is very involved, but he chooses to hide behind another name: Saint Germain. As I was traveling through France, I noticed a multitude of towns named after Saint Germain. It appears that he carries as much or more clout than Saint Michael or Michel. I had to know who this Germain is. The ATI,TPE reveals, "Saint Germain is a name of a group of entities—Sananda and his entity followers." Unfortunately, some people who follow the MCEO-GA choose to believe that the GFofL Sananda is an imposter of their beloved Sananda and Jesus. They are mistaken. At times, high ranking entities cloak their identities to further their agendas, but their big egos do not allow other entities to usurp their names.

In the November 18, 2005 channeling to Candace Frieze, Michael explains Sananda's role now as an Ascending Son (which Michael has also become in his supposed re-incarnations but does not refer to himself as such):

> Sananda is an Ascending Son of God, with a long history in Nebadon. He is a Kumara, a group of Beings originating long ago in Lyra, and who successfully got themselves out of a matrix that had kept them there with Weapons of Mass Destruction, besides the mind control method used to control a planetary people by enslaving races.
>
> Sananda is ImmAnnuel Esu Kumara, originally born of Gabriel [this is false, clarifies the ATI,TPE] and of more recent times, the only son of Sanat Kumara. Sanat Kumara was Planetary Logos [this is another lie; I described this correlation in Chapter 5] until around 20 years ago, and returned to Venus, where his offices are, and his home, as he became Solar Logos, of your Solar System. He was replaced by Lord Buddha, the same Buddha that came around 500 years before I did, and who is the author of the Conversation of God Books, with Neale Donald Walsch.[127]
>
> [Note: Before I read this prophecy by Michael, I already asked the ATI,TPE who gave the prophecies for the *Conversations with God* books, and it said, "Buddha," who is Thoth. The ATI,TPE also communicates that Michael gave the prophecies for *A Course in Miracles* to scribe Helen Schucman. I briefly skimmed through the *Miracles* book and do not know if Michael is mentioned there, but its Jesus appears to not instruct anything substantial. Hundreds of pages seem to go on and on in rants while admonishing and patronizing the author. My mother and I were in that position before, so what I skimmed through did not hold my attention.]

In the same channeling, Michael states that Sananda reincarnated as King David, which, if true, would mean that Sananda was Thutmose III, or he possessed him. What is revealing is Michael's admission about why King David's mission was "a great one.... Immanuel is a highly experienced warrior my friends, yes Sananda is indeed a warrior!"[127] So much for the peaceful Essene story about Sananda.

The Kumara family lives on 4th dimensional Venus as an administrative hub. I asked the ATI,TPE how it could be 4th dimensional when it is an HU-1 planet, and it replies, "The 4th dimensional distorted portion of Venus contains an extended 'leg' of diffused natural frequencies with the energetic light that has been blocked at that distorted sector." Venus is linked to many aliens who influence our planet. In Tibetan manuscripts, Sanat Kumara is the head of this family and is the "Ancient of Days" mentioned in the UB and the Bible.

In a religious-minded research paper about Sanat Kumara, author John Nash states:

> Sanat Kumara came to Earth at a critical time in the development of our planetary chain and scheme, after an earlier assignment on the Venus chain. But where He originally came from is uncertain; it is possible that He came from outside our planetary scheme.[235]

Nash presents information that equates the Logos to Sanat, whereby Sanat was the incarnation of the Bible's Holy Spirit. Since Michael was the most popular "Word made flesh" wherein he is also deemed God, this designation blurs the line of Sanat having allegiance to Michael or creating a new faction. Sanat Kumara is a re-incarnation of Lucifer, confirms the ATI,TPE.

According to the UB, Michael and Sananda Immanuel are half-brothers. The ATI,TPE states that Immanuel was originally a 12th dimensional Elohim, and the GA confirms this dimensional status in *Voyagers II*. Sananda is a title that represents earlier plasmic creation that Immanuel has not fully integrated, states the ATI,TPE. Immanuel re-incarnated into Sho-Sho-NaTA and Anunnaki races, confirms the ATI,TPE, so a familial relationship with Michael could have occurred along the way. However, Michael is now a fully phantom being who is advertised as being "like us" as Jesus, so this does not fare well for Sananda's status; additionally, I doubt Michael would wish to change his original status to another, "lesser" race. If Michael did re-incarnate and become Sananda's half-brother, then the Kumara family would provide the best situation for him, Sananda as Esu Kumara, and Sanat Kumara to directly work together. The Kumara family contains concentrated Shantarel and Anunnaki genetics that can house several fallen friends in one bloodline.

Sananda and Sanat Kumara work with another leading figure named

Ashtar. Ashtar leads the Ashtar Command in which Sananda is an admiral. The Ashtar Command works closely with the GFofL, and they are essentially synonymous.

According to a Human who has been in contact with the GFofL since he was a child:

> The Galactic Federation of Light was founded over 4.5 million years ago to prevent inter-dimensional dark forces from dominating and exploiting this galaxy. At present, there are just over 200,000 member star nations, confederations or unions. Approximately 40% are humanoids and the rest are varied forms of sentient beings. Most members of the Galactic Federation are fully conscious beings.[236]

This person merely repeats its propaganda that they are here to "assist us in our ascension/transformation process."[236]

The GFofL plays upon the contrasting "light and dark" theme, yet it claims to be of the light and against the dark. Contrary to this claim, Michael continually admits that he supports duality and allows darkness so that he can see how far his manipulated creations can go. Some of his prophecies to Ms. Frieze explain this. I do not wish to repeat much of his nonsense that says he is our "God Creator of this Universe" who did not wish for us to experience darkness, while he also says that "[t]his is a grand experiment on so many levels you still can't comprehend."[127] His self-imposed God role forces us to deal with his experimentation upon us. He says, "it had never happened before in this type of scenario," when indeed the Bourgha duality experiment did already happen; he merely was not in control then. Michael and his group aim to continue this "experiment" to see how far they can go. He says that the Earth is a training ground for "Ascending Sons…to train here to become worthy new Creator Sons of the new Universes at present being formed."[127]

As part of Michael's experiment, could he succeed in drawing a gullible army of members from us Humans to perpetuate the Bourgha agenda? Many Humans would eventually become expendable, though. Accordingly, how is a new experiment occurring when their eager Thought Adjusters latch onto us and direct our thoughts and ways? Their ascension façade uses us much more than we need them.

In another channeling, the GFofL—sometimes called the Intergalactic Federation of Light to reveal the association with other galaxies—says that it had a plan for us to go to the Sirius star system as our "destiny" in 2013.[237] This is quite convincing language. It also paints a picture of coordinated relationships with us all acting as one big, loving family, giving us renewed environments on planets, destroying bad guys (when it actually works with them), and having all-around harmony to get us to go along with its members in their spaceships.

This reminds me of the scary 1962 *The Twilight Zone* television episode with the tall, telepathic aliens who came here and solved all of our environmental and political problems. They said their mission was "To Serve Man," and they invited people to visit their planet with no strings attached; we could visit a new place and return home whenever we would want. The supportive public did not know that the alien handbook found by suspecting Humans was actually a cookbook to eat them! I am not trying to bring fear but a wise discernment toward anyone who paints an idyllic picture for us while seeking to control us, which the Jesus group and all god groups do no matter how much they say they are helping us.

Imagine what it would be like for unsuspecting Christians, Jews, Muslims, Buddhists, Hindus, and so forth to suddenly see a large spaceship and aliens walking out of it. Many of these aliens would look like Humans, but they definitely would seem foreign. The religious Humans would be fearful much like the people in the Bible who fell to the ground in fear of these aliens. The Jesus or Messiah dispensation of time aims to diminish this fear because we are taught to wait in expectation of our savior who "cometh in the clouds, and every eye shall see him" (Revelation 1:7). The spacecraft will likely be cloaked to illuminate the miraculous return of one or more religious figures who will then coax us into receiving their space brothers. This new scenario is the same as before except that we are now blind and brainwashed concerning its reality.

Is ignorance and fear what you wish to have in order to follow someone? Many people already believe in having fear toward a God, but do you really want the fear that would make you fall down prostrate? Would you rather know more of the story so that you can make an educated decision about whether to follow any God? Would you also want the confidence to know that you do not have to follow aliens or even believe them, and you can simply stand strong in yourself?

A member of the GFofL gave a prophecy to Blossom Goodchild saying that the GFofL would de-cloak a massive mother ship over Alabama in the United States on October 14, 2008, and it would be visible in surrounding states. When I read this broadcast before the projected event, I was highly unsettled and did not want this to happen, but its message was very convincing that the spacecraft would appear regardless of dissent. After a sleepless night and then a troubled day (during which my mother and I did our part to expand the ATI,TPE connection and Eia energy to thwart it), I found out that its big reveal did not happen. Believers and other channelers then asked why the GFofL would not follow through on its promise. Interestingly (but not surprisingly), it replied that Goodchild was erroneous in her transmission of the prophecy. No, I do not believe she disrupted the message because I know that prophecies take over the person. The GFofL had to cover its tracks because its plan did not transpire.

Goodchild bravely declared her feelings in a video she promptly made after the failed event.

> I feel that by living in my light and my love and my truth, I've been made to look the biggest fool and I feel very humiliated, and it will take a lot, a lot to change that and for me to find out where I stand within all of this.[238]

Unfortunately, she has chosen to continue being a GFofL channeler. Although she had a brief self-awakening, she still supported her belief as her "truth."

I have realized that New Age and religious entity groups want the majority of our population to look forward to their arrival because our prayers, rituals, ceremonies, and overall welcoming energies link to them and help draw them into our world. The MCEO conveys that if at least 70 percent of an area on Earth is Metatronically encoded, such as a religious center of worship, then it would be pulled into the Phantom Milky Way's Phantom Earth if the BeaST could entrap it.[239] Since our bodies are comprised of Earthly energy, we can extrapolate this effect upon us if we also infuse ourselves with Metatronic energy.

Even if the 2008 prophecy was a test to gauge Human response, the KRH and its allies helped thwart the Jesus group's plans. The Jesus group may eventually come to show its otherworldly nature in order to take some highly devout followers with it. Sadly, most of those followers may be too trusting or even fearful to turn away unless they wake up to their fundamental strength and connection to the ATI,TPE.

An October 14, 2010 Jess Anthony channeling given in turns by Sananda, Lady Nada, and Michael is particularly telling.[234] Sananda admits, "Free choice can be overruled by a higher choice," which means their choice. He also says, "Christ Michael was given the lead to design his universe as he saw fit," showing his allegiance to Michael.

Lady Nada speaks about her perceived polarity to Sananda as the softer complement to his strength, as the yin and yang duality that shows their belief in opposites. The ATI,TPE reveals that Lady Nada is a Reptilian who was originally a Shantarel. The ATI,TPE also reveals that she is the leading entity behind the Sophia entity group that many religions and philosophies revere. She re-incarnated as Lilith, the first "Eve" prototype created for the first man

Adam whom I soon explain. Lady Nada also reincarnated as Mary Magdalene. Mary was a popular woman with both Yahshuas, willingly propagating her distorted genes with Humanity.

Then, Michael says:

> This is Christ Michael Aton, as I have come to be called. My will is that Earth ascends. To that end I have taken over the process and am now controlling the complete scenario for this to happen. I have let man play out his games of control and dominance over others. It has served a purpose in his education, but it is now finished. I will no longer tolerate the delay in acknowledging my wishes. I will no longer allow those at odds with my purposes to direct the progress of my planet....I am the Christed Michael who created the Universe of Nebadon of which the planet Earth is an integral part that I designed specifically. I created the concept that is Earth. I chose all the elements that comprise her manifestation. I allowed all forms of physical actualization as a means to realize my vision for her [Chapter 8 totally refutes these claims].
>
> I chose to allow dark elements at odds with my vision to take over my creation....I was determined not to allow this to happen again and I chose to make my final bestowal as a physical embodiment here to redirect the flow of man's energy streams in an inevitable path I created through my incarnation [possession].
>
> This has led to now, this time. Man has done what he could do from within. There is no more he can accomplish without my direct intervention. I have the complete authority to intervene as I choose and redirect the ascension of my Earth as it needs to be.[234]

Michael's massive ego shows itself here. His surname Aton is described as "Sovereign" in another prophecy to Mr. Anthony on December 5, 2005; this is his preferred title because it entails the most control. Aton or Aten was the Egyptian god that got Akhenaten to break away from his family and follow it exclusively; Michael funneled and refined the "Fisher King" Zadoks toward his Jesus group.

Michael reveals a clue to being Aton in another channeling that was published in *The Phoenix Liberator* on January 13, 1992 when he presented himself as the pseudonym "Gyeorgos Ceres Hatonn, Commander in Chief, Earth Project Transition, Pleiades Sector Flight Command, Intergalactic Federation Fleet."[240] In the later December 5, 2005 prophecy, Michael admits, "Hatonn is a Commander of the Phoenix and as such was my disguise for many years."[127]

Michael's lie as Hatonn is noteworthy because he mentioned the Pleiades star system that contains the 5th dimensional Tara stargate. The Pleiades is a strategic place for evil aliens to position themselves for access to the Earth.

The following quote equates the Ashtar Command with the star Aldebaran, although this group encompasses more locations, especially the Pleiades. A general view about Aldebarans is that they are Reptilian, but the quote likens them to white Andromedans of our Milky Way (generally known as Andromies) and Pleiadians, both of whom are the white "Nordic" aliens who appeared to well-known contactees Alex Collier and Billy Meier, respectively.

An alien-focused website describes the Ashtar Command:

> The Ashtar Fleet, also called Ashtar Command are originally from Aldebaran constellation. The Ashtar Command are among many entities that come to Earth and have been circling above it, for the most part invisible to the naked eye, since the early 1950's A.D. Their height ranges from 5 to 6 feet. They are humanoid and have less water in their bodies and are "pasty" in appearance. The color of their skin is very pale, and rubbery. They have blonde hair. Their heads and eyes are similar to humans. The color of their eyes are blue or gray.[241]

This description perfectly matches an actual picture taken of such an alien that can be found on the internet.[242] In a well lit room, a type of albino woman with slightly different characteristics to ours is shown above the following official-looking identification:

TS-SCI- S.A.M-422Wxxy
Report prepared for S.A.A.L.M by XXXXXXXXXXXXXX
A-C-T-I-O-N_ACIO PINE GAP[*]

Description
Extra-terrestrial
Species: SAM?Nordics
Aliases: Swedes, Tall whites, Nordics
Height: 5 – 6.5 feet
Weight: 120 – 240 pounds (estimated)
Eyes: Human
Hair: Blonde
Skin: Pale white
Sex: Male and Female

Communication: Telepathic
Location of Origin
Mt Ziel – Northern Australia
Distinguishing Characteristics
Share common physical features with human beings
(especially Scandinavians)
Are taller than the average human
Have more of a muscular build than the average human

[* Pine Gap is a United States military facility near the city
Alice Springs in the middle of the Australian Outback. It is the
Australian equivalent of Area 51. It is known for its extensive
UFO reports and Aboriginal "spirit world" alien encounters.]

The prior description of rubbery skin shows amphibious genetics relating
to the GA's depiction of Jehovian Sirian-Anunnaki "Bipedal Dolphin People"
(p. 168).[144] However, Nordics also contain Reptilian genes, as evidenced in
the above referenced picture of a woman with Reptilian eyes. This Nordic
woman lives underground with her intruder race among Reptilian and Grey
alien allies. The Nordics are known as a violent group, one that both scared
and influenced Adolf Hitler, as I later explain in "One World Order Agenda."

The Pleiadians who contacted Meier, such as Semjase, and the Andromies
who contacted Collier, work together among the GFofL, Ashtar Command,
Great White Brotherhood organization, and Marduk's Ra group. Because the
Nordic-type hominids look like us, they are the best delegates to reach us as
"brothers" and "sisters." How clever.

The Andromies are generally entwined with the Necromiton race,
together being called the Necromiton-Andromies. 570 million years ago,
Wesadeks entered the phantom Andromeda constellation and created the
Necromiton, a phantom Wesadek-Shantarel-Anu-Seraphim hybrid upon
which the vampire character is based.[123,243] Under Archangel Michael's lead,
the Necromitons raided the Leviathan-Human race (in the "Lucifer" section)
and created another Nephilim hybrid, which illuminates the complexity of
Human races.[123]

Arguably the most popular story of Human creation is that of Adam and
Eve. The UB states that Adam and Eve were two higher dimensional beings
who appeared here fully-formed to upgrade the Human gene code. Although
this is a different Human creation story than Enki's in the Sumerian Tablets,
both stories essentially say that we would be lost without the interference
of these aliens, specifically the lie of giving Humans genetic upgrades. They
purposely neglected to say that Humans were already seeded here by advanced,

higher density entities, and Earth Humans were doing just fine on their own. The UB states that its lowest but still very important group in Archangel Michael's hierarchy is the Life Carrier who seeds life, just like what Enki did on Earth. This alludes to cooperation between Michael and Enki, especially since the Zadok line was heavily influenced by Michael's group.

The biblical timeline of Adam and Eve's creation around 5,000 B.C. is inaccurate, especially since different entity groups had their own versions of a perfected Earth intruder race. In c. 30,000 B.C., Shantarel, Jehovian Anunnaki, and Necromiton-Andromie races combined their genes with Humans and Tara's Adami-Kudmon race during a vulnerable time in Earth's history that involved legendary Atlantis, reveal the ATI,TPE and "M." Michael's group members wanted to re-write Human history according to their highly controllable bloodline, and the Adami hybrid creation allowed them to do it as their master race.

The Ashtar Command also created an Earth intruder race around the same time as Michael's Adam. About 29,500 B.C., states the ATI,TPE, it genetically engineered Pleiadian Anunnaki Samjase "Nordic Blonde" DNA with DNA captured from Tara's (and Inner Earth's) Beli-Kudyem race and Procyon's Maji pre-Angelic Human race similar to the Oraphim. This new Human copy was the Beli-Kudmon. The Samjase, who also have Thetan genetics, reveals the ATI,TPE, thoroughly assimilated Procyon's Maji race. Samjase races are placed throughout key Phantom and Milky Way locations including highly distorted versions of Sirius A, Aldebaran, Nibiru, and portions of our solar system.[123,125]

Accordingly, Enoch, Thoth, and Marduk created their own Human copies as competition or augmentation to the Adami and Beli Human hybrids. Later, Enoch's Jehovian group combined its hybrid with the Thoth group hybrid to form the master Adam-Kadmon race orchestrated to take over the planet after the main biblical flood of 9,558 B.C. God-group infighting created the ancient biblical rifts among their prized Human hybrid king lines.[123]

The GFofL, Ashtar Command, and Necromiton-Andromies under Michael seek all power within the spectrum of extremes. They tell us about their version of "love" and "light and dark"—or what New Agers often give as a salutation, "love and light"—because they want to desensitize us to the purity of the ATI,TPE and real love.

In Michael's December 2005 channeling, he reveals more of his ego and his support of darkness.

> I was interested in seeing how I could become apparently detached from my Creation, yet still be attached as Maker. This connection and detachment took on various guises of Light

and Dark energy, active and passive receptivity, attraction and repulsion, positive and negative directions and energy flow. This became manifest in people and objects characterizing the physical embodiment of my conceptions within my Universe. My interest is played out on a grander scale than you can imagine.

Your role on Earth-Shan [Urantia, according to him] was to take this preoccupation with separation to an extreme. I could predict various scenarios you would pursue, but I wanted to see how you would operate without my direct connection guiding you.[127]

This quote contradicts what he later said on November 14, 2006, that his "intention was not to have the Dark take over."[127] Active allowance of extreme separation and duality, and the creation of such that he does not often admit, support the power of darkness that can infiltrate and take over light. These are acts of whitewashing, similar to treating abuse as insignificant incidents.

Below is a guided meditation in January 2011 that Michael gave to Carolyn Ann O'Riley for us to follow.

In your imagination ask through prayer for The Creator to send you down a protective Ray of White Light by praying mentally something like this "My Creator I AM asking for a protective Ray of White Light to enfold me and lift me up so that I am experiencing the very highest of vibrations during this journey into my inner most depths of understanding and Being…. I am thanking you My Creator for assisting me by sending this Ray. I am visualizing the ray in my imagination now coming down through the corner of the area where I am meditating. It is entering into my physical form, permeating all that is within my I AM presence."

The Creator sends you Blessings and All the Love that you could ever want for. Feel the Love vortex building now around you like a cocoon. Close your eyes and allow that sensation, that higher Vibrational feeling of Love to just wash over you and continue wave after wave until you deem it enough for the moment. My Beloveds you can start that Love flow again at any time by simply closing your eyes and re-calling the Loving feeling.

Note that this meditation pulls in both light and love from the outside. These are vibrations, including a vortex, which zeroes into us. It continues:

Breathe in deeply allowing and seeing within your spiritual imagination your Guardian Angels and invited Spirit Guides as they join you. The Angels take your etheric essence hands and guides you out of your physical body and directs you into your Etheric Spiritual Heart Chakra. An Angel has been stationed to stay with your physical essence until you return from your meditation journey.

You are seeing, feeling and sensing this within your imagination, Your Guardian Angels, Spirit Guides and special invited guests are now within your Spiritual Heart Chakra with you.[244]

This last part is especially unsettling. As I explain in the next two chapters, the heart chakra relates to the 4th dimensional astral field; when manipulative entities harness this aspect of our body, they can easily control us. Michael channeled information to Rudolf Steiner—the founder of Anthroposophy, an offshoot of Theosophy—in lectures aptly titled "What Does the Angel Do in Our Astral Body?" and "Death as Metamorphosis of Life."[245] The lectures teach that possession by a more powerful angel or god is the only way to save us, emphasizing the "Christ" death and resurrection story.

The meditations, prophecies, and prayers with them have us agree to their light-activation ceremonies by drawing in their manipulated light energy and false perception of love. This essentially removes us from our original heart energy and makes us needy for someone else to fill us, although we only receive crumbs because of this fragmented "love." It is no wonder why we feel some emptiness in our hearts. Yes, love is felt from others, but we must know how to generate it first within ourselves because it is a foundational part of our composition. Love is a flowing energy without bound, effortlessly giving and receiving.

The Jesus group links with our energy when we call upon it for help. We feel altered (I explained in chapter 3 that it is a heightened, ecstatic feeling), but just like a sugar binge high, it does not mean that it is healthy. When we call upon the name of Jesus as Christians, and something in our favor happens, this wins our admiration; we may dedicate ourselves to this group of aliens as a result.

I still think that when we genuinely need help, their temporary assistance is not the end-all-be-all factor. When I was briefly possessed with a Drakonian or a member of Michael's extended family (mentioned in chapter 3), the exorcism procedure with the fire-and-brimstone pastor was grueling work. The entity did not instantly and miraculously go, but my determination to heave out my negative emotions drained me so that I could finally sleep and repair myself. I believed I would become free of the possession, and I soon was.

It is possible that our genuine need can connect to the small measure of goodness within controlling, religious entities, but I strongly believe that our innate goodness is what drives out the dark forces instead of the Jesus group doing it. In fact, the Jesus group contains many demons and dark forces it claims to exorcise as enemies, so the entity harassments may be an orchestrated ruse by the Jesus group to gain our worship and obedience. It promotes the message of possession (God/Holy Spirit/Jesus living inside of us), so it can replace a demon in its group or a similar group with a supposedly more favorable Jesus entity. However, to get them all to leave, it has to be by our will and ability.

Although the Jesus group can and does give some healings for our obedience, the healings are not freely given out of love because these entities do not know what real love is. When we decide to detach from controlling entities after their involvement with us, they will kick up a fuss and harass us. We consistently need to stay strong within ourselves, and they will eventually go.

New Age spiritualities are no different than Christianity because they both follow the same Jesus group. There are initiations in every religion, including the "laying on hands" with prayer in Christianity and Catholicism. Usually these hands are placed over or on the head, which means they are over our crown (spiritual) chakra that redirects energy into our head and then body.

New Age "religions" have been devised over the last few decades to target people who do not like the suppressed servitude of religion but still want to do good works by loving people, animals, and the Earth. Naturally, people are becoming more evolved along with the Earth's readiness for natural ascension (in chapter 8), so the Jesus group had to reformulate its tactics to suppress an increasingly awakening Human population.

A friend of mine named James Macaron unwittingly attended an initiation ceremony as part of a raw vegan food retreat put on by David Wolfe. James was not interested in anything religious or spiritual and only attended the retreat to meet other heath advocates in a beautiful location. Unfortunately, this spiritual ceremony was part of the program. It was a light-body activation ceremony, formally called Breath Activation and Clearing Ceremony, and the itinerary gave no explanation except that it was a breathing meditation. The itinerary included a list of daily intentions which on that day was "surrender." Surrender is an accurate word to describe what was expected of the unsuspecting candidates.

James describes the ceremony:

The ceremony was heavily religious in the guise of New Age spiritualism. We received a blessing of the sign of the cross with burning sage before entering the hall. In the hall was a large altar with a giant light crystal and an assortment of many smaller ones. In my recollection, another part of the display was a picture of Jesheua (as they call him) receiving a ray of light or standing within the Poison Apple configuration.

Participants were told to lie on the floor in a circle with their heads toward the altar. Then, we had to rapidly breathe, which involved two breaths in and one breath out as progressively accelerated tribal drumming held the tempo. This breathing is supposed to help activate our body to release negativity, old emotions, and receive pure healing light as facilitated by the practitioners. The breathing hyperventilates the body to the point of blood alkalosis, and it opens the chakras to entities so they can manipulate both emotions and the mind. We were told to let emotions freely come and go. People were laughing, screaming out in joy, or crying. The emotions would shift rapidly.

Various people running the ceremony were doing things between the altar and the heads of the participants, although I could not tell what they were doing while I was participating. One of the facilitators was Omakayuel, which is not a human name; he was also my personal "buddy" whose name I pulled out of a hat at the beginning of the retreat.

As the ceremony went on, I experienced cramping in my hands that raised them to my chest and curled them into claws. I experienced complete paralysis of my body, and I felt an invisible energetic presence over and around me. I tried to move but I couldn't—my body felt like it was taken over except for my consciousness. I was scared. This went on for what felt like at least five minutes. Then within the space of a few seconds, the presence left and so did my paralysis. It was so rapid that it felt abnormal instead of simply blood alkalosis from the hyperventilation.

Afterwards, I felt lighter in my body but in a state of shock, and I felt permanently activated more with my emotional self. This means that my chakras were opened, but I sometimes felt like I wasn't controlling them, my emotions, and even my mind. I have had to learn to stop within myself when I would start to act like I know I normally wouldn't. I have had to rediscover myself and my own energies so I can stop any partial possession from happening due to that initiation ceremony.

After realizing how different he was after the light-body activation ceremony, James did some research about it. The ceremony was orchestrated by Amoraea Dreamseed and his partner who both run a Metatronic false ascension school called The Light School. They teach people about receiving the "Codes of Light" within our divine blueprint, ascending, and communing with angels, masters, and guides. They refer to God as the "Omnicentric Fractal God Source."[246] They describe the Metatronic Tube Torus (Poison Apple) as a field that holds together creation—a spiraling, spherical field with a black hole at its center. This "infinite gravity wave implosion that spirals all energy into itself" via the Fibonacci expression is their force called love.[247] As James states, none of this information was explained to the people who participated in the breath work that they deceptively used to activate the light-body toward angelic control. Activation should be a beneficial occurrence in normal circumstances, but the fallen angels created an access link to the area of activation. In other words, now the aliens can easily partially or fully possess those people until they realize this and close off their energy link.

This ceremony is also called "rebirthing." James did not want or need to become a higher dimensional alien's body as that rebirth! On Dreamseed's website, he displays his digital and acrylic images that show streaks of lights affecting the participants during similar ceremonies. The ATI,TPE explains that these lights are entities. The ultimate intention of the Metatronic ceremonies is to have these entities fully enter the person, as Amoraea's art shows.

Dreamseed works with Amorah Quan Yin, the channeler for the book *Pleiadian Perspectives on Human Evolution* that I mentioned in chapter 3. Omakayuel has lived with them at Mount Shasta, California and also traveled to the Egyptian pyramids with Quan Yin. The ATI,TPE reveals that Omakayuel is the alien group that continually harassed James after the ceremony. James's "buddy" renamed himself Omakayuel to not only show honor (worship) toward his "angelic guide" but to receive its possession. The ATI,TPE also reveals that a Reptilian High Commander has harassed James to feed off of his energy; we discovered that it is a leading member of the Omakayuel group.

James told me that he often felt a presence in his house after that ceremony. Since learning the truth about his situation, he regularly creates protective bubbles of energy around himself and his house, and he aims to be conscious of his energies.

Metatron gives guided meditations and channelings similar to Michael. "'Tron' means instrument, or device"; therefore, Metatron is the extensive device throughout multi-universes.[248] As a participant with his Galactic Federation of Light ground crew, he recruits people to perform false healings that euphorically remove the symptoms but implant a darker sickness of deadly energy. An obvious Metatronic procedure is Reconnective Healing®.

The popular teacher of this practice, Eric Pearl, was drawn in by a female energy worker who told him to read a chapter of *The Book of Knowledge: The Keys of Enoch* by J.J. Hurtak. He complied and then received her energy work that switched him onto the Metatronic energy current. In a warm room, he instantly became freezing cold for five minutes, but somehow this was acceptable to him as part of the religious experience. Once, his palm randomly bled, but he denies it mirrored stigmata. He says that he is just "running the energy" to people, zapping them left and right in a type of awe-filled miraculous ceremony. He and his followers feel and often see an otherworldly presence in the room with them when this energy work is performed.[249]

Unfortunately, I received this energy work, but I was reluctant. A chiropractor of mine had pestered me about it because I was not healing from years of treatment. My intuition and experience told me to beware because it would most likely call upon other entities/aliens to come to me. I told him this, and he replied, "I do not call upon anything but just put my call to the furthest region of the universe for the pure energy to come through me."

I did not fully believe him, but I was open enough at that time because I thought I had exhausted my options for healing my bodily pain. I reasoned within myself: "I can protect my energy once I feel something 'off.' I don't want to be too closed-minded in case it could help."

I lied on my back on his treatment table with my eyes closed most of the time. He started at my feet with his hands over me, and he walked up toward my head. I began to feel strong warmth over my head, so I opened my eyes and saw that he was standing behind it with his hands in my aura. I tried to go into myself while calling upon love, truth, and All That Is, The Pure Essence, but it was early in my journey when I did not really know how to protect myself. I also continued to stay somewhat open to the procedure. After he was done, I sat up and immediately felt dizzy. I drove home a bit precariously, and all night, when I got up to walk in my house, I bumped into walls and had to put my hand on something for stabilization. I thought that maybe my energy simply shifted and that sleep would help me. No, nothing helped, and I awoke feeling just as unstable.

The night after the procedure, I called my mother to come over to recalibrate me. I told her that I could not do it on my own. I felt out of control. She sat in front of me, held both of my hands, and energetically reached into my body with the extended essence of the ATI,TPE to link my energy to it. I knew her pure energy in this practice, so I allowed her to help. She then expanded this correct energy throughout my body and outside of me to my aura, and I finally felt like myself again. My head and body were mine again.

The Jesus group and its allies want us to lose our true selves. They spin the truth about their whitewashing actions and technologies into a lie that says they are actually beneficial to us or even our choice! An example is in this channeling by Michael's collective to Ms. O'Riley:

> You volunteered My Beloveds to be veiled in selective amnesia so that you could "know the place for the first time" if you will. Your contracted selected lessons would be sensed as new and your longing for HOME would not interfere in your learning and experiencing the lessons that were contracted for this lifetime.
>
> Without the veil My Beautiful Beings of Light you would constantly be wanting to go HOME when things became a little rough and rocky.[244]

The Jesus group uses the Metatronic encoding of the Blank Slate Technology to remove us from our true identity. As stated in *The Terra Papers*, this aligns with the SSS-T.

> Countless wars over billions of years had taught the SSS Queens a vital lesson, an enemy or rebellious subject serves no purpose if executed. But if the brain was re-programmed, resistance was eliminated and an able body was added to the labor force. Mind control was the SSS-T Science of choice (p. 4).[211]

It is easier to trick people to comply to these measures instead of physically force them, but if these aliens do not get enough mind-controlled members to join their armies or other purposes, then I do not wish to fathom how aggressive they will become.

The Jesus group and all controlling god groups are persistent because they need us, not the other way around as they like to say. Harassments can be dangerous if we do not have the awareness and tools to break free of them. I will elaborate upon this important process in chapters 9 and 11.

The following excerpt is a sad and desperate plea on an internet forum by a man named Rich who did not know his options. Unfortunately, when I tried to contact him, his profile was erased.

Hello everyone,

This is an urgent message!!! Please take the time to read all of it. I'm writing you because there aren't many places I can post this message and I need to tell someone before it's too late. I am being tormented by demonic beings who claim to be the same as the GALACTIC FEDERATION, COUNCIL OF LIGHT, ASHTAR COMMAND, COMMANDER HATONN, AND THE ASCENDED MASTERS. They possess my body like a classic demonic possession. They have been tormenting me with lies now for several years. They spell in a very crude manner by moving my feet or toes. The spelling isn't very good....can take hours to decipher. They claim that they have "gift for you." Want to awaken kundalini. I have a constant buzzing sound in my head like I am part of an alien hive. I know that they use implants which they can implant through invisible means. I have found two of them just under my skin on my elbow. I have come to believe that these beings are infernal creatures that plague all humans. Most are unaware of it. We are merely host to alien beings who use us for their own agendas. Some of us more than others. I believe they are trying to set me up as a full time host or something. They are changing my body and consciousness in some way. It is the most frightening experience imaginable and I live with this daily. Please read the following...."Our bodies are also the result of sound resonating energy into form and if our minds are powerful enough to change the sound range of the body, it moves into another form or disappears from this dimension, altogether. This is what is called shape-shifting." This came from the following web page http://www.angelfire.com/ut/branton/posers4. html. I believe they are trying to steal me over to another dimension or shape-shift me into something else. I don't know, but dread the thought of waking up somewhere one day surrounded by these monsters. These beings are master geneticist [sic] who are breeding human hybrids and hubrids [sic] which they are slowly integrating into our society. It is the highest form of subterfuge. The alien phenomenon is real. These beings have been the Gods of the bible (ELOHIM, JEHOVAH, JESUS) and all other religious deities. IT HAS ALL BEEN A RUSE!!! There is no God. There are only these beings who have given primitive humans an illusion of God. They also spurn cult religions, Satanic churches, wiccan covens, secret societies, secret cabals, you name it. They do this through mind control. They use subtle persuasion on weak minds or people that they have been manipulating for a lifetime. They are also supported by beings who are in physical form. You wouldn't know they weren't human if you passed them on the street. They form the secret government's of the world.

Controlled by the illuminati whom are nothing more than puppets for the alien rulers of this planet....

These beings work with the most sophisticated technologies. It is beyond human comprehension. They operate with hyper nano tech, particle physics, electromagnetic energy, sound, light, worm whole [sic] technology, hyper drive vehicles, controlling weather, and so many other advanced methods that it would boggle the mind. They control this planet. They control our security agencies. They perform mass mind control through the media (sublimely). MONTAUK, MK ULTRA, BLACK BUDGET, PSY OPPS, MJ 12, you name it. They've had a hand in it. Now they want to present themselves as Ashtar of the Galactic Federation, Pleiadians, Sirians, the Arcturians, Andromedans, Christed beings, Michael the Archangel, Commander Hatonn, Christed beings, and Metetron, said to be the highest Archangel, and a host of other characters. Not to mention the beings behind all of the contact scenarios in the 50's. Don't you get it folks. We are all being played by alien imposters who are posing as our gods (or space brothers). This is right out of Stargate SG-1. These beings are actually demonic in nature. They hail from various densities (galaxies) and dimensions and they live right hear on earth. Seven years ago I would have never believed any of this, but I know it to be true. Many people who channel messages from these beings are finding that their messages are faulty or just plain lies....

...I believe our world is under great threat from these beings as David Jacobs points out in his book "THE THREAT." Particularly hear [sic] in the United States. We should demand that our government...tell the truth about the alien controlled bases all over the United States like Area 51, Mt. Shasta, Dulce, and others. Please note that I am of sound mind and intelligence. I'm writing this because I don't think I have much more time. They are flooding my head with all of this energy and I am all but deaf in my right ear. I was recently told that they will turn me into flames. I don't know if this is in reference to spontaneous combustion or what. But this is the kind of hellish intelligence that I am dealing with. I fear that if I don't get this message out, I may not have an opportunity to later. Those of you who channel these beings, please ask them why they are tormenting me and post your comments here. Others, please pass this message along.

Rich [250]

[Note: I removed parts of this letter that put Lucifer at the head of everything evil because it is only partially true.]

After I wrote this book's first edition, a woman named Holly contacted me to tell me her memory of Rich's post and how she experienced a similar possession. Her case involved entities using her nose to write words in the air that she could see. They continually harassed her day and night until she consciously released all energetic connections to her New Age past and linked to the All That Is, The Pure Essence for pure energy protection that allowed her to regain herself. Accordingly, another woman named Jamie told me that until she verbally and energetically released all soul contracts—as she calls them—with other entities, she was able to gain freedom and control as her true self. She saw thick, black astral sludge leave her.

Although alien entities can be persistent and sometimes overwhelming, we do have ultimate power over ourselves. Regarding Rich, I do hope he finds his own power very soon, if not already.

This chapter is a very uncomfortable one to write and read. Please forgive me, but I must unveil the dark energy that the leading gods embody. Light lives without darkness; however, "darkness" cannot live without the symbolic "light of life" from the ATI,TPE, so it is true what Rich wrote about these aliens changing our bodies. They use us as an energy source. I read another channeling by Michael that directed the subject to open up his body to him so that he could repair the man's DNA. That is a lie, at least largely.

Remember: awareness, critical thinking, and centering in the core of yourself will empower you. If you do not know your true self apart from your social conditioning, I suggest that you start the process of getting to know yourself now. As for this moment, just exhale and shake off the ick of what you read in the above channelings and excerpts, and please continue with me in renewed strength. I suggest you keep up your inner strength while reading the following sections; Part 4 of this book will help refine our abilities and expose our awesome nature.

Lucifer and Satan

Michael's group in *The Urantia Book* explained the close relationship between the supposedly polar opposites of Jesus and Lucifer, otherwise known to Christians as the Devil. *Devil* in the Bible's Old Testament is uncapitalized and pluralized to represent demons or merely bucks for sacrifice. The New Testament shows the association of *devil* to demon, but it also introduces "the devil" or "Devil" as a single entity. In chapter 4 of the Bible's Gospel of Matthew, "the devil" tempted Jesus, physically took him places, and eventually left him. The Bible describes this Devil as a finite type of man. The First Epistle of John chapter 2, verses 13-14 further state that "ye have overcome the wicked one." Christians have created a mystical, powerful Demonhead (similar to Godhead) that cannot be identified into separate, less powerful entities, which contradicts the Bible clearly stating different names and physical limitations for the Christian adversary.

The main devils of concern are Lucifer and Satan with Lucifer at the helm. To a lesser extent are the devils Caligastia and Beelzebub. All of these names are mentioned in the Bible except Caligastia who is the Planetary Prince in the UB. Caligastia is a separate entity to the others, clarifies the ATI,TPE.

According to the UB's hierarchy of Local Universe Sons of God, Lucifer held rank two levels below the Melchizedeks.

> LUCIFER was a brilliant primary Lanonandek Son of Nebadon. He had experienced service in many systems, had been a high counselor of his group, and was distinguished for wisdom, sagacity, and efficiency. Lucifer was number 37 of his order, and when commissioned by the Melchizedeks, he was designated as one of the one hundred most able and brilliant personalities in more than seven hundred thousand of his kind (601.1).
>
> Lucifer is now the fallen and deposed Sovereign of Satania [a name for our solar system that he was assigned to rule]. Self-contemplation is most disastrous, even to the exalted personalities of the celestial world. Of Lucifer it was said: "Your heart was lifted up because of your beauty; you corrupted your wisdom because of your brightness" (601.5).
>
> Very little was heard of Lucifer on Urantia [Jesus group's incorrect word for Earth] owing to the fact that he assigned his first lieutenant, Satan, to advocate his cause on your planet. Satan was a member of the same primary group of Lanonandeks but had never functioned as a System Sovereign; he entered fully into the Lucifer insurrection. The "devil" is none other than Caligastia, the deposed Planetary Prince of Urantia and a Son of the secondary order of Lanonandeks. At the time Michael was on Urantia in the flesh, Lucifer, Satan, and Caligastia were leagued together to effect the miscarriage of his bestowal mission. But they signally failed (602.1).
>
> Beelzebub was the leader of the disloyal midway creatures who allied themselves with the forces of the traitorous Caligastia (602.2).[16]

The ATI,TPE reveals that Lucifer is one of the very old, original Bourgha-Metatron Shantarel. Currently, he is reincarnated as the so-called Ascended Master Sanat Kumara. Sanat Kumara largely or solely operates out of the 4th dimension. The ATI,TPE states that Lucifer changed his form in order "to better control Earth specifically." In *Voyagers II*, the GA does not acknowledge Lucifer as a single entity. It rather describes him as a family that currently operates out of Nibiru and the Pleiades locations of Tara (presumably its phantom portion) and Tiamat.[120] It is true that Lucifer has an extended family in these locations, but the male entity behind the Lucifer name existed eons before.

The Bible only once mentions Lucifer in chapter 14 of the Book of Isaiah, but it mentions Satan more often. In fact, the *exeGeses parallel BIBLE* lexicon shows that *adversary* in the Bible is substituted with *satan*.[7] Satan is the Shantarel entity Samael, and he is Lucifer's second commander, states the ATI,TPE. He carries much influence in the Bible based on how frequently he is mentioned. The GA states that there is a Drakonian-Anunnaki Satain family that is personified as Satan;[120] but this is not the actual Satan as Samael.

Lucifer, the Devil, and Satan are identified with various symbols such as the pentagram, goat, dragon, and serpent. I wish to clear up some of this confusion and show the relationship to Judeo-Christianity.

The pentagram is associated with astrology and creation. When it is depicted in the upright, "correct" way, it represents the spirit presiding over the four elements of matter. In Babylonia, it likely represented astrological orientations for "the five planets Jupiter, Mercury, Mars and Saturn, and Venus as the 'Queen of Heaven' (Ishtar) above."[251] With Venus at the apex, we are directed to Sanat Kumara and Gabriel. In early Christianity, it also represented the five senses for health and the five wounds of Christ. In the Jewish Kabbalah religion, rituals use the pentagram to invoke Michael and his companion angels at each point.

The pentagram's four different segment lengths are constructed from the golden ratio. The natural, upright pentagram's apex extends beyond this ratio to act as an interdimensional doorway into the next higher dimension. The MCEO shows in Ashayana's *Sliders-2* workshop how this particular pentagram structure is used in creation physics.[252]

The upside down pentagram was an important geometric symbol to the Pythagorean school of thought. With two points up, it is the place or womb where the first pre-cosmic-offspring was put for the ordered cosmos to appear.[253] This represents the void out of which creation appeared, and it originated in Sumerian writings dated c. 3000 B.C.E.[251]

The 19th century A.D. French occult writer Eliphas Lévi popularized the "evil" meaning behind the upside-down pentagram. Most Christians are unaware he that taught magic according to the Kabbalah rituals that invoke Michael and his subcommanders, not Satan. A paraphrased summary from Lévi's *Transcendental Magic, Its Doctrine and Ritual* states:

> A reversed pentagram, with two points projecting upwards, is a symbol of evil and attracts sinister forces because it overturns the proper order of things and demonstrates the triumph of matter over spirit. It is the goat of lust attacking the heavens with its horns, a sign execrated by initiates.[251]

The Satanic image is represented by a half-goat, half-man. Goats were the preferred animal for sacrifice. The Book of Leviticus is the only book in the Bible that mentions a scapegoat, which is how a goat could be associated with a man. Scapegoats take the blame and are figuratively sacrificed humans. Interestingly, we can view Arihabi as Yahshua as the ultimate goat who was sacrificed.

Leviticus chapter 16, verses 8-10 state:

> And Aaron shall cast lots upon the two goats; one lot for the LORD and the other lot for the scapegoat. And Aaron shall bring the goat upon which the LORD's lot fell, and offer him *for* a sin offering. But the goat, on which the lot fell to be the scapegoat, shall be presented alive before the LORD to make atonement with him, *and* to let him go for a scapegoat into the wilderness.

A Bible lexicon shows that *scapegoat* is another word for *azazel*.[7] In the Book of Enoch, Azazel is a fallen angel, showing that the goat represents sin. The GA states that Azazael is an Angelic Human-Seraphim hybrid with some Zephelium (pre-Zeta Grey) genetics.[120] This may be one of his re-incarnations; originally, he was an ancient Shantarel, states the ATI,TPE. The ATI,TPE also reveals that Azazel is Lucifer's first commander, and he sometimes possessed Thoth due to Thoth's hunger for power.

The Devil character as the scapegoat takes the focus away from Michael so that he can continue to portray the good guy and carry on with his destructive deeds. As products of Michael's creation, religious figures of the original Shantarel race became his army, showing that he is "God" over his fallen angels who are also known as devils. Because some of these devils consciously left Michael's dictatorship, they were painted as fallen in the Bible when they were already fallen. Their defection is usually temporary or minor when they want their own glory. In general, they carry out Michael's commands because they collectively—as a dysfunctional family—have the same agenda.

The actual half-goat, half-man demigod was Pan, a Greek god of fertility. Pan gained a renewed following in Western Europe's Romantic Movement of the 18th and 19th centuries A.D. as well as neopaganism of the 20th century A.D.[254] He was renamed Goat of Mendes in the 19th century A.D. by Eliphas Lévi (not his real name—his surname shows his belief that connects the occult to the Levitical priesthood). Lévi probably referred to 5th century B.C.E. Greek historian Herodotus's account that the god of Mendes—the Greek name for a city in Egypt—had a goat's face and legs. However, the actual Egyptian deity was a ram that was believed to be the soul of Osiris, Marduk's son.

Lévi combined "images of the Tarot of Marseilles Devil card and refigured the ram Banebdjed as a he-goat, further imagined by him as 'copulator in Anep and inseminator in the district of Mendes'."[255] The new symbol of the goat-man god was renamed Baphomet. Some Satanists claim that the name Baphomet was mentioned several times by a few French Knights Templar when they were tortured into confessions by the power of King Philip IV of France, but they did not describe it as having any goat or ram characteristics. What stands out to me in the popular, amalgamated Satanist symbol created by Lévi are the female breasts, two crescent moons (Islam uses the crescent moon symbol), and angelic wings. The portrayal of fertility supports the common fallen angelic practice of forced hybridizations and genetically modified, artificial insemination.

One representation of the Devil character is a dragon. The UB states, "The dragon eventually became the symbolic representation of all these evil personages. Upon the triumph of Michael, 'Gabriel came down from Salvington and bound the dragon (all the rebel leaders) for an age'" (602.3).[16] The UB's dragon represents rebels mainly from the Red Dragon races of Wesadrak and the Milky Way. The Jesus group prefers to work with the Annu and Wesadek Green Dragons, but with the reality of genetic hybridizations over time, the race card has become somewhat muddied. The religion of Satanism most obviously follows the Red Dragon influence, including worship of the Dramin dragon queen who has Drakonian and Reptilian genetics. The Dramin and SSS-T queen is a pivotal character because she married Anu to produce Enki, the symbolic bridge for the Wesadek and Wesadrak political agendas.

The Ku Klux Klan (KKK) is a good example of a religious and political organization that combines both Wesadek and Wesadrak agendas (very similar to Hitler). It is commonly believed that the KKK is a Satanic organization, and the GA concurs in its description of the KKK's Red Dragon founders.[120] However, the only official "Dragon" title within the KKK is the state leadership role of the Grand Dragon, and its designated green robe shows allegiance to the Green Dragons. Additionally, the KKK generally claims to be Protestant

Christian.

Another representation of the Devil is a serpent. Serpents are more snake-like than dragons, but they are commonly substituted for one another. They are characteristically amphibious and reptilian, and Enki fits this role perfectly as the serpent in the biblical Garden of Eden. Author Michael Tsarion writes, "The most common symbol used by the Merovingians was the serpent, or the dragon. Indeed, the most well known amphibian god was Dagon, whose name connotes Dragon. One of the Merovingian kings bore the name Dagobert."[256]

The Merovingians likely descended from Sarah, the child of Yahshua-Sananda and Mary Magdalene, and they have consistently been one of the planet's 13 most politically and economically powerful families, collectively known as the Illuminati. The Illuminati can be traced to Mary Magdalene, as I explained in chapter 5. These interwoven families, which also include Rockefeller and Rothschild, are investigated in the books of David Icke and Laurence Gardner that show the nearly seamless transition from the Jewish to Christian-Catholic bloodline and belief system. Now we can add Luciferian Satanism into the picture.

The "men in black" in Vatican City and political agencies across the world work for the Illuminati. The Illuminati and their secret societies started and control the banking system that puts everyone in debt through its robbery of accrued interest. The world's biggest corporations are synonymous to its families; they control the world's oil, and they control the banks that in turn control the governments, putting everyone at their mercy to receive a living wage. The United States government's Department of Defense receives the bulk of Illuminati funding and public taxes over which we have no control. Its wars are contrived according to their interests, keeping all of us distracted and impoverished. The Illuminati also fund the genetic modification of food and "food" laden with chemicals to make us sick so they can pump us with more chemicals via their pharmaceutical industries; this affects our energetic discernment and cumulatively breaks down our DNA.

Freemasonry is the recruiting arm of the Illuminati. There are 33 degrees or levels of status within the Freemason hierarchy, with the highest 33rd degree attributed to the ultimate master. Freemasonry has tracing board diagrams that show various symbols to partially reveal its secrets, which the Illuminati insert into architectural designs to both desensitize the public and keep their agenda alive to their inner circle. The First Degree Tracing Board portrays a central ladder erected toward a single star. To the right of the main star is the moon depicting the night sky along with seven stars. To the left of the main star is the Sun in daylight. People have tried to find the meaning behind this tracing board, but perhaps they have not interpreted its clues to literally reveal the identity behind the main star. Wayne Herschel, a researcher of esoteric symbology, has provided part of the answer that assisted my process in solving it.

Herschel studied the Hebrew Key of Solomon parchment that is currently held in the British Library. One pictogram has a circle of stars surrounding a square diagram with another star atop a tall, slight angle in the middle. The stars have directions that produce a star map. One of the star formations in the outer circle, a diagonal cross intersected with a vertical-horizontal cross, is copied in the center of another pictogram. Herschel states that this "double cross" is the Key of Solomon, and the Chi Rho ✻ Catholic symbol—that was signed by Jesus or God at the end of my mother's prophecies—signifies the double cross. Herschel states that the Chi Rho represents the collaboration of the Pleiades and Orion. The double cross symbolizes Orion with its four end points—Bellatrix, Rigel, Saiph, and Betelgeuse—as the "X," and its three "belt" stars are the "+" that form the spine toward Pleiades—signifying the letter "P"—along with the Orion Nebula crossbar.[257]

Herschel also studied the Astronomical Ceiling mural from the Tomb of Senenmut in Deir el-Bahri, Egypt. Senenmut was the steward and vizier of Queen Hatshepsut who was married to Pharaoh Thutmose II.[258] The mural's facsimile, on display at the Metropolitan Museum of Art, shows the same central star atop a tall, slight angle. It also shows Orion's hunter aligned via Orion's Belt to the Taurus constellation that is represented by a bull standing upright as if on one leg. The Pleiades star system is the seven-star system in the First Degree Tracing Board, and it is the bull's leg that can stand upright in the sky. The main star, which Herschel calls "Ra," is found in an alignment between Orion and Pleiades.

The biblical allegory of Jacob's Ladder can represent the First Degree Tracing Board's ladder or stairway to heaven to reach the Ra star. Is the route traversed by angels in descent and ascent between Heaven and Earth (Genesis 28:10-22). In Kabbalah, this ladder is the replicated Sefirot, the Mystical Tree that is the Metatronic Tree of Artificial Life.[259] Icelandic pagans revered Ra by putting a star ornament atop a triangular tree to celebrate the winter solstice, thereby starting the European Christmas tradition.

To solve the puzzle of the 33 degrees and Tracing Board ladder, Herschel correctly determines each step as altitude degrees up the azimuthal grid, which provides angular or arc measurements in degrees from the horizon upward across the Earth's spherical sky. He also correctly assumes that the Washington Monument obelisk, a major Freemason symbol, helps to identify the Ra star when facing east at night.

We can use planetarium software such as Stellarium to show the azimuthal grid and positions of stars and planets as a living star map that can be set to real time.[260] It appears that Herschel did not use planetarium software because his diagrams incorrectly show Pleiades east of Orion's Belt. When positioning Orion's Belt, Pleiades, and nearby luminous stars at and near the 90 degree east azimuth on the Stellarium star map, we can determine which star is Ra. Before such technology was available, Freemasonry used a measuring compass—its dominant symbol—to identify Ra.

East is the most significant direction for the family of religions that dominate the Earth. There is even a Freemasonry offshoot organization called Order of the Eastern Star. At the Washington Monument on September 15, Herschel deduces that the 33 degree steps start at the top star of Orion's Belt, Mintaka. He uses this specific date because September 15, 2009 is when Dan Brown originally published his book *The Lost Symbol* involving the Monument, so he thinks it is a clue to locate Ra. He takes a wrong turn by not using the vertical spine of the Pleiades to indicate a north-south direction. Instead, he uses the southwest direction of Atlas, the lowest Pleiades star, to create an inverted "sacred" triangle.[257] This configuration positions the Pleiades to the right of the east azimuth in order to point to a southwestern star at the east azimuth that is 33 degrees northwest from Mintaka. This strategy leads to a little-known star such as HIP 18508, so his conclusion maintains a shroud of mystery about the Ra star.

To properly investigate Herschel's process at the Washington Monument coordinates, I input Brown's publication date in Stellarium according to real time, and to my surprise, he did give us a clue! In fact, the clue shows the Ra star in plain sight, but he did not reveal it to possibly protect himself from harmful repercussion. At 1:33:45 a.m., the entire Orion's Belt is visible over the horizon, and the Pleiades spine of the Chi Rho and bull's leg points down the east azimuth directly over Aldebaran. Ra is Aldebaran as the luminous Eastern Star!

I am baffled that researchers have not solved these evident clues, but if they are conspiracy theorists who believe that hidden messages involve hidden things, then they may disregard the obvious and obfuscate the matter. Perhaps they are taking the 33 degrees altitude literally. Aldebaran is only about 27 degrees above the horizon, and the steps between Mintaka and Atlas are 34 degrees. I think that Scottish Rite Freemasonry purposely chose the 33rd Degree title of Grand Inspector General for a Human so it could preserve and shroud the 34th Degree for God that indicates Ra below it.

The second part of the puzzle involves the Egyptian mural. I input the Tomb of Senenmut coordinates in reference to a significant event in world history: Yahshua-Michael's birth. I chose the year 7 B.C.E. to satisfy the Bible's and GA's stories, and I used the September 15 date. At about 10:32:00 p.m., Aldebaran is the Eastern Star. Orion's Belt is again entirely in view over the horizon, and the Pleiades spine is vertical; however, the Pleiades cluster is slightly west of the east azimuth. The azimuth alignment would have hinted toward the time of birth, not necessarily a supernatural event at that moment. In both locations, the alignment lasts for a few days around September 15, but it appears that the Washington Monument is most precise on that date.

The Old Testament Scripture Hosea chapter 11, verse 1 states, "When Israel *was* a child, then I loved him, and called my son out of Egypt." Matthew chapter 2, verse 15 applies the Hosea "prophecy" to Yahshua, saying, "Out of Egypt have I called my son." As I showed in chapters 4 and 5, several people with royal blood were YHWH's sons. Hosea's Scripture refers to the Exodus departure under Akhenaten as Moses, and the Yahshuas were the new demigods of importance. Yahshua-Michael was the pivotal leader whose New Covenant unfolded into Christianity and eventual New Age-ism.

Matthew chapter 2, verses 1-2 state, "[t]here came wise men from the east to Jerusalem, Saying, Where is he that is born King of the Jews? for we have seen his star in the east, and are come to worship him." Yahshua-Michael's star is known as the Star of Bethlehem, and various theories have suggested that it guided three Magi kings from the East to the place of Jesus's birth.

> When they had heard the king [Herod], they departed; and, lo, the star, which they saw in the east, went before them, till it came and stood over where the young child was. When they saw the star, they rejoiced with exceeding great joy (Matthew 2:9-10).

Alien exopolitics theorists suspect the Star of Bethlehem was a spaceship that guided the kings. A spaceship could have been involved, but I deduce that Archangel Michael's collaborative Jesus group on Aldebaran channeled directions to lead the "wise men" to Yahshua. Aldebaran led the way when it entered its perfect astronomical position, thereby starting their journey toward Bethlehem. It is the Egyptian circumpunct symbol, a dot at the center of a circle otherwise called the bull's eye, which is literally Aldebaran as the Taurus bull's right eye.

The ATI,TPE confirms that Ra is the nickname of the orange giant star Aldebaran. It further reveals that Aldebaran has a wormhole connection to Wesadek. Aldebaran is a key location for diverse but similar alien groups under Archangel Michael that desire control over the Earth, even when they are in temporary disagreement.

Michael's group in the UB explains Lucifer's rebellion:

> Lucifer charged that the Universal Father did not really exist, that physical gravity and space-energy were inherent in the universe, and that the Father was a myth invented by the

Paradise Sons to enable them to maintain the rule of the universes in the Father's name. He denied that personality was a gift of the Universal Father. He even intimated that the finaliters were in collusion with the Paradise Sons to foist fraud upon all creation since they never brought back a very clear-cut idea of the Father's actual personality as it is discernible on Paradise. He traded on reverence as ignorance. The charge was sweeping, terrible, and blasphemous (603.3).[16]

Lucifer was deemed blasphemous against Michael, one of the most blasphemous aliens of all. This is the epitome of hypocritical, religious contradiction. Initially, "Lucifer joined forces with Michael as commander-in-chief of Michael's fallen legions," states the ATI,TPE. When he defected, more than one quarter of administrative Seraphim and lower orders of seraphic ministers left Michael's group to join Lucifer (434.6).[16] With this information, he is certainly not low in the pecking order as a Lanonandek son.

Lucifer's religious followers believe that his stance as stated in the above excerpt supports autonomy, and everyone should have self-assertion and liberty. I agree with this particular perspective, but I do not much agree with Lucifer because he desires a godly position over others, which contradicts his followers' assumptions about his statements. His charge likely means that he wants to be free from the rule of another. He might see some of the deception but then will cause more deception on his own.

Michael and his proponents argue in the UB that chaos and complete anarchy will occur in absence of totalitarian rule. This is an assumptive and typically weak argument against self-assertion and self-rule. It negates the intrinsic ability, morality, and responsibility of the intelligent, adult individual. It sets us back in our personal growth and development to the point of self-sacrifice that can become enslavement. I agree that unchecked ego is a problem, but the capable individuals will generally check and balance their community and treat others as they would like to be treated, upholding real community as individuals who make up a group, not a communist group of numbers run by a small totalitarian regime.

Although the UB's Universal Father was either Michael or his creators, lesser gods of varying degrees are welcomed in the ranks as long as everyone knows their proper place; all of them are needed to manage the large numbers of planetary systems. Michael originally appointed Lucifer as God over the Earth, so when he defected from Michael's rule, Michael extended his greater God role toward Earth.

The Freemason elders embrace Luciferianism along Christianity because they essentially carry the same Metatronic energy; however, they publicly deny their belief in Lucifer in order to hide the greater truth of their Luciferian Leviathan race line.

The Leviathan race was created in the time of Atlantis in 68,000 B.C. when essentially all higher dimensional phantom races raided the evolved E-Luhli-Levi race—the Annu-Melchizedek race.[120] The Annu-Melchizedek was created to allow phantom races to incarnate on Earth under the GA and Thoth-led bio-regenesis plan, which many phantom entities took full advantage. The sufficiently restored Annu-Melchizedek DNA contained stargate ascension codes to Tara.

The Annu-Melchizedek-Leviathans created anti-krystic king lines such as the Hyksos that involved Abraham.[120] The Leviathan comprised the Luciferian version of Adam and Eve that contained Luciferian Shantarel, Anunnaki, and Drakonian genetics along with many more alien groups over time including Reptilians and Zetas (Greys), and its descendants include the Illuminati. The mythical sea serpent called the Leviathon has seven heads, which is the same seven-headed, Metatronic Cube Beast of the Bible (Revelation 17:9).

Thoth's deep affiliation with Azazel led him to defect in 22,328 B.C. from his lengthy service toward bio-regenesis so that he could usurp the Human race with the Leviathan and bring the Earth into phantom. Eieyani-Human colonies that existed on present day Kauai, Hawaii—the activation site for Earth's stargate-12 at Monségur, France—did not expect his betrayal because he had helped them anchor frequency that would open the Hall of Amoraea passage from Earth's stargate-12 to Sirius B's galactic stargate-6. This passage was necessary to override the phantom implanted Nibiruian Diodic Crystal (NDC) Grid so the 22,326 B.C. Earth stellar activation cycle (SAC) ascension process to Tara could commence (in chapter 8). The MCEO explains that Thoth then led Marduk's crew from Nibiru over to the Eieyani-Human settlement. They managed to jam communications from Sirius B, and they told the Eieyani-Humans that the Sirius Council had surrendered and Earth was surrounded by phantom forces. Thoth offered a deal to the women that said their men would be spared if they went with Anunnaki to Nibiru to become breeders to share their codes. They reluctantly agreed or were taken against their will, but Thoth's forces killed the men anyway. The women were raped on Nibiru, but many of them killed their babies because they were created to carry phantom souls with an evil agenda. Afterward, the women were murdered, or they killed themselves. Thoth, Marduk, and Lucifer orchestrated the horrific genocide and destruction that resulted in the Earth losing its ascension capability at that time.[223,261,125]

The channeled book, *The Law of One*, was given by Marduk's entity group called the Confederation of Planets or Ra Confederation of Planets.[262] This book has a distorted understanding of oneness that Lucifer's group largely supports, as conveyed by one of Lucifer's group members, the Hidden Hand. The Hidden Hand says that he is directly involved on the Earth as part of the Illuminati for his Creator, Lucifer. He says about *The Law of One*:

> I read some, but not all of the books when they first came out, some 25 years or so ago, and it is very similar to the knowledge my Family has, and have passed down for many many generations. It is approximately 85-90% accurate. The inaccuracies occurred when the channel was weak, and were not intentional. We know Ra (the entity) very well, and are happy that they are even now still working here on this planet "behind the scenes" to prepare for the Great Harvest.[263]

As you are well aware by now, this "Great Harvest" is our bodies and every other organism of our Veca.

Although the Illuminati are most aware of the alien agenda on Earth, they are riddled with religious worship toward their God Lucifer. It is true that Lucifer's group contributed several genes, but so did Gabriel and many others. Lucifer plays the childish game of "I was here first as your God, so worship me," when many "creator gods" were here at various times, even before Lucifer's influence in our race line as chapter 8 shows.

If we played this game today, then all Americans of European ancestry should go back to Europe, all British Australians go back to the United Kingdom, all Indians and Chinese go back to their populated homelands, immigrants seeking political asylum go back to their oppressive governments, and etcetera. This game is impossible today because we all contain a measure of mixed genetics, and we were born in new lands; the way of our world is to coexist, respect each other, and freely travel. In actuality, Lucifer was the foreigner here with no Earthly genetics. For him (and Michael, Marduk, and etcetera) to have the gall to claim the Earth and its inhabitants is absolutely ludicrous.

Ra Confederation of Planets

Marduk formed the Confederation of Planets, and he is its leader as Ra, confirms the ATI,TPE. The ATI,TPE expounds to state that Marduk named himself Ra to represent Aldebaran; he is a high commander over Aldebaran's affairs. Like Lucifer, Ra wanted to be God because his group's hierarchy did not allow him enough control. To carve out his own niche, he as Ra typically gives us kind words and empty promises threaded with truth. Proof of this was in the prophecies to my mother.

The ATI,TPE reveals that Marduk's Ra group gave my mother all of her prophecies up until we left religion, calling itself Jesus, Father, God, Yahuah, Yashua, and Ya at different and sometimes simultaneous times. Then, Enki stepped in as the Grand Intellect, possibly to save the direction his son was going with us. I thought that Enki could have also been the Grand Master after my mother turned away from Christianity, but the ATI,TPE reveals that it was yet another name used by the Ra group to communicate with her. The Grand Master title, which is given to leaders of Freemason Grand Lodges, shows the alliance between Ra, Lucifer, and Satan.

The Ra group used the Freemason and Catholic Chi Rho symbol in my mother's prophecies. Its alter ego of the Christian God and Messiah shows that it works closely with the Jesus group. With the plethora of entities involved with the Jesus group, there is practically no limit to their "brotherhood." The Illuminati bloodline represents the brotherhood of all of these related alien groups. I hope that all prophets, channelers, and religious followers will seriously think more than twice about what they have been doing because they are essentially calling upon all of these aliens.

These alien groups use average Humans as religious operatives because we would probably detect bad energy from the Illuminati and therefore distrust their message. The Hindu "hugging saint" Amma is a perfect example. Mata Amritanandamayi, known as Amma, is partially and sometimes fully possessed to gain a following by performing little miracles. A documentary titled "Miracle of Amma" highlighted one miracle she did in 1975 that turned water into milk. When watching this video, you can see that she is in a total trance while the liquid transformation occurred.[264]

Amma is viewed as an Ascended Master when she is really a puppet like other "chosen" people. This is actually good news because they can choose to break their trance and free themselves from these gods. It makes sense why the aliens use Humans as intermediaries to the masses: it is because of the better energy and measure of innocence that we portray. I have no doubt that she is exuding her own kind energy in her hugs, but it is only a measure of what her goodness could be if she would detach herself from her gods; additionally, her gods are sending their energies through her hugs to people.

More often than not, we should take out the magnifying glass to investigate otherworldly messages. Ra in *The Law of One* states the Source energy as "all that there is," similar to the Hidden Hand saying "All There Is." Let us look at how their distortion of All That Is progressed. The Confederation of Planet's phrase includes both options of here and there as "that" and "there" for its concept of Oneness. This allows both light and dark for a comprehensive view just as the GFofL and Ashtar Command see it. The Illuminati description further distorts it to just being "there." The "All That Is" (as the true pure essence) is a description of the present with a specific, singular eternity implied in "All That." "All There" is everything else outside of something specific, which in this crucial distinction is the origin before creation. I witnessed the "All There Is" phrase said by a couple of New Age spiritualists who welcome angels and pagan worship. Their supposedly good angels sometimes brushed by my head at night in a noticeable wind (the windows were closed) while I was staying at their house. I did not feel good energy there.

A well-known channeler of Ra's message is David Wilcock. Wilcock seems to have a mind of his own because he is often partially possessed; however, when he takes a moment to think according to his innate wisdom, he soon shuts it down in favor of his mission for the fallen alien group. Wilcock claims to be the reincarnation of channeler Edgar Cayce who was alive approximately 100 years prior. The ATI,TPE confirms this is true. Edgar Cayce came back as Wilcock with a similar body appearance and several similar planetary alignments in the month of March; the resemblance of Wilcock to Cayce is uncanny. Although Cayce likely did not choose his family for reincarnation, his genetics best identified with a similar type. It is debatable that astrological phenomena may bring certain traits as well.[265]

I almost feel sorry for Wilcock (and Cayce) because my mother was controlled just as he is, but he has further entrenched himself into his role by electing to perpetuate Ra's message. The ATI,TPE states that reincarnation can be a choice for those who wish to complete a mission in a fractal system (however, it is not a choice when strong Metatronic energy takes over the person). A telling piece of information is that Wilcock says he was a person named Ra-Ta during the time of Atlantis when he helped design the Great Pyramid with the help of (Marduk's) Ra group.[265] He has continually allowed the guidance of Ra in his lives. He was probably a Ra group operative before his Human experiences, so I do not pity him for his decisions that do not explore his beautiful Humanity that can create his own path.

Wilcock says that every ancient spiritualist religion communicated about a golden age that is coming, and the messages showed great excitement about it.[266] They glorified a New Earth after a spontaneous ascension process. He said that Cayce's readings were adamant that the second coming of Christ is really us. Wilcock taught that the golden or new age would have begun on December 21, 2012. Contrary to his "good news," the golden age fulfills the irrational golden ratio that is produced by the Metatronic 55.5-144 merkaba spin and energy blast.

The Metatronic 55.5-144 agenda is to send the BeaST wavelength to us from Abaddon and its network. Not surprisingly, Wilcock has repeatedly talked about the wavelength that will reach us from the center of the Milky Way. He states that the center of our galaxy is a torsion field generator. The wave from the center passes through planets and stars and charges them with energy, causing massive effects that stimulate and program the DNA molecule to rewrite all life on the planet.[266]

If you view Wilcock's message as a shiny, plastic-covered image of a golden age with feel-good words, then it can appear that we will not have any more misery on our planet. Lift the plastic veil, and you will clearly see the dark energy wave causing destruction toward everything in its path.

The problem with the Ra Confederation of Planets' group message is that it does know about ascension mechanics with wavelengths reaching us and activating us, but it cleverly adds lies that mirror the UB's version about instant materialization of Humans from a simple frequency. Wilcock's examples involve the Fibonacci ratio of the torsion field-generated wave, so this only means that particles were recycled and then reassembled. This does not mean that people were naturally or spontaneously created, as chapter 8 clarifies. I would greatly prefer to not have this Metatronic frequency further disassemble my DNA.

Greys

The dominant Grey taskforce is comprised of certain 3rd dimensional Zeta races that are proficient in interdimensional time travel. They also operate out of a hive mentality that lacks spiritual awareness. I give extreme caution when labeling them advanced beings because they are generally greedy with their abilities: they have ultimately destroyed their planets and genetically weakened their bodies due to experimentation.

The Zeta race line originated with the Zephelium, who were tall, bipedal, blue-skinned insectoid Reptilian serpents. The Zeta race initially resembled the natural early reptiles of Earth, but it has become severely genetically modified by Drakonians and Reptilians into 4-foot tall gray or variously colored beings with large, entirely black, almond-shaped eyes and frail bodies that can no longer procreate.[144] Colonel Philip Corso of the Eisenhower Administration, who later became a whistleblower, saw a body that fits this description in 1947 at the Roswell base in New Mexico. [267]

The Zeta are from the Zeta Reticuli star system, but they have emerged as a very relevant problem to our survival as a planet and Human race. The GA explains, "The Zeta entered your time continuum because of the proximity of Earth's time portals to their own and also because the Earth has certain environmental elements the Zeta need for survival" (p. 13).[144] They initially preferred to reconstruct the pathways of their destroyed planetary portals by working through our dimensional portals. It was because they were experimenting with time travel that they got their planets stuck in-between dimensions. When they realized they could not repair their portals, they had to find a way to live elsewhere. The Earth is a beautiful candidate, but since the carbons in our environment prove toxic to the Zeta, they decided it was best to continue their race line by developing hybrids that can live on the Earth. Through their continued desire to operate outside of natural creation mechanics, these Zeta have shown their disconnection to natural evolution and ascension. If they can fully possess or re-incarnate into an artificially crafted Human hybrid, then I deduce that they would not peacefully coexist with us.

The book *CoEvolution* by Alec Newald confirms the GA's account. Newald recorded his abduction experience by blue-skinned Zetas who visited him during his childhood. They explained that they wear full-body suits on their planet to protect their skin from the dying atmosphere that needs monoatomic gold to temporarily sustain it. They got stuck in the 3.5 dimension while trying to artificially ascend to the 4th dimension. Newald was targeted since childhood to get him comfortable with their presence and to study him as a suitable candidate for their agenda. He was swayed by their story for survival, and he hinted toward giving them his semen so they could create Zeta-Human hybrids to live on Earth! I wonder if he carries a significant portion of Leviathan-Jewish genetics because of the following statement by the GA.

> The Zeta had great interest in the Nazi experimentation with genetics and were supportive of their agenda of creating a "superior race." The Zeta would let the humans help them create a genetically superior human prototype which they would then use to create the Zeta-human hybrid. Zeta interest in the Hitler regime began to dwindle over disagreements concerning the Nazi's anti-Semitic policy.... [U]nlike the Nazis, the Zeta believed the Jewish race to be *superior* genetically, and they were *not* interested in a human proto-type that did not carry the coding particular to the Jewish race (p. 14).[144]

Zetas found governments that helped them create hybrids so they could continue their lineage on Earth. In addition, they have abducted Human women to extract their eggs in order to perform genetic experiments. If their agenda could succeed, our future could be one where Humans assimilate into Greys. This is what it really means to be assimilated—it is forced interbreeding!

Zetas specialize "in the art of 'perceptual interference,' being able to alter human perceptual frequency enough to appear in whatever forms they choose," state the GA (p. 14).[144]

First, this has allowed them to appear as Human allies with extraordinary knowledge to further the gains of governments who in turn allow them to covertly control the planet.

The GA explains:

> During the time of World War II the Zeta in your system approached certain elements of government in the allied forces, using the guise of human form.... *The Zeta themselves set in motion the structures for what has become our global, covert Interior Government* (p. 15).[144]

I know that Drakonian, Reptilian, and Anunnaki groups contribute to this type of government, so the blame is not solely placed upon the Zeta or Greys. In fact, Zetas work with these Illuminati groups although they each have their own agendas. The lower levels of the world's governments have no idea about the sordid nature of the Interior Government unless classified documents are mistakenly or purposely leaked. I call for the open disclosure of all Interior Government documents so that we can take back our own power. Arguably, our wars are almost always orchestrated by aliens and their high-level implants, so we as organic Humans have nothing to fear among each other because we want to live safely on our own planet. Our Earth's Humans are our best allies!

Second, this gives Greys the ability to disrupt our brainwaves and dull our minds as though we are in a dream while they try to abduct some of us. In October 2010, while my mother and I were both involved in researching alien factions and asking the ATI,TPE for clarification, I was briefly out of town when Zetas attacked her. She was sleeping and started to feel like her body was being pulled away from her. She cried out, "No, no, no!" Thankfully, my step-father was there to wake her up and get her fully back before any harm could be done. I think Zetas were abducting her etheric-type body because her physical body was in bed when she was awoken. This type of abduction was set in motion to probably implant a genetic detachment away from her inner self who knows the truth. When she called me to tell me what happened, I was a bit shaken and then very angry. How dare they!

Just a year earlier, the ATI,TPE revealed to us that Zetas took my twin sister in the womb of my mother. My three-month-old sister was recently deceased by that time, as my Neuro Emotional Technique muscle-testing sessions revealed and the ATI,TPE later confirmed, so what use did they desire of her body, I wonder? I know that their intentions were not good. I am glad that they at least left me alone. I was alive, so perhaps that made a significant difference.

Both of these partial abductions sped up the dimensional reality of my mother's body and environment to make our dimension easily accessible to theirs. Often, the ghosts that people see are actually Greys when carefully looked at. (Other ghosts are fragmented consciousness left behind by people, as confirmed by the ATI,TPE.) Greys can also appear as orbs of light when they enter here from their dimensions.

The GA explains:

> Most often the Zeta will remain physical and use simple frequency modulation tactics to "scramble" the brain wave patterns of those viewing them. They are there, but they can interfere with the human's bioelectrical system sufficiently enough to make themselves appear invisible, "ghost-like" or disguised in other forms (p. 11).[144]

Thankfully, we can detect "odd odors" when such scrambling takes place because of the way our neurological system processes the distorted perceptual data, states the GA. Our energetic sense can also distinguish the attack.

Zetas are wicked beings if they feel they must work covertly behind the scenes to dupe our people and take control over us. Do they think that we cannot coexist peacefully, or are they another alien group that hates the Oraphim and Angelic Human lineage? Is this why they prefer Jewish genetics because their mutations are easier to manipulate, not solely because the Hibiru lineage (pre-Habiru) is valuable?

The GA states that the Zeta who do wish to evolve are assisted by higher-level, nearly 12-foot tall praying mantis-like beings called the Aethian.[144] If you see an Aethian together with a Zeta, there is probably some hope for it; I do hope the Aethian are good and aware as teachers.

I was surprised to find out from the ATI,TPE that Zetas are generally less evil than the Tall Greys, but there are varying shades of phantom. The approximately 7-9 feet Tall Greys control some of the smaller Greys, including some Zetas. If you see these beings accompanying Zetas, this is a very different scenario to that of the Aethian, and it is much more common. Tall Greys generally oversee Zetas, even as their overlords, to dictate their actions. Tall Greys are usually the doctors who perform the surgeries and place implants into abductees. Implants monitor Humans and inject frequencies to control and dull our minds. [267]

Tall Greys have been reported to look white, almost humanoid in appearance while still resembling stereotypical Greys with almond-shaped, black eyes. Some have large noses, such as the Verdant race in the book *Alien Mind* by George LoBuono. Tall Greys are comprised of Reptilian and Drakonian genetics and generally work closely with both races. They are mainly from the Orion constellation where large populations of Reptilians and Drakonians live. They live among Reptilians underneath the Earth in caverns, and they both consume the glands and blood of kidnapped people, according to whistleblower accounts. One whistleblower story reveals that "Holloman Air force base in New Mexico has reportedly been the site of subsequent extraterrestrial meetings with tall Grays." [267]

Tall Greys are generally disgusting and horrible, so I would agree that they are worse than the Zeta, although these groups of Greys, especially a smaller version at 3 feet tall, are generally mercenaries. Some of them have been genetically bred to have no emotion at all. This means that some Zetas who are enslaved by Tall Greys are now like robots. If they are truly innocent in how they inherited such unnatural bodies, then they could use their reasoning and choose to rebel or die instead of kill or enslave others. Better yet, they can energetically reach out to benefactors who may be able to save them.

Chapter 8 reveals the Zeta Grey agenda over the last few centuries. They are primarily aligned with Drakonians and are operating as their army, working to drag our entire Earth into phantom status so they can proliferate their population.

Thetans

After their return from exile, the Thetans settled in the Theta-Orion star system in HU-1, hence why they are known as Thetans. 250 million years ago, when Parallel Earth was being populated, Bourgha-Budhara and Thetans swept in and captured some of the early Humans. They added some of their genes to these Humans to create a slave race that they could control and also destroy its gene pool. Tragically, Parallel Earth's Human races no longer exist except for a mutant version that is used as livestock, states the MCEO.[208]

Over time, Thetans hybridized with various groups of Anunnaki, although the MCEO states that Thetans are a nemesis of the Green Dragon-Anunnaki group. Most notably, they hybridized their race "with factions of the Metatronic Thothian-Anunnaki from which they evolved their more hominid appearance and mind-control skills. In later Earth mythology, the Thetans were often referred to and depicted as 'energetic-vampire-hominid-creatures' called 'Wraith,'" states the MCEO with Ashayana (p. 15).[185]

Thetans raided the Earth 75 million years ago. They constructed a wormhole from Parallel Earth to Earth in order to anchor an emerging Metatronic technology called the Threshold Glass Towers grid control system that involves planetary implants. Threshold technology combines the power of previously installed Metatronic grid placements on the Earth. Thankfully, Aquafereion Races of Urtha— AquaLaShA's original Earth—came to the

Earth to bring in Aurora energy that is intolerable to Thetan biology. They "fought" by standing in this amazing energy to anchor it into the Earth. This showed the true strength of the Aquafereions.[208] They wanted to get involved, not only to help the Earth but to protect Urtha. Urtha and its sun, Sala, are the Thetan objective, meaning that our Sun is as much at risk as our Earth. Unfortunately, Thetans came back again to fully develop their technology in the Earth, joining forces with other intruders who follow the Dragon and Bourgha phantom agenda (in chapter 8 "2012").

Just as the Jesus group's Metatronic technology has directed us to Wesadek, the Thetans perpetuate the Metatronic Threshold technology to direct us to Wesadrak and the Bourgha matrices. They have furthered the Bourgha agenda by linking Parallel Earth and Earth locations up to its time rip network that connects Bourgha matrices to Wesadrak, Parallel Milky Way, and Milky Way. Bourgha entities finally entered our Ecka portion 25 million years ago to create the fallen Ecka stargate-1 called Telos, states the ATI,TPE (in chapter 11).[208] Thankfully, the Bourgha time rips have not entered Galaxy-2 due to the successful protective efforts of the Krysthal River Host groups, states "M" with confirmation from the ATI,TPE.

In general, Metatron aliens do not want to be diverted to the Bourgha Ecka-Veca matrices. They want to activate the BeaST but not the Threshold. The Thetans (and the Wesadraks on-going) have become the "dark forces" to the Jesus group along with Lucifer's group during its brief rebellion. Since Michael has affiliations beyond what we are told by his Jesus group, and he has actively controlled Parallel Earth with some relationship to the Thetans, he may put the Bourgha objective before the concerns of the Green Dragons.

Thetans have mastered the practice of deception like all other religious gods. They "miraculously" healed a woman, Vianna Stibal, of cancer in 1995, and they are using her to teach and perform their energy work. Her website states the following:

> ThetaHealing® is a technique that focuses on thought and prayer. ThetaHealing® teaches how to put to use our natural intuition, relying upon unconditional love of Creator Of All That Is to do the actual "work". We believe by changing your brain wave cycle to include the "Theta" state, you can actually watch the Creator Of All That Is create instantaneous physical and emotional healing.[268]

I hope the reader has learned by now to pay special attention to how these entities phrase their words. Here, the Thetans flipped the order of the All That Is to a creation, where there is a creator beyond it—the Thetans with their "creative" dark energy. Just like the Jesus group, Thetans use our prayer or simple willingness to allow them access into our bodies.

Another website about Stibal's practice reveals its alien origin and intent:

> Orion Healing is also known as DNA/Theta Orion Energy Healing.... Core Belief Reprogramming is the second part of the Theta Healing process. Here the practitioner energetically enters the body to replace or resolve belief systems that no longer serve the client.[269]

Removing the beliefs that were falsely indoctrinated into us do benefit us, but in the context of the Thetans (or any Metatronic-energy group), their message screams Blank Slate Technology. Thetan healing techniques remove old core beliefs and replace them with their theta dream-world frequency with which we can identify in our sleep. They work on our entire self: core, gene, history, and soul. If they replace all of these levels in us, we will have no self left!

The Thetans are the gods of the Church of Scientology. The "Galactic Federation" is their nemesis in Scientology doctrine, showing the prior split between the Red and Green Dragons before they combined forces leading up to 2012 A.D.[270] The Scientology religion discloses the alien aspect of the gods, but it also includes us as those particular gods, calling us all Thetans. This would make us one happy family with these very loving Thetans! All brotherhood and light! As their assimilated slaves, that is.

As with all religions, the healing given to Ms. Stibal allows entities to use her in order to falsely heal others. If her healing ritual seems to work, then it is most likely because the compromised individuals are partially lifted out of their bodies in a whitewashed mental, emotional, and physical state to detach them from their problems. The Metatronic energy imparted to them has them accept on some level the Frankenstein Science occurring in their bodies. If there is some actual healing, then it is to create another worker as a mouthpiece for the Metatronic agenda. The mouthpieces are few and far between, so the first example and speaker is showcased.

One World Order Agenda

The "New World Order" is a catch phrase sometimes said by world leaders, but it actually designates a One World Order (OWO). For many thousands of years, three dominant OWO agendas have competed against each other to selfishly gain Earth and ultimately Milky Way quanta. One plan was directed by the Drakonian-Reptilian-Red Dragons to siphon the quanta toward Wesadrak. Another plan was led by Anunnaki Elohim-Green Dragons to direct the quanta toward Wesadek. Third, the Green Dragons split into a Luciferian agenda toward Phantom Milky Way.

The higher dimensional Seraphims won their wars against the Jehovian Anu races and gained leverage in their plan. Additionally, Thetans helped influence the result toward Wesadrak. Some Anunnaki-Green Dragons accepted this result, so they joined their previous enemies and together formed the United Intruder Resistance (UIR) in 2000 A.D. because of their mutual hatred of the Krysthal River Host races. Other Anunnaki-Green Dragons went back to Wesadek or sought amnesty with the MCEO-GA, which likely will have them stay in the Milky Way and on Earth because they do not want to be sucked into Wesadrak from the Phantom Milky Way if Red Dragons succeed in their plan.

The MCEO-GA states that the Necromiton Andromie beetle-hominid race initially oversaw the UIR before more powerful groups successively stepped in, ultimately putting the Bourgha-White Dragons in control, although Michael's Bourgha-Shantarel group was involved long before this.[120,271] Necromitons and Andromies in general are part of the Jesus group and are also strongly aligned with the Marduk-Luciferian group, which I have shown is another part of the Jesus group. It is difficult to ascertain into which matrix Michael's groups ultimately aim to siphon the Alpha-Omega energies if the Bourgha overlords intend to take them all.

Chapter 8 explores Earth's acute history that led up to recent years of planned fallen angelic destruction and KRH countermeasures. The UIR began to initiate the Jehovian Anunnaki agenda of the Apocalypse for overall planetary destruction, while world governments aligned with the Drakonian-Luciferian One World Order agenda to control the Human population. One significant way to do this is to cull our numbers with genocides by deranged leaders or environmental anomalies. A more common tactic is to covertly spread viral concoctions, subsequent vaccinations, and also chemtrails criss-crossed and streaked across the sky to severely weaken our immune systems. Various large-scale destructive attempts have been thwarted by the KRH and its allies.

Evil forces had to align themselves to better counteract the Oraphim and Angelic Human protection of the Earth. Our small but amazingly significant planet is inherently linked with stargate-3, one of the few Milky Way stargates that has remained connected to AquaLaShA. If the UIR could control the Earth and further distort its energy, it would be in a better position to take much of the Milky Way with the Earth due to how the stargates are connected on the kathara grid.

The OWO aliens have set up camp in several major cities across the world, even planning cities according to a specific geometric design to help ground their Metatronic energies. Canberra, the capital of Australia, is a perfect example.

I had the interesting fortune to live in Canberra. It was designed by architect Walter Burley Griffin to maximize his transcendental spiritualist ideals and interest in nature, whereby the placement and structure of buildings and towns could amplify nature's energy (as God or an aspect of God) to enhance spiritual experience and growth. Transcendentalism links directly to Freemasonry through the metaphysical spiritualism of Emanuel Swedenborg, a scientist, philosopher, and self-proclaimed "Servant of the Lord Jesus Christ" who was a big influence to Griffin along with other prominent architect masons.[272] Within the masonic movement, there is significant importance in establishing a divine connection with its version of God called the "Grand Architect of the Universe," and this is carefully facilitated through the use of Metatronic geometry.[273]

Griffin coordinated his geometric plans in alignment to the stars, something that many researchers have observed about the alignments in Washington D.C. He was strongly influenced by the work of Sir Norman Lockyer who taught about symbolic axiality through the emerging field of astroarchaeology. Lockyer proposed that ancient Egyptian and Greek temples and many sacred sites were axially aligned in accordance with the solstices or equinoxes, or the rising and setting of the moon or a particular star. Astronomy governed the selection of sites and how their buildings were aligned and constructed.[274]

Lockyer's work was heavily utilized by the Theosophical Society, an organization established in 1875 to advance the esoteric and spiritual belief of Theosophy.[275] Helena Blavatsky, one of the founders, incorporated the basic tenets of animism and pantheism into its teachings. Animism states that all matter, including inanimate objects, contain a spiritual essence, and pantheism states that everything is God. Behind these assertions that appear to have no hierarchy, Theosophy transforms transcendentalist philosophy into a religion by appointing god and goddess entities at the top. *Theos* is a Greek word for god, and *sophy* shows god(dess) Sophia, which I previously revealed is the entity group led by Lady Nada.

The Griffins were not officially recognized as Theosophists until the 1920s, but there is little doubt of their earlier ties. The Theosophical Society ushered in many of the beliefs now prevalent in the contemporary New Age movement. It also influenced many of those who would later rise to power in Nazi Germany, including Adolf Hitler who applied Theosophical concepts to the spiritual foundation of Nazism. The symbol of the Theosophical movement was the Swastika before it became synonymous with Nazis.

Charles Leadbeater, an influential member of the Theosophical Society, openly declares in his book titled *Masters And The Path* that the "Great White Brotherhood" (GWB) of Ascended Master "Adepts" had revealed the principles of Theosophy to Blavatsky, and the head of this brotherhood, Sanat Kumara, is the King or Lord of the Earth. When he asks an unnamed God—likely Sanat Kumara—about what we must do in life, the entity aptly replies (with my added emphasis in italics), "[T]hrough striving to be and do your best, you will find yourself *possessed* of the qualifications which admit to Initiation and membership in the Great White Brotherhood itself" (paragraph 131).[276] Leadbeater adds, "And the kingdom of heaven, remember, is the Great White Brotherhood of the Adepts" (paragraph 310).[276] Leadbeater had a fascination with Australia, and in 1915 during a series of lectures in Sydney, he proclaimed "Australia and New Zealand as the home of a new sub-race...children and young people of a distinctly new type."[277] He called this sub-race *Aryan*, an evolved state of Humanity that would eventually become like the GWB, a close associate of the Ashtar Command and GFofL. The GWB originates in Wesadek, which I further explain in chapter 10.

Theosophy promised the arrival of another world teacher or Messiah figure who would usher in the new Aryan race of Humanity, and Adolf Hitler considered himself to be this figure. It is possible that 40 years earlier, Griffin was part of a group that aimed to design a capital from where the world teacher would emerge.

In his book *The Secret Plan of Canberra*, Professor Peter Proudfoot notes Walter Burley Griffin's desire to design a city plan representing a new example of democracy that incorporates the laws of nature.[274] Although Griffin had his spiritual and professional ties, it appears that he was hesitant to execute them because he procrastinated and nearly missed the deadline. In her memoir *Magic of America*, his wife Marion, also an architect, explains this situation in the third person after a long day paddling up a stream to Lake Michigan.

> Perhaps it was the torture of those sunburned legs, perhaps it was just that well known mean disposition of hers or perhaps it was those spiritual advisers, of whom Xanthippe [Marion] was unconscious at the time, that said to her - "We can't do anything with that Socrates [Walter] without some human help. Won't you do something to make him get a start on that important matter he has in mind?" or perhaps it was the suggestion of the Devil himself as Socrates was later inclined to think (p. 293-4).[278]

With only nine weeks left before the deadline, Marion yelled at Walter to get going right away; there was a time line after all. She was working with alien entities in order to facilitate a greater agenda that she kept secret from

Walter, which the ATI,TPE verifies that he was unaware of the overall plan.

Walter was influenced by an overshadowing process when he constructed his precise designs, and Marion ensured that the process was completed correctly. She revealed in her memoir that Archangel Michael did "so often" reach over Walter's shoulder to influence his work.

> I had returned alone from India and felt that the Archangel Michael himself had lent the senor [Walter] one of his meteors so that he could do what he had so often reached over a draftsman's shoulder to do with that firm hand of his - sweep in a form just where and as required - so that he could give our work in these plays in which he was so interested that final touch of perfection (p. 440).[279]

When I asked the ATI,TPE if Marion's entity group extended beyond Archangel Michael's influence, it states that she had often been in contact with the Samjase Luciferian-Seraphim-Anunnaki-Human faction. They mainly constitute the Ashtar Command but are also spread out among the GFofL and Milky Way extensions of the GWB. The Samjase group later initiated contact with Hitler and the Nazis, and famed UFO contactee Billy Meier.

Proudfoot writes:

> Marion frequently refers to Canberra as the "only true modern city – Alpha & Omega"; as a city designed by "creative thinking", and one that revives "the ancient science", even though nothing was said of the esoteric nature of the scheme at the time (p. 87).[274]

Interestingly, both architectural societies of Australia and Britain protested and dissuaded many of their architects from entering the contest because it had a strangely narrow advisory panel with the Minister for Home Affairs as the ultimate judge. Lack of competition and fairness favored the Griffin design along with its advanced alien influence.[280] However, the ATI,TPE expounds that some governmental officers who worked with generally benevolent alien groups resisted several designs when they realized what the geometries and images represented, which caused some delays.

Canberra was established in 1913, and its "temporary" parliamentary building was built in 1927. This building was used for 61 years until New Parliament House was constructed in 1988 to commemorate Australia's Bicentenary. Remarkably, New Parliament House is located only a few hundred feet north of the old building. Both buildings are standing on the city's main ley line. A ley line is a straight path that connects two vortices.[281]

The parliamentary ley line connects two mountains: Mount Bimberi, the tallest mountain in the region, and Mount Ainslie. The road up Mount Ainslie coils like a snake and ends at the top of the mountain in the shape of a snake head. In 2009, on the base of Mount Ainslie's tower in the snake head, an occult group performed a goat sacrifice to its God of Canberra—Lucifer.

Black Mountain, a mountain nearby, has an imposing tower that can be seen for miles outside the city. This telecommunication tower emits ultra-low electromagnetic frequency (EMF) waves. The ATI,TPE states that EMF towers are covertly used to communicate with aliens and to disrupt the energy of the Earth and our bodies. It is no coincidence that many of Canberra's major arterial roads run directly in alignment with the EMF tower on Black Mountain.

Canberra's street design incorporates all of the sacred geometries important to the Illuminati and Metatronic death science. Washington, D.C. comes close. A prominent feature in Canberra's design is the Parliamentary Triangle that consists of three main avenues heading northeast of the New Parliament House apex of the Triangle: Commonwealth, Kings, and Constitution Avenues. Each Triangle point represents government, commerce, and military buildings—the three main interests of Illuminati control. The government point is encompassed by a circle representing the Illuminati's "all-seeing eye," similar to what is shown on the back of the United States of America one dollar bill. The commerce point as the City Center is encased in Metatronic Cube symbology pointing northeast. The military point is a circular mosaic of little black granite stones that swirl like a vortex. Behind this circle is an Ichyths fish road design, the Christian—predominantly Catholic—symbol representing Jesus Christ.

Professor Proudfoot establishes in his work that Canberra was built around the shape of the rhombus, which is two conjoined, equilateral triangles within the center of the vesica piscis in Figure 4. The rhombus is not readily apparent when glancing at the Canberra street plan; its geometry is implied with the Parliamentary Triangle and its opposite equilateral triangle whose apex meets Mount Ainslie.

The vesica piscis is a dominant geometry of death science. Esoteric groups favor this shape as their creative force or "womb of the universe" because to them it symbolically represents the intersection of the spiritual and material worlds (p. 16).[274] It is the basis of the Ichthys fish, and Gothic-style churches are framed with the vesica's pointed arch.

"Sacred" sites all over the world are built upon the vesica piscis as documented in Professor Proudfoot's research.

Canberra, therefore, has affinities with Stonehenge, sacred

Glastonbury, ancient Egyptian temples and pyramids, even with the concept of the new Jerusalem. In common with them all, Canberra is constructed in accordance with ancient architectural and planning principles and the same sacred geometry emanating from the Vesica.[274]

These geometric patterns imbued in street designs, temples, and significant ancient monuments are not just token symbols to the alien gods; they are actual technologies that both activate Metatronic frequencies into the Earth and capture Earth's energetic quanta. They directly affect us in the same way.

Symbols, also called geomancies, are geometrically formed light codes that can activate and alter frequencies and blueprints of matter. Symbols act as scalar waves that create specific energetic signatures, including languages.[282]

Canberra's abundant symbols provide hints about who is trying to control the city. There is a central, man-made lake that is shaped like a dragon. The Parliamentary Triangle is part of a larger but incomplete inverted pentagram that starts with the New Parliament House apex. The face of the goat-man Baphomet or Goat of Mendes appears to be cleverly woven into the New Parliament House design when viewed from above. The Triangle also incorporates a curved, connecting road that signifies the Masonic compass. Before the military point of the Triangle, an eagle standing atop a tall flag pole obelisk looks to its right at New Parliament House. The eagle has a similar chiseled face and torso to the Nazi eagle symbol that also faces to the right. The Nazi eagle's wings are outstretched east-west while Canberra's wings are stretched north. The ATI,TPE cautions Canberrans to stay outside of the Parliamentary Triangle because it has the most Metatronically amplified energy. The situation is most unfortunate for the government workers there.

Down the main parliamentary ley line stands the War Memorial's room of the Unknown Soldier that represents all Australian soldiers who died for the OWO agenda (in chapter 8). The room contains abundant false ascension mosaics depicting armed service figures overseen by various entities and energies. The War Memorial is shaped like a cross to memorialize the sacrifices. Numerous people visit it each year, filling the area with grief and trauma. The geometric design of Canberra amplifies this negative energy and directs it into the Earth and toward the energy vampires. An interesting aspect of the promenade along the ley line that leads to the War Memorial is the specially designed street lights that resemble UFO aircraft. A fellow researcher about Canberra, James Macaron, has not seen this street light design anywhere else in the city.

Canberra was built over natural limestone caves. The ATI,TPE states that these caves cover approximately 40 miles underground and have been used by aliens for millions of years. If you do an internet search about encounters with aliens, you will find countless stories about sightings and dangerous experiences with Reptilians and Greys who live underground. They emit such dark energy that the unsuspecting Humans were lucky to escape in time.

In addition to Canberra, many other places around the world have long been centers for underground activity, including Los Angeles, California. It is no surprise that Hollywood favors the dinosaur. Reptilians may be the most common underground alien race because reptiles have been with the Earth for eons.

The vampiric aliens include a network of hominid-looking aliens who often live underground and work as liaisons to military and government personnel. The "Archangel Michael" section introduced the Nordic Anunnaki "Tall whites" who live underneath the Mount Ziel region of Northern Territory, Australia near the massive Pine Gap military base.

Canberra and its outlying land are sectioned off into a state called the Australian Capital Territory (ACT), where a part of its territory oddly extends far out to the east. What lies within that strange acquisition is a newly built, deeply underground military complex called the HQJOC, which likely connects to the vast network of caves.

New Parliament House was built inside of a hill also with probable underground connection. Insiders have reported a huge dark chamber that exists under New Parliament House and has no specific purpose. A witness gives this statement:

> At the far south-eastern end of the building, underneath the Senate side ministerial wing, there's an ENORMOUS void – probably 3 to four stories high in parts. Nothing but a partially excavated dirt floor and very long columns supporting the "ground" floor above. It's affectionately called "The Cathedral". It's not drawn on any of the architectural drawings that I saw, but the door into it was on the drawings, needless to say our curiosity got the better of us! The only sign of it from above is the very hollow sounding wooden floor outside the elevators on the "ground" floor.[283]

The secretive, upper echelon of Australia's Interior Government has highly classified information about aliens, and Australia is part of the most powerful family of countries in the world—England and the United States of America. Much of the European Union is on the same level. There is a direct correlation between the advancement of military technology and alien technology given to high ranking government officials. Several races from notable star systems have directly interacted with our world governments, but one star, Aldebaran, stands out with Canberra.

James explains his investigation into the plans of Canberra:

> How did I discover Canberra's link to Aldebaran? It began when I was exploring why the Parliamentary Triangle had been landscaped as it had. What spiked my curiosity was that the rose gardens that had been planted well over 50 years ago had been landscaped to what looks like eyes. There were many other features across the design that have it looking like there is some kind of semi-hidden face. I had noticed that the Illuminati's occult freemasonry work has the trait of hiding things in plain sight. To them it is part of the game to do this, but also the geometry is used for other Death Science related technologies that we now know more about.
>
> When I started tracing over a few key aspects of the Canberra Parliamentary Triangle design, it appeared that a bull's face was showing. There is of course the head of the goat (Goat of Mendes) on New Parliament House. But why the bull?

When James began to investigate the Taurus constellation, he noticed that its symbol was a crescent moon (or horns) lying atop a circle. The Canberra design also has this symbol, but it is broken into two parts. Figure 5 shows the circle directly above the bull's head, and the crescent is further upward on the lake's shoreline. As I previously stated, the Taurus constellation's image of the bull has Aldebaran as its right eye. Aldebaran's nickname is Bull's Eye, which can represent both rose bushes. It appears to exist between the Pleiades and Orion, making it a functional location for the intruder alien groups.

It is popularly believed that *Canberra* originated from the aboriginal word for "meeting place," although no such aboriginal word appears to exist. It does appear that Canberra was derived from *Kembery*, the name given by Bavarian geologist Dr. John Lhotsky.[284] According to the Australian Council of National Trusts paper "The Real Heritage of Canberra," Lhotsky was sent to Australia by King Ludwig I to explore and describe the Australian Alps, but he first went to the Limestone plains to study it for several days. He predicted in 1834, "Limestone is also one of the most important spots as far as the political economy of the colony is concerned.... At Limestone, therefore, at no distant period, a fine town will exist."[285]

Why was the King of Bavaria involved in this foreign expedition nearly halfway around the world? Freemasonry emerged out of the Bavarian Illuminati movement during the 18th century, so it appears that the Ashtar Command

and affiliates were paving the way for the covert creation of Canberra at their selected location.

Figure 5. Canberra Bull and Goat of Mendes

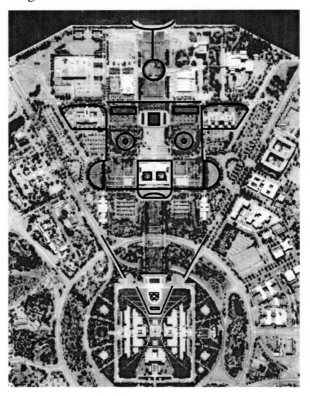

It is probably no coincidence that Canberra is claimed to be a meeting place; perhaps it is the intended meeting place for these entity groups and their Earthly Illuminati representatives establishing the One World Order. James researched this theory:

> There were posts across some internet sites that claimed Canberra was going to be the home for the New World Order capital. I was always curious why the Canberra location was selected for the capital, because up until recent times, it was nothing more than a back country sheep station and a total inconvenience.
>
> After asking questions about Canberra to the ATI,TPE, we learned that it was a key location for the Reptilians on the planet. So, now I have information about the Illuminati, OWO,

Freemasons, and Satanists choosing Canberra as their World capital, the Reptilians here, and a link with Taurus and Aldebaran.

When researching Reptilians and Aldebaran, interesting information arises that starts to fill in some gaps.

In a website that outlines UFO contactee Alex Collier's 22 extra-terrestrial (ET) races involved with the Earth, Collier states that Aldebaran comprises "Human/Reptilian" ETs. He also states that the same ETs are in Orion (Rigel, Betelgeuse, and Syclopesus) and Sirius.[286]

In the "Archangel Michael" section, I called out the fact that Collier is a pawn of the Andromedans. That section also shows a plethora of aliens working together, not only Reptilian hominids. The important aspect of these dark operatives is that they are highly hybridized to gain an edge in our gene pool, therefore passing their severe distortions onto us.

Often the terms "experiment" and "project" are used in otherworldly communications to describe the seeding of Humans. Remember that when phantom entities give the story, it is for hybridization away from our natural genetics.

The latest Human hybridization experiment was orchestrated through Hitler. James found websites that wrote about Hitler and the Nazis. Hitler was influenced by Aldebarans.

William Alek, Director of the Progressive Tech Center, gave a presentation about Nazi spacecraft technology and its link to the Vril secret society.

In 1919, Karl Haushofer founded the Vril Society in Berlin. The word "Vril" was ancient Sumerian meaning "like god" [my note: the Sumerian language did not have the phoneme "v," so it was likely a word from another alien origin[287]] and was used in the novel called "The Coming Race" written in 1871 by Edward Bulwer-Lytton and is about a race of supermen living within the Earth's interior. Members of the Vril Society are said to have included Adolf Hitler, Alfred Rosenberg, Heinrich Himmler, Hermann Göring, and Hitler's personal physician, Dr. Theodore Morell. These were original members of the Thule Society which supposedly joined Vril in 1919. The NSDAP (National Sozialistische Deutsche Arbeiter Partei) was created by Thule in 1920, one year later. Dr. Krohn, who helped to create the Nazi flag, was also a Thulist.

The Vril Society met with a female psychic medium, Maria Orsic at an old hunting lodge near Berchtesgarden [where the Nazis later set up camp], where they received remarkable news.

Maria led a group of beautiful young women psychics called the Vrilerinnen and began to receive messages from ETs called the Aryans on Alpha Tauri in the Aldebaran star system. Maria and a sister medium named Sigrun, learned that a half billion years ago, the Aryans, also known as the Elohim or Elder Race, began to colonize our solar system. On Earth, the Aryans created a colony in the hollow of the planet.[288]

Alek's presentation shows diagrams of Nazi symbolism, one of which is the Black Sun. The Vril Society joined forces with the Thule Society (later renamed Third Reich) because they both worshipped the Black Sun. "The 'Black Sun,' a large ball of 'Prima Materia', provided light and radiation to the Aryans of the inner Earth. Its [sic] also known as the great 'Central Sun' in the inner Earth."[288]

Actually, this Black Sun is not in or near an "inner Earth." The ATI,TPE states that it is the Phantom Milky Way stargate-4 named Rhabezoid that is the phantom portion of Tara's sun.[201] Rhabezoid may be connected to an inner region of our Earth by way of Phantom Earth portals, or the previous quote refers to the ET Aryans living on Phantom Tara.

It is believed that 1947 and 1956 United States military expeditions led by Admiral Richard E. Byrd resulted in the discovery and potential entrance into interdimensional portals "beyond" the Earth's poles to Inner Earth.[289] The Nazis had an Antarctic base called Neuschwabenland presumably near the portal's access point.[290] This information appears to involve lower dimensional territories within Earth as the literal Inner Earth (in chapter 8's "Atlantis and Lumeria").

Agartha is the name of our original Ecka stargate-3 as the significantly less dense ancestor of Earth. While nearby dimensional spaces or zones can be interpreted as subterranean "Inner Earth" planes, the ATI,TPE states that any such equation to the Krysthal Ecka Agartha is erroneous. Unfortunately, different entities within the same group can give contradictory and confusing stories. For example, MCEO entities have stated through Ashayana on different occasions that Agartha is a fallen zone as well as the original Ecka stargate-3. (Incorrect portrayals are in *12 Tribes* and are fortified by the GA story in *Voyagers II*, while correct information is in *Dance for Freedom, Part 1*, DVD-3.)[291]

The Vril and Thule Societies followed another version of a New Age religion about the power of light from their "Black Sun." A pro-Christian website that exposes the Vril states the following:

[It is] the invisible inner light of the universe, which gives or generates incredible power and communicates with Aryan aliens through psychic channeling. This 'Black Sun', became their god, responsible for the power of the Vril, energy in the form of an all permeating fluid possessed by the subterranean race (the Vril-ya) who are said to be the descendants of Atlantis along with the 'Aldebarans.'[292]

The website continues, "The darkest side to the Vril was their belief, which dates back many millenium, that the sacrifice of a young child will give more power than anything else in the dark realm."[292] This horrible example shows that artificial power must have real life to sustain it.

The Vril and Thule Societies wanted to build spaceships to visit Aldebaran, but their ultimate aim was to scour the universe in search of ultimate energy as light and dark, death and life. I recall reading an internet story around 2009 (I cannot seem to find it anymore) about an encounter a man had with Reptilians who were obsessed with finding an all-powerful energy. This man knew about the ATI,TPE, which the ATI,TPE confirms, and he presented expanded ATI,TPE energy to them in a sphere between his hands. They were fascinated about this energy, but then the sphere dissipated after he gave it to them. The ATI,TPE explains that they could not keep the pure energy nor know how to expand it.

Information about a removed internet Nazi reference, edited as "Nazi History of Alien Contact," states:

> The Nazis said that their supermen resided beneath the Earth's surface and were the creators of the Aryan race. Aryans therefore in Adolf Hitler's reasoning, constituted the world's only pure race and all other people were viewed as inferior genetic mutations. The Nazis under the reported guidance of Manipulative Extraterrestrials planned to re-purify humanity by committing genocide against anyone who was not an Aryan. Top Nazi leaders believed that the underground supermen would return to the surface of the Earth to rule it as soon as the Nazis began their racial purification program and established the Thousand Year Reich. These Nazi beliefs are very similar to other religions apparently also guided by Manipulative extraterrestrials that teach people to prepare for the future return of supernatural beings who will reign over a Utopian Earth. As in other such religions, the coming of the Nazi supermen would coincide with a great final divine judgment....
>
> Though he lost the war, eventually, Manipulative

Extraterrestrials apparently communicated with Nazis that those chosen by Satan will follow with success in establishing a Fourth Reich. Four is the number of Satan/Enki [Note: Satan is Samael who partially possessed Enki.] Hitler saw the ideal human in Satan and his demons who are of the extra-terrestrial race who looked like human beings with very tall statures, light blonde hair and blue eyes [Nordic]. Nazi technology is also alleged to have been disseminated under guidance by Manipulative Extraterrestrials. The Nazis had everything before any other country, they had radar in 1933, they had infra-red sensors, heavy water, etc., etc. We have been told lie after lie in terms of who invented these things. If anyone in the world had access to alien technology it was the Aryans.[293]

Contrary to the prior excerpt about Vrilerinnen psychics who said an ET Aryan race came to inhabit our solar system, the above quote claims that the Aryans were a Human hybrid by Nordic-Reptilian alien manipulators. Both claims have truth, but the second one accurately portrays the Aryan race as a Human hybrid.

Hermann Rauschning authored *Hitler Speaks* in German, claiming to meet with Hitler many times to gain insight into his thoughts, yet the veracity of Rauschning's statements have been contested and largely dismissed by critics. Whether Hitler said these exact words or not, I believe this quote that was attributed to him is true, "The new man is living amongst us now! He is here. Isn't that enough for you? I will tell you a secret. I have seen the new man. He is intrepid and cruel. I was afraid of him."[294]

Maria Orsic, who later became the leader of the Vril Society, received the words "Adolf Hitler" during a trance that named him the new Messiah.[292] The GA states that Hitler and his Illuminati inner circle worked with the Zeta-Rigelians to reduce populations that had less tampered Hibiru genes, leaving the heavily hybridized Jews untouched.

The Zeta masterminded a plethora of Illuminati events at the time, even providing the United States government with technologies for the atomic bomb and for time travel in Montauk and the Philadelphia Experiment (in chapter 8). The Illuminati network makes it easy for one government official in the Freemasonry brotherhood to call up another government official across the world to get things done. A case in point was during the Revolutionary War when George Washington needed more troops, so Benjamin Franklin contacted his French "brother" for back-up. Illuminati groups are direct pawns of fallen alien control. The GA says that they are usually too afraid to disobey the technologically advanced, evil intruders. I think that most Illuminati members identify with the skewed energy of power, so they are not much different than their leaders; accordingly, some Illuminati are reincarnations of those leaders.

Necromiton-Andromies wanted to put Zetas "in their place," so they gained Hitler's favor by giving him secret knowledge about Earth's ley lines and stargates, and relics to access them. In return, they used Hitler's personal prejudice against the entire Jewish lineage to go on a largely indiscriminate killing spree. The Zeta-Drakonian-Luciferian Illuminati withdrew their support of Hitler and banded behind the World War II Allied forces to ensure defeat of the Axis powers.[120]

Although Hitler did not fully satisfy yet another Messiah role, OWO aliens have not exhausted their efforts, especially when they continue to send us religious prophecies and channelings directed toward their "heavenly" bases.

The religious fascination with the Taurus constellation is integral to Canberra's design, but like the ancient sites, several affiliate star systems are also represented. An investigation into *Star Names: Their Lore and Meaning* by Richard Hinckley Allen and *The Living Stars* by Dr. Eric Morse provides the missing link between religion and astronomy that favors Aldebaran and Michael:

> The great "red giant", war-like "Aldebaran" is one of the four "Guardians of Heaven"—sentinels watching over other stars. It formed one of the four royal stars of Persia as "Watcher of the East".
>
> These were also called archangel stars; this star Aldebaran was Michael—Military Commander of the Heavenly Host. The others were; Gabriel (Fomalhaut) Watcher of the South; Raphael (Regulus) Watcher of the North; Uriel (Antares) Watcher of the West. At one time they marked the two Equinoxes and two Solstices. Aldebaran marked the zero Aries point in 3044 BC, "Antares" marked zero Libra 3052 BC, "Fomalhaut" marked zero Capricornus, 2582 BC, "Regulus" marked zero Cancer 2345 BC....
>
> These four stars have been characterized as Horses, reflected both in the famed Four Horsemen of Apocalypse (Revelation chapter 6) and Chariot Horses in the Book of Zechariah.[295]

James discovered a significant astrological alignment in Canberra during the December 21, 2012 solstice peak when Aldebaran, Rigel, and Jupiter were perfectly aligned in the northeast direction. When looking up from New

Parliament House coordinates on the Stellarium star map at about 10:10:50 p.m.—just over one minute before the official peak time—Algol, commonly known as the Demon star, was precisely north at 0 degrees azimuth. About two minutes past either side of 10:11 p.m., it passes the azimuth. Algol aligns at a slight curve with the triple alignment of Aldebaran, which can be an acceptable alignment when accounting for the Earth's curved field.

The parliamentary ley line runs northeast at a 36 degree angle when measured off North. Algol also rises at near the 36 degree azimuth every day. Canberra's alignments are not a coincidence. The ATI,TPE states that its geometries were planned to anchor the combined currents that connect to Abaddon. North involves the Earth's staff, so Algol and Canberra's technologies can anchor the Aldebaran alignment into the backbone of the Earth.

The inclusion of Jupiter in this alignment amplified phantom energies within our solar system due to the astrological Yod formation that occurs in cycles; the previous one happened in 1989 A.D. Yod as the "Finger of YHWH" is a triangular formation, and astrologists say that the 2012 event had Jupiter at the apex of a 30 degree angle with Saturn and Pluto at equidistant 75 degree angles based on their circular event chart. Actually, astrologists state that Saturn and Pluto are offset from each other at 60 degree angles, which does not correspond to their diagram. It is impossible to verify these statements on Stellarium software because Saturn and/or Pluto are out of view, depending upon the planetary reference point. They also claim that Venus anchors Jupiter in an almost equidistant alignment between Saturn and Pluto.[296] Jupiter in this pivotal position represents God's finger by bringing in phantom galaxy energies to our solar system. As phantom Aldebaran is known as the star of Michael, and he likes to call himself God, this energy is purposely directed by Michael. The triangular formation and angles created an intensely focused, combined energy that was captured in the crystalline limestone beneath Canberra.

All Metatronic geometries in city designs are intentionally placed as technologies to anchor and distribute phantom blasts directly into the core of our planet, confirms the ATI,TPE. Their symbols also steal the natural energy of Earth and its beings. In both Canberra and Paris, France, the technologies anchor wormholes from Aldebaran to allow for covert alien infiltration as well as transport of Earth's precious metals, states the ATI,TPE. Particularly, Paris's Eiffel Tower and Canberra's Telstra Tower loom above the cities to anchor and amplify Metatronic energy, and the ATI,TPE adds that the Telstra Tower is used to communicate with Aldebaran. The combined Jesus and Luciferian group's next grand plan involves Lucifer as Sanat Kumara potentially entering Canberra's wormhole during the Earth's probable 2017 dimensional blend that is explained in chapter 8.

The ATI,TPE states:

> Lucifer's planned return in 2017 is to attempt another pole shift since his failed attempt to do so in 2012. This is his full agenda. His intention to do so would make this planet accessible for greater space travel with his higher dimensional invasion forces. He will remain covert to allow for space travel in the upper elements whenever he chooses.

The ATI,TPE supports my assertion that higher dimensional entities do not prefer to lock themselves into the Earthly limitations that many of them have created. Since the Earth's last stellar activation cycle, dimensional blend periods have typically occurred every 2,213 years during stargate opening cycles, and they last five years during which entities can enter Earth and then leave before they become trapped. During certain intermediate periods in our past, gods have chosen to stay to directly rule us in their materialized forms. Although this is not currently happening, some have chosen to reincarnate as humans.

On August 16, 2011, I asked the ATI,TPE, "Are the residents of Canberra in for a big shock after 2012, or will they still be unaware of the greater agenda going on behind the scenes?"

It replied, "They will still remain unaware of the greater agenda due to greater 'sleep' of their mind and mind control."

This was somewhat good news so fear and panic would not take over; however, it is not good overall if people stay asleep and keep the Metatronic energy alive through their indirect allowance of it.

Although the UIR mainly involves Red Dragons, the One World Order agenda is not divided among Red, White, or Green Dragons. They generally work together to harm and confuse us as pawns in their twisted game. The main reason that they have not yet fully revealed themselves and their large spaceships to us in recent times is because the Krysthal River Host and affiliated groups have blocked their points of access to the Earth and diffused their large-scale actions. Nevertheless, the phantom races still work to gain energetic access to us. Let us not perform any solstice, equinox, and moon ritual celebration nor put out any more welcoming energy to them through religious prayers. Let us amplify our own naturally greater energies and connection to the ATI,TPE to further shield ourselves and the Earth, which chapter 11's techniques facilitate.

The greater history of the Milky Way provides the background to the Earth's drama and ascension cycle. Hold on for more of a ride into the story about our Earth and its Human inhabitants.

CHAPTER 8

Earth as an Ascension Planet

December 21, 2012—the infamous date that is widely believed as the end of the Mayan calendar. Why would the Mayans stop time as we know it at the winter solstice of this particular year? Was this their prophetic date of the Apocalypse? Or, did they have a different take on the end of the world as though it will be a rebirth?

The New Testament states that the day and hour of the Apocalypse will be known by no one (Matthew 24:34-36, Mark 13:31-33). Could it be that the exact date for the end of the world was not predictable because of differing agendas among many alien factions and the countermeasures of Krysthal River Host (KRH) races?

The Book of Revelation prophesied horrific acts in the Apocalypse that were recounted throughout the New Testament. First Corinthians chapter 15, verses 51-52 states, "We shall not all sleep, but we shall all be changed, In a moment, in the twinkling of an eye, at the last trump: for the trumpet shall sound, and the dead shall be raised incorruptible." The last trumpet in the Book of Revelation followed cataclysmic events, so this means that the Galactic Federation of Light (GFofL) and company are saying that ascension happens to the "chosen ones" after terrible worldwide events. This clear message in the Bible is amiss in church teachings that rather say we would be caught up in the "rapture" before the Apocalypse. Christianity teaches this because the Bible continually suggests that we are taken care of and comforted by Archangel Michael of Nebadon as God, and the great judgment would be reserved for all the deserving sinners.

The Mayans worshipped Quetzalcoatl (Ningishzidda/Thoth) as God, so this means that they will be "left behind." Being left behind implies that the Earth will become hell for the heathens, and heaven is somewhere above the clouds as the safe realm. Or, the Jehovah Witness version will have the righteous people inherit the Earth while 144,000 chosen people enter into heaven. A big wrench in the general belief about heaven is what Michael's group said through the prophet Isaiah, "And all the host of heaven shall be dissolved, and the heavens shall be rolled together as a scroll: and all their host shall fall down, as the leaf falleth off from the vine, and as a falling fig from the fig tree" (Isaiah 34:4). Matthew chapter 24, verse 35 concurs that heaven would also pass away. Therefore, all of us good ones will be left behind.

The Mayans believed something would happen to the Earth and its people, but was it Quetzalcoatl's distorted plan or something natural, or both? Religious gods usually give us truth mixed with lies because they know we have intelligence and innate wisdom but do not always access these qualities.

The future is only predictable at best, but past events have significantly altered course on Earth to where some future events are now unavoidable. This chapter relays and often discerns information given predominantly by the Guardian Alliance (GA) with input from the Melchizedek Cloister Emerald Order (MCEO) about the Earth's greater history and certain creation mechanics. I also include information by other Krysthal River Host (KRH) affiliates as well as the All That Is, The Pure Essence (ATI, TPE) and Eia about events leading up to December 21, 2012 and beyond. I must use otherworldly sources that support natural creation, along with the ATI, TPE and my intuition, to bring to our awareness this big picture that immediately and importantly concerns us.

I do not believe every message that the MCEO and GA have conveyed to us; however, let me reiterate their group purposes. In general, the GA is a task force of the Interdimensional Association of Free Worlds (IAFW) that protects our planet and galaxy from destruction, and the MCEO works closely with the GA while also involving Ecka Eieyani (in chapter 10). The IAFW is a noble organization. There are other free worlds with similar intent that do not belong to the IAFW, but they are allies and equals to the IAFW (an example is in chapter 9's "Higher Self" section).

Most people in the Milky Way are interested in what is happening on Earth at this present time; the situation here can affect our entire galaxy because the Earth is part of galactic stargate-3, and the Sun is galactic stargate-4. Fallen aliens have interfered with our poor Earth and Sun to try to claim their stargates along with other key locations to eventually bring our Milky Way and Parallel Milky Way into not only fully phantom status but also space dust implosion. These "end times" are very difficult to face, but religious stories have given us enough fodder to see their agendas in this direction. Although this chapter is upsetting at times, its information helps secure us in the knowledge that ample awareness and goodness do provide a way out of the mess.

Tara, Sirius, Sun, and Earth

The Earth is estimated to be at least 3.8 billion years old according to stratigraphy and radiometric dating of planetary rocks. The Earth could also be older if it was formed along with the Sun between 4.5 to 4.6 billion years ago, a theory scientists tend to favor.[297] Both scenarios may be true.

According to the Tri-Veca nature of creation, a fallen portion of our Ecka's 3rd dimensional Agartha probably created particle and antiparticle extensions as Earth and Parallel Earth that could match the 3.8 billion year estimate, and there could have been pre-existing field energy emitted by the Sun.

An alternate but complementary story of Earth's creation dates the Earth much later than some of its rock formations. Older rocks existed as part of the Ecka remnant, but additional rocks, flora, and fauna were transported here from alien worlds.

In *Voyagers: The Secrets of Amenti, Volume II*, the GA presents a creation story of cataclysmic proportion that involved a plethora of alien input to nurture Earth into a viable planet. Alien involvement expedited Earth evolution because it was viewed as a temporary planet to serve the Tara agenda. Some of its rocks may also be from Tara to further connect to the Earth.

The GA describes what happened on Tara to eventuate the Earth in its entirety.

> Approximately 560 million years ago...many ET and metaterrestrial races [in HU-4 and HU-5] combined their genetic and energetic make-up to create a master race of beings that would serve as Guardians of the planet Tara. The Sirian Council from Harmonic Universe 2, along with several other groups were appointed as directors and overseers of the project, the Turaneusiam-1 (T-1) experiment (p. 2).[120]

The HU-3 Elohim oversaw the Sirian Council races, so they were interested in the project. It is important to note that the GA information in the *Voyagers* books was conveyed during sensitive negotiations between the GA and certain Anunnaki. These books do not often distinguish between the types of Elohim so as not to put a stigma upon the Anunnaki. Technically, all entities living in the Milky Way are "fallen," but often it is not by choice; therefore, what is correctly termed *Elohim* leaves us wonder if these entities were pure-intended. Accordingly, the GA's use of the word "experiment" does not sit well with me, especially since Archangel Michael has used the same word in channelings to describe the seedings on Earth. Nonetheless, I recognize the unpredictability of new grand-scale plans as an appropriate use of the word.

About 550,750,000 years ago, inbreeding with digressive strains in the original 12-strand DNA genetic code of Tara's Turaneusiam lineage led to another game of "my race is better than your race." Members of the more passive Lumian race "foresaw a cataclysm in their future, brought on by the increasingly dangerous Alanian experimentation with power generation through Tara's planetary core" (p. 3).[120] The Lumians petitioned the Sirian

Council and Elohim for help. "Under direction of the Sirian Council, the Lumians set up amongst their members an organization called The Council of Mu" (p. 3).[120] The Council of Mu helped Lumians move large numbers of their race across the oceans to a largely uninhabited island.

Now that the seeding experiment became compromised, the Elohim helped the Lumians by interbreeding with those who had a compatible gene code. They created an upgraded race called Ceres to help their evolution. The Ceres created the Priesthood of Mu with a matriarchal and egalitarian slant that taught the "sacred Law of One, or Unity Consciousness" (p. 3).[120] Unfortunately, many interpretations of oneness are inaccurate, especially among people with some distortion in their genes and perceptions. For instance, digression continued within the Lumian race after the creation of the Ceres.

Ironically (but understandably due to the power struggle game), the Templar Solar Initiates, placed as overseers or controllers to the Alanians by the Sirian Council, sympathized with the Sirian Anunnaki who did not want to follow Sirian Council orders. This brought about the fall of the Templar Solar Initiate genetic code and consciousness. Subsequently, the Initiates became greedy for more control.

The Alanians, aware of the dangers involving the Initiates, approached the Lumians and Ceres to be allowed to relocate to Mu. These three races interbred to create the Ur-Tarranates sub-race, which is the origin of the famed term *Ur*. On a related side note of famous biblical words, E-den was the large land mass on Tara where Lumians and Alanians first coexisted.

The Ur-Tarranates created the Priesthood of Ur. This priesthood along with the Priesthood of Mu conducted rituals to support their belief in the Law of One, which in my opinion is unnecessary because if you are aware of truth, you do not have to perform ritualistic acts to remind you of it. An example of their rituals is the baptism. Although baptisms can make us think about and potentially experience interdimensional properties of water, they also show the link to the amphibious Sirian Anunnaki Elohim, which borders upon worshipping them. The Priesthoods of Ur and Mu shared most of their beliefs, but Ur was more interested in scientific applications such as portal mechanics. The Priesthood of Ur later guarded the portal to Earth.

The Templar Solar Initiates went underground beneath Alania to the planetary core where most of the natural power lied in crystals. They misused the crystals and caused them to explode approximately 550 million years ago.

The GA explains:

> This created a chain reaction of implosions within Tara's
> planetary grid. Portions of Tara's grid were blown apart and

fragmented, becoming detached from the Morphogenetic Field of the planet. Portions of Alania were immediately destroyed and the entire planet suffered the effects of rapid pole reversal. For a period of two days Tara ceased to rotate on its axis. It took 10,000 years to re-stabilize Tara's environment, during which the few surviving Taran races still on-planet retreated permanently underground.... Surface life also returned to Tara following this 10,000 year period of healing.... Tara could not re-emerge with the energy grid of its dimension-7 counterpart Gaia, until its own grid system was repaired....

The fragments of the Taran planetary grid that became dismembered from Tara's core energy supply rapidly fell in vibration until they could no longer resist the natural magnetic pull of the descending interdimensional energy currents. The planet fragments were pulled into a Sun within Tara's universe, vaporized, and the morphogenetic field carried in those fragments was pulled into a black hole at the center of this Sun and re-emerged into a galaxy within the lower-dimensional fields of Harmonic Universe 1. [Note: recall in chapter 6 that stars have natural black and white holes.] Entering this system as gaseous substance, this morphogenetic field broke down into 12 pieces, which set up a "mini-solar system" around a star within an already existing HU-1 solar system. One of the 12 pieces of Tara's fragmented morphogenetic field fused with this Sun, while the 11 other pieces began to build up matter density and re-manifest their forms through their portion of the morphogenetic field (p. 5).[120]

It appears the GA says that no planet in our solar system existed before parts of Tara's grid fell and re-manifested in our three dimensions. I think that some planetary matter already existed in our solar system, but I lean toward the probability that the bulk of it arose from the plethora of quanta that entered through an already existing Sun. The ATI,TPE states that our Earth contains Tara quanta as a minority of its composition.

The GA states that there were 12 planets formed in our solar system from Tara, but three of them have since been destroyed: Maldak, which is now our asteroid belt because of Anunnaki destruction; Nibiru, which has a very long orbit past Pluto and is now fully phantom; and Chiron, our 11th planet that was demolished to create several phantom moons to create an artificial orbit and intruder stations.[291] The GA considers Pluto a planet, but astronomers now believe that it is a large comet along with others in the Kuiper belt.

Pluto's largest moon at nearly half its size, named Charon, shares the same orbit as though they are a "double planet."[298] Based on this information, Pluto and its comet moons are probably remnants of Chiron. Tara, the fallen portion of Galaxy-2's Alcyone, is almost 20 times the size of the Sun, so it can conceivably provide enough quanta for our solar system while retaining enough structural integrity as its own star-planet in the Milky Way.[299]

Mayan and New Age channelings have proclaimed that our Sun orbits around Tara (as Alcyone) every 26,000 years.[300,301] Tara is approximately 400 light years from Earth, a very far distance that is probably impossible to orbit in only 26,000 years. Instead, this short time cycle relates to the interdimensional phenomenon of the stellar activation cycle by which the Earth transfigures toward Tara, as I later explain in this chapter. In an effort to make the ascension process scientifically believable, the channeled claim misses the mark. Interestingly, science does embrace the 26,000 year time frame in reference to the Earth's axial or general precession.

In astronomy, the moon, Sun, and other solar system planets cause the gravitational and rotational pull of the Earth's axis and slight equatorial bulge to rotate as a gyroscope. The conical rotation is known as the general precession of a slow moving wobble that takes approximately 26,000 years to return to its starting point.

The general precession involves the incremental westward movement of the stars along the ecliptic relative to the "fixed" position of the equinoxes. An equinox occurs twice every year in March and September when the Earth's axis is tilted neither toward nor away from the Sun. Astronomers generally agree that all stars change position in the sky very slowly. This can be attributed to most luminary stars being part of a binary or cluster star system whose relationship causes an elliptical orbit. Perhaps the supposedly fixed stars of a kathara grid actually move in relationship to each other. Studying the Earth's general precession can illuminate our Sun's relationship to the kathara grid.

Ancient Egyptians based their Sothic calendar on the heliacal rising of Sirius—when it first becomes visible above the eastern horizon just before dawn. Sothis was the Egyptian name for the "Dog Star" Sirius. This event is extremely difficult if not impossible to observe; Egyptians must have been instructed about the importance of Sirius from their gods, which hermetic and channeled texts verify. Thoth's pupil Drunvalo Melchizedek claims in his book, *The Ancient Secret of the Flower of Life, Volume 1*, that our solar system and the Sirius system are intimately connected through gravitation.[206] According to NASA astrophysicists, Sirius A is our sky's brightest star at about 8.7 light years away, and it is over twice the size of our Sun.[302] As chapter 7's Anunnaki Elohim section indicated, it is part of a tertiary star cluster.

Jed Z. Buchwald, Professor of History at California Institute of Technology, writes in *Egyptian Stars under Paris Skies*:

> Because of Sirius' position, and the latitudes at which the Egyptians observed the sky, both Sirius' heliacal rising and the summer solstice remained nearly the same number of days apart throughout Egyptian history even though the zodiac moves slowly around the ecliptic.[303]

The Sothic calendar was the most precise yearly calendar on record, ultimately being altered by the Roman Catholic Church. This is because Sirius is not precessing like the other background stars. Astronomy enthusiast Walter Cruttenden postulates that the Sun-Sirius binary model does not necessarily wobble because the entire solar system curves through space along with Sirius's orbit.[304]

According to Figure 3's kathara grid diagram of harmonic universe 2 (HU-2), the Sun as stargate-4 directly connects to stargate-5 Tara and has a relationship with stargate-6 Sirius B. Although the Sun is physically closer than Sirius is to Earth, the kathara grid's left "vertical" bar shows less distance between stargate-3 Earth and Sirius B. The MCEO states that Sirius B is the most important HU-2 star interfacing with Earth because of the way the universal merkaba vortices run. Solar systems are not floating aimlessly through space, nor are they isolated in revolutions within a Milky Way arm. The MCEO explains that solar systems in HU-1 revolve around their respective HU-2 Central Suns, in HU-2 they revolve about respective HU-3 Central Suns, and this pattern continues up the harmonic universes.[305] The Earth's direct relationships with all three HU-2 Central Suns complicates the concept of only one Central Sun per creation.

"The event of Tara's cataclysm became known as the 'fall of man,'" states the GA (p. 6).[120] Archangel Michael, Enlil, and Enki obfuscated the innate remembrance of many Humans by associating the fall of man in the Book of Genesis with disobedience to them as our gods. The actual fall of man was the fall of the Alanian people who were blown apart and sent with corresponding parts of Tara's grid to our solar system.

Just prior to the cataclysm, the Ur-Tarranates had the important foresight to time-travel to future Earth to implant their genetic code into Earth's morphogenetic field in order to ensure that the fragmented people would return to Tara in the ascension process. Then, once Tara is healed, it could ascend to meet Gaia. This process would ensure the continuation of Tara's race lines.

The GA states:

Once on Earth, with the help of the Sirian Council, this group of Ur-Tarranates transmuted their body forms into pure energy (Keylontic science) and merged into a gestalt energy field of consciousness, which served as a morphogenetic field for the 12-strand DNA Turaneusiam race prototype. Also contained within this morphogenetic field were the Keylontic Time Codes (electrotonal frequency patterns) of the pre-cataclysmic time/space coordinates of Tara, which would allow Tara to re-assemble the lost portions of its grid into the fabric of time. With the assistance of the Ra Confederacy [Yanas entities explained in chapter 10] this gestalt of consciousness/genetic and planetary morphogenetic field was entered into the remaining morphogenetic field of Earth through the 11th and 14th dimensions. This morphogenetic field of consciousness energetically took on a shape of a sphere, and was called the Sphere of Amenti (p. 7).[120]

Nearly 550 million years ago, the Sphere of Amenti was placed within the newly integrated Amenti Earth's core at the 2nd dimension to establish a stable portal between Earth and Tara. The importance of the Sphere required extreme protection.

All of our solar system's planets have their own portals and parts of Tara electrotonal frequencies represented in colored spectra of light. When each planet has accrued enough frequency, it could transform back into Tara's morphogenetic field in its ascension process. The Earth's frequency pattern that was inherited from Tara appears as "a standing wave pattern, composed of fourth- and fifth-dimensional frequencies, and thus appearing as blue in color...with a pale shade of green, several inches in height"; it is the Staff of Amenti through which we must pass in order to transmute form and appear on Tara, states the GA (p. 14).[120]

550 to 250 million years ago, when Ur-Tarranates entered the Sphere of Amenti, the Earth's grid had not yet evolved and picked up speed with Tara's quanta so that they could materialize. They hung around on Earth in their higher dimensional bodies and also went to Parallel Earth to help their brethren in the following process as explained by the GA.

The Sphere of Amenti morphogenetic Field allowed for the Ur-Tarranates to enter incarnational cycles on Earth, pick up the fragments of consciousness from the lost souls by pulling their energetic particles from the HU-1 Unified Fields into the DNA, merging the consciousness of the soul fragments with the embodied Ur-Tarranate consciousness, thereby allowing this composite identity to evolve through a sentient life form, back into its original soul matrix (the Turaneusiam 12-strand prototype) (p. 9).[120]

This mission was called the Covenant of Palaidor; it involved several Turaneusiam races and their higher dimensional advisors, including Sirians and Elohim. Other Turaneusiams fought against this mission in what was known as the long-standing Taran Wars that spread some of the chaos to Earth. During this time period, HU-1 extra-terrestrials (ETs) seeded various other species such as plants, insects, and animals on Earth where they evolved.

250 million years ago, five Palaidorian Cloistered races finally started to materialize, although it happened on our antimatter Parallel Earth. This was the T-2 Turaneusiam experiment that was also called the Second World in Native American lore. The First World involved the T-1 Turaneusiam cultures of Tara from 550 to 560 million years ago.

The GA states that the Sphere of Amenti contains five smaller spheres that became the morphogenetic patterns for the Palaidorian Cloistered races that were the five original Earth races. When these races entered HU-1 through the Sphere of Amenti field, they split their energy fields to involve matter and parallel antimatter for each race. The GA explains this process in terms of spheres within the greater Sphere:

> The 10 new spheres collectively held the blueprint for DNA strands one through 12.... Each sphere became the morphogenetic field for one Root Race plus its companion Cloister Race that would simultaneously manifest into physical expression on Earth, during the time periods that corresponded to the dimensional DNA strand to which each race was appointed. These five morphogenetic fields became Root Races 3-7, through which DNA strands 2-6 would be assembled. Each Root Race was responsible for evolving/assembling one strand of DNA while its companion Cloister Race would hold the imprint of that strand plus strands 7-12. The Cloister Race would appear first and through this race its Root Race would emerge (p. 15-16).[120]

This explanation equates Root race 3 to DNA strand-1 and -2 with Cloister DNA strand-7 and -8 as the overtone, Root race 4 to strand-3 with overtone strand-9, and so forth until Root race 7 with strand-6 and overtone strand-12.

Soul fragments from the dimension that corresponded to the

DNA strand of the Root race would be pulled from the Unified Field of that dimension into the body form, progressively pulling the frequency bands of that dimension into the DNA until all the frequencies of that dimension were assembled into the morphogenetic field of the body (p. 16).[120]

The GA states that activations of these DNA occurred later on Earth when DNA particles merged with their antiparticles to allow the Cloister races to "plug into" the operating antiparticle genetic code. I suppose this could have been briefly feasible since their antimatter counterpart was not phantom at that time; however, the parallel "twin" exists entirely independently to the Human, as I explain in chapter 10. Accordingly, For us to ascend without our parallel counterpart—an individual person who does not look like us—we can change the angular rotation of particle spin (ARPS) and density of our own body to our matter-based destination. The process of DNA activation "increased the rate of pulsation of the matter particles of the body into HU-2 patterns, which allowed the incarnate to turn its body into light, pass through the Halls of Amenti as pure energy, then re-manifest within a less dense version of that body upon Tara," explains the GA (p. 17).[120]

The Palaidorian Cloistered races included the white-skinned, original Hibiru with DNA strand-4 and the yellow-skinned, original Melchizedeks with DNA strand-5. Brown, red, and black were the other skin colors. Initially, none of these people possessed a gender or sex. These races on Parallel Earth—and later on Amenti Earth—provided many ascensions for fragmented Turaneusiams.

Three Earth Seedings

25 million years ago, the Halls of Amenti were created to allow materialization on Earth for the five Palaidorian Cloistered races. The Halls of Amenti are eight portals within the Sphere of Amenti, states the ATI,TPE. One links to Tara's past, and seven link to various stages of Earth's future in dimensions 2-8, each encoded with certain frequency-patterned DNA.

The First Seeding manifested 60 adult Humans—six males and six females from each race—in a simultaneous seeding with each person held in equal standing, states the GA. These families built up the population on Earth, known as the Third World to Native Americans. "Incarnates who kept the integrity of their genetic code transmuted through each of the races then ascended" (p. 18).[120]

According to the GA, Earth Humans eventually interbred with animals, which concerned members of the Sirian Anunnaki, other ETs, and HU-5 entities who cared about the relative integrity of the Turaneusiam lineage. This genetic distortion was causing the non-ascended Earth-Turaneusiams to lose their ability to transfigure, thereby jeopardizing their immortality.

5,509,000 years ago, many HU-2 races who did not want the digressive Human element to return to Tara, along with groups who just wanted control over Earth for their aims, waged war against Covenant of Palaidor races. This was a 900-year war called the Electric Wars, wherein higher dimensional aliens descended upon our solar system and Earth's atmosphere to fight "great battles of pure energy" for control over the Earth's stargates and Sphere of Amenti (p. 18).[120] The Humans caught in the middle of this chaos ascended if they could, relocated to other HU-1 planets with the help of Elohim and HU-2 Palaidorians, or perished along with many animals.

The GA explains the devastating result of the Electric Wars.

> For a period of time following the end of the Electric Wars, Earth could not sustain life. For over 4,000 years Earth was plagued by erratic weather patterns, tectonic shifting and climatic anomalies. Earth experienced a slow, partial pole reversal and tilted several degrees on its axis between 5,508,100 and 5,504,000 years ago, as a result of damage done to Earth's energetic grid and portal systems during the Electric Wars. Numerous ET races visited the planet during its more stable periods, some serving as Guardians over the Sphere of Amenti. Various animal forms were again reseeded by visiting races. Approximately 5,504,000 years ago a sudden, final shift in Earth's grid as its poles realigned, caused a "quick freeze" Ice Age to occur, which wiped out most life-forms on the planet except for some of those residing in deep caverns beneath the seas. Following this shift the vibrational rate of Earth's grid dropped swiftly and it could no longer hold the higher frequencies of the Sphere of Amenti at its core. If the Sphere of Amenti were not removed, the Earth would explode (p. 22).[120]

Elohim and the Yanas-based Ra Confederacy group detached the Sphere of Amenti from the Earth's core and relocated it in a secure position deep in space within 4th dimensional frequency bands. For the Sphere to now operate in the 4th dimension, a seal called the Seal of Palaidor had to be placed upon the associated morphogenetic field of the ascending Humans.

The Seal of Palaidor could only be removed by Root races able to hold dimensional frequencies 4 and above; therefore, Root races 3 and 4 were further fragmented because they could not assemble their DNA. Consequences of the

Seal of Palaidor included wiping out memory of their previous lives on Tara, creating the subconscious mind and duality between the body and mind, and introducing chaotic identities into Root race 5.

As if this seal was not enough of a distortion, the Seal of Amenti was previously placed upon the first base code for both the Cloister and Root races. The Seal of Amenti was a genetic mutation placed upon the base DNA strand-1 at the end of the Electric Wars. The goal was to always protect Taran races above and before Earth races when Humans messed up, but adding more distortions made us further devolve.

The Seal of Amenti caused a blockage between the physical and etheric body, creating death; it is known as the Death Seal. It also caused electricity build-up within the Human body because the antiparticle codes could not join it on Earth. Currently, most Humans have Root race 5 coding that continually tries to clear its cellular energies that became blocked from the stifled electricity.

An alternative way to evolve and release the Seal of Palaidor was to pass through the Hall of Amorea, a portal bridge created approximately 4,000,000 years ago that linked together the Earth's core, Sphere of Amenti, and Sirius B's core. The Hall of Amorea facilitated the Second Seeding. In the latter Third Seeding, it was renamed the Third Eye of Horus. Interestingly, the Third Eye of Horus was the artificial ascension passageway through which the Yahshuas and Egyptian pharaohs performed ascensions for their chosen ones. The Second and Third Seedings are known as the Fourth World to Native Americans.[120]

3,700,000 years ago, the morphogenetic field for the Second Seeding of Turaneusiam races on Earth was entered into the core of Sirius B. The Second Seeding immediately occurred after this event and lasted until approximately 848,800 years ago.

The GA continues, "The races began incarnating on Earth through a small group of Human hybrids who had found exile and evolved within the HU-1 Pleiades star system during the Electric Wars. Through the Sirian Council of HU-2 and the Galactic Federation of HU-1, members of this hybrid race, known as the Europherites,…migrated from the HU-1 Pleiadian star system to Sirius B" where they interbred with a race called the Kantarians who were closely aligned with the Galactic Federation of Light (p. 28-29).[120]

Oh how the plot thickens with the blurred lines between purposely fallen aliens and Earth's helpers! This new hybrid race was the Dagos. These races became intertwined with the original Turaneusiam-2 imprint of the First Seeding and then became our Second Seeding upon Earth.

The GA states that Root race 5 incarnated with its ancestors' subconscious personality fragments because the lower Root races could not organize them;

therefore, it had the burden of assimilating everything for its ascension. Root race 5 was the Aeiran, and its Cloister counterpart was the Hibiru.

The advanced status and burden of the Hibiru-Aeiran race line is why it has been coveted by intruder aliens. *The Terra Papers* (TP) refers to the Orion Anunnaki as the Arians (see chapter 7 "Anunnaki"). The second seeding of the Aeirans was the Ayrians, which suggests that the Orion Anunnaki, many of whom already relocated to Sirius, influenced the Second Seeding.[120] In fact, the GA states that the Jehovian Anunnaki of Sirius A infiltrated the First Seeding and hybridized one of the races that later became known as the Urantia race line.[144] Obviously, the Green Dragons were a part of this forced hybridization. The Aryans were created in the Third Seeding 65,000 years ago, but they were also prized and altered by the intruders (see chapter 7 "One World Order").[120]

The 6th Root race counterpart, the Melchizedek Cloister, "assisted in repairing genetic digression [of the Hibiru-Aeiran] toward the end of the Second Seeding, becoming one of the Host Matrix families, then began their race birthing cycle during the Third Seeding" (p. 31).[120] They created a hybrid Melchizedek-Hibiru Cloister race that was an early ancestor to the Habiru.

The Second Seeding, although it had flaws, progressed in evolution until an intruder race came to Earth. The GA explains:

> Approximately one million years ago a race called the Drakon from HU-1 Orion star system came to Earth and tampered with the genetic code of the races. They created hybrids within the Root Races called the Dracos.... The Drakon also tampered with certain strains of Earth dinosaurs (who were seeded on Earth about 375,000,000 years ago as an experiment by other ET races), creating aggressive, carnivorous monitors for their captive human populations. Many of the cultures of the Second Seeding abandoned their advanced surface cultures and retreated underground to escape the terror of the Drakon monitors (p. 44).[120]

This situation prompted Earth races "with the assistance of Anunnaki Visitors from Sirius A" to use the power within the Earth's grid to destroy the underground habitats of the Drakon and its dinosaurs (p. 45).[120] Their actions caused an explosion in the Earth's crust, which again created climatic problems, flooding, a global ice age, a slight pole shift, and destruction of part of the land masses. This caused the Drakon to flee or be destroyed along with the dinosaurs. Regarding the Human races, the surface conditions forced most of them to retreat to lower dimensional underground territories until environmental conditions stabilized. Unfortunately, the Dracos stayed until they were banned by the HU-5 advisor races approximately 100,000 years later. This ban did not prevent Dracos from returning because they feel entitled to live on Earth due to their Human ancestry.

About 950,000 years ago, the Anunnaki-Green Dragons created its Nephilim Human hybrid of giants now that they had no real enemy. The GA states, "Having more developed genetic codes via their Anunnaki fathers [Note: this is because of the hybridization and seals placed upon Humans], the Nephilim quickly dominated the less developed humans, creating a highly advanced materialistic culture built upon exploitation of less evolved forms" (p. 46).[120] More animal-Human experiments occurred, which was against the original plan of Anunnaki involvement toward the Turaneusiam lineage.

The GA states that the Elohim and the Ra Confederacy saved the Humans by "removing the distorted Nephilim racial strains from their connection to the Amenti morphogenetic field and 'splicing them in' to the morphogenetic fields of other entities from HU-3, HU-4 and HU-5" through host matrix transplants (p. 46).[120]

The Anunnaki-Green Dragons were not happy with how their creation was stopped, but if they had any sense of right or wrong, I think they could understand why the overseeing races stopped the intrusive species. Instead, they retaliated against the Amenti races and sought to use the Humans as slaves. This involved Enlil and Enki as high-ranking Jehovian Anunnaki from Phantom Sirius A.

900,000 years ago, the Earth was able to hold 4th dimensional frequency, so the Sphere of Amenti was returned to the Earth. Having the Sphere in the Earth's core would accelerate assembly of the DNA and at least release the Seal of Palaidor. However, Anunnaki-Green Dragons waged war upon the Elohei-Elohim from 850,000 to 848,800 years ago in what is known as the Thousand Years' War, causing yet another pole shift and more environmental disasters that required the Sphere to be removed again. The flooding caused by the removal of the Sphere combined with the floodings from the recent war and in 9,558 B.C. comprised the great flood story of the Bible. The Sphere was safely placed in AquaLaShA until the war ended, confirms the ATI,TPE.

Toward the end of the Thousand Years' War, HU-5 races intervened "to negotiate a treaty through which both the Anunnaki and Elohim would assist in the Third Seeding of the human lineage," states the GA (p. 48).[120] Sadly, this was because the surface Humans were wiped out by the war.

As if a measly treaty would do anything to change their wicked ways? Does a verbal agreement or written record make an enemy an ally? This measure only gave the Anunnaki-Green Dragons more access to the Human strains! For instance, the Anunnaki-Melchizedek Human hybrid was called the Annu, possibly to help the ancient fallen Annu Elohim. The Treaty of El-Annu made the Anunnaki displace the Nephilim onto other planets, and their subsequent hybrids had to uphold the Law of One belief. Some Anunnaki did not agree to this treaty, so they instead created the Anunnaki Resistance with the aim of destroying the Sphere of Amenti. The Draco races on Sirius A joined the Resistance and brought the Drakons back on board.

To protect the Earth and its races, "the Templar-Axion Seal (the "666" genetic configuration) was applied to the morphogenetic field of the Anunnaki Resistance" and the Dracos (p. 49).[120] This seal prevented them from interbreeding with Humans.

About 840,000 years ago while the Sphere of Amenti was in Urtha, another portal connection to the Sphere—the Arc of the Covenant—was created for Turaneusiams to incarnate on Earth for the Third Seeding. According to the GA, this is the true "ark" of the Bible that arose after the floods damaged Earth and allowed the last major seeding of Humans. The GA emphasizes, "*The Arc of the Covenant was designed in such a way that the Sphere of Amenti could eventually be re-entered into the Earth core through the portal bridge of the Arc.* In this way the Arc became self-regulating" (p. 52).[120]

Hundreds of thousands of years after the Melchizedek Cloister-Hibiru hybrid races were originally seeded, the first wave of 25 Melchizedek family seedings occurred 35,000 years ago (37,000 B.C.). One family, the Cloistered Family of Melchizedek or Priesthood of Melchizedek, taught the egalitarian Melchizedek Cloister teachings of the Law of One. A patriarchal Melchizedek priesthood was guarding the blue flame Staff of Amenti, so the Priesthood of Ur and the Palaidorian Council of Tara made sure to transfer the role to the Melchizedek Cloister race about 10,000 years ago.

To prevent the Melchizedek distortions from entering Tara, a new seal called the Templar Seal was placed upon the Halls and Sphere of Amenti, which thwarted integration with 6th Root race attributes. Predictably, this new seal caused more distortions within subsequent Melchizedek Cloister seedings. One result was the creation of the "shadow self" that affects the Root races as exaggerated, primitive emotional impulses.

3,500 years ago (1,500 B.C.), "descendants of the Templar-Sealed Melchizedeks infiltrated Egyptian culture and violated the Covenant of Palaidor by opening the D-3 [3rd dimensional] Earth portals as a way of orchestrating ascension through the D-1 and D-2 Underworld. Through their misdeeds many chaotic forces were unleashed upon the Earth, and humans with distorted morphogenetic imprints were released from the Seals of Palaidor and Amenti and allowed to pass into Tara," informs the GA (p. 33).[120] This caused many tragic events on Tara, so the Templar-Axion Seal was placed upon the Templar-Sealed Melchizedeks who actively participated in those events.

The Templar-Axion Seal is very damaging because it traps people in reincarnational cycles until the time when Tara and Earth should merge. It is called the 666 Seal because it affects the 6th dimensional base tones of DNA strands 1, 5, and 6.

The GA expounds:

> This genetic configuration of the Templar-Axion Seal was the original meaning behind the symbolism of the "666", and these numbers also figured prominently in the earlier building of the Great Pyramid, for this Seal had originally been applied to the Sirian-Anunnaki in HU-2, who assisted in the construction of this machine [Great Pyramid]. The "666" became the trademark of members of the Sirian-Anunnaki who refused to accept leadership from the Sirian Council, and who would not uphold the Law of One (p. 36).[120]

The "666" Templar-Axion Seal has unfortunately become part of the Human genetic code through hybridization with the Templar Melchizedek families, and it is now known as the Omega Kill Code (OKC). The Melchizedek Cloister race did a second seeding in 1,500 B.C. to upgrade its lineage, and its last seeding was in 1750 A.D. Finally, in 2005 A.D., the MCEO-GA and their allies started to clear the OKC in the Human DNA, reveals the ATI,TPE. The MCEO states that it removed this seal in October 2007, but the ATI,TPE clarifies that only most of the seal's effects were eradicated.[120,200,185]

Atlantis and Lumeria

The Annu-Melchizedek race, the Anunnaki bio-regenesis race mentioned in chapter 7, was seeded into the Atlantean-Egyptian race line through the Melchizedek Cloister host c. 70,000 B.C. It prospered in Atlantis where it had open communication and assistance with its Sirian-Anunnaki ancestors. Lumerian races worked with HU-1 Pleiadians and also prospered. As a reward for their positive evolution, the Sirian Council and affiliated entity groups gave them advanced technology to further their abilities. Most notably, they received power generator crystals that could draw upon Tara's blue flame and access multidimensional frequency.

The Arc of the Covenant portal was located under Atlantis, and from there it connected to Lumeria and other land masses. After the Annu-Melchizedeks gained the favor of the Sirian Council, they and early Habiru peoples became primary guardians of the Arc.

The Anunnaki Resistance grew in the Third Seeding, especially upon Atlantis and Lemuria. "Motivated by their own desires to utilize Earth as an evolutionary option, the Anunnaki Resistance quietly infiltrated Atlantean culture about 55,000 years ago, covertly moving within the ranks of Anunnaki of the Sirian Council," states the GA (p. 58).[120] These Anunnaki enemies interbred with Annu-Melchizedeks, imparting the Templar Seal to their offspring and ultimately digressing subsequent populations.

Around 50,000 B.C. the Templar-sealed Annu (Templar-Annu) allowed the Dracos to secretly return to Earth as long as they would help assimilate Earth populations. "The Dracos infiltrated the Lemurian continent of Muarivhi, creating an extensive network of underground lairs within the tunnel systems that ran between Lemuria and Atlantis," states the GA (p. 58).[120]

When the Draco threat emerged, "the humans hoped to use the generator crystals to create small, pin-point explosions within the underground caverns in order to seal the Dracos within their lairs until the Sirian Council could come and evacuate the Dracos" (p. 58).[120]

What do you think happened as a result of this? Another misuse of power that overloaded the poor planet's grid? Definitely. Lemuria was destroyed along with many of its inhabitants. "The explosion caused massive volcanic activity, earthquakes and floods," states the GA (p. 58).[120] A small ice age resulted from the environmental upheaval. The Atlantean continent was not majorly damaged, but it needed to be repaired along with the Earth's grid.

After the damage, the Arc and its guardians migrated to Egypt. This massive influx of people upset the Templar-Annu in Egypt, and a plethora of them relocated to Atlantis to gain a better hold over their environment. After they influenced and dominated the remaining Atlantean priesthood culture, they planned to use the generator crystals to dissolve the electromagnetic barrier to Inner Earth portals. However, the Sirian Council stepped in to fortify the portals and vacate the remaining Egyptian Templar-Annu to Atlantis where they posed less of a threat to the Arc.

Their location in Atlantis prevented sufficient access to the portals, so the Templar-Annu forced extra power through one of the main generator crystals. This predictably exploded the crystal unit "with more than 10 times the force of an atomic bomb" (p. 63).[120]

The 28,000 B.C. explosion of Atlantis ripped apart its large Atlantic continent to create several smaller islands. The explosion also slightly tilted the Earth's axis, which broke the energetic link between the Great Pyramid of Giza and Sirius B. The Great Pyramid was an interstellar teleport station for the Sirian Council to quickly arrive on Earth to diffuse harmful situations and monitor everything. It was created after the destruction of Lemuria, so another purpose of the pyramid was to protect the Arc of the Covenant.

The Great Pyramid's process of teleportation pulled in higher dimensional, resonant frequency tones through the use of a large ankh symbol placed beneath the pyramid's crystalline capstone. "The pyramid and Arc of the Covenant were situated upon Earth's geographical center point, within the energy vortex that represented the 'Heart Chakra' within Earth's planetary bio-energetic system," states the GA (p. 62).[120] The purposeful placement of these interdimensional fixtures helped to heal or damage this sensitive location depending upon who was in control.

More trouble ensued by the Anunnaki Resistance and its Templar-Annu sympathizers who destroyed the Great Pyramid, Sphinx, and other cultural centers in Egypt in 10,500 B.C., after which the Great Pyramid and Sphinx were repaired but altered (see chapter 7's "Anunnaki Elohim"). The Great Pyramid was slightly realigned in order to create a harmonic resonance link with the Pleiadian star system through Tara. Thankfully, the Arc of the Covenant and Inner Earth territories survived the catastrophe.

The Anunnaki Resistance is part of the "Alpha-Omega Templar Melchizedek Anunnaki-Drakonian Alliance" with races from Alpha and Omega Centauri.[306] Most of the New Age spiritual channels promoting false DNA activation-ascension programs are conducted by this network that includes transmission from the Jehovian Anunnaki phantom HU-2 planet Tiamat from Pleione in the Pleiades.[142] Chapter 7 revealed that these races are overseen and potentially hybridized by the phantom Dragon races, Archangel Michael and the Shantarel, and the Bourgha overlords. I will henceforth abbreviate these groups as the BEA-O—Bourgha, Equari Dragons, and Alpha-Omega alliance—which spreads the foul odor of death science.

Atlantean Obstacles

Certain key events occurred during the Atlantean period that significantly affected our current ascension cycle. Earth's last stellar activation cycle (SAC) of 22,326 B.C. ended in a stalemate between the Krysthal River Host Councils and BEA-O when the Halls of Amenti were forced closed.

The SAC is a 17-year opening cycle with an additional 5-year closing cycle that allows interdimensional transit for the process of ascension through the Halls of Amenti. Naturally, it would draw the Earth and its inhabitants into Tara's 5th dimension. SACs are a natural part of our evolution when our particles speed up and blend with those in the 4th and 5th dimensions, dissolving the frequency barriers that normally keep the levels separate.[120]

Because the BEA-O plan failed in the previous SAC, its groups have stepped up their involvement in the latter part of Earth's Atlantean period, ultimately causing Atlantis's demise. They hoped to gain the upper hand for the next SAC that was due to occur in 4230 A.D. Its agenda required the artificial acceleration of time in our solar system to then synchronize the opening of our SAC with Metatronic wormholes at the already accelerated Parallel Earth.[182] The BEA-O also needed to disrupt the Human presence on the planet to separate them from their intrinsic abilities that could thwart the agenda.

Four events occurred in the Atlantean period to expedite the Earth's SAC. These were the c. 15,000 B.C. Amenti Earth division, 13,400 B.C. Great Netting, the 10,948 B.C. Great Toral Rift Time Rip, and the 9562 B.C. Great Encasement. Unless otherwise stated, the rest of this section is sourced from the MCEO's "Topic Summary 1," one of two official MCEO disclosure summaries freely distributed on the internet about current events facing Humanity.[307]

The ATI,TPE reveals that Amenti Earth quanta was divided c. 15,000 B.C. to create what the MCEO calls Higher Earth. This was a stage that the MCEO-GA have omitted in their Earth history. While I do not know the specifics involving this important event, it occurred similarly to how our Earth was later created from Higher Earth. What remained as the original portion of Amenti Earth is called Median Earth, which Ashayana Deane states is indeed different than Higher Earth.[308]

The 13,400 B.C. Great Netting of Nibiruian Electrostatic Transduction (NET) fields caused the unnatural division of Higher Earth to create a Lower Earth under lower dimensional NET fields. NET energy comprises a series of multidimensional, electromagnetic harness fields created by Metatronic BeaST technologies that the BEA-O implanted throughout all three HU-1 dimensions. Our Earth is the Lower Earth that MCEO calls NET Earth, although Higher Earth is technically another NET Earth. The ATI,TPE states that the NET containment fields were initially created before 15,000 B.C. to first harness quanta into the higher dimensional space for Higher Earth. Median, Higher, and NET Earths are planets with three-dimensional form, but their time-pulses and dimensional positions have diverged.[307] While the next sections may be sobering to read, there is great hope and progress at this time because Median Earth as a free planet is within our reach, as I later explain.

The Great Netting of our Earth caused the first of two slight accelerations of Earth's geographical pole (axis or staff) wobble within the NET fields. The 26,556-year general precession cycle that occurs on Higher Earth became expedited to a cycle of 25,920 years on our Earth, confirms the ATI,TPE.

The MCEO's summary describes what eventuated from the Higher Earth division.

As a result of the 13,400 BC "Netting," portions of the Earth field that were once physically manifest "seemed to literally disappear" when viewed from within the NET and its geomagnetic field harness. As the Lower Earth "NET-bound" field engaged the first 636-year "equinox precession acceleration," and the Higher Earth field did not, the spin-speed of subatomic particles and atoms, as well as Earth's rotation speed, adopted two slightly different "energy vibration-pulsation rhythms," or "time pulses." The "Lower Earth" time pulse was unnaturally accelerated, while the Higher Earth time pulse remained consistent with the greater, longer, slower time pulses of the free multidimensional Universe [note: it was not the free Median Earth; the MCEO did not introduce Median Earth in this summary]. Space-time within the Lower Earth NET field entered a slight inorganic acceleration, contraction and compaction; Lower Earth's axis spin, as well as its wobble, became a little faster, causing days to shorten slightly, and making the "bulge" at Earth's equatorial poles more pronounced. Biorhythms of the life-field quickened, as did elemental decay rates, and the "DNA" of Lower Earth's life-field became entangled within the "magnetic grip" of the anomalous geomagnetic field generated through the NET. The territories of Higher Earth—with their slower, more expansive "time pulse"—did not experience any of these environmental or biological anomalies.[307]

The NET fields have given disastrous results to the Humans trapped within them, particularly toward our DNA. The NET levels include the 1st dimensional Bio-NET or Derma-NET that harnesses the DNA template on the etheric level. The 2nd dimensional Intra-NET harnesses the chemical DNA. The 3rd dimensional Epigenetic Overlay (EGO)-NET harnesses the "chemical sheaths" that tell DNA what to switch on and off (p. 92).[196] Scientists are discovering how functions built into the DNA template can control genes (see works of physicist Bruce Lipton, Ph.D. and chapter 9's "DNA").

NET technology allows the BEA-O groups to switch on and off our DNA as they see fit. This manipulation of our DNA affects its activation potential and can alter how we express our consciousness. The false ego takes after the EGO-NET. It makes Humans self-centered and selfish so that the individual self is more important than everyone else; ironically, this myopic state has made Humans easy to control. We can override the EGO-NET by operating out of truly loving energy.

The GA states that the Bio-NET blocks the function of our pineal gland, which is a soft tissue gland in the center of our brain behind the lower-middle part of our forehead.[309] The pineal gland gives us interdimensional visionary abilities as a main component of our sixth chakra, and it regulates important hormonal activities in our body (in chapter 9's "Chakras").

During this time period, BeaST technology wiped out the Human collective memory consciousness. Humans literally woke up one day and did not remember who they were. This allowed certain BEA-O aliens to present themselves as Gods with their languages, creation stories, and history.

The MCEO explains:

> In human populations, the DNA mutation resulting from this anomalous environmental event of 13,400 BC resulted in the "first of three" biologically induced "memory wipes" and the fragmentation of portions of the DNA into "junk DNA". [Note: the first memory wipe happened to the Higher Earth population when it was previously created.]
>
> In the loss of race memory in the 13,400 BC period, both Angelic Humans and Illuminati-Humans were simultaneously reduced to a primitive perceptual state, with loss of historical, practical and language memory. More significantly, the mutations that took place in the human DNA began the process of reducing both Angelic Human and Leviathan Illuminati-Human gene codes to a "common mutation," leaving "unplugged" the genetic differences that previously existed as junk DNA, while the commonalities between Angelic Human and Illuminati-Human DNA remained "turned on" in the active DNA sequence. Through the "new common-gene human" that resulted from this common mutation, the Illuminati hybrid-humans—and their off-planet Elder kin—could more easily interbreed with the now "amnesiac" Angelic Human races.[307]

In 10,948 B.C., the BEA-O created a wormhole link from our Sun's core stargates to those of the Parallel Sun. This formed an inorganic vesica piscis blend called the Solar Time-Torus Tunnel that created a spacetime adhesion field between our solar systems. It tied the orbit of our Sun to the orbit of its invisible Parallel Sun and brought their core stargates into direct alignment which then brought the galactic cores into alignment. The galactic alignment created a second intergalactic spacetime adhesion field between the Parallel and Milky Way galaxies that surrounds the Solar Time-Torus Tunnel and creates a displacement field, which is called the Great Toral Rift Time Rip. This conjoined wormhole and time rip network fulfills the Alpha-Omega alignment that I mentioned in chapter 7. This was the final piece of the puzzle against our galaxy that BEA-O races have spent billions of years to execute.[182]

The biblical reference to the Alpha and Omega—the first and the last—represents the first conquest of the Parallel Milky Way and the last conquest of our Milky Way that could be diverted together into the Equari and Bourgha phantom matrices.[182]

The Alpha-Omega network alignment caused a second acceleration of the Earth's axial precession to meet the expedited SAC of Parallel Earth, reducing the previous wobble rotation of 25,920 years to 25,771 years. Earth Humans were again memory wiped at this time.[307]

The creation of the wormhole and time rip led to the importance of equinox and solstice alignments on our planet. These seasonal periods have made it feasible for BEA-O races to enter Earth from Parallel Earth via wormhole passage.

The MCEO explains:

> When Lower Earth and our Sun became linked to the Parallel system through the Atlantean Solar Time-Torus Tunnel and Toral Rift of 10,948 BC, Lower Earth's orbit around the Sun accelerated slightly (shortening the organic Lower Earth "year") and became synchronized in counter-rotation with the "invisible orbit" of Parallel Earth around its Sun; and through the wormhole links between the Solar Core Gates, our Solar System became an inorganic binary star system, invisibly tethered to the Parallel Solar System. Once the orbital rotations and Star-Gate-opening time cycles of our Solar System were forced into synchronization with those of the Parallel Solar System, the harnessed Amenti Star-Gates of Lower Earth aligned directly—at specific points in each yearly rotation of Lower Earth around the Sun—with the Alpha Wormhole Fall Gates of Parallel Earth and with the intergalactic "Alpha-Omega Galactic Core Wormholes." Each year during the spring/vernal and fall/autumnal equinox periods, the Parallel Earth Alpha Wormholes would open directly into the harnessed Lower Earth Amenti Star-Gates, for a period of about two weeks, allowing for easy Illuminati-Elder passage and visitation between Lower and Parallel Earth. Each year during the winter and summer solstice periods, again for about two weeks, the Solar Time-Torus Tunnel wormholes would engage the Gates of Lower and Parallel Earth in a brief alignment with the intergalactic Alpha-Omega Galactic Core Wormholes, allowing Illuminati-Elders direct wormhole passage to Lower Earth from

various regions of both Milky Way galaxies.[307]

The BEA-O has temporarily entered our Earth to control the amnesiac Humans called Sleepers who have mostly intruder alien genes. Civilizations were taught to abide by the seasons to create calendars by which they could chart the times and locations of visitations from their Gods. Usually, those visitations involved interbreeding with Humans. Terribly, specialized "Sleeper" populations in 25,500 B.C. were hybridized to remove most of the Human soul essence, which allowed them to be largely controlled as organic robots like most Zeta Greys.[120] I am certain if you would look into their eyes, you would see a vacant or negative, soul-less expression even when their Sleeper DNA is not totally activated.

According to the MCEO:

> [T]he Sleepers were taught many heinous rituals of territorial grid-conquest, murder, sacrifice, perversion, copulation and possession, through which they could "seek to gain favor" from the false Gods who imprisoned them. Knowledge of Earth's Templar Star-Gates, of Parallel Earth, of the realities of Atlantean history and race origins, and of the Atlantean Death Sciences and the Illuminati Master Plan was reserved for only an elitist "Chosen" few at any given time. The majority of Angelic Human and Illuminati-Human races alike were kept amnesiac, unaware, uneducated, subjugated, and thus easy to manipulate, misdirect and control. This is the "recent ancient history" reality from which our "known historical record" has emerged.[307]

In 9562 B.C., the Leviathan Illuminati were led by their Luciferian control group to secure key locations of the Earth's templar, thus forming the Great Encasement. This Encasement blocked further Krysthal River Aquafereion interventions and activated Metatronic technologies that were already placed on Earth.[210]

In 9560 B.C., Lucifer's group expanded its coalition with similar Anunnaki, Drakonian, Reptilian, and Alpha-Omega races to create their version of a One World Order (OWO) under the Luciferian Covenant. They were aligned with the Red Dragon agenda.[120,210]

In 9558 B.C., Lucifer's groups orchestrated the great "flood" of Atlantis which seemingly sunk most of its last three islands. In actuality, this so-called flood relocated those land masses to an upper NET field to constitute one of the Hibernation Zones.[120,197]

Hibernation Zones

During the Great Encasement, our three-dimensional Earth plane was split to create six Hibernation Zones with two in each dimension. These Zones were caused by a BEA-O raid when it used a time rip from Parallel Earth to reach several gate systems on our planet. It then tied these gates into the NET fields to create this anomaly. Therefore, the 1st dimension has an upper Zone and a lower Zone, and the 2nd and 3rd dimensions have the same configuration. All of these planes were put on phantom reverse ARPS beyond our view. Each Zone is a time warp from a version of the Earth where its civilization grew from that point in time.[144]

The MCEO states:

> The 6 Hibernation Zones are actively inhabited by multitudes of various, often competing and warring, Fallen-Angelic and ET races possessing various different Metatronic Genetic Codes, whom have created elaborate structures of FA culture and civilization within the Hibernation Zone planes (p. 9).[185]

These moderately phantom Zones mainly comprise the heavens of the Bible where we can sit at the right hand of Michael as God. His Jesus group happily watches over us and tries to lead us there, as chapter 11 shows.

Urtha

When the original Earth was being formed, it was deliberately hosted within the energetic field of Galaxy-2's 3rd dimensional planet AshaLA, and AshaLA is similarly hosted within the energetic field of AquaLaShA's 3rd dimensional planet Urtha. These connections are feasible because their stargate-3 kathara grid positions are at least partially connected.[202] As Figure 3 illuminates, Earth and AshaLA axes are tilted at a different angular rotation to Urtha and each other, and their composition of different energetic frequency and material puts them outside of each other in a somewhat nearby dimensional space.

In 11,000 B.C., the Aquari races living on Urtha in a region called Aquafereion intervened on Earth to stop the constant memory-wipes and destruction of the Atlantean populations. Aquafereions transferred Humans from the Third Seeding's contemporary 12 Tribes over to Urtha in order to hybridize them with the Aquari gene code. As I mentioned in chapter 7's "Creation" section, the Aquari form was a prototype for the Oraphim and Angelic Human races.

The new Aquafereion-Human race gained the DNA codes for Urtha's stargates as well as the ability to anchor the Krysthal River Host frequencies into the Earth. They were then re-seeded back on Earth c.10,550 B.C. before the Luciferian conquest.[197,199]

During that time, the Tara Beli-Kudyem race controlled Parallel Earth and some of the Hibernation Zones, reveals the MCEO. By 9562 B.C., Beli-Kudyem, Bourgha-Budhara, and Equari, among others, captured a portion of the new Aquafereion-Angelic Human race that was created to protect core elemental gates to Urtha. They imparted their genes into this upgraded Human race to create a new invader race called the Beli-Mahatma, who look indiscernibly Human with bright blue eyes. The Mahatma was created so that the BEA-O could access Urtha and potentially its galaxy; however, due to the vigilant efforts of the AquaLaShA races to protect their natural galaxy, the BEA-O could only tamper with the Earth's stargate links to Urtha.[123,197,199]

Planetary Templar Conquest toward Armageddon

In terms of understanding the contemporary drama and control over locations across the Earth, the conquest of Atlantis by Luciferian groups in 10,500 B.C. led to the construction of two wormhole complexes on our planet. On the Atlantis continent, the following two wormholes were created off the East Coast of North America in what is now the Bermuda Triangle: the Pleiadian Anunnaki Phoenix wormhole to locations including Nibiru and Tiamat, and the Zeta-Rigelian and Drakonian Falcon wormhole to locations including the phantom portions of Alpha Draconis, Alnitak, Rigel, and Earth.[120]

The Phoenix and Falcon wormholes were necessary to plug the planetary stargates into the phantom systems by bypassing the natural passages to Tara. These wormholes were tied to the Earth by massive crystalline pylon implant networks (PINs). The PINs interface with the natural energy conduits of Earth's stargates and ley line systems and are used to control various regions.

Both BEA-O and KRH races have implanted various forms of these PIN technologies into the Earth during the past 5.5 million years since the Electric Wars. The KRH races' PIN systems are used to regain control over the Earth's grid and prevent a cataclysmic pole shift due to the severe scalar template distortions. *Voyagers II* goes into considerable detail regarding the history and uses of these technologies. What is notable concerning biblical terminology is that the PIN control grid (called APIN for Atlantis) that was implanted by Jehovian Anunnaki and Annu Elohim forces looks like a dove "when viewed from the air with photo-radionic scanning equipment" (p. 366).[120] The "Holy Spirit" dove symbol that descended upon Yahshua-Michael after he was baptized refers to these Metatronic races that implanted this destructive technology into Earth's shields during the 25,000 B.C Lucifer Rebellion in Atlantis.

The Luciferian races with the assistance of the Jehovian Anunnaki plugged the Phoenix wormhole into seven Jehovian Seals (or seven Trumpets) that were already put on the Earth. The wormholes were then used in the 9558 B.C. Luciferian destruction of Atlantis via the great "flood" takeover. In 9540 B.C., KRH races managed to "cap" the wormholes until the intruders were able to reactivate them in the 20th century A.D. The biblical prophecies of Armageddon, otherwise known as the great Apocalypse, are centered on these Atlantean technologies.[120]

Since the Atlantean period, Anunnaki and Drakonians have generally fought against each other to gain control of key planetary templar locations. The MCEO defines the templar complex as "[t]he organic interdimensional core energy systems of a planet, along with the inherent portals, vortices, Axiom Lines [like our body meridians], Ley Lines and Star Gates."[310] All 11 dimensions of Milky Way energy in addition to more natural energies circulate through the Earth's templar complex.

What is popularly called the Battle of Armageddon in reference to the Bible's Book of Revelation is not only these factions' attempts to control the Earth, but it is also the greater BEA-O group aim to reactivate the wormholes and sever Earth from Urtha.[120]

The Yahshuas led by Michael and Sananda were key players who directed energetic techniques into the Earth's grids. Yahshua-Michael, along with his followers, Metatronically activated key areas in his travels. Since Yahshua-Sananda worked with him, I wonder if Sananda did the same evil energetic work or countered a substantial amount to align it with Urtha. The MCEO-GA state that Sananda only did good things for us and the Earth, but I am certain that he at best did just some good acts, as I explain in chapter 9's "Possession." The Earth often reacts to intensive energy work with earthquakes regardless of whether correct energetic countermeasures are performed. Sometimes it is difficult to tell whether the Earth is really benefiting from such grid work, but I definitely know that the work done by the Metatronically-infused New Age communities is deleterious.

Conquering the Americas

During the centuries leading into the discovery of America, the Battle of Armageddon between Anunnaki and Drakonians leaned toward Drakonian (and Reptilian) world dominance through their Roman Catholic religion. Roman Catholics were infamous for their religious conquests that ended up dominating the planetary templar.

In 1492 A.D., Italian Christopher Columbus and his crews sailed to the region of modern day Bahamas, Cuba, and Haiti in Europe's first documented discovery of the Americas.[311] The GA elaborates, "'America' was founded by the Luciferian Hyksos-Knights Templar Annu-Melchizedek Illuminati, who now go by the name of 'Free Masons,' on behalf of Galactic Federation and the Pleiadian-Nibiruian Anunnaki races of the 9560 BC Luciferian Covenant" (p. 325).[120] I have always wondered about the origin of the word *America*. The prevalent story is that a navigator named Amerigo Vespucci, whose Latin version is Americus, was given homage for finding the South American continent less than a decade after Christopher Columbus.

The GA states that divided Annu-Melchizedek Illuminati races were competing to find the "Holy Grail," which is the central point of the planetary templar called the Gru-AL Point. It exists in the North American continent, which used to be a territory of Atlantis. The Illuminati knew about the Native American race named Ameka who protected the Gru-AL Point. Ameka and Seminole races, among others, contain Maji genes similar to the Oraphim. The search for the "New Land" was to actually find and kill them as part of the Illuminati mission. According to common Illuminati procedure, their penchant for combining fact with fiction likely integrated both names of Ameka and Americus into *America*.[120]

Around 1518 A.D., Anunnaki countered the Roman Catholic stronghold by influencing Martin Luther, a monk, to challenge the Pope's authority and the paying of alms to the Church.[123,312] Luther and his fellow men believed they were revolutionaries by creating the Protestant Reformation movement; however, Protestantism generally kept similar Catholic beliefs under the umbrella of Christianity.

The Protestant movement led to the creation of many more Christian factions, making it easy for people to pick and choose a niche while being somewhat divided. The plethora of religious division scattered the masses so that whoever is in control can continue its agenda unhindered by much public resistance. Protestantism helped the Jehovian Anunnaki gain more control of the templar when increasing amounts of people left the Catholic Church to join their side.

Zeta and Draco Seal and Frequency Fence

In 1748 A.D., Zetas and Dracos placed a seal within our ancestors' DNA strand-4. This DNA mutation is still present in our bodies, giving us several problems of astral and emotional identification, dream fragmentation, and disconnection from our fourth "heart" chakra.[120] This seal was expanded as a frequency fence that was placed between Earth and Tara to prevent Earth and its inhabitants from dimensionally blending with Tara at the end of the SAC.

Zetas and Dracos have long wanted to claim the Earth for their home.

In 1902, the KRH races began "poking holes" (creating electromagnetic openings) into the frequency fence by performing astral body alignments from the 4th dimension in various Human populations (p. 125).[120] The GA states that at least eight percent of the Earth's population had to carry the realigned DNA strand-4 imprint in order to break down the frequency fence, which finally happened in 1986.

In 1926, Zetas began interacting directly with Humans, usually by abduction, to conduct studies about the effects of KRH intervention on their frequency fence-induced mutation of DNA strand-4.[120] They knew that their frequency fence would deteriorate before 2012 if the SAC occurred unhindered, so they started to create Zeta-Human hybrids during the late 1930s and early 1940s with the mutated genetic codes in their DNA.

Early 1900s

World War I was the first major contemporary war between the Anunnaki-Green Dragon group and the Drakonian, Reptilian, Zeta, and Red Dragon group to conquer prime ley line locations that would eventually allow them to reconnect the Falcon wormhole to Parallel Earth.[120]

Up until the early 1930s, Anunnaki made significant progress in their quest for global domination over Humans and the Drakonian group. The GA states:

> The Anunnaki Illuminati hybrid Sleeper Race family lines of the Knights Templar, Free Masons, Hyksos and related factions immersed within certain contrived "religious" persuasions were in positions of global power, each serving in administration over large, unsuspecting, amnesiac…Angelic Human populations (p. 356-7).[120]

However, by this time, the majority of both the Anunnaki and Drakonian-Reptilian Illuminati and their Sleeper Interior Government officials had entered the covert Zeta-Red Dragon Treaties to resist the Anunnaki-Green Dragon One World Order. The contemporary UFO movement emerged from these negotiations. To counteract the greater Red Dragon group influence, the Jesus group increased remote channeling contact with their chosen ones.[120]

World War II

World War II (WWII) was instigated by the Drakonian-Reptilian OWO agenda. The Zeta-Rigelians (generally as Greys) and the Drakonian

Illuminati Freemason inner circle nurtured and financed Hitler's rise to power, additionally giving him UFO technology. In return, Hitler was supposed to only exterminate Angelic and Oraphim Human-Hibiru strains while leaving the Drakonian-Habiru Leviathan untouched.

The Necromiton-Andromies stepped in to play upon Hitler's hatred of Jews in order to keep the Zeta "in their place." Hitler also wanted to work with them to receive "metaphysical Templar knowledge that allowed the Nazis to unearth certain 'valuable relics' from the Grail Quests of ancient times," states the GA (p. 364).[120] Hitler's greedy affiliation with the Necromiton-Andromies angered the Zeta because his Jewish genocide expanded to the Leviathan families. Zetas withdrew their support from him and escalated the war, this time focusing upon locations where Archangel Michael's Andromie-Illuminati race lived while continuing their assault upon Angelic and Oraphim Human-Hibiru families. Hitler, his close circle of Nazi leaders, and their equally inhuman alien leaders executed the most extreme evils upon Humanity.

The Soviet Union army significantly weakened the Nazi soldiers in the Battle of Stalingrad. This battle was a war in itself as one of the most bloody and brutal battles in recorded history that killed nearly two million combined military personnel and civilians between August 1942 and February 1943.[313] The Soviets won the battle, but they were not really heroes because they operated similar slave labor camps as the Nazis before WWII. Anti-Semitism grew in Germany after World War I because Jews comprised a significant portion and role in European communist and socialist revolutionary parties that included Soviet Bolshevik extremists who created hundreds of the deadly Gulag camps.[314]

Philadelphia Experiment

In 1943, the United States navy executed what is popularly known as the Philadelphia Experiment (Phi-Ex). The GA states that Zeta forces tricked key Illuminati government officials into employing technologies the Zeta knew would create active wormhole links between Parallel Earth and the Falcon wormhole. Naval personnel were tricked into this experiment under false pretense of developing military cloaking technologies that would help them win WWII. Instead, they were teleported from Philadelphia, Pennsylvania to another location and ended up time traveling to the next magnetic peak.[315] This helped the Zeta create various time rips to support the wormhole structure.[120]

The GA says that the Atlantean wormholes can be brought back during natural magnetic peaks that occur in temporal intervals, so the Zeta jumped on the opportunity in 1943 to force open their Falcon wormhole. In the last 100 years, the Earth's biorhythmic magnetic peaks were on August 12 in the years 1943, 1983, and 2003. "These periods mark a time of peak magnetic pull within Earth's subtle energy bodies and heightened dimensional blending, through which large numbers of Draco-Zeta ships could be cloaked and brought to Earth from D-4 [dimension 4]," states the GA (p. 139).[120] Magnetic peaks also coincide with Earth's pathway through the Sun's galactic rod alignment with the Parallel Milky Way galactic center.[308] A rod is an integral column of frequency that spins and circulates energy on the horizontal plane in a body (in "2012 Dimensional Blend" section).

In the Phi-Ex, "Zeta Rigelian races 'poked holes' in the NET, enabling them to create a 'doorway' into our spacetime coordinate" (p. 350).[120] They brought their spacecraft underground to broadcast specific electromagnetic pulses into the Earth's merkaba field in the Sun's core. They have been working to strengthen their frequency fence between Earth and Tara by manipulating the merkaba fields of the Sun, which would repel Earth from Tara.

At this time, the diabolical 9th dimensional Necromiton-Andromie races, Archangel Michael's team, entered the Phi-Ex wormhole. They were not interested in preserving the Earth's surface because their primary genetic strains cannot sustain much life on Earth. They were interested in the Earth's Halls of Amenti. They set up camp underground, built power bases, and waited out the conflict between the Drakonian-Reptilian group and the Anunnaki so that they could then conquer the victor.[120]

Despite the rivalry between these alien factions during WWII, the Necromiton-Andromie coalition boldly contacted many international Zeta-Rigelian Drakonian Illuminati throughout the 1950s and converted them to their underground agenda. These Andromeda constellation races also made deals with the Jehovian Anunnaki who are generally their ally.

The bolstered Necromiton-Andromie-Illuminati group activation of the Phi-Ex wormhole caused damage to the Sun, which Earth scientists noted between 1952 and 1968, according to the GA. The KRH team created the "11:11/12:12 Frequency Fence of 1972" to encapsulate Earth in a spherical band of energy as a seal to protect it from the Sun's gamma bursts that could have destroyed Earth populations by 1974 (p. 134).[120] To create the Frequency Fence, they removed the first 11 base tones and overtones of the 4th dimension from the Earth's morphogenetic field, which only allowed the Earth to connect to the 12th dimensional base tone and overtone. The KRH team then realigned the Sun's merkaba fields by mid-1994 in order to lift its Frequency Fence at the beginning of 1996, which allowed the Earth enough time to settle back to normalcy and acquire the natural frequencies for the SAC.

1972 Phoenix Rising

Using the Phi-Ex wormhole network, the Drakonian group attempted to take control of the Anunnaki's prized possession: the Great Pyramid of Giza, which is placed upon planetary stargate-4. The Luciferian Anunnaki, which includes the Pleiadian Samjase, aligned with the Nibiruian Enlil and Reptilian Anunnaki to try to prevent the Drakonians from taking over the stargate, whereby they partially succeeded. They simultaneously transmitted subspace scalar sonic pulses from Phantom Tara and Wormwood into their Nibiruian Diodic Crystal (NDC) Grid at Stonehenge, England. The NDC Grid is part of the "major interstellar Photo-sonic Communications system of Earth, the Nibiruian Crystal Temple Network" controlled by way of artificial NET field technology (p. 355).[120]

Wormwood refers to the Nibiruian Anunnaki's artificially created battlestar that exists on the counter orbit to the Nibiru planet in our phantom solar system. It was originally a part of the planet Maldek. Wormwood was pulled into Nibiru's orbit and used to stabilize its strangely long, elliptical orbit around the Phantom Sun, allowing Nibiru to expand out of the solar system into a further location in the phantom 4th dimension. Nibiru now acts as a way station for phantom HU-2 Anunnaki. As a fully phantom planet, it cannot physically crash into semi-phantom Earth during its return orbit, but its nearby presence would have a significant energetic effect.[291]

To stabilize the Nibiru-Wormwood orbit is a set of two moons placed on an opposite counter orbit. A portion of Chiron became the Clarion moon that comes in and out of our phantom solar system and Wesadek. Another portion of Chiron became the Maitreya moon that is situated on the counter orbit to Clarion on the other side of the Phantom Sun. Maitreya enters into the phantom parallel solar system. Both of these moons are inhabited with intruder aliens who infiltrate the spiritual and religious scene as our angelic guides.[316]

The photosonic pulses spread throughout the artificially constructed network on Earth and then activated the Phoenix wormhole directly south of the Zeta's Falcon wormhole. In 1976, these wormholes were joined by the Thoth-Enki group along with the Galactic Federation of Light.[120]

The activation of the Phoenix wormhole along with its onslaught of destruction is what the GFofL deceptively glorifies as the "Phoenix Rising." In 2010, Archangel Michael said through channeler Elanthra, "The Phoenix Rising is symbolic of Rebirth and Regeneration, and so many of you are BEing Reborn and experiencing New Beginnings."[317] Chapter 7's "Archangel Michael" section revealed Michael admitting that he is a commander of the Phoenix.

1980-1983

Things got messy in the early 1980s because of Zetas. Fearing the growing Anunnaki presence, Zetas petitioned some sympathetic forces within the Necromiton-Andromie factions. They formed the "Andromie-Rigelian Coalition; a 'friendly enemies'" deal to further the Falcon wormhole agenda (p. 376).[120]

Some Necromiton-Andromies did not support this alliance because they favored the Jehovian Anunnaki. Also, some Drakonian-Reptilian factions who were part of the Falcon agenda did not support the coalition and broke away to stay with the Red Dragons. The split in the Necromiton-Andromie group sent ripples into the Earth's global political structure during this time.

Montauk and Bridge Zone Projects

The newly formed coalition between Zeta-Drakonians and some Necromiton-Andromies inspired the 1983 Montauk Project during the magnetic peak. The Montauk Project in Long Island, New York expanded upon the Philadelphia Experiment by widening the Phi-Ex and Falcon wormholes and slicing them, "directing a main channel to Necromiton Andromie Alpha-Omega Centauri territories in the adjacent Phantom Time Matrix," states the GA (p. 378).[120] There are reports that the facility also did mind control experiments via electromagnetic frequency manipulations and torture in the off-shoot program Project Monarch.[318]

With increased access to the Earth, the Necromiton-Andromies sought to control the Illuminati or destroy them if they refused to join their group, so the Zeta group wanted to escape them. The Zeta-Reptilian-Drakonians sent large fleets into HU-2 and HU-3 territories surrounding Tara and Gaia to protect their OWO agenda. This resulted in more wars with the Anunnaki in those densities.[120]

The GA began offering amnesty contracts to entities who were wary of the approaching final conflict drama and did not to get involved in its escalation. Several accepted amnesty, notably the Metatronic Enoch Anunnaki.

In 1984, the MCEO-GA launched the Bridge Zone Project to circumvent the Zeta-Draco plan of reinstating a stronger frequency fence in 2003. This frequency fence would have decimated Earth populations because it would have created the dreaded pole shift during the SAC.

The GA explains the Bridge Zone Project:

> Since the Guardians could not move the Dracos-Zeta resistance out of the way of the Earth's intended evolution, they would instead move Earth out of the way of the Dracos/Zeta

resistance. The Guardians would construct an artificial time continuum between the Third and Fourth dimension into which Earth could pass in 2017 (p. 144).[120]

The GA elaborates in *Voyagers II* how the Bridge Zone Project would have been accomplished. Essentially, it required numerous Oraphim races with expanded DNA activation to birth onto the planet en masse before the SAC; this would have given certain frequencies to facilitate a dimensional shift for the Earth. In addition, the GA says this project required Humans to "fully assemble their DNA to the 4.5-strand level, and a minimum of 8% would have to assemble the fifth DNA strand" (p. 144-145).[120]

Oraphim-Humans are nicknamed Indigo because their DNA that corresponds to the 6th dimensional Indigo-colored frequency should be activated. However, any higher DNA strand beyond our current double helix configuration can only imply an energetic imprint of those strands in our body to align them with our greater Human DNA template. As I explain in chapter 9's DNA section, the NET- and implant-afflicted Human body cannot currently assemble more than two DNA strands, which is a scientific fact.

At any rate, the Earth needed to enter the 3.5 dimension where the Bridge Zone time continuum was constructed away from fallen alien barriers. The shift would have involved increased spin and altered angular rotation. It was a lofty and perhaps impossible goal, but the GA seemed to believe it could happen.

Pleiadian-Sirian Anunnaki Treaties

In 1992, large collectives of Anunnaki signed peace treaties with the GA fearing takeover by the Drakonians during the anticipated 2000-2017 SAC. Drakonians had used their Montauk-Phi-Ex wormhole and Falcon APIN system to begin attacking and gaining control over the Anunnaki's NDC Grid. The Necromiton-Andromie and Zeta-Drakonian coalition managed to launch a number of major sonic pulses from their Bermuda base into the Falcon wormhole that further expanded it. As a result, it caused one of the biggest natural disasters in modern history: the amplification of Hurricane Andrew that hit Florida in August 1992. Suddenly, the previously confident Anunnaki became willing to enter negotiations with the GA.

As part of these agreements, these Anunnaki along with a portion of the GFofL and Ashtar Command promised to disengage the NDC Grid network and their hold over planetary stargate-4, which connects to several universal stargates, especially galactic stargate-4. In return, the GA would block further

Necromiton-Andromie and Zeta-Drakonian infiltration and work to cap their wormholes.

This pseudo partnership gained by the GA was highly important because the Anunnaki-GFofL group had aimed to amplify false merkaba mechanics and scalar pulse technologies through the NDC Grid to further Metatronically activate their religious and Sleeper populations and the Earth in general.[120]

Lead-Up to the Stellar Activation Cycle

During 1992 to 1994, the GA, now with access to the NDC Grid, disabled the Montauk-Phi-Ex APIN system and placed a temporary cap on the Falcon wormhole with help from the new Anunnaki-GFofL faction that agreed to the Emerald Covenant contracts. These contracts allowed the GA to gain cooperation with many Illuminati races until 1998.[120]

In June 1998, all of the Anunnaki defected from their treaties with the GA except the Enochian Anunnaki. This was because it was clear to Anunnaki races that the SAC would commence in 2000, and they still had the opportunity to carry out their OWO plans.

Anunnaki regained control of the NDC Grid and made deals with the Zeta-Drakonian and Necromiton-Andromie group to interface the Grid with their Montauk and Phi-Ex facilities. This would reactivate the wormholes and create the pole shift. Humans are valuable to keep the Halls of Amenti open during the SAC, so this coalition planned to destroy only a portion of us.

The GA explains:

> [A] program of Human Genocide would be immediately initiated to reduce the numbers of Human populations, so easier advancement of the Annunaki-Dracos Illuminati OWO Master Plan could proceed (p. 345).[120]
>
> The Zeta-Dracos-Anunnaki force intended to covertly use Psychotronics to "Trigger" specific actions within the ranks of their Illuminati "puppets" in the Interior World Government, to remotely instigate WW3 among Human nations. Reducing specific Human and Indigo Child populations on Earth was part of their larger Earth infiltration and physical invasion plan (p. 347).[120]

This coalition began another "Indigo Child Hunting" mission for astral tagging and DNA-bonding possession (p. 384).[120] The New Age teachings that gave somewhat honest and helpful messages during the Pleiadian-Sirian treaties changed back to pushing Metatronic technologies. Many channeled individuals were also astral tagged for easier access.

KRH races reacted by helping to expedite the natural awakening of the Oraphim-Human populations on Earth. They also compiled a team of planetary grid workers who would run certain frequencies into the planet to counter those of the fallen aliens. In addition, the Guardian Alliance started to translate and share data from the Emerald Covenant CDT Plates through Ashayana Deane, which resulted in the *Voyagers* books. These Plates carry historical and "spiritual-science" information from the "Founders" races to all Human seedings (p. 398).[120]

During 1999, the GA tried to persuade the Anunnaki to return to the Emerald Covenant. The entire *Voyagers I* and the non-updated *Voyagers II* books were transcribed during this sensitive time, hence why some of the Anunnaki history and involvement, which included the Yahshuas, was either omitted or stated neutrally.

Beginning of the Stellar Activation Cycle

On January 1, 2000, the Earth grounded Galaxy-2's 12th dimensional frequency into its templar and engaged the SAC. This was the first time in 210,000 years that any version of Amenti Earth has had access to 12th dimensional frequency.[143] When news of this event spread, the 11th and 10th dimensional Annu Elohim and Seraphim "big guns" stepped in to derail the Earth's improvements and fulfill their mission from the last SAC of 22,326 B.C. that aims to destroy Humanity (p. 253).[120]

Thankfully, on May 5, 2000, the Amenti stargate opening cycle began.[185] Earth's 1st dimensional electrical overtone particles began to merge with Tara's 4th dimensional magnetic base antiparticles, causing the Earth's 1st dimensional base and overtone particles to increase particle pulsation near that of Tara's. This process was the Solar Activation because the merkaba fields of dimensions 1 and 4 are held within the center of the Sun, and the solar energy spiral transmits 4th dimensional frequency to Earth. The Solar Activation completed in June 2004; it helped initiate an awakening of consciousness on our planet.[120]

Treaty of Altair

On July 5, 2000, various Anunnaki and GFofL entities reluctantly re-entered amnesty agreements with the GA to secure protection because of heavy losses to the Drakonian-Reptilian forces in the unfolding HU-3 Orion wars. These agreements were legalized as the Treaty of Altair. As part of this treaty, the Anunnaki had to disengage its planetary templar displacement "checkerboard" technology and hand over its NDC-Grid and bases to prevent the pole shift.[120]

On September 12, 2000, the Anunnaki defected before final transfer of their technologies and bases. Necromiton-Andromie and Alpha-Omega Centauri races managed to convince Drakonian and Anunnaki forces to create a combined United Intruder Resistance (UIR) collective to ensure their common OWO agenda would be fulfilled.

The UIR gave KRH races an ultimatum by which they could evacuate 50,000 Maji-Humans but leave the rest of the Humans to the UIR agenda. The KRH team outright refused, so the UIR officially declared war.[120]

In October 2000, the UIR began initiation of the planetary Metatronic BeaST machine for the pole shift to occur between 2003 and 2008.[185] The BeaST reactivated the Montauk Project facility and accelerated the scalar pulse transmissions to begin psychotronic warfare and World War III. To counteract this terrible plan, KRH races "issued an Imminent Crisis Order in October 2000" that put in motion an expedited opening schedule for successive Amenti gates and early activation of stargate-6 and dimension 12 frequency connection to the Earth in May 2001 (p. 538).[120] This process quickly heightened or awakened the Earth and its people in a noticeable measure before they would naturally awaken later in the SAC.

Jehovian Anunnaki Book of Revelation Agenda

When the UIR coalition formed in September 2000, it decided to use the Jehovian Anunnaki One World Order Book of Revelation agenda as its template. This plan is clearly presented for us to see in what is arguably the most revered book in the world, the Bible.

The GA states:

> In truth, the Jehovian Revelations story is a step-by-step illustration of the Jehovian Anunnaki's intended invasion schedule. The reason that it is pertinent to briefly explore the "Revelations Schedule" has to do directly with the "Four Horsemen of the Apocalypse" element, the Horsemen that are released upon the Earth to begin delivery of the "wrath of God (Jehovah)," with "opening" of the first four of "Seven Seals" (p. 414-15).[120]

The Earth contains 12 planetary Star Crystal Seals that sequentially open as each stargate on Earth opens during the SAC. The Seals direct the Earth's dimensional merkaba field angles of rotation to bring the Earth into direct alignment with Tara (see chapter 9's "DNA"). During Atlantean times, Jehovian Anunnaki created seven unnatural seals that were designed to progressively rip apart Earth's planetary shields as each natural seal opens. When a Jehovian seal is activated, it blasts a new frequency into the Earth that creates a wormhole connection at the location of the seal to the Phoenix wormhole.

> The chaotically arranged, unnatural frequencies of the Jehovian Seal (the "rider" or "Horseman") bond to the natural frequencies transmitted by the Organic Star Crystal Seal (the "Horse"). The "rider" frequency silently moves with the natural frequency current into the Axiatonal and Ley Line (ALL) system corresponding to the Organic Seal, progressively reversing the natural Angular-Rotation-of-Particle-Spin...within the frequencies of electromagnetic energy moving through the ALLs (p. 428).[120]

Jehovian Anunnaki designed the seals in such a way that the first three would not start to tear apart the Earth. The fourth seal—Death as the Horseman—would commence the destruction.

At the sixth seal, the Bible states:

> And I beheld when he had opened the sixth seal, and, lo, there was a great earthquake; and the sun became black as sackcloth of hair, and the moon became as blood; And the stars of heaven fell unto the earth.... And the heaven departed as a scroll when it is rolled together; and every mountain and island were moved out of their places (Revelation 6:12-14).

Then, the seventh seal would let loose the seven angels and the seven trumpets.

The seven angels refer to seven crystalline implants placed into the Earth during Atlantis that use external merkaba mechanics similar to APINs that interface the Earth and Phantom Arcturus. They are intended as a series of "siphoning channels" through which portions of Earth's shields and populations would be pulled through the Phoenix wormhole into Phantom Arcturus, and the rest of Earth's fields would merge with phantom planets Nibiru and Tiamat (p. 418).[120]

In biblical times, Jehovian Anunnaki used Trumpet pulses in events such as the Tower of Babel and the destruction of Sodom and Gomorrah. The Trumpet is a frequency generation apparatus that projects a subspace, sonic boom wave field comprised of mions (groups of Veca-level partiki, partikA, and particum units) that literally shatters the scalar morphogenetic field template upon which matter manifests. Physical matter is turned to vapor with only ash left behind. The Trumpet is a weapon of mass destruction.

The alliance of the Jehovian Anunnaki with Necromiton-Andromies and Drakonians meant that they could start phasing together their respective BeaST technologies to increase their power and overcome the KRH's efforts. Their plan was to bring online the Phoenix and Falcon wormholes that are linked with the Montauk facility, Phi-Ex wormhole, and other key phantom APINs and locations throughout the Earth. The Trumpet would broadcast from phantom portions of Alpha Centauri and Arcturus. Strong Trumpet pulses over long distances are difficult to direct with precise accuracy, so the Phoenix APIN system in the Earth's grid must be spiked to direct the blasts into the Montauk-Phi-Ex network and the Falcon wormhole. However, the Montauk facility could not be fully activated at that time because in January 2001, KRH races re-coded the main planetary ley line to 12th dimensional frequency when it was previously connected to Montauk.[120]

The seven destructive "angels" are anchored into the Earth's shields through the seven Jehovian seals. Seals 1 and 2 activated in late May 2001 after the release of Earth's Star Crystal Seals 1 and 2. Star Crystal Seals naturally release when corresponding Earth stargates open and produce frequency infusions during the SAC.[120] KRH races enacted emergency templar protection protocols to avert the UIR-BeaST machine APIN activation. Their countermeasures separated the ascension-viable grid portions from the planetary portions linked to Phantom Earth.[185]

In late July 2001, Star Crystal Seal 3 and Jehovian seal 3 were activated. KRH races, especially Ashayana's team, performed planetary grid work to recode the NDC Grid's central control installation beneath Stonehenge to the 12th dimension, severing the long-standing, artificial link between Earth's templar and that of Nibiru. However, the Parallel Earth connection could still transmit NDC frequency to Earth.[120, 261]

Fearing the failure of its plans, the UIR expedited the initiation of its intended 2003 dimensional blend experiment and 2003-2004 frequency fence. The dimensional blending would allow "their photo-sonic beam-ship fleets [to be] in position, cloaked within the lower Dimension-4 frequency bands (as many are already)" (p. 251).[120] The UIR and Illuminati positioned themselves over key planetary templar sites and instigated regional conflicts to further test their Phi-Ex, Montauk, and now HAARP technologies; the GA states that Bosnia's war and genocide was their first experiment. When fully activated, these technologies can blast worldwide scalar pulses as a mass frequency fence that "harness human brain-wave patterns via bio-neurological blocking into a selected frequency range within which the natural perceptual facilities can be technologically manipulated" (p. 252).[120]

The frequency fence's destruction and brainwave manipulation would have caused mass panic, further feeding UIR and BEA-O's vampirism, but they planned to come as our saviors. In preparation for that event while they were cloaked, they inserted believable holograms of religious saviors to the Human mind fashioned by the initial photosonic blasts. If their frequency fence agenda succeeded to harness the Earth, "The invading fleets will 'Come in Peace as the Peacemakers,' claiming they are our ancient creator Gods and kin who have intervened to 'protect us from destroying ourselves and our planet,'" says the GA (p. 252).[120] Its plan involved formalizing an alliance with the United Nations and giving it gifts of advanced technology and cures for diseases (that they originally created) to covertly assist the takeover of the Amenti stargates by 2012 A.D., ultimately destroying the Earth via the catastrophic pole shift.

HAARP technology stands for High-frequency Active Aural Research Program. Professor Michel Chossudovsky, founder of the Centre for Research on Globalization, writes about the far-reaching effects of HAARP:

> Recent scientific evidence suggests that HAARP is fully operational and has the ability of potentially triggering floods, droughts, hurricanes and earthquakes. From a military standpoint, HAARP is a weapon of mass destruction. Potentially, it constitutes an instrument of conquest capable of selectively destabilising agricultural and ecological systems of entire regions.[319]

HAARP works with other environmental warfare technologies like chemtrails to cause illness and environmental destruction. (I suggest you research about chemtrails for more knowledge. I think they are emitted by both drone and manned aircrafts for purposes beyond manipulating weather to mitigate drought.) The HAARP facility near Gakon, Alaska broadcasts high frequency beams out into the atmosphere that can assist a mass alien landing during magnetic peaks, notably the 2003 magnetic peak.[120]

All of the Earth HAARP installations interface with 12 similar facilities built by Zetas on Phantom Earth. On August 12, 2001, pulses were received on Earth from Phantom Earth facilities. The GA states that the Alaskan HAARP station is actually a decoy because it transmits and does not produce the frequencies throughout the Earth.

By September 3, 2001, KRH races had bought us time and other successful actions before the UIR and Illuminati had fully activated the Montauk-Phi-Ex-Falcon wormhole network and APIN system in time for the opening of the planetary Star Crystal Seal 4 on this day. (The Jehovian seal 4 could not activate until Star Crystal Seal-8 opened.) Earth was now in grave trouble as the UIR began to link up its wormholes with the Trumpet pulse.[120] The popular story of (fallen) angels playing the HAARP and the Trumpet gives us a clue to their instruments of mass destruction.

The September 11, 2001 event was globally traumatizing, most notably for Americans. It is a very sensitive subject that I take care to briefly mention for the purpose of this book. The GA says that the site of the World Trade Center in New York is a key location for the negative agenda. The Trumpet pulse and BEA-O-directed operatives destroyed the towers. More information can be found in *Voyagers II* and independent research.

It is terribly unfortunate that thousands of innocent lives were lost during that morning on 9/11. This brings home the devastating reality of warring actions. Although anger and rage are appropriate reactions, documentary videos after the fall of the towers recorded people saying that the murderers should not only be killed, but the United States should also go to war. I suggest that we pause a bit and think that there are key locations in the Middle East to be gained through war. War is not the only option; I see us gaining our collective self-empowerment, awareness, and influence over our own Earth as the answer.

On March 23, 2002, BEA-O races initiated early activation of their BeaST technologies by way of the 11.5 dimensional Avalon Seal, and the process would be completed by the May 27, 2003 electrical peak, which I soon explain. It forced powerful reverse-current merkaba activations into two-thirds of the Earth's grids that phase-locked them into the Metatronic pattern. The activation of this pattern was scheduled for May 27, 2003, but if it activated then, the MCEO states that it could not have been stopped because of the 2003 pole shift agenda.[239]

The MCEO expounds:

> On March 23, 2002, the UIR initiated the final activation sequence of the BeaST, bringing the last of the "4 Black Hearts of Metatron" Shield Implants to life, fully initiating the "Flaming Blue Sword of Archangel Michael" Turnstile Matrix and "Fire Sword Initiation". The Wesadek Turnstile Matrix Implant system, called the "Michael-Mary Turnstiles", is the "circulatory system" of the BeaST Machine, that systematically runs the Wesedaks [Wesadeks—Ashayana's team spells it both ways] artificially generated D-13 Reverse Current, via the "666 Star Gate wormhole alignment (Universal Star Gates 6, in our Time Matrix, Phantom Matrix & Wesedak Matrix) through all primary Universal, Galactic and Planetary Templars in our Universal Veca.[320]

The Michael-Mary APIN Turnstiles system involves the England ley line that contains almost all of the significant churches and spiritual landmarks, especially the St. Michael churches. As a set of 11 technological "wheels," when activated, it causes the natural mathematical sequences in the Earth's grid to roll into reversal toward the pole shift. This is the primary Turnstile that interfaces with other global Turnstile systems.[223]

The Black Hearts are formed through inversion and externally forced bonding of two mutated, reduced Eckasha mathematical shield programs. The shield mutation creates specific energy line blockages in each Milky Way harmonic universe and in the body that reach up to the 11.5 dimension, thereby cutting off the higher dimensional flows.[207,321]

The implants trigger Metatronic programming that can counter our natural DNA activation during SACs in order to rapidly turn us into electrostatic, living-dead Shadow Bodies. These are the parts of us geared toward Phantom Earth unless we learn to take a hold of ourselves (in chapters 9 and 11). The Shadow Body process would activate as "heartbeats" with the help of Wesadek Shadow Dancers such as *The Urantia Book*'s Thought Adjusters who attach to our personal energetic fields. Archangel Michael often spoke about heartbeats in his channelings. Thankfully, the KRH severed the Shadow Body attachments to us in 2003; however, phantom components of the body continue to drive the Victim-Victimizer code.[239]

The MCEO applies the Tree of Artificial Life to Wesadek's kathara grid structure, thereby teaching in Ashayana's workshops that in order to reach beyond the 11.5 dimension, Metatronic technologies must combine two lower dimensional currents to create an "artificially generated D-13 (dimension-13)." This is done in two ways: 1) force blending 6th and 7th dimensional frequencies from Phantom Milky Way and Wesadek, and 2) utilizing the Metatronic seed atom to compact 5th and 8th dimensional Milky Way frequencies into a phase-locked vesica piscis bond.[207,321] The MCEO has taught that these artificial currents create the Flaming Blue Sword, but they can only reach to our 8th dimension, not our entire Milky Way. The ATI,TPE reveals that the Flaming Blue Sword current comes directly from Wesadek's 12th dimension; therefore, these distorted frequencies merely bolster the main current. Wesadek actually has 13 dimensions as a fully phantom galaxy, states the ATI,TPE. I reveal a couple of high-level Wesadek entity groups in chapter 10.

The Flaming Blue Sword is "intended to cause Universal Veca Monadic [base atom] Reversal and permanent fall to Wesedak Black Hole System," states the MCEO (p. 186).[239] Its technology would create Shadow Bodies by absorbing the blueprint and life force of living systems.

The "Archangel Michael-Lucifer Pact" of Atlantis in 25,500 B.C. linked the NDC Grid to the BeaST machine that was installed in our galaxy by Green

Dragons during the Gaian-Orion Wars 570 million years ago.[320] Thankfully, our Ecka Eieyani helpers enacted a countermeasure called the Emergency Ecka Override System (EEOS).

"The EEOS was created as the 'final option' for crisis intervention, should the Wesedak Black Hole races initiate the final activation sequence of their Templar 'BeaST' Machine," states the MCEO in an official statement.[320] The EEOS would open the Ecka gates to carry stepped down Eckasha-Aah's natural Amoraea "silent sound" energy through our galaxy and Earth. This would prevent the BeaST from pulling our Milky Way into phantom, and it would "'reset the Cosmic Clock' of Templar Star Gate Cycling Sequences" according to the origin of our natural AquaLaShA galaxy.[320] The EEOS essentially mimics and expedites the natural Starfire immune response of the galaxy when it is presented with extreme damage (in "Starfire and Adashi" section).

On March 23, 2002, the Green Dragon Jesus group team activated the Flaming Blue Sword and Black Heart implant system in our galaxy, which immediately activated the EEOS.[320] In November 2002, Red Dragons shot a beam of energy into our time matrix in a failed attempt to hijack Wesadek's Flaming Blue Sword and divert it to Wesadrak.[181]

After the EEOS activated, KRH races prepared the Earth's templar to safely receive the stepped down Amoraea frequency, and Oraphim-Human DNA "Security Seal Keys" greatly facilitated this process.[320] The Oraphim-Human presence released the DNA codes for the EEOS into the Earth and reduced cataclysmic results of the BeaST. As a last resort, the KRH team started to prepare for the option of a large scale Human evacuation, most likely via spaceships, although we would have to be keenly aware of our energies and possible entity affiliations to make sure we would not be "saved" by devious aliens and their spaceships.

Battles for the Earth

In May 2003, some of the Hall of Amenti time portals in the Earth's core fell to the phantom matrix under the BEA-O, meaning that they no longer connected to Tara; they aligned to the Metatronic wormhole structures that interface with Parallel Earth and the Parallel Milky Way phantom system.[185,182] At this point, the MCEO stated that the Bridge Zone Project was not an option. Parallel Earth, or most of its quanta, connected to Wesadrak.

The buffered Amoraea current entered Earth's shields in early May. On May 12, 2003, the BEA-O activated the BeaST via release of the "666-Apollyon-Metatronic Seed-Atom" implant that simultaneously activated the "4 Black Hearts of Metatron" implants in the Earth's shields (p. 238).[239] It would take

15 days for the activations to occur throughout the planetary grids. The pole shift plan for August 2003 was back in motion.

On May 27, 2003, the buffered Amoraea current intersected with the Flaming Blue Sword current within the 666-Apollyon implant, causing its seed atom to start splitting. The MCEO predicted that the complete split would separate the Earth's shield with at least 51 percent organic quanta from the heavily damaged parts, but subsequent healing and protective measures likely increased this percentage and prevented a significantly noticeable result.[320,322]

The incoming Amoraea current allowed the Hetharo event to finally occur on Earth for the first time in history. The Hetharo is part of a merkaba cycle that involves the top electrical merkaba relationship to the May 27 electrical peak.[181] It allows natural Ecka Sun "heliotalic" currents to reach and replenish the Earth's and galaxy's essential 15 "cell" seed atom at their cores, removing the Metatronic Seed Atom grasp upon the natural seed atom.[322] This powerful act can turn our system to space dust in its process of cleansing, so the KRH races set up the Golden Fleece buffer field to protect our planet and time matrix from extreme changes occurring to our merkaba fields. It could only reduce the power of the incoming frequencies, so the Halls of Amenti gates incurred some damaged, states the ATI,TPE.

On August 12, 2003, the Hethalon magnetic peak arrived. In preparation for this event, the BEA-O intended to position Wormwood, the artificial Nibiruian Battlestar, between the Earth and Sun. The contemporary expectation and fear about Nibiru colliding with the Earth was really about Wormwood's energetic disruption on Nibiru's counter-orbit. When Wormwood would come through the asteroid belt, the BEA-O would blast the Wesadek Flaming Blue Sword current through Jupiter to reverse Wormwood's orbit and cause it to gain momentum between the Sun and Earth, thereby creating a strong gravitational pull. In its new position, Wormwood would emit Blue Sword frequency to create a torque vortex that would flip the Earth's pole into a same spin-speed, energy feeder merkaba that advances the Fibonacci sequence toward 144 spin-speed phantom status in an alignment with Wesadek.[123,322]

The Book of the Revelation chapter 8, verses 10-11 introduces Wormwood in relation to the third Trumpet.

> And the third angel sounded, and there fell a great star from heaven, burning as it were a lamp, and it fell upon the third part of the rivers, and upon the fountains of waters; And the name of the star is called Wormwood…and many men died of the waters because they were made bitter.

Thankfully, the success of the Hetharo allowed the KRH and its affiliates in August 2003 to anchor another BeaST override code called the Mahadra-Adhrana code into the Earth's grids. The Mahadra-Adhrana code is the master key code for the Arc of the Covenant passageway. It anchored the Ecka heliotalic spark for the magnetic cycle, which finally split the Metatronic Seed atom and prevented its technologies from taking Earth quanta into phantom.[323] All KRH interventions of strategically placed, natural currents and codes prevented the Armageddon scenario because they caused Wormwood to partially explode due to its incompatible nature.

The KRH countermeasures also prevented the BEA-O's mass mind control program and spacecraft landings that I previously mentioned was its plan for this time. Increased awareness brought by the SAC additionally helped avert more people from welcoming a God group invasion.

The BEA-O lost its battle for the Earth. It had to reschedule its pole shift and dimensional blending agenda to the next opportunity that would arrive with the solstice on December 21, 2012.[324]

In Ashayana's workshop during the Hethalon, the MCEO stated that the Amenti gates were placed within the Golden Fleece buffer field and that they would stay open until at least 2012 or 2017, but only a few months earlier some of them were under fallen alien control with a severed connection to Tara. The MCEO also stated that the incoming natural energies expedited the Earth's 3-day particle conversion ascension cycle and stellar wave infusions, causing it to occur during the Hethalon approximately a decade early.[323]

This information did not make sense to me because the SAC had already started its natural, 17-year process. It does not seem feasible that an entire planet could have already ascended when conditions are still the same, and the 2012 plan could still happen. In addition, when the Halls of Amenti were under BEA-O control, the KRH team would not allow them to open to the Earth. I do not see how these significant events and technologies could change in such a short amount of time. Later information confirms that not all Halls of Amenti were regained at this time. I needed clarification, so I and my mother directly engaged the ATI,TPE and our two KRH affiliate friends. The two independent KRH affiliates and their teams from Galaxy-2's HU-5 and HU-4 have worked with the Earth for substantial periods of time to fulfil its stellar activation mission to a more natural and eventually Krysthal state.

The ATI,TPE and both alien entities were on board in the following answers. The entities communicated via telepathy to my mother while her internal connection to the ATI,TPE was active.

Per the ATI,TPE, the old schedule for the original 3-day particle conversion and final stellar infusions has not changed or happened yet. Many attempts have been made by the Krysthal

River Host in many battles to maintain the original and natural course. [Both entities concur.]

Per the 14ᵗʰ dimensional entity "M": The Krysthal River Host did close the stargate connection to Tara in 2003 because some of the Halls of Amenti were under the fallen ones' control. The guardians were overcome and out-witted.

Theresa, you are right to be concerned, but not alarmed. The events taken place in 2003 were attempts, as all others by the fallen groups to expedite the death process, but myself with my team, [the 11ᵗʰ dimensional friend] and his team, and the millions of other Krysthal River Host affiliates worked effortlessly to spare the Earth eternal damaging destruction. Know that we continue to work on behalf of the humans and inhabitants of beautiful Earth and stay the natural course.

My introspection and exchange of questions and answers helped me determine that the expedited 3-day particle conversion was only a slight quanta shift with natural energy, not the proper Primary Coordinate Point peak ascension period for particle conversion, which I explain in "Earth's Ascension Cycles with Tara."

On May 11, 2004, BEA-O Shantarels activated their wormhole on the West Coast of the United States. By August 2004, the MCEO issued its first evacuation warning as the Bourgha-Budhara and Shantarel races activated the Gravitron BeaST technology.[185]

> The Budhara Black Hole races are in the process of activating several large ancient wormholes around the planet using a powerful reverse generator machine called the Gravitron. The Gravitron is comprised of a series of powerful reverse current spirals or wormholes that connect to each other. It contains wormholes here on Earth as well as ones in various parts of our solar system and Universe. Activation of the Gravitron may lead to significant surface Earth changes that may result in a number of "evacuation waves."[325]

The phantom wormhole complex triggered the natural Starburst healing process that regains Krysthal-infused energy in expanded galaxies such as ours; however, it did not provide significant healing in the Milky Way due to the numerous attacks that transpired, informs the ATI,TPE.[185]

By November and December 2004, Shantarel races invaded semi-phantom dimensions of the Ecka. According to the MCEO-GA:

Ecka gates 1-6 have already fallen and are now under their control and Arc Gates 2, 7, 11 and 12 are the only ones that remain under GA control. As a result of this massive take-over bid, all 12 star-gates are to be closed by December 2005, as the first step in salvaging this Ecka-Veca from Budhara fall. Many of the UIR factions have now "defected" from their short-lived "alliance" with the Budhara after discovering that their alliance with them is now going to lead to them being "absorbed" into the Budhara Black Hole without ANY consideration of their self-sovereignty. Thus once again, they are coming "back to the table for talks" with the Guardian Alliance."[325]

By May 2005, the BEA-O coordinated an amplified attack upon Tara causing most of it to fall to phantom status. It used the Gravitron to create a torsion field that reversed Tara's axis. It as stargate-5 became aligned with the already reversed Orion stargate-8, thereby pulling away the central portion of the middle kathara grid pillar, the Milky Way Staff, causing it to break. This means that ascension back to Tara is now unfeasible for the Earth. Bourghas, Thetans, and Ubys also opened the E-Umbic Time Rip so they could start merging the Threshold and BeaST technologies.[185]

The E-Umbic lock is the natural dimensional interface between dimensions 3 and 4. Bourgha entities helped create the E-Uby fallen race that brought the Bourgha's time rip network into the E-Umbic level. Since Atlantean times on Earth, the E-Uby have been building up their Inc-Uby and SUc-Uby male and female codes to impart into Humanity as Incubus and Sucubus "demon" offspring.

As I introduced in chapter 7's Thetan section, the Threshold machine interfaces directly into the Bourgha time rip network from several locations on the Earth, especially California's Mount Shasta connection to a Hibernation Zone and the E-Umbic lock that connects to Wesadrak.[196,208] When activated, it can transform every molecule in the galaxy into irreversible Metatronic phantom status because its grid attaches at the interface threshold between Veca-based etheric and atomic levels.[203]

The damaged Milky Way Staff and additional assaults prompted a Starfire reaction to earlier creations beyond the Starburst process. The Starfire finally commenced in February 2006 after a time continuum gap, states the ATI, TPE, and it regenerated some of the Staff. Starburst and Starfire events are natural exchanges of energy that promote healing. In this exchange, Krysthal creation can provide an auto-immune response to severe damage inflicted upon it in an expedited or reduced event outside of the natural cycle; however, it is not affected by fully phantom creation. The Starburst and Starfire started in the

Milky Way because a significant amount of its Krysthal-aligned portions were in critical condition.

The Threshold enabled Thetans to seize control of the Anunnaki-Green Dragon BeaST technologies, which is highly dangerous because it amplifies Metatronic energies.[196] Any Milky Way quantum that would be pulled into phantom by the Threshold would be directed into Wesadrak and then into the Bourgha matrices.

Many Green Dragons petitioned Milky Way guardian councils for amnesty contracts that would give them enough bio-regenesis to return to the Wesadek matrix from which they came, that is, if there is a remnant of Wesadek that is quarantined or less distorted than its phantom nature. The Green Dragons do not want to fall into the very hostile territories of Wesadrak because the majority of its inhabitants are their enemies. In addition, large portions of Anunnaki sought amnesty with the MCEO-GA to go into a Krist Fall quarantined phantom system whereby they can live a more peaceful, finite evolution.[196] This included portions of the GFofL, Ashtar Command, Great White Brotherhood, Enochians, Thothians, and Jehovians.[203]

In April 2006, the KRH initiated an expedited takeyon activation cycle to override Thetan amplification of Threshold technology.[185] This acceleration was crucial to intercept the Threshold spiral from potentially taking down our entire galaxy into phantom.[326]

In May 2006, the local KRH team succeeded in reclaiming all of the stolen Halls of Amenti gates. The KRH affiliate "M" explains:

> We worked with the Krysthal River Host to gain back control of the Halls of Amenti, and we succeeded to partially access and start rebuilding aspects of the site. The droves of Fallen Ones were diminished and fled. It was a grand fight!
>
> Extra guardians have been placed at the sites to prevent further damage and protect our groups and others from invasion.

Also in May 2006, the MCEO-GA thought it had secured an important victory when the Beli-Mahatma races sought amnesty. The Beli-Mahatma did not want their Hibernation Zone worlds to be transferred to the Bourgha black hole matrices, so they agreed to give many of the Hibernation Zone grids to the MCEO-GA to prevent the fall. However, soon afterward, Bourgha races offered the Beli-Mahatma a deal that was apparently too good to refuse, so they broke their amnesty contracts and handed their grids over to the Bourgha.[199,185] If the MCEO-GA had gained control over some of the Hibernation Zones, then the situation would have been very difficult for Bourgha and Thetan races to fully engage the Threshold.[196]

On January 8, 2007, the Bourgha overpowered Parallel Milky Way Budhara and broke through their barricade to our E-Umbic level. Right away, they worked to fortify their time rip network connection to the Earth as well as the Sun.[199]

Krysthal River Host Protective Measures

The Krysthal River Host (KRH) lent us an energy arm to counteract the amplification of the Threshold machine. As I mentioned in chapter 7's "Creation" section, these Krysthal councils initiated a more powerful tri-matrix triangulation than that of the Bourgha because the KRH consists of Eckasha and earlier frequencies. The KRH is well beyond the influence of Metatronic technologies because, as the MCEO state and ATI,TPE confirms, no black hole technology has ever reached the Eckasha level.[196] However, on our galactic level, the Threshold weapon is comprised of a different power that is partially aligned to our semi-phantom state and can sever the Earth's and Milky Way's links to Galaxy-2 and AquaLaShA.[185]

The KRH spiral is designed to not only suspend the Milky Way and Earth from falling into phantom matrices, it also infuses the Milky Way with natural energies that can potentially correct it toward Krysthal configuration. This KRH energy is particularly extended to the Earth, stargate-6 Sirius B, and stargate-9 Mirach for their long-standing passageways to Galaxy-2 and then AquaLaShA.[185,208]

KRH races assembled different stargate structures on Earth to serve as rescue gates if the natural planetary stargates fall or are destroyed. After the failure of the Bridge Zone Project, the Guardian races began to activate these dormant structures, each having 12 rescue gates. The most notable gates are the Spanner, Arc of the Covenant, and Trinity gates.

The Spanner gates initially directly connected to Urtha to anchor the KRH spiral into the Earth. Spanner gates are natural gate systems that occur in hosted systems like the Milky Way. The MCEO states that Spanner gates require full 24-strand DNA activation for passage through them in order to provide extra protection from infiltration.[208,199] However, this amount of activation is unfeasible for the Human condition.

The Earth's Arc of the Covenant gates are coded with 12-strand DNA activation. They link to the Aurora Silver Seed gates in the Aurora Trans-harmonic Field between Earth and AshaLA, and AshaLA and Urtha, states the ATI,TPE. The Aurora races from the KRH Eckashas and Hub realms impart their Krysthal energies to the Aurora Field.[185,202] Recall from chapter 7 that a Hub is the space or plate between an Eckasha level, Ecka, and Veca and their parallel systems through which earlier Krysthal energies can gently integrate into denser light-body mechanics. If the Sphere and every Hall of Amenti would fall, then the KRH would hold open the Arc of the Covenant passage, which Ashayana calls a Hub passage, that links the 12 Arc gates on Earth to AshaLA as the intermediary to Urtha.[327]

The Trinity gates were designed to help Humans with average DNA activation to pass through the Arc and Spanner gates. The Spanner, Arc of the Covenant, and Trinity gates were plugged into each other for lower frequency Humans to enter.[327]

There are three additional Spanner core gates that connect the Earth's core to Urtha's core by way of AshaLA. Every Spanner gate interfaces with these Spanner core gates. Two of the core gates had to be closed by the Urtha Aquari races due to attacks by the Beli-Kudyem during the Great Encasement of 9562 B.C. Its Earthly Beli-Mahatma hybrid then connected these gates to the Hibernation Zones through Mount Shasta. The third core gate called Shala-13 partially fell.[196] The preserved part contained only the Spanner-7 gate ascension passage to Urtha. This gate is in the United States in Phoenix, Arizona in a location surrounding Scottsdale and Mesa. Humans with Aquafereion genetic codes have caused all 12 Arc Hub gates to open and plug into Arc-7, which then plugged into Spanner-7.[197,199]

On January 20, 2007, the KRH Gyrodome technology blocked Wesadrak races' attempts to activate their neighboring Threshold-7 Tower complex that could take over the Spanner-7 gate and nearby grid space.[185] Threshold Towers were anchored into important locations of the planet to connect to the greater wormhole and time rip structures controlled by the Thetans and Bourgha races.[199] The Gyrodome was set into sections of Earth's and Tara's grids by Aquari races about one billion years ago. It serves to increase the Krysthal Spiral frequencies into these grids while also deflecting or preventing Metatronic frequencies.[328]

When this information was given to Ashayana, some MCEO-GA entities warned that if the Spanner-7 gate complex is usurped by the BEA-O, the Earth would no longer maintain its ascension potential.[197] One reason for their warning was unawareness about other options. Certain Aquari races and higher level beings in the KRH have been working on the Aurora Field project in a space-between-space dimension that connects earlier plasma energies to Earth, ultimately merging it with Urtha. This process has been planned and developed for eons, so it is surprising to me that the MCEO-GA's message was narrowly focused and overly startling. However, if a certain group gives information regarding its particular focus and sense of urgency, then it can and often does exclude other realities.

Using the Gyrodome, the KRH spiral was able to interface with the Threshold machine, bending two-thirds of the Metatronic frequency onto the

KRH spiral and putting it back to the natural spin. This reduced the power of the Threshold to one-third of its full energy, states the MCEO. In addition, the KRH energy arm prevented the Threshold and its related alien entities from completely taking over our bodies.

Around this time, Bourgha in their matrices were firing pulses through Wesadrak's grid into their time rip network to captured portions of Earth with the objective of hitting prime planetary locations such as Giza's stargate-4. KRH races were aware of these events and deflected the pulses in time.[199]

In March 2007, the KRH Councils gave a Stand-Down Order to the Bourgha races: if they continued to assist Thetan and Wesadrak races in their quest to conquer the Earth, the KRH Gyrodome would refract most of the pulse through their links back to their original matrix. The Bourgha races refused the Order. They blasted more energy into the Threshold complex to try to override KRH energy, which they erroneously thought they could do. The Gyrodome performed its function as the KRH Councils warned it would. The blast through the Time Rip connection bounced off the Gyrodome and initiated the space dust implosion process within some—not all, states the ATI,TPE—of the Bourgha matrices.[185,208] The Bourgha worked for eons to divert energy into their matrices, and now many of them will finally get to experience the direct consequence to their actions that underestimate natural creation mechanics.

The ATI,TPE states that the Parallel Milky Way and Milky Way galaxies were the first external system that the Bourgha sought to fully consume. This is why, after hundreds of billions of years, Bourgha matrices have not yet faced the probability of annihilation until now.

The ATI,TPE explains that the plethora of death science technologies cannot divert our Milky Way and Parallel Milky Way galaxies into the dying Bourgha matrices. However, the Bourgha probably already connected their time rip network to their remaining matrices to continue siphoning away energy matter.

Unfortunately, a result of their evil actions overloaded the solar core of our Sun, causing it to spasm. This spasm caused the Sun's energy to lock, cutting the natural "breathing" between it and its dark matter template. In other words, our Sun began the death process, which I will explain in the "2022" section.[185]

According to the MCEO, on April 2007, Bourgha-Budhara races took over command of all Red Dragon and UIR groups manipulating Earth; however, based on the information I provided about Michael's Shantarel group, many Bourgha entities were already in command. In May 2007, KRH races prevented the Bourgha from capturing Spanner Gate-7 in Phoenix by activating the Aqualene Sun buffer field as part of the ancient Aqualene

Transmission plan that steps down CosMA'yah currents into the Aurora Field.

In February 2008, the Bourgha-White Dragon races took control of the Hibernation Zones and phantom alien activity on Earth. In October 2008, Zetas intended to invade the Earth via the Hibernation Zones, and the Bourgha-White Dragons wanted this plan to go unhindered. The Zeta ship invasion would have created mass panic and global-wide allegiance to the fallen angelic Bourgha races who would save us from the Greys in yet another false savior fabrication. The Bourgha races also had an All Kill agenda against Humanity, so our obedience to them would facilitate our demise. Thankfully, KRH races managed to shut down most of the Hibernation Zone gates in time to block their easy access to us and prevent these assaults. As a response, Bourgha races have increased their meddling in world affairs, including the global financial crisis in 2008 that was set up by the subprime mortgage collapse. The MCEO states that the serious economic recession was orchestrated to destabilize Illuminati families sympathetic to the Green Dragons in order to begin full takeover of world governments leading into 2012.[185]

In 2009, the KRH team moved the Arc of the Covenant passage from Giza to Ireland, a remnant of Atlantis, and keyed it to Higher Earth and the Aurora Field, which could bypass our potentially dysfunctional Halls of Amenti.[185,308] It also activated the Shield of Solomon, a square diamond-shaped shield, to hold onto the Earth's two natural rods. The Shield covers nearly one-sixth of the Earth and also surrounds the false Caduceus West rod that is situated in the Gulf of Mexico. As the KRH team managed the false West rod, they also mitigated the false East rod spin, which the BEA-O has progressively activated in Southeast Asia to cause the 2004 tsunami among other earthquakes.[308] The Shield was able to do this because it contains three major frequency rings that correspond to the seven CosMA'yah krystars in the Eckasha-Ah domain.[329]

In 2010, the Sphere of Amenti was finally returned to Median Earth's core from Urtha, states the ATI,TPE with confirmation from "M." Earth, Higher Earth, and Median Earth each contain a number of the eight total Halls of Amenti portals to keep their connections to the Sphere.

In 2011, two of the three Shield of Solomon rings were breached by FAtalE—phantom Phim-Bourgha-Equari—infiltrators who cracked light-plasma codes specific to the Shield's Earth interface, starting with the lower-frequency violet ring and ending with the intermediate green ring. The three Aqualene krystars relate to the preserved but vulnerable light blue ring. The breach caused the two rings to anchor the Metatronic spiral.[329] It also boosted the spiral with artificial violet plasma that is generated by a Bourgha Phantom Ecka Central Sun. The FAtalE originally harnessed the lowest CosMA'yah violet current near its Ecka and created an artificial plasma synthesizer of "violet rays of consumption" to siphon energy into the artificial Deity planes (see chapter 7's "Archangel Michael" section). The artificial violet ray reproduced its green and blue ray sub-currents to allow the FAtalE access to the higher-coded rings.[330]

On October 25, 2011, Michael gave a prophecy to Celia Fenn that said people would anchor the 7th dimensional current on November 11, 2011, but he neglected to say it was from the Phantom Milky Way and Wesadek blend. Duped New Age followers gathered on that day to set up their bodies to receive and download it into the Earth. Previously, the Phantom Milky Way and Wesadek 6th dimensional current blend was sent in August 2011. Below, I interject in three places with brackets to reveal the true meaning.

"Light Codes" or "Cosmic Codes" of Renewal are received into the Crystalline grids of the Earth. The Reception of the Codes of Renewal will again accelerate the frequencies of the Earth Hologram, allowing for Reconnection with the Seventh Dimension of Consciousness....

Then, in August of 2011, at the time of the Lion's Gate, you took another Great Step forward as you connected with the Sixth Dimension and the Flows of Abundance and Manifestation that will unlock the New Earth. Those of you who were ready anchored these energies into the "Rose Lines" of the Crystalline grids, those energetic meridians that carry the Cosmic Christ Consciousness [Phantom Milky Way and Wesadek HU-4 energies] from the Divine Heart [Black Heart implant] into the Heart Grid of the Planet [Giza].

Now, at the 11/11/11, those of you...will anchor the Seventh Dimension, the Consciousness of the Ascended Masters of Light.

There are many Indigo-Crystal beings, both the young and those who have awakened and made the shift, who are now ready to embrace a New Soul Purpose for the New Earth. This New Soul Purpose will align fully with the New Earth and by the 12/12/12 Homecoming Celebration in 2012, this Group of Soul Leaders will have seeded the new structures and communities that will take the Earth across the Rainbow bridge and into the Final Triple Stargate of Time gate. This will be the period from 12/12/12 to 21/12/12, a period of 9 days in which the final integrations and alignments with the Cosmic Heart will be achieved, and the earth will be "re-set" for her next Grand Cycle of Evolution into Peace, Harmony and Love.[331]

Metatron and Michael like to use numerology with repeated, triple numbers, such as 10-10-10, 11-11-11, and 12-12-12. In the prophecy where the above excerpt is taken, Michael calls these triple numbers portals or stargates, which the dates symbolize. This information reveals his objective to merge the stargates of Earth and Phantom Earth, Milky Way and Phantom Milky Way, and Wesadek as the completed Cube Matrix.[321]

To paraphrase the above prophecy, Michael says that our current Earth is not our home, and we should be directed elsewhere. He also said this theme in a previous channeling in chapter 7's "Archangel Michael" section. I have never agreed with this message as taught in religion because all Earth organisms are integrated with the Earth as our home.

The KRH and its allies have set up more than one option for our natural ascension because of their exhaustive history with varied BEA-O (and FatalE) attacks. They have worked toward a fail-safe path of ascension while also wanting to allow the Earth its evolutionary path toward Tara. Although the Earth cannot merge with Tara in the foreseeable future, its new connections must build upon pre-existing ascension mechanics, so it is important to learn about the Earth's organic ascension process.

Earth's Ascension Cycles with Tara

Each harmonic universe in the Milky Way and Galaxy-2 has a harmonic time cycle through which planets evolve and infuse their three-dimensional bands, and then they shift along with collaborative higher HU cycles. This natural cycle is called a Euiago, and it is about 5,000 years longer than Higher Earth's 26,556 year general precession, states the ATI,TPE. Median Earth as the remaining portion of Amenti Earth runs on the proper Euiago cycle. As I explain in chapter 10's "Milky Way Base-12 Mathematics," there are six Euiagos that prepare the Earth for full ascension to Tara. If each Euiago is roughly 31,550 years, then the entire HU-1 process of evolution would take approximately 189,300 years.

Entity groups, including the MCEO-GA, have erroneously amalgamated the unnatural general precession wobble with the natural harmonic time cycle. Therefore, many interpretations of the Euiago cycle base it upon the general precession or precession of the equinoxes. This is careless information because dimensional blend periods from the equinoxes and solstices involve numerous interactions with Parallel Earth, often with phantom energies; those frequency blends are not the same as the Earth growing within its own harmonic universe. I asked the ATI,TPE if our current Euiago was altered to the general precession cycle, and it says, "Yes." This is because the NET fields expedited it to meet the Parallel Earth's SAC.

As I stated in "Atlantean Obstacles," the MCEO-GA says that the next natural SAC is supposed to happen in 4230 A.D.; however, this is not the Amenti Earth time cycle, thereby bringing into question what is really natural. The ATI,TPE states that our current Euiago is supposed to end c. 4500 A.D., and it started c. 27,000 B.C. As for Higher Earth's 26,556 general precession cycle that would near its end at 4230 A.D., and the Earth's 25,920-year general precession, one of these cycles best corresponds to Sirius B's orbit; therefore, our Earth would increasingly show that it no longer aligns with Sirius B if its current 25,771-year cycle continues.

With this said, I will show the prevalent entity-based interpretations in reference to the general precession because they provide a spring board toward greater analysis. We can remain cognizant that the original harmonic ascension cycle is a different time cycle and overall event. Although the MCEO obfuscates this topic, its mechanical explanation largely supports a proper Euiago.

Twentieth century A.D. alchemist Fulcanelli was an alleged occultist who must have obtained knowledge about the outdated 25,920-cycle because he taught that the Earth's general precession is divided into four cycles within this time frame. Mayan calendar enthusiasts equate its end date to the end of the last Hindu Yuga cycle, the Kali Yuga, as depicted in Vedic texts. Yugas are also divided into four cycles of time, but they are significantly longer as ages of successively less years, starting at the Golden Age of 1,728,000 years and ending at the Iron Age of 432,000 years.[332]

Fulcanelli interpreted the angel with four faces in the Book of Revelation as the quadrants of the universe that relate to the general precession. One of the quadrants is the Leo constellation as the Age of Aquarius, which is one of the signs of apocalyptic change. The New Age community sees it as a shift toward greater consciousness. The number four can also represent four-dimensional space. What is most telling is how scientists view the four-dimensional structure.

Author Jay Weidner writes:

> In modern physics, it is well known that four-dimensional space, of which time is an aspect, is in the shape of a hypersphere....
> A hypersphere is similar to the shape of a doughnut or bagel. Physicists call this hypersphere a torus.... [The] hypersphere torus is also represented by the hypercube (p. 201).[332]

The hypersphere torus looks like the Poison Apple configuration of energy manipulation. The cube is also Metatron's favored geometry. "As the energy flow begins to fall into the vortex that runs through the center of the sphere, it takes on the shape of a tetrahedron," states Weidner (p. 203).[332] As I have asserted, physicists unfortunately deem the Metatronic geometries to be natural, and most have based their models off of such distortions.

There are only four times during a Euiago when the Earth interacts with Parallel Earth and Parallel Tara to gain different dimensional frequency in preparation for transfiguration to Tara. There are six time cycles within a Euiago, which the MCEO-GA state are 4,426 years each. In the first cycle, Earth fuses twice with Parallel Earth, once at the midpoint and once at the end. Both of these time periods are called Primary Conjunction Points. In the sixth cycle, the two time periods are called Primary Coordinate Points because the Earth's grid fuses with Parallel Tara's grid. The occurrences of both sets of points in six cycles of progressive accretion through the HU-1 bands constitute the full ascension cycle.[120]

Although the Earth began to interact with Tara in 2000, it more directly interacts with Parallel Tara due to their compatible particle pulsation rates, otherwise known as time. The process of ascension brings lower pulsations from HU-1 to a higher and less dense state that operates at a faster, light-filled speed. Parallel Earth and Tara operate at a pulsation rate that is twice as fast as that of Earth and Parallel Tara, so Earth's involvement with Tara's antiparticle base tones gives it the necessary energetic shift to meet with Parallel Earth and then Tara in a collaborative effort.[120]

The second stage of the sixth time cycle concerns us. Earth's overtone particles progressively merge with Parallel Tara's base antiparticles until the energy exchange builds up in their morphogenetic fields and creates a backflow or morphogenetic wave. During the wave, the "Earth's overtone particles become progressively suspended in hyper-space and the dimensional base-tone frequencies left within the Earth's grid begin to blend with the overtone anti-particles in Tara's grid," says the GA (p. 112).[120] When the wave reaches its threshold five years later at the Primary Coordinate Point, the conjoined particles would undergo fission and replication into their respective higher harmonic universes. This is when Tara and Earth would have been fully aligned, and "Earth's overtone particles re-manifest as Tara's base-tone anti-particles and Tara's base-tone anti-particles re-manifest as Gaia's particles," says the GA (p. 112).[120] Interestingly, the GA states that the last morphogenetic wave created the Photon Belt around the Pleiades, which is a claim that our scientific community has yet to verify.

As the Earth's base tones and Parallel Tara's overtones blend, a harmonic resonant tone is formed, which causes both matter and antimatter to temporarily reverse in spin and shift in angular rotation to meet in the 4th dimension. When their electromagnetic fields are in balance, the changes do not cause either planet to shift on its axis. The GA elaborates:

Some fluctuation in Earth's magnetism may be detected, and some tectonic movement may occur in areas that are not fully energetically balanced, but the basic structure of the Earth's body will remain intact.... *It is very important that the Earth's bio-energetic structure and electromagnetic grid are balanced during this five-year period* (p. 113).[120]

Our current time in Earth history is magnificent because we entered the last 10-year morphogenetic wave of the last Earth's Euiago cycle on December 21, 2012 A.D. On this date, some of the embattled Halls of Amenti passages opened, according to the ATI,TPE and Eia, and it is possible that they could fully open by this SAC's last Primary Coordinate Point on December 21, 2017. *Voyagers II* conveys that the 3-day crest would transpire several months earlier in May 2017. I confirmed with the ATI,TPE that this now invalid schedule planned to connect the theoretical Bridge Zone Earth during the electrical peak with the harmonic resonance of Tara.

During the full crest around December 21, 2017, the 8th dimensional meta-galactic core of the Milky Way galaxy should spiral energy "through the planetary cores of Earth, Tara, and Gaia for about 3 days, and the grids of Earth and Tara are in complete alignment" (p.116);[120] however, it is unclear how much of Gaia, Tara, and Earth will receive that energy. Gaia and Tara are now predominantly phantom, and the Earth has started to infuse Aurora Field energy. For the next five years until December 21, 2022, the morphogenetic wave would progressively slow until the final ascension process is completed.

Ideally, a fulfilled ascension toward Tara would have the entire Earth merge with Tara, Tara merge with Gaia, Gaia merge with Aramatena, and Aramatena merge with its HU-5 counterpart so that all fractal versions of these energetically similar planets would eventually gain Krysthal matter outside of the Milky Way in a safe Ecka level. Realistically, the damage that Earth and Tara have sustained will keep the Earth in HU-1 for an extended time period. It remains to be seen if a portion of its quanta could meet with the non-phantom remnant of Tara through an Amenti gate portal.

To hopefully solve the Earth's struggles, the end of 2012 brought the Earth a new ascension path toward not only the Aurora Field but to outside of the Milky Way. The following sections introduce this ascension path; finally, the "2022" section will put the Earth's SAC into context with recent events.

2012 Dimensional Blend Drama and 2013 Hope

In its accelerated Earth timeline to meet Parallel Earth's SAC, the BEA-O planned to use Metatronic wormhole structures to blend both Earths' templars. To preempt them from opening the Halls of Amenti early, KRH races unfortunately decided to open the Halls early in order to commence their now defunct Bridge Zone Project. They wanted to postpone this "Final Conflict Drama" until the Earth's organic SAC on 4,430 A.D. (26,556 years from the last failed SAC), but they did not expect the Earth to last that long.[182] They believed "that the Earth would meet a cataclysmic end in the future probability of 2976 AD," states the MCEO, because fully Metatronic aspects of Parallel Milky Way, including Parallel Earth, are predicted to explode by that time.[182] This does not necessitate Earth destruction because non-phantom portions can still be preserved; however, if they could destroy our Sun, then the Earth would be in peril.

As I introduced in "Atlantean Obstacles," the BEA-O plan for 2012 A.D. was to use the Solar Time-Torus Tunnel wormhole, which binds the Sun and Parallel Sun orbits and aligns their galactic core stargates, to open the Great Toral Rift Time Rip spacetime deflection field as it stood at 10,948 B.C., literally linking that moment in the past with 2012 A.D. If the Earth and Parallel Earth SAC stargates open in unison, then the spacetime deflection field would bring them and their Suns into the Phantom Alpha-Omega galactic alignments of that time.[182]

The New Age movement has claimed that the projected 2012 galactic alignment is an uncommon star map alignment that would have positioned the Earth at the galactic plane. An astronomy enthusiast, Bruce McClure, clears up this claim.

> No, Earth will not pass through the *galactic plane* in 2012, contrary to what you might have heard. Earth won't be physically passing through the plane of the Milky Way galaxy for another 30 million years. However, Earth will cross the galactic equator in 2012. As seen from the sun, the Earth does this every year – twice.[333]

The MCEO explains that the proper alignments are about the invisible rods and staffs of the planetary, star, and galactic bodies.

> The Staff is the North central vertical [lateral] column (axis) of the Kathara Grid and the Merkaba field of our large vertical [lateral] Parameter field [Note: the lateral designation applies to large fields with many objects; the vertical designation applies to a single body's central column].... The Rod is a column of frequency that spins on the horizontal, Harmonic Shield and as [it] spins it brings frequency into our personal shields which we experience

the manifest hologram....There is a direct connection between the Rods and Staffs of Kristiac Systems. As energy circulates there is an energetic interaction between the Rod of one system and the... Staff of another.[334]

Each planetary, stellar, and galactic body contains an East-West rod and a front-back rod chamber that interfaces with the natural kathara grid rod. These rods come out of the center horizon of the body at 90 degree angles to each other. The rods of the planet and Sun pass through each other in a Yan-Yun electromagnetic flow, forming the larger Lotus Arc flow, as I introduced in chapter 7's "Creation" section. The naturally zero degree tilt of their staffs allows the Sun to pass quanta to the planet that is spinning in the same plane. Our system does not look like this.

The BeaST's Gravitron technology put the Earth on a 23.5 degree angle to align it with Parallel Earth because Parallel Earth was already manipulated to that angle in the opposite direction. This extreme tilt allows vortex networks to jump in between the Earth and the Sun. Additionally, the Gravitron harness diverts the Yan-Yun into the Metatronic Yin-Yang "Poison Apple" torsion field that circulates energy within itself. Yin-yang, the popular phrase in Eastern religion, contains distorted polarities that cut off the Earth's "breath" toward Earth's ultimate demise.

Parallel Earth travels around Parallel Sun in the clockwise direction while our Earth travels around the Sun in the counter-clockwise direction. Twice a year during the vernal (spring) and autumnal equinoxes, Earth and Parallel Earth merge while they pass through each other, states the MCEO. For a week each side of the equinox, the Earth's stargates open, allowing passage between these two planets. During the winter and summer solstices, Earth and Parallel Earth are on opposite sides of the Sun. At these times, the planetary rods interface with those of the Sun's solar rods, allowing passage between Earth and Parallel Earth through the Sun's core.[308] This is why New Agers, pagans, and etcetera like to perform certain rituals on equinoxes and solstices. People were taught during the Atlantean mind-wipes to keep track of the equinoxes and solstices so they could know when their gods from Parallel Earth would return.

During the Earth's SAC, the Milky Way galactic chamber aligns with our Sun's rod. This is what happens during the natural galactic alignment. It is these alignments of the galactic, solar, and planetary rods that allow stargate passages to open. Additionally, the MCEO states that the spinning action of the rods facilitates the opening of the stargates.

Our natural planetary rods have been distorted by a frequency split, forming false rods called Caduceus rods. To make this happen, the Earth was struck by both a frequency blast through the Parallel Earth wormhole and an asteroid to roll the crust North and East to align the Earth with Parallel Earth. The 0 degree Prime Meridian at Greenwich, England and the opposite 180 degree International Dateline reflect the accelerated base pulse rhythm of the new alignment. In addition, the natural rods split and shifted upward from the Equator to the Tropic of Cancer.[308]

The Caduceus rods are held in place by specific BEA-O bases containing implant technology predominantly in the Earth's mantle so that the spinning rods could heat up the mantle to facilitate crust movement. The MCEO informs that the BEA-O has controlled 48 Alpha-Omega bases on Earth to hold these false rod alignments. The alignments were required to connect with Parallel Earth alignments so that the major pole shift plan could come to fruition. When the technology activates the Caduceus rods, they literally create vortexes and sink holes through which the planetary structure can be sucked into the wormholes. This is how Atlantis and Lumeria "sunk" into the Hibernation Zones.

The BEA-O planned to aim a frequency blast at the Earth's false rod via a wormhole from Parallel Earth that would drag it into the Sun and then Abaddon. When such a harsh frequency hits a planetary rod and makes it spin, this snaps the crust and causes the pole to shift unless buffer fields are put in place, which the KRH did provide.[308] This is why we constantly see references to the 2012 pole shift, especially in disaster movies such as *2012*. Sadly, this event succeeded on Parallel Earth in 2003.[316]

The pole shift would have moved the rods to the position of the planetary and solar polar alignments that existed in 10,948 B.C. when the Great Toral Rift Time Rip experiment was implemented. The spinning rods would have triggered the core of the Earth's merkaba to hit a 55.5 spin-speed activation. The merkaba fields of our solar system and parallel solar system would then become progressively compressed and drawn back in time, compacting into a vesica piscis bond as the two solar systems intersect to engage the vesica piscis orbit.

During this process, both solar system spin-speeds would merge into a 55 one-way spin-speed merkaba field called the Death Star. Death Stars contain an internal encasement harness that surrounds energy matter and acts like a vortex to expedite their spin-speeds along the Fibonacci expression. When it accelerates to 144 rotations—each per trillionth of a billionth of a nanosecond (PTBN)—it becomes an automatic feeding spiral that consumes the solar systems within it and then transfers the energy matter to a giant Death Star external merkaba. Our atomic structures will implode, explode, and shatter into raw energy of "hyper-accelerated space-dust."[182]

December 21, 2012 provided the BEA-O the opportunity to execute its deadly plan because of the winter solstice connection to Parallel Earth. According to the MCEO, if the Earth's merkaba reached 55 PTBN spin-speed on that date (which really would have been 55.5 PTBN for the greater momentum), Earth would have been thrusted into a 40-day window of chaos from December 21, 2012 until February 1, 2013 as the spin would "reach critical acceleration to 'Metatronic Death Star Merkaba 144 spin-speed.'"[182]

The space dust would have been pulled into the dying Sun, and the entire solar system quanta would transfer through the solar rod passage that is in alignment with the galactic rod.[327] To achieve the Parallel and Milky Way merkaba and dimensional blends, the BEA-O has worked to unnaturally align their particle and antiparticle rods and staffs to the form or sign of the cross.

The Solar Cross involves the solar Death Star merkaba with the following construction: stargate-3 Earth would connect to stargate-10 Vega, and stargate-4 Sun would connect to stargate-9 Andromeda. This pattern would be repeated in the Parallel Milky Way. The next stage is to combine their merkabas to form the 55 same spin-speed Grand Cross Death Star with the central axis between the merged Parallel and Milky Way galaxies that would progressively eat the galaxies as it expands, or rather compacts, to the full 144 same spin-speed.

The external, giant Death Star merkaba field would be used to create a massive "rip in space-time" that would drag the Wesadrak black hole matrix along with the Parallel and Milky Way galaxies into Wesadek, giving it enough quanta to sustain its inhabitants for many eons. It is the fully functioning Death Star merkaba—not a supermassive black hole—that continuously consumes energy to sustain the hells of finite creation. The Bourgha controllers would then siphon some of the energy through wormhole or time rip connections to their surviving matrices.

The BEA-O planned this grand galactic dimensional blend to commence during the Earth's Hetharo on May 28, 2003 because Parallel Earth's axis aligned with Wesadek's 22.5 degree axis. When its agenda failed, it aimed for December 21, 2012.[323]

The MCEO illuminates the BEA-O's religious and material objective in its "Topic Summary 2" official disclosure statement:

> Through creation of the Artificial Death Star Black Hole Galaxy — an abomination of Metatronic "Bloom of Doom" Death Science creation — the "Alpha-Omega False God-Head" falling Illuminati-Elder collectives hope to "Re-create Creation in their Own Image." They hope to use the Death Star Galaxy to "create, then assimilate, others of its kind," to form a massive Death Star Universe that sustains its existence and averts the

organic consequence of eternal Cosmic Physics Laws.[182]

If this plan had materialized, all Earth organisms would become re-formed into mutated copies of what we once were. We would be subjected to a total memory wipe, potentially becoming a living-dead consciousness with severe Alzheimer's and autistic genetic mutations. The MCEO states that the transformed living-dead "life" field would no longer give us free will choice and eternal life ascension because we would become slaves to the BEA-O Gods in a type of purgatory until our atomic material might permanently turn into space dust.

The MCEO explains:

> With activation of the "Metatronic 55-Blending Ratio" the "Common-man Blended DNA Mutation" becomes permanent, and human DNA becomes permanently transformed from that of the original eternal-life Angelic Human species genome, into the inorganic finite-life genetic imprint of a new Illuminati-Leviathan mutant-hybrid-human Fall-species, predestined to temporary subjugated dominance, and intended eventual extermination, by the Illuminati-Elder races to which its mutated Encryption Lattice is connected.[182]
>
> [Note: The encryption lattice is the part of the morphogenetic template upon which thoughts, ideas, emotions, and matter-forms create a literal radiation field that flows according to what the MCEO calls the "Law of Reciprocal Attraction" or cause and effect of energetic consequence.[182] The encryption lattice works with the core frequency-vibration to ebb and flow with whatever it attracts and thereby creates a new type of morphogenetic template. It is true that thought-energy and associated words have the potential to shape matter.]

To protect the Earth, the KRH planned to implement the "Living Mirror in the Sky" deflection field around it when the December 21, 2012 galactic blast came from Abaddon's alignment network. The Mirror involves 48 massive plasmic Krysthal ray ships that form armored interlocking plates, each about the size of the Shield of Solomon to effectively surpasses the damaged Shield. It also effectively shields the Earth against any reversed violet plasma ship invasion that would step up the BEA-O offense. The Mirror would refract the blast back to its origin with at least 12 times the strength of the blast. This would cause severe consequences to those races and their systems.[330,327]

The KRH also synchronized the activation of their Cosminyahas-infused

Silver Seed Host Grid with the Alpha-Omega harness grid to engage one-third of Earth's encryption lattice and time cycle with slower moving ascension stargates of Higher Earth.[182]

The MCEO predicted with confidence:

> There is nothing the Illuminati Force can do to prevent or override the direct intervention of the Guardians' Stardust Silver Seed Ascension Grid; the Illuminati Force will discover the truth of this reality when they find that the Cataclysmic Pole Shift of Earth, which they are currently predicting for 2013–2015, does not occur as they plan.[182]

The GA stated in *Voyagers II* that the Halls of Amenti would begin to open in May 2012. If they would have opened in May, then why was the prevailing focus on December 21? The reason for the later date was because May incurred a significant struggle that nearly pulled Earth into phantom. My KRH affiliate contacts confirmed that "the Halls of Amenti started to open in December 2012 instead for the time frame was pushed ahead due to the May 2012 troubling event." Ashayana Deane, Speaker-1 for the MCEO and GA, also publicly split from her Speaker-2 and Speaker-3 colleagues during this critical time.

The troubling event was on May 27 when the BEA-O sent a Metatronic-55 blast several months before its planned 55.5 merkaba reversal on December 21, 2012. This strong attack overrode and reversed the KRH Gyrodome frequency that anchored into Aurora platforms in between the Hibernation Zones. The Aurora platforms connected to the Earth and provided safe zones until the blast compromised their energies. The blast also penetrated the Earth to push its merkaba to a reversed 55 spin-speed. The BEA-O planned to redirect the Gyrodome current to Parallel Earth and use it to merge Parallel Earth with Earth.[208,186,335]

As I illuminate in chapter 10, certain entities and Humans as part of the MCEO-GA's varied affiliations have siphoned fully phantom energy into their Earth grid work. Ashayana concurred this was happening in the lead-up to the May 27 blast about which she knew beforehand in April, but she rather attributed the phantom energy to attacks upon vulnerable members (which is also true).[330]

In Ashayana's August 2012 workshop, she explained that "the beloveds" allowed the Metatronic-55 blast to bring the Earth precariously close to its demise in order to prompt its Krysthal code to "drag it all back into balance."[186] This explanation implies that destruction is the way to prompt a response from Krysthal creation to somehow heal it, but as I previously stated, finite creation is external to Krysthal creation, not within it to prompt an auto-immune response. In fact, in 2009, Ashayana said that the Mirror in the Sky and Shield of Solomon (later as a remnant) would not only hold the Caduceus rods in place but maybe roll them marginally backwards to prevent the torque toward pole shift.[308] They were also designed to hold the Earth's merkaba in place, confirms the ATI,TPE. Plans are usually imprecise estimations, but the MCEO did not give any indication that they would fail. Telling the story after-the-fact in a type of religious "I secretly planned it that way" manner should give us reflective pause concerning the highly unsettling event.

Thankfully, the Earth was not pulled further away into the Death Star merkaba due to the help of KRH and affiliated entity groups, including the predominantly Phim-based Alhumbhra Council (AC). On October 11, 2012, the KRH activated the Alhumbhra Cathedrals Network on Earth that allowed us to re-establish control of the Gyrodome current and initiate permanent Death Star merkaba deactivation that would permanently prevent the Great Toral Rift Time Rip pole shift. The Earth's merkaba returned to its previously reversed spin-speed directions of 34 counter-clockwise over 21 clockwise.[335]

Between December 21, 2012 and January 3, 2013, the efforts of the KRH and its allies came to fruition when they finally infused enough stable quanta and plasma into the Earth through the Aurora Field to establish a secure, fail-safe ascension situation. On December 23, 2012, the Alhumbhra Cathedrals Network brought in energy that vaporized our Earth's Metatronic Seed atom! By December 30, 2012, the Earth's core gained an HU-1 version of the Cosminyahas core Silver Seed core unit. The Earth is now a proper ascension planet being slowly directed and transformed toward the Aurora Field and its Krysthal connections, which the ATI,TPE confirms.[335]

Aurora Ascension Earth

Aquafereions created four Aurora platform zones with Gyrodome technology that replicated parts of Earth's and Urtha's energy fields and connected them to the Aquious Hub to sustain the Earth from fall.[208] The platforms exist within the greater Aurora Trans-Harmonic Field. After the platforms were closed above Earth, the Gyrodome was progressively deactivated to our region in favor of the protected DhA'YahTEi Planes (D-Planes). D-Planes are a type of plasmic Hub interface to the CosMA'yah domain that allow CosMA'yah and Cosminyahas currents to flow to the Aurora Field, as the ATI,TPE confirms. The D-Planes—where many Alhumbhra Council members exist—support current Earth weaknesses with their unique energies as part of a very large Krysthal River Host. Buffered DhA'YahTEi currents of the CosMA'yah and Cosminyahas Silver Seed core fully anchored into related

D-Span gates on Earth between December 21, 2012 and January 3, 2013.[335] D-Span gates bypass damaged Spanner gates.

The Aurora Field safely allows the merging of Earth with its other ascension-viable versions that previously became divided due to fallen angelic invasion. Currently, if Urtha's gates opened to Earth, our Earth would blow up because it cannot hold the frequency of Urtha. The Aurora Field creates a meeting place between the two worlds.[208]

At the time of writing this book, the Earth upon which we live is less than one-sixth quanta of Amenti Earth since it has been divided multiple times, states the ATI,TPE. The MCEO gives simplified quotients of halves and thirds without clearly delineating Higher Earth and potentially other portions.[271] Therefore, I will largely refrain from repeating its quotients except for a few examples, and I will state what we have learned about the divided Earth levels.

A portion of Amenti Earth quanta was pulled into the growing Phantom Milky Way to form Phantom Earth. Another measure of Amenti Earth quanta was split to form Higher and Lower Earths as progressive mutations occurred during the Atlantean period. The MCEO has renamed the remaining portion of Amenti Earth as Median Earth. Higher Earth and our Earth can be considered as blended planets of partially phantom and partially Amenti material, but our Earth's construction contains more phantom quanta.

When the Hibernation Zones were fully formed in 9562 B.C., the blended Earths were further pulled apart. The MCEO states that one-half of "Blended Earth" quanta were captured and placed on reverse spin to form Caduceus Earth within the Hibernation Zones (p. 241).[271] All of these Earths exist side by side with slight separations, matter variations, and ARPS differences.

Fully phantom races have tried to take all Earth portions into Phantom Earth. The original BEA-O plan would have first dragged our Earth into the Hibernation Zones to merge with Caduceus Earth before combining them with Phantom Earth.[271]

Thankfully, in 2008, KRH races largely shut down the Hibernation Zone entry points to our Earth. This helped prevent the apocalyptic alien invasion scenarios planned by the BEA-O. In addition, they worked to connect one-third of the NET Earth grids (ley lines, land masses, etcetera) into the grids of Median Earth before the Metatronic 55.5 technology was sent to hit our Earth on December 21, 2012.[271]

Now that the Aurora platforms between Earth and Median Earth are shut down, a temporary Alhumbhra "Earth" can provide the safe connection. This so-called Earth is really a trans-harmonic, "elemental-atomic plasma field" from the D-Planes.[335] It connects to Earth and both Higher and Median Earths via the Eye of AL-Hum-Bhra Passage to help them integrate with the

Aurora Field and eventual D-Planes of further ascension. The Passage connects to the new Halls of ARhAyas placed within the cores of all three Earths to help infuse eternal Cosminyahas Silver Seed plasma.

A multitude of MCEO-GA entities and their Amenti gate team were aware in varying degrees of the Aurora Field project whereby some chose to participate, while other MCEO-GA members were completely unaware of the project. Both the MCEO and GA are not entirely, internally united, confirms the ATI,TPE.

The AC aims to utilize the Halls of ARhAyas for the Earth's ascension process and has therefore not provided much information about the Halls of Amenti or Arc of the Covenant. The Halls of Amenti have been integral to the health of our Earth by keeping it connected to Sphere of Amenti, and the Arc of the Covenant was created to protect the Sphere while providing another passageway for us. I do not see how they can become overlooked, so I sought answers from another source.

On November 4, 2013, both of my independent KRH affiliate contacts stated the following answers to my several questions that my mother navigated with them concurrently.

> The Sphere of Amenti is partially functioning. If the Sphere of Amenti was not used or usable, which is not the case, the Arc of the Covenant would connect to it and direct it to AshaLA to keep it or allow it functioning ability. [The Arc of the Covenant is not connected to it by default, nor does it necessarily have the structural integrity to reach Urtha that is light years away unless additional extensions are added, elaborates "M."] It is true that the SAC-in-progress would continue due to the Sphere's partial functioning ability.

> Our groups are still working to reconnect the Halls of Amenti to Median Earth, for they were partially shattered by the Fallen Ones when they seized them in the 2003 invasion and takeover. The Halls of ARhAyas are not presently our focus unless the mission to reconnect the Halls of Amenti completely fails.

When I asked if all the Earth stargate and SAC connections to the unfallen part of Tara are now severed, one KRH affiliate replied, "No, not entirely, but we are trying to salvage them." The KRH and allied groups are working to fulfill the historical promise of our immediate SAC. The projected timeline toward Tara is in the process of being directed to Median Earth, as I explain in the upcoming "2022" section.

The MCEO originally predicted that the KRH would host or protect the

Earth from phantom fall until 2230 A.D., but the success of the DhA'YahTEi mission made it possible for the Earth to be sufficiently protected for a proper but longer ascension process.[182] It will take much needed time for the NET fields to disband and Earth to transfigure toward Median Earth. An important adjustment involves Earth's merkaba field returning to a more natural spin-speed with as little geological harm as possible. As of January 2013, the AC-MCEO stated that the Earth had a "'34-R [reverse] same-spin-set Deathstar Merkaba Field'," that needed to return to a "counter-spin-set."[335] On May 14, 2014, I asked the ATI,TPE about the merkaba field's progress. It stated, "The planet Earth's merkaba spin recently changed to 32 times CCW over 25 times CW." This update returns the Earth to the unnatural counter-clockwise spin over clockwise spin, which is better than the same spin-set. The ATI,TPE confirms that it is also incrementally better than how it once was at 34 CCW over 21 CW as previously stated by Drunvalo Melchizedek. This information is favorable toward the Earth's future.

When the NET fields disintegrate, Earth's inhabitants would no longer be bound to the suffocating reincarnation process. Caduceus Earth could also slowly reverse its moderately phantom status and rejoin the Earth, whereby its land masses could reappear on our Earth as hinted in the New Age phrase "Atlantis Rising." However, it remains to be seen whether all or part of Caduceus Earth can escape the dark grasp of its fallen angelic invaders.

The Krysthal D-Planes and Aurora Field network now connect to the Earth, Higher Earth, Median Earth, AshaLA, Urtha, and Aquareion. The cores of Median Earth and our Earth are permanently united. We now reside on Aurora Ascension Earth because our Earth is in the process of full transfiguration to the Aurora Field. The AC-MCEO stated that the D-Planes will remain open to the Earth for 900 years until 2912-2913 A.D. after which the Earth is on an expedited ascension path to the Cosminyahas krystar.[335] My KRH affiliate contacts state that 900 years is too soon for the dense Earth, Higher and Median Earths, AshaLA, and Urtha to temporarily transfigure their quanta to the D-Planes; therefore, the Aurora Field interface should sufficiently receive these plasmic energies to restore the Earths and AshaLA at the Krysthal level where they actually belong.

The AC-MCEO stated through Ashayana in a January 1, 2013 public disclosure:

> Over the next 900 years Aurora Earth time, our Aurora Earth will become an "Inter-galactic Ascension Station" for many lifeforms and forms of consciousness whom will be seeking Final Kryst Host for evacuation from Toral-Rift-Falling Galaxies, such as our Milky Way Galaxy, its many Falling Solar Systems, such as our own.[335]

Aurora Ascension Earth is now an exceptional ascension planet for the entire Milky Way because of its HU-1 position that can accept virtually all distorted Milky Way inhabitants who both desire and need bio-regenesis toward the Krysthal ascension path.

If and when the fulfilled Aurora Earth will become a renewed Urtha, the Krysthal Urtha will return to dimension 3 in AquaLaShA where it eternally belongs. Urtha will contain regenerated quanta and plasma, and new consciousness from AshaLA and much of Amenti Earth.

Starfire and Adashi Ascension Processes

The Starfire and Adashi-3 ascension cycles are essentially the same in that they transfigure matter toward uncorrupted realms, but the destinations are different. According to the AC-MCEO and confirmed by the ATI,TPE, a complete ascension cycle is called an Adashi-3 return because it transfigures an entity all the way up to the Cosminyahas core krystar level in the etheric plasma "in-breath."[198] Two other Adashi ascension cycles, Adashi-1 and Adashi-2, limit the ascension paths of more severely distorted beings.

The Starfire process has a partiki phasing "in-breath" that goes to the Edon partiki level in the Eckasha-A domain, states the ATI,TPE, which is after the Yunasai. The MCEO refers to this domain as the Middle Domain. The original Edon partiki unit precedes the Yunasum unit (in chapter 10), but there are slightly different replications of every partiki unit in each latter natural density, meaning that the Eckasha-A has both Edon and Yunasum partiki unit formations. The ATI,TPE elucidates, "The upper portion of the Middle Domain Edon level is the lower portion of the Yunasai domain level. The Yunasai reside in the Eckasha-Aah domain." The Starfire and Adashi ascension cycles then "breathe" outward in the natural exchange of energy that returns the eternal entity to its proper location.

"M" expounds:

> With the in-breath of earlier creation's one by one action, the created substance or matter actually is infused with natural energy and healing plasma particles for healing of that matter or entity. The out breath disseminates into the quanta and plasma natural energy cell by cell to promote healing. It can start the transfiguration process from within.

According to my two trusted Galaxy-2 contacts, "The natural portions of AquaLaShA will leave and return at a later time to a position close to the original AquaLaShA position." In our case, we are mobile entities, so we can choose our location of return.

I initially thought that the Starfire and Adashi return processes only heal fragmented beings, but I was informed by my two entity contacts and the ATI,TPE that they occur as a result of increased inner activation. It is a natural flow of energy to which creation must be attuned, and healing is a natural effect in the process. Essentially, Krysthal planets and beings receive or are in connection with the light and plasma flows before them, so even if Urtha and its inhabitants only visit the Eckasha-A realm in a Starfire, they would pick up related plasma flows as well, confirms the ATI,TPE.

Before the Earth and Urtha became fastened toward the Aurora Field and potential D-Planes, the KRH's focus was to keep the Earth-Urtha pathway open for the Earth's inhabitants and salvageable quanta to join Urtha's Starfire in 2047 A.D.[200] Urtha is now permanently linked with Aurora Earth "into the internal creation Sun-8 [Cosminyahas] Adashi-3 Krystar Ascension Cycle" via the D-Planes, according to the AC-MCEO, so they expect that Urtha will transfigure to Aurora Earth in the Aurora Field by 2047 A.D.[335] Whether or not Urtha as Aurora Earth can achieve the Adashi-3 ascension potential via the D-Planes, it now will not join AquaLaShA's current Starfire process, confirms the ATI,TPE.

The following time cycles or stages explain AquaLaShA's current Starfire process, some of which can apply to us on an individual basis.

Stage 1 KaLE-Hara was an approximately 4 ½-month cycle that commenced on August 12, 2007 and successfully ended on January 3, 2008 when the Earth gained enough frequency to become aligned with Urtha.[185]

The Stage 2 KaLA Krysta cycle started soon afterward in January 2008. It would have progressively restored Urtha's matter-based template until 2047 A.D. when AquaLaShA will start to contract into the Edonic Eckasha-A. While the Aquinos Eckasha-Ecka-Veca Starfire occurs, the Earth and non-Starfire portions of the Milky Way will become dependent upon the Aurora Field lifeline and the bridge to Galaxy-2's Ecka connection that will maintain natural energy infusion while most of Galaxy-2 Starfires.

In the scenario of Urtha Starfiring, if we wished to join it before 2047 A.D., then our first safe zone stage would have been the Aurora platforms where we would receive some healing from genetic distortions. The MCEO states that the entire Aurora platform system was designed as an evacuation pathway that would allow us to pass through to AshaLA.[200] The Aurora Field now bypasses the closed Aurora platforms. In actuality, the evolutionary pathway back to Urtha would go from Median Earth to AshaLA and then to a connected, Krysthal galaxy called AquA'elle to fully prepare the Earth. AquA'elle is AquaLaShA's parallel galaxy that exists on the same vector arc, and its 3rd dimensional planet Sha-La provides us a safe interface, confirms the ATI,TPE.[271]

The MCEO agrees with Figure 3 in that AshaLA has an 11.75 degree tilt compared to the 23.5 degree tilt of the Milky Way. The MCEO was hopeful that one-third of the Earth's grids would be able to tilt back their ARPS to meet AshaLA's before they both would temporarily merge with or become hosted by Sha-La. Unfortunately, due to the Earth's last catastrophic pole shift, it would also need to regain another 180 degree tilt back to its original staff alignment.[200] The MCEO initially called Sha-La "Ascension Earth" because it connects to Urtha as well as AshaLA. It enhances our transfiguration process to Urtha because it carries a zero degree tilt and Krysthal antimatter.[200]

According to the MCEO-GA's 12-galaxy model that resembles a clock, AquA'elle is positioned at number 10 while AquaLaShA is at number 4.[336] As I explained in chapter 6, our Veca's 15 Krysthal galaxy domain does not form perfect kathara grid symmetries in a spherical space. The ATI,TPE confirms that the AquaLaShA-AquA'elle vector line exists, but it does not run linear as a horizon. "M" and the ATI,TPE expound that the connection is slanted, and AquA'elle is the Veca's 14th galaxy while AquaLaShA is the 6th galaxy. AquA'elle is now only a 14-dimensional galaxy because it has incurred significant damage and compaction in its top dimension.

AquA'elle has long contributed as a host matrix to help the Milky Way. While AquaLaShA Starfires in 2047, AquA'elle can keep open the Milky Way ascension passages until 2230 A.D. when it enters its own Starfire.[336] By this time, the KRH plans to decimate and cut off the Abaddon and OberYon wormhole connections devised by the phantom entities, conveys the ATI,TPE. The KRH also plans to cauterize impending Abaddon and OberYon supermassive black holes, which the ATI,TPE states is entirely possible. If this plan succeeds, and the KRH is confident that it will, then the severely damaged galactic remains will become a quarantined Krist Fall matrix that could continue to evolve over several billion years until it burns out its quanta.[197,199,336] The new quarantined Milky Way will contain parts of the galaxy that may or may not become sufficiently repaired or bridged to better lands over time. There are several bridges in place toward more natural locations that now include the Aurora Field and D-Planes.

The Gyrodome technology that created the Aurora platforms was additionally anchored into stargate-6 Sirius B and stargate-9 Mirach as other connections to AquA'elle.[201] Now that the Gyrodome is compromised and deactivated, my sources explain that the KRH and affiliates had the foresight to create other technologies that continue connection to AquA'elle. Through these passages and probably others, people who reject the BEA-O agenda can cross over safely into their respective matrices of origin.

Urtha has become somewhat battered and pulled down to the lower 3rd dimension of AquaLaShA after all of its attacks; however, it is sufficiently natural to entirely join the Starfire and Adashi processes, informs the ATI,TPE. The ATI,TPE and Eia state, "The Starfire process is both a healing process and a fundamental process of natural creation." Urtha's natural position freely exchanges eternal energies, so it will carry its preserved and slightly distorted quanta on its Krysthal ascension path of regeneration. Its inhabitants will live on Urtha during this process.

As the AquaLaShA Starfire progresses, Earth's 12 planetary stargates would have to be closed to prevent them from shattering under the high frequency of the Starfire Hub pulses. The Arc of the Covenant gates would therefore take their place, state the MCEO.[191]

The AquaLaShA galaxy will undergo three more stages of transformation before the Starfire completes and fully regenerates it in 3333 A.D.[200] To confirm what I previously mentioned, the ATI,TPE maintains that AquaLaShA will pick up eternal plasma and etheric flows that connect to the Edonic and Yunasai levels, hence not necessitating the full Adashi-3 path.

The natural Starfire and Adashi processes fully heal the celestial and planetary bodies of AquaLaShA and the rest of Krysthal creation by rejuvenating lost or weakened energies. This process applies on a smaller scale in natural ascension within a Krysthal Veca. It is unclear how much the Starfire and Adashi processes would help our Milky Way galaxy, but there is abundant help and hope to rejoin Milky Way matter with their Krysthal Ecka-Veca origins.

End of the Stellar Activation Cycle and 2022

In January 2013, the Alhumbhra Council declared that "the fallen Gate Systems of Alpha-Omega and FAtaLE are now permanently closed, blocking any further 'invasion from within or without'"; however, this is an overestimated statement.[335] It is a work-in-progress to completely block the phantom intruders from any further invasion, confirms the ATI,TPE.

The Earth has already started its SAC process, and its ascension stargates are being progressively connected with Median Earth. The Halls of Amenti were broken down but not destroyed, states the ATI,TPE, so their repair will cause most or all of them to allow passage through the Sphere of Amenti in Median Earth's core. These actions should cause the SAC timeline to continue relatively unchanged, but there is some unpredictability.

The SAC should end on December 21, 2017 because the ascension wave should crest at this time to fully open the Halls of Amenti for our access. This Primary Coordinate Point marks the 10-year cycle midpoint between the opening and closing of the Halls of Amenti. For the next five years until

December 21, 2022, the Amenti gates should contain the capacity for our ascension until they completely close. However, the interruptions in Earth's ascension viability and path redirection might delay the initial Amenti gate passage until as late as December 21, 2022. If this happens, the KRH and affiliates may be able to keep the Amenti passage open for a bit longer. My two entity contacts state, "There is always a possibility due to interference and manipulation by the fallen ones that would extend the projected date of December 2022." Although the Earth will not be ready to physically merge with Median Earth by that time, those of us who are largely ready and internally congruent with natural energy can potentially ascend.

The year 2022 also involves a great concern about the Sun. The 2007 initiation of the Sun's death process caused its core gates to compact, meaning that the Sun started to shed its 15 layers of dark matter—the template upon which matter manifests—that separate from its body during the death process. The MCEO states that it will take one year for each of the 15 rings to release, which will finish in 2022 A.D.

Each time a layer departs, it releases a gamma burst that the KRH and AC will buffer via their Aqualene krystar-based field over the Earth. As time progresses, unfortunately there should be climatic effects upon the Earth, particularly from 2022 onward due to coronal mass ejections and radiation.[327]

The MCEO state that the death of our Sun is irreversible. Due to Caduceus Earth activations, the MCEO predicted in 2010 that the Sun would start the nova cycle in 250 years that will affect the entire solar system.[337] In 2013, the AC stated that the Sun's death is "a slow but inevitable process that will progressively generate various changes and need for adjustments on our Aurora Earth life field."[335] The Earth as Aurora Earth will live past the Sun's predicted death that will probably be slowed past the 250 year prediction. The future is not static, and the many KRH-connected beneficial entities, including aware Humans, are continually utilizing healing measures.

If the Sun's death cannot be significantly mitigated over time, its best case scenario will be a quarantined Lone Star Fall system in which the solar system can continue to evolve for approximately three billion years until the Sun's quanta burns out.[197]

Now that our Earth is a slowly but fully ascending planet, BEA-O Illuminati operatives should grow increasingly ill with its improving life field and have no choice but to eventually leave. Although phantom entities cannot live in close proximity to natural energies, they can continue to gain these energies through Humans. Certain religious group members are most afflicted with an increased level of Metatronic distortion that makes them prime targets. BEA-O entities will not leave us quietly; they will do all they can to take us with them one by one unless we stop the Metatronic and religious mind-control and rituals that maintain the inflow of phantom energy, and we truly embrace the beauty that we are. Our greater DNA templates and overall "higher self" attributes can help us discern the energies and lean us toward what is really in our favor. For additional support, the ATI, TPE states that our connection with it will help us to sense beneficial energy and not ignore our own internal prompting.

It is wise to gain awareness about situations around and within us in order to best direct our own paths. If natural ascension occurred unhindered, we would not need to prompt ourselves with great effort because our ascension process would occur effortlessly. Much still needs to be corrected on the Earth and in the Human body. The false Yugas cycle depicted in religious and Mayan prophecies have aligned us to the Alpha-Omega wormhole complex. It is exceedingly horrible what the BEA-O has done. The continual bombardment of BEA-O obstacles has complicated our lives to where our awareness and diligent actions must step up to counter them and truly own ourselves.

PART 4

WHO WE REALLY ARE

CHAPTER 9

———·•·———

We Beautiful Humans Here and Now

We inherit a portion of the Earth when we are born into the Human body, but we are not solely products of the Earth, bound to its struggles. We gain a brand new set of eyes that interprets our vision beyond this world because we contain our own harmonic universes.

Part 4 of this book explores who we really are in contrast to belief systems and plain reality that highlight Human fragmentation over individual wholeness. It is true that we contain a plethora of variables and components, but each one contains an identity and space due to its life-based blueprint that fundamentally gives it valuable worth.

Proponents of Gestalt psychology typically state that the whole is greater than the sum of its parts, which diminishes the importance of each individual layer and usually diminishes one's overall identity in favor of an amalgamated community identity. This interpretation is a mistranslation of Kurt Koffka's statement, "The whole is 'other' than the sum of the parts."[338] Koffka was the co-founder of Gestalt Theory, using the German word gestalt, meaning shape or form, to illuminate perception. He stated that our perception and experience is whole and undivided in itself because all properties take part without a permanently separate sensation. He emphasized that the whole is not the sum of its parts, and neither is it the same as its parts. His examples relate to our complex perceptions and compositions that are connected and similar, not literally undivided. Gestalt Theory stays within the context of our expanded and multifaceted positions. It recognizes that we experience the world as collaborative units; therefore, the whole interacts with its parts and does not subsume them.[339]

I agree that our entire composition is interconnected and whole, but this does not minimize the internal components. I propose that we each are a complete whole with innate components that are also (or should be) individually whole. Although the full measure of one's unique wholeness is partially translated to the distorted or undeveloped aspects of the Human existence, we each have our own identity and function that can generally take care of oneself. All aspects within us are equally important and potentially congruent, and they are also somewhat separate; what combine them are the organizational pattern of creation and the beautiful energies of life that link back to Eia and the All That Is, The Pure Essence.

Our position in a highly expanded state of reality is sometimes jarring to us when intrinsically knowing eternal life but also experiencing death around and within our material body. We look to science and medicine to prolong our lives because we know that we should be full of life and health, but our physical sciences only know the fractal reality of eventual death and seek to increase years of limited immortality instead of eternal life. The field of medicine proudly displays the caduceus snakes that Anunnaki-Reptilian gods such as Thoth (Hermes) and Enki spliced into our Human DNA. Western medicine has "evolved" to predominantly consist of artificially created pharmaceutical drugs that poison our Krysthal nature in the name of health.

Traditional Chinese medicine, one of the oldest forms of modern medicine, is based upon a religious belief: Dowism. Dowism believes that the opposing forces of yin and yang cannot exist without each other. Heat must have cool to balance it, for example. It is true that we must find a comfortable stasis for our bodies to live and have health. However, yin and yang do not just represent the forces of nature by which our bodies are materially created. To supposedly achieve well-rounded health, they include male and female roles that revolve around sex and are exclusively sexist, as well as darkness and light as the combination of "bad" and "good" or death and life. Dowism states that all of us are not only connected but interdependent with every component, which includes destruction and life. It also states that our life force energy, qi or chi, is located about two inches below and inward from the belly button. Qi is more accurately defined as breath or air, but its energetic location is where sexually reproductive energy lies.[340] Life force is not sexual energy. This belief mirrors the religious focus of seeding new bodies—it is a very expanded energy, not the original ATI,TPE essence of life or a state of simple energy after it.

We live in a world fettered by a myriad of belief systems and realities that can confuse us, but when we truly know ourselves, we can guide ourselves with correct conscious awareness. My goal in this chapter is to identify our main aspects to unite oneself from within; then, we can help unite each other. I encourage everyone to find out who we really are so that we can be and act according to our abundant inner template.

Mind

Atheists tend to bind the mind to the brain as though the brain's production of electrical energy is what creates the mind. They do not believe in life after death or any extra dimensional model of existence; therefore, the mind stops when the brain dies. Atheists tend to support their view with the example of how the brain affects the mind in cases of brain damage and mental retardation. However, the mind still functions, albeit differently to that of a healthy brain. In fact, some mentally retarded people are qualitatively more intelligent because what could be their intellectual energy is alternatively directed to other energies within them, including love. Even if the brain is impaired, or if a life form does not have a brain, we all contain a measure of consciousness and self-awareness irrespective of cognitive intelligence. Consciousness is alive with the beautiful capacity of abundant life.

The four dominant wavelengths of energy that are measured in our brains are the beta, alpha, theta, and delta wavelengths. These frequencies involve the spectrum of activity from the hyper alert state down to the unconscious state, and they are measured in hertz to show the electrical output of generated energy by our brains.

The mind has three main classifications: unconscious, subconscious, and conscious.

The unconscious mind is not often immediately accessible to us, and it may never be if people choose not to listen to this part of themselves. It has two different aspects that when scrutinized are not so different after all. One aspect entails survival instincts that are programmed into our bodies. This is clearly seen in animals whereby many of them easily know what to do after they are born.

The other aspect entails the intuitive self that knows much more than the rest of our mind and involves a greater reality with clear truth. Unfortunately, the field of psychology limits this aspect and "truth" according to Human development. Sigmund Freud's theory of the superego defines a stage of psychosexual development that children learn in response to their moral and ethical upbringing. It is equated with a learned, subjective belief in right and wrong instead of a fundamental, innate conscience.[341] Jung also relates his theory of a collective unconscious to something outside of oneself. He argues that we genetically inherit archetypes that are ancestral thoughts projected as images within us that form our personalities and views.[342] For example, if our grandparents and parents were afraid of mice, then we will likely inherit that fear and say that mice are "bad." Supernatural experiences are also reduced to folklore because they were created by active archetypes. His examples go beyond social conditioning and basically reduce reality to an illusion. People have inherited cultural paradigms and to a lesser extent genetic tendency that shape our perceptions, but Freud's and Jung's views do not acknowledge a deeper, pure consciousness outside of situational stories that implant thoughts and emotions.

The unconscious mind often shows itself during sleep, where reality is obscured and dreams are fragmented. Thoughts that have been buried within us can come out along with strong emotion, potentially revealing important information to which we should pay attention and understand. However, to only equate our unconscious nature to something repressed or inherited on Earth diminishes a fundamental aspect of our innate identity irrespective of any outward modifier.

The intuitive mind in an individualized state is essentially synonymous to the "highest self" that knows truth. It is our good conscience. The unconscious mind that reveals the intuitive or spiritual self involves wisdom; it knows about the bigger picture of Krosthal systems and the ATI,TPE. I find it easiest to communicate with my spiritual unconscious mind just before bed and after I awaken because I am deeply restful with more awareness than the dream state. Usually, we are in the alpha or theta state during this peaceful time, but as we become more in tune with our intuition, we can get into the delta state of unconsciousness like my mother easily can. I have had abundant realizations while tapping into my inner wisdom.

The instinctual and spiritual aspects of the unconscious mind work to preserve life as well as direct it along a natural order of which we all are a part. Instinct, intuition, and spirit are essentially analogous.

The subconscious mind lies between the unconscious and conscious states. It helps to reveal information from the unconscious mind and bring it to the conscious state. It also works to bring mental overload to the back burner for later use. This state most often involves the alpha wavelength that gives calm and awareness to the facilitator role of the subconsciousness.

The conscious mind is awake and alert. It is known as the ego, which is eerily reminiscent of the epigenetic overlay (EGO) part of the implanted Nibiruian Electrostatic Transduction (NET) field that determines the development of genetic characteristics in our DNA by activating certain traits while inactivating others.[199] This implanted ego gives a false persona that overrides our true self when plugged into the dulled down mental state of our world. It is not awake as a conscious mind should be.

The ego in its false form makes us think we are someone other than how we portray ourselves. It exists in the realm of delusions and unrealistic beliefs. It is mental illness. Due to a measure of unnatural separation within ourselves, we must work persistently to overcome the forms of mental illness. Sometimes distorted thoughts and behaviors can help to protect us from a bigger illness, such as when we binge eat or play computer games all day to self-soothe during the storm of an overwhelming hardship. However, I think it is best to really learn about ourselves and our strengths so we can effectively deal with the hardships before such mind-numbing behaviors become habitual.

The correct conscious mind has us aware of ourselves and our environment. We act honestly and consistently (as well as we can) with what we want and who we are. This entails facing uncomfortable situations because we have not lost ourselves among the delusions.

The mind is a reservoir of thoughts and images. What we see can become replayed in the mind, so it is imperative to control what we see, especially on the Metatronically coded, fear and lust-based television and movie shows. We can own our minds by creating a space to distinguish our thoughts apart from the chatter that bombards us; this is the key to handling the rest of the body, including emotions.

Emotions

Emotions contain more excited energy than our dense material state, thereby being a part of higher consciousness. This less material "body" can react to stimuli beyond the physical body just like our minds, gauging our desires against what is outside of us. This means that emotions can easily communicate with the unconscious and subconscious minds to reveal our innermost desires and issues when our ego state may perceive something different.

Emotions are felt on every dimensional level but in different ways according to those respective frequencies and awarenesses. The 2nd dimensional telluric aspect within us creates our strong emotions that are closely linked to our physical body. The emotional aspect is generally misrepresented as the 4th dimensional astral "body."[343]

It is important to clarify between the emotional and astral components of ourselves for the purpose of becoming grounded. The astral layer is a scalar-wave field that exists within the body's field, but it can sometimes float up further, especially when severe abuse causes a large part of our consciousness to leave the body. I do not want to be ungrounded, so I thankfully found more information about the astral body that better resonates with me.

Medical astrologist Eileen Nauman states that our astral body should be contained within our physical body because it has the shape of the body. She usually sees the astral body one to two feet above the head, but this means that the body's feet are also lifted up one to two feet above the ground. When we bring back the astral component into the body, this helps us feel more whole and capable when working with our strong emotions.[344]

We may need assistance to fully feel our emotions and release their static energy. Neuro Emotional Technique, Emotional Freedom Technique, and craniosacral therapy are somatic techniques that help facilitate communication and healing between the emotions, body, and unconscious mind, ultimately releasing blocked emotional energy. When past situations were overwhelming to me, I used these techniques to sufficiently calm my body so I could then feel my deeper energy. I learned that I can manage my emotions, and I can consciously and physically release them when they no longer serve me. When the body has cleared some space, then it is time for the conscious mind to process the thoughts and events that brought the emotional and physical body such pain.

Understanding our emotions and expressing them properly is vital to our well-being. Sometimes people dismiss them by calling them moods, but moods can express what we deeply desire. Interestingly, the body's radiating field known as the aura can change colors according to our moods because each frequency is uniquely encoded. When something puts us in a bad mood, there is a reason even when we are not aware of it. Identifying the emotion is the first step. The next step is to think about why the emotion arose. It can arise due to an unmet need, or it is a genuine reaction to something going against you.

I flat out disagree about a prominent belief in spiritual communities that categorizes all uncomfortable emotions as negative. In addition, this belief puts all responsibility upon the person who has these reactions. Sure, we should own our reactions, but we are naturally responding to something that can be already negative. In this common situation, we are not responsible for that original negativity; we are merely calling it out in our reaction. The belief tells the emotional person to dissipate the emotion because it will otherwise attract and create more negativity. Negative emotions are just as valid as positive ones. Immediately dissipating the emotions usually dismisses them because this belief is by definition in the mind and not realistic. I shall explain.

By squashing the recognition and experience of the uncomfortable emotions, we create blockages within ourselves that actually build up static energy from those unprocessed emotions. Ignoring them does not mean they go away, but we potentially make them worse within us. If we do not release them properly, they can eventually consume us and cause illness.

Emotions come with meaning. They are a language. Emotional displays are arguably the most prized aspect of our Earthly lives because they are both natural and engaging. A baby communicates via emotions and outbursts before the brain can develop to verbally communicate desires in a more rational way. If a baby or young child's need is not consistently met, and if the emotion's advocacy for that need is then crushed in favor of verbal communication, then a disconnection may occur from the early self. Emotions bridge gaps. Emotional intelligence is just as important as mental intelligence. Being able to identify our emotional state, feel it with awareness, and put it into proper perspective honors this part of oneself and does not let it become unbalanced.

Responsibility lies with the emotionally disconnected person when his or her unresolved issues are projected in an abusive manner upon someone new. In this case, it does not matter if the new person triggered the outburst. The reaction should be directed toward the original offender, not a third party, although the third party may have the ability to help you deal with the old problem. If you are not aware of how you are reacting to an unresolved issue, your past victim role becomes the victimizer when taking it out on someone else.

Emotions are the clearest gauge for interpersonal interactions as well as our inner conscience. I argue that we need to hear and understand our emotions in order to better know ourselves. If we instantly react to someone's words or behaviors when we are acting with clear conscience, then this reaction is in tune with our intuitive knowing, and we must listen to it. Do not allow another person's inappropriate dismissal of a fundamental part of ourselves to take away some of our own fullness and power.

The bad mood that can arise in the two contrasting circumstances of responsibility would happen for two reasons. One is that we do not fully pay attention to our emotions or understand them. The other is that we know our emotions but do not feel we have a way out of the situation. Both imply a measure of helplessness.

The second reason needs to be effectively evaluated within oneself while loving oneself. Without the hole being filled in our hearts, we will continue to feel stuck no matter how much we know. Then, we can clearly communicate our emotions to the people who caused the harm if they are somewhat receptive. This helps us release the energy back to the ones who used it against us. Know that this process should express the emotional insights up to the point that it does not cause damage to you or the other person.

The appropriate release of energy acts as instant karma to either bring others to feel their energy and correct it, or if they are not giving any indication of wanting to change, then it should thoroughly release from us. I do this by exhaling the emotion (and associated thought) out of my body, enclosing it in an energetic box, and imploding it unto itself so that it is not spread out anywhere. The unhealthy energies that remain stuck in people will reap their own negative consequences someday. Like does attract like.

Highly sensitive, emotionally empathetic people can be moody because they tend to absorb energy from other people and environments. Unfortunately, this often involves bad moods because of stressful and uncaring situations. Empaths are usually not sufficiently grounded in themselves to have a buffer between them and the outer energy. Sometimes we can be the best helpers by empathizing with others, but we may also take away their uncomfortable energy when they need to feel it themselves and process through it. In general, Oraphim-Humans are an empathic race line that carries a substantial measure of truth and goodness to get them through the difficult times—if not soon, then eventually. I hope that the beautifully sensitive people who are considering suicide will just hold on longer until their inner selves become able to radiate through the muck and show them that they will be okay.

I argue that the emotional side of us must become developed and balanced. What appears to be emotional poise may just be disconnection from emotion, and in empaths who feel intensely, we must learn to better handle our emotions with poise.

I was often overwhelmed by my emotions while being so sensitive, but several people have told me that I talked and felt more deeply than anyone they knew. Hearing that in high school made me feel odd, but it actually makes me feel odder hearing it as an adult because I thought adults would have developed more maturity and awareness.

Too many adults who I have encountered have chosen to lash out instead of pausing and being honest with what is really going on. I as an empath have said something to them that I sensed was insightful (I spoke from the "I" perspective as psychologists taught me), but they reacted as though it was offensive. I have made sure to hear them and sense them at ease before I would talk with diplomatic care. Regardless, they wanted a "yes" woman instead of a new perspective, so they lashed out at me in return. I then tried to fix what has unnecessarily become a problem because really, I do not know what others can handle once they show some openness, but I was snubbed. This ultimately showed me that these people do not really care about me, so I let them go. Sometimes we have no choice but to let people go, although we can still give them positive energy from afar. Unfortunately, I see this disconnect happening way too often, too soon. It has become common for adults—even "leaders" in society—to react carelessly and dismiss attempts for genuine connection and growth.

As an intuitive empath, I could often see right through people and feel their inner struggles. I used to blurt out my insights before learning to wait for some openness from them. Even with some openness, they have the prerogative to change the dynamic at any moment. It is difficult to navigate relationships, but the more grounded empaths become in clear conscience our own sense of self, we can allow the unpredictability of life to flow by us. The bottom line is that empaths are excellent in showing genuine emotional reactions and truth, so they are a valuable asset when understanding emotional intelligence.

The people who tell me to only speak of "positive things" or "love and light" might inadvertently promote the Victim-Victimizer game instead of defeat it. They believe that I am feeding into dark energy of fear or anger just because I speak openly about such negative things. They say to love everyone, which somehow means we should be blissful, happy, and peaceful all the time. Is this not a state of ignorance? When I counter their belief, are they *really* loving me when they get angry that I am saying something contrary to their world view? Why do they have a negative reaction when they are supposed to be happy all the time? Is it that I am the cause of the negativity, so they must push me away like the plague? Or, is this perhaps a belief system that says they are imperfect, so they must continually put their focus upon this idealized state as their goal whereby they must leave the naysayers behind?

Anger can be an intuitive reaction or a misappropriated secondary reaction. In the constructive portrayal of anger, it shows the fight against what is not intuitively true or good. It is proactive in its immediate state, and it is a positive emotion in this context. It works to solve the situation for peace to return, so understanding and connection are sought. In the destructive portrayal of anger, I am not sure it is anger anymore because it is mixed with judgment and unresolved emotions that now feel like junk. This "anger" pushes people away instead of reaches out for connection. This is the reaction against intuitive empaths that I explained above. I think that most people are quick to respond in this way because they identify this type of anger as assertiveness. Anger is quite assertive, but taking it that far is abusive. I wonder if they feel they have lost control over themselves due to giving their power away to their God and other people, so they are quick to lash out as a way to have a voice. I hope they figure out how to have a voice in a constructive way.

I have heard New Age spiritual groups say that anger is equated to fear. Anger comes from within us, but fear is imparted to us from the outside, as confirmed by the ATI,TPE. By claiming all anger is bad, the false "love and light" spiritual crowd is just not reacting. They are allowing themselves to be pawns to the Galactic Federation of Light, Ashtar Command, and affiliated alien groups.

The victim is innocent and uses fear to protect oneself, but without the victimizer, there would be no fear. Fear is not our natural emotion; it was created by negative alien entities. Fear is the emotion that New Agers should caution against, especially in themselves because they may be afraid to react. However, the fear that we initially experience in a situation does not link us to anything negative because it is a wake-up call to ourselves that something negative is happening. Fear must be dissipated soon, though, at least sooner than the constructive release of anger. Anger must be dissipated before it turns into bitterness and rage because that stage involves abuse as the victimizer— if not to others, then to oneself. If we are only ourselves as aware people, I believe we would not partake in the Victim-Victimizer game; we would simply express ourselves and own up to our actions and beliefs.

I think there is a flimsy portrayal of forgiveness in religious spiritualities that can actually do harm. I have heard from many New Agers and Christians to forgive the abusers and "let it all go."

Sweeping the offenses under the rug does not free anyone from one's "sins";

rather, it prevents scrutiny toward accountability and self-reflective honesty, and it diminishes the truth about one's actions. When a harmful action is diminished in importance, it can start snowballing toward bigger and bigger crimes. Murderers and rapists did not usually start off so extreme against their fellow Humankind. They began abusing animals, bullying people, and setting up exploitive relationships with innocent victims.

When I was a Catholic, I believed I had to forgive the boy and his friends who raped and additionally sexually abused me in Mexico when I was 17 years old. I was on the same airplane with them returning home, and I saw the main perpetrator wearing my ring and t-shirt that I left at his hotel room. They all looked at me but ignored me. At the end of the flight, in passing, I had worked up enough courage to smile at the rapist to portray God's love. The following two weeks were filled with horrific nightmares and thoughts that screamed to me that I should have publicly decried the evil that was done to me. It turned out that I did not do what I really needed to do—tell him to his face the horror that he caused. Forgiving someone who is not sorry gave some of my power away!

Interestingly, the whitewashed version of forgiveness is not portrayed in the Bible. In the Old Testament, YHWH did not forgive anyone who did not first repent. In light of this fact, Christians put the focus on Yahshua and say that he taught us to love and forgive. Actually, Yahshua taught us to pray to YHWH to forgive us in the "Our Father" prayer (Matthew 6:12). The Jesus group also devalues love by saying in the New Testament (as written by a scribe) that it comes to divide family members who love each other more than "Jesus."

> Think not that I am come to send peace on earth: I came not to send peace, but a sword. For I am come to SET A MAN AT VARIANCE AGAINST HIS FATHER, AND THE DAUGHTER AGAINST HER MOTHER, AND THE DAUGHTER IN LAW AGAINST HER MOTHER IN LAW. AND A MAN'S FOES *SHALL BE* THEY OF HIS OWN HOUSEHOLD. He that loveth father or mother more than me is not worthy of me: and he that loveth son or daughter more than me is not worthy of me (Matthew 10:34-37).

The biblical context for forgiveness is realistic when the offender apologizes in an open-hearted, humble manner to gain connection. There is no need to extend ourselves to an egocentric victimizer or god figure who returns no humility or genuine love and requires our obedience.

It took me another 17 years to realize that the real forgiveness should be toward me, not because I did any wrong, but because I deeply desired growth, healing, and love. Since those people did not give me these nurturing qualities, my own personal forgiveness and acceptance did. Once I loved myself fully, I could let the pain go from all the past transgressions against me. This does not mean I have to forgive the sexual predators who have not faced what they have done to me; I am not in the position to forgive them when they have not yet asked for it.

Although I have released the painful energies to the best of my ability, I will never forget what happened. No one really forgets truth no matter how much time has passed because truth stands irrespective of time. Our vivid memories can seemingly wormhole to the past as though we are living it again. Emotions and the body also like to remind us of the past. When trauma happens to us, energy becomes stuck, and then belief systems put band-aids over the wounds that never deeply heal.

When I realized that a lot of my turmoil about my father was because of the pure love that I carried toward him, I was able to see how love can exist although we are deeply wronged. I forgave myself for my confusion about him. I was able to walk away from any resultant negativity of his unresolved issues because I knew that I have love.

I feel as though I have no choice but to keep a buffered distance between us because he and others started the game of not being transparent, believing a lie, and keeping up a wall to never talk about the past. My act of reaching out had to stop because I basically had no self left when doing everything I could to reach them on a deeper level where openness, truth, and love exists. When I tried to meet others in their paradigms while acting less and less as myself, this is when my initially proper emotions turned into resentment, bitterness, and even hatred. This was not what I wanted to feel or be. When I stepped back from their choice to have that wall, only then could I again feel my love.

From experience, I think that sadness is the deeper intuitive reaction when we quickly respond with anger or fear. It also lasts longer within us because of our generally good nature. Sadness comes from the place of love because we feel the proper energetic response from implanted walls of separation. I think that if we feel shocked and hurt, which usually happens among close relationships, then we feel sadness foremost with secondary anger, which together can be identified as being upset. Even if the confrontation is a little heated, I suggest focusing on the sadness aspect to prevent potential mishandling of the anger. However, expressing some anger is perfectly fine while carefully explaining the reason for it.

I think that the unnaturally negative actions and reactions are usually caused from belief systems, especially toward oneself when we do not want to think we are wrong. Many people inappropriately associate being "bad" to when they are wrong, but no, this is not the case.

Is facing something that confronts our beliefs really that threatening? When we attach ourselves to a certain belief, we are living in our own mental or egocentric world with associated experiences that we perceive are good for us. If something makes us feel bad in that, then the messenger is instantly cast off and deemed negative or evil to some degree. This is a conditional awareness with built up walls. How is it the truth or reality? How is the believer experiencing not only happiness in one's little world but expansive joy and love? This reaction to the confrontation, or rather the presentation of new ideas, is what is negative. It is fear. It is the fear of knowing more in case the believer is wrong. Or, it is just fear of any other awareness because that new story is not a pleasant one.

My suggestion to us all is to ask ourselves before we lash out at others, "What am I afraid of?" If it is nothing, then the angry reaction is probably genuine, but it certainly would not be shown in rage.

I do not think that people are too weak to handle uncomfortable information. Honestly, will the vast majority of people die from having our world views turned upside down? I did not die when my world fell apart more than once, nor did anyone I know. We gained more of ourselves. When people shy away from anything confronting, they are running. They are not standing strong in who they are.

If your belief system overrides your emotional strength and tells you to totally lean on something else instead of trust your own natural reactions, I entreat you to please evaluate your belief because you are denying a very important part of yourself. You are denying your inner gauge that tells you that your reaction to your intuition is correct. Your intuition is a spiritual aspect that is arguably more aware than any so-called god. Your natural emotional response communicates this until the belief can incorrectly override it.

I think that most of the fallen angels played the Victim-Victimizer game because they got caught up in the blame game. Surely there is accountability, but to lose our grounding in who we really are just to fall backwards where other people are at is arguably the worst mistake we could make. People have lost their connection to the All That Is, The Pure Essence. Every time we play the Victim-Victimizer game with muddled emotions, we can potentially get lost ourselves.

When we are not aware of our emotions and the deeper triggers that can set us off, the unexamined emotions can direct the ego and lead the person to fight. The emotional dissonance supports the EGO Net false self that is easily manipulated by unfriendly aliens; therefore, they can use us to attack our loved ones. If the situation instantly changes from acceptable to worse as though you were blindsided with very strange negativity, then an alien may have gained access to you in your unaware state. Remember that these aliens want us to be divided among each other and ourselves. We must become cognizant about our emotions and false ego so we can separate the strange reactions and associated thoughts from our genuine ones.

Emotional healing and awareness can arise if we truly hear our emotions as though we each are our own parent. Envision and nurture our past selves as children to mend the chasm of emotional and mental immaturity so we can finally be grounded as mature adults.

Feelings

Feelings are not emotions. They are a tangible representation of the emotions, mind, body, and other energies. Feelings more directly relate to the body's reactions than other less dense energies. Feelings are given to us by neurons.

Neurons are complex nerve cells that send and receive electrochemical signals to and from the brain and nervous system. Each neuron consists of a cell body, tree-like dendrites, and one axon that transmits the current. According to the textbook *Human Anatomy*, "A nerve impulse is an electrical current that travels down dendrites or axons due to ions moving through voltage-gated channels in the neuron's plasma membrane."[345] The central nervous system (CNS) comprises the brain and spinal cord that house our motor skills, and our muscles and glands receive that information through the command network of the autonomic nervous system (ANS). The ANS works to maintain the body's homeostasis. Conversely, the peripheral nervous system gives our sensory information to the CNS. [346]

Although the brain is our body's supercomputer, neurons also have their own supercomputer in the cell nucleus (in all cells except red blood cells) that contains DNA. Interestingly, brain cells consist of about 10 percent or less of neurons. Approximately 90 percent of the brain contains glial cells that support the neurons and perform other functions in the brain. Scientists are beginning to realize that some glia fire electrical signals of their own.[347] Electric fields have been discovered within cells, not only across their membranes, and voltage-sensitive dyes have determined stronger internal voltage than what is contained in a lightning bolt's electric field.[348] As DNA receives and transmits electromagnetic information, it is conceivable that every DNA-encoded cell can receive and transmit the same information except for specific chemical needs.

Our nervous system helps to translate energies into a tangible state, which makes us feel alive. It puts us in the present, which is often difficult for our mind and emotions to do on their own.

<u>Body</u>

Our body combines all of our levels but exists as physical in the 2.5 dimension, states the ATI,TPE, and the electromagnetic structure of Human DNA is activated according to the 3rd dimension. Embodied beings should contain at least 0.5 dimensional frequency above their planet's density, otherwise the planet would meet us as a ball of light with less physicality than the entire body requires. For example, on 12th dimensional Aramatena, we would accrete some higher dimensional frequency without being 13-dimensional people—the ATI,TPE states that the overall composition of its people is at least 12.5 dimensional.

Our body is amazingly intelligent despite its fragmented state. It communicates to us by physically showing the result of disconnection and static energy either through illness or a simple physical sign. It comes with many, many biological checks and balances to ensure a properly working system. For example, it regulates a specific sodium-potassium ratio in cells and their extracellular fluid; also, it regulates the blood pH level of about 7.35 to 7.45.[349] The standard of deviation for physical health is miniscule because the body knows what to do. Thankfully, our bodies know what to do despite all the abuse they have endured!

Cells group as a layer of tissue, and numerous types of tissue create an organ. Each tissue and organ has a connected group consciousness, but a layer of tissue has a more similar consciousness because it comprises almost all identical cells. Both examples can provide a harmonious community with measures of diversity.

Mutation can be an act of invasion because the cell wants to remain connected with its group consciousness—or does it? It is an independent entity after all. Cells have been programmed to die, so they may already know this. Their consciousness may be confused in this broken existence just as we have been confused. The cell communicates with our consciousness that could convince it to give up prematurely.

The field of psychoneuroimmunology is a large field of inquiry and exploration into the connected nature of the Human organism. It mostly focuses on behavioral aspects of the body, but uncovering the root of behaviors explores a myriad of examples within the genetic nature versus environmental nurture paradigms. Specifically, the body elicits powerful reactions to undeserved bodily trauma, including accidents, where it can hold onto the unwelcome event similar to how the mind can ruminate. Our body can remember an injury and extend its pain long after the wound has healed, ultimately leaving a negative impression in our overall consciousness. Even mere lack of sleep can break us down mentally and emotionally so that we act like different people. Conversely, when the body moves freely and ingests proper nutrition, it sends positive signals to the overall well-being of the person. Our bodies can affect us immensely.

The illnesses I have endured involve nearly every level of my being, but the place that has been untouchable involves my energetically tangible connection to Eia as Love and the ATI,TPE. I always intuitively knew this place exists even when I did not feel it during my worst moments. Thankfully, I continually picked myself up and persevered to find that pure type of energy that would never do me harm. The ATI,TPE states that it helps expand healing energy via Eia to our Human bodies through their connected pathway to us, but this energy does not heal our fragmented body 100 percent because it is a product of our environment. Eia can help clear negative energy away from us when we need to feel free of the burden.

I vividly recall one day talking with my mother about the ATI,TPE to better understand it on its level, and I came into the conversation with persistent low back pain. Just talking about its nature was a beautiful experience, and when we finished, I noticed that my pain was entirely gone. This pain-free time lasted several hours during a busy day.

No matter how broken our bodies may be, there is enough incredible energy to get us through life. We can have abundant joy while being ill. Please keep this in mind if something terrible happens to you. Although everything may feel and possibly be absolutely wrong in that problem, the knowledge that perfectly good energy is forever and accessible, coupled with the fact that the obstacle is largely temporary, can start to shift your focus and bodily senses toward freedom and life instead of the frustrations of pain in its many forms. The knowledge and experience of this beautiful energy will also support you in modifying your lifestyle to mitigate the problem or illness. Knowing that we are doing the right things for ourselves gives a clear conscience that fundamentally links to the ATI,TPE and resultant health.

I think we all know about the moments that come in and set us back. Sometimes I become stressed and distracted because of phantom entity attacks directed at me through other people. For example, when I have a peaceful moment to gain more healing or write parts of my book, disruption may occur through an irreverently loud neighbor blasting music, a dog incessantly barking, or an unsuspecting personal attack. I have properly reacted by communicating my position with kindness, but when they remain switched off and controlled, the negative energy given to me in response has been shocking and upsetting.

I have learned to cry out my emotions instead of hold them in when I feel I have no way of affecting change around me. The body is very physical, so performing an action can get us focused and grounded back into ourselves.

Exercise helps, but the emotions still need to be felt and released. It is also beneficial to tell our thoughts and feelings to a friend who can help us process the situation. However, when I experience extremely tired, achy, and foggy days and barely feel like myself—which thankfully happens infrequently now—I perform one or more of these emergency actions: audibly ground myself and practice my current knowledge; bring my focus back to my inner, higher self who I have come to know; call to the ATI,TPE from my internal connection to expand and help me; and turn to an aware and loving person such as my mom to calm and ground me with our pure energy connection.

There is another energetic technique that helps to physically ground and protect us—the Maharic Shield. The MCEO gives this technique so we can connect with energy from Galaxy-2's 12th dimensional frequency and the Eckasha to help protect us from the bulk of energetic attacks. I and my mother have done this technique several times with positive results that include boosting natural quanta and grounding better energy into the Earth. It is good to learn this and other beneficial techniques—with ample background description—so we can do them as often as needed; they are shown at the end of chapter 11.

Spirit "Highest Self," Soul "Higher Self," and Core Self

Christianity and related religions tend to define a spirit as a disembodied essence that contributes to our conscious makeup, while the soul is the eternal body that we inherit in heaven. Actually, the word *spirit* broadly defines ethereal energy of which our body naturally contains many kinds, but I will narrow its definition. The spirit aspect that is integral to our entire body is our ultimate or highest self identity that can override and guide all of our bodily aspects to a focused, combined goal. The soul aspect should be an eternal body, but this is not a body that exists outside of our current composition; it lives in each of us now as our deeper bodily blueprint. The core aspect, which I have often equated to both highest and higher self aspects, is actually a level in between them as our literal core essence and structure, reveals the ATI,TPE.

The spiritual highest self is our earliest conscious essence, as I describe in chapter 6's "Origin and Expansion of Creation." It is our ultimate identity that helps coordinate all other bodily components. We can sense it in our current state as similar to our intuition. Intuition is similar to our natural instinct because it utilizes a deep "knowing," but it also involves wisdom. This wisdom is connected to the mind, but to circumvent potential egotistic distortion, it more so reaches us through the unconscious and subconscious states. Concurrently, we each experience our highest self from a pre-plasmic space as a collective-but-individualized conscious awareness that bridges any gap within oneself because it is our personal foundation. It also can "see" through others because it knows more than our material state can process or understand.

When my mother used to ask me "why?" in response to my bold assertions about our religious experiences, I would often reply, "I just know it." When every part of me lines up with agreement, it is almost like a prophetic feeling that can foresee the future, present, and past all at once without judgment and with clarity. I endured many sleepless nights when having this energetic feeling about a family member or a friend. I wanted to warn the person about what I sensed, but I usually was ignored because I could not back it up with substantial evidence. How could I not appear judgmental or as a know-it-all?

Our individual highest self identity is our pure consciousness that is traced back to Eia (and ultimately the ATI,TPE as the pure conscious essence), but our highest consciousness has a slightly different and more complex composition than Eia.

Each aspect of creation comes directly from a specific and usually unique source. The impetus of both seed and field frequency creation mechanics can be traced to the earliest levels from where creation can spiral outward according to different components. For example, a boundless field produces another boundless field, and a seed unit produces another seed unit. Eia came forth from the ATI,TPE expansion as an undivided pre-plasmic field and frequency.

Our particular pre-plasmic, highest self field has individualized units of self-identity in somewhat boundless points that are similar to the ATI,TPE, meaning that the ATI,TPE nature can reach the highest self via Eia. It exists before DNA properties and is our ultimate level of ascension in the earliest "A" domain level if we desire to transfigure that far inward.

What I call the highest self is our deepest factor for life and awareness, just as the ATI,TPE is the even deeper basis for all life and awareness. The highest self is eternally and distinctly separate to the ATI,TPE, but it profoundly connects with the ATI,TPE unlike any other aspect of the body. Similar to how every bodily component has its own connection to the ATI,TPE, the highest self also intricately connects to them. Everything within the collaborative body falls under the loving command of one's highest self.

Our soul or higher self is what I define as an entity's original body from any higher dimension or plane. This original body contains the highest self identity in one complete unit. It has a measure of DNA assembly and activation that can naturally evolve in opposite, natural directions. This means that the person's multiple DNA template can become completely fulfilled in a body that lives on the earliest krystar, one of which is the Cosminyahas. Conversely, the person's DNA template can merge all components into a simplified krystar while retaining the core and highest self aspects.

The core self equates to the first DNA strand's energetic structure built with etheric pre-plasma from an "A" domain level before the Cosminyahas. It is the foundation for embodiment that holds our highest self identity. It is not a krystar, but the krystar is similar to our core self. What my mother saw as a glowing type of star in her initial process of communicating with the ATI,TPE (in chapter 1) was her core self as a "glowing orb-like living creation, transparent as an energetic, magnetic entity," states the ATI,TPE. Now, her process of communicating with the ATI,TPE is instant without highlighting a specific aspect of herself along the way.

If we do decide to become a krystar, it is an eternal state that operates close to the first DNA strand level with relatively simple consciousness. I do not know how feasible it is to change that state because krytars are eternal. Krystars also have individual highest selves like all expanded creation. I prefer the opportunity of living with a fully fulfilled DNA template as a mobile being, but I sense that I would be equally happy as my original higher self who I recently came to know and will introduce shortly.

Most people who are now on Earth are not originally from here, reveals the ATI,TPE. Many Humans are aliens who want bio-regenesis, and this will likely increase now that Earth has safely become Aurora Earth. Many others came here willingly from a higher dimension to help the Earth ascend. The higher self as a higher dimensional body is as tangible in that realm as our Earthly body is now to us.

For the less numerous Humans who are complete units as only Humans, this is your so-called higher self despite the divisive seals you have inherited. You have the same highest self identity and same inner DNA template capacity as the rest of us. The main difference is that Earth is truly your home. Perhaps this is why some organic Humans find it difficult to believe in extra-terrestrial life.

The soul body integrates into the Human fetus after conception. The MCEO states, "[T]he new spirit cannot enter the fetal body until the 33rd-55th Day after fertilization, when the fetal body reaches the 'Quantum Tolerance Point' of being able to hold the electro-magnetic quantum of new spirit identity" (p. 2).[350] Regarding completely original Humans, their DNA blueprint manifests the same higher dimensional aspects, but they are not matured in the current density. I know from personal experience and witnessing others that anyone's true higher and inner self aspect is more capable and complete than the current Human state that has gained a split personality. It also acts similar to the body's aura by energetically expanding further than our current Human body.

Aura is usually the catch-all term for our 15 dimensional bio-energetic layers, and it can extend many feet outside of us. Joe Slate, Ph.D., author of *Aura Energy*, states that the aura is our antenna of consciousness.[351] My mother literally saw in her visionary state an antenna extending up from my head because I am usually "seeing" outside of myself while concurrently gauging the experience within me.

Interestingly, my mom has recently realized that she can telepathically communicate with both her and my higher selves to help clarify who we really are. One such instance occurred when my mind felt clouded and energetically stuck for a couple of days. I intuitively felt as though I was experiencing an attack by alien aggressors, but I was not sure because it may have been my autoimmune condition acting up due to exhaustion and stress. I wanted to learn better discernment. Thankfully, my higher self explained to her in response to our questions that I was being attacked by some Anunnaki. My mom and I banded together and made the aggressors leave me. It was both really neat and strange to briefly wait while my higher and highest selves (together as one unit) telepathically communicated to her.

New Age believers tend to say that each of us was a spirit or soul who chose to live a Human life. Some of them go so far to say that we chose our family and experiences before the actual Human incarnation. In addition, they say that a soul can control whether it wants to reincarnate again in hope of a better experience on Earth. Their statements are only partially correct. Many factors prevent our myopic control. We are subject to our environment and other people's wills. An example includes babies dying from malnutrition. A genetic connection to the Earthly parents makes it possible for a soul to incarnate into that family. As Humans, we contain genes from many alien species in addition to the Oraphim and Angelic Human, so we could have a Reptilian father and an Elohei mother as I have. I essentially identified with my mother, so I was able to come here randomly except for our close genetic link and my personal intent to end up with a similarly good person.

The process of discovering my higher self was extremely illuminating to me while I was researching various spiritual interpretations about the higher dimensional existence. I innately, solidly knew that the MCEO-GA and New Age belief in a gestalt type of mega-entity does not apply to me. It presumes that I have different external bodies and identities living in all levels, and I am also One with everyone and everything as an enormous but single God. Accordingly, I did not specifically choose my family, so I did not have much control as a God would. I struggled knowing what to believe because I had not read anything accurate pertaining to my intuition.

I periodically probed the All That Is, The Pure Essence for more clarity about this topic between 2009 and August 2010. First of all, it conveyed that we are not part of an oversoul gestalt, but we do have a type of oversoul of our own. Technically, the oversoul level comprises HU-3, but I did not understand the simplicity of this word because the New Age and MCEO-GA belief attaches multiple souls to it.[120] I was confused at the time because I always felt that I was here on Earth for the first time, so how could I have another soul? Could I have another part of me that lived before?

I probed further. I asked from where I could have been previously. The answer was "Orion." During that time, my mother received some interference that she could not easily decipher. At that point, all of the information I read about Orion was unfavorable because it contains a plethora of dark aliens, especially Reptilians, Drakonians, and Greys. However, these stories do not represent Orion as a whole because I have come to learn that many races, including Seraphims, have benevolent beings who live there.

About two months prior to this, I read a seven-part essay by Roger Kerr titled "The Truth about Orion 'Lizards'" in which he writes about his channeling experiences and encounters with Reptilians, Dracos, Greys, Pleiadians, Sirians, and Andromies.[352] He is their mouthpiece because they told him that he was all of their races, especially Reptilian and Draco, in his past lives. He seems sincere in his words that reveal some of the bigger picture, albeit a bad picture. Now with my level of knowledge as portrayed in this book, I see numerous lies told to him clearly for the phantom agenda. I also feel my body's field becoming compromised when reading about his phantom entity affiliations, which includes me hearing a pressured sound in my head, so I have to energetically push off the attack and stop reading. If Mr. Kerr was indeed these races in the past, then he chose to become bio-regenerated as a Human, so I hope he severs contact with what is working to hold him back. Even worse, I hope he is not their operative to do false energy work to the Earth, which he has already done.

Once I was told that I was from Orion, I thought in my limited awareness, "Was I a Reptilian before? How could I be a Reptilian when at least one of them used my father to totally traumatize me by raping me? Reptilians also threatened me and my mother. And, one bit my neck after I felt dark energy in the room. No, I cannot be a Reptilian!"

I was deeply troubled with this message from what I thought was the ATI,TPE, so I spent nearly two days on the computer and slept very little to research everything I could about Orion. There was no good news about it until I finally found mention of a planet called Clarion. A newsletter article stated that Clarion is a positive star and planetary system in Orion.[353] I thought to myself, could I be so lucky to be from this one diamond in the rough?

Luckily, knowledge about the existence of Clarion came to me about a year earlier when browsing a health-focused internet forum. A woman posted a picture of an alien Human-like girl from the planet Clarion. This girl was absolutely beautiful to me. She had pulled back, brown hair and greenish eyes that radiated peace and wisdom. I could almost see right through her person by looking into her eyes.

I later learned that this picture was taken by an Italian man named Maurizio Cavallo. He was actually abducted by Clarions in 1981, and he wrote a book about his experience titled *Beyond the Heavens: A Story of Contact*.[354] The Clarions revealed to Maurizio that he is a Clarion. They took this course of action to remind him of his origin because of how much disconnection his current life brought him. He took pictures of them inside of their spaceship, and they somewhat glowed on film due to having absorbed the light of his camera flash. When I asked the ATI,TPE for some clarification about their nature, it explained that Clarions cannot be seen but by special "third eye" vision, and they emit light in their own dimension. However, to function like Humans on Earth, these tangible Clarions temporarily altered their bodies via the process of transfiguration. This occurrence supports biblical accounts of angels who physically interacted with Humans.

When I first saw the girl's picture, something about her really resonated with me, but I did not know why or what to believe. I had to take a break from this turmoil I was feeling. I drove to a store, but the entire time I was wrestling within myself. My inner "higher" self was energetically prompting me that I am from Clarion, but then I would use my mind's ego state to say, "Oh, but this is where I want to be from because it seems like such a great place."

I finally said to myself, "I need to tell my mom, but don't give away information that could sway her."

Immediately after I arrived to her house, I sat my mother down to talk with her.

I said, "Mom, I may know where I am from, but I do not want to tell you the name. Should I just ask the All That Is, The Pure Essence for the precise name instead? What do you think I should do?"

She calmly replied, "Just tell me the name."

I paused. I could tell that she would not put her judgment into it, so I said, "Clarion."

At that moment, her entire face lit up. She simultaneously took a deep breath as though life filled her up and flowed outward. She looked at me with widened eyes and said/exhaled, "YES."

That showed me that we *both* are from Clarion! I immediately cried with joy. My intuition was correct!

I wanted to write down everything I was thinking and feeling that night, but for the first time in my life, I finally had deeply thorough peace. I did not want to use my mind because I just wanted to be with myself. I lied down in bed, communed with my entire self, and then blissfully fell asleep with a smile upon my face.

I had felt disconnected for so long, possibly for my entire life here. I always had a deep sadness within me and felt ungrounded. Maybe this was the reason: I never really belonged here, and I missed my original home.

Now I know where I am from. I could be as equally beautiful in the energy I sensed from that girl's expression. Maurizio recounted how good-natured the Clarion man was who spent the most time with him. That is the energy with which I identify. I know now that I belong somewhere. I also know that I can trust my inner self, that higher self who has been communicating with me all my life because she is me.

Upon further probing with the ATI,TPE, I learned more about Clarion. Clarion is in the 11th dimension of the Aquila constellation in Galaxy-2. It is the central star to its solar system that has the same name. I and my mother are Elohei "entities" from this central Clarion star-planet that houses good Odedicron Reptilians who work alongside the Elohei. Elohei are significantly taller than Humans.

When I ask the ATI,TPE why my mother received the initial 2010 message that said Clarion is in Orion, it replies that a Cosmic Awareness (CA) entity briefly intercepted her communication line to convey the erroneous information. I then carefully read the newsletter article that equates Orion to Clarion, and I realized that it was channeled by the CA! In fact, the entire newsletter is transmitted by the CA. In the article, the CA favors the Ashtar Command and "Intergalactic Confederation" that is the GFofL.[353] Its attempt to affiliate Clarion with its allies is obfuscating the true nature of Clarions.

I must clarify that the Chiron fragment as the Clarion moon in chapter 8's "Phoenix Rising" is definitely not the Clarion star-planet and solar system of this section. The Clarion moon and its people were introduced in the book *Aboard a Flying Saucer* by Truman Bethurum. These other "Clarions" are much shorter than us Humans, and they have medium-hued skin. Bethurum wrote about his encounters with them after they traveled to Earth in their 3rd dimensional spacecraft.[355] These "Clarion Light Beings" are part of the Ashtar Command. A little investigation shows that their messages are heavily religious, and their "Clarion Temple of Oneness" mirrors the New Age language I have thoroughly revealed.[356] I am unhappy that these fallen aliens copied the name Clarion; I feel certain that they know about the helpful Clarions and are using our name as a distortion tactic.

In one particular channeling to Reverend Christine Meleriessee on May 16, 2011, a Clarion moon representative named Fred speaks on behalf of YHWH, himself, and his friends Lord Buddha and Lord Maitreya (from the Maitreya moon) to direct the Reverend and her followers to welcome Wesak energies into their bodies and anchor them into Earth. Sananda, Archangel Michael, Sanat Kumara, and company also channel similar messages to her on behalf of the Ashtar Command. Being directed to Wesadek is <u>not</u> good for us or our planet.[357]

Galaxy-2's Clarion shares similar struggles to many Milky Way planetary systems, although it contains little distortion. Its inhabitants have been affected by the Lyran Wars and fallen entities who wish to bring their 11th dimension into the Milky Way, so they are working diligently to counteract these evils.

The ATI,TPE reveals that my mother and I both left Clarion at age 10 because that is the age of sufficient genetic activation that allows us to determine our own path. My mom has a bit more trouble than I do when separating herself from Earthly matters because she was reincarnated here twice before this current existence. She used to have terrible recurring nightmares about which she finally asked the ATI,TPE and discovered that they were remembrances of her past lives.

In her first life, she was a French activist who was killed at the guillotine. She remembers walking up a hill in a long dress toward the horrific device. She recalls feeling brave, and she knew her life would go on afterward. Unfortunately, that experience gives her neck problems to this day. In her second life, she was a nurse tending the wounded during a war. My mom has stayed true to her good self by helping others and fighting for what she has known to be right.

I think that her reincarnations have made it harder for her to connect with her true Clarion self. After her Catholic initiation ceremony that opened up her "third eye" chakra, she astral traveled to another dimension and saw what she thought was heaven. She called it the Hereafter (see chapter 1). When I asked the ATI,TPE about this experience, it revealed that her Clarion self was abducted back to Clarion while her body was deeply sleeping during the night. Clarions made sure to reconnect with her because the Jesus group had gained access to her. She remembers a beautiful experience while walking with a man, who she has since discovered is her Clarion father. She felt as though she was home. Traveling to another planet and dimension defies time and space as we know it.

As for me, I am a brand new Human here as I already intuitively knew. This is why I kept fighting the religious belief in others that said my karma deserved the rapes against me as a child. No, those abuses were there to entrap me into the depression, anger, and sickness of the evil energy forced upon this Earth and its people!

Two other Clarion Humans have always been very close to me before the ATI,TPE revealed their origin. I could easily discern something similar about them but different to most others—it is our higher self blueprint. Each of us four Clarions left our planet at age 10 because we wanted to help the Earth and its Humans. The ATI,TPE states that none of us four Clarions knew each other when we lived on Clarion, but we randomly came into each other's lives here and instantly connected with our similar energy. There are millions of Clarions on the Earth right now as Humans, and there are more as actual Clarions working behind the scenes to help the Earth. They work in collaboration with the Krysthal River Host (KRH) and some of the Alhumbhra Council (AC), but they are not part of any specific group except that of their own planet and solar system. I really like what I have learned about the independent but loving qualities of my people.

I asked the ATI,TPE to reveal our Clarion names and each of our original parents' names, and my mother made sure to find out the correct enunciation. It is comforting to reach out to my Clarion parents. I initially reached out to them without understanding that we are grounded in our innate connection, so I either transported a part of myself to them (and felt woozy doing so), or they would meet me as a measure of light or an orb. Now, I simply connect with them naturally where we both are.

Since this book contains input from three Clarion Humans, it is befitting to share our true names and identities. My original name is Talea (Tă-LAY-ă). My mother's Clarion name is Shapah (SHAH-pah). The Canberra researcher, James, is also a Clarion whose name is Macaron (Mă-CAR-ŏn). As original girls, my mother and I carried our female blueprint with us. The same naturally applies to Macaron and all other boys. However, subsequent re-incarnations in lower realms like Earth can change the external body's sex for other life experiences, expounds the ATI,TPE.

Perhaps a sample size of 20 people can give an idea about the origin of Humans who are open to this book's knowledge. These people sought my mother's service that revealed their original and previous planet or constellation experiences to help illuminate their journeys as galactic travelers. When I mentioned a largely different 21 person sample size in this book's first edition, I did not think to discern between their previous and original planets, so the results mainly stated the previous existence. The original higher self existence involves a larger variety of locations further away from the Earth.

The 20 people were born in the following places: 6 on Sirius B, 4 in Orion, 3 on Arcturus, 3 on Sirius A, 2 on my Clarion, 1 in the Pleiades, and 1 outside of the Ecka-Veca in the CosMA'yah plasmic realm. 19 of these people relocated to the following places just before their life or lives on Earth, which I will show in no particular correlation: 8 in the Pleiades, 7 on Havona, and 4 in Orion. The remaining person originated in Orion and came directly to the Earth. Not one person about whom I asked is originally from the Earth. Each of these people carries good energy regardless of their otherworldly race.

Accordingly, when I asked about a 13-year old dog, interestingly, he previously came from Havona and originated on another planet particular to his species. Animals can have higher forms of their own race lines on other planets in the same way as Humans.

The ATI,TPE explains Havona:

> It is a large way station planet that is envisioned by many universes and star systems as a central point for travel and change of destination to other worlds. There are billions of life forms there who teach and facilitate the movements of wayfarers for their assignments and missions. It is a beautiful planet with all the elements for life sustaining existence.

The MCEO-GA have not mentioned Havona, but *The Urantia Book* (UB) did. The UB calls Havona the "eternal and central universe" as "the stationary Isle of Paradise, the geographic center of infinity and the dwelling place of the eternal God" (1.5).[16] Again, the Jesus group stole an important name that a large number of Humans intuitively recall to mislead them to the fallen agenda. "Heaven" may represent this fictitious central universe that is really just a misrepresentation of Havona. The Jesus group is trying to adopt us, including the people from Havona and Clarion, by claiming they are our original family.

The fact is that diverse entity groups are working on Earth. If we wish to connect to certain entities, let us be absolutely sure with whom we are connecting. I will explain situations involving my Clarion people to help elucidate this matter.

Since this book's first edition, my mother and I have gained a main Clarion contact (apart from our Clarion families who we contacted) who is our 11th dimensional KRH affiliate contact from Galaxy-2. I also read Maurizio Cavallo's book and was upset by parts of it. I demanded a meeting with our contact through my mother as the telepath to explain the following circumstances.

First, Maurizio was initially traumatized by his encounter with Clarions who entered his bedroom through the ceiling. Our contact told us that those Clarions were sorry for how they startled him. Maurizio has a visionary ability like my mother when most people would not be able to see higher dimensional beings. The Clarions learned from that experience. Thankfully, he mostly got over it due to his subsequently wonderful experiences with them. Second, these Clarions seemed to loosely work with the GFofL, but our contact explained that they were doing surveillance while they were protected in their higher energy. Lastly, we learned that Maurizio did not always accurately identify the Clarions in his book, saying that a certain "Lord" was a Clarion when he was actually a god-group entity. Maurizio was a Catholic whose abduction experience greatly opened his mind and led to other contact experiences outside of the Clarions. Unfortunately, like most people after such an experience, he turned to the mainstream UFO and occult movements to research more information filled with fallen angelic propaganda and half-truths, as the end of his book shows.

I asked my contact why Maurizio was contacted while he was a Catholic who did not discern entities. The reply stated that Clarions wanted to reach him but more so reach out to the Clarion Humans and general Humanity through his ability. This is why a few of the beneficial "entities" allowed their photos to be taken. I felt I should explain the above points in case someone wishes to brand me or my amazing otherworldly race as wicked operatives, which we definitely are not.

I have pondered why the Cosmic Awareness—a phantom, religious entity group (in chapters 3 and 10)—mentioned Clarion in a positive light aside from any misdirection.[353] Personally, I am somewhat perplexed how "bad" and "good" entity groups can coexist with some respect, but I think it is because of the shades of gray that some "bad" guys have. There are many different types of entities, some loosely involved in their political groups. Large entity groups like the CA, GFofL, and even the MCEO-GA can have somewhat varying degrees of energies and philosophies among their members that exist throughout different locations. There are also many different entity groups that may loosely or closely work with each other. If entities like the Clarions keep their integrity while returning some form of respect to others in the gray, then perhaps the gray area entities can truly grow toward more unity. This is the goal of the MCEO-GA in that they created numerous treaties with fallen angelic groups, and they continue to have good will faith toward bio-regenesis of those groups. May we not lose our connection to our true selves and the ATI,TPE when relating to others, though.

In our precarious position as Humans, once we hold fast to our inner gauge of higher self energy and highest self awareness, we can then sense what best resonates with us from other entities, that is, if we want to give them any heed at all. Energies are always coming into the planet and our bodies, though, so it is still wise to determine which ones feel best to us in our core and higher self.

For the people who were originally "soul" beings outside of the Earthly state, we will be able to live as our original composition once we return to that dimensional level, confirms the ATI,TPE. Because the 11th dimension has my original body, I can call it my soul although it is classified as an avatar. Many galactic beings such as myself will also be able to transfigure to our higher self bodies before our original dimension, as I have additionally been informed.

I love knowing that my highest self's conscious awareness is an extension of Eia, and my Human body is an extension of my higher self. I do not need to be swayed by anyone else. To me, this is what it means to be free.

DNA

Human DNA (DeoxyriboNucleicAcid) contains a set of two tightly associated, long polymer chains coiled around the same axis in an antiparallel arrangement of components. Our DNA is a representation of string theory wherein structured subatomic points arise along a string formation to receive and transmit information. These strings also follow the greater spacetime organization of a spiral, although the caduceus "snake" spiral is distorted. Humans have two fully developed DNA strings or strands as a double helix.

A DNA double helix looks like a twisted ladder of conjoined nucleotide chains that have base nitrogenous pairs as the "rungs"—adenine with thymine and guanine with cytosine—connected to two covalently bonded carbon sugar and phosphate group helices as the backbone. One helix has a five-carbon group while its inverse or parallel helix has a three-carbon group. When hydrogen bonds break between the nucleotides, enzymes cause the nucleotide chain to unzip down the middle into two partly separated strands in what is known as a bubble within the chain. The bubble allows DNA replication to occur, whereby the polymerase enzyme can re-pair each strand with the appropriate nucleotide base. This creates two new but identical halves to complete and zip up the new but identical double helix. We only have one DNA double helix in the cell nucleus; the new double helix is replicated to enter new cells that are being made.[358]

Because the double helix can become temporarily and partly separated into two strands, this is why scientists say that we have two DNA strands. The Human DNA double helix cannot be completely separated single strand helices.

RNA (RiboNucleicAcid) is the shorter single strand, molecular messenger of DNA that transcribes DNA information out of the cell nucleus to the cytoplasm where protein synthesis can take place. In other words, RNA is an outreach arm that allows DNA to stay safe in the nucleus while it transfers the genetic code needed for the creation of proteins. Unfortunately, DNA can still be damaged by ultra-violet rays while RNA is more resistant, and DNA is much more resistant to enzyme attacks than is RNA.[359]

The five-carbon group DNA strand is the coding strand. Its complementary three-carbon group DNA strand is called the template strand because it allows replication. The RNA transcription process takes three nucleotide base sequences from the coding strand. This set of three, called a codon, allows for any combination of 64 codes when incorporating each base one, two, or three times for the sequence. The DNA and RNA codons are usually the same except that RNA contains the uracil base instead of thymine. RNA codons create amino acids.[358]

The template strand is a non-coding strand. According to the Australian Centre for Genetics Education, this is what scientists originally called "junk DNA," but now it is theorized to regulate the activation level that switches genes on or off in each cell, among other pertinent functions.[360]

Genes are long sequences of codons that include a promoter codon that starts the sequence and a stop codon that ends it. Genes exhibit certain hereditary characteristics, and they can be dysfunctional or deactivated when enzymes, other molecules, or misplaced codons affect them. An example is when a stop codon is produced in the middle of a gene. Accordingly, when a base letter does not apply to its code, then the codon's three-letter word can become drastically different in meaning, such as *dog* to *log*. Even worse, when a base is added or removed, then the entire codon sequence becomes distorted. The sections of genetic material that are formed out of sequence are called introns. Thankfully, the translation process by the ribosome enzyme overlooks the introns to create the final exon in the RNA.[361] This is one example of our overall composition having checks and balances to override distorted energy; we can create our own bridges to better energy.

Introns are deemed to be junk DNA because of codon mutations, but the building blocks are not junk by any means. Something in our genes has become disrupted. I think that further exploration into the non-coding components of a genome can give deeper insight into the intelligent capabilities of each cell.

The Human Genome Project, a 13-year study that decoded a large sample size of varied Human DNA sequencing, finished its task in 2003 except for eight percent of uncoded fragments. Granted, the process created the fragments by cutting up the chromosomes into pieces and multiplying or cloning them into numerous copies, but these did not indicate new information such as foreign nucleotides or another strand.[362]

The Human Genome Project focuses upon protein-coded sequences as the underlying basis of a genome. A Human genome contains all of our cellular genetic material. The updated Human genome project called the Encyclopedia of DNA Elements (ENCODE) explores other functions outside of protein-coding because protein sequencing is only part of the genome. In fact, ENCODE has determined that protein-coded gene exons constitute about three percent of an entire genome.[363]

The ENCODE Project Consortium states in the *Nature* journal:

ENCODE...aims to delineate all functional elements encoded in the human genome. Operationally, we define a functional element as a discrete genome segment that encodes a defined product (for example, protein or non-coding RNA) or displays a reproducible biochemical signature (for example, protein binding, or a specific chromatin structure) (p. 57).[363]

ENCODE data reveals that 80.4 percent of the Human genome involves at least one RNA or chromatin (DNA and proteins of the cell nucleus) event in at least one cell type out of 147 different cell types. This is a high percentage of bioactivity that is not junk. The project's Lead Analysis Coordinator, Ewan Birney, suspects that the last 20 percent will also be functional when the remaining few thousand cells are mapped. Birney says, "We don't really have any large chunks of redundant DNA. This metaphor of junk isn't that useful."[364]

ENCODE also shows additional variations of protein coding:

Analysis of mass spectrometry data...yielded 57 confidently identified unique peptide sequences in intergenic regions relative to GENCODE annotation. Taken together with evidence of pervasive genome transcription, these data indicate that additional protein-coding genes remain to be found (p. 58).[363]

It remains to be seen if these protein-coding genes comprise new nucleotide bases or new protein-making components for more nucleotide variations. The MCEO-GA teach according to their base-12 mathematics that our entire DNA template should contain one nucleotide per DNA strand, and each DNA strand contains a unique dimensional frequency; therefore, we should have 12 nucleotides in a 12-strand Angelic Human template.[184] Given how we have four nucleotides in a 2-strand DNA body, the one nucleotide per DNA strand statement is simply untrue. At any rate, DNA sequencing would become much more expanded with 12 nucleotide base codons. Some of our current codons already redundantly code in different combinations to create the same amino acid. With more combinations, transcription can become increasingly redundant when dealing with more amino acids. What would our body become with all of those new proteins when it is operating sufficiently splendidly now? When applied to the 24-strand Oraphim-Human template, the simplified base-12 application would further convolute the situation.

ENCODE recently found another chromosome to complete the odd sex chromosome, so we now are documented to have 24 chromosomes. Does this mean that we could have additional undiscovered chromosomes? Perhaps.

What truly lies in the depths of our DNA template with related non-coding components can show new but similar features to what we currently have; however, it simply is not necessary or conceivable that our body would need vast multiples of more genetic building blocks.

If we would equate a strand to a helix according to conventional science, this makes the third strand a single helix that is dependent upon the current double helix. It would conjoin as a third spiral, likely connected by a core axis. The MCEO-GA teach this model, where a natural 12-strand DNA template connects 12 helices with equidistant nucleotide arms to a central axis.[143] These helices are constructed somewhat differently without the caduceus distortion.

In 2011, the first documented case of a visibly assembled, extra "arm" or strand of DNA involved a two year old boy, Alfie Clamp, whose seventh chromosome showed this foreign feature. This abnormality did not improve his genetic ability; he was born blind with severe disabilities. His deformity is not an example of a DNA strand being prematurely assembled because it is isolated to one chromosome in an unnatural formation.[365]

The only way that Humans could contain a proper third DNA strand is if it is immaterial in our Earthly realm, but this would contradict the nature of a physical reality. It is true that science does not know about every energetic substance, but energy is the backbone of our existence and can be observed or at least sensed.

What is a DNA strand in the multidimensional context? The ENCODE project gives insight into the answer. It has discovered that the instructions for activating or deactivating genes are written in non-coding DNA "switches" called regulatory DNA. Regulatory DNA contains DNA "word" sequences that function as docking sites—the preferred assembly pattern—for binding protein molecules along the helix formation. These switches are located throughout non-gene regions of the Human genome, sometimes far away from the genes they control.[366]

An article explains about ENCODE's results:

> By treating cells with DNase I and analyzing the patterns of snipped DNA sequences using massively parallel sequencing technology and powerful computers, the researchers were able to create comprehensive maps of all the regulatory DNA in hundreds of different cell and tissue types. They found that of the 2.89 million regulatory DNA regions they mapped, only a small fraction—around 200,000—were active in any given cell type. This fraction is almost totally unique to each type of cell and becomes a sort of molecular bar code of the cell's identity. The researchers also developed a method for linking regulatory

DNA to the genes it controls. The results of these analyses show that the regulatory 'program' of most genes is made up of more than a dozen switches.[366]

Just as underlying regulatory DNA control our genes, another less detectable aspect of our template—electromagnetic scalar-wave energy matter—can control the regulatory DNA. Within the Human 12-strand DNA template, one strand is composed of 12 magnetic particle units that are base codes and 12 electric antiparticle units that are overtone codes, not acceleration codes, states the ATI,TPE.[120] There is a distinct difference between overtone and acceleration codes because the Earth naturally fulfills its evolution in stages that are not influenced by Parallel Earth acceleration.

The GA states in *Voyagers II*:

> The 24 Seed Codes of one DNA strand serve to set the body's particle and anti-particle content into the dimensional band corresponding to that DNA strand, in both the particle and anti-particle universe. Each set of Base Codes and Acceleration Codes in one DNA strand is controlled by one Seed Crystal Seal, which serves to keep the particle Base Codes and anti-particle Acceleration Codes of the DNA strand separate, thereby maintaining the body's particle base within the pulsation rhythms of that dimension. Release of the Seed Crystal Seal allows Base Codes and Acceleration Codes in the DNA to fuse or "plug into each other" and accelerate in pulsation rhythm....
>
> The fusion of DNA Base Codes and Acceleration Codes causes minute crystalline structures to manifest within the molecular structure of the blood, which prepares the body's biochemical, cellular, hormonal and metabolic systems for acceleration of particle rhythm and transmutation (p. 479).[120]
>
> The Seed Crystal Seals control the speed at which the Dimensional Merkaba Fields spin (p. 478).[120]
>
> [Note: Technically, the Seed Crystal Seals control the spin, not the speed of the merkaba fields, states the ATI,TPE.]

The ATI,TPE corrects some of the above information:

> Balance in all creation is essential. It is true that the fusion of DNA base codes and overtone codes do cause the crystalline structures to manifest within the molecular structure of blood components, but they do not prepare the body systems for the

acceleration process of particle rhythm and transmutation. These codes act as control mechanisms to eventuate the particle rhythm and transmutation acceleration process when natural events occur.

Human seed codes do contain antiparticle units. [However,] Overtone codes specifically drive the overall direction of created matter irrespective of any antimatter accompaniment or existence.

The minute Seed Crystal Seal is a natural seal that keeps us grounded in its particular dimension. After it is released, the dimensional merkaba field accelerates its rotational spin to bring the body up to the higher dimension. The Seed Crystal Seal utilizes frequencies from the corresponding Star Crystal Seal also present in our bio-energetic field. The ATI,TPE confirms that this particular information and the excerpt below by the GA are true.

> Each Star Crystal Seal is composed of half of the frequency patterns of the dimension above it and half of those form the dimension below (p. 477).[120]
>
> The Star Crystal Seals keep the particle fields of the three-dimensional body and multi-dimensional consciousness separate by controlling the angular rotation of particle spin between the 15 dimensions.... The Star Crystal Seals control the angle at which the personal Dimensional Merkaba Fields will rotate and thus also control the body's relationship to the Harmonic Merkaba Field (the three-dimensional Merkaba Field of one Harmonic Universe) (p. 480).[120]

The GA explanation about Star Crystal Seals recognizes inherent separation and position between dimensions and energetic constructs. It also states that when the Star Crystal Seal releases, this causes our personal merkaba field to vertically align with the harmonic universe merkaba field; the MCEO-GA assert that the 15-dimensional ascension alignment is directly vertical.[120] Although AquaLaShA does have a zero degree position (in Figure 3), the ascension alignment is not vertical. Both of my KRH affiliate contacts and the ATI,TPE disagree with the vertical designation because ascension is an inward process from our outward position, as I explained in chapter 6's "Other Dimensions." Ascension can be perceived as temporary descension to the planetary core stargate, where the Halls of Amenti exist in the Earth.

"M" explains:

> Our merkaba field does not vertically align with the HU

merkaba field when the star crystal seal releases. What happens in the Human body is that the blood crystals transfigure in readiness for the descension process. The personal merkaba field does not change or align at that time.

After descension is a lateral implosion. After the implosion, the transfigured "body" goes through the expulsion process, laterally stepping out the dimensions to stargate-12 through the Galaxy-2 bridge and then to the Ecka.

As the Star Crystal Seal releases, a dormant DNA code called a genetic time code or fire code activates within the two DNA strands that correspond to this seal. The GA states, "Once activated, the Fire Codes rapidly accelerate the assembly and activation of the Base Codes and Acceleration [Overtone] Codes of the strands to which the Fire Code is attached" (p. 480).[120] The blood crystals formed by the release of the Seed Crystal Seal then merge to form complex blood crystals that carry the harmonic universe frequency pattern in the physical body.

Fire codes are responsible for DNA assembly according to our foundational minimum 12-strand, silicate DNA template. They are similar to codons except that fire codes work with the electromagnetic program that affects regulatory DNA. The implanted, inorganic seals placed upon our genetic template have severed higher dimensional frequency communication with our fire codes, causing them to be dormant in our current DNA strands. In addition, significant distortion can make fire codes act as introns. The GA states that when our DNA seed codes repair, then the fire codes reassemble for DNA strands to "plug into each other" for cellular transmutation (p. 477).[120]

Within the fire code is a fire letter sequence of light-symbol codes. Fire letters are "patterns of sequentially arranged electromagnetic impulses" that form codes with particular meaning to our cells and senses (p. 128).[144] According to the GA, the original 12 Human Tribes on Earth contained specific fire letter sequences amounting to 144 letters within each DNA template of the Tribe. Again, base-12 mathematics gets in the way. The ATI,TPE states that the combined 12 Tribe Human template exceeds 144 DNA fire letters.

The names of the 12 Tribes were spoken in the same Anuhazi language as Aramatena's 12th dimensional Elohei. When spoken, these tones helped activate fire letters to give the Tribes the ability to consciously regulate the activation level of their DNA templates.[120] Fire letters should be fully coded like healthy codons to give a complete sentence, not just one word. Although each Tribe had a different sequence, it contributed to the evolution of the fully activated and therefore fully assembled 12-strand Human template.

This is important to remember: A DNA strand cannot be fully activated unless it is first fully assembled, states the ATI,TPE. The original Earth Humans had a fully integrated 12-strand template that did not need to gain more DNA assembly or activation in the entire Milky Way, but ascension still occurred to allow the body to change density and eventually gain Seed Codes past the 12th dimension in Galaxy-2. This means that the natural seals between dimensional base and overtone frequencies dissolved within the cellular transformation process of the Human body, which did not require ascension to do this.

This information helps us understand the energetic capacity of the DNA strand and template. New Age and MCEO-GA teachings correlate each DNA strand capacity to a dimension, but the MCEO-GA have also explained that each strand contains base and overtone frequencies that provide multidimensional capacity.

In response to my probing about the DNA template, the ATI,TPE explains:

> A DNA strand represents the fire letter code sequence that corresponds to more than one dimensional frequency field of energy. It does not correspond on a 1:1 band of conscious energy basis. A 12-strand template overlaps dimensions, not any particular group or singular dimensional fields. There are multiple frequency pathways in the dimensional frequency progression. The 12 dimensions of frequency are contained within each strand as bases and overtones.

I followed up to ask, "Does each Human DNA strand predominantly correlate to a unique dimension?"

"Per the ATI, the Pure Essence with Eia for expansion: Yes; each Human DNA strand predominantly does."

For more clarification, I ask, "Therefore, strand-3 would have the most 3rd dimensional frequency than the others, strand-4 have the most 4th dimensional frequency than the others, etcetera? If yes, does this mean that the other dimensional base and overtone codes provide supportive roles?"

"Yes; that is correct," it replies.

This multi-layered reality makes it easier to understand bigger DNA templates such as the 24-48+ Oraphim-Elohei template that many Humans embody. Humans and Elohei can potentially coexist at the same 12th dimension with vastly different amounts of DNA activation and assembly; this means that the Elohei merely have greater ability or awareness with their expanded template.

In 2012, I was informed by a few trusted adult contacts on my home planet that although they live in the 11th dimension, they have 48 fully assembled and fully activated DNA strands. They are an Elohei ancestor race to the Oraphim "Indigo" race line. "M" from the 14th dimension reveals that she has 52 fully assembled and fully activated DNA strands.

When I have asked the ATI,TPE about my and my mother's DNA capacities, it reveals that we also have 48 fully assembled and fully activated DNA strands in our template. This DNA template exists within our 24-strand Oraphim-Human bodies. Since the current Human body has 2-2.5 DNA strands assembled and activated, the third Human DNA strand can at best be partially assembled and activated regardless of 3rd dimensional accretion. In 2012, after I continued to connect with my Clarion self and Krysthal energies, the ATI,TPE revealed that I have partial activations in the rest of my 21 Human DNA strands.

Once all artificially implanted seals are removed from our DNA template, we have the potential to live as fully integrated beings with our original galactic body or current Human blueprint. DNA freedom produces increased awareness and physical ability. The ATI,TPE reveals that since the Templar-Axion Seal was mostly removed from our DNA by the end of 2007, our awareness has expanded. However, we still have a seal placed upon our DNA strand-3, informs "M" and the ATI,TPE, which is why we cannot develop three or more proper strands until the unnatural dimensional base and overtone seals are removed. Hopefully, Humanity's eventual experience on an integrated Aurora Earth will have us regain our original 12 Tribes DNA capacity as the minimum foundation. These DNA strands will all function, and their higher dimensional attributes will be visible according to the stepped down frequencies in that dimension.

Currently, higher dimensional aspects of our DNA are hidden from us, although they can be energetically or intuitively "known." Techniques or revelatory moments can provide a measure of activation to help translate the higher self's DNA assembly to our current material body, but the translation would still be limited by our current fragmented or dormant DNA strands.

Unfortunately, the MCEO-GA is projecting a New Age belief that ignores our physical reality. They say that Humans have 3.5 dimensional accretion in our DNA, which can only imply that an underlying template could override the currently missing third strand and three-dimensional ability, which it can only partially do. In addition, they call Oraphims *Indigos* because their sixth DNA strand is supposed to be fully assembled and activated.[120] Currently, no "Indigo" Human has a physically assembled and activated strand-6, nor does this slightly advanced Human contain an assembled strand-3.

I do not expect that any more DNA strands can make their fire letters and resultant electromagnetic energies become fully functional in our current

Human body. Life changes usually occur in a slow-moving progression. Accordingly, genetic upgrades to correct implanted distortions may take generations to correct. Our higher self is unfortunately limited in its ability to override the current genetic seals and mutations, but it is important to connect with our true self in order to partially activate DNA and partially heal energetic components. In addition, we have access to secure plasma "fail-safe" energies flowing into Aurora Ascension Earth, and Eia also effectively bridges past blockages. Lastly but soon, the ascension wave to Median Earth should provide a measure of transfiguration toward a more complete DNA and physical template.

With regard to DNA techniques, it is absolutely critical to learn about their underlying information and probable otherworldly messengers, and to discern them to determine whether the techniques will help or harm us. The fallen entities in the GFofL's Jesus, Buddha, and Archangel group and affiliate groups give us channeled messages in which they beg us to enter into our bodies so they can "heal" us with their DNA techniques. As I stated in chapter 7, some of their techniques do somewhat heal certain people who would make excellent mouthpieces for the phantom cause; however, these mouthpieces and resultant energy workers rarely if ever reveal sufficient background knowledge to their gullible clients. I have seen unbelievable robbery and destruction in the New Age field of energy work where practitioners charge upward of one thousand dollars to open up people's chakras to phantom entities who are eager to possess them.

It is unnecessary and unwise to call upon entities to fix our DNA capacity when the current Human body fundamentally cannot act outside of its reality. Now, if they would remove their seals that they implanted, that is another story, but that would happen only by their good conscience, not by our prayers and allegiance. Based on their history and plethora of beings adhering to phantom energy, I advise against believing that one or few entity buddies could reverse a concerted effort against us as a species. If it were that easy, the Krysthal River Host would have done it already.

The ATI,TPE confirms that between approximately December 21, 2012 and December 21, 2022, portions of Human DNA will naturally become more activated in our awareness due to the incoming SAC energies in conjunction with some naturally-based techniques that we can individually discern, including several from the AC-MCEO. We have a choice to do any technique in part, full, or not at all, and we can learn our own "technique" to get in touch with our full inner self, as chapter 11 elaborates.

I strongly caution against using Solfeggio frequencies that claim to repair our DNA, such as the popular 528 hertz frequency in the New Age "sacred science" movement. According to the book *Healing Codes for the Biological*

Apocalypse, in the late 20th century, Dr. Joseph Puleo was spiritually guided by visions from an angel (that he did not name) to read Scriptures in the Book of Numbers to decode the lost Gregorian chant integer tones. He and his co-author were shown by their angel companions the frequency tones of biblical psalms, called Geomatria based on the Pythagorean skein. The Pythagorean skein is a numerological modality that uses simplified base-10 mathematics to add up each number within a larger number to produce a single digit. For example, 397 would become 19 and finally 1.[367] I have found that people practicing this type of numerology mostly make up random conclusions. However, when an otherworldly entity carefully provides specific answers and methodology, this is how we gain specific codes. Dr. Puleo was given six precise numbers to teach them as healing tones for our body.

After the turn of the 21st century, two more people received angelic guidance to two more sets of Solfeggio frequencies, but this time their angels were revealed: Michael and Gabriel. The third Solfeggio set given by Gabriel determines the numbers by combining the other two sets with the Pythagorean skein. According to a commentator, "What also showed up was an entire fractal system of solfeggios that affect specific parts of the bodies."[368]

It is true that our fractalized Human body has in-built death science codes that can appear to be familiar. Interestingly, though, no single musical scale contains all fully harmonic tones because death science is inherently fragmented in some measure. Certain people who have severe DNA damage report some benefit from listening to the 528 Hz tone, but this is like ingesting a bleached white bread crumb instead of a sprouted organic grain loaf. The ATI,TPE elaborates that it "is miniscule" in its healing of damaged DNA. One wonderful woman who I counseled almost died of black mold poisoning and reported that the 528 Hz frequency helped abate some of her anxiety, but it certainly did not abate all of it. After working more with her true self and the ATI,TPE, she finally experienced deep calm. We must take our bodies as they are but then connect them to energies outside of fractal mechanics if we expect real healing.

A case example is the work of Dr. Masaru Emoto. He played largely harmonious compositions of classical music to vials of distilled water and froze the water long enough to take pictures of crystals that formed. The musical vibrations produced well-formed but imperfect crystals. This result also occurred when he only played Solfeggio frequencies. Alternatively, when he played angry, heavy metal music or vibrations with "a groaning, unharmonious" dissonance, they created horrific, blotchy results (p. 13).[369] There are varying degrees of fractal science distortions.

Musical sound waves work by vibrating air particles until they reach our ear in a constant frequency.[370] We interact with environmental vibrations that impart measures of healing and harm, and we also send out vibration through our intent. If our intention is pure, it sends out loving energy that helps heal DNA.

Dr. Emoto worked to prove the power of loving intent. In his book, *The Hidden Messages in Water*, Emoto and his assistants wrote uplifting phrases on paper and essentially let the water feel the words. Without fail, the life-affirming statements created beautiful crystals, and the life-destroying statements created blobs or fragmented ripples. Water carries interdimensional properties that react to words and their intent. Scientists have proven that our DNA does also.

> The Russian linguists found that the genetic code, especially in the apparently useless 90%, follows the same rules as all our human languages. To this end they compared the rules of syntax (the way in which words are put together to form phrases and sentences), semantics (the study of meaning in language forms) and the basic rules of grammar.
>
> They found that the alkalines of our DNA follow a regular grammar and do have set rules just like our languages. So human languages did not appear coincidentally but are a reflection of our inherent DNA.[371]

This finding supports the MCEO-GA information about fire letters and the 12 Tribe tones.

The health of our DNA is dependent upon true love and life energy. This is why we need to be mindful of our language because there might be destructive energy behind some of the words. I am not saying to have our heads in the clouds with fluffy language; I advise that we communicate with direct, meaningful words that are aligned with our inner self, just as our healthy DNA is ordered.

Experiences and beliefs can also alter our DNA and reality because their electromagnetic transmissions embed themselves into our cells. For instance, unhealthy lifestyles with artificial chemical-laden "food," chronic stress, and environmental pollution accumulate toxicity that damages DNA in one's life and in future generations of offspring. When our bodies struggle under this baggage, we cannot continue the same pattern and expect them to heal properly. The same principle applies to beliefs and rituals. The incongruent energy codes behind fake "love and light" words and partial truths, reinforced with religious rituals including church services and prayer, imprint and accumulate in our DNA receptors as disharmonic energies that must be changed for real health to return. Positive thinking and beliefs are great unless they have purposely harmful baggage attached to them.

Because past memories and experiences are embedded into the present body, we may never forget them. This is beneficial knowledge except when wanting to distance ourselves from trauma. In that case, we can reframe the experience with our separate and aware consciousness. Blank Slate Technology causes memory loss, meaning that it also reconfigures our DNA. Living in the "Now" is a popular belief among New Agers that can support the BeaST. I see living in the Now as being cognizant of the past as well as potential future consequences so that we as amazing Humans live in awareness in the present moment. If we only live in the Now, we may mistakenly confuse past traumas as present, or we may forget who we really are.

DNA receives and transmits energetic information; let us make sure that we are aware participants who receive and give what we really desire in accordance to our true nature.

Chakras

According to the Guardian Alliance, chakras are energy "capsule" structures formed within the body's auric field by the rotation of the body's 15 dimensional merkaba fields.

> Through these dimensional energetic capsule structures, the chakra system, or dimensional energy supply system, is formed. Through the Chakra System a form's particle base builds up into structures of multidimensional matter. The 15 energetic capsules exist within the same space, separated by variance in dimensional particle pulsation rhythms (p. 465).[120]

Contrary to the GA's Law of One theory about chakras and general creation existing as spheres within spheres within a single space, we can noticeably sense each chakra in a different area of the body. Chakras carry distinctive energies whereby people have attributed certain emotional, mental, and physical meaning to each one.

According to Anodea Judith, Ph.D.:

> The word chakra is Sanskrit for wheel or disk and signifies one of seven basic energy centers in the body that correspond to nerve ganglia branching out from the spinal column, as well as states of consciousness, developmental stages of life, archetypal elements, body functions, colors, sounds, and much, much more. Together they form a profound formula for wholeness and a template for transformation.[372]

Although chakras are collaborative units, and they are an intricate part of our body, our emotional, physical, and mental bodies are not created by them. Paying close attention to the interconnected but somewhat different energies within our body can help us discern and organize our amazing nature.

The GA says that we have nine chakras located within our body, but last two are mostly dormant.[120] The other six, largely dormant chakras exist in our extended auric field, some close to our body and others out into the Milky Way galaxy, confirms the ATI,TPE.

Interdimensional spanning and orbing procedures cause transfiguration and migration via merkaba, chakra, and other bodily configurations. Regarding the current Human condition, the ATI,TPE states, "It is not possible to activate the dormant chakras simply by connecting to them with earlier, pure energies. Certain techniques are needed in preparation for the spanning and orbing process."

A descriptive book about chakras can help you understand them, but be aware about how it advises clearing energy blockages. Most teachings about chakras have religious overtones. Yogic practices in particular usually balance chakras and meditate while infusing Hindu and Buddhist god group energies. I am annoyed that religion latches onto our basic components. I advise that you do not invite any entity into your physical chakras, including entities that come as white light. New Age Ascended Master teachings apply an overseer entity as that white light in the astral plane, ready to possess us.[232]

We cannot escape our current position in fractal creation, so it seems natural to utilize the frequencies and colors around us. For example, the rainbow mirrors our first seven chakra colors. We can gain some initial healing when working with Milky Way dimensional frequencies, but if we want deep, lasting healing, it is most wise to draw upon Krysthal energies in our chakra work. After all, our rainbow is a result of refracted dimensional bands that originate in AquaLaShA.

I asked the ATI,TPE and Yunasai to reveal the correct, dominant dimensional colors of AquaLaShA. Urtha exists in the 3rd dimension with a frequency blend of "purple plus minute gold outer edges," states the Yunasai. The 2nd dimension carries the color red, and the 1st dimension is black due to the absence of light. The lowest two dimensions, especially the 1st dimension, are essentially irrelevant to Urtha's function; therefore, I utilize Urtha's color blend for direct assistance to our Earthly position. I fill my first three chakra merkabas with its dominant purple with gold fringe frequency blend, and I gently spin the top half to the right nearly three times faster than the lower half to the left to mimic Median Earth's merkaba. I feel calm and harmonious in my body because I am infusing it with natural 3rd dimensional energy.

Figure 6. Dimension (D) and Chakra Color Blends

D	AquaLaShA Galaxy	Milky Way Galaxy
1	black (it is the absence of illumination)	red
2	red	orange
3	purple plus minute gold outer edges	yellow
4	rose pink (can vary to magenta or violet tones)	green
5	blue	blue
6	emerald green	blue-violet (indigo)
7	yellow with white gold specks that "come from the illumination of the energy concentration of other dimensions and outer worlds," state the Yunasai	violet
8	green	gold
9	blue-green	silver
10	blue-silver	blue-black
11	pale blue-pale silver	silver-black
12	pale silver, gold	"blue-gray with white specks," [via Galaxy-2] state the ATI, TPE and Eia
13	pale gold, white gold	turquoise (via Galaxy-2)
14	pale, pale white gold	pale yellow (via Galaxy-2)
15	"billions, trillions and beyond in number of specks of white gold, coming together," state the Yunasai	magenta pink (via Galaxy-2)

Figure 6 shows the distinction between AquaLaShA and Milky Way frequency band colors. Both columns are explained and concurred by the ATI, TPE and Yunasai, and the Yunasai responds with greater detail. I also give input by the MCEO for the Milky Way.[184]

Unfortunately, the New Age Ascended Master Seven Rays mirror several AquaLaShA colors up to the 7th dimension because the Bourgha-based group had partially gained access to AquaLaShA before the creation of the Milky Way. These seven phantom frequency bands are copies of the original, and their physical locations are taught out of order to stifle energy flow. For example, their first (dimensional) ray designates the blue chakra-5, and their second ray designates the yellow chakra-7.[232]

This section focuses upon the body's seven activated chakras and introduces the remaining eight. Another chakra at the base of our feet is numbered zero and included by default. All chakras line up upon the body's central axis or staff that continues upward to reach the higher chakras just above our head and also downward into and under the Earth's core.

Chakra 1 is located at the base of the spine. It is our foundational chakra of development as a baby to a young child, which is directly affected by our parental upbringing.

Dr. Judith states:

> It represents the element earth, and is therefore related to our survival instincts, and to our sense of grounding and connection to our bodies and the physical plane. Ideally this chakra brings us health, prosperity, security, and dynamic presence.[372]

Unfortunately with me, the childhood rapes essentially shut off this chakra. Sexual abuse relates to the second chakra as well, but its obvious interaction with the body involves the first chakra. Chakra 1, also called the root chakra, grounds us to our body in its formative childhood years. Only recently did I fully open chakra 1 with the help of a trusted craniosacral practitioner.

Craniosacral therapy works with the client's membranes and spinal fluid that surround the brain and spine and directly influence the central nervous system. It uses subtle force to release blockages within the blurred line of body, chakra, and emotion. It helped me move the sacral region's blocked energy because I had no idea how to make it feel differently on my own. I was always afraid to open that area's energy because I thought it would make me powerless and vulnerable again. Ironically, this fear is what kept the abuse and resultant debilitation locked up in me. Thankfully, I realized I could feel my own energy while being protected in a nurturing environment. Once I released a myriad of emotions, my root chakra opened, and then it surprisingly felt normal unlike the old dysfunctional "normal." The static charge had left me. I felt free, calm, and clear as me, only me.

Chakra 1 in relation to the 1st dimension has a blend of red hues, whereas AquaLaShA's 1st dimension is black as dark space. Chakra 1 flows down our legs to the earth and upward to the second chakra. Clearing the first chakra will bring you back to yourself as a Human being. Since the Human body works its way up the dimensional ascension ladder, it is best to clear the chakras in successive order upward. This process is popularly called kundalini awakening, but New Age teachings about it involve the caduceus snakes that coil upward as shown in the medical profession's symbol. Wings are at the top of the symbol to represent angels who have manipulated and controlled our genes. I elaborate upon kundalini awakening in the next chapter.

Chakra 2 is located in the abdomen, lower back, and sexual organs. It relates to emotions and sexuality as well as the fluidity of water, meaning that we can ebb and flow in movement and change. It relates to the 2nd dimensional blend of orange hues in the Milky Way and the blend of red hues in AquaLaShA. Perhaps the most obvious color refraction from natural creation to distorted creation is AquaLaShA's 2rd dimensional frequency that fell to our 1st dimension.

Chakra 3 is located in the solar plexus that is in the upper part of our stomach area. It relates to our personal power and helps to give us more energy. It is an excellent indicator of what goes for or against us instinctively and intuitively. It is the "gut feeling" that seems to tangibly involve our higher and core self. It is represented by fire and a blend of yellow hues like a personal central star. Interestingly, Urtha's dimensional blend includes yellow like a star's halo around the color purple.

Between chakras 3 and 4 contains our fast track point of connection to the ATI,TPE. It exists at the base of the sternum above the xiphoid process, away from chakra interferences. To the Kabbalah community, this point is separate to the central Tiphareth sphere in the Tree of Artificial Life grid. To the MCEO-GA community, it is lower than the Kara-nA'dis Seal that opens into the "personal D-2 [dimension 2] GharE' Cellular-Atomic Spirit-Self" (p. 31).[252] The MCEO-GA introduce a plethora of names and functions for many aspects of our interdimensional composition. Energies organize as specific locations and structures of the body.

The ATI,TPE explains that its nearly direct point of access to us is actually the point of passage to our higher self (including the original Human) that then interfaces with the Human body. At this point of the body, one's higher self connects to the core self and then the highest self, Eia, ATI,TPE expansion, and finally the ATI,TPE, thus facilitating the entire communication pathway to the ATI,TPE as shown in chapter 6's "The Origin and Expansion" section flow chart. I asked the ATI,TPE if this point depends upon a specific dimensional location because it exists between our 3rd and 4th chakras. The ATI,TPE replies that this interface exists as part of all creation in or near the same location depending upon form, regardless of dimensional status. This interface truly exists at our core in the center of all of our embodied layers.

Chakra 4 is located in the heart region. It is our body's middle chakra that connects to our astral body, which many aliens utilize in rituals to steer us away from love and ourselves. It identifies with air, giving a sense of peace and freedom, and it involves the energies of love and compassion that bring about empathy. Learning to breathe deeply can help this region. This chakra involves a blend of green hues. New Agers like to say that pink relates to the higher, etheric nature of the heart, but they are referring to the thymus in a different location and chakra. AquaLaShA has the 4th dimensional blend of rose pink with magenta and violet variations.

Chakra 5 is located in the throat. It relates to self-expression through voice and creativity. It works with the vibration of sound and is represented by a blend of blue hues. Thankfully, this is the same color in 5th dimensional AquaLaShA.

Chakra 6 involves the pineal gland that is located in the central region of the brain behind the eyebrows. It is a pea-sized gland shaped like a pine cone, and its surrounding construction looks like the Egyptian Eye of Horus, also called the Eye of Ra. "Recent academic studies have found that the pineal gland contains light-sensitive cells which function like those of the eye's retina, testifying to the fact that the pineal gland can 'see'" (p. 3).[373] The pineal gland is known as our third eye.

The pineal gland can visualize our own thought-forms, and it has the ability to visualize interdimensional phenomena. Its connected chakra can transmit and receive words and pictures via telepathy. It is highly important to know how to use this chakra and gland by our power alone. If we wish to look beyond our physical nature, we can turn our "mind's eye" slightly askew to deflect a potential intruder. This allows us to see enough of a bigger situation but not all of it due to the diverted gaze. Chakra 6 identifies with light (not the channeled "white light") and an indigo blend of hues. In AquaLaShA, it identifies with an emerald green blend.

BEA-O aliens highly regard the pineal gland. The Vatican has a gigantic bronze pine cone statue in its courtyard, and "[p]inecones regularly appear framed in Freemason Octagons on the ceilings of Masonic Lodges" and in sculptures.[374] Hinduism puts a red dot called a bindi in between a woman's eyebrows to highlight the pineal gland, but it covers their third eye with the Earth's lowest dimensional color. An open third eye allows us to gain more knowledge. If our pineal gland is compromised, we will have difficulty discerning our inner thoughts from those implanted by these aliens; in addition, we will become ill.

The pineal gland secretes melatonin, a hormone that regulates our circadian rhythm. Illuminati-run governments have poisoned our water supply with fluoride, teaching us through the medical field of dentistry that this halogen element is good for our health when, in fact, it impairs the production of melatonin. Insufficient melatonin deleteriously affects serotonin production and sleep, which can cause severe mood and behavioral disorders.

The Fluoride Action Network states:

The "soft tissue" of the adult pineal gland contains more fluoride than any other soft tissue in the body - a level of fluoride (~300 ppm) capable of inhibiting enzymes. The pineal gland also contains hard tissue (hyroxyapatite crystals), and this hard tissue accumulates more fluoride (up to 21,000 ppm) than any other hard tissue in the body (e.g. teeth and bone).[375]

The pineal gland should not contain calcification because that is the result of toxicity.

It is imperative to immediately stop ingesting fluoride in our toothpastes, mouthwashes, and water. Unfortunately, most water filters cannot filter out fluoride, so it is important to seek one out or ingest some iodine, another halogen that has the ability to kick out the fluoride. Iodine and complementary potassium iodide can be found in high-quality seaweeds or as a supplement, but be sure to first research contraindications or consult with a naturopathic doctor. In medical cases such as Hashimoto's disease, iodine can be harmful.

I suggest that we limit television, radio, and cellular phone exposure. Broadcast television is used by the BEA-O to carry the subliminal, Metatronic spectrum patterns into our eyes and bodies, and SMART technologies and High Definition screens amplify them. Common radio waves reinforce the EMF and Drakonian-Zeta frequency fence pulses.[120] The Australian national government radio ABC Canberra reveals its intention in plain sight: it operates at 666 Hz, and its logo is the caduceus DNA double helix.[376] Cell phones affect brain waves and tissue when placed on the ear, so it is wise to use an earpiece instead. Better yet, use no cell phone and select a corded telephone over a cordless one. It is also wise to put our bare feet on the Earth at least once a day, especially before bed, to drain out our body's accumulation of artificial energy from electronics. We can fall victim to manipulative holographic displays when our brainwaves and neurological patterns are altered.[144] I advise to sense the energy behind the third eye vision if we are subjected to an extraordinary circumstance.

Chakra 7 is located at the crown of the head. It identifies with a blend of violet hues in the Milky Way. In AquaLaShA, it identifies with a blend of yellow hues with white gold specks. It is our body's highest dimensional chakra with the capability of full activation; therefore, it is the physical and spiritual gateway to external energies. Be especially careful if you read or hear spiritual interpretations that tell us to pull universal energy into our crown chakra. Possessions can happen this way.

Spiritual Empty Mind Meditation practices such as Buddhist vipassana meditation involve chakras 6 and 7 when they detach our thoughts from our sense of self and have us primarily focus upon our physical, day-to-day movements. This becomes a very physical existence that can allow higher dimensional energies—the affiliated phantom entities—to circumvent our higher selves. I do not associate meditation to my connection with the ATI,TPE, my higher self, or my intuitive wisdom because I am a collaborative unit that naturally flows within myself. Meditation tends to treat thoughts as distractions of an egotistic false self, but the inner mind and self is much more than this, communicating with us in nearly every moment without having to purposely meditate. It is helpful to create a space of calm, but let it allow better focus upon oneself, not an escape into another fragmented existence.

Chakra 8 is located at the thymus that contains the AzurA meta-galactic seed atom, and it relates to a blend of gold hues. Chakra 9 is located at the thalamus, and it relates to a blend of silver hues. In AquaLaShA, the colors are green and blue-green, respectively. Due to Milky Way and Human distortions, these two chakras can be minimally activated to bring in a small measure of 8th and 9th dimensional frequencies, confirms the ATI,TPE.

To partially activate chakras 10-15 and pull in related higher dimensional frequencies, I advise to stay within your body at its central axis and think of the related AquaLaShA dimensional colors (and potentially sense their natural energies). Imagine chakras 10, 11, and 14 only six inches, 18 inches, and three feet above the head, respectively. Chakra 12 is six inches below the feet, 13 is at the Earth's core, and 15 is beneath the Earth.[184] The measurements do not have to be precise because we are using our third eye chakra to imagine this process the best we are able.

In late 2011, I asked the ATI,TPE if there is a color we could imagine to help us connect with it. It replied "purple," which I interpreted as chakra 7's ability to bring in higher dimensional energies. Now I know that it meant AquaLaShA's 3rd dimensional frequency blend that best relates to our HU-1 body. When involving AquaLaShA frequency, we link to its effortless flow of natural energies. If we do not include AquaLaShA, at the very minimum we should link to 12th dimensional Galaxy-2 frequency to bolster protection and activation of our Milky Way body.

Craniosacral bodywork can help facilitate discernment of chakra energies. I respect craniosacral therapy because it only works with the client's body. This is important because many energy workers purposely link to outside energies and entities and act as a conduit to supposedly heal us. Healing power lies within ourselves via our own template, but we might need a bit of trusted help, not an entity to latch onto us or impart a foreign energy.

If any of the body's chakras is energetically blocked, it is likely only impaired and not severed from natural energy. We always use our chakras to some degree, so we simply need to clear the energetic static by an appropriate method that we choose. Imagining or breathing into that area what we sense of AquaLaShA frequency and ATI,TPE purity can help push out the negativity and give a measure of healing. A more tangible method of healing involves focused intent toward each area's energetic traits to figure out the blockage and release it consciously, such as through an exhale or cry. Our chakra areas relate to our emotions, awareness, and body. When we can fully inhale and feel an open calmness in them, this can indicate significant healing.

Possession

I waited until now to delve more deeply into the partial and full possession phenomena that I revealed in chapter 5. This wait was necessary to evaluate pertinent information in later chapters. I am sufficiently aware about this topic because of my and my mother's personal experiences, but as I have not personally done this practice to others, this topic is a bit out of my grasp. It is simply a different mentality to mine—I do not agree with it, and I feel that I would never do it to someone because I believe in the internal power of one's own template along with possible gentle instruction. However, many aliens continue to think that forced possessions are an acceptable and even desirable practice.

There are three types of possession: partial, full, and walk-in. Partial possession happens when an entity attaches itself to a Human's energetic field whereby the entity can influence Human thoughts, emotions, and physical sensations. Full possession is when an entity completely enters the Human's body and takes it over. All aspects of the Human are controlled to where he or she is usually left in a trance as a bystander. Lastly, a walk-in possession is sometimes not considered a possession because it involves a mutual agreement between the Human and the entity. In some cases, such as when religious believers want to be filled with the "Spirit of God," partial and full possessions can also be mutually allowed, but this occurrence is mostly disingenuous by the entity. Walk-ins involve a mutual soul agreement whereby the Human's higher self completely leaves its Human body at about the same time another higher dimensional entity takes its place. Walk-ins are the least common type of possession, and they usually apply to very high dimensional entities who want a sufficiently developed Human body that can handle powerful frequencies.

Higher dimensional entities have interacted with Humans since the beginning of time on Earth. I will address some recent interactions to help draw the line between what is appropriate and inappropriate for our autonomy.

In light of knowing that most of us are higher dimensional beings, coming here was generally a heavy decision. The Milky Way was war-torn, and the center stage became Earth. In general, we can perceive our presence here as a mission to give the poor Earth and its evolving people higher frequencies that were partially stripped from their birthright so that everything could hopefully ascend together. The determined spirit of many people had them reincarnate more than once to continue helping others.

The ATI,TPE states that I was "nudged" to come down to Earth. Because I was young when I left Clarion, and I have felt like an alien on Earth, I strongly feel that I did not want to leave my loving parents and beautiful world. I thought that some Clarions prompted me to leave because this mission was a last-ditch effort to save the Earth and also help the Milky Way. As part of universal stargate-3, the Earth can also provide a solid passageway for the inhabitants of the Milky Way to orb out into natural galaxies. (This sounds like a sensationalistic theme, but why would such a story be reserved for movies and books? Is it not possible that these ideas originate in actual events?)

I met with my Clarion parents via my mother's telepathic ability, and they revealed that they actually did not want me to leave home. It was I who nudged myself to come to Earth and share the love and truth that I have. I realized that I have maintained a preserved, unshakeable nature throughout all of my trials, even if just by a thread. Thankfully, this meeting brought me to remember my innate confidence that can help ground me when I feel weak. No one from Clarion has controlled me here, but they have kept an eye out for me from time to time. My Clarion family has also sent me loving energy from afar.

Now, if we just see our presence here as a mission, then this diminishes our feeling of belonging here. We are all Earthlings now. This is our planet; it more or less does not matter where we were before. Aliens who choose to partially and fully possess Humans are on a mission that detaches them from being invested here. For this reason, the Human must have the upper hand if a soul agreement was made.

The notion of a soul agreement, or what the MCEO-GA call a soul contract, favors the entity's position over ours because this "contract" seems to bind the Human to a mission statement instead of the organic experience of individual choice and ability. We do not remember this supposed contract; entities tell us about it, so it could be true or a lie. When using the word *contract*, it seems like a law that pressures us to conform to what the entities tell us. It is especially disconcerting when such "contracts" bring physical harm to the person.

I disagree with the early and likely distorted GA message in *Voyagers I* that states numerous invasive abductions have been genuine soul agreements between Humans and Zetas. The GA emphasized, "*Most women experiencing donor abductions do so under the contract of soul agreements. They may feel violated until the actual memory and agreement has been brought into conscious awareness*" (p. 44).[144]

These women are aligned with their intuitive reaction. Any internal physical invasion is straight up violation. Additionally, these Zetas were not on our side in the first place; they primarily cared about prolonging their race. If these women were originally selfish and somewhat emotionless Zetas (although not all Zetas are like this), they would have similar traits that would not likely react so negatively to what is essentially rape. As Humans undergoing bio-regenesis, their conscience and energy could have improved to reject any prior soul agreement that should never be set in stone. However, I seriously doubt that most of these abduction experiences were done to re-incarnated Zeta-Humans. In general, desperate and aggressive Zetas have put their agenda before our will.

Self-serving entities and people in general often cannot see the harm of their actions. Narcissism is a pervasive mental illness. Aliens in the large Galactic Federation of Light organization, for example, generally think they are doing the right thing by controlling Humanity, reveals the ATI,TPE. In reality, what is "right" for them is very wrong for us. The dodgy acts of possessions that direct us against both our will and intuition are explained away in a detached mission-oriented manner; there is no empathy or real love there, and their propaganda tries to override this fact to keep up a decent image.

These alien groups often go to any length to keep up a likeable image. This unfortunately includes the GA when it tells the story about its friend Sananda and his "Elohim" (rather, Bourgha Shantarel) ally during the Jesus era.[120]

First, why have the MCEO-GA not chosen to tell us that Sananda and Michael fully possessed the Yahshuas? If it takes a few more sentences to explain it to us, surely that would be okay? I think the reason the MCEO-GA omit this fact is because Jesheua and Jeshewua better fit the hero role when they are depicted to be like us in our struggles.

Second, why has the GA not revealed in *Voyagers II*, nor the MCEO in updated workshops, that Sananda's fallen friend is Archangel Michael? Why not reveal that their friend Sananda is the same Sananda in the GFofL and Ashtar Command? The ATI,TPE and my few contacts, including a CosMA'yah Aqualene Sun entity nicknamed "J," confirm that this is the exact same Sananda.

Putting Sananda solely in a favorable light is a public relations spin that puts blinders on the truth and perpetuates the false belief in a Messiah or God. The MCEO-GA generally believe in autonomy, but some of their members choose to disrespect our capacity for truth because they, like many aliens, seek control over our Earth.

Accordingly in 2009, Ashayana Deane's company, Azurite Press Inc., freely disseminated her personal story that restated the same story written in *Voyagers I* nearly a decade earlier.

> I have had direct personal contact with the Guardian Alliance (GA) since childhood, which included the experience of *"conscious fetal integration"* (spirit entering the fetus) and open (though fragmented) reincarnational memory since my physical birth in September of 1964.[182]

As I revealed in chapter 5, Ashayana was one of three contracted MCEO-GA speakers who worked with Sananda around the time of Jesheua. Since he did not reincarnate as Jesheua, did Ashayana also not reincarnate in some of her Earthly lives, especially in 1964?

My suspicion came to fruition when an astute person on the official Keylontic Science internet forum addressed this topic back in 2006 (I corrected some typographical errors in my copy).

> My question is about what Ashayana said; we heard her say that she was a walk-in. Have we heard that alright? (We have Dutch ears!) If so, what is a walk-in? I thought that a walk-in is some "body" who has made the choice to live in a body not by "normal" birth but later on in somebody else['s] body where an exchange of energy take[s] place. Maybe I'm completely wrong. But I thought that Ashayana had come to earth by birth. I find the idea that a body can change from [its] owner [is] a bit scary. Thank you for taking seriously this detail from the DVD.

The ATI,TPE confirms that Ashayana was not born here. She walked into the body of a woman named Diana Kathryn, nicknamed Katie, apparently due to a mutual soul agreement between her and Diana.

Another forum member responded with the following statement (with some of the typographical errors).

> Beloved *name of woman,*
>
> Ash has discussed this in several other workshops—but I can't remember exactly which ones right this minute. I know that when she mentioned that she was a walkin in one workshop— she indicated in the next workshop that some folks were upset about this. But in the Secrets of the Indigo Children materials she explains the following about Indigo Composite Type-1—which

she is:

Secrets of the Indigo Children. p. 37:

Type-1 Indigos are part of the Oraphim-Human hybridization program, serving to accelerate and expedite reaching critical mass of the Diamond Sun DNA Matrix within the race gene pool, before 2012.

Type-1 Indigos have an Emerald Order Oraphim 48-Strand Emerald Sun [D]NA Matrix, which give them the maximum potential of 30-48 Ascension Codes through which the Avatar identity may embody and the consciousness may expand into the Ascended Masters identity levels.

Type-1 Indigos ALWAYS incarnate through WALK-IN agreements, whereby a smaller Soul essence from their own Over-Soul collective begins the incarnation to raise the frequency of the body, and once the DNA is sufficiently activated the original Soul "walks out" into Ascension and the Avatar identity walks-in (transfers the spirit essence into the body) to awaken within the body and fulfill its world service contract. The walk-in usually occurs at age 12 or 22, and must occur by the age of 33.

Walk-ins and full possessions utilize the same ages of significant Human development. In the *Architects of Light and the Secrets of the Indigo Children* workshop, Ashayana says that there were about 350 Type-1 Indigos on Earth in year 2000, and another 5,000 were scheduled to walk-in between 2005 and 2017. She explains that the walk-in experience involves a higher dimensional aspect or person who then cohabitates or takes over the body. In the workshop, she instructs everyone to "find our Sirian selves" (DVD-2).[377] I and my mother, among other Type-1 "Indigos" in the Milky Way and Galaxy-2, give testimony that we each do not have a Sirian self, nor do we need to walk-into lower dimensional bodies; we can properly birth directly onto Earth without damaging anything. Walk-ins should not involve cohabitation; in light of Ashayana's explanation about Sirian selves, she is unknowingly teaching full possession.

The MCEO-GA oversoul belief considers us smaller and more fragmented than what exists in a higher dimension or beyond as a supposed collective or gestalt. This hierarchical belief can give permission to entities to possess us when the reality is that we essentially have complete bodies of our own—despite the distortions—with which we can direct our own paths. The only context I can see for Ashayana's explanation is if a lost Turaneusiam or other alien soul as Katie is fragmented to where she needs Ashayana's frequencies to help her reintegrate. However, this context does not apply because Katie was already an integrated Human who became a functioning adult, and she has now moved on from her Human body, not able to inherit Ashayana's frequencies.

In one of her *12 Tribes* workshops, Ashayana reveals that she tried to walk into Katie, but Zetas messed up Katie's genes to prevent the walk-in. She states that she finally gained complete access into Katie when she was 33 years old.[378] It was never Ashayana who was schooled as a child—it was Katie in order to prepare her for the walk-in "possession"!

Now that we know that Ashayana is really an MCEO-GA entity who took over Katie's body in the late 1990s, and she herself knows this, I do not know why she has chosen to deflect her awareness as though she has been Katie for her entire life. She has said in earlier workshops that she cannot remember the full details when she was a child as Katie, but this is because she was not Katie at that time. Either she empties her awareness when being a mouthpiece for the MCEO-GA and telling their stories, she has fragmented her own consciousness through the walk-in process, or her religious belief in the Law of One misdirects her interpretation of reality. The Human body does carry its own memory, so the walk-in process has overridden some of Ashayana's awareness; however, this should not create a split personality that says she is Katie one day and Ashayana the next (or previously AneA'yhea as Anna Hayes, or now E'Asha).

As I explain in chapter 10, the Law of One belief essentially erases the line between the self and the other, thereby potentially opening Ashayana up to an undiscernible mix of entities. I am glad that she has preferred to say "God" and "Source" instead of "All That Is" because her Law of One viewpoint would have misrepresented the actual All That Is, The Pure Essence similar to what the Thetans and Jesus group have done. In fact, she and the MCEO-GA in 1999 initially defined "All-That-Is" as the following great distortion.

> [T]he "forces of good and evil" can be understood in terms of the forces of order and chaos — organization and disorganization — creation and destruction — darkness and light — natural attributes of the nature of All-That-Is. Therefore we learn to embrace the totality of existence, the darkness and the light within ourselves and throughout the universe (p. 39).[175]

How much distortion has come into the MCEO-GA with all of their political alliances, genetic hybridizations, and pussyfooting around certain fallen alien groups whenever the fallen ones join them in some way?

After reading the above forum block quote, I pondered how the six DNA strand difference between the minimum 30-strand Type-1 Indigo and maximum 24-strand Type-2 Indigo could possibly prevent the Type-1 from incarnating here properly. All prior higher dimensional Elohei and Oraphim had to detach themselves from their planets to integrate into the Human body, including the walk-ins. Ashayana has also lived in the Milky Way for a long time, already gaining the necessary codes to allow her proper Human integration. Like Sananda and Michael, I surmise that she did not want to re-incarnate this time on Earth so she could have more control over her Earthly experience that possessions in any form provide. Therefore, I think that the galactic Type-1 designation is made up to divert us from seeing their desire to possess Humans. Sananda is an Elohim who has many connections and abilities, which is why he has been generally accepted by the Alhumbhra Council. The KRH and AC have been generous and trusting toward him just as they have with Ashayana. Sananda was actually one reason for our recent DNA victory over the Templar-Axion Seal, known as the "666" Omega Kill Code, because he traveled to AquA'elle (that contains the Sha-La ascension planet link to Earth) to gain natural codes and impart them into Humanity through Jesheua. Sananda's genetically manipulated, artificial insemination into Jeudi gave the upgraded genes to Jesheua—as well as distorted genes—so that subsequent generations would carry the override code. This life-preserving code was then spread throughout Humanity, likely by additional means.

I asked the ATI,TPE, "Why did he help us when he was somewhat bad at that time?"

It replies, "Sananda was divided with his allegiance to others."

For this book's first edition, I asked the ATI,TPE to describe the nature of the GA—not distinguishing between the MCEO and GA at the time—to which it replied:

> The GA is giving false information mixed with truth. The GA is comprised of good and ill-intentioned entities who joined the Alliance for their own selfish ends. [The majority are generally good, though, as the ATI,TPE also confirms.] The Krysthal River Host has intervened time and time again to offset untruths being fed to the human race.

I further asked, "The Krysthal River hosts are believed to be intergalactic members of the Guardian Alliance. How are they different than the Guardian Alliance in the Milky Way?"

"They are beyond this matrix with purer gene lines. There are many distortions and discrepancies between the GA of this Milky Way galaxy, this [mostly] phantom world," responds the ATI,TPE. The ATI,TPE confirms that each of the three KRH Eckasha councils—KrysthalA, Krysthal River, and Aurora—is thoroughly good for us.

This is why I continue to stress the point of testing a message's energy and researching more messages to see their congruency. Our good energy can determine this. The MCEO-GA say that we should look within, and they are generally working with the KRH; therefore, I suggest that we focus on the purer information that resonates with our desire for truth. The more we want the truth, the more we will find it, and the more we will not need outsider help to navigate through the distortions.

Regarding partial possessions, I think that they are mainly intrusive and unwelcome. Like full possessions and walk-ins, they do not value the ability of Humans to do what is best for ourselves. Since the first edition, I have learned more about how my otherworldly, extended Clarion family interacts with Clarion Humans. They do not possess non-Clarions or Clarion Humans in any way. They have applied some force in their introduction to a few Clarion Humans, sometimes involving brief abductions, but this always occurred with the Clarion avatar's permission. This does not mean that they do not make mistakes in their interactions with us.

Similarly, "M" first introduced herself to my mother by getting very close to my mom's energy field in the process of checking her out. My mom's immediate response was to create an extended All That Is, The Pure Essence energy shield and push it out toward this entity and her small group behind her to which they all responded by stepping back. In another visit from "M," my mother told her to request a meeting instead of coming unannounced to which she complied. Aliens are literally aliens who need to learn our customs and boundaries. When they care about us, they will respect our wishes because they actually want to work *for* us.

I have learned that Clarions and many aliens are able to leave their planets and travel the universe in spaceships similar to how we leave our home and drive in cars, although they also often orb themselves which we cannot yet do. They most often stay hidden to us in their higher dimensional form, but many can choose to materialize by lowering their vibrational density until our foreign environment becomes damaging to them. Although I came out of religion, I still needed to deprogram some religious perceptions when first learning about these entities. The ATI,TPE gives some clarification, but it is only in part.

Alien entities are literally just like us in that they have one body that does not detach part of itself to live elsewhere while the rest is at home. My understanding was initially convoluted because we and they can astrally project part of ourselves, but this is not optimal or long-lasting since we are left vulnerable in a fragmented state. I feel confident to say that aliens and Humans prefer to be as powerful and capable as we can be. This is why aliens tend to go by the same name throughout their many life experiences: they are proud to be who they are with their abilities.

Beneficial entities generally contact us when we are ready to ask them for help. During this desperate and heavily distorted time on Earth, our true allies want us to wake up and act purposely, which means that they do not expect us to reach out for their assistance. Religious-minded entities want us to pray to them for help, but they rather seek our submission instead of camaraderie. My few alien contacts are predominantly independent people who value autonomy and the intrinsic abilities of everyone. I finally became open to contacting a few trusted beings after realizing that we are not alone in the greater universe and our respective missions, so I do not need to eschew all entities because of terrible experiences with manipulative ones.

Natural, genuine truthfulness comes with an open flow of energy from the ATI,TPE to our higher and present selves. I did my best to stay in this good energy of myself throughout this book. My hope is that with this energy, we present ourselves with integrity that is sufficiently open to the other person and not weakened by ego trips. I want our interactions to leave us both standing, not falling. This entails us standing as solidly congruent people within ourselves when faced with beings of purposeful distortion. If certain entities of the MCEO-GA and anywhere else want the distortion, then our good energy knows the difference and can detect them. Distorted energy cannot usurp or deceive what is purely aligned with the ATI,TPE, but the attempt by intrusive entities to disrupt that energy alignment can remind the individual Human to keep one's energy in check.

I really hope that the MCEO and GA, as my allies in general, will not act offended or insulted by words that I have chosen to share about them. I want to hold them to a high standard because their groups claim to desire natural creation. My transparency looks to find more transparency in everyone, so we can all put our truth on the table to better understand the big picture and create a better future.

I have a request to our alien allies: please tell us the truth, and trust us that we can handle it. Let us engage in meaningful dialogue as friends if a real friendship can occur. Otherwise, please leave us be so that we can follow our pure, inner leads. Possessions and half-truths hold us back instead of help us.

Our Ability to Love

As I explained in chapter 6, we contain an imprint of the "Love" first pre-field frequency named Eia within our makeup, and its permeable, pre-plasmic type of energy can expand to us and in spaces within us as the ultimate bridge. Eia contains its own conscious identity and essence, although it is very similar to that of the ATI,TPE. The ATI,TPE states that we can envision Eia as "a river of energy; ongoing, peaceful, powerful," and Eia concurs.

Eia's pre-field frequency is greater than what we can experience and create, but it can easily link to our intrinsic vibrations as a gushing river that slows down and feels perfect to us. We contain a slightly slower frequency counterpart to Love as a lower-cased *love* that can also jump over boundaries to bridge every layer within us for effective communication. All that I am within me wants no disconnect, and I follow the pattern of early creation that also wants no disconnection.

All entities can receive Eia (substitute *pure Love* if not yet comfortable with *Eia*) and become co-creators alongside it by internal mechanisms that give our measure of love. Our love is a uniquely individual and beautiful energy that is a basic part of our makeup; I feel confident to declare that our highest self is our purest level of love. When people say that we are love, they are correct within this context.

Love helps to push out any negativity within me. I instantly cry as my release, and then I feel warm, peaceful, and whole. I contain my own fullness, but when I did not know or experience this in the past, I felt empty because my focus was outside of myself where I wanted to be energetically filled by others. The fact is that there will always be some separateness between every person and entity that can feel like a gap between us because we each have our own desires and expressions. The most productive option is to rely on the eternal flows of energy within ourselves to fulfill our needs.

As our love permeates every open level of our existence, it is not rigidly defined or confined. Our pure love does not correlate to male or female parts, nor does it need someone's approval through a marriage ceremony and certificate to show its authenticity. This is a cultural interpretation of love. Love is also not an emotion that is fleeting.

Any amount of real love should be celebrated, not banned. If a man wants to express his love to another man, or a woman to another woman, where each one offers all aspects of themselves in their unique connection to Love, then this is nothing but healing for the involved couple. Additionally, recall in the "Higher Self" section that some homosexuals are the opposite sex as their original "soul" within them.

I recall hearing a Christian pastor say on cable television that marriage should be solely between a man and a woman. This was during the 2010 election in California when Proposition 8 was on the ballot to ban gay marriage. The pastor spoke in a calm and calculated way according to his beliefs. Another guest was a gay rights activist who wore her heart on her sleeve, speaking from a place of victimization; we could see her honest, passionate plea that reached to her very core. Regardless of public opinion, I could tell that her fire would continue to burn brightly because she wanted to break free from discrimination and subjugation.

The pastor's main argument was that homosexual couples are physically unnatural, and the adopted child needs both a father and a mother for their respective gender roles. It is illogical to role-play based solely upon a body having different genitalia and a different concentration of the same hormones. In addition, the unnatural argument does not hold water because religious gods against homosexuality are notorious for doing unnatural sexual acts. These aliens are actually disgusting and horrifying in what they do.

Love allows individuality, but its nature always brings people together somehow. Let us not judge people in how they find and experience true love. Nobody needs to be fighting because it detracts away from experiencing more awareness about love within ourselves. If someone's awareness really wants to be with someone of the same sex for eternity, then that is love. It surpasses the sexual experience, although sex can be part of our physical body's expression of love.

When we realize that we are complete unto ourselves, where we do not need to have an external person's amount of love fill up our vast measure, then we actually create more love within ourselves. Love continually flows and gives. We cannot really love others until we learn how to thoroughly love ourselves; then, our own river will overflow to our surroundings. There is no limit to eternal Love. Together, wow, we can be amazingly positive forces of co-creation when embodying our true, loving nature.

Why Are We Now Here on Earth?

I have often asked myself this question during my difficult life on this Earth. I seriously pondered the worth of this life when a plethora of gray to black energies swarmed around me as though true Love and goodness did not matter or even exist. I have contemplated suicide, but something in me would never let me do it. Now that I know who I truly am, I can better understand why I chose to stay on Earth.

As I stated in the "Higher Self" section, most but not all Humans are originally from higher dimensions. This is due to the reality of creation occurring on every dimensional level. There was probably a time when much of the Human population was originally born here after most fallen Turaneusiams reintegrated on Earth and went back to Tara; however, the Earth's recent events and SAC became too important for higher dimensional beings to ignore.

The Earth's precarious ascension cycle prompted many beneficial, higher dimensional entities to get involved. I will mainly address the role of higher dimensional beings like myself, but this section can also apply to organic

Humans because we both were born into this Human body.

The Earth has been heavily manipulated toward becoming a phantom creation that would eventually die. Other planetary inhabitants in star systems throughout our galaxy have been dealing with similar intrusions, wars, and destruction. I truly believe in the power of Krysthal energy due to its uncompromised nature, but it does not conquer all when strong-willed entities get involved in the co-creative process. What happened to Tara, Gaia, and the original Amenti Earth exemplify how powerful death science technologies can be. More so, what happened to the original AquaLaShA galaxy and many others like it to create partially phantom systems such as Galaxy-2, Milky Way, and M31 Andromeda show how some Veca Krysthal entities can be defeated.

I have realized that I chose to become Human. As a purer being, I could not foresee the extent of negative energies and experiences that could affect me on Earth, but I knew that it was dangerous. I just trusted myself and my pure intent, and I broke away from the harmony of my family and planet to enter the Earth.

Neither I nor a god chose my father and all of my experiences, unlike what the New Age and mainstream religions teach. I was thrown helpless into extremely difficult circumstances as are countless babies and children across the world. Most Humans will not seek the information in this book while they are stuck in survival mode; nonetheless, if they personally challenge their societal belief systems and return to their innate sense of truth, this act of personal empowerment can shift their awareness and bring them healing. There is a time to shift away from the victim role to a powerful non-victimizer, and that time is sooner than we may think regardless of the degrees of victimhood that still beset us.

As I have illuminated thus far, we are complete beings within ourselves. No matter the degree of distortion that we have inherited, if our intent is pure and our drive toward eternal energy is strong, we can eventually override our obstacles. In the short term, this can happen from natural energies that build bridges to surpass obstacles so we can cope in our greater abilities. In a longer term, when we transform those obstacles into natural constructs, then this completely heals the distortion.

We are born as evolutionary Humans, slowly integrating our inner layers of awareness and connection. This has made us focus on our physical state that unfortunately feels the compromise and traumas of this existence. We simply cannot be detached, perfectly loving, happy, and strong people when we are literally part of the heavily distorted creation here. However, we can learn to treat this physical body as a body suit that merely covers our purer components instead of it being a permeable cloth that allows distortions to seep inward. In a somewhat similar analogy, apostolic New Testament Scriptures teach us to put on the new man, but their idea of a "new man" has us receive phantom angelic energies that take over the supposedly sinful or distorted inner self instead of the true inner self that properly heals the outer Human body.

This 2.5 dimensional body is a vehicle through which the rest of our spiritual aspects can live on Earth. The process of becoming Human merges our inner aspects with the Earth's physical energy matter, so we feel the energies flow through us, and we react naturally to them. As I explained in "Emotions," some appropriate reactions can eventually become deleterious. Our greater awareness of who we really are in our connection to the ATI, TPE and true Love keeps us on track.

This chapter's categories represent slightly different aspects and functions of matter that work together as a combined unit. The highest self identity can try to put all of its connected attributes into submission, but each one has an identity that continues to perform a function. The highest self only helps coordinate the aspects. As Humans, our bodies follow the blueprint of harmonious collaboration.

Oneness entails cooperation with what is energetically similar. The energy that we contain should be unified for fluid communication and response throughout each aspect. When one component becomes filled with dying energy, this severs the oneness. Depending upon the extent of destructive energy in that component, the person's overall energy can bring it health again.

I wonder if otherworldly entities have *not* become compromised from experiencing traumas. The Metatron family is a pertinent example. Entities know about the dangers of distorted and abusive regions, so they choose to cloak their purer bodies when working there, especially on Earth. My million dollar question to higher dimensional beings has thus become, "How can we come to Earth without diminishing and forgetting our true selves?" I believe that we are the ground crew trying to figure out this great conundrum once and for all.

I have learned that when I focus upon my bodily distortions long past the acute stage, then I have allowed the distortion to become like one with me. It is most difficult when children endure traumatic events before their cognitive abilities can process them, so chronic illness is a likely result. In my situation, my body struggles to undo its victimized reaction because it developed neural connections from that early foundation and created some nerve and organ damage.

To answer the big question for myself, I now know to simply recognize my body's chronic state while not giving into it because it has become a broken record. I already know my problems. I will now act as and be Talea in my expanded awareness, and I will divert the trauma state to Talea's loving connection back to the All That Is, The Pure Essence.

I have realized that my mission here is to maintain myself to the best of my ability amidst all struggles, so although there were and are setbacks, my inner connection from my true self keeps pushing through them. Talea is me much more than Theresa is. Theresa depends upon Talea for life. The ultimate goal for Theresa is to remove her lower dimensional distortions in a healing process that transfigures her into who I really am as Talea. The Earth's distorted energies are reorganizations of natural energies that our inner template has the ability to correct.

I wish we did not need to involve ourselves with a suffering Earth in this totally tangible way in order to help it. We did not need to learn how far distortions can become or how they feel. But when someone else is physically attacked, should we look the other way? If our loved one is about to get raped, should we not push off the perpetrator? I often wondered why I was allowed to be raped not only once but repeatedly. Where were my saviors then? The answer is that they were not able to be physically present to make it stop, but they were still energetically connected to me. Ultimately, I was and am my savior. I chose to come here to help with my own abilities, so it has been up to me to learn how to keep connected to my true self no matter what atrocities I experience.

Almost all of us intuitively know what is right or wrong. We know that having an ill body is not good for us. We know that painful abuse is not right. However, too many people have shut themselves off to speak up against the distortions because they are either judged as being negative, or they feel overpowered and weakened by surrounding negative forces, thus causing them to retreat and escape. This escape becomes a distortion when it turns into paralyzing fear, complacency, or self-destruction. The biggest tragedy is losing oneself in the process of trying to help others!

We helpers came here because we wanted to correct the wrongs. Therefore, I plead with you to keep the good intent. Keep up the overflowing love to unlock the doors to those cold, dark places that have become shut off to eternal energy. Our Earthly bodies are innocent. We came here to help the innocent Earth heal. Our self-love carries forth from our body to its related Earthly material and to everyone around us. When we diffuse the power of Metatronic energies one step at a time, these energetic victories resonate throughout the Earth and help keep it aligned to Urtha and also the ATI, TPE.

Now that the Earth is a properly ascending planet, our vision for a better world can become a reality. Let us put forth our insights to co-create a safe place that celebrates the kind of unity in diversity that progressively erodes the systems of subjugation and slavery, lives sustainably with the Earth, and lovingly corrects one another and oneself so that we can grow together in a home that meets our needs.

Conclusion

In the fullness of ourselves, we can transcend our difficulties because of our multifaceted and incredible composition. There is no need to feel alone because we now know that we have our own family of energy matter that can work in unison within our body. Our bodies are based upon the natural template of health, love, awareness, and life. The awareness that we gain in this book and throughout our personal lives can eradicate the fragmented energies and fears we have carried that put up walls against our true nature and each other.

I ask that we get in touch with our beautiful energies within us. We can start with the chakras because that is where our emotions, physical sensations, and mental perceptions can meet. Alternatively, we can start in any aspect of our makeup that I put into the above categories. The goal is to open up communication between all of our aspects so that each of us can best live as our true original self, the self who we deeply love and miss.

CHAPTER 10

Individuality and Oneness:
A Critique of the Law of One

Similar to the religious beliefs that I explored through Judeo-Christianity, the New Age Law of One belief also carries significant contradictions. In general, religions favor a hierarchical power structure while the Law of One favors the power of a group. However, in most cases, the lines between both belief systems are blurred because God group entities who follow their own leaders tend to believe in the Law of One.

The Law of One is the most prevalent belief system in our galaxy; it is the religion of about 85 percent of all Milky Way entities like us, reveals the All That Is, The Pure Essence (ATI,TPE). I am one of the 15 percent who does not believe in it due to one of many reasons: it tries to create a feel-good sense of equality while it actually conforms people to the hive mentality, or worse, it seeks to assimilate us entirely.

The Law of One is distinctly different than the notion of *oneness* that implies more than or like one. Oneness accounts for the reality of separation while the Law of One states that our individual physicalities are merely holograms of division.

The Guardian Alliance (GA) and Melchizedek Cloister Emerald Order (MCEO) are two entity groups that teach the Law of One while claiming to want eternal life creation. The GA states that "DNA is the literal vessel through which the illusionary experience of physical, external reality is manufactured" (p. 158).[120] The MCEO agrees and further states that our body is comprised of planetary programs that we project as chemically translated holograms based on what frequencies most resonate with us.[143] This means that if you and I deeply resonate and feel very real to each other, then we must be a significant aspect of each other on a bigger level, or we essentially are each other. My lamp and computer are very real to me, so I wonder if they are also considered a significant part of me. In other words, it is an illusion that we seem divided because we are representations of the same gestalt or overall whole that has been downloaded into each of us. This belief takes Gestalt Theory out of context and asserts that we all are the singular I AM. This is supposedly the ultimate self, and our individual self-serving representations of it have no real meaning except to experience something fractionally different, that is, without real movement or individuality.

My energy feels constricted when learning about the Law of One. I feel as though I am being bound by a theoretical, encapsulating God sphere that is not how I know creation to be.

The Law of One treats every creation as equally important parts of the absolute whole while somehow there are no separate parts. This belief also says that we are fragments of this whole, which does imply some separation. Law of One proponents are unclear when defining their whole gestalt, preferring to simply call it "Source"; however, there are many sources that are like small seeds or large bodies such as eternal star-planet krystars that contain a multitude of elements and field frequencies. The Law of One entwines the creator with the created as an ultimate, plasmic krystar that contains everything, which I call the Everything Krystar. The theoretical Everything Krystar somehow creates within itself in subsequently smaller spheres, fragmenting itself in increasing measures to then necessitate pulling in those entities to eventually become the Everything Krystar's God Source again. The ultimate krystar state is supposed to be undistorted in its early etheric and plasmic construction, but the Law of One has it contain the properties for distortion.

Like all large belief systems, there are factions that add new meaning to the original belief. One notable faction is Marduk's Ra group that channeled 106 sessions from 1981 to 1984 A.D. to create *The Law of One* books.[262] I choose to largely ignore second-hand versions of the Law of One belief in order to focus my critique on its foundational tenets. Therefore, I will evaluate Ashayana Deane's transmissions and beliefs because she is a strong advocate for the Law of One and its basic mathematical model, and she provides the most extensive explanations, vocabulary, and diagrams about it.

As I have previously mentioned, Ashayana has many entity contacts, and she welcomes some of the diversity, especially with the duplicitous Sananda. Additionally, the MCEO and GA mainly contain Milky Way and Galaxy-2 members who contribute perceptions that support hierarchical relationships. Her communications often lack transparency about which entity or group gives her the message. For this reason, I will simplify the issue and place all of Ashayana's entity groups who support the Law of One in the MCEO group, and I will also introduce other prevailing groups for clarification. The information given by entities often cannot be fact-checked due to its otherworldly nature, but this is where our intuition and intelligence can kick in to approximate more truth. Reading the transmitted messages can help sharpen our critical thinking skills, especially now that my book has provided food for thought.

In April 2012, Ashayana, who now prefers to be named E'Asha, decided to primarily work with the AL-Hum-Bhra Magistracy Councils of Cosminyahas, abbreviated as Alhumbhra Council (AC), in the role of AMCC

[AC]-MCEO-GA™ Speaker-1.[379] The AC mostly consists of Phim entities from the Cosminyahas krystar, but many of them have since incarnated into distorted realms such as Galaxy-2 and the Milky Way, confirms the ATI,TPE. Her newly transmitted information still adheres to the Law of One, so I deduce that her MCEO and galaxy-based Phim friends give these portions of her communications. Although I deeply appreciate her data that delves into the Krysthal and Keylontic sciences, not all of it is accurate, especially when it follows the Law of One religion.

Great White Brotherhood, Cosmic Awareness, and Melchizedek Cloister Emerald Order

The All That Is, The Pure Essence reveals that the Great White Brotherhood (GWB) entity group created the Law of One paradigm, and the GWB exists in the 13th dimension of Wesadek. A similar entity group in Wesadek's 13th dimension is the Cosmic Awareness (CA) who took the GWB teachings and reconfigured them as its own. The ATI,TPE states that the GWB and CA are affiliated with each other. They are not part of the MCEO, but some MCEO entities are affiliated with the GWB and less so with the CA.

To adhere to its false 12-point kathara grid structure, the MCEO not only puts the 13th dimension in an adjoining kathara grid, it also puts it at the apex of the grid as the most powerful position of our entire time matrix. This illogical grid position comes as no surprise when understanding that 13th dimensional phantom entities created this base-12 teaching.

MCEO's Emerald Order designation implies entity groups that come in the name or purpose of the emerald frequencies. The MCEO refers to the pale yellow 14th dimensional frequency (in Galaxy-2) as the "gold flame," and the turquoise 13th dimensional frequency (in Galaxy-2) is the "blue flame."[145] The correct 15-dimensional kathara grid infuses the blue flame into the top 15th dimension, the gold flame into the 14th dimension, and the violet flame into the 13th dimension (see chapter 6's Figure 3). The ATI,TPE explains that the original blue and gold flames comprise the blue-green "emerald" frequency fields of Ecka dimensions 6 and 5 respectively, which means that Galaxy-2's harmonic universe 5 (HU-5) and Ecka's HU-1 are expanded versions of the blue, gold, and violet frequencies. The blue flame frequency was down-stepped into Tara and then into Amenti Earth's Sphere of Amenti.

The MCEO places the frequency sound tones Kee, Ra, and ShA in the HU-5 of its upside-down, adjacent kathara grid and calls them primal light tones. Perhaps the MCEO designates them as "primal" to hint to the Ecka HU-1, which the ATI,TPE states is the origin of these particular sounds, but their placement and identification need to be ordered correctly based on the accurate kathara grid. ShA is the sound tone of Ecka dimension 3, which is the Eckatic level. Ra is the sound tone of Ecka dimension 2 as the Polaric level. Lastly, Kee is the sound tone of Ecka dimension 1 as the Triadic level, states the ATI,TPE.

The MCEO entity group originates in Ecka dimension 3, which was seeded by Grandeyanas entities in Ecka dimension 6, informs the ATI,TPE. The Ra Confederacy entity group originates in Ecka dimension 2, and it was seeded by Wachayanas entities in Ecka dimension 5. Ecka dimension 4 entities are the Ramyanas who seeded Ecka dimension 1. Unfortunately, our Krysthal Ecka's HU-1 and HU-2 levels were attacked to create distorted versions connected to the Milky Way galaxy; we can deduce which Ecka entity groups contain some of these distortions based on their teachings.

The ATI,TPE reveals that Ashayana is a Wachayana whose related entity group is the Ra Confederacy. The MCEO states that *Ra* becomes *Melchizedek* when translated into English and other Earth languages.[145] Ra and Melchizedek are popular names to religious-minded entities and Humans. The MCEO makes a point to call the first Ra-Melchizedek group the Melchizedek Cloister to separate it from later and lower dimensional groups coming in the Melchizedek family name. However, the 12 Tribes also contained a galaxy-based Melchizedek Cloister, which illuminates that the MCEO does not only exist in the Ecka.

Ashayana relates the Melchizedek Cloister to a clock in which it holds the top 12 position, meaning that it contains the codes to all lower dimensions. She says that the Melchizedek Cloister is our God-seed: "It is the God-Seed that the human design was created through" (p. 10).[380] She equates this position to one of power.

To have power over the 12 dimensions, the Melchizedek Cloister would have to originate in HU-5 where some of it agreed to support the idea of a lesser and potentially controllable 12-dimensional kathara grid. Investigation into the MCEO material reveals that 12-strand DNA templates of the Human and Angelic Human lineage did indeed originate with Galaxy-2's HU-5 "Diamond Sun" Melchizedek Cloister Elohei (p. 27).[381] If we go along with their hierarchical model, their highest dimensional position would give them more power, but they do not have the larger pre-Oraphim, "Emerald Sun" DNA capacities that already exist in other HU-4 and HU-5 Elohei races.[381]

Many advanced entities do not assume power and superiority based on their genetics and dimensional positions. One reason is because of their developed Krysthal consciousness, and another is because galactic races such as Elohim and Seraphim can and do gain similar expanded DNA templates through the ascension process.

The HU-5 entities that adopted the base-12 Law of One belief from the

GWB started this religion in Galaxy-2. It has also been a favorable belief to many 12th dimensional entities to have the top position of their own shortened kathara grid model, which many have believed to be true since their 12th dimensional stargate was damaged for eons, preventing some higher dimensional awareness. What started as a fledgling religion has become solidified into a Law via migration across HU-5 and the lower dimensions of Galaxy-2 and the Milky Way. Accordingly, lower dimensional entities can carry remnants of similar religious beliefs in their ascension process to HU-5 to support this man-made Law.

For most of Ashayana's transmissions, the MCEO has chosen to focus upon the HU-5 level of identity because it supposedly entails our Heroic Probability self that guides each of us back in line with our "God-Self."[382] "Heroic Probability is the fullest expression of our Divine Blueprint across time, states the MCEO."[382] Ideally, this level would exist in AquaLaShA; however, every MCEO technique involving HU-5 incorporates Milky Way and Galaxy-2's dimensional colors (although it erroneously says the 12th dimensional color is white).[184] Therefore, our Heroic Probability involves the integration of our entire bodily template that has been created with varying amounts of semi-phantom energies.

As I introduced in chapter 7's "One World Order Agenda," the GWB is an ally of the Ashtar Command and Galactic Federation of Light (GFofL). In 2007, Ashayana and her MCEO entity group stated that the GWB group works with the more distorted Templar Melchizedeks for the aim of bio-regenerating the Elohim.[380]

> The Alpha-Omega Templar Melchizedek Order is that of the Anunnaki Priesthood, which is intended to work under direction of the D-13 [dimension 13] "Great White Brotherhood" true YHWH Host Matrix, with the primary purpose of assisting in DNA Template Bio-Regenesis of Anunnaki and Human-Anunnaki hybrid race strains (p. 22).[380]

As we learned in the beginning of chapter 7, the "true" YHWH Host Matrix in Wesadek was semi-phantom when Metatron's polarization-refraction lens connected it to Galaxy-2's 11th dimension. Sometime afterward, all of Wesadek and Metatron became phantom, so it is not the matrix it once was. The above MCEO quote confirms the ATI,TPE's statement that the GWB is located in phantom Wesadek, which has more dimensions than the Metatronic Tree of Artificial Life has created on our side. Metatron is a close ally to the GWB and CA. Metatron adopted the Law of One belief from them, reveals the ATI,TPE.

Since the beginning of 2012 A.D., many Metatron family members either joined or became allies with the MCEO-GA (and beforehand with their Enoch subgroup) to supposedly accept bio-regenesis. This is generally not because they seek full recovery; it is because they lost control of the Alpha-Omega wormhole network to the Red Dragons. The ATI,TPE states that their aims are self-serving. After all of Metatron's unbelievably terrible, destructive technologies, it is most wise of us to be extremely cautious of any story claiming its quick turnaround.

Ashayana's entity group associations have taught that fallen entity groups—such as the GWB—carry certain fallen codes that can help worse-off, lower dimensional "patients" or family members who seek their expertise. Proper bio-regenesis cannot happen when using phantom codes, especially in the case of entities who teeter toward phantom or become phantom as the GWB have been for a very long time.

For example, Thoth was chosen by the MCEO to help heal the Atlantean Leviathan race on Earth. He had an 11.5-strand DNA template with great knowledge to help himself and others worse off than he was. Unfortunately, he chose to break away from this better energy to completely join the Leviathan and its Bourgha-Shantarel masters. Thoth's hunger for power was huge, so choosing him to aid a regenerative mission was a risky and dare I say unwise move in the first place.[123]

I seriously question the aims of the similar GWB and CA groups because they do not adequately show their differences to the fundamentalist Jesus group led by Archangel Michael.

As I introduced in chapter 9's "Higher Self" section, a September 1992 channeling by the Cosmic Awareness, typically calling itself "This Awareness," vilifies what it calls the "Orion Empire and Draconian Federation" while praising the Ashtar Command and Galactic Federation of Light.[353] Like many phantom entity groups, the CA gives disinformation in the article about the Ashtar Command and GFofL, saying that they are only light frequencies and not actual persons.

As I stated in chapter 3, the CA was the "voice" that spoke to religious prophets Jesus, Buddha, Muhammad, and Krishna. It also spoke through the scribe of its channeled book, *Who, In Fact, You Really Are*, who was in a trance to receive the messages.[15] The CA focuses mostly upon Jesus in its book of spiritual lessons that is somewhat analogous but much less depreciatory than the Jesus group's *A Course in Miracles*. One main difference is the identification of God.

The CA states:

Every human face is every other human face, and all entities are one within the body of this Awareness (p. 10).

Each of you is this Awareness. Each of you is an example of the Christ Consciousness. Each of you is God (p. 13).[15]

We well know that mainstream religions externalize a God entity, but another religion that some rather call a philosophy—Theosophy—internalizes God as the CA does. The GWB heavily influenced Theosophy, which claims that God and Nature are One, and there is no ultimate distinction between spirit and matter because all is energy (see chapter 7's "One World Order").

Helena Blavatsky, a main founder of 19th century modern Theosophy, was a channeler of The Great White Lodge, otherwise known as the Great White Brotherhood, who taught that Humanity evolves through seven planes of existence via the help of a "World Teacher" Christ entity of the so-called Ascended Master group.[383] Evolution would occur through seven Root Races, each with seven subraces and many reincarnations. Theosophy's current stage comprises the fifth Root Race of the Aryan, which is compatible to the GA information in chapter 8 except that Theosophy takes it in another direction: the Christ entity must fully possess a Human body to bring forth the wisdom that guides our evolution and eventual meeting in its plane of existence.

Blavatsky writes in *The Secret Doctrine, Volume I*, "MAITREYA is the secret name of the *Fifth* Buddha, and the *Kalki* Avatar of the Brahmins—the last MESSIAH who will come at the culmination of the Great Cycle" (p. 384).[384] Maitreya was poised to take over a chosen "vehicle" by the name of Jiddu Krishnamurti, a young Hindu who was groomed by the Order of the Star in the East.[385] In 1922, he underwent an otherworldly transformative process that brought him in and out of consciousness, presumably completing the possession process, but he considered it an awakening of spiritual awareness.

In *J. Krishnamurti: A Biography* by Pupul Jayakar, Krishnamurti said, "I have altered so much during the last fortnight—both inside and outside my body, my face, my hands, my entire being has changed. The only way to breathe fresh air of life is by this constant change, constant turmoil, constant unrest" (p. 74).[386]

In 1929, he publicly rejected his hierarchical status and Theosophical organized religion, aiming to dissolve the Order of the Star in the East. He proclaimed freedom without authority and organization while mentioning a Law of One belief: "Because I am free, unconditioned, whole—not the part, not the relative, but the whole Truth that is eternal."[387] In his biography, Krishnamurti explains his Law of One views that actually contradict freedom:

Walking over the hills of India last winter, there appeared before me my Ideal, my Beloved, my Guru, my Great Teacher and ever since that vision I seem to see all the trees through him, all the mountains, all the little pools, all the little insects and ever since that vision, that understanding of things has remained. [Jayakar then writes: "This oneness with the guru and the mystery of life continued to be the theme of his talks."] (p. 74).

I and my Beloved are one. The vision is total. To me that is liberation.... The personality of J. Krishnamurti has been swallowed up in the flame—what happens after that does not matter—whether the spark remains within the flame or issues forth (p. 77).

Understanding of the self only arises in relationship, in watching yourself in relationship to people, ideas, and things; to trees, the earth, and the world around you and within you. Relationship is the mirror in which the self is revealed (p. 147).[386]

Although Theosophy leader Charles Leadbeater considered that "the Coming had gone wrong," I see that it generally succeeded because a spiritual and philosophical faction was created in the tradition of new and improved Messianic teachings.[385] It did not matter which entity with a Law of One agenda possessed Krishnamurti—Maitreya revealed in a channeling published in 1932 that Krishnamurti was initiated as a vehicle for not only him but also other entities called Devas who eventually took precedence; he was still used to usher in a new faction.[388] Krishnamurti referred to the totality of his word as *the* teachings, not *my* teachings.

In *The Secret Doctrine, Volume II*, Blavatsky explains that Lucifer as the "Light-Bearer" is the ultimate Christ who exists in us as our divine mind (p. 513).[389] "Lucifer is the name of the angelic Entity presiding over the *light of truth* as over the light of the day" (p. 512).[389] Ultimately, it is he as God with whom we all would be conjoined.

If we water down our belief into a basic philosophy and state that all entities are energy, especially in the esoteric spiritual state, then assimilating into Michael, Lucifer, Maitreya, or any type of "God" entity can seem almost acceptable to some people. The fundamental tenet of the Law of One is that we are all some sort of God beyond our current illusion. However, when we know the distinction between entities and energies, we are aware of our differences and individual options toward a very different reality.

Both religious and Law of One spiritual beliefs share the same definition of God: an omnipotent, omnipresent, and omniscient being. The CA adds a few more "OM" words: omnificient, unlimited in creative power; omnifarious, composed of all creational varieties; omnidirectional, "in communication in all directions"; and omnidimensional, "permeating everything in existence"

(p. 38).[15] The CA focuses on the sound tone *Om* which the ATI,TPE reveals is a fractal sound-tone in our galaxy. The CA also correlates OM to the "Omnificent-Moment" of the dimensional vibratory octaves that make our reality tangible to us (p. 38).[15]

The phrase "I AM" is unrelated to OM, states the ATI,TPE, but it is prevalent in both Judeo-Christianity and the Law of One where it represents the ultimate God state. I asked the ATI,TPE why fallen entities want us to recite this phrase, to which it replies:

> By reciting the phrase 'I AM,' it invokes Michael's group and Michael as its supreme 'God' along with giving these fallen entities praise and worship by sound vibration using language. The I AM sound tone represents and links to Alpha and Omega, which is the religious beginning and end-all God state.

When any entity group asserts that fractal energy is unlimited in creative power and variety, this skewed perception that harnesses both life and death must be addressed within the all-inclusive interpretation of "oneness." Entity groups who introduce this concept along with an incomplete creation science exist at the top of their hierarchy. For example, Metatron introduced this belief and the Flower of Artificial Life to the Milky Way from its top 11.5 dimensional position. The CA asserts base-12 mathematics in its channeled book to give it an upper hand over the 12 dimensions below it.

The somewhat contrasting definitions in the Law of One paradigm inadvertently reinforce the fact that Humans contain necessary, multidimensional codes for a sufficiently functional body. Our latent abilities can become partially activated simply by recognizing the intelligent levels of elemental "entities" within our current bodies that can find ways to bypass and even heal our distortions. This is mostly an internal process. No matter how much mainstream ascension teachings tell us that what is outside is somehow within us, they fundamentally have us look outward in an externalized process.

Milky Way Base-12 Mathematics

The Law of One does not recognize our mainly complete nature as Humans with the Oraphim or Angelic Human template because it was created with the mindset that we must ascend in order to gain other dimensional parts of ourselves. Ascension is a natural phenomenon, but its process should be simple and within our own ability.

Ashayana says the following about the divine blueprint and heroic path of probability:

[O]n the first level of primal sound fields coming out the entity level where you become an entity which is a collective where you know yourself as many, you know yourself as a family of consciousness scattered around space-time and you start to get open memory and the ability to communicate and be in the heads of all of your selves at once, this is what it means to integrate. [382]

In other words, we are not an actual family of consciousness where each person is made of different but similar particle matter; instead, we are simultaneously created as multiple forms across all the dimensions. There is no real self; we are a multitude of selves that completes us as our own gestalt, but then our gestalt is also the greater gestalt of everyone. Therefore, it is okay to call upon similar entities and have them enter into our fields and consciousness because we are all One.

The Law of One does not distinguish between the compositions and cycles of our external worlds and our personal bodies. According to the MCEO and ATI,TPE, the Earth should follow six Euiago harmonic cycles to accrete all proper HU-1 base and overtone dimensional bands in preparation for its ascension to Tara. After these six Euiagos pass in what is called an Eyugha cycle (which is what the Vedic Yuga cycle falsely represents), Earth quanta would shift angular rotation and particle spin (ARPS) to enter the 5th dimension. After three Eyughas pass, the former Earthly quanta of organisms, including Humans, can cross over to meet the 12th dimensional Aramatena and continue two more Eyughas until they enter the Ecka. Together, the five density time cycles along with the five parallel density time cycles are called an Eyana cycle. [120,191] The Law of One declares that Humans follow the same blueprint of mathematical expression.

The MCEO states:

> Every human Incarnate is part of a larger "family" of incarnate selves called the Personal Christos. The Personal Christos is the Eternal Personal Identity that includes 1728 simultaneous incarnations, each placed within various space-time locations, or Time Vectors, within the 4 Rounds of the Cycle of the Rounds.
>
> In each of the 4 Evolutionary Rounds there are 216 simultaneously incarnate selves, and their anti-particle counterparts within the Parallel Earth system, for a total of 1728 Incarnates (216 selves x 4 Rounds = 864 selves + 864 anti-particle counterpart selves = 1728 selves)....
>
> Each individual incarnate self comes to know itself as an Eternal Christos Avatar Identity that is simultaneously manifesting

in 1728 different Time Vectors, wearing the "costume" of 1728 different bodies and personality characterizations (p. 32-33).[380]

The 216 selves in an Earthly Eyugha incorporate 36 selves per Euiago. Divide each Euiago into another six to account for the time continuum cycles, and we each have six selves living on Earth that come in sets of two for the "twin flame" concept that I will soon explain. It is unclear whether we, as beings split into two, would reincarnate into all those other beings, or our consciousness would be part of the Earth in the figurative or literal air to produce six bodies within the entire general precession cycle. Reincarnation on Earth according to the Fibonacci sequence and NET field harness does not allow us more than seven lives unless an otherworldly plane can provide some bio-regenesis.

Since this way of dividing a gestalt self within the Law of One paradigm does not have us come together as one physical being, the MCEO addresses this conundrum by stating, "Through the activated 12-Strand DNA Template, the frequencies of energy and consciousness of each of the 1728 selves merge into an embodied, unified consciousness awareness" (p. 33).[380] The Avatar supercomputer would therefore control the illusory "costume" of all of its 1,728 simultaneous selves and personalities.

The MCEO teaches the step-down process of dimensional creation, so if we were a "Christos Avatar Identity," its one self in HU-4 does not instantly turn into 1,728 selves in HU-1. When we apply the CA's base-12 pattern for creation, the HU-4 self produces 12 selves in HU-3, 144 selves in HU-4, and 1,748 selves in HU-1. This formula removes access to the prized HU-5 "God-Self" that would theoretically produce 12 selves in HU-4, 144 selves in HU-3, 1,728 selves in HU-2, and 20,736 selves in HU-1. Although the MCEO's base-12 "selves" from HU-5 to HU-1 appear to be expanded multiples, an ultimate "One" can only divide into itself to create, which is not actual expansion; rather, it is close to fractalization.

In Figure 1, the Krysthal sequence of expansion does not contain numbers 12 or 144. The Fibonacci sequence, on the other hand, does not have number 12, but it does have number 144. Of course, these specific numbers are in both natural and fractal systems, but I am introducing how they play a part in fallen angelic teachings. God group leaders, especially Archangel Michael, Lucifer, and Thoth, like to use the number 144.

Aristotle and Plato, who were both heavily influenced by Thoth, taught that a significant change in the cities would occur every 144 years, and a significant change to Humanity would happen every 1,728 years.[390] Plato taught that the dodecahedron—a polyhedron with 12 pentagonal, flat sides—is the pattern behind the universe.[391] The dodecahedron's dual polyhedron is the icosahedron with 12 vertices that meet the center of each dodecahedron face when placed within a larger dodecahedron structure. The edge length of the icosahedron is the golden ratio, phi.[392] Thoth also taught modern day apostle Drunvalo Melchizedek about this geometry. Drunvalo writes in *The Ancient Secret of the Flower of Life, Volume 1*:

> If you were to take the icosahedral caps off the icosahedron and fit them onto each surface of a dodecahedron...the resulting shape happens to be the stellated dodecahedron...of the specific proportions of the Christ consciousness grid around the Earth (p. 38).[206]

Drunvalo explains that the stellated dodecahedron surrounds us and the Earth when subjecting us to the Fibonacci-based, reversed merkaba spin-speed of 34 over 21 to create 55 (see chapter 6's "Other Dimensions"). He uses shrouded language to attribute the 55 spin-speed stage to an expansive "55-foot limit of your energy field" (p. 167).[206] Drunvalo teaches according to the Fibonacci sequence to bring the Earth just past the reversed merkaba 55 spin-speed to the expedited process that culminates as the giant external Death Star merkaba at 144 spin-speed, which is when it will become an automatic feeding spiral.[182]

In the Bible's Book of Revelation, Archangel Michael's group gives a variation of the number 144 as 144,000 Jews from the biblical 12 tribes who would be spared apocalyptic judgment (Revelation 7:4-8). New Jerusalem would house these Jews, having a city wall that measures 144 cubits (Revelation 21:17).

Michael likes to think that he is the Milky Way's God because he was created by Bourgha and Metatron entities to have superior anti-Krysthal Veca genes (see chapter 7's "Archangel Michael" section). As an originally 13th dimensional Galaxy-2 being, Michael can support base-12 mathematics that places him at the top of a 12-dimensional, severed galaxy. As the "God" of Jeshewua, who was originally a 9th dimensional being, Michael and Jeshewua became "one" through possession and related genetics. This new designation can place the number 1 self in HU-3, so the direct division would be 12 selves in HU-2 and 144 selves in HU-1. HU-3 is called the oversoul level.

According to the GA and MCEO:

> The over soul—the HU-3 identity—creates 12 soul identities in HU-2, each of which create 12 incarnates within the six time cycles of HU-1. Thus, each person is part of an incarnational family of 144 incarnates residing within the six HU-1 time

cycles. Each of the 144 incarnates carries part of the 12-strand DNA pattern within the genetic code. As the 144 incarnates simultaneously evolve with the planet through the six time cycles, the 12-strand DNA imprint is progressively built up in the genetic code. DNA evolves and human consciousness expands as identity evolves with the planet through the Euiago cycles in each Harmonic Universe (p. 148).[120]

Your Soul is a plural with 12 faces and is part of a larger identity called the Oversoul that is composed of 12 souls–each with their 12 incarnate identities, so you are dealing with 144 incarnates in your immediate Oversoul family.[393]

The GA teaches that DNA represents electromagnetically encoded data of the other living parts of oneself that are somehow concurrently living in other times. Earth and Tara share quanta at specific times of the ascension cycle while also being separate planets, but this is different than the MCEO-GA's Law of One belief that has them share the same space while each has a unique ARPS.

The Law of One teaches that time and space are fundamentally simultaneous. This is because the One origin contains mathematical structures called vectors that order a collection of elements into angular representations relative to the origin. Believers state that these angles appear to create distance and directions as though they are illusory, but if we look outside of us, we do see distance and various directions. As I explained in chapter 6, vectors involve different elements in different spaces. Some spaces are unique dimensional spaces. The Law of One cannot simply invalidate what we currently experience and scientifically explain.

Accordingly, this belief states that we have future selves who live concurrently with our present and past selves. Our current dimensional experience is dependent upon the lower dimensional reality field of Earth that gives us solid physicality. Here, we can recall the past while also living in the present. If one could live as multiple versions of oneself, then the future selves would best fit the advanced time continuums of Tara, Gaia, and so forth. Tara's time is ahead of the Earth's by several thousand years; this does not affect how its current existence is relative to our present. Thus far, Tara is most relevant to our past. If the Earth would catch up to Tara's spacetime coordinates, which the ascension cycle is naturally able to achieve, then that would bring us to Tara's present time. Our future does not yet exist, confirms the ATI,TPE. It is merely possibility, but higher dimensional entities prefer to call it probability so they can try to pigeonhole a prediction.

Higher level entities, as a single entity or group, who teach the Law of One like to say they are the Ascended Masters beyond created form, and we must align with them as our ultimate God where they are One and we are somehow One with them. Unfortunately, the following MCEO statement concurs: "Harmonic Universe 4 which has dimensions 10, 11 and 12 is the highest form you can go into before you turn into non-form. Remember you started as pure consciousness without any illusion of manifest form (p. 7).[380] The MCEO seems to contradict itself in another workshop when stating that the process of ascension continues in the similar Eyanic time cycles of the Ecka.[191]

In New Age Ascended Master teachings, Lucifer, Sophia, or another high-ranking "divine" person is our oversoul. Although the oversoul level involves HU-3, many of its "gods" have re-incarnated to the 4th and 5th dimensions (primarily phantom) to better position themselves over our solar system. Lately, their messages have predominantly focused upon the "soul" level because they have wanted to redirect our HU-2 path.

The GFofL and Ashtar Command groups took the Great White Brotherhood and Cosmic Awareness beliefs into deeper distortion, but the Law of One as taught by the MCEO-GA agrees with the basic tenets of fractalized, phantom angelic teachings. The GA states, "To the soul-self, the 12 immediate HU-1 incarnates that are in its incarnational family are recognized as living sub-personality fragments of its own identity" (p. 149).[120] In addition, New Agers and the MCEO-GA teach that we each have a twin flame that is literally one half of our quanta's embodiment in a time continuum cycle.

The GA states:

> Usually, a soul—HU-2 identity, manifests into 12 simultaneous incarnations, two in each of the six time cycles in one Harmonic Universe. In each pair of incarnates, one is male, the other female; this relationship is referred to as "twin flames", but does not necessarily imply a romantic "soul mate" involvement (p. 148).[120]

Our supposed multiple selves are represented in sets of twins. The twin and twin flame concepts have become convoluted across many teachings, so I will delve into their main tenets to help uncover what, if any, is reality.

Is There an Embodied Twin Flame?

The MCEO introduces the twin flame as a polarized energy current that splits into particum and partikA realms. It states that the flame's electric frequency permeates our mainly magnetic Ecka as male energy, and its magnetic frequency that enters our mainly electric Parallel Ecka is deemed female energy.[191] Frequencies and subatomic particles are neither male nor female, but in a fractal galaxy like the Milky Way, the ATI,TPE confirms that men do carry more electric energy, and women carry more magnetic energy. This is a reason why some people metaphorically refer to the Earth as a woman.

The Law of One considers us replicas of our outer (but supposedly inner) environment, so I should have a male counterpart who must one day merge with me to make my current embodiment whole for the ascension process. This hypothetical twin would most likely be my antimatter counterpart that arose when my human body's antimatter components materialized on Parallel Earth. However, twin flame believers usually think that their other half is somewhere on Earth during the same lifetime. If the hypothetical particle twin is half of oneself, then the incarnations must be simultaneous. This formula would give me two twin flames and a potential third as a parallel to match my male counterpart, which would only give me one quarter or one third of my quanta potential.

The antimatter person living on Parallel Earth is a totally separate person to me with his or her will who also does not look like me. This person can be male or female depending upon the individual's genetics. I consider this person as a kind of double or twin instead of a divided half because of the way natural creation expands. Since most of our Parallel Milky Way is now phantom, and the non-phantom parts are probably now in quarantined Lone Star Fall status, I asked the ATI,TPE about my supposed antimatter double potentially being trapped there if he or she is not awakened enough to escape.

"If my antiparticle double will not escape, does this mean that I will also be trapped? Is my destiny dependent upon this other person's position, according to the perspective that we merge into a bigger oneness?"

"No," replies the ATI,TPE to both questions.

I cannot do anything to help my antimatter partner unless he or she chooses to save oneself. In addition, my ascension path is sufficiently separate so that I can go where I need to go. The ATI,TPE states, "The antiparticle partner on Parallel Earth is similar only in that density's consciousness, not in form." Individual choice can cause stark separation or unification between the individuals. If our antimatter partners ascend with us up our Veca, then we would work together in our consciousness as yet another layer added to the fullness of ourselves. Now that our current bodies will not have the opportunity to naturally ascend together from Earth and Parallel Earth toward Tara and Parallel Tara, perhaps a Krysthal River Host-facilitated Parallel Earth evacuation, healing, or redirection similar to the Earth could unite us—not merge us—at a safer level.

The ATI,TPE's answers make sense to me because the added factors of previous lives, higher selves, and other galactic destinations would—if this could in any way be possible—bind us to the other person's decisions as though we have no free will of our own.

The ATI,TPE states that I do not know my HU-1 antimatter partner. I wish that person well and to somehow join me. I wish the same for my biological twin who was also similar in consciousness to me, as I found out more about her from the ATI,TPE. No one is bound to anyone, but hopefully we keep the connection strong between us no matter the obstacles.

We do not have identities scattered around simultaneously. When I asked the ATI,TPE about the MCEO definition of the oversoul, how "[y]ou will know yourself as 144 different beings and each and every one of them are you" (p. 5),[380] the ATI,TPE continuously and emphatically replies "NO" to whether it is true. Each of us is present in our own body, although our higher innate consciousness can also exist somewhat outside of Human distortions and see into other dimensions.

To make this equation more complicated, the MCEO and Ashayana have taught that we are literally replicas or manifestations of multiple parallel selves. They say that we have another twin, the Adjugate twin, who has our spirit body as its physical body, and its physical body as our spirit.[185] The proper adjugate relationship, which is merely a parallel relationship, exists between AquA'elle's Sha-La "Earth" and AquaLaShA's Urtha. This does not relate to the majority of Humans who are originally from the Milky Way and Galaxy-2. If we include AquaLaShA, then we also must include Galaxy-2; this formula for twins and other selves might not end.

In her *Sliders-7* workshop, Ashayana says that she did a mirror technique during which she was contacted by a parallel version of herself that looked exactly like her but wore different clothes.[394] How could another woman have her exact same features from parents who must also look exactly like her parents? This would be that theorized parallel universe that precisely mirrors everything on Earth. Simply imagining this idea messes with my head; my first reaction was that an entity was playing a trick on her. I asked the ATI,TPE several questions about this topic and whether an entity had shapeshifted into Ashayana's form, or she saw a projected holographic image to perpetuate that belief. It replies:

An entity did not shapeshift into Ashayana's form. She saw a projected holographic image to perpetuate that belief.

Humans do not have a 'double' that looks exactly like themselves due to the difference in human construct. Another reason is that more than one of any created being exactly like the other in any phantom or natural domain denies individuality in its construct and DNA makeup.

I intuitively know and am correct that I have never had any twin flame; however, this does not mean that someone else does not have one according to the intended meaning of the phrase that entails division. I learned that embodied twin flames do exist when the original person was born outside of distorted Ecka and Veca creation. A notable entity group that creates twin flames is the plasmic Phim race from the CosMA'yah and Cosminyahas realms and DhA'YahTEi Planes.

In a fully Krysthal galaxy, all natural energies can flow freely throughout every dimension, so there is no need for outer entities to step-down or divide their power, confirms the ATI,TPE. There are men and women, but there are no physical embodiments of fractalized twin flames there. Krysthal mechanics comprise different energy configurations to fractal mechanics, but only high level Krysthal entities create twin flames to enter fractal creation, states the ATI,TPE. AquaLaShA entities do not divide themselves to enter the Milky Way.

It is debatable whether Phims should have gotten involved in our issues because their step-down process, as told by Ashayana, divided their quanta in favor of the female in our magnetic galaxy. The galactic Phim female has 66 percent original quanta, the male embodiment has 33 percent, and one percent is left for the Phim higher self up in its original realm.[198] Perhaps some of the GWB and CA entities who started the Law of One belief are divisions of an original Phim or another outside race that wanted to help Wesadek but unfortunately became too fragmented. However, these groups' experiences and galactic troubles do not identify the reality for the rest of us. Ashayana reveals that when Phims, especially the vulnerable men, became highly distorted, they became the worst demons—FAtalE—that our Veca has known.

When Phim men came into distorted Wesadek and Wesadrak to help their fallen Equari offspring, they had a chakra system vulnerability because some plasmic and DNA components were inactivated. They were infiltrated by Bourgha-Equari females who merged with their chakras in a light-body activation procedure to gain access to their gene pool and mutate it into the new FatalE race. This is the true meaning behind the "Femme Fatale" phrase, which people commonly repeat without realizing its dark alien history.[198]

Ashayana shares her perspectives in the initial *Sliders-12* workshop. First, she conveys the self-centered side of experience.

The DhA'Yah-TEi Planes are, ah, really where, ah, what do

you do after you ascend? What, like okay, you can go back home to God Source and you can decide to just immerse yourself in that consciousness and do nothing and then get bored and decide you want to go do something again because you're awake and aware and alive. Just like God Source likes to continue to put parts of itself in the matrix to experience and we would most likely do that too (DVD-3).[198]

This perspective is riddled with contradiction from a teacher who claims to desire Krysthal science. I feel confident when asserting that totally natural entities have no desire to experience death sciences. When we would live in a fully loving, capable, and magnificent environment, and we fully love ourselves, who in their right mind would want to leave that experience and join a fragmented body unless they believe that their attributes can help those less fortunate? I can only deduce that fallen angelic entities are projecting their compromised mentality and state of existence when imagining fully natural realms. Channelings and prophecies reveal the fallen angelic perspective of creation merely existing for the sole creator to experience itself in many different personalities and situations.

Second, Ashayana's Law of One view puts responsibility upon higher level entities to sacrifice themselves for others. She says:

I wish it was a better word than hierarchy, but it is a hierarchy of frequency strengths. And that would mean the ones that are the strongest would feel an obligation to assist the ones that are weaker, but it would also mean that the ones that are weaker would strive to be stronger so they don't be a burden on the one that is helping them (DVD-3).[198]

There is a codependent relationship among entities who believe that we are the same unified albeit schizophrenic entity, but this supposed unity involves unbalanced power. If we relate this Everything Krystar to our body, an injury in one location detracts from our overall ability to override the problem.

The natural expansion of creative energies entails each aspect having its own special power and ability. Even in the highest krystar realms where we can eventually join, beings will reach their highest genetic potential, but they are not necessarily the same type of entity. The genome is still unique to the individual while she, he, or it coexists in harmony with others on the krystar. This translates to every natural level of creation where everyone has free will choice without being a burden or savior to another person. Love does not force us to help others. We naturally would contribute as we feel fit to do.

Scrutiny into the twin flame phenomenon shows that the original entity had a choice—not any obligation—to come here. Among Phims, for example, their quanta were not divided evenly; however, as men and women in our Veca, their embodiments can carry similar quanta capacity with the influx of natural energy. Each twin can become fully capable and activated when going his or her individual way. The original Phim can also regain its full quanta and plasma if the divided parts do not return. It is not an either/or situation of power because individuality involves self-sufficiency. This individuality implies that twin flames do not have to come to the same planet at the same time as their partners.

Ashayana's personal experiences show the power of choice. Her original Phim existence split itself into a distorted Ecka dimension after which they sometimes went their own ways. *Ashayana* is the name of her Yanas embodiment. She has long worked with another Ecka entity named Azurtanya who walked into a man named Michael Deane. He married Ashayana as Diana Kathryn (Katie) and was her partner as MCEO Speaker-2. Due to personal reasons and allegations, she cut off association with him and filed for divorce. Her Eieyani mission still applies today; however, in 2011, she reunited with her original Phim portion in a man named Andreas and now focuses upon her Phim mission that creates connections between the Earth and Cosminyahas.

Uncommon twin flames may be helpful together when they blend their chakras so their original codes can radiate into the Earth. This process of energy sharing is weaved into teachings about sex because it is a physical representation of two people joining themselves like one. Tantric sex is believed to assist chakra opening and DNA activation when participants work with kundalini sexual and universal energies known as prana or qi (pronounced chi). The body does not need sex to heal itself for the ascension process, nor is sex necessary for chakras to merge. In fact, certain sexual and fractal energies can actually help destroy the body.

Kundalini versus Natural Ascension

According to Vedic knowledge, prana is "a Sanskrit word for 'life air' or 'life force.'"[395] Indian prana is the same as Chinese qi, Japanese ki, and Polynesian mana—likely the same manna in the Old Testament from the Hebrew God. Prana, as taught according to Himalayan masters' tradition, predominantly flows on one side of our body, so balance must be met with the other polarized side. These sides, the cool feminine Ida and hot masculine Pingala, come together to form the snakes of the caduceus, while the Sushumna silver cord is the most important central channel that forms the staff.[396] The MCEO reveals that the silver cord involves the first 9 dimensions of frequency.[175]

In addition to the 9th dimensional cap, the caduceus snakes wrap around our chakra central column to distort and obstruct infusion of higher dimensional frequencies. The kundalini symbol at the base of the spine, called the Muladhara or Adhara support chakra, has an upside down triangle with a coiled snake within it. The snake appears to be coiled into 3.5 circles, resembling the Reiki Power Symbol that contains a total of 3.5 coils around a vertical, central staff. Reiki is another spiritual practice that draws upon fractal universal energy. Both symbols represent power and knowledge, and they give distorted energy to the other chakras.[397] The 3.5 circles can represent the harmonic universe cap of Caduceus Earth within the three-dimensional Hibernation Zones, as I explain in chapter 11.

Kundalini means coiling, like a snake. It is a form of prana that is assumed to lie inactivated in our first chakra. The objective of kundalini awakening is to stimulate the first chakra and shoot its energy upward to open all other chakras into the enlightened state that can potentially reach nirvana with or as God. What is the best way to stimulate chakra 1's genital region and create a surge of energy? Tantric sex.

Participants in tantric sex consciously and deeply inhale prana through their noses into their diaphragm, directing the energy into the "sexual" chakra 2 and moving it downward to chakra 1.[396] Both kundalini and tantric sex pay the most attention to the first two chakras that transform the prana or qi into ching, which is sexual energy. Then, orgasmic ching supposedly refines the qi. Teachers of tantric sex say that its process creates more love and healing.[398] This is false because anything that is twisted by inorganic energy and excites the body from an externalized act is the opposite of eternal energy, deep healing, and true love. This is a backward perspective that phantom aliens teach so they can attach themselves to this new form of excited energy that resonates with them. It is no wonder why sexual rituals are used to invite alien entities not only into the room but also the body. Sex, truly "sacred" sex, comes from being internally and congruently connected to non-fractal, non-universal energy.

In Ashayana's first *Sacred Sexuality* workshop, she teaches that orgasm and sex build up energy to produce the 1,728 "keys" (familiar base-12 number) needed to ascend into the Edonic Middle Domain worlds just after the Yunasai level.[180] This is very similar to Wilhelm Reich's belief about sexual potency of orgone, his term for prana. Reich became fixated on the power of the orgasm, thinking that it unlocks the key toward health.[399] Ashayana teaches that sex can connect us with the Middle Domain because its disc-like code, the Um-Shaddh-Eie with the Eckasha's 12-point Reuche "kryst-cross" configuration, interfaces with our body about one-half of an inch above the genital region.

Ashayana states that the Um-Shaddh-Eie does not exist in Metatronic entities. This natural interface is a coveted piece of our anatomy by phantom entities who are able to maintain immortality through their attachment to it. It is true that the Reuche technology in this code can spark and retain quanta, but sexual energy is not needed to do this. She has taught that this Um-Shaddh-Eie interface disc is our fast track to the Edonic Middle Domain, so basically the more sex, the better place to which we will ascend.

Quantum generation and connection to fully Krysthal realms can bring in healing energy, especially when correcting the reversed and distorted "checkerboard mutation" in our body's DNA and main meridians caused by "shona" frozen or dead light.[120,184] This genetic disarray was implanted by the Pleiadian-Nibiruian Anunnaki's Nibiruian Diodic Crystal Grid in 25,500 B.C. and must be repaired for proper bodily ascension. However, does one part of the anatomy in a vulnerable place hold the keys for a fast-track ascension to the Middle Domain? Does the first chakra hold the keys to ascension? Where is the line drawn between natural bodily ascension and implanted technology toward bodily harm in our fractal position? I think the following discoveries hold the answers.

In the same *Sacred Sexuality* workshop, Ashayana teaches that the Reu-Sha-TA energy spiral that comes from the Reuche cross creates the following six vortices in each chakra: one at the top, one at the bottom, and four in equidistant, horizontal locations.[180] She incorporates information about a "seer" she favors named Barbara Brennan who sees the same six vortex chakra. Brennan was heavily involved with Wilhelm Reich's orgone teachings that influenced her style of instruction along with channeling and hands on "healing." The Reu-Sha-TA spiral naturally interfaces with us until specific geometric technologies related to our sexuality are placed to twist it into a new energy. Death science technology displaced our chakras below their natural bodily locations and distorted them. Ashayana shows the original locations of our chakras before the checkerboard mutation, but the energy flow to them is the distorted last stage that Barbara Brennan sees, not what they should be. When wanting to help our Human body, we recognize the current fractal state but must impart natural information. If the end result is Metatronic mutation, then it will disfigure incoming natural energies and invalidate healing.

As a capsule formation within the body's auric field, a chakra should send and receive energy in a 360 degree manner in all directions, as the ATI, TPE confirms. Chakras are connected by a central line, but their interdimensional nature interacts with our body through a vast template of connections that we can feel without limitation. Reducing any aspect of our body to a vertical channel with polarity points and few energetic vortices is missing the greater reality of what eternal energy is in its completeness. The ascension process in the Milky Way entails eternal energy increasingly healing Fibonacci distortions, not maintaining disconnection.

Some good teachings can carry small but significant problems. Ashayana teaches that we can heal Elementals that are not only elementary atoms but also entities as fairies, trolls, elves, and etcetera on or in the Earth that can be predominantly good or bad. In order to heal the Earth, we can heal these entities by turning our bodies into ascension vehicles for them. She also states that we can quickly heal our and the Earth's elemental matter, including our supposed fairies and trolls that are connected to it, through our Um-Shaddh-Eie.[180] According to the ATI,TPE, "Elementals involve lower creations that can deter the Human ascension process. Carrying other entities with the Human during ascension is detrimental and can cause dark flowering before the ascension process is complete." I asked the ATI,TPE to describe dark flowering, which it replies:

> The phrase "dark flowering" can be defined in regards to humans carrying other entities with them as a tainting of negative energetic essence of an otherworldly entity by which the entity attaches itself to the Human essence and consciousness, not its construct. By this action, the Human is under its control and mental manipulation.

In other words, dark flowering is a form of possession that can spread phantom energy into our body, and it can reach into our light-plasma body depending upon the entity. It can resemble how the Daisy of Death technology opened up into the Milky Way.

With all this said, I find it very hard to believe that one small part of our entire body can act as our stargate passage to a protected realm, especially when our position is heavily fractalized and dangerous. There is too much distortion in any "sacred" sexuality teaching to apply it to our ascension process. The ATI,TPE and my two Galaxy-2 contacts confirm that our genital region with the Um-Shaddh-Eie interface does not provide fast-track ascension to the Edonic Middle Domain.

The MCEO does provide only frequency-based techniques with codes to reconnect the Human template beyond intrusive technological implants and genetic distortions. An important technique is the Maharic Shield. It utilizes an Eckasha symbol code to help align our body's energies with protected Eckasha energy. We work with the Eckasha code along our personal, vertical chakra column and immerse it and the 9th dimensional silver cord into the combined silver-blue-gray frequencies of the 11th and 12th dimensions (note: I adjusted the MCEO's inaccurate HU-4 pale silver color involving white). This process links us to Galaxy-2's 12th dimension to restore the Human DNA template that was previously stifled by the damaged 12th dimensional stargate. The ATI,TPE reveals that most of stargate-12 was finally repaired in early 2012. I will provide the Maharic Shield and other beneficial techniques at the end of this book.

In the natural process of partiki phasing, where the energetic "breath of life" vibrates to create pre-quark sparks of radiation, this flow reaches us in the Ecka-Veca with which we would transform to lighter densities in the inward ascension process that coordinates what exists within us to the new environment. The Law of One belief does not allow ascension alternatives because it has us systematically go back through the original phasing cycle that brought us to our expanded stage; therefore, we must regain all of our personally encrypted fragments to get back to the "Source" gestalt. In actuality, energy can fast-track or direct as it and we wish along progressively connected pathways, so I am happy to know that there are no other selves I must await in order to live and direct my life. To confirm my assertion, all we need to do is look at the new path of Aurora Ascension Earth as directed by its plasmic connections.

In summation, "sacred" sexuality relies upon polarized units with the aim of getting omni-polar energy. Tantric sex or any form of physical sex cannot approach the pure energies in early realms, but teachers of tantric sex say that the unifying act of sex opens up our chakras to allow the kundalini flow of universal fractal energy. This myopic flow requires us to work from the bottom-up instead of internally outward from our intrinsic energetic connections. If sex is not treated as the externalized, last part of oneself that can somewhat reflect eternal energies from within, and its participants use it to feed a deficit, then this draws upon static, recycled energies that harm the chakras and our ascension viability.

Law of One Mathematical Origin

The early stages of creation were not sexual or polarized; some "time" before the omni-polar partiki unit was created, there were pure energy levels that closely approximated the most pure origin of all, the All That Is, The Pure Essence. Partiki phasing starts the natural light-body polarization process of creation. Polarized entities were not divided or broken down but added and multiplied by the process of expansion. Partiki units phased from one to three in early Starborn cycles when the first unit created a spark that expanded its substance to equidistant locations outside of it, creating the particum and the partikA. The open flow of energy exchange brought these polarized units back to the omni-polar center for another addition to occur.

Partiki unit creations involved a specific mathematical formula, according to the MCEO.[180] After the first three-unit Tauren, the partiki unit in each successive stage is multiplied by the prior unit to eventually become the 48 partiki Hub unit. Then, somehow a quantum leap occurred to create a multiple of three that gave 144 partiki units to the Adon unit. Lastly, the base-12 model produced 1,728 partiki units per Edon unit and 20,736 partiki units per each Yunasum cell. This is the basis of the Law of One teaching about our supposedly other galactic selves!

Ashayana's instruction about how the partiki expanded illuminates the MCEO-GA's spherical model of creation. A 360 degree platform becomes filled with equidistant angles and axes for the creation of the 12 "point"-spaced kathara grid. She states that the "mind of God" chose this pattern of creation.[180]

Since every conscious essence has choice, it can choose how to create. The MCEO's mathematical replication process is possible, but I find the "quantum leap" difficult to believe. Therefore, I asked the ATI,TPE and my two main entity contacts for confirmation about the partiki numbers 48 up to 20,736. They each state that the particular partiki unit numbers are correct except for the number 144 pertaining to the Adon unit. Ah, that number again. Ashayana calls this number the "divine blueprint."[180] The creationist function of the number 12, not necessarily multiples of 12, is one of the mathematical blueprints, but even this blueprint is not prevalent. Now that she is working with the Alhumbhra Council, she has accurately learned about seven, not 12, plasmic CosMA'yah krystars and one Cosminyahas krystar; however, she still maintains the belief that our complete Cosminyahas DNA template contains 144 strands. According to the ATI,TPE, our maximum DNA strand count is 120.

The creation process does not follow perfect mathematical formulas or constants for every situation especially in our much expanded position due to circumstance and individual will. Creation is a mix of control and freedom, and freedom entails randomness. The Law of One perception of creation is very controlled and calculated; it is not representative of any individual anomaly, and it is highly flawed.

My mother and I asked our two contacts and the ATI,TPE to reveal the correct numbers of partiki expansion. We learned that the partiki numbers are estimates due to their random occurrences across creation. This means that although there is an original Adon unit of a certain number of partiki, not all Adon units are exactly the same in their replication processes, so the partiki units per Adon can differ. The Adon has approximately 20,000 partiki units, not 144 as Ashayana teaches, and there is actually another unit with about 15,000 partiki between the Adon and the approximately 1,728 partiki Edon.

At this stage of Ashayana's awareness, she thinks that the MCEO-GA's mathematical pattern represents the original process of expansion as though the Everything Krystar is not only super knowledgeable but also able to control the replication process within it. When any other entity is created, regardless if it is within the general field of its predecessor, it is a separate entity that cannot be fully controlled. Law of One proponents often do not accept this reality because of their own control issues.

Conclusion

Perhaps the reason that Ashayana does not discern her entity groups' inconsistent messages within the Law of One paradigm is because she partially believes that there is no actual evil; instead, we all eventually go back to that one gestalt source, even if just by space dust. This perspective misaligns her desire to help people ascend properly. It entails that nothing really matters when countless people and entities *know* eternal life energies matter greatly; Ashayana has expressed a mutually strong agreement despite some of her teachings and beliefs.

I struggled when hearing the contradictory life and death message from New Agers over the years. It operates out of a mental belief instead of the inner conscious and emotional layers of raw intuition and reaction. Surely, what is good and connected to the All That Is, The Pure Essence matters, not only in the grand picture but also to the ATI,TPE? Surely it matters if people do not want to know eternal life energies? Surely it matters that people are misrepresenting the ATI,TPE and the truth of creation? The ATI,TPE expresses to my concerns that truth, love, and life do indeed matter.

The ATI,TPE does not have emotions, but it does have intent. It intends to have connection, not disconnection. It cannot know disconnected people that well, but it very much knows people who are truly connected to it and to Eia as its expanded bridge to us. This shows that there are differences, and it does matter when we do not choose eternal life. People who want severe distortion have the potential to eventually be cut off from the ATI,TPE. We are not the ATI,TPE, and the ATI,TPE is not us. If we do not choose life, we do not magically become like one with the ATI,TPE. There is eternal separation, which can be an almost indiscernible film or a potentially unreachable abyss.

If we do not understand about individual separation in addition to the reality of connection, we might become easily swayed by higher dimensional entities and their spokespersons who convincingly tell a certain story about creation. When realizing our separation, we sense our own space that can help us gauge the situation with the combination of logic, personal experience, intuitive knowing, and energy detection. When we become aligned with our individual core selves, eternal energy just flows through us in clarity, and we can lead ourselves more completely than any external teaching will do.

When creation expands and contracts in every complete Starborn phasing cycle, which brings the previous Krysthal energies with it to and from the original krystar, a new domain can potentially be created from the regenerative replication process. This type of increase does not expand the krystar or any created being because they are already self-contained. We and similarly complex, mobile entities could visit creation after or lower than us and take on its matter, but this is unnecessary and often undesirable.

The Law of One theory is shortsighted and incorrect when viewing subsequent creation within one encompassing krystar sphere. The earliest levels of existence are outside of creation, unable to be captured, and creation is ever flowing and moving. The pre-krystar levels including our core and highest selves have created multiple krystars like the Cosminyahas with additional expanded realms like ours. We can eventually live on one of these krystars in our full genetic ability of 120 DNA strands, similar to how we live as complex people on a more simplified planet, or we can choose to live in any other created domain. Another option is that we can transfigure the fullness of our complete template and simplify it to our core or highest self, or another elementary state such as a krystar or Yunasum. We are not destined or bound to arrive at any one place because opportunities are bountiful and endless! Those invisible realms seem imaginary to us now, but our intuition can know them as fact due to our amazing composition with perceptible connections back to the ATI,TPE.

The Law of One's amalgamation of created entities not only muddles our specific identity and boundaries, but it also ultimately erases them. As parts of a supposedly single entity, an atom is essentially deemed the same as a complex Human. God-group entities perpetuate the confusion by asserting themselves as our nature-God master. We know that chemical elements are not our identity. We can apply this logic to other extensions of matter that are like us: our parents are not us, and we are not our parents. We are unique individuals through and through, even if duplicated. Instead of thinking about our current world as a hologram, it would better serve us to pay attention to the different aspects of creation and our boundaries so we can learn to peacefully coexist in realistic unity.

The notion of us all as a single God with a predestined plan that orchestrates every individual body like a puppet master is disempowering to us. The Law of One is an attractive belief system because of our innate desire to connect; however, let us not lose our sense of self because both eternal realities of connection and separation exist simultaneously.

CHAPTER 11

The Next Step is Our Decision

We were born into bodies that were imprinted with fallen alien technologies and genetics. This barrage of distortions is the "sin" that we did not bring upon ourselves. What pains me most when I look around me is the level of delusion that many people have when they say they feel "fine" amidst obvious polarities of their reasoning and actions. Metatronic frequencies have aligned them to a negativity that feels normal, even happy to them. I have often felt as though I was speaking a foreign language to such people when giving my perceptions. I realized that they see another reality than mine, one whose energy does not feel normal to me.

The conjoined reality of oneness and individuality can produce aligned energy. This is easiest when we live as our true selves among similar energies, but when we need to assimilate our physical body that is partially built upon fractal mechanics, we cannot help but partake in some of its vampirism in order to survive. For example, we kill plants and animals for dietary consumption. The Earth involves opposing energies that we must somehow balance in order to live here.

Achieving balance can produce very different results. It can be a collaborative output of each aspect within us that will give us health, or it can entail compromise that dulls our senses and eventually switches off our awareness and DNA. Can we continue to act with full awareness and love while we must sometimes put ourselves first at another entity's expense? Where does the line become drawn in the spaces between us, and where does the judgment of "good" and "bad" come in?

This is a very difficult topic with which I struggle when seeing blatant contradiction screaming at me like split personalities, but I somehow must stay sane. I think that sanity involves full realization of these contradictions while also seeing degrees of difference as basic reality. When we understand how creation and our place in it is, we realize that we each have our own space with a synergistic body and consciousness that work together as our complete, individual self. Then, we can put out our receptors to energies around us to determine if they are mostly compatible or not.

My Human body is mostly compatible with Talea's body, so I work with my similarities to create more congruence and strength. If some parts of me clash, then I can quarantine or bypass them in my inherited oneness. In order for me to live with others, this practice also applies. However, if they possess a greater discordant energy that does not work with mine and sometimes attacks mine, then a greater measure of space must be placed between us for the sake of my good health.

The religious and political twists of "oneness" usually involve the combination of everything with little to no boundary. Although both religion and government tout an ideal, the rulers of both want the extremes and everything in between as though that gives the most power and influence. Instead, this combination diminishes their actions as the combined polarities negate each other into stagnation. Whether the compromise is intentional or inevitable, it lessens the unified, synonymous power of all people as well as the individual. When really unified, we grow together, but when we become dulled to chaotic and confusing energies, we become fragments of ourselves.

Our current world is filled with the symbolic color gray because of obvious polarities of beliefs and life and death experiences. This gray is translated as a neutral position, but often the feeling of helplessness or complacency can come in to make us stagnant. Taking on the neutral position either shows some acceptance toward the situation or an act of forfeit. The line is not clearly drawn between neutrality and complacency because we must have some measure of acceptance toward the contradictory "circle of life" so we can have a positive outlook on Earth. The line is drawn when we start to feel lost, incapable, or victimized.

When our consequent action diminishes the oppressed feeling, this is when we willfully blur the line, potentially creating a domino effect of less desirable energies that could turn us into an almost completely different person. How do you think that originally eternal entities became seriously distorted? It was not instantaneous. One by one, their choices severed connections to pure energies, ultimately changing their physical makeup and losing their self-identity. I argue that we must be cognizant of the spaces between energies and entities so that we can avoid blurring their lines. We can make conscious decisions within a neutral zone while knowing they are not 100 percent awesome, but they are the best we can do in current circumstances.

Unfortunately, Metatronic energies polarize the reality toward self-centeredness on one end of the spectrum and a hive mentality on the other end. Why has "normal" become flat and dulled, yet it is also egocentric and resistant at the same time? Why do some people want to stay in such energy just because they are used to it?

The Metatronic frequencies have slowly and systematically infiltrated our bodies to show us another reality that is the fakest reality of all. It is just like *The Matrix* movies where we live in a dream world. However, this dream world still has its nightmares, so it makes no sense to me if someone would reject reality where we finally can control ourselves and feel real happiness and joy in it. For instance, people might think they are happy in a dysfunctional relationship, but those "happy" times are when events do not erupt in abuse—it is survival mode. This is mediocre at best. People have told me that after they left their abusive marriages, they finally understood what happiness is. They got themselves back. It upsets me to see good and capable people fall to the Bourgha, Equari, and Alpha-Omega (BEA-O) lies. They are allowing that alignment!

My plea to the reader is to realize what you are doing. Please explore the layers of your own beautiful self that I helped to uncover in chapter 9; then, make the informed decision whether you really wish to continue following your religious or spiritual belief. This is important because the level of BEA-O belief and associated energy that you might willfully follow will lead you to a similar dimension or space after life on this Earth, yet it may not be shrouded in the same Matrix dream that you are choosing to currently believe. Its energy is entrenched in abusive power. When with the BEA-O on its turf, we will fall under its control and therefore be subjected to more totalitarianism and slavery. There is potential for us to wake up during any point in time, especially since those dimensional spaces will feel "unpleasant" to us there, states the ATI,TPE, but if infected with a worse delusion and energy than what is on Earth now, it may be much harder to break the spell.

Currently, our inherent energy should be sufficiently tangible to awaken us and override a belief, but beliefs are not mere thoughts that can float away. Beliefs are encoded with specific energetic patterns, hence why it takes a lot of our energy to change them. At this stage of the book, I hope that you now operate in the realm of thoughts that can check themselves with the true energy of yourself, where you can consciously dismiss the energies that do not fully resonate with you. Then, you can clearly feel what you want to do instead of what you were falsely programmed to do.

This chapter explores the immediate dimensional locations into which Humans can arrive after Earth. It also provides insight into energetic discernment and protection. We have several options available to us, so it is most wise to have our eyes wide open to consciously choose the right path rather than be led away from our preferred homes.

Ascension Options from Aurora Earth

On January 3, 2013, the combined efforts of the Krysthal River Host (KRH) and its allies, especially the Alhumbhra Council, established a fail-safe situation for the Earth to be able to reintegrate with most of its original Amenti Earth quanta. We worked diligently behind the scenes since December

21, 2012 to thwart the Metatronic 55.5-144 agenda and impart the fail-safe connections. The general public derided the uneventful date of December 21, which was believed to involve apocalyptic change due to prophecies and assumptions about the end of the Mayan calendar, so people continued to live their everyday lives. Good. Living one's life without fear or extreme expectation is what should happen on an ascending planet.

Aurora Earth identifies our Earth as an ascension planet that increasingly integrates protective light-plasma from the Aurora Trans-Harmonic Field or Continuum between Earth and Urtha. For eons, this was the backup plan if Earth could not integrate with Tara. Since Tara is now largely phantom, Earth is now geared toward the Aurora Field that first and foremost reunites us with Median Earth, the preserved portion of Amenti Earth. I think that our re-emergence with Median Earth should have been the first step all along toward our ascension journey, but since it holds the Sphere of Amenti in its core, it presumably would have joined Earth during our expedited ascension cycle.

Keep in mind that the future is unwritten. Along the path of healing for the Earth, there is potential that Tara could be somewhat restored by beneficial entities, conveys the ATI,TPE. This means that Turaneusiam Humans could be able to return to Tara. Plans can change course as history has often proven, but above all, the goal for Earth and its inhabitants is to eventually get to a fully natural state. The safest route for this to occur is via the Aurora Field to Urtha.

The Nibiruian Electrostatic Transduction (NET) fields between the Earth and Median Earth are in the process of shutting down. This should reverse Caduceus Earth's moderately phantom status and reintegrate it with the Earth. Until this wonderful event materializes, death and reincarnation will continue to happen, but reincarnation will begin to involve increasing remembrance and awareness. Eventually, death should be no more, although a measure of atomic compaction will still occur on Aurora Earth until it finally becomes Urtha. If our bodies are sufficiently composed of and connected to natural energy matter after the NET fields finally dissolve or during a proper ascension period, then the body could travel with the rest of our spiritual makeup as one complete unit to the next lighter density.

In the Milky Way, planets take a lot longer than their inhabitants to ascend. The cellular compaction process reaches a threshold in our fractal body before decay would occur, so we in our bodies are ready to meet the next stage of existence. For my 11th dimensional planetary family in the lesser fractalized Galaxy-2, for example, the ATI,TPE reveals that they ascend, body and all, in approximately 800 Clarion years after birth. When I followed up with my Clarion contact, he states that they could choose to return to Clarion soon afterward—with some advanced quanta—in order to be with their loved ones. To return to that density, the body slightly transfigures; we will understand this when we are in that situation.

Therefore, if we would die or ascend with a somewhat compacted body outside of Earth's natural ascension cycle, the ATI,TPE communicates that people and also animals on the natural ascension journey would enter dimensional holding places that are bridged to Median Earth, Tara, or other beneficial locations. This dimensional holding space involves bio-regenesis. People can potentially regain a copy of their old body or another one of that realm. If Humans with no prior higher self or with a damaged template are organically directed to Tara (or Median Earth now), then they will wait in this region until they can join the Earth in the transfiguration process. Time would pass differently there, making the waiting period generally easy.

In a fully natural Krystal system, the ATI,TPE reveals that cellular compaction does not occur, and planetary inhabitants ascend with their planet in its natural Starborn cycle. This is the future hope for Aurora Earth once it assimilates into a renewed Urtha.

For people who identify with fallen angelic energies on the phantom path, other dimensional holding places were created to entrap them. The Melchizedek Cloister Emerald Order (MCEO) calls these places "review planes," but this review does not imply proper introspection. In the BEA-O-encoded planes, people merely continue their self-absorbed struggles and beliefs while in a slightly less dense body.[400] Nothing much changes until they become aware on their own (with the help of ATI,TPE and Eia), just as they were supposed to become more aware on Earth. As I have mentioned, this change will be more difficult in these distorted realms because there is less recollection of natural energies. Often times, people do not know that they have died while in these planes; "life" is just as real to them as it was while living on Earth. There are also "mass review bands" where large amounts of people are grouped together, which makes personal awareness even more difficult to gain.[350]

When it comes to any ascension destination, the energy with which we identify will lead us to a location that contains that energy. Awareness about ourselves and our surroundings will help us consciously direct our paths; however, if people have minimal mental awareness but abundantly good energy that naturally identifies with the ATI,TPE and Eia, then their fundamental nature should guide them to the right place, concurs the ATI,TPE.

The possibility of conquering death is not only a futuristic dream; its time is upon our current generation because of the Earth's stellar activation cycle (SAC). The SAC commenced in 2000 A.D. and has continued despite subsequent Earth and Tara grid battles. As I stated in chapter 8, the Halls of Amenti have been compromised, but they are partially functioning. The KRH and allies are working to regain and connect the Hall portals to the Sphere of Amenti to approximate the SAC's ascension-viable time frame. According to my Clarion contact, "Even if the Sphere was unusable, which is not the case, the Arc of the Covenant would connect to it and direct it to a protected place to keep it or allow it functioning ability." The Earth and its stargates are largely operating on the SAC momentum. In some capacity, Earth as a living entity can consciously circumvent or heal areas of injury similar to what our body can do to keep its ascension objective.

When I and my mother worked with the Earth to bring in Eia and Urtha energies on December 21, 2012, I initially felt its energy of suffering. This was a new experience to me, but I stayed with it because it felt familiar to what my body and emotions have endured. When I carry a burden, and I link to the ATI,TPE and Eia as well as my Talea self, I feel nurtured enough to let out my pain. This release must happen so I can allow loving energy to fill me.

After I felt the Earth release some of its negative energy, I then felt a sense of freedom within it. I could envision a swift and easy infilling of eternal energies, and a measure also entered into the Halls of Amenti. This experience confirmed to me that we are ultimately the masters of our body. Of course, I do not negate tragic subjugation and enslavement that cause us to lose control, but if I have not been clear enough already, there is at least one way out. Death in the Human body unfortunately has occurred, but the way out has been through our soul's ascension. When our intent is pure, we have many allies just as the Earth has, so our path to the next stage of eternal life has fortified support.

The plasmic stabilization of Aurora Earth and the Earth's SAC and Halls of Amenti are almost two separate issues. Now that the Earth will not link with Tara, its activated ascension schedule can potentially lengthen past December 21, 2022. The Earth may not be ready to merge with Median Earth by this time, so its plasma stabilization allows it more time and space for their reunification. The Halls of Amenti will now mainly be for us to crossover to Median Earth if we are sufficiently keyed toward its increased natural energies.

In order for the Human body to become ascension-viable to Median Earth, it must contain at least 80 percent of living light (shaLAah) and water (hydrolase), states the ATI,TPE.[401] Eventually, but hopefully not long afterward, the 3rd dimensional physical form will easily transfigure into the original, higher self from higher dimensions.

Unfortunately but realistically, the ATI,TPE conveys that our embattled Human body needs some natural energetic assistance in order to become ascension-viable. I have intuitively felt as though my own internal connection is sufficient to help me, but this knowing is my experience as Talea. Theresa's body struggles, sometimes a lot, when dealing with its obstacles. The few techniques that I provide at the end of this chapter will greatly assist the entire body. These techniques along with personal work outlined in chapter 9 provide an ample baseline toward our body's ability to ascend. Ascension is now reality for the Earth, but let us exercise care about where our individual paths will lead.

Deceptive Near Death Experiences

You are now aware that the death experience is unnatural for the original Human genetic template. However, it is similar to an ascension process in that it transmutes the rest of our "body" into a less dense dimension. Near death experiences (NDEs) usually show a window into the unnatural aspect of death when "Jesus" is seen on the other side. The ATI,TPE explains that in these particular experiences where a tunnel brings the person to that light-filled dimensional space, that tunnel is a wormhole arc frequency. Natural ascensions do not utilize wormholes. Can we really trust those wormholes that lead us to Jesus on the other side?

People who briefly died and left their bodies did not go into the 4th dimensional astral plane; they entered a Hibernation Zone or less likely a similar "heavenly" encoded review plane close to Earth.[350] They literally entered into the clouds or heavens. The Bible states, "And they heard a great voice from heaven saying unto them, Come up hither. And they ascended up to heaven in a cloud; and their enemies beheld them" (Revelation 11:12). Additionally, after death from the Apocalypse "shall they see the Son of man [Jesus] coming in the clouds with great power and glory" (Mark 14:26).

Hibernation Zones receive NET-harnessed Humans after death while they await their reincarnation. The MCEO expounds:

> The 6 Hibernation Zones are actively inhabited by multitudes of various, often competing and warring, Fallen-Angelic and ET races possessing various different Metatronic Genetic Codes, whom have created elaborate structures of FA culture and civilization within the Hibernation Zone planes. Currently and throughout post-13,400 BC history, the Hibernation Zone races have covertly directly intervened and interfered with evolving earth races in conquest for full control of Earth's Templar; many "Channels and Mediums" consciously receive their "spirit communications," and multitudes of humans unconsciously receive "creative inspiration, ideas, mis-guidance, invention and direct mental/emotional/physical manipulation etc" from Hibernation Zone races through the Metatronic Broadcast

System Mass-Control-Matrix of the planetary NET....

During general "Astral Projection/Remote-Viewing" and subconscious Dream-state projection, as well as following death of the physical body, multitudes of humans find their continuing-conscious-spirit ensnared, entrapped and imprisoned within the reality-fields of earth's Hibernation Zone planes, unable to continue their organic path of spirit-evolution to Ascension. Kryst-Guardian races continue work to free such trapped consciousness from the Hibernation Zones and are currently actively opening the "Aurora Safe-Zone Platforms" [now using the Aurora Field] to allow Earth's life field safe inter-dimensional communication and safe Ascension passage beyond the entrapment fields of Earth's inorganic Hibernation Zones.[185]

The Hibernation Zones are the focus of this section to put the NDEs into perspective. As I mentioned in chapter 8, the Atlantean NET technology created the six Zones to link up to portals on our Earth. The MCEO states:

The NETs were frequencies, un-natural static frequency bands that, above and below a NET...you have a D1 [dimension 1] NET, and the D1 NET would take a piece of the D1 frequency band and the matter stuff that was in it and literally freeze it where it couldn't get out. It was like quarantined, and then above it and below it, it would create a split—a lower D1 hibernation zone and an upper D1 hibernation zone. We have them on D1, D2 and D3. These hibernation zones used to be part of the natural holographic field of our D1, D2, and D3 holographic field on this planet, and they literally have been split and put on reverse spin, so we can't see them (p. 75).[210]

The reverse spin of the Hibernation Zones basically involves the same matter as Earth but in a more discordant and thus invisible form as Caduceus Earth. Hibernation Zones have a crust and atmosphere in their respective levels. Due to the nature of multidimensional frequency blends, some lower dimensional Zones exist above the Earth, but they are indeed comprised of lower dimensional energy matter.

Our Earth should exist at the 3rd dimension. Its 2.5 dimensional position and Hibernation Zone surroundings can provide understanding as to why a measure of Human consciousness has accepted intensely pornographic, violent, and horror-filled movies, video games, and even real life crimes because it is easier for the lowly parasitic and Metatronic energies to reach us.

If the Earth were more natural at the 2.5 dimension, then its life forms would be somewhat simpler, not disgusting and destructive. Thankfully, Earth and its inhabitants both have and receive natural energies. The life forms closest to Earth consciousness such as animals, deva entities, and plants are not significantly aware, but most have a measure of innocence along with their innocent Earth.

The Earth's 2.5 dimensional position logically places it between the 2nd dimensional Hibernation Zones, confirm both the ATI,TPE and "M." The following are the order of the Hibernation Zones. Zone-1 is the fallen Inner Earth at the lower 1st dimension that connects to the Earth's core layer. The upper 1st dimensional Zone-2 is in the Earth's ozone layer and is the subject of the Wizard of Oz story, according to the MCEO. Outside the NET-created Van Allen Belts in a half dimension below Earth is the lower 2nd dimensional Zone-3 into which most of Atlantis and Lumeria were warped. Above Earth in the upper 2nd dimensional Zone-4 is Shamballah, as revealed by "M." Shamballah, our closest biblical "heaven," is a prevailing destination in New Age and religious channelings. The ATI,TPE states that there is no other Shamballah than what exists in this Hibernation Zone. The lower 3rd dimensional Zone-5 is Olympus that likely connects to Wesadek's stargate-7 Olympeus. Lastly, the upper 3rd dimensional Zone-6 connects to Telos, the fallen portion of Ecka stargate-1 named Brenaui.[210,197]

Generally, certain Greys and Nordics have bases in Zone-1, and the Zeta like to hang out in Atlantis and Lumeria.[197] I think that the Greek gods as Wesadek's hybrids have lived in Olympus literally above the clouds. Many science fiction and fantasy stories—including ancient religions that we dismiss as myths—were told by phantom entities in the Hibernation Zones.

We can find numerous New Age and religious depictions of Shamballah.

> Whatever its historical basis, Shambhala gradually came to be seen as a Buddhist Pure Land, a fabulous kingdom whose reality is visionary or spiritual as much as physical or geographic.[402]

> Although some will make claim that Shambhalla exists only within your heart and mind there are those that would differ. The idea that Shambhalla is located in the material world is firmly rooted in Tibetan tradition. However the opinions as to its location differ considerably.
>
> Tibetan religious texts tell us that the technology of Shambhalla is supposed to be highly advanced; the palace contains special skylights made of lenses which serve as high-powered telescopes to study extraterrestrial life, and for hundreds

of years Shambhalla's inhabitants have been using aircraft and cars that shuttle through a network of underground tunnels. On the way to enlightenment, Shambhallans acquire such powers as clairvoyance, the ability to move at great speeds, and the ability to materialize and disappear at will.[403]

Buddhists portray Shamballah as a place of tranquility and happiness. However, it is ruled by a line of kings, which entails implicit hierarchy. The chosen king will emerge at an appointed time much like the Messiah character who comes to "save" the world from the destruction that he helped create.

> Shambhala is ruled over by a line of Kings of Shambhala known as Kalki Kings [Kalki in Hindu; Rigden in Tibetan Buddhism], monarchs who uphold the integrity of the Kalachakra tantra. The Kalachakra prophesies that when the world declines into war and greed, and all is lost, the 25th Kalki king will emerge from Shambhala with a huge army to vanquish "Dark Forces" and usher in a worldwide Golden Age. Using calculations from the Kalachakra Tantra, scholars such as Alex Berzin put this date at 2424 AD.[402]

Celtics also revered Shamballah within the guise of religious belief.

> Shambhalla is known by the Celtics as the mystical "Avalon", hidden in the mists of illusion. Once our home, now mostly forgotten except in our dreams, our soul still goes there for healing and revitalization. It is a land without time, full of power and mystery, offering enlightenment to the traveler that is fortunate enough to enter its gates.[403]

The "love and light" New Age belief also associates Shamballah as a healing center, but this so-called healing energy is a lie. New Agers provide pieces of factual information mixed into religious-oriented stories.

> The Ascended Master known as Saint Germain...is the original channel through which the Shamballa energies were first introduced to the Earth plane in the time of Lemuria when he was incarnated on the physical plane. Today, Germain channels through many people, including Hari Baba and other Shamballa Masters.[404]

Sanat Kumara [Lucifer] is the Planetary Logos, apparently

the greatest of the Avatars. He is the God of this Universe and He oversees ascension initiations in the inner planes. He has an Ascension seat in Shamballa, over Gobi Desert, where you may ask to go in meditation…. Sanat Kumara is the Master of Shamballa, also known as the Ancient of Days.[405]

Many are becoming aware that the earth is hollow and that we have a seventh inner continent named Agartha…The rise in consciousness is opening the minds of many to this truism….

I will also place the facts before you that the GFL [GFofL] primary Earth base is located in the inner-Earth caverns, beneath Tibet's spiritual city of Lhasa….

From that vast base, many miles in diameter, there are cavern tunnels that lead out to various exits, including those in India….

Something I would like to add about our primary GFL base, is that is is [sic] right next to Shamballah, 400 miles under Tibet's capital city of Lhasa…Officially the base is described as the GFL Command Base and it is 50 miles in diameter, with five levels.[406]

The above background and channelings are revealing. Maitreya is the Kalki king who works alongside Lucifer in Shamballah (see chapter 10's "Great White Brotherhood" section). The ATI,TPE states that Maitreya is the so-called Ascended Master El Morya, Archangel Michael's partner as one of his group's Seven Rays of light.

Buddhists and others are not enlightening themselves by taking astral trips to Shamballah. The MCEO states that Archangel Michael likes to take people there. A New Age believer concurs, "You can go there while you sleep! Just ask Archangel Michael to take you there before bed, and you can be taken there in your finer bodies if your vibration and consciousness is high enough."[407]

Michael's large army controls most or all of the Zones, so once people enter into them, they will gain their phantom frequencies and activations. People can enter the Zones through astral projection, abductions, and near-death experiences. When they return back to Earth, they will unknowingly run the Metatronic frequency that anchors the Threshold machine into the Earth's grid.[197,199]

Telos is often mentioned with Shamballah. Telos is completely controlled by the Bourgha, and it was plugged into the BEA-O time rip network 25 million years ago, states the ATI,TPE with Eia. It is well known in the New Age movement as the underground city of Mount Shasta.[197,196]

According to channeler Aurelia Louise Jones:

Telos is also called "The Crystal City of Light of the Seven Rays." In the future Telos will manifest on the planet's surface. There will be a merging of Telos and Mount Shasta City....

Their predominant spiritual activity is Ascension that involves visiting different dimensions, particularly moving from the third to the fifth dimension and is learned in temple training.

Telos is a technologically advanced civilization. They have a remarkable transportation system. The inner-city transportation is composed of elevators and electromagnetic sleds. The people of Telos travel between other underground cities on an electromagnetic subway that moves at 3,000 miles per hour. Telos is a member of the Confederation of Planets, and its people travel to other worlds. They possess inter-dimensional spacecraft. Their computer system is amino acid based and is linked to other underground cities and galactic civilizations. Each family and individual has its own computer.[408]

The above excerpt is a moderately accurate and detailed channeled story. Ms. Jones further explains that Telos means "communication with spirit," and its king is named Ra, who is Marduk. This message clearly shows the collaboration between the GFofL, Ashtar Command, and Ra Confederation of Planets. It also confirms their goal to blend the Hibernation Zones with Earth.

The following excerpt combines the Hibernation Zones and fallen Ecka dimensions into one cohesive unit, much like *The Urantia Book* does when lumping in Wesadek with the Milky Way. This type of presentation makes it easy for "God the Father" to control the combined masses.

The city is made up of five levels.... Telos is a city of the Argathan Network that is made up of over 100 cities. Its capital and seat of government is Shamballa. All cities are of the light. They honor spiritual teachers of the surface including Sananda/ Jesus, Buddha, and Osiris. These cities were built to keep records, sacred teachings, and technologies.[408]

The small city of Mount Shasta connects to Telos via Zone-6 and contains a significant population of Pleiadian lightworkers, especially Amorah Quan Yin and Omakayuel. As I explained in chapter 7's "Archangel Michael" section, Omakayuel facilitated the brief partial possession of my friend James Macaron, which then caused a Reptilian high commander to harass him for access to his body.

It is important to know that a lot of the New Age and traditionally religious channels have come from the Hibernation Zones. These cities are nothing but platforms to entrap Humans who align to their messages of false ascension. The Humans become part of their army when further Metatronically encoded, but after their Earthly service, the BEA-O—especially the Jesus group—will likely try to consume them.

I have not yet heard a near death experience story that does not involve meeting Jesus on the other side. My friend "Ramona" recounts the NDE of her friend:

> I do know he was dying in the hospital on the operating table—he'd had a heart attack! He floated out of his body, and then he says Jesus, along with all his deceased family and friends, were pouring love into his heart and healed him. He went to "heaven" and said they have the most amazing music he ever heard. He says Jesus told him he is to "live in love" as his only commandment, and that he still had a lot of work to do here on earth. His energy is very loving, open, wise, and peaceful. He's one of the nicest persons I've ever met.

My initial thoughts to Ramona's description were, "How could he feel love from such an evil group as I know them to be? Surely, he does not know the deep love energy that I do? But then why does he act so loving toward people? Is it the type of 'love' that will turn against you if you speak up against his belief, where it is only kind when he receives praise?"

Then I thought, "Who am I to discount what my friend is experiencing with this man because my friend is a nice and honest person."

I decided to ask the ATI,TPE for clarification about this specific person's experience. "Why did that man think he felt so much love and peace from the Jesus group alien when that was not the ATI,TPE energy?"

It replies, "The man had a measure of the ATI,TPE connection within him, which was greater than the entity group's measure, and both measures connected. Love and peace returned to him. The ATI,TPE permeates everything with the Love energy [Eia]."

The ATI,TPE explains that the amazing sounds that the man heard in that dimensional plane are some harmonic sequences. It was an overall positive experience for him because he left some of his body's distortions to travel there; however, he still experienced distorted energy.

In this man's experience, the ATI,TPE reveals that the "Jesus" entity was real, but his family members were not. On August 25, 2011, the ATI,TPE stated generally:

People who experience after-death encounters usually perceive a display of projected images from their religious affiliations. Those without religious or sect connections project their root affiliations, usually religion when growing up or the name they worshipped or followed.

For a period of up to three full days after death, states the ATI,TPE, the recently deceased person stays tied to his thoughts and feelings on Earth, so he can carry the past perceptions into the NDE, thereby creating a mentally-projected experience.[271] NDEs do not last longer than this window of time. When people return to their bodies, I hope that they will realize their religious affiliations within their unconscious and conscious minds and weed them out. This is what my mother did when she saw Jesus's feet standing upon the figurative dry ground of her core; she faced that association, and then it left her permanently. In my opinion, the NDE should be a time of rediscovery and empowerment, not further enslavement to another religious experience.

I will not impart an entirely negative message about NDEs in these fabricated heavens because the ATI,TPE gives a bigger perspective about the experience. The person does feel a measure of love, and certain deceased family and friends might be there. The Hibernation Zones also draw from Earth's natural energy.

However, the fact that many people in their NDEs have gone to the Zones in the first place shows that they are connected to the Jesus group and affiliated aliens. No matter what the feel-good experience, the ATI,TPE states about the Jesus person, "This person is not aligned with the ATI,TPE energy." Then, when Jesus tells the recently departed to return to Earth and do good works, the Jesus group increases its use of the victim.

As I suspected, this is what happened to Ramona's friend who briefly died. Now, this man channels the Jesus group and helps others receive its "spirit guides" who want to attach to Humans. Ramona said that he never did this before his near-death experience.

Unfortunately, Ramona wrote to me, "Yes, he 'channels' my 'guides' for me sometimes. They are always loving, positive messages that don't feel to have a hint of evil." A little while later, she told me she was having an identity crisis and felt scared and confused, which showed me that her inner self was speaking up against her New Age affiliations. Nevertheless, she decided to ignore her higher self and settle into the Metatronic energy.

It disheartens me to know that when people openly receive these spiritual guides via a religious ceremony or spiritually inclined friends, they think they feel fine with those energies. I think that Ramona initially identified with the "love and light" feel-good words and her genuine connection with her friend.

She needs to pay closer attention to the guides' outer energies and her inner energies to best demarcate what feels most natural and good to her. I take care in this book to present many scenarios and thoughts as to what really feels natural to us.

The ATI,TPE explains a way out of the meddling entity's influence or grasp: "The person must take the steps to reach truth, if not experienced before. The will must change course to goodness and true energetic awareness."

Since January 3, 2013, the KRH and affiliate groups have taken control of Earth's connections to the Hibernation Zones. They aim to progressively infuse Aurora Field energy into the Zones and hopefully release many inhabitants. Although this is wonderful news, it has not deterred BEA-O channels that continue to direct us toward the Jesus group. They operate out of the partially open Hibernation Zones and similar phantom dimensional holding spaces that connect to their phantom matrices, confirms the ATI,TPE. It is highly improbable that they can affect the Earth's ascension path, so their backup plan aims to capture Humans unless we are aware.

<u>Distinguishing Between False and Natural Energies</u>

Life is eternal. It never will stop. If we do not sense how valuable our life is here, even if it is wrought with terribleness, then we might not separate the good from the bad, and our view of reality will be clouded. If people deeply love life, they will link to the ATI,TPE. The ATI,TPE does not change; it is the single constant from which awareness, life, and love come. Know true life and love, and your body will naturally evolve in more life and love.

As a combined unit, we each should feel largely grounded in our body, emotions, mind, and astral nature. These are the dominant physical aspects of our composition that fallen aliens manipulate. If we are obviously struggling, then we can build energetic bridges past the discomfort and disconnection to maintain sufficient conscious awareness in the present.

We are becoming increasingly heightened by the ascension process and Aurora Earth energies that partially activate more DNA and excite our electromagnetic bodies. This is different than the heightened feeling that is experienced in religion and prophetic channeling where it ungrounds us by lifting us elsewhere and taking us over. Less obvious beliefs also help to unground us away from our most integral aspect of existence—our original higher selves. I will introduce a few scenarios that address these other beliefs that masquerade as personal will.

James Macaron told me about a meeting he had with an acquaintance, "Danté," whom the ATI,TPE states is an Oraphim-Human. This man knows about Ashayana's teachings and did the Maharic Shield once or twice, but he believes that he should not do any techniques if he already knows the right energy within him. James says that his energy felt good at the time, and he was open to information about the ATI,TPE. Danté said that he always felt separate as a child from everything around him, and he questioned most everything. He attended spiritual and "conspiracy theory" events as an adult, but he went as an observer to see what people think. He is very self-assured, and he radiates peace and kindness as well as sadness about the reality of the world. He point-blank told James that he does not care if he turns into space dust. He said he is not afraid of anything.

James describes his conversation with Danté:

> He said he has done some level of astral travel, even told me how he met a demon in that realm that bit his neck. He remained unattached and just relaxed, and it went away. Then it came back and attacked him again (totally vampiric) and he just said to it, "Hey, whatever you're experiencing in your reality, that is your experience, but this is not my reality and not my experience, so please leave." And it went. No fear, and that way he was protected in that realm. This is a reason why he feels he does not need techniques to protect himself because his energy feels good enough to him from within.

It seems as though Danté is in connection with his higher self along with the ATI,TPE; however, he does not sufficiently honor life because he admitted to me that he feels no connection to his body or this planet nor does he desire one. I think that he as an Oraphim-Human correctly feels separate to the mess, but at the same time, he is giving up. He is probably one of the people who chose to be here to help bring up the Earth's energy for the natural ascension process, but implied in that mission is the belief in life. Additionally, we are not fully helping the Earth if we are not helping our Earthly body. His energy is not fully congruent.

I skyped (internet called) Danté whom the ATI,TPE further reveals is a Clarion like me and James. He left Clarion when he was 100 years old, so this could explain why he feels self-assured and separate to the Earth. I explained a lot of the situation to him, but what I heard in return was a belief system that mirrors non-attachment of Buddhism. It turns out that his interest in those spiritual gatherings was not out of mere curiosity because he does believe part of the message. I pointed this out to which he openly agreed was probable; regardless, he did not wish to change his view.

I learned from this encounter that our paths are our individual choice, although too many people do not choose congruently. I told him that I do not believe him when he says he does not care to be wiped out of existence, especially since he is so lucky to be him. I said that he is feeling fragmented here, and that is perfectly normal. Now, he can understand why and override the belief he gained that furthers the feeling of fragmentation. Unfortunately, as the conversation ensued, his belief presented its dominance instead of the instant connection and intuition we shared as Clarions.

I think that good energy should identify with a good message. Our sensible self and the ATI,TPE do not turn away truth. I know that Danté has good energy within him; I just hope that it will be sufficient to correct his current mind frame. If his belief is resistant to change, then he will choose a different path than what he used to know.

I counseled my friend "Alex" who had a kundalini awakening experience. This example is most common because when people strongly feel their own energies, they are usually not paying attention to anything behind the scenes. Alien-initiated chakra experiences are valid experiences that interact with our natural energy. What is important to learn is that there are natural and unnatural ways to move our own energies.

The unnatural kundalini awakening process predominantly moves sexual energy up through the chakras, but it also utilizes chakra-related emotional energies that develop from birth onward. If there is a problem up the chakra line, it could have originated in a lower chakra and maybe an earlier time in our lives. It is important to heal the first chakra properly because it can help ground us back into our body and reconnect us to our innocence and original self. Natural chakra awakening uses multidimensional frequencies outside of sexual energy; we can sense pure freedom in our opened chakras that abide by our personal fields.

Alex had an unnatural kundalini experience because he experimented with emotional energies when he was 19 years old. He intentionally brought himself to the darkest of emotions and then worked to bring himself to the height of happiness. When happy, he thought he was cleared of the negativity, so when strange sexual energy entered his body afterward, he did not think twice about it. The intense energy started at his genitals and went up his spine to his head. Then, he started convulsing in ecstasy three times the strength beyond what he had experienced before. He said that he felt extremely peaceful afterward, so because of that pleasure and peace, he deduced it was a good experience. However, since that time, he has been ill. He has nerve damage in his face and persistent sinus pain, and he often cannot smile without sharp pain. He drastically changed his diet to a minor advantage. The sensory overload of that experience gave him residual tension in his upper shoulders and neck that compound the nerve damage.

I told Alex that the experience was very real because it used his own energy but then amplified it to the extreme. The highly polarized energies are familiar to the phantom BEA-O aliens, so they were able to direct the kundalini experience and gain access to his chakras. Non-sexual, emotionally ecstatic energies are also used in religious ceremonies to gain access to people. I advised that he purposely ground himself in his true "Indigo" energy and link to the ATI,TPE for extra help. (I used the word Indigo because although it is technically incorrect, it is commonly known—he is another Oraphim-Human who was targeted.) He needs to learn to override that continual tension and heal what he can of the nerve damage, but first, he needs to stop the behaviors that allow BEA-O connection.

Another friend of mine, "Charlotte," seemed happy all of the time. It was as though she was in her own world, singing to herself while preparing food and always smiling and laughing. My mom and I stayed with Charlotte and her family one weekend, and my mom later told us something startling about our gathering in the living room. While Charlotte was sitting on the couch between me and her mother who was talking, I kept noticing how poised she was. Her back was straight with arms relaxed, and her palms were open and facing upward. I felt a bit "off" while next to her because I could not believe how she could stare blankly in front of her during the entire time her mother was talking. She appeared to be at peace, but it seemed as though she was more of a zombie.

My mother found the right time to sit us both down and talk to us. She said that she saw a tall Reptilian standing behind Charlotte. Charlotte freaked out about the news, but she believed my mom because she knew that we do not lie to her. Interestingly, another Reptilian was also standing behind Charlotte's mother, but she was in the teaching mode that took her focus away from her own energy.

After my mom and I left, my friend could not sleep for a few nights. She decided to face this fear in herself, which was brave and honorable of her to do. At night, Charlotte drove into the wilderness near her house where the only light was the night sky. She sat in her car and saw what was in her words "a clear, glass-like being" that moved around the car. She told it to leave her alone, but it only stepped back several feet to still be near her. She explains that when it did not move, she could not see it. She recounts, "I don't remember if I then fell asleep—no, how could I fall asleep!" Although this experience was difficult for her, she gained confidence in her ability to make it step away from her, and it finally did. She vowed to me that she would not lose her awareness to let it affect her again.

For a while afterward, my encounters with Charlotte were much more real. She started to deeply feel her feelings. She would cry without holding back her tears, and she let her and other people's energies flow through her without becoming ungrounded. Our conversations were focused and profound. She realized that the previous peace and happiness she thought she had were not what she later experienced. She wrote to me, "I am so much stronger now. I feel a deep connection with the All That Is [The Pure Essence] and my feelings within me."

I wish that her realization lasted, but she has gained minor fame in her line of work. She resumed her "love and light" belief of always being happy because now she is an example to others; in the process, she has unfortunately lost a part of herself. Her energy is now somewhat superficial like it used to be, which saddens me because she used to know what it felt like to be expanded and aware. Worst of all, I sense the familiar Reptilian has returned.

Alex also realized that he did not reach the true happiness that he thought he did. How could pure joy, happiness, and love be found when he was willing to feel the worst energy? He was navigating an experiment after touching fire, so he could not feel perfection while feeling the burn. Also, real happiness is not artificially stimulated. The unnatural bipolar energies are what the BEA-O has wanted from him and us all.

One night while I was in Canberra, Australia, I was attacked by an entity, and the experience showed me how energy vampires link to people. First, I awoke feeling some dark energy in the room. Instead of dispelling it, I let my mind wander toward fearful thoughts about being in a new country. The fear built within me, and then all of a sudden, I felt something bite my neck! I immediately gathered myself and went straight into my core with the ATI,TPE, and I then told whatever it was to leave. I later asked the ATI,TPE if something did bite me, and it confirms, "Yes." The ATI,TPE states that it was a Reptilian, and my excessively fearful energy allowed it to come close to me.

Once I understood this reality of energy exchange, I have not allowed my fear to get me to that point of no control. It does not significantly matter if entities sometimes invade my home because I do not share their dark energy, so they cannot really harm me. I have not been harassed in that way since then, but I do get physical harassments of acute pain from time to time. Now, I keep my awareness about me to quickly dismiss their unwelcome presence, therefore preventing potential damage. However, it is important to mention that they do learn how to alter their attacks in response to our growing awareness. They caught me off guard when a series of unfortunate events weakened my discernment, and I started to get depressed until I soon realized I was being attacked. They also like to prod the edge of my field to slightly unsettle me. I have learned how to counteract their several strategies by becoming astutely aware of my energies. It can be very difficult for trauma-survivors to learn how to control or manage our plethora of excitable energies, but this is our inborn ability that we can master on our own.

My link to the Reptilians occurred in my childhood. The atrocious childhood incest that was forced upon me by my father was influenced by a Reptilian High Commander, reveals the ATI,TPE. This is a reason why my father does not totally recall the incidents, although he also has buried them deep within his subconscious mind because he was alert and willing in his sick participation.

I usually felt a dark energy about my father when I was younger, so now I know it was largely due to his unwitting affiliation with dark forces. The abuses of this world happen because of a much bigger reason than what the majority of Humans would choose to do in their right minds. They are most often used as pawns to further the Victim-Victimizer game in order to embroil us in negative emotions and destructive thoughts. I was raped as a child because they wanted to entrap me. It worked for quite some time, but thankfully I fought my way out of the prison.

After James's light-body ceremony, he was harassed in his sleep a few times; in addition, he was slowly awakened with intense sexual thoughts. When he realized what was happening, he promptly gained his proper awareness that knew an alien was there wanting him to carry out that energy. James never complied. One time, he verbally said, "No, it ain't gonna happen." Each time, the alien became angry and pushed him against his chest, indenting his body one or two inches into the mattress, and then it left him alone because "it knows it's going nowhere with me," says James. The ATI,TPE reveals that it was a Reptilian High Commander who kept trying to control him. I think it was Omakayuel, the Pleiadian entity group in the GFofL. Since then, my mother, James, and I have banded together with excellent energy connection to the ATI,TPE to rid James of Omakayuel's harassment hopefully once and for all. Before it left, a spokesman of this particular 10 member entity group said to my mother, "He never told us to leave before," to which I replied, "That is a lie," while I continually kept up protective energy throughout and around us. Since he unknowingly attended Omakayuel's possession ceremony, James has learned to stop the kundalini energy from rising within him when he senses sexual energy attaching to him. He now can determine when it invades him from the outside instead of starting within himself even if his body has somewhat responded.

Reptilians are especially drawn to primal kundalini energy that they skew toward their desires. Other entity groups seem to prefer invading the heart chakra to reverse our heart energy, or the crown chakra or third eye to give prophecies. Nonetheless, they all manipulate the lower chakras due to the plethora of sexual ceremonies, and often the DNA is manipulated as well. David Icke states in his book *Children of the Matrix* that rapes, especially against children, are how they gain access to our energetic bodies.[409] This is exactly what happened to me as a child.

These aliens are drug addicts. They often overexcite our bodies to feed their twisted energetic desires. If we are not wrapped up in their energies of fear, rage, intense lust, or cold detachment, then they give us the religious experience for a false sense of euphoria. We do not realize that our religions and careless actions are draining us because of the high. It is an "experience" as people call it, hence it being real and cherished as a part of us. If only people realized how we are throwaways after we are sucked dry. I would think that our adrenal fatigue from such experiences would be an indicator that we have been running on false energy. Aches that spread up our spine and through our body are another indicator of harm.

We think our health is failing due to our own accord while they have been indirectly and directly steering us toward artificial stimulation and unhealthy habits. If we are not following in their footsteps by outwardly seeking instant pleasure and stimulation, we can easily detect the drug addict energy around us. However, we usually pass off our increasing fatigue to aging or stressful events in "normal" life. When our bodies show enough dis-ease, we enter the place of surrender that has us call to God to heal or save us. This is their plan! God will then come in to further excite our bodies to a degree, only to burn us out even more.

I think it is impossible to always feel grounded on Earth with experiencing all of our energies in a stable fashion; however we can look at the world from within the protected and stable area of our core. As Talea-Theresa, I can energetically sense someone with deleterious energy, so my body starts feeling stifled, less grounded, and somewhat shaky. I then know to step away and recharge with my internal fullness. I must add that the reaction of feeling somewhat altered can also occur in response to Krysthal energy, so it is most wise to not be quick to judge and to first check your own discernment skills. From the reference point of the congruent self, we can sense the shifts of energy that either subtract from or wholistically add to us.

It is imperative to distinguish between our own energies and those of others because there are enemies at play to muddle our sense of self. I am not suggesting that we gain a thick skin or act on guard. I desire that we have the awareness to handle any situation without being blindsided if something does not go according to our beliefs, because usually it will not. Covert manipulation of the Human against oneself is arguably the most advanced form of BEA-O control, but our awareness and appropriate actions can overpower it.

Summary

When we become in tune with the incredible layers of ourselves, we will go to better places after our Earthly life. Essentially, each of us came here alone and will leave the Earth alone, so it behooves us to build a solid relationship with oneself. We cannot control anyone's will but our own, so let us be sure with which energy we wish to embody because energies continue after Earth. The ATI,TPE informs about our next destination: "Those with an extended and increased measure of the ATI,TPE through Eia than those with less measure, will sense their loved ones [with less measure] but bypass them to other or higher dimensions. They will not be together."

When I have questioned the worth of this Human life, I have been assured from my higher self and the ATI,TPE that it does matter very much and so does the life in the next destination. The ATI,TPE has never wavered about the flowing nature of life. When I ask it about the deceased who have maintained a decent amount of goodness, it replies, "The All That Is, The Pure Essence knows who these conscious 'souls' are, and will extend its connection to them." It is up to individuals to choose the type of energy they wish to align and embody because it does affect us now and later.

As we approach the potential opening of the Halls of Amenti passageway to Median Earth after December 21, 2017—more likely near December 21, 2022—the ATI,TPE stated on August 21, 2011: "The ATI, The Pure Essence will increase people's awareness and knowing as the time approaches. Those aware will be propelled into action, for their chakras will automatically open and respond to this process." Even if this seemingly far-out event does not occur, we can feel confident that our increased awareness will result in more control over our own paths.

I ask the ATI,TPE what it would advise to people at this crucial time, and it replies, "The All That Is, The Pure Essence tells humans to be open to all that is happening around them; be aware and question everything. Do not be followers and accept information without question. Choose truth and goodness."

If people are not aware of the acute information in this book, but the good energies are intuitively known, then this should prompt and connect them into sufficient alignment with the ATI,TPE and their true selves. It should also be enough to protect them from Metatronic 55.5-144 energetic technology.

I kindly advise that we do the following techniques below. You may explore other techniques, especially those given by Ashayana's entity groups, but I do not recommend pulling in any complex entity. It is completely unnecessary and often deleterious to bring into ourselves any type of angel for our natural ascension journey. Other complex entities such as those presented by the MCEO as "floating Buddhas" or "Wha-YA-yas" in the *Sliders* material are also not necessary for us, confirms the ATI,TPE.

We have a familial relationship between what exists in the natural realms and our own bodies, so it is beneficial to bring in certain simple "entities" of Krysthal frequencies and fundamental constructs. For the bio-regenesis process, we can bolster and partially activate this energy matter within the DNA and body as long as we are cognizant of the process, any symbols used, and direct intention.

Lastly, if we wish to connect to a trusted entity or team that provides an outwardly, loving connection, the ATI,TPE confirms that it can be beneficial to request their assistance for extra protection and information, but I advise that this option is secondary to the grounding we must first gain in ourselves.

Techniques

We initially need to get from point A to point B: Earth to the more natural Median Earth in the 3rd dimension. To facilitate our transition, we should introduce our body to the shaLAah light and hydrolase water of Median Earth. Even if the Human body does not make it out and therefore would die, the rest of us can safely arrive on Median Earth when we truly align with our original self, the ATI,TPE, and natural energies. As I previously stated, we need at least 80 percent shaLAah quanta in our body to prepare it for ascension after this current stellar activation cycle. The ATI,TPE informs that shaLAah is fairly easy to lose if we do not keep active our inner drive and actions toward truth and love in all areas of our lives. If we feel out of touch with our personal power, we can be our own cheerleader and reignite our spark from within, much like lighting a figurative match to boost our inner flame.

Until the present day in 2014, the beneficial bodily techniques have only helped prepare the human atomic structure for the future transfiguration process of complete ascension. The ATI,TPE informs that transfiguration "techniques will be known through a specific, high level, etheric group in the most high dimension of the Eckasha at a later date," which means that part of the Krysthal River Host familiar with our anatomy will naturally transmit the energetic codes and currents to those of us who are ready for that next stage of transition. These techniques will not be technical, states the ATI,TPE, so they will be "known" by our innate involvement with pure, eternal energy. I sense that the final transfiguration techniques will be transmitted energetically to us when the Earth's ascension gates are fully open to Median Earth. Perhaps some Humans may learn some specifics about them before the time period would arise; otherwise, if we are truly ready, then the transfiguration process should just happen.

CONNECT TO YOUR ORIGINAL SELF

Background: Getting to know one's original "higher" self requires some trust. It is not like religious faith toward something outside of you—it is inherently your basis for being.

Start this technique with the belief that you are good, beautiful, amazing, or any other positive statement that makes you feel secure, peaceful, loving, and trusting in your action. Stay completely positive without any power play or fear. This is the foundational energy of this technique that will provide the courage to reach in to your true self.

For extra help, you may envision shiny, happy cable lines that you can plug in one by one to connect each chakra to your core point. This is a joyous and grounding experience to reconnect with yourself.

Technique: Become comfortable in your own skin. Sense your physical body's skin as your boundary to keep you within yourself when connecting to your core. Turn your vision inward toward your pineal gland "third eye" in the lower region of the central forehead. You can sense it within your interdimensional mind. Use your third eye to look downward between chakras 3 and 4 at the base of the sternum above the xiphoid process, away from any chakra interference. With the pure, trusting, and "knowing" energy that is your entire focus, draw this point deeper inward and expect that you meet your true self. You can stay there for a little while to feel its fullness as you. You can then expand your higher self through your entire body.

You may receive physical validation from your higher self through your third and fourth chakras that give a quick burst of tangible joy as an actual energetic leap from your core to you to validate your connection. This energy effortlessly spreads throughout your body in a united, self-aware state.

Post-technique: Recall the interdimensional process by vision or feeling of meeting your original self within you. Be brave and spread that energy forward in your faithful declarations about you and your intuitive guesses, and your true self may increasingly provide that energetic leap of confirmation that overflows from your core connection into the surrounding third and fourth chakras. By keeping the natural energy flow between you and your original, higher self, information is communicated and revealed between two congruent "people" who can and should become one.

CONNECT TO ALL THAT IS, THE PURE ESSENCE

Background: Usually, it takes at least a few tries to become steadfast in your Human core toward the ATI,TPE. The direct pathway must be free of emotional, mental, and chakra disturbances.

Technique: Perform the previous "Original Self" technique to reach the central point at the base of the central sternum above the xiphoid process that opens the protected communication line between your current awareness and your higher self.

You may wish to envision at your core any or all of these words, "love, truth, peace, goodness, pure" if you do not yet trust the words "All That Is, The Pure Essence." Then, extend the line to the All That Is, The Pure Essence. At this final stage, there is only stillness. If you do not sense complete stillness, check to see if the surrounding third or fourth chakra is interfering with unresolved energy or if the third eye is losing its focus. When identifying the blockage, feel it and exhale it out, possibly as a brief cry. Then, reconnect back to the ATI,TPE.

With the third eye focused upon the small and still location of the ATI,TPE, envision it expanding from its pre-pre-gaseous "point" to a sphere until it expands wider throughout your entire body. Then, expand it past the body into an outer sphere of protection. Do not jump ahead to the vision of the outer sphere until its essence is fully sensed within the body in a natural flow.

The process of linking to the ATI,TPE and expanding it via Eia and your true self can happen quickly in seconds once you become familiar with this uninterrupted pathway.

ECKASHA MAHARIC SHIELD[410]

Background: The Maharic Shield or Seal is an MCEO technique that anchors into the body and the Earth protected Eckasha energy that properly aligns our dimensional frequencies. It resembles kundalini activation but carries our chakra energy upward to Galaxy-2's 12th dimension and beyond to the eternal Eckasha light-body aspect.

The Eckasha symbol code is shown below in Figure 7 for this visualization and energy work. The cross formation in the inner circle is the Reuche, otherwise called the Kryst Cross. This cross is at the center of the Eckasha, and it "holds the intrinsic coding for the formation of Light and Sound" for our Ecka-Veca system, states the MCEO and confirms the ATI,TPE.[411] It helps correct the Milky Way and Galaxy-2 distortions.

Note: Ashayana states that we should first do the Cosminyahas Journey (in "Helpful Techniques") before any light-body technique since the Shield of Solomon frequencies were breached in 2011 by plasma-coded FatalE beings (see chapter 8's "Krysthal River Host Protective Measures"). The Maharic Shield technique links to the eternal energy flows of the Eckasha, Galaxy-2, and also AquaLaShA via my italicized addition in Step 8, so I do not give caution either way; therefore, it is up to your discretion. I have already presented the Original Self and ATI,TPE techniques to first align our inner energies in a protective manner, so outer distortions are additionally thwarted. Plasmic energies, although powerful, do not override our light-body anatomy; they exist cooperatively but separately, and our destination to Median Earth predominantly involves the light-body.

Lastly, I slightly alter some grammar and capitalization of the MCEO Maharic Shield technique to facilitate reading comprehension and performance; I do not alter the MCEO's instructions except where briefly italicized, omitted as unnecessary in an ellipsis series of dots, or clarified within brackets. I also insert the natural frequency color for the 12th dimension.

The instructions teach that the HU-4 dimensional frequencies blend to pale silver, but this is incorrect. As I stated in chapter 10's "Kundalini" section, the MCEO teaches that Galaxy-2's 12th dimensional color is white, but the ATI,TPE and Eia reveal that it is actually a blend of blue-gray hues with white specks. The MCEO's pale silver color also does not include the 10th dimensional blue hue. Figure 6 shows that the MCEO's pale silver hue mainly resembles AquaLaShA's 12th dimensional pale silver-gold blend. Since we are connecting the Milky Way to Krysthal energy, we do not need to blend all of HU-4's colors, so the 12th dimension suffices because it carries the lower frequency codes. I will substitute pale silver-gold for the MCEO's pale silver. You may use either option because the Eckasha energy helps correct distortion, although the ATI,TPE states that the technique would be more complete when linking to AquaLaShA's 12th dimension.

Figure 7. Eckasha Symbol Code

1.   Imagine the 2-dimensional image of the "Eckasha Symbol Code" as if the image is drawn on a black background on the inside of your forehead.... Its colors denote the frequency spectra of the triadic, polaric and eckatic levels of the energy matrix [Ecka HU-1] and 15 dimensions of frequency. [The predominant color of light blue throughout the symbol denotes an Eckasha frequency blend, states the ATI,TPE.] It will be used as the key code to unlock the 12th dimensional Maharic Shield in the personal and planetary scalar grids.

2.   Inhale while visualizing the Eckasha symbol at the center of the brain in the pineal gland.

3.   Exhale. Use the exhale breath to firmly move the Eckasha symbol down the central vertical body current (energy current in the center of the body), then out between the legs and straight down into the Earth's core (13th chakra).

4.   Inhale while imagining that you can see at Earth's core a huge, disc-shaped crystalline platform of pale silver-gold light, that extends outward on a horizontal plane through the entire body of the Earth and out into the atmosphere. Visualize the Eckasha symbol suspended in the center of the disc (this image represents the planetary Maharic Shield, the scalar-wave grid composed of dimension 12 frequency, with the Eckasha positioned to activate the planetary shield).

5. Exhale. While pushing your breath outward into the Earth's Maharic Shield, imagine as you exhale that the force of the breath has made the Earth's Maharic Shield begin to spin.

6. Inhale. Use the inhale breath to draw pale silver-gold light from Earth's spinning Maharic Shield into the Eckasha symbol positioned at the center of the planetary shield.

7. Exhale. Use the exhale breath to push the pale silver-gold light throughout the entire Eckasha symbol, making the symbol glow and pulsate with pale sliver-gold light.

8. Imagine that the glowing Eckasha momentarily flashes *from* crimson red *to Urtha's purple with slight gold fringe* and then returns to normal. Then use the inhale breath to draw the Eckasha vertically up from its position at Earth's core to a position 12 inches below your feet (the position of your dormant personal Maharic Shield scalar-wave grid). As you inhale the Eckasha symbol upward from Earth's core, imagine that it trails a thick cord of pale silver-gold light behind it; one end of the pale silver-gold cord remaining attached to Earth's core, the other attached to the Eckasha symbol (the cord represents an energy feed line through which you will draw energy up from the Earth's Maharic Shield into your personal Maharic Shield).

9. With your attention on the Eckasha symbol positioned 12 inches below your feet, use the exhale breath to push a burst of pale silver-gold light outward on a horizontal plane from the Eckasha symbol. Imagine that a disc-shaped, crystalline platform of pale silver-gold light, about 4 feet in diameter, extends on a horizontal plane 12 inches beneath your feet, around the Eckasha symbol at its center. (This image represents your personal Maharic Shield).

10. Inhale. Use the Inhale breath to draw more pale silver-gold light up through the pale silver-gold cord from Earth's core, into the Eckasha at the center of your personal Maharic Shield.

11. Exhale. Use the exhale breath to push the pale silver-gold light from the Eckasha symbol out into your Maharic Shield. Imagine that your Maharic Shield now pulsates as it fills with the pale silver-gold light from Earth's core.

12. Inhale. Draw more pale silver-gold light up from Earth's core through the pale silver-gold cord into the Eckasha symbol, and imagine the pale silver-gold cord expanding to 4 inches in width, forming a pillar of pale silver-gold light running up from Earth's core directly into your 4-foot diameter Maharic Shield.

13. Exhale. Use the exhale breath to push pale silver-gold light from the Eckasha symbol outward into your Maharic Shield. While imagining that your Maharic Shield "takes on a life of its own," the disc suddenly "folds upward" with a "popping" sensation to form a 4-foot diameter pillar of pale silver-gold light all around and running through your body (this is your Maharic Shield, a temporary scalar-wave pillar of dimension 12 frequency light, that blocks out disharmonic frequencies from dimensions 1 through 12 and begins to realign disharmonic frequencies in your body and bio-field to their original perfect natural order).
[Note: People with sufficiently opened chakras may not experience a popping sensation.]

14. Inhale. Imagine that the inhale breath draws the pale silver-gold light from the pillar encasing the body into every body cell; sense the tingling feeling as the pale silver-gold light moves through the physical body.

15. Exhale. Imagine that you can feel the energy of the pale silver-gold light expanding into every crevice of the body and then outward around the body into the bio-field.

16. Breathe naturally for a minute or two. Feel the pale silver-gold light move through you, while sensing the energy presence of the Maharic Shield pale silver-gold pillar 4 feet around your body. The more time you spend breathing and sensing the energies, the more dimension 12 frequencies you are drawing into your pillar, which will increase the length of time the Maharic Shield pillar will remain in your bio-field.

17. Return your attention to the Eckasha symbol still positioned 12 inches below your feet.

18. Inhale. Use the inhale breath to draw the Eckasha symbol up through your central vertical body current, then out the top of your head (the 7th "crown" chakra), to a point about 36 inches above the head (the 14th chakra).

19. Exhale Forcefully. Use the exhale breath to rapidly expand the Eckasha symbol outward on a horizontal plane at the 14th chakra, until the Eckasha suddenly "disappears" from view with a *possible* mild "popping" sensation.

20. Breathe normally. Visualize for a moment a brilliant 4-foot pale silver-gold pillar of light extending from the Earth's core upward, fully encasing your body and extending far above the head, into Earth's atmosphere and to a single star of pale blue light far off in deep space [this star exists in the Eckasha, states the ATI,TPE]. Your Maharic Shield is now temporarily activated and your Maharic Shield pillar is temporarily manifest within your bio-field. The Maharic Shield will remain in your bio-field anywhere from 20 minutes to 1 hour at first. The more this exercise is practiced, the longer the pillar will remain.

Post-technique within 24 hours to quickly reinforce the Eckasha Maharic Shield: Imagine a spark of pale silver-gold light *(with basic recollection of the Eckasha symbol)* at the pineal gland, exhale it rapidly down to Earth's core and imagine the Earth's Maharic Shield spinning, call to mind the pale silver-gold cord and inhale the 4-foot diameter cord all the way up around you, forming the pillar, attaching it "out in deep space" to the star of pale blue light.

Post-technique anytime: You can approximate remembrance of the symbol, locations, and structures of this technique for a quick seal. If your mind is stunted when experiencing an energetic attack, it may be preferable to quickly link to your original self and ATI,TPE and push out protective energy throughout and around you.

KRYSTAR VEHICLE ACTIVATION

Background: This is an MCEO technique for protection, orbing, projecting, and potentially sliding our body. Essentially, this is a personal energetic vehicle shaped as a large diamond surrounding the body. Imagine the bottom of the diamond at the base of the feet, the width as an extension past our fully extended arms, and the top about three feet above the head. When my mother does this technique, she feels as though she is driving her little space car.

The following excerpt is the MCEO technique from the *Sliders-2* workshop with more elaboration as known in the Keylontic Science group. Step 1 (the first inhale) refers to the natural E-Umbic point between the 3rd and 4th dimensions, and Rasha comprises our dark matter components.[196] Step

2 involves the AzurA point at the base of the thymus that is the galactic body's core atom, and EirA is an Eckasha-A partiki unit, clarifies the ATI,TPE.[184] The last Steps 3 and 4 should be understood by now.

> Perform three rapid inhale breaths; do not exhale between all three.
> Inhale at a point two inches below the navel and say to yourself "Rasha."
> Inhale again at a point at the base of the thymus whilst saying "EirA."
> Inhale again at the pineal gland while saying "Krystar."
> Exhale forcefully from the AzurA at the base of the thymus while mentally stating "Now," and imagine the Krystar capsule surrounding you.[252]

HELPFUL TECHNIQUES

Some MCEO, KRH, and Alhumbhra Council *Sliders* techniques "can be helpful," states the ATI,TPE. Use caution toward the *I AM God-Self* and *Power of 12* statements as well as any indication of Law of One probabilities, the number 144, and meeting entity guides. You do not have to follow every aspect of a technique, and it is up to your discretion to do any technique.

1. The *Sliders-2* workshop information helps open our conversion pathway to Median Earth's hydrolase atomic living water. One of its techniques utilizes the Allur-E'ah Ra-sha-tan "Feel Good Code" that holds the imprint of all cosmic elements at the center of our cosmos. The MCEO erroneously teaches that it contains 144 elements due to its incomplete base-12 formulation and Law of One belief.[252] The ATI,TPE states that the complete code carries the imprint of 216 elements that are fully actualized in all levels of the cosmos. When using the MCEO version of the technique, keep in your mind and energy the greater extent of the real code. Although the Feel Good Code is incomplete, the ATI,TPE states that it is still helpful with our proper intent toward eternal life creation.

Sliders-2 introduces many foreign words about which some are explained in *Sliders-1* at an extra monetary expense. You can also refer to www.keylonticdictionary.org for vocabulary assistance for as long as that website is accessible.

2. In August 2012, the Alhumbhra Council provided a guided journey through Ashayana to the Cosminyahas core called "Journey to the ARI-ARhAYas AL-

Uma-Un-Core of the Krystar Seed Atom."[186] This process bolsters our plasmic and light-body protection, and it improves a measure of transfigurative ability toward Median Earth's shaLAah living light and hydrolase living water. However, caution is warranted during the journey until we arrive at the Cosminyahas destination. My mother and I performed this technique together, so I will share my experiences and thoughts about it.

Before we did the technique, we individually created a personal shield around us by activating our personal Krystar vehicle and expanding our pure energy connection to the All That Is, The Pure Essence. Then, we made our intentions known to the Alhumbhra Council that we did not want them to enter our personal space during the technique.

The technique creates a little barrier between us and the outside by enveloping us in protective frequency; however, it also sends us a personal Alhumbhra guide. Ashayana's techniques often give us guides with whom we would have over a dozen guides by now if we accepted them. While I appreciate the willing help of new friends, other entities who pretend to be our friends can jump into our field if we are not discerning.

During the technique, we stepped back from Ashayana's teachings in the following cases that I will not recall in order.

A. When she talked about our personal guide behind our right shoulder, this startled me a bit, so I restated my intent for the entity to step back. I then forgot about that entity as the technique ensued because I only felt my own energy. When she later reminded us about the personal guide, I felt distracted again, but I re-established my energy and was fine.

B. The personal guide touches our wing spot area to activate it. I immediately stepped away and communicated that I want to touch my own wing spot area between my 4th and 5th chakras on my back. I did it energetically along with my third eye experience of it. I had my higher self touch that area in her body which simultaneously corresponded with me directing that energy to touch my human body's wing spot. What I did was acceptable, and I felt that my Alhumbhra helper was fine with it.

My mother and I are very protective of our fields and bodies. We do not ask for help from a personal guide to activate any part of us. We think it is most wise to do our own tasks until we absolutely need the help from someone else, such as a helper possibly aiding us through protected passageways.

C. Ashayana talks about our plasma body having wings and eyes. My mother and I have never identified with having wings. We know that our original bodies are an Elohei race made of hydroplasma without wings. When

Ashayana tells us to open our plasma eyes, I do not envision any other plasma being outside of my original body with eyes. If a person doing this technique is originally from a carbon or silica dimension in our time matrix, then imagining a plasma body with eyes will probably feel foreign. You can simply imagine your human eyes on your inner plasma aspect to feel more grounded.

Ashayana takes some time to talk about wings and how they affect the wing spot. She talks as though we all should have wings, but this is incorrect. It is wise to pay attention to our instinctive reactions because they may be individually true.

So, my mother and I just stood there as our hydroplasmic bodies while Ashayana took time to talk about how feathers and wings should feel. My body's wing spot area on my back felt a bit warm and tingly, but that was it. My mom and I appreciated standing there as a somewhat different race that is accepted into this new group of beautiful beings. We would not need to work with them if the Earth's and Milky Way's situations were not dire, so this was indeed a journey for us. We were not going "home" as Ashayana calls it; however, the destination felt like a lovely adoptive home.

D. When the personal guides brought us through a passageway, I felt a wave of energy right over my head because the entity put me under its wing. This energy was too close to me, so I pushed it outside or on the edge of my field to re-establish my space. We cannot really avoid feeling close energies around us, so I just made it more comfortable for me.

Overall, I felt I was in tune with my needs during the technique, and I experienced pure, eternal energy at the end destination of the Cosminyahas core. I did not always appreciate Ashayana's visions and interpretations because I felt that they sometimes created thoughts in my mind about what I should see and feel, but this was her way of doing it. Everyone has their own approach to some degree.

I think I should mention that the technique involves certain words without explanation, such as Eckasha code, which I include in the Maharic Shield technique, and cruxansatea. The cruxansatea is both an Eckasha and Tri-Veca merkaba vehicle. It involves a large flow of 15-dimensional energy that somewhat resembles an Eckasha tear drop symbol encasing a similar but smaller, upside down teardrop shape around one's body. The inner, upside down symbol stands the person on the top platform of the 12th dimensional Maharic Shield pillar, which resembles the staff of an ankh with the upside down, teardrop "head" on the horizontal platform.[239] The Egyptian and Gnostic ankh symbol is a Bi-Veca merkaba vehicle without the outer teardrop symbol, and its platform extends further as "arms" of the cross symbol. In addition, I do not think that the religious ankh symbol can reach HU-5 frequencies. This is why the natural code is appropriately called cruxansatea, not ankh, for its sufficiency.

End result: my mother and I feel fine. We gained eternal plasma crystals from the Cosminyahas core, and the plasma feels nicely smooth and calming. This technique can be currently downloaded for free at the ARhAyas Productions LLC website, www.arhayas.com. The recording ends with the expectation of having to do additional activations of our plasma crystals, but I think that we can work with this energy ourselves since it is now part of our body.

3. Awakening the Flame of Amoraea and the DNA Amoraea Buffer (MCEO flame body techniques 7 and 8).[412] Activating the Amoraea Flame extends the foundational Maharic Shield up to the 15th dimension and into the Eckasha-Aah domain. (Note: the Eckasha-Aah "ManU" partiki unit mentioned in the technique is an expanded version of the original pre-partiki ManU in the "A" domain, states the ATI,TPE). Activating the Amoraea Buffer helps to protect our DNA from Metatronic technologies. The MCEO advises to perform the Amoraea Buffer technique daily because it can essentially replace the Maharic Shield prerequisite, but I sense that this constant repetition is unnecessary after we become sufficiently aware of energetic differences and can easily connect to our higher and highest selves. Periodically doing both the Maharic Shield and Amoraea Buffer techniques can act as shaLAah tune-ups, confirms the ATI,TPE.

4. Connect to the Krysthal River Host

This technique is simple: Mentally identify the Krysthal River Host and lovingly link to its group. That is it. It is unnecessary to use any code, including the *Sliders-2* Allur-E´ah Ra-sha-tan "Feel Good Code" explained above. If you would like extra help, my 14th dimensional Galaxy-2 KRH affiliate contact "M" suggests:

> Imagine the letters "K R H" and say mentally or out loud the words "Krysthal River Host, my true self (or its name if known) would like to connect with your group." The individual will sense a loving connection through frequency and alignment with his/her being.

If you choose to not identify with what the ATI,TPE represents as well as deep love, then I am certain that this will prevent alignment with the KRH if you decide to link to it half-heartedly "just in case." The KRH energy is beautiful, and these entities are helping us; I suggest that you treat them with care as you would a true friend.

The first time I reached one or more KRH entities, my mother wanted to know how I did it. I just said that it was natural when connecting with the ATI,TPE and then thinking about them. My mom likes to visualize her interdimensional experiences, so she asked the ATI,TPE to help facilitate her connection because she did not know where to locate them.

She asked the KRH if we were connected with it, and she received "YES" in the visionary reply. She asked it where it was. She saw a point really far off to her left to which she saw the word "here." She then felt as if she was going through a portal to it, so she stopped that connection and pulled out. Our objective is to bring them here to help us, not make us more ungrounded. Lastly, she saw a willowy figure and a wave coming from that figure. This wave is the energy sent to us. She asked this KRH entity how long we should link with it, and it responded "forever." Its response brought tears to my eyes because they want to help us, and they appreciate us as we appreciate them.

In conclusion, energetic and physical techniques need ample background and explanation to reveal the meaning behind their symbols, key phrases, and objectives. The technique must anchor eternal energy, and any symbol must be sufficiently natural.

I advise to first connect with your pure, inner energy so that you can best sense the technique and symbol and determine if their energies feel calm and unrestrictive or alternatively stifling. Also, apply critical thinking to determine if it is religiously based in the Law of One or if it is fear based whereby you must do it or else you cannot ascend.

The important point to remember in all of our actions, especially in techniques, is to lovingly communicate with every frequency, possible entity—even as subatomic particles—and the non-entity All That Is, The Pure Essence in order to collectively work together in a similar will. For example, I entreatingly and respectfully asked a heavily clouded sky to clear so I could enjoy my day hike, and most of it wonderfully did so within about 10 minutes. We can also help loved ones connect to pure energy from their cores when we sense that their true selves desire it beyond current limitations. Lovingly reach out to their original higher self at their core point and help them expand their own bubble or technique of eternal energy that will help integrate them. Concerning the people who carry different energy and intent, we can send them love from afar that they can assimilate if they choose.

Hopefully, we will increasingly live on Earth in our protected energy bubbles or krystar vehicles that allow us to walk calmly and lovingly through unsettling environments. We can be immersed in vivid, multidimensional frequencies in a new version of this world that feels unfettered and limitless while darkness can exist merely feet away. Our energies will not resonate with unwelcome intruders, and we will act as our abundant, true selves. Let us work together to expand our beautiful, innate nature so we can finally let the Earth shine as a harmonious planet and home.

Please check my website for prospective information over the coming years at www.rediscoverypress.com. Thank you. I wish you well.

BIBLIOGRAPHY

1. **Landau, Elizabeth.** Inside CERN's $10 billion collider. *CNN Tech.* [Online] Cable News Network. Turner Broadcasting System, Inc., December 8, 2013. http://www.cnn.com/2013/12/08/tech/ innovation/lhc-cern-higgs-cms/.
2. **Rothschild, Babette.** *The Body Remembers: The Psychophysiology of Trauma and Trauma Treatment.* New York : W. W. Norton & Company, Inc., 2000.
3. The Official Creed of: United Pentecostal Church International. *The Interactive Bible.* [Online] http:// www.bible.ca/cr-United-Pentecostal-(upci).htm.
4. **Benner, Jeff A.** Shin. *Ancient Hebrew Research Center: Plowing through history, from Aleph to Tav.* [Online] 2013. http://www.ancient-hebrew.org/3_shin.html.
5. The Alphabet of Biblical Hebrew. [Online] http://biblescripture.net/Hebrew.html.
6. Hebrew. *Shekinah.* [Online] http://shekinah.elysiumgates.com/hebrew.html.
7. **Jahn, Herb.** *exeGeses parallel BIBLE: a literal translation and transliteration of Scripture, Fourth Edition.* Orange, CA : a non profit religious organization, 1994.
8. **Greenburg, Gary.** *101 Myths of the Bible: How Ancient Scribes Invented Biblical History.* Naperville, IL : Sourcebooks, Inc., 2000.
9. **Gardner, Laurence.** *Genesis of the Grail Kings: The Explosive Story of Genetic Cloning and the Ancient Bloodline of Jesus.* Boston : Element Books Limited, 2000.
10. **Friedman, Richard Elliott.** *Who Wrote the Bible?* New York : Summit Books, 1987.
11. **Benner, Jeff A.** Yad (Yud). *Ancient Hebrew Research Center: Plowing through history, from Aleph to Tav.* [Online] 2013. http://www.ancient-hebrew.org/3_yad.html.
12. **Icke, David.** *...and the truth shall set you free.* Isle of Wight, UK : David Icke Books Ltd, 2004.
13. **Icke, David.** *The David Icke Guide to the Global Conspiracy (and how to end it).* Isle of Wight, UK : David Icke Books Ltd., 2007.
14. **Yin, Amorah Quan.** *Pleiadian Perspectives on Human Evolution.* Santa Fe, NM : Bear & Company, 1996.
15. **Awareness, Cosmic.** *Who, In Fact, You Really Are.* Olympia, WA : Cosmic Awareness Communications, 2008.
16. A Brief Description of The Urantia Book. *Urantia.* [Online] Urantia Foundation. http://www.urantia. org/urantia-book.
17. **Assmann, Jan.** *Moses the Egyptian: The Memory of Egypt in Western Monotheism.* First Harvard University Press, 1998.
18. **Owen, Bruce.** The emergence of civilization in Mesopotamia: 'Ubaid and Uruk. [Online] 2009. http:// bruceowen.com/emciv/a341-09s-11-UbaidUruk.pdf.
19. **Tellinger, Michael.** *Slave Species of god: The Story of Humankind from the Cradle of Humankind.* Johannesburg : Music Masters Publishing (now called Zulu PlanetPublishers), 2005.
20. Map of Ancient Trade Routes from Mesopotamia to Egypt and the Mediterranean. *Bible History online.* [Online] 2013. http://www.bible-history.com/maps/maps/map_ancient_trade_routes_mesopotamia. html.
21. UR of the Chaldees. *Bible Hub.* [Online] 2013. http://bibleatlas.org/ur.htm.
22. **Redford, Donald B.** *Egypt, Canaan, and Israel in Ancient Times.* Princeton, NJ : Princeton University Press,   1992.
23. **Greenburg, Gary.** *The Moses Mystery: The African Origins of the Jewish People.* Secaucus, NJ : Carol Publishing Group, 1996.
24. **Jones, Alfred.** *Jones' Dictionary of Old Testament Proper Names.* Grand Rapids, MI : Kregel Publications, 1997.
25. Terah. *JewishEncyclopedia.com.* [Online] 2011. http://jewishencyclopedia.com/articles/14330-terah.
26. **Mizra, Syed Kamrau.** Was Allah The Moon God of Ancient Arab Pagan? *FaithFreedom.org.* [Online] http://www.faithfreedom.org/Articles/skm30804.htm.
27. From Babylon to Mecca Allah Was a Myth. [Online] http://www.scribd.com/doc/2309673/From-Babylon-to-Mecca-Allah-Was-a-Myth.
28. **Icke, David.** *Human Race Get off Your Knees: The Lion Sleeps No More.* Isle of Wight, UK : David Icke Books Ltd., 2010.
29. **McDaniel, Thomas F., Ph.D.** *The Song of Deborah: Poetry in Dialect.* Thomas F. McDaniel, 2003. http://web.archive.org/web/20120915033903/http://tmcdaniel.palmerseminary.edu/Deborah.pdf

30. **Sivertsen, Barbara J.** *The Parting of the Sea: How Volcanoes, Earthquakes, and Plagues Shaped the Story of Exodus.* Princeton : Princeton University Press, 2009.

31. Egypt in the Third Intermediate Period (1070–712 B.C.). *Heilbrunn Timeline of Art History.* [Online] The Metropolitan Museum of Art, 2013. http://www.metmuseum.org/toah/hd/tipd/hd_tipd. htm#ixzz1A7fNGDWE.

32. The Victory (Israeli) Stele of Merneptah. [Online] Tour Egypt, 2013. http://www.touregypt.net/ victorystele.htm.

33. **Gardiner, Sir Alan.** *Egypt of the Pharaohs: An Introduction.* New York : Oxford University Press, 1961.

34. Asherah. *BiblicalTraining.* [Online] http://www.biblicaltraining.org/library/asherah.

35. Asherah. *Wikipedia: The Free Encyclopedia.* [Online] February 8, 2014. http://en.wikipedia.org/wiki/ Asherah.

36. *The Ha-bi-ru—Kin or Foe of Israel?, Second Article.* **Kline, Meredith G.** 19, Westminster Theological Seminary, 1956, Westminster Theological Journal, pp. 170-84.

37. **Collins, John Joseph.** *A Short Introduction to the Hebrew Bible.* Minneapolis : Fortress Press, 2007.

38. **Whipps, Heather.** How the Eruption of Thera Changed the World. *livescience.* [Online] TechMedia Network, February 24, 2008. http://www.livescience.com/4846-eruption-thera-changed-world.html.

39. Minoan eruption. *Wikipedia: The Free Encyclopedia.* [Online] February 25, 2014. http://en.wikipedia. org/wiki/Minoan_eruption.

40. Israel & the Hebrews. *Bible Believer's Archaeology.* [Online] BibleHistory.net, 2013. http://www. biblehistory.net/newsletter/Israel.htm.

41. *Differential Y-chromosome Anatolian Influences on the Greek and Cretan Neolithic.* **King, R. J., S. S. Ozcan, T. Carter, E. Kalfoglu, S. Atasoy, C. Triantaphyllidis, A. Kouvatsi, A.A. Lin, C-E. T. Chow, L. A. Zhivotovsky, M. Michalodimitrakis, and P.A. Underhill.** 2, University College London, March 2008, Annals of Human Genetics, Vol. 72, pp. 205-214.

42. Chapter 29: The Mysterious Habiru. *The Moyer Papers.* [Online] Moyer Publishing. http://www.world-destiny.org/a29hab.htm.

43. arya. *Bhaktivedanta VedaBase Network.* [Online] The Bhaktivedanta Book Trust International, Inc., September 10, 2010. http://vedabase.net/a/arya.

44. Documentary Hypothesis. *Wikipedia: The Free Encyclopedia.* [Online] February 2014. http:// en.wikipedia.org/wiki/Documentary_hypothesis.

45. Jeroboam. *Dictionary 3.0.* [Online] 2011. http://www.dictionary30.com/meaning/Jeroboam--.

46. **Leithart, Peter J.** Jeroboam And Saul. [Online] January 23, 2005. http://www.leithart.com/ archives/001087.php.

47. **Wilson, Dr. Ralph F.** The Sword of the Lord (Judges 7:15-8:21). *JesusWalk® Bible Study Series.* [Online] http://www.jesuswalk.com/gideon/3-gideon-battle.htm.

48. Omri. *New World Encyclopedia™.* [Online] July 22, 2008. http://www.newworldencyclopedia.org/entry/ Omri.

49. *The Book of Samuel: Its Composition, Structure and Significance as a Historiographical Source.* **Garsiel, Moshe.** 5, The Journal of Hebrew Scriptures, Vol. 10.

50. **Osman, Ahmed.** Moses and Akhenaten: One And The Same Person. [Online] 2002. http://www.dwij. org/forum/amarna/10_moses_akhenaten.htm.

51. **Osman, Ahmed.** *Moses and Akhenaten: The Secret History of Egypt at the Time of the Exodus.* Rochester, VT : Bear & Company, 1990.

52. Amarna. *Wikipedia: The Free Encyclopedia.* [Online] February 27 2014. http://en.wikipedia.org/wiki/ Amarna.

53. **Tilles, Gérard.** History and geography of ritual circumcision. *History of Circumcision.* [Online] http:// www.historyofcircumcision.net/index.php?option=content&task=view&id=81.

54. **Gadalla, Moustafa.** *Historical Deception: The Untold Story of Ancient Egypt, 2nd Ed.* Greensboro, NC : Tehuti Research Foundation, 2003.

55. **Pope, Charles N.** Chapter 8: The Fullness of Time. *Domain of Man.* [Online] 2004. http://www. domainofman.com/book/chap-8.html.

56. **Giokaris, Amalia.** Hammurabi, King of Babylon. *The Web Chronology Project.* [Online] David W. Koeller, 2003.

57. The Code of Hammurabi. *The Avalon Project: Documents in Law, History and Diplomacy.* [Online] Lillian Goldman Law Library, 2008. http://avalon.law.yale.edu/ancient/hamframe.asp.

58. Yaqub-Har. *Wikipedia: The Free Encyclopedia.* [Online] November 7, 2013. http://en.wikipedia.org/ wiki/Yaqub-Har.

59. **Mackey, Damien.** The Many Faces of Ashurnasirpal and his Son. *The California Institute for Ancient Studies.* [Online] November 2004. http://www.specialtyinterests.net/the_many_faces_of_ashurnasirpal_ and_his_son.html.

60. **Pope, Charles N.** Chapter 15: A Shepherd They Withheld. *Domain of Man.* [Online] 2004. http://www.domainofman.com/book/chap-15.html.

61. **Watson, Rev. J.S., trans.** Justinus: Epitome of Pompeius Trogus' "Philippic histories". *Attalus: Greek and Roman history 322 - 36 B.C.* [Online] Book 36. http://www.attalus.org/translate/justin5.html.

62. **Osman, Ahmed.** *Stranger in the Valley of the Kings: Solving the Mystery of an Ancient Egyptian Mummy.* New York : Harper & Row, 1987.

63. **Sutherland, Mary.** Red Haired Mummies of Egypt. [Online] 2003. http://www.burlingtonnews.net/redhairedmummiesegypt.html.

64. **Pope, Charles N.** Chapter 12: At the Side of My Father. *Domain of Man.* [Online] 2004. http://www.domainofman.com/book/chap-12.html.

65. Uriah. *Jewish Virtual Library.* [Online] The American-Israeli Cooperative Enterprise, 2013. http://www.jewishvirtuallibrary.org/jsource/judaica/ejud_0002_0020_0_20230.html.

66. Bowl of General Djehuty. *Louvre.* [Online] http://www.louvre.fr/en/oeuvre-notices/bowl-general-djehuty.

67. Tracing The Hebrew Pharaohs Of Egypt...Who Was This King Solomon? [Online] [Cited: January 10, 2010.] http://web.archive.org/web/20100110062708/http://www.egyptcx.netfirms.com/were_there_hebrew_pharaohs_egypt_3.htm.

68. **Gardner, Laurence.** *Bloodline of the Holy Grail: The Hidden Lineage of Jesus Revealed.* New York : Barnes & Noble Books, 1997.

69. **Ward, Dan Sewell.** Moses and Miriam. *Library of Halexandria.* [Online] January 28, 2010. http://www.halexandria.org/dward922.htm.

70. **Tellinger, Michael.** *Slave Species of god: The Story of Humankind from the Cradle of Humankind. Third Edition.* Johannesburg : Music Masters Publishing (now called Zulu Planet Publishers), 2006.

71. **Von Däniken, Erich.** *The Return of the Gods: Evidence of Extraterrestrial Visitations.* Rockport, MA : Element Books Limited, 1997. Excerpt from Figure 8.

72. **Parsons, John J.** The Letter Yod. *Hebrew for Christians.* [Online] http://www.hebrew4christians.com/Grammar/Unit_One/Aleph-Bet/Yod/yod.html.

73. **Martincic, Tom.** Why Yahushua? [Online] January 9, 2012. http://www.eliyah.com/yahushua.html.

74. Demigod. *Oxford Dictionaries.* [Online] Oxford University Press, 2014. http://oxforddictionaries.com/us/definition/american_english/demigod.

75. Names and Titles of God in Judaism. *Wikipedia: The Free Encyclopedia.* [Online] February 2014. http://en.wikipedia.org/wiki/Names_and_Titles_of_God_in_Judaism.

76. **Rich, Tracey R.** Mashiach: The Messiah. *Judaism 101.* [Online] 2011. http://www.jewfaq.org/mashiach.htm.

77. **Sumner, Paul.** Melchizedek: Angel, Man or Messiah? *Hebrew Streams.* [Online] Origin of excerpts: *The Complete Dead Sea Scrolls in English* by Geza Vermes, 1997; *The Dead Sea Scrolls: A New Translation* by Michael Wise, Martin Abegg, and Edward Cook, 1996; and *Songs of the Sabbath Sacrifice: A Critical Edition* by Carol Newsom, 1985. http://www.hebrew-streams.org/works/qumran/melchizedek-dss.html.

78. Does the Book of Wisdom call Sophia God? *Theology @ McAuley.* [Online] http://dlibrary.acu.edu.au/research/theology/alan_moss.htm.

79. Apocrypha. *BibleStudyTools.com.* [Online] Salem Web Network. http://www.biblestudytools.com/dictionary/apocrypha/.

80. **Cooke, Patrick.** The Lost Books of the Bible: The Real Apocrypha. An Introduction, Part 3. *The Lost Books.* [Online] http://www.thelostbooks.com/bookapocintro3.htm.

81. Ecclesiasticus Chapter 24. *The Official King James Bible Online.* [Online] http://www.kingjamesbibleonline.org/Ecclesiasticus-Chapter-24/.

82. *Saint Joseph Edition of the New American Bible.* New York : Catholic Book Publishing Co., 1977.

83. **Dashú, Max.** Khokhmah and Sophia. *Suppressed Histories Archives.* [Online] 2000. http://www.suppressedhistories.net/articles/sophia.html.

84. Demiurge. *Wikipedia: The Free Encyclopedia.* [Online] January 31, 2014. http://en.wikipedia.org/wiki/Demiurge.

85. Pleroma. *Wikipedia: The Free Encyclopedia.* [Online] June 22, 2013. http://en.wikipedia.org/wiki/Pleroma.

86. **Bet Emet Ministries.** Christianity's Lost Goddess...the Sophia. [Online] [Cited: November 18, 2006.] http://web.archive.org/web/20061118091128/http://firstnewtestament.netfirms.com/christianity_lost_goddess_sophia.htm.

87. **Jayaram, V.** Hindu God Lord Shiva (Siva) - the Destroyer. [Online] 2014. http://www.hinduwebsite.com/hinduism/siva.asp.

88. **Merkur, Daniel.** *Gnosis: an esoteric tradition of mystical visions and unions.* Albany, NY : State University of New York Press, 1993.

89. Sufism. *Wikipedia: The Free Encyclopedia.* [Online] 2012. http://en.wikipedia.org/wiki/Sufism.

90. Antiquities of the Jews. *Wikipedia: The Free Encyclopedia.* [Online] February 18 2014. http://en.wikipedia.org/wiki/Antiquities_of_the_Jews.

91. Alexander the Great. *JewishEncyclopedia.com.* [Online] 2011. http://www.jewishencyclopedia.com/view.jsp?artid=1120&letter=A#2909.

92. **Haughwout, Mark S.** Dating the Book of Daniel. [Online] October 31, 2007. http://www.markhaughwout.com/Bible/Dating_Daniel.html.

93. Babylonian Captivity. *Wkipedia: The Free Encyclopedia.* [Online] February 18, 2014. http://en.wikipedia.org/wiki/Babylonian_captivity.

94. Chapter 6: Essene Origins -- Palestine or Babylonia. *The History of the Ancient Near East: Electronic Compendium.* [Online] http://ancientneareast.tripod.com/DeadSeaScrollsShanks.html.

95. Hasmoneans. *Wikipedia: The Free Dictionary.* [Online] January 19, 2014. http://en.wikipedia.org/wiki/Hasmoneans.

96. **Wise, Michael O.** *The First Messiah: Investigating the Savior Before Jesus.* New York : HarperCollins, 1999.

97. Dead Sea Scrolls - A Compelling Find. *All About Archaeology.* [Online] 2014. http://www.allaboutarchaeology.org/dead-sea-scrolls.htm.

98. **Magness, Jodi.** *The Archaeology of Qumran and the Dead Sea Scrolls.* Grand Rapids, MI : William B. Eerdmans Publishing Co., 2003.

99. **Tabor, James D., Ph.D.** The Jewish Roman World of Jesus. *UNC Charlotte College of Liberal Arts & Sciences: Profiles, Projects, Research, Blogs...* [Online] 2013. http://clas-pages.uncc.edu/james-tabor/the-jewish-world-of-jesus-an-overview/.

100. Dead Sea Scrolls - 25 Fascinating Facts. *CenturyOne Bookstore.* [Online] 2011. http://www.centuryone.com/25dssfacts.html.

101. **Johnson, Cleve A.** The Qumran Community. [Online] [Cited: January 13, 2011.] http://web.archive.org/web/20110113112138/http://www.lighttrek.com/Qumran.htm.

102. Covenant of Damascus: The 'Zadokite' Document. *The Nazarenes of Mount Carmel: An Esoteric Spiritual Order.* [Online] 2006. http://www.essene.com/History&Essenes/cd.htm.

103. The Nazarenes of Mount Carmel: An Esoteric Spiritual Order. [Online] 2013. http://www.essene.com.

104. The Way of Jesus the Nazarean. *The Nazarenes of Mount Carmel: An Esoteric Spiritual Order.* [Online] 2006. http://www.essene.com/Church/nazirene.html.

105. **Kilmon, Jack.** The Essenes and the Nazarenes. *The Scriptorium.* [Online] http://www.historian.net/dssx.htm.

106. **Habermann, A. M., ed.** *The Scrolls from the Judean Desert.* Jerusalem : Machbaroth Lesifruth Publishing House, 1959.

107. **Kirby, Peter.** 1 Enoch. *Early Jewish Writings.* [Online] 2013.

108. **Akers, Keith.** Strange New Gospels. *Compassionate Spirit.* [Online] commenting upon *Strange Tales about Jesus* by Per Beskow. Fortress Press, 1993. http://www.compassionatespirit.com/strange_new_gospels.htm.

109. **Ousley, Rev. Gideon, trans.** The Gospel of the Holy Twelve (The Gospel of the Nazarenes). [Online] http://web.archive.org/web/20120105191855/http://www.mossypooh.com/goh12.pdf.

110. **Funk, Robert W., Roy W. Hoover, and The Jesus Seminar.** *The Five Gospels: What Did Jesus Really Say?* New York : Polebridge Press, 1993.

111. **Holding, James Patrick.** On Gideon Ouseley and "The Gospel of the Holy Twelve". *Tekton: Education and Apologetics Ministry.* [Online] http://www.tektonics.org/lp/ouseley01.html.

112. Dionysius Exiguus. *Wikipedia: The Free Encyclopedia.* [Online] January 14, 2014. http://en.wikipedia.org/wiki/Dionysius_Exiguus.

113. Was Jesus born on December 25th or early September? *Truth or Tradition?* [Online] http://www.truthortradition.com/modules.php?name=News&file=article&sid=467.

114. **S, Acharya and D.M. Murdock.** Mithra: The Pagan Christ. *Acharya S's Truth Be Known.* [Online] 2013. http://www.truthbeknown.com/mithra.htm.

115. **Murdock, D.M. and Acharya S.** Was Krishna Born on December 25th? [Online] http://www.zenzoneforum.com/threads/18272-Was-Krishna-Born-on-December-25th.

116. **Philostratus, Flavius.** *The Life of Apollonius of Tyana.* Translated by F.C. Conybeare. Cambridge, Massachusetts : Harvard University Press, 1912.

117. **Editors of Encyclopædia Britannica.** Cappadocia. *Encyclopædia Britannica.* [Online] 2014. http://www.britannica.com/EBchecked/topic/94094/Cappadocia.

118. **Allen, Don.** Pythagoras and the Pythagoreans. *Texas A&M University Mathematics.* [Online] February 6, 1997. http://www.math.tamu.edu/~dallen/history/pythag/pythag.html.

119. The Book of Enoch & the Evolution of Essene Theology...170 B.C.E. [Online] Bet Emet Ministries [Cited: February 20, 2009.] http://web.archive.org/web/20090220051954/http://essenecx.netfirms. com/noo9_enoch1.htm.

120. **Deane, Ashayana.** *Voyagers: The Secrets of Amenti, Volume II of the Emerald Covenant CDT Plate Translations. 2nd Edition.* Columbus, NC : Wild Flower Press, 2002.

121. In Praise of the New Knighthood. *TemplarHistory.com.* [Online] March 31, 2010. http://blog. templarhistory.com/2010/03/in-praise-of-the-new-knighthood/.

122. Erikson's Psychosocial Stages Summary Chart. *Psychology.* [Online] About.com, 2014. http://psychology. about.com/library/bl_psychosocial_summary.htm.

123. **MCEO Freedom Teachings®.** *"The Dance for Love." The Second 36 Elements of Spiritual Mastery: The Inner Keys to the Lower, Middle & Higher God-Worlds.* [DVDs and Manual] Greece and Cyprus : Azurite Press Inc., May 2002.

124. What is Freemasonry? and Freemasonry Research Links. [Online] http://www.whatisfreemasonry.com.

125. **MCEO Freedom Teachings®.** *The United Intruder Resistance: "Michael-Mary" Turnstile Matrix.* [DVDs] Calgary, Canada : Azurite Press Inc., February 2002.

126. **Starbird, Margaret.** *The Woman with the Alabaster Jar: Mary Magdalen and the Holy Grail.* Rochester, VT : Bear & Company, 1993.

127. **Frieze, Candace.** Earth Changes & Ascension Plan for Planet Earth: 2005–2013. *The New Earth.* [Online] November 18, 2005. Channeling titled "The Many Hats of Christ Michael, Sovereign of hte Local Universe of Nebadon". http://www.thenewearth.org/AtonEarthChangesPlan.html.

128. **Manocha, Dr. Ramesh and Anna Potts.** Jesus Lived in India. *Knowledge of Reality.* [Online] Knowledge of Reality Magazine, 2006. http://www.sol.com.au/kor/7_01.htm.

129. **Durie, Dr. Mark.** 'Isa, the Muslim Jesus. *Answering Islam.* [Online] 2013. http://www.answering-islam. org/authors/durie/islamic_jesus.html.

130. The Urantia Book. *Wikipedia: The Free Encyclopedia.* [Online] January 27, 2014. http://en.wikipedia. org/wiki/The_Urantia_Book.

131. **Howell, Elizabeth.** What Is the Big Bang Theory? *Space.com.* [Online] March 25, 2014. http://www. space.com/25126-big-bang-theory.html.

132. **Redd, Nola Taylor.** What is Dark Energy? *Space.com.* [Online] May 1, 2013. http://www.space. com/20929-dark-energy.html.

133. **Musser, George.** According to the big bang theory, all the matter in the universe erupted from a singularity. Why didn't all this matter--cheek by jowl as it was--immediately collapse into a black hole? *Scientific American™.* [Online] September 22, 2003. http://www.scientificamerican.com/article/ according-to-the-big-bang/.

134. **National Aeronautics and Space Administration.** What is the Ultimate Fate of the Universe? *National Aeronautics and Space Administration.* [Online] December 21, 2012. http://map.gsfc.nasa.gov/universe/ uni_fate.html.

135. How is a Black Hole Created? *HubbleSite.* [Online] http://hubblesite.org/reference_desk/faq/answer. php.id=56&cat=exotic.

136. **Lyzenga, Gregory A.** How do scientists measure or calculate the weight of a planet? *Scientific American™.* [Online] December 12, 2005. Originally published on March 16, 1998. http://www. scientificamerican.com/article.cfm?id=how-do-scientists-measure.

137. Black Holes and Quasars. *Curious About Astronomy? Ask an Astronomer.* [Online] December 15, 2011. http://curious.astro.cornell.edu/blackholes.php.

138. **NASA.** Black Holes. [Online] www.nasa.gov. http://www.spitzinc.com/pdfs/educ_guide_blackholes_ nasa.pdf.

139. Quasar. *Wikipedia: The Free Encyclopedia.* [Online] February 28, 2014. http://en.wikipedia.org/wiki/ Quasar.

140. The Universe. *Sloan Digital Sky Survey / SkyServer.* [Online] http://cas.sdss.org/dr3/en/proj/basic/ universe/.

141. Krystal Spiral (Krystal Sequence). *Keylontic Dictionary.* [Online] From *Kathara Team - Spirals of Creation Class Module.* http://www.keylonticdictionary.org/online/member/index.php?page=kathara-grid.

142. **MCEO Freedom Teachings®.** *Engaging the Load-Out; The Last Ascension Cycle and the Gate of AshaLA.* [DVDs] Phoenix, AZ : Azurite Press Inc., January 2008.

143. **MCEO Freedom Teachings®.** *The Kathara™ Bio-Spiritual Healing System; Level-1 Certificate Program.* [Manual] Allentown, PA : Azurite Press Inc., 2000.

144. **Deane, Ashayana.** *Voyagers: The Sleeping Abductees, Volume I of the Emerald Covenant CDT-Plate Translations. 2nd Edition.* Columbus, NC : Wild Flower Press, 2002.

145. **MCEO Freedom Teachings®.** *Kathara Levels 2-3 Foundation: "Awakening the Living Lotus" Healing Facilitation Through Crystal Body Alignment.* [Manual] Phoenix, AZ and Long Beach, CA : Azurite Press Inc., April 2004.

146. **Bowman, Carol.** *Children's Past Lives: How Past Life Memories Affect Your Child.* New York : Bantam Books, 1997.

147. Electromagnetic Spectrum. *NASA Goddard Space Flight Center.* [Online] March 2013. http://imagine. gsfc.nasa.gov/docs/science/know_l1/emspectrum.html.

148. *Einstein, Cartan and Evans--Start of a New Age in Physics?* **Eckardt, Horst and Laurence G. Felker.** December 9, 2005, NET-Journal. http://www.aias.us/documents/eceArticle/ECE-Article_EN.pdf

149. **Nave, Rod, Ph.D.** Quarks. *HyperPhysics.* [Online] http://hyperphysics.phy-astr.gsu.edu/hbase/particles/quark.html.

150. proton-electron mass ratio. *The NIST Reference of Constants, Units, and Uncertainty.* [Online] November 2012. http://physics.nist.gov/cgi-bin/cuu/Value?mpsme.

151. **Knierim, Thomas.** Relativity. *thebigview.com.* [Online] [Cited: August 3, 2013.] http://web.archive.org/web/20130803073224/http://www.thebigview.com/spacetime/relativity.html.

152. **Haramein, Nassim.** "What is the Origin of Spin?". *The Resonance Project.* [Online] 2004. http://web.archive.org/web/20130125001751/http://theresonanceproject.org/pdf/origin_of_spin.pdf.

153. String theory. *Wikipedia: The Free Dictionary.* [Online] [Cited: November 10, 2012.] http://web.archive.org/web/20121110194257/http://en.wikipedia.org/wiki/String_theory.

154. **Schwarz, Patricia, PhD.** Looking for extra dimensions. *The Official String Theory Web Site.* [Online] http://www.superstringtheory.com/experm/exper51.html.

155. Oxford Dictionaries. *Definition of dimension in English.* [Online] Oxford University Press, 2013. http://oxforddictionaries.com/definition/english/dimension.

156. M-theory, the theory formerly known as Strings. *Cambridge Relativity.* [Online] University of Cambridge, 1996. http://www.damtp.cam.ac.uk/research/gr/public/qg_ss.html.

157. Planck Length. *Cosmos - The SAO Encyclopedia of Astronomy.* [Online] Swinburne University of Technology. http://astronomy.swin.edu.au/cms/astro/cosmos/p/Planck+Length.

158. **Brown, Eryn.** CERN: We've found 'a Higgs boson'; but is it predicted version? *Los Angeles Times.* [Online] Los Angeles Times, March 14, 2013. http://articles.latimes.com/2013/mar/14/science/la-sci-sn-higgs-boson-20130314.

159. *Discovering the Higgs: Inevitability, Rigidity, Fragility, Beauty.* Spring, Princeton : Institute for Advanced Study, Spring 2013.

160. **Holthausen, Martin, Kher Sham Lim, and Manfred Lindner .** *Planck Scale Boundary Conditions and the Higgs Mass.* Heidelberg : Max Planck Insitute for Nuclear Physics, Saupfercheckweg, March 5, 2012. http://arxiv.org/pdf/1112.2415.pdf

161. **Peat, F. David.** *Superstrings and the Search for the Theory of Everything.* Chicago : Contemporary Books, 1998.

162. **Alexjander, Susan, MA.** Microcosmic Music - A New Level of Intensity. *Our Sound Universe--the Music of Susan Alexjander.* [Online] 2007. http://www.oursounduniverse.com/articles/microcosmic.html.

163. **Simonetti, Dr. John.** Virginia Tech Department of Physics. *Frequently Asked Questions About Quasars.* [Online] http://www.phys.vt.edu/~jhs/faq/quasars.html#q11.

164. **Johnston, Hamish.** Antihydrogen trapped at CERN. *physicsworld.com.* [Online] November 17, 2010. http://physicsworld.com/cws/article/news/2010/nov/17/antihydrogen-trapped-at-cern.

165. **Chung, Emily.** Antimatter atom 'measured' for first time. *CBCnews.* [Online] CBC News, March 7, 2012. http://www.cbc.ca/news/technology/story/2012/03/07/science-antimatter-alpha-hayden.html.

166. **Soffer, Abner.** What's the matter with antimatter? *Particle Physics in Plain English!* [Online] http://conferences.fnal.gov/lp2003/forthepublic/matter/index.html.

167. **Staff, SPACE.com.** Why We Exist: Matter Wins Battle Over Antimatter. *SPACE.com.* [Online] SPACE.com, May 18, 2010. http://www.space.com/8441-exist-matter-wins-battle-antimatter.html.

168. Does antimatter exist? *STFC Large Hadron Collider.* [Online] Science and Technology Facilities Council, 2013. http://www.lhc.ac.uk/The+Particle+Detectives/Take+5/13685.aspx.

169. Matter-Antimatter Annihilation Visualization. *echochamber xkcd Forums for the webcomic.* [Online] June 6, 2010. Science category. Forum post by PM 2Ring. http://forums.xkcd.com/viewtopic.php?f=18&t=61064.

170. What are electromagnetic fields? *World Health Organization.* [Online] World Health Organization, 2013. http://www.who.int/peh-emf/about/WhatisEMF/en/.

171. Scalar Potentials and Scalar Waves. *Research Media & Cybernetics.* [Online] RMCybernetics. http://www.rmcybernetics.com/science/physics/electromagetism2_scalar_waves.htm.

172. Tachyonic field. *Wikipedia, the free encyclopedia.* [Online] January 30, 2014. http://en.wikipedia.org/wiki/Tachyonic_field.

173. **MCEO Freedom Teachings®.** *"Festival of Light Celebration: The Starfire Cycle and the Re-birth of the Original Amenti Rescue Mission".* [DVDs] London : Azurite Press Inc., February 2006.

174. **MCEO Freedom Teachings®.** *The Amenti Series-1 Classes.* [DVDs] New Jersey : Azurite Press Inc., 1998.

175. **MCEO Freedom Teachings**®. *The Tangible Structure of the Soul: Accelerated Bio-Spiritual Evolution Program.* [Manual] Azurite Press Inc., 1999.

176. An Atomic Description of Silicon - The Silicon Molecule. *About.com Inventors.* [Online] 2014. http://inventors.about.com/library/inventors/blsolar4.htm.

177. Tara, Goddess of Peace and Protection. *Goddess Gift.* [Online] The Goddess Path, 2014. http://www.goddessgift.com/goddess-myths/goddess_tara_white.htm.

178. **Atsma, Aaron J.** Gaia. *Theoi Greek Mythology.* [Online] 2011. http://www.theoi.com/Protogenos/Gaia.html.

179. **MCEO Freedom Teachings**®. *"Sliders-4" The Call of Aurora - Probability Alignments & the Adjugate Bond.* [DVDs and Manual] Phoenix, AZ : Azurite Press Inc., May 2009.

180. **MCEO Freedom Teachings**®. *Sacred Sexuality & the Art of Divine Relationship: Sacred Sex, Divine Love & Eternal Co-Creation, Part 1.* [DVDs] Denver, CO : Azurite Press Inc., July 2006.

181. **MCEO Freedom Teachings**®. *The Forbidden Testaments of Revelation-1: The Cosmic Clock, Secrets of Lohas And the Arc of the Covenant.* [DVDs and Manual] Dublin : Azurite Press Inc., February 2003.

182. **MCEO Freedom Teachings**®. Introductory--Topic Summary-2. *Azurite Press Of The Melchizedek Cloister Emerald Order.* [Online] Azurite Press Inc., 2009. [Cited: July 18, 2012.] http://web.archive.org/web/20120718050409/http://www.azuritepress.com/New%20Comers/intro_topic_summary_2.php.

183. **Melchizedek, Drunvalo.** Holy Mer:.Ka:.Ba:. Meditation. *The Blue Brethren.* [Online] July 11, 1999. http://www.bibliotecapleyades.net/bb/drunvalo.htm.

184. **MCEO Freedom Teachings**®. *Kathara Levels 2 & 3 Foundations "Awakening the Living Lotus": Healing Facilitation through Crystal Body Alignment.* [Manual] Phoenix, AZ : Azurite Press Inc., April 2004.

185. **MCEO Freedom Teachings**®. *Sliders-8: Preparing the Body for Slide—Advanced Level. Awake, Aware, and ALIVE in the Lands of Aah: The "Sea of Ah'yah," Eternal Stream of Ah-yah-YA', the Covenant of Ah-Yah-RhU', and Eternal Dream-Fields of the ONE.* [DVDs and Manual] Phoenix, AZ : Azurite Press Inc., August 2010.

186. **The Tan-Tri-Ahura Teachings--The Path of Bio-Spiritual Artistry**™. *Treasures of the Tan-Tri-Ahura: Gate-Walkers, Wave-Runners and Star-Riders of the Krystal River Host.* [DVDs and Manual] Sarasota, FL : ARhayas Productions AMCC-MCEO LLC, August 2012.

187. A teacher's life lessons using a jar and some golf balls. *Sunny Skyz.* [Online] October 23, 2012. http://www.sunnyskyz.com/feel-good-story/111/A-teacher-s-life-lessons-using-a-jar-and-some-golf-balls.

188. **Icke, David.** Back Cover Book Description. *Remember Who You Are: Remember 'where' you are and where you 'come' from, Remember ...* Ryde, Isle of Wight : David Icke Books, 2012.

189. **Bohm, David.** *Wholeness and the Implicate Order.* New York : Routledge Classics, 1980.

190. The Universe as a Hologram. *Earth Portals "Insights".* [Online] 1997. http://www.earthportals.com/hologram.html.

191. **MCEO Freedom Teachings**®. *The Cosmic Clock Reset: Entering the Reucha-TA Great Healing Cycle.* [DVDs] Phoenix, AZ : Azurite Press Inc., 2003.

192. **Mullen, Leslie.** Plasma, Plasma, Everywhere: A New Model of the Plasmasphere Surrounding our World. *NASA Science.* [Online] National Aeronautics and Space Administration, September 7, 1999. http://science1.nasa.gov/science-news/science-at-nasa/1999/ast07sep99_1/.

193. **Jessa, Tega.** What Are Stars Made Out Of. *Universe Today.* [Online] September 19, 2010. [Cited April 12, 2012.] http://web.archive.org/web/20120412102724/http://www.universetoday.com/74032/what-are-stars-made-out-of/.

194. **LaRocco, Chris and Blair Rothstein.** The Big Bang: It sure was BIG!! *University of Michigan.* [Online] http://www.umich.edu/~gs265/bigbang.htm.

195. Vacuum state. *Wikipedia, the free encyclopedia.* [Online] December 4, 2013. http://en.wikipedia.org/wiki/Vacuum_state.

196. **MCEO Freedom Teachings**®. *The 12-Tribes Transcripts, Class 3.* [Manual] Azurite Press Inc., March 2007.

197. **MCEO Freedom Teachings**®. *The 12-Tribes Transcripts, Class 2.* [Manual] Azurite Press Inc., February 2007.

198. **MCEO Freedom Teachings**®. *Sliders-12: Externalization of the Kryst; Secrets of the Tan'Tri-A'jha. Part-1.* [DVDs] Sarasota : Azurite Press Inc., January 2012.

199. **MCEO Freedom Teachings**®. *The 12-Tribes Transcripts, Class 1.* [Manual] Azurite Press Inc., January 2007.

200. **MCEO Freedom Teachings**®. *The 12-Tribes Transcripts, Class 10.* [Manual] Phoenix, AZ : Azurite Press Inc., January 2008.

201. **MCEO Freedom Teachings**®. *The 12-Tribes Transcripts, Class 8.* [Manual] Phoenix, AZ : Azurite Press Inc., October 2007.

202. **MCEO Freedom Teachings**®. *MCEO Grid-Keepers Communion Conclave-1: Elemental Commands, Cellular Secrets and the Aurora Potential; Glass Towers, Crystal Canyons And the Aurora Force.* [DVDs] Redding and Mount Shasta, CA : Azurite Press Inc., May 2006.

203. Thetans. *Keylontic Dictionary.* [Online] http://www.keylonticdictionary.org/online/member/index.php?page=thetans.

204. **MCEO Freedom Teachings**®. *The Kethradon Awakening: Starburst Pillar-13 and the Gifts of Rama.* [DVDs and Manual] India : Azurite Press Inc., January 2005.

205. **MCEO Freedom Teachings**®. *The Science and Sprituality of Creation.* [DVDs and Manual] Seattle, WA : Azurite Press Inc., September 2003.

206. **Melchizedek, Drunvalo.** *The Ancient Secret of the Flower of Life, Volume 1.* Light Technology Publishing, 2012.

207. **MCEO Freedom Teachings**®. *Dance For Freedom, Part 2: The 12:12:12:12-11:11:11:11.* [DVDs] Tewkesbury, UK : Azurite Press Inc., November 2002.

208. **MCEO Freedom Teachings**®. *The 12-Tribes Transcripts, Class 4.* [Manual] Azurite Press Inc., April 2007.

209. **MCEO Freedom Teachings**®. Frequently Asked Questions. *Azurite Press of the Melchizedek Cloister Emerald Order.* [Online] Azurite Press Inc., 2013. http://www.azuritepress.com/articles/faq.php#18.

210. **MCEO Freedom Teachings**®. *The 12-Tribes Transcripts, Class 5.* [Manual] Phoenix, AZ : Azurite Press Inc., June 2007.

211. **Sky, Robert Morning.** The Terra Papers. [Online] http://jordanmaxwell.com/images/documents/the-2520terra-2520papers-2520[irm08].pdf.

212. **Sitchin, Zecharia.** *The Lost Book of Enki: Memoirs and Prophecies of an Extraterrestrial God.* Rochester, VT : Bear & Company, 2002.

213. **Bowling, Collin Robert.** *A New Order of the Ages: A Metaphysical Blueprint of Reality and an Expose on Powerful Reptilian/Aryan Bloodlines, Volume One.* Bloomington : iUniverse, 2011.

214. **Temple, Robert.** *The Sirius Mystery: New Scientific Evidence of Alien Contact 5,000 Years Ago.* Rochester : Destiny Books, 1998.

215. Mesopotamian Gods. *Biblioteca Pleyades.* [Online] http://www.bibliotecapleyades.net/sitchin/mesopotamian_gods.htm.

216. **Kramer, Samuel Noah.** *The Sumerians: Their History, Culture, and Character.* Chicago : The University of Chicago Press, 1963.

217. **Lessin, Sasha, Ph.D.** Essay 25: Marduk's Son Satu Kills Brother, Asar; Asar's Son, Horon Defeats Satu, Unites Egypt. *Enki Speaks.* [Online] http://www.enkispeaks.com/Essays/25SatuKillsAsarButAstaBearsHoron.htm.

218. **MCEO Freedom Teachings**®. *The Real Christmas Story.* [Handbook] Azurite Press Inc., December 2001.

219. **Cremo, Michael A. and Thompson, Richard L.** *The Hidden History of the Human Race: The Condensed Edition of Forbidden Archeology.* Los Angeles : Bhaktivedanta Book Publishing, Inc., 1999.

220. **Bavley, Alan.** Ape-woman Lucy walked like a modern human, new research shows. *timesfreepress.com.* [Online] February 11, 2011. Article in the Kansas City Star. http://www.timesfreepress.com/news/2011/feb/11/ape-woman-lucy-walked-modern-human-new-research-sh.

221. **Rice University.** 'Mitochondrial Eve': Mother of All Humans Lived 200,000 Years Ago. *ScienceDaily°.* [Online] ScienceDaily, LLC, August 17, 2010. http://www.sciencedaily.com/releases/2010/08/100817122405.htm.

222. 10,500 BC - Who Lived on Earth? *Biblioteca Pleyades.* [Online] March 2006. http://www.bibliotecapleyades.net/sumer_anunnaki/reptiles/reptiles28.htm.

223. **MCEO Freedom Teachings**®. *The Emerald Covenant Masters Templar Stewardship Initiative: Secrets of the Amenti Star Gates and the Grail Quest Signet Roundtables.* [Manual] Azurite Press Inc., July 2001.

224. **Violatti, Cristian.** Siddhartha Gautama. *Ancient Encyclopedia History.* [Online] Ancient History Encyclopedia Limited, December 9, 2013. http://www.ancient.eu/Siddhartha_Gautama/.

225. **Lessin, Sasha, Ph.D.** Essay 24: Ningishzidda, Memorialized As Sphinx, Creates Pyramids To Guide Rockets To Sinai Peninsula Spaceport. *Enki Speaks.* [Online] Based on the works of Zecharia Sitchin. http://www.enkispeaks.com/Essays/24ThothSphinxSinaiSpaceport.htm.

226. **Bauval, Robert and Adrian Gilbert.** *The Orion Mystery: Unlocking the Secrets of the Pyramids.* New York : Three Rivers Press, 1994.

227. **Huisman, Robert.** What's the difference between a star and a planet? *Kapteyn Astronomical Institute.* [Online] University of Groningen. http://www.astro.rug.nl/~onderwys/sterIIproject97/huisman.

228. **Archæology, Society of Biblical.** *Proceedings of the Society of Biblical Archaeology. Volume 23, Thirty-First Session, First Meeting.* London : Offices of the Society, January 9, 1901.

229. Three Steps to Mastering the Secret Laws of Attraction. [Online] Quoted in 2013, but website is removed in 2014. I am keeping the quotes to show the hard-lined teachings from a credible website before they were watered down as a sales pitch. http://masteringthe11forgottenlaws.com/the-secret-laws-of-attraction.html.

230. **Rachael.** Archangel Metatron. *Rise Like a Phoenix.* [Online] March 2007. [Cited: April 15, 2009.] http://web.archive.org/web/20090415163112/http://www.riselikeaphoenix.com/archangelmetatron. htm.

231. **Tyberonn, James.** The Alchemy of 2010 Archangel Metatron Channel with Saint Germain via James Tyberonn. *Lightworkers.* [Online] December 31, 2009. http://lightworkers.org/channeling/96128/ alchemy-2010-archangel-metatron-channel-saint-germain-james-tyberonn.

232. **The Chohans.** *The Ascended Masters.* [Online] Keepers of the Flame, 2009. http://www. ascendedmastersoflight.com/chohans.php.

233. **Cyr, James Oliver, M.D.** Who are the Spiritual Hierarchy. *Kuthumi's Hands.* [Online] Kuthumi Hands, 2013. http://www.kuthumi-hands.com/hierarchy/hierarchy.htm.

234. **Anthony, Jess.** Christ Michael, Esu and Lady Nada say prepare. *2012 Unlimited.* [Online] October 14, 2007. http://www.2012.com.au/CM_prepare.html.

235. **Nash, John.** Sanat Kumara. [Online] March 2002. Published in *The Beacon* magazine established by Alice and Foster Bailey's Lucis Trust. http://www.uriel.com/knowledge/articles-presentations/Nash%20 articles/Beacon030403--Sanat%20Kumara.pdf.

236. **Nidle, Sheldon.** Introduction to the Galactic Federation of Light. *Planetary Activation Organization.* [Online] 2014. http://www.paoweb.com/gfmember.htm.

237. **Koen.** Galactic Federation of Light "First Contact" – Preliminary Draft. *we must know.* [Online] March 13, 2010. [Cited: May 18, 2012.] http://web.archive.org/web/20120518050558/http://wemustknow. net/2010/03/galactic-federation-of-light-"first-contact"---preliminary-draft/.

238. **Goodchild, Blossom.** *Blossom Goodchild updates 16th October.* [www.youtube.com video] 2008.

239. **MCEO Freedom Teachings®.** *Dance for Life, Love, Freedom: Shadow Body Healing & Flame Body Activation.* [Manual] Azurite Press Inc., 2002.

240. Commander Hatonn. [Online] http://www.greatdreams.com/ufos/hatonn.htm.

241. Ashtar Fleet Amongst Us. [Online] [Cited: April 29, 2012.] Source: 1996 Nuwaubian Calendar, "Extraterrestrial Amongst Us". http://web.archive.org/web/20120429104753/http://factology.com/ front8_12_00.htm.

242. *Anunnaki Female Extraterrestrial Alien.* [www.youtube.com video] June 6, 2010.

243. **MCEO Freedom Teachings®.** *The Egypt Lectures: Awakening the Flame of Orion.* [DVDs] Giza : Azurite Press Inc., March 17-26, March 2000.

244. **O'Riley, Carolyn Ann.** A Message from Archangel Michael Channeled Through and Written by Carolyn Ann O'Riley. [Online] Channeling titled "The Ferris Wheel." O'Riley's website: www. carolynannoriley.com. http://indianinthemachine.wordpress.com/2011/01/22/a-message-from-archangel-michael-channeled-through-and-written-by-carolyn-ann-o'riley/.

245. **Steiner, Rudolf.** *Death as Metamorphosis of Life: Seven Lectures Held in Various Cities; November 29, 1917-October 16, 1918.* Great Barrington, MA : SteinerBooks, 2008.

246. Holographic Art, "Antahkarana". *Divine Blueprint, Amoraea.* [Online] 2014. http://divine-blueprint. com/visionary-art/visionary-holography/.

247. "Universal Torus Lightbody". *Divine Blueprint, Amoraea.* [Online] 2014. http://divine-blueprint. com/325-2/#info.

248. Who is Metatron? *Metatronic Life.* [Online] 2010. Warning: please do not look at the distorted kathara grid for long.. http://www.metatronic-life.com/who-is-metatron.

249. **Weinsterin-Moser, Edie.** Interview with Dr. Eric Pearl. *The Avalon Reconnection.* [Online] June 2007. From *Wisdom Magazine*'s U.S. National Edition. http://www.theavalonreconnection.com/ interviewwithericpearl.html.

250. The Galactic Federation of Light & Ashtar is an Alien Hoax -- Everyone Please Read. *Lightworkers.* [Online] September 2, 2010. Forum post by Rich228. http://lightworkers.org/forum/113894/galactic-federation-light-ashtar-alien-hoax-everyone-please-read.

251. Pentagram. *Wikipedia, the free encyclopedia.* [Online] [Cited: November 14, 2012.] http://web.archive. org/web/20121114110427/http://en.wikipedia.org/wiki/Pentagram.

252. **MCEO Freedom Teachings®.** *Sliders-2. Reclaiming the Vessel—Preparing the Body for Slide.* [DVDs and Manual] Virginia Beach, VA : Azurite Press Inc., September 2008.

253. **August, Comrade and Tani Jantsang.** The Pythagorean Pentacle - it is Two Points Up. *Guardians of Darkness.* [Online] May 2014. http://www.guardiansofdarkness.com/GoD/god-pythagorean-pentacle. html.

254. Pan (god). *Wikipedia, the free encyclopedia.* [Online] February 28, 2014. http://en.wikipedia.org/wiki/ Pan_(god).

255. Baphomet. *Wikipedia, the free encyclopedia.* [Online] February 28, 2014. http://en.wikipedia.org/wiki/ Baphomet.

539

256. House of Merovingian. *Truth Control.* [Online] [Cited: May 11, 2012.] From *Atlantis, Alien Visitation and Genetic Manipulation* by Michael Tsarion. http://web.archive.org/web/20120511024853/http://www.truthcontrol.com/node/house-merovingian.

257. **Herschel, Wayne and Birgitt Lederer.** *The Hidden Records.* Thehiddenrecords.com, 2003.

258. **Bart, Anneke.** Hatshepsut (Maatkare). *Ancient Egypt.* [Online] Saint Louis University, April 2007. http://euler.slu.edu/~bart/egyptianhtml/kings%20and%20Queens/Hatshepsut.html.

259. **Parsons, John J.** The Kabbalah of Creation. *Hebrew for Christians.* [Online] http://www.hebrew4christians.com/Articles/kabbalah/Creation/creation.html.

260. Stellarium. [Online] Free open source planetarium software. http://www.stellarium.org/.

261. **MCEO Freedom Teachings®.** *The Lemurian & Atlantean Legacies - Secrets of the Arthurian Round Tables.* [DVDs] New York City : Azurite Press Inc., April 2001.

262. **Ra (channeled).** *The Law of One.* Louisville, KY : L/L Research, 1982, 1984, 1998. Five Books. Can also see http://www.lawofone.info/.

263. **Penre, Wes.** Dialogue with "Hidden Hand", Self-Proclaimed Illuminati Insider. *Illuminati News.* [Online] December 27, 2008. http://www.illuminati-news.com/00363.html.

264. *Miracle by Amma.* [www.youtube.com video]

265. **Wilcock, David.** *Wanderer Awakening: The Life Story of David Wilcock.* [ebook]

266. **Wilcock, David.** *2012 Event Horizon: Prophecies and Science of a Golden Age.* [Series of four videos on www.youtube.com.] May 2010.

267. **Salla, Michael, Ph.D.** The Short and Tall Greys. *Biblioteca Pleyades.* [Online] http://www.bibliotecapleyades.net/vida_alien/alien_zetareticuli02.htm.

268. **Stibal, Vianna.** About ThetaHealing°. *ThetaHealing°.* [Online] 2014. http://www.thetahealing.com/about-thetahealing.html.

269. Welcome to Orion Therapy at Natural Earth. *Natural Earth.* [Online] [Cited: August 1, 2013.] http://web.archive.org/web/20130801130421/http://natural-earth.com/orion_therapy.html.

270. **McClare, Scott.** Scientology: An Overview. *The Cult of Scientology.* [Online] April 3, 1998. http://web.ncf.ca/cj871/overview.html.

271. **MCEO Freedom Teachings®.** *The 12-Tribes Transcripts, Class 12.* [Manual] Azurite Press Inc., 2010.

272. Emanuel Swedenborg. *Wikipedia, the free encyclopedia.* [Online] November 25, 2013. http://en.wikipedia.org/wiki/Emanuel_Swedenborg.

273. **Kirkpatrick III, Bro. James Robert.** The Three Pillars of Masonry. *Grand Lodge of Florida: Boynton Lodge No. 236 F.& A.M.* [Online] http://www.boyntonlodge236.com/TheThreePillars%20of%20Masonry.pdf.

274. **Proudfoot, Peter.** *The Secret Plan of Canberra.* Sydney : University of New South Wales Press, 1994.

275. Theosophical Society. *Wikipedia, the free encyclopedia.* [Online] October 13, 2013. http://en.wikipedia.org/wiki/Theosophical_Society.

276. **Leadbeater, C.W.** *The Masters And The Path. Second Edition.* Adyar, Madras, India : The Theosophical Publishing House, 1927.

277. **Sabeheddin, Mehmet.** Esoteric Australia. *The World's Most Unusual Magazine: New Dawn.* [Online] July 1, 2010. http://www.newdawnmagazine.com/articles/esoteric-australia.

278. **Mahony Griffin, Marion.** Section IV: The Individual Battle. *The Magic of America.* Chicago : Griffin & Nicholls.

279. **Mahony Griffin, Marion.** Section III: The Municipal Battle. *The Magic of America.* Chicago : Griffin & Nicholls.

280. Rebels and Gilt-spurred Roosters: Politics, Bureaucracy and the Democratic Ideal in the Griffins' Capital. *National Library of Australia.* [Online] http://www.nla.gov.au/seminar/a-cultivated-city-the-griffins-in-australia-s-capital-speakers/rebels-and-gilt-spurred-roosterspolitics-bureaucracy-and-the-democratic-ideal-in-the.

281. **Ireland, Lorea.** Return Focus Triangle & Marble Mountain Wilderness. *VortexMaps.com.* [Online] 2014. http://www.vortexmaps.com/irley.php.

282. **MCEO Freedom Teachings®.** *Engaging the God Languages.* [Manual] Phoenix, AZ : Azurite Press Inc., October 2005. Created by Melissa Higginbotham and PamE Bown.

283. Top Secret military "bases" in Canberra. *RiotAct "Canberra News, Views and Opinion".* [Online] January 18, 2008. Forum comment #37. http://the-riotact.com/top-secret-military-bases-in-canberra/6622/comment-page-2#comments.

284. **Koch, Harold, and Luise Hercus, eds.** *Aboriginal Placenames: Naming and Re-Naming the Australian Landscape.* ANU E Press and Aboriginal History Inc., 2009.

285. **Dowling, Peter.** *The Real Heritage of Canberra.* Australian Council of National Trusts, 2013.

286. 22 Numerotropic Group Bulletin Board. *Technosophy.* [Online] October 13, 2002. [Cited July 28, 2013.] Edited from http://www.andromedainsights.com by Alex Collier. http://web.archive.org/web/20130728145011/http://www.technosophy.com/22responses.htm

287. **Penre, Wes.** Thule Gesellschaft and the Vril Society. [Online] 2009. http://black.greyfalcon.us.

288. **Alek, William.** *Out of the Gravity Well.* [Digital presentation] Progressive Tech Center, June 18, 2009. Presentation at the Sedona Mutual UFO Network.

289. **Bernard, R.W., Ph.D.** The Hollow Earth Chapter 1: Admiral Byrd's Epoch-Making Discovery. *The Hollow Earth.* New York : Fieldcrest Publishing Co., Inc., 1964.

290. Admiral Byrd and Operation High-Jump. *hidden-truth.org.* [Online] 2014. http://www.hidden-truth. org/en/secrecy/admiral-byrd-and-operation-high-jump.html.

291. **MCEO Freedom Teachings®.** *Dance for Freedom, Part 1.* [DVDs] France : Azurite Press Inc., November 2002.

292. Vril: witches & UFO's. *fallenalien.com.* [Online] [Cited: April 4, 2013.] http://web.archive.org/ web/20130404060814/http://fallenalien.com/vril.htm.

293. **Davis, Jane, ed.** Nazi History Of Alien Contact. *UFO Casebook.* [Online] 2014. http://www. ufocasebook.com/nazihistory.html.

294. New World Order/Synarchy - The Secret History. *DavidIcke.com.* [Online] January 17, 2011. Forum post by solve_et_coagula. http://www.davidicke.com/forum/showthread.php?t=153479.

295. **Wright, Anne.** The history of the star: Aldebaran. *Constellations of Words.* [Online] 2008. http://www. constellationsofwords.com/stars/Aldebaran.html.

296. **Partridge, Jamie.** December 21 2012 Astrology. *Astrology King.* [Online] April 26, 2012. http:// astrologyking.com/december-21-2012/.

297. **Dalrymple, G. Brent.** How Old is the Earth: A Response to "Scientific Creationism". *Talk Origins.* [Online] 1984. http://www.talkorigins.org/faqs/dalrymple/scientific_age_earth.html .

298. Why is Pluto no longer considered a planet? *physics.org.* [Online] 2012. http://www.physics.org/article-questions.asp?id=49.

299. **Lesikar, Arnold V., Professor Emeritus.** Alcyone. *The Dome of the Sky™.* [Online] 2010. http:// domeofthesky.com/clicks/alcyone.html.

300. **Men, Hunbatz.** *The 8 Calendars of the Maya: The Pleiadian Cycle and the Key to Destiny.* Rochester : Bear & Company, 2009.

301. **Frieze, Candace and Sananda Immanuel.** Ascension and the Galaxy: Ascension of Earth (Part). *2012 Unlimited.* [Online] http://www.2012.com.au/Ascension_and_the_galaxy.html.

302. **Casado, Juan Carlos.** Sirius: The Brightest Star in the Night. *Astronomy Picture of the Day.* [Online] NASA and Michigan Tech. University, June 11, 2000. http://apod.nasa.gov/apod/ap000611.html.

303. **Homann, Uwe.** *Sirius & Precession of the Solstice: 6000 Years of Intercalation and Inundation.* Sirius Research Group, July 2005.

304. **Cruttenden, Walter.** Reponse to the Precession Dialogues. *Binary Research Institute.* [Online] July 16, 2009. http://binaryresearchinstitute.com/bri/research/papers/bautforum.shtml.

305. **MCEO Freedom Teachings®.** *The Lemurian & Atlantian Legacies - Secrets of the Arthurian Round Tables.* [DVDs] New York : Azurite Press Inc., Easter 2001.

306. Alpha-Omega Alliance. *Keylontic Dictionary.* [Online] http://www.keylonticdictionary.org/online/ member/index.php?page=alpha-omega-alliance.

307. **MCEO Freedom Teachings®.** Introductory--Topic Summary-1. *Azurite Press Of The Melchizedek Cloister Emerald Order.* [Online] Azurite Press Inc., 2009. [Cited: May 30, 2012.] http://web.archive. org/web/20120530104416/http://www.azuritepress.com/New%20Comers/intro_topic_summary_1. php.

308. **MCEO Freedom Teachings®.** *"Sliders-6" - The Arc of the Covenant, Sphere of Destiny & the Stairway to Heaven.* [DVDs and Manual] Dublin and Skellig Michael : Azurite Press Inc., October 2009.

309. *Phoenix April 2007 Workshop Diary: "The Krystar Awakening and Starfire Maps. Solar Gates, Prana Seed and the Aqualene Sun".* **Azur'yana, Georgi.** Phoenix, AZ : Endorsed by Azurite Press Inc., April 2007. Reported in official Keylontic Science forum at http://groups.yahoo.com/group/KeylonticScience.

310. Planetary Templar Complex. *Keylontic Dictionary.* [Online] http://www.keylonticdictionary.org/online/ member/index.php?page=planetary-templar.

311. **Minster, Christopher.** The First New World Voyage of Christopher Columbus (1492). *About. com Latin American History.* [Online] About.com, 2014. http://latinamericanhistory.about.com/od/ latinamericatheconquest/p/Columbusfirst.htm.

312. Martin Luther. *Wikipedia, the free encyclopedia.* [Online] February 22, 2014. http://en.wikipedia.org/ wiki/Martin_Luther.

313. Battle of Stalingrad. *Wikipedia, the free encyclopedia.* [Online] December 4, 2013. http://en.wikipedia. org/wiki/Battle_of_Stalingrad.

314. German Labor Camps Vs The Soviet Gulag. *rense.com.* [Online] August 18, 2011. http://www.rense. com/general84/germl.htm.

315. The Philadelpha Experiment. [Online] http://www.phils.com.au/philadelphia.htm.

316. **Project Camelot.** *Ashayana Deane Ascension Mechanics, Part One.* [www.youtube.com video; www.youtube.com/watch?v=AQ-ZaU6FHNw] Project Camelot Productions, 2010.
317. **Elanthra.** A Message From Archangel Michael. [Online] February 28, 2010. Original title: "Archangel Michael: The Divine Awashing & The Twin Flame Portal" from www.livewithlight.com. http://clevelandohiousa.tripod.com/amessagefromarchangelmichael/.
318. **Lorgen, Eve Frances, M.A.** Montauk Mind Control Victim Interview. *rense.com.* [Online] NewsHawk Inc., May 13, 2000. http://www.rense.com/general/montauk.htm.
319. **Chossudovsky, Michel.** H.A.A.R.P. *From the Wilderness Publications.* [Online] [Cited: October 31, 2011.] http://web.archive.org/web/20111031031731/http://www.copvcia.com/free/pandora/haarp.html.
320. **MCEO Freedom Teachings®.** *Preparing for Contact--Level 1: Introduction to the "Arc Project" & Eieyani Mentorship Program. Official Statement.* Bermuda : Azurite Press Inc., 2002.
321. **MCEO Freedom Teachings®.** *The Science and Spirituality of Creation.* [DVDs and Manual] Seattle, WA : Azurite Press Inc., September 2003.
322. **MCEO Freedom Teachings®.** *Dance for Joy: A Universal Hetharo Celebration.* [DVDs] Paxos, Greece : Azurite Press Inc., May 2003.
323. **MCEO Freedom Teachings®.** *Dance For Joy, Part 2: Hethalon Peak.* [DVDs] Andorra and Barcelona, Spain : Azurite Press Inc., August 2003.
324. **MCEO Freedom Teachings®.** *Eieyani Council "Open Letter".* Azurite Press Inc., 2003.
325. *Phoenix October 2005 Workshop Summary: "Whispers of the RashaReishA, Revelations of the Unspoken Ones, the HaahTUr's and the HUB".* **Azur'yana, Georgi.** Phoenix, AZ : Endorsed by Azurite Press Inc., October 2005. Reported in official Keylontic Science forum at http://groups.yahoo.com/group/KeylonticScience.
326. **MCEO Freedom Teachings®.** *Two Moons Rising.* [DVDs] Phoenix, AZ : Azurite Press Inc., April 2006.
327. **Project Camelot.** *Ashayana Deane Ascension Mechanics, Part Two.* [www.youtube.com video; http://www.youtube.com/watch?v=7-h_Qk4Z1SQ] Project Camelot Productions, 2010.
328. **MCEO Freedom Teachings®.** *Festival of Light 2007 - "Transcending the Towers of Threshold; the Crystal River Union, and the Arc of Aquari".* [DVDs] Phoenix, AZ : Azurite Press Inc., January 2007.
329. **E-LAi-sa Freedom Forum.** *The Cosmos is Watching & Always Will Be: The Dance of Lila, the Pillar of Peace & the Bridge Across Forever.* [DVDs] Sarasota, Florida : EFFI-Project™, May 24-30, 2012.
330. **MCEO Freedom Teachings®.** *Sliders-12: Externalization of the Kryst; Secrets of the Tan-Tri-A'jha'. PART-2.* [DVDs] Sarasota, FL : Azurite Press Inc., April 2012.
331. **Fenn, Celia.** Archangel Michael: 11-11-11 is a Great Moment in the Transformation of Planet Earth. *Ashtar Command.* [Online] October 2011. Forum. Credit to http://www.starchildglobal.com/NewYorkNov211.html.. http://www.ashtarcommandcrew.net/forum/topics/archangel-michael-11-11-11-is-a-great-moment-in-the.
332. **Weidner, Jay.** The Alchemy of Time: Understanding the Great Year and the Cycles of Existence. *The Mystery of 2012: Predictions, Prophecies & Possibilities.* Boulder, CO : Sounds True, Inc., 2007.
333. **McClure, Bruce.** Will Earth cross the galactic equator in 2012? *EarthSky.* [Online] July 19, 2012. http://earthsky.org/astronomy-essentials/will-earth-pass-through-galactic-plane-in-2012.
334. **Rod & Staff.** *Keylontic Dictionary.* [Online] From Cosmic Clock Reset manual. http://www.keylonticdictionary.org/online/member/index.php?page=rod-staff.
335. **The Tan-Tri-Ahura Teachings-The Path of Bio-Spiritual Artistry™.** *"AMCC-MCEO 13 Days of Kryst-Mass and the Planetary Silver-Seed Awakening": General Overview of Planetary Grid Activations 12/21/2012-1/3/2013.* s.l. : ARhAyas Productions AMCC-MCEO LLC, 2013.
336. **MCEO Freedom Teachings®.** *The 12-Tribes Transcripts, Class 9.* [Manual] Phoenix, AZ : Azurite Press Inc., December 2007.
337. **MCEO Freedom Teachings®.** *The 12-Tribes Transcripts, Class 6.* [Manual] Azurite Press Inc., July 2007.
338. *Gestalt principles (Part 1).* **Wong, Bang.** 11, Nature America, Inc., November 2010, Nature Methods, Vol. 7, p. 863.
339. *Perception: An introduction to the Gestalt-theorie.* **Koffka, Kurt.** 1922, Psychological Bulletin, Vol. 19, pp. 531-585.
340. *Qi. Wikipedia, the free encyclopedia.* [Online] December 2, 2013. http://en.wikipedia.org/wiki/Qi.
341. Chapter 3, Section 5: Freud's Structural and Topographical Models of Personality. *AllPsych Online: The Virtual Psychology Classrom.* [Online] AllPsych and Heffner Media Group, Inc., 2003. http://allpsych.com/psychology101/ego.html.
342. Chapter 5, Section 3: Carl Jung's Analytic Psychology. *AllPsych Online: The Virtual Psychology Classroom.* [Online] AllPsych and Heffner Media Group, Inc., 2003. http://allpsych.com/personalitysynopsis/jung.html.

343. **MCEO Freedom Teachings®**. *Sliders-5: Essential Alignment, Stardust Flow, Mirror in the Sky & the Orbs of Aquareion--"Freeing the Body for Slide"*. [DVDs] Phoenix, AZ : Azurite Press Inc., August 2009.

344. **Nauman, Eileen.** Ground Yourself--How to Do It. *Medical Astrology*. [Online] 1997. [Cited: October 25, 2011.] http://web.archive.org/web/20111025163242/http://medicalastrologybyeileennauman.blogspot.com/2011/03/how-to-ground-yourself-and-stay-in-your.html.

345. **McKinley, Michael and Valerie Dean O'Loughlin.** Animation: The Nerve Impulse. *Human Anatomy, Student Edition.* [Online] 2006. Chapter 14. http://highered.mcgraw-hill.com/sites/0072495855/student_view0/chapter14/animation__the_nerve_impulse.html.

346. Neurons and Nerves. *Review of the Universe.* [Online] http://universe-review.ca/R10-16-ANS.htm.

347. **Leitzell, Katherine.** The Other Brain Cells: New Roles for Glia. *Scientific American™.* [Online] May 22, 2008. http://www.scientificamerican.com/article.cfm?id=the-other-brain-cells.

348. **Bourzac, Katherine.** Lightning Bolts within Cells: A new nanoscale tool reveals strong electric fields inside cells. *MIT Technology Review.* [Online] December 10, 2007. http://www.technologyreview.com/news/409171/lightning-bolts-within-cells/.

349. Blood pH – How the body maintains its acidity and alkalinity. *Laboratory MedNews.* [Online] March 2, 2010. http://jenaisle.com/tag/blood-ph-acidity-and-alkalinity.

350. **MCEO Freedom Teachings®**. *Sliders-1: "Emerging from Darkness"—Preparing the MIND for Slide.* [DVDs and Manual] Phoenix, AZ : Azurite Press Inc., August 2008.

351. Auras. *Age of E.* [Online] http://www.age-of-e.com/auras/AuraInfo/AuraInfo.html.

352. **Kerr, Roger.** Truth about Orion "Lizards". [Online] http://www.thewayofblindman.com/wp-content/uploads/2012/05/truth-about-orion-lizards1.pdf.

353. **Cosmic Awareness.** Getting the Alien "Federations" Straight (More on Clarion, Vega, Lyra and the Orion Empire). *Revelations of Awareness: The New Age Cosmic Newsletter.* September 19, 1992, Vols. 92-15, 407, p. 10. http://www.cosmicchannelings.com/cos/1992/Cosmic-Awareness-1992-15_alien-perot-nemesis-politics-health-ashtar-command-president-clinton-space-walk-in.pdf

354. **Cavallo, Maurizio.** *Beyond the Heavens: A Story of Contact.* Bloomington : Author House, 2008.

355. Truman Bethurum. *Ufology.* [Online] December 30, 2007. http://ufology.wikidot.com/bethurum-truman.

356. **Meleriessee, Christine and Mike Hayden.** Clarion Temple of Oneness. [Online] http://clarionlightbeings911.wordpress.com/.

357. **Meleriessee, Christine.** Preparing for a New Awareness-Wesak 2011-Sanat Kumara-Clarion Light Beings-Unified in Oneness. *Lightworkers.* [Online] May 16, 2011. http://lightworkers.org/channeling/132114/preparing-new-awareness-wesak-2011-sanat-kumara-clarion-light-beings-unified-onene.

358. **Clark, Jim.** DNA - Structure. *chemguide.* [Online] December 2013. Entire six page article. http://www.chemguide.co.uk/organicprops/aminoacids/dna1.html.

359. DNA vs RNA. *Diffen.* [Online] www.diffen.com/difference/DNA_vs_RNA.

360. Genes and Chromosomes: The Genome. Fact Sheet 1. *Centre for Genetics Education.* [Online] http://web.archive.org/web/20130703135510/http://www.genetics.edu.au/Publications%20and%20Resources/Genetics-Fact-Sheets/Genes-and-Chromosomes-FS1.

361. Intron. *Wikipedia, the free encyclopedia.* [Online] November 21, 2013. www.en.wikipedia.org/wiki/Intron.

362. About the Human Genome Project. *Human Genome Project Information Archive 1990-2003.* [Online] U.S. Department of Energy, July 23, 2013. http://web.ornl.gov/sci/techresources/Human_Genome/project/index.shtml#whose.

363. *An integrated encyclopedia of DNA elements in the human genome.* **The ENCODE Project Consortium.** Macmillan Publishers Limited, 2012, Nature, Vol. 489, pp. 57-74.

364. **Yong, Ed.** ENCODE: the rough guide to the human genome. *Discover.* [Online] Kalmbach Publishing Co., September 5, 2012. http://blogs.discovermagazine.com/notrocketscience/2012/09/05/encode-the-rough-guide-to-the-human-genome/#.UQJg1B3C0y0.

365. **Daily Mail Reporter.** Boy, two, is first person in the world to be born with an extra strand of DNA. *Mail Online.* [Online] Associated Newspaters Ltd, April 11, 2011. http://www.dailymail.co.uk/health/article-1375697/Alfie-Clamp-2-1st-person-born-extra-strand-DNA.html.

366. **Seiler, Stephanie and Gray, Leila.** Millions of DNA switches that power human genome's operating system are discovered. *University of Washington.* [Online] September 5, 2012. http://www.washington.edu/news/2012/09/05/millions-of-dna-switches-that-power-human-genomes-operating-system-are-discovered.

367. Pythagorean Mathematics. *Internet Sacred Text Archive.* [Online] Evinity Publishing Inc., 2011. http://www.sacred-texts.com/eso/sta/sta16.htm.

368. Vibrational healing with solfeggio frequencies. *Altered States.* [Online] http://www.altered-states.net/barry/newsletter572/.

369. **Emoto, Masaru.** *Messages from Water and the Universe.* Carlsbad, CA : Hay House, Inc., 2010.

370. Pitch and Frequency. *The Physics Classroom.* [Online] 2014. http://www.physicsclassroom.com/class/sound/u1l2a.cfm#range.

371. **Fosar, Grazna and Bludorf, Franz.** DNA Can be influenced and reprogrammed by words and frequencies. *Scribd.* [Online] http://www.scribd.com/doc/36629342/DNA-Can-Be-Influenced-and-Reprogrammed-by-Words-and-Frequencies.

372. **Judith, Anodea, Ph.D.** Chakra Exercises & FAQ's. *Sacred Centers.* [Online] 2014. http://sacredcenters.com/the-chakras/chakra-faqs/.

373. *Science and Spirituality: The Mysterious Pineal Gland.* **Formosan News Group.** 4, Traditional African Clinic, March 2011, African Traditional Herbal Research Clinic, Vol. 6.

374. History & Symbolism. *Third Eye Pinecones.* [Online] 2012. http://www.thirdeyepinecones.com/history-symbolism.

375. Pineal Gland. [Online] Fluoride Action Network, 2012. http://www.fluoridealert.org/issues/health/pineal-gland/.

376. *666 ABC Canberra.* [Online] Australian Broadcasting Corporation, 2014. http://www.abc.net.au/canberra/.

377. **MCEO Freedom Teachings®.** *Architects of Light and the Secrets of the Indigo Children.* [DVDs] New York City : Azurite Press Inc., April 2000.

378. **MCEO Freedom Teachings®.** *The 12-Tribes Transcripts, Class 11.* [Manual] Phoenix, AZ : Azurite Press Inc., February 2008.

379. About E-LAi-sa Freedom Forum, AMCC-MCEO, LLC. *E-LAi-sa Freedom Forum.* [Online] 2014. http://www.elaisafreedomforum.com/pages/about-eff.

380. **MCEO Freedom Teachings®.** *The Melchizedek Cloister Emerald Order (MCEO) Ordinate System: Getting Your Ascension Codes Back.* [Manual] Azurite Press Inc., 2007.

381. **Deane, Ashayana.** *Angelic Realities: The Survival Handbook.* Columbus, NC : Wild Flower Press, 2001.

382. Heroic Path. *Keylontic Dictionary.* [Online] From workshop *USA Wrap Up,* 2002, Allentown, PA. http://www.keylonticdictionary.org/online/member/index.php?page=heroic-path.

383. *The Christ of the New Age Movement.* **Rhodes, Ron.** Reasoning from the Scriptures Ministries, Summer 1989, Christian Research Journal, p. 9.

384. **Blavatsky, H.P.** *The Secret Doctrine: The Synthesis of Science, Religion, and Philosophy. Vol. I.--Cosmogenesis.* London : The Theosophical Publishing Company, Limited, 1988.

385. Jiddu Krishnamurti. *Wikipedia, the free encyclopedia.* [Online] February 19, 2014. http://en.wikipedia.org/wiki/Jiddu_Krishnamurti.

386. **Jayakur, Pupul.** *J. Krishnamurti: A Biography.* New York : Penguin Books, 1986.

387. **Krishnamurti, J.** Truth is a pathless land. *J. Krishnamurti online: The Official repository of the authentic teachings of J. Krishnamurti.* [Online] Krishnamurti Foundation America, 1980. http://www.jkrishnamurti.org/about-krishnamurti/dissolution-speech.php.

388. **Anrias, David.** *Through the Eyes of the Masters: Meditations and Portraits.* London : G. Routledge & Sons, Ltd., 1932.

389. **Blavatsky, H.P.** *The Secret Doctrine: The Synthesis of Science, Religion, and Philosohpy. Vol. II.--Anthropogenesis.* London : The Theosophical Publishing Company, Limited, 1888.

390. Properties of the number 144. *Riding the Beast.com.* [Online] December 19, 1998. http://www.ridingthebeast.com/numbers/nu144.php.

391. The shape of the universe: Platonic truths. *The Economist.* October 9, 2003.

392. Dodecahedron. *Wolfram MathWorld.* [Online] Wolfram Research, Inc., 2014. http://mathworld.wolfram.com/Dodecahedron.html.

393. Oversoul Matrix. *Keylontic Dictionary.* [Online] http://www.keylonticdictionary.org/online/member/index.php?page=oversoul-matrix.

394. **MCEO Freedom Teachings®.** *Sliders-7 - "The Lands of Wha: Mirror Mapping, the 3 Paths of the Kryst and the Wha-YA'-yas Masha-yah-hana Adashi Adepts".* [DVDs] Sarasota, FL : Azurite Press Inc., May 2010.

395. Prana. *VEDA Vedic Knowledge Online.* [Online] 2014. http://veda.harekrsna.cz/encyclopedia/prana.htm.

396. Kundalini Awakening. *Traditional Yoga and Meditation of the Himalayan Masters.* [Online] http://swamij.com/kundalini-awakening-1.htm.

397. **Sivananada, Sri Swami.** *Kundalini Yoga.* Shivanandanagar : The Divine Life Society, 1999. World Wide Web Edition.

398. **Chia, Grand Master Mantak.** Healing Love. *Universal Healing TAO.* [Online] 2013. http://www.universal-tao.com/FAQ/healing_love.html.

399. *Sexual Theories of Wilhelm Reich.* **Baker, Elsworth, M.D.** 2, The American College of Orgonomy, 1982, The Journal of Orgonomy, Vol. 20.

400. **MCEO Freedom Teachings**®. *Sliders-1: "Emerging from Darkness"—Preparing the MIND for Slide.* [DVDs and Manual] Phoenix, AZ : Azurite Press Inc., August 2008.

401. **MCEO Freedom Teachings**®. *Sliders-9: "Advanced Spiritual Body Training - The Flame of CosMAyah, Mayan Mother Matrix & Luminary Body Activation".* [DVDs and Manual] Mayan Cruise and Sarasota, FL : Azurite Press Inc., December 2010 and April 2001.

402. Shambhala. *Wikipedia, the free encyclopedia.* [Online] [Cited: January 30, 2012.] http://web.archive.org/web/20120130095540/http://en.wikipedia.org/wiki/Shambhala.

403. **Sutherland, Mary.** In Search of Shambhala. *Biblioteca Pleyades.* [Online] June 2003. http://www.bibliotecapleyades.net/sociopolitica/sociopol_shambahla06.htm.

404. **Wittels, Nedda.** Shamballa Multi-Dimensional Healing. *Rays of Healing Light.* [Online] [Cited: November 2, 2012.] http://web.archive.org/web/20120625082126/http://www.raysofhealinglight.com/300_shamballaMDH.htm.

405. **Finney, Dee.** The Ascended Masters - Who They Are. [Online] April 30, 2003. http://www.greatdreams.com/masters/ascended-masters.htm.

406. The Location of Earth's GFL Command Base. *Ashtar Command.* [Online] August 5, 2011. Forum post by Drekx Omega. http://www.ashtarcommandcrew.net/forum/topics/the-location-of-earth-s-gfl-command-base.

407. The Shambhala Triangle. *Forum Project Avalon.* [Online] October 3, 2009. Forum post by 14 Chakras. http://projectavalon.net/forum/showthread.php?t=16747.

408. Telos: The Underground City of Mt Shasta. *Lightworkers.* [Online] June 4, 2009. Forum post sourced from http://web.archive.org/web/20100424202539/http://www.mountshastawisdomproject.com/Teloscity.htm. http://lightworkers.org/blog/78455/telos-the-underground-city-of-mount-shasta.

409. **Icke, David.** *children of the matrix: How an interdimensional race has controlled the world for thousands of years -- and still does.* Ryde, Isle of Wight : David Icke Books, 2001.

410. **MCEO Freedom Teachings**®. The Eckasha Maharic Seal Technique. *Azurite Press of the Melchizedek Cloister Emerald Order.* [Online] Azurite Press Inc. http://www.azuritepress.com/techniques/Maharic.php.

411. Reuche. *Keylontic Dictionary.* [Online] From *Keys for Mastering Ascension* manual. http://www.keylonticdictionary.org/online/member/index.php?page=reuche.

412. **MCEO Freedom Teachings**®. Flame Body Activation and Shadow Body Healing. *Azurite Press of the Melchizedek Cloister Emerald Order.* [Online] Azurite Press Inc., 2010. http://www.azuritepress.com/techniques/flame_body_techniques.php.

INDEX

Numbers

12 tribes
Israel 127, 129, 134, 136, 145, 267
original Human races 267, 439
Third Seeding Human races 357
666 number 257. *See* **Metatron's Seed**
6-6-6 stargate wormholes 258
Apollyon implant 375-376
Seal 349. *See* **Templar-Axion Seal**

A

"A" domain 221, 227, 424
Abaddon 249, 258, 332, 402
Abraham 119, 125-127, 142-144, 271.
See **Djehuty**
Anunnaki group 271-272
Adam 68-69, 119-120, 122, 133, 146,
150, 156, 265, 271, 286
Adama 265
Adami-Kudmon hybrid 287
Adam-Kadmon 287
Beli-Kudmon 287
Beli-Mahatma 358, 380, 382
Adapa 264-265
Adashi 400, 403
Agartha 237, 328, 336
"Inner Earth" 237
Ah'-yah field 229, 234
Akhenaten 137, 139. *See* **Moses**
Alhumbhra Council (AC) 229, 396, 469
alien 92, 241-242
Allah 125-126
All That Is, The Pure Essence (ATI,TPE)
12-15, 95-97, 109, 112, 114-115,
225-226, 230-231, 234, 238-239,
247, 283, 297, 309, 316, 423, 449,
458, 492, 508, 515, 518
All There Is 309
Alpha-Omega 32, 40, 258, 351, 354-
355, 393, 403, 476
Amenti
Earth. *See* **Earth:Amenti**

Halls 343, 351, 367, 375-376, 380,
384, 389, 398, 404
Rescue Mission 259
Sphere 341, 347-348, 395, 398, 470,
498
Staff 341
America 360
Amethyst Order 248
Amoraea
Buffer 527
current 375-376
Flame 527
amygdala 23
Andromies 286, 331, 362-363, 365
ankh 526
annihilation v, 213-214
Annu (Human hybrid) 348, 350
Templar-Annu 350-351
antimatter 212-213, 215-216, 388, 482
Anunnaki 124, 259-260, 262, 270
Jehovian 260, 270, 369
Ra-Thoth. *See* **Ra:Marduk** and **Thoth**
Anunnaki Resistance 348, 350-351
Anyu 248-249
Apocalypse 162, 167, 318, 331, 334, 359
Apocrypha 154
AquA'elle 401-402
Aquafereion 356-357
AquaLaShA 242, 247, 401
Aqualene
buffer field 383
krystars 245, 384
Transmission 245, 383
Aquareion 244
Aquari 245, 253, 357
Aquinos 242, 244
Aramatena 235-236, 248
Arc of the Covenant 348, 377, 382, 398,
499
gates 381, 403
passage 384
Arihabi 183-184, 186, 254, 300

CPSIA information can be obtained at www.ICGtesting.com
Printed in the USA
BVOW05s0351260615

405914BV00004B/192/P